Oracle Press™

OCP Oracle Database 11g: New Features for Administrators

Exam Guide (Exam 1Z0-050)

ORACLE®

Oracle Press™

OCP Oracle Database 11g: New Features for Administrators

Exam Guide (Exam 1Z0-050)

Sam Alapati

New York Chicago San Francisco Lisbon London Madrid
Mexico City Milan New Delhi San Juan Seoul Singapore Sydney Toronto

Cataloging-in-Publication Data is on file with the Library of Congress

McGraw-Hill books are available at special quantity discounts to use as premiums and sales promotions, or for use in corporate training programs. To contact a special sales representative, please visit the Contact Us page at www.mhprofessional.com.

OCP Oracle Database 11g: New Features for Administrators Exam Guide (Exam 1Z0-050)

1234567890 DOC DOC 0198

ISBN: Book p/n 978-0-07-149683-4 and CD p/n 978-0-07-149684-1 of set 978-0-07-149682-7
MHID: Book p/n 0-07-149683-1 and CD p/n 0-07-149684-X of set 0-07-149682-3

Sponsoring Editor Timothy Green	**Technical Editor** April Wells	**Production Supervisor** James Kussow
Editorial Supervisor Jody McKenzie	**Copy Editor** Nancy Rapoport	**Composition** Apollo Publishing Services
Project Editor Laura Stone	**Proofreader** Susie Elkind	**Illustration** Apollo Publishing Services
Acquisitions Coordinator Jennifer Housh	**Indexer** Karin Arrigoni	**Art Director, Cover** Jeff Weeks

To the twins, Nina and Nicholas.

ABOUT THE AUTHOR

Sam Alapati (Irvine, TX) is an experienced Oracle DBA who holds the Oracle OCP DBA (11g) certification and the Hewlett-Packard UNIX System Administrator certification. He currently manages Oracle databases at the Boy Scouts of America's national office in Irving, Texas. Previously, Sam worked for AMR Holdings (Sabre) and the Blanch Company in Dallas. Sam was a Senior Principal Consultant for Oracle Corporation in New York, working with NBC and Lehman Brothers. In addition to being a professional Oracle database administrator, Sam has also taught Oracle DBA classes for many students and college-level courses at Kansas State University, University of Texas at Austin, and Rutgers University.

About the Technical Editor

April Wells (Austin, TX) is an experienced Oracle DBA who holds multiple OCP DBA certifications. She currently manages Oracle databases and Oracle data warehouses at NetSpend Corporation in Austin, Texas. Previously, April worked for Oracle Corporation in Austin as on-site support at Dell; at Corporate Systems in Amarillo, Texas; and at US Steel in Pennsylvania and Minnesota.

CONTENTS AT A GLANCE

1   Installing, Upgrading, and Change Management   1

2   Diagnosing and Resolving Problems   77

3   Intelligent Infrastructure and Database Security   147

4   Automatic SQL Tuning and SQL Plan Management   213

5   Automatic Storage Management and Partitioning
    Enhancements   263

6   Performance Enhancements   321

7   RMAN and Flashback Enhancements   383

8   Oracle SecureFiles and Miscellaneous New Features   449

    About the CD-ROM   491

    Glossary   493

    Index   507

CONTENTS

Acknowledgments . . . . *xv*
Introduction . . . . *xvi*

1 Installing, Upgrading, and Change Management **1**

Installing Oracle Database 11g 3
   Changes in the Optimal Flexible Architecture 3
   Automatic Diagnostic Repository 5
   Changes in the Installation Options 6
   New Database Components 7
   Role and Privilege Changes 7
   An Oracle Database 11g Installation 8
New Features in Database Creation 10
   Summary of New Initialization Parameters 10
   DBCA Enhancements 12
   Using the DBCA to Create a Database 13
Upgrading to Oracle Database 11g 19
   Moving Data as Part of the Upgrade 19
   New Privileges for Storage Management 20
   Upgrading to Oracle Database 11g 20
   Exercise 1-1   Scripts to Run for Upgrading a Database 31
Real Application Testing 32
   Database Replay 33
   Exercise 1-2   Procedure for Capturing and Replaying
   a Database Workload 47
   The SQL Performance Analyzer 51
   Exercise 1-3   Testing SQL Performance Following a Database
   Upgrade 61
  ✓ Two-Minute Drill 63
 Q&A Self Test 68
   Lab Question 71
   Self Test Answers 72
   Lab Answer 75

2 Diagnosing and Resolving Problems **77**

Automatic Diagnostic Repository 80
   The Structure of the ADR 81
   ADRCI 83

Incidents and Problems 88
    Incident Packaging Service 90
    Exercise 2-1   Creating an Incident Package
    with ADRCI 95
Support Workbench 96
    Viewing Critical Error Alerts 96
    Examining Problem Details 98
    Collecting Additional Diagnostic Data 98
    Creating a Service Request 99
    Packaging and Uploading Diagnostic Data 100
    Tracking the Service Request 102
    Implementing Repairs 103
    Closing Incidents 103
    Generating a User-Created Problem 103
    Viewing the Alert Log 104
Health Monitor 105
    Running a Health Check 106
    Exercise 2-2   Running a Health Check with Input
    Parameters 107
    Viewing the Health Monitor Reports 110
SQL Repair Advisor 110
    Using the Support Workbench 111
    Using the DBMS_SQLDIAG Package 111
    Exercise 2-3   Exporting a SQL Patch to Another
    Database 114
Data Recovery Advisor 115
    Failures 117
    Repair Options 118
    Using RMAN to Manage the Data Recovery Advisor 119
    Proactive Checks 126
    Managing the DRA with Database Control 130
    New Parameter to Detect Database Corruption 131
  ✓ Two-Minute Drill 135
Q&A Self Test 138
    Lab Question 142
    Self Test Answers 143
    Lab Answer 146

3   Intelligent Infrastructure and Database Security **147**

Enhancements in AWR Baselines 148
    Managing Baseline Templates 149
    Renaming a Baseline 152
    Setting AWR Baseline Metric Thresholds 152
    Moving Window AWR Baselines 155
    Managing the New Baseline Features 156
Controlling Automated Maintenance Tasks 158
    Predefined Maintenance Windows 159
    Managing the Automatic Maintenance Tasks 159
    Implementing Automatic Maintenance Tasks 163
    Configuring Resource Allocation for Automatic Tasks 163
    I/O Calibration 164
    Exercise 3-1 Calibrating I/O Resources 164
Database Resource Manager New Features 167
    Per Session I/O Limits 168
    Pre-Created Mixed Workload Resource Plan 172
Using New Oracle Scheduler Features 173
    Lightweight Jobs 173
    Exercise 3-2 Creating an Array of Regular Scheduler Jobs 177
    Remote External Jobs 178
    Scheduler Support for Data Guard 184
Security Enhancements 185
    Secure Password Support 186
    Configuring Fine-Grained Access to Network Services 190
    Encrypting Tablespaces 194
    Creating the Oracle Wallet 195
    Creating an Encrypted Tablespace 196
    Restrictions on Tablespace Encryption 198
    ✓ Two-Minute Drill 201
    Q&A Self Test 204
    Lab Question 207
    Self Test Answers 208
    Lab Answer 211

4   Automatic SQL Tuning and SQL Plan Management ... **213**

Automatic SQL Tuning Advisor 214
    SQL Profiles 216

Limitations   217
The Automatic SQL Tuning Process   217
Exercise 4-1 Using Enterprise Manager to Access
the SQL Tuning Advisor   222
Interpreting Automatic SQL Tuning Reports   223
Data Dictionary Views   224
SQL Plan Management   225
SQL Plan Baselines   226
Capturing SQL Plan Baselines   227
Fixed SQL Plan Baselines   235
SQL Plan Baseline Attributes   235
Managing SQL Plan Baselines   237
The SQL Management Base   238
Managing SPM with the Enterprise Manager   240
SQL Access Advisor Enhancements   240
New Procedures   240
Partitioning Recommendations   242
Publish Points   243
Running a SQL Access Advisor Job Using PL/SQL   243
Using Enterprise Manager   249
Using the Cursor Cache to Get SQL Access Advisor
Recommendations   251
✓ Two-Minute Drill   254
Q&A Self Test   257
Lab Question   259
Self Test Answers   260
Lab Answer   262

**5 Automatic Storage Management and Partitioning
Enhancements** **263**
Automatic Storage Management New Features   264
ASM Architecture   264
ASM Fast Mirror Resync   265
ASM Preferred Mirror Read   269
ASM Scalability and Performance Enhancements   272
New SYSASM Privilege   274
ASM Compatibility   275
Changing ASM Disk Group Attributes   279
New Manageability Options for Commands   280

Exercise 5-1   Using the md_backup and md_restore
      Commands   288
Partitioning Enhancements   289
      Interval Partitioning   290
      System Partitioning   295
      Virtual Column-Based Partitioning   298
      Reference Partitioning   301
      Composite Partitioning Enhancements   307
   ✓ Two-Minute Drill   312
Q&A Self Test   315
      Lab Question   316
      Self Test Answers   317
      Lab Answer   318

6   Performance Enhancements **321**
Automatic Memory Management . . . .
ADDM Enhancements   322
      ADDM for Real Application Clusters   322
      New DBMS_ADDM Package   324
Automatic Memory Management   328
      SGA, PGA, and the MEMORY_TARGET Parameter   329
      Exercise 6-1   Using Automatic Memory Management   331
      Monitoring Automatic Memory Management   332
      DBCA and Automatic Memory Management   333
Enhancements in Optimizer Statistics Collection   334
      Statistics Preferences   334
      Partitioned Tables and Incremental Statistics   337
      New Sampling Technique   338
      Deferred Statistics Publishing   338
      Extended Statistics   341
Result Cache   347
      Result Cache Memory Pool   347
      Managing the Result Cache   348
      Caching SQL Results with a Result_Cache Hint   348
      Using the DBMS_RESULT_CACHE Package   350
      Using Dynamic Performance Views   353
      The SQL Query Result Cache   354
      The PL/SQL Function Result Cache   357
      The Client Query Result cache   359
Adaptive Cursor Sharing   362

How Adaptive Cursor Sharing Works 364
Monitoring Adaptive Cursor Sharing 365
✓ Two-Minute Drill 369
Q&A Self Test 373
Lab Question 376
Self Test Answers 377
Lab Answer 380

7 RMAN and Flashback Enhancements **383**

RMAN Enhancements 384
Active (Network-Based) Database Duplication 384
Parallel Backup and Restore of Large Files 392
Archival (Long-Term) Backups 394
Fast Incremental Backups 398
Improved Block Media Recovery Performance 398
New Persistent Configuration Parameters 401
Backup Failover to Non-Flash Recovery Areas 404
Recovery Catalog Management 405
Merging Recovery Catalogs 405
Virtual Private Catalogs 408
New Flashback-Related Features 413
Flashback Data Archive 413
Flashback Transaction Backout 427
Exercise 7-1 Using the TRANSACTION_BACKOUT
Procedure 430
✓ Two-Minute Drill 433
Q&A Self Test 438
Lab Question 442
Self Test Answers 443
Lab Answer 447

8 Oracle SecureFiles and Miscellaneous New Features ... **449**

Oracle SecureFiles 450
Enabling SecureFiles 451
Capabilities of SecureFiles 452
Storage Options for SecureFiles 453
Creating SecureFiles 454
Managing and Monitoring SecureFiles 456
Migrating to SecureFiles 457

Online Enhancements   458
   Locking Enhancements   458
   Minimal Invalidation of Dependent Objects   460
   Creating a Parameter File from Memory   461
   Hot Patching   462
Miscellaneous New Features   463
   Invisible Indexes   463
   Shrinking Temporary Tablespaces   465
   Tablespace Option for Creating Temporary Tables   467
   PL/SQL and Java Automatic Native Compilation   467
   Exercise 8-1   Setting Up a PL/SQL Program Unit for
      Native Compilation   468
   OLTP Table Compression   472
   Direct NFS Client   473
   ✓ Two-Minute Drill   480
Q&A Self Test   483
   Self Test Answers   487
   Lab Answer   490

Appendix   **About the CD-ROM** **491**
   System Requirements   491
   Installing and Running MasterExam   491
   MasterExam   492
   Electronic Book   492
   Help   492
   Removing Installation(s)   492
   Technical Support   492
   LearnKey Technical Support   492

Glossary **493**

Index **507**

ACKNOWLEDGMENTS

I wish to acknowledge the excellent technical editing of the book by April Wells. Thanks to April's careful and expert technical vetting, I've been able to avoid errors and improve the quality of the presentation.

In the last few years, over the course of writing three books for Oracle Press, Timothy Green, Senior Acquisitions Editor, has also become my friend. Tim's sagacious replies to queries as well as excellent counsel and encouragement have been extremely helpful. I also thank the excellent help and support provided by the Acquisitions Coordinator, Jennifer Housh.

I appreciate the terrific job done by Laura Stone, the Project Editor, in seeing the chapters through all the editing and production stages with great patience, skill, and cheer. Laura has shown great alacrity and exceptional understanding at various stages of the manuscript to keep the workflow moving steadily. Exceptional copy editing by Nancy Rapoport has significantly enhanced the style and presentation of the contents of the book. I'm also grateful to the great proofreading by Susie Elkind. I'm lucky to have friends at work such as Myra Riggs and Dabir Haider. Myra always finds time to talk about just about anything, and I can always count on her help and advice. Dabir has been a source of help and support ever since he joined us last year. I couldn't have taken care of business without the kind help of Leticia Salazar, who has gone out of her way to help me in numerous ways throughout the last year—thanks, Leticia! My buddy Mark Potts has been a true friend over the years and I'm grateful to him for all his help. My colleagues at work, Lance Parkes and Rob Page, are always helpful, and I acknowledge their kindness as well. I'm fortunate to work with David Jeffress and Dave Campbell, two exceptional managers, and thanks go out to both of them. I would also like to express my appreciation for Dan Nelson and Debra Kendrew for their friendship and caring.

Finally, I'd like to extend my profound thanks to both of my families. I'm grateful to Mom; Dad; and my two brothers, Hari Hara Prasad and Siva Sankara Prasad; for their love, affection, and support. Thanks also to Aruna, Vanaja, Ashwin, Teja, Aparna, and Soumya for their love and kindness over the years. I wish to acknowledge the enormous debt I owe to my wife, Valerie, who had to fill in the void left by my absence from the home front during the writing of this book. Finally, thanks to Shannon and the twins, Nina and Nicholas, who always love it when we get to look at the first copies of a newly printed book!

INTRODUCTION

Oracle Database 11g offers several highly powerful enhancements to the management of Oracle databases. Oracle databases are the leading commercial databases in the world today, and it's a great challenge as well as a matter of pride to certify in the latest flagship offering of the Oracle Corporation. For more information about the Oracle certification exams, requirements for certification, or recertification, please visit Oracle's certification web site (http://www.oracle.com/education/certification).

This book will help you in your endeavor to upgrade your Oracle OCP DBA certification to the latest level—Oracle Database 11g. It is a study guide for Oracle Database administrators who plan to take the OCP Oracle Database 10g: New Features for Administrators Exam Guide (Exam 1Z0-050). This exam is also known commonly as the DBA "Upgrade" exam because you can upgrade to the latest Oracle Database 11g OCP certification from the Oracle10g OCP certification. In order to take this exam, Oracle Corporation must have already certified you as an Oracle10g OCP.

If your goal is to update your credentials, you can do so by diligently working through this book, doing all the exercises and practice tests. However, your goal should ideally reach beyond passing the exam. Ultimately, you'll need to use the new skills you learn in your present job, and the only way to do so is by clearly understanding the nuances of the various enhancements offered by the Oracle Database 11g release. To this end, I've designed this book as much more than a simple exam guide, by carefully introducing the topics and discussing them in sufficient detail to provide you with a solid understanding.

Some of you, I'm sure, are tempted to just learn the minimum necessary to pass the upgrade exam. However, I urge you to delve deeper into the new release by testing the new features on your own and exploring the many new capabilities of the Oracle Database 11g release. In general, Oracle certifications are voluntary, in the sense that in most cases they are not prerequisites for a job working with Oracle products. The real value of certification comes in the mastery of a wide range of capabilities of the Oracle database software. As the first chapter shows you, it is easier to install the new Oracle software than ever before. Therefore, you really don't have any excuses for not installing the Oracle Database 11g software on your workstation or a test server and exploring all the new features. I've found that testing the various features is the best way to understand and remember the nuances of the new features, including the usage of the new commands and SQL statements that help implement the features.

In This Book

This book is organized to serve as an in-depth review for the OCP Oracle Database 11g: New Features for Administrators Exam for Oracle professionals who already are certified OCPs. Each chapter covers a major aspect of the exam; all the OCP official certification objectives are carefully covered in the book.

On the CD-ROM

The CD-ROM contains the entire contents of the book in electronic form, as well as two practice tests that simulate the real Oracle Database 11g OCP certification test. For more information on the CD-ROM, please see the appendix.

Exam Readiness Checklist

At the end of this introduction, you will find an Exam Readiness Checklist. I constructed this table to allow you to cross-reference the official exam objectives with the certification objectives as I present and cover them in this book. The checklist also allows you to gauge your level of expertise on each objective at the outset of your studies. This should allow you to check your progress and make sure you spend the time you need on more difficult or unfamiliar sections. I've provided a reference for each objective exactly as Oracle Corporation presents it, including the section of the study guide that covers that objective, as well as a chapter and page reference.

In Every Chapter

This book includes a set of chapter components that call your attention to important items, reinforce important points, and provide helpful exam-taking hints. Take a look at what you'll find in every chapter:

- **Exam Watch** notes call attention to information about, and potential pitfalls in, the exam. As I mentioned earlier, I took the new OCP exam and received my certification. I took the Beta exam in December, 2008—it had over 170 questions, so I know something about what you will go through!

- **Exercises** are interspersed throughout the chapters, and they allow you to get the hands-on experience you need in order to pass the exams. They help you master skills that are likely to be an area of focus on the exam. Don't just read through the exercises; they are hands-on practice that you should be comfortable completing. Learning by doing is an effective way to increase your competency with a product.

- **On the Job** notes describe the issues that come up most often in real-world settings. They provide a valuable perspective on certification- and product-related topics. They point out common mistakes and address questions that have arisen from on-the-job discussions and experience.

- **Inside the Exam** sections toward the end of each chapter are designed to anticipate what the exam will emphasize. I provide pointers regarding key topics to focus on, based on my own exam experience. You can get a leg up on how to respond to actual exam questions by focusing extra attention on the contents referred to in the Inside the Exam sections.

- The **Certification Summary** is a succinct review of the chapter and a restatement of salient points regarding the exam.

✓
- The **Two-Minute Drill** at the end of every chapter is a checklist of the main points of the chapter. You can use it for a quick, last-minute review before the test.

Q&A
- The **Self Test** offers questions similar to those found on the certification exam. The answers to these questions, as well as explanations of the answers, can be found at the end of each chapter. By taking the Self Test after completing each chapter, you'll reinforce what you've learned from that chapter, while becoming familiar with the structure of the exam questions.

- The **Lab Questions** at the end of the Self Test sections offer a unique and challenging question format that, in order to answer correctly, require the reader to understand multiple chapter concepts. These questions are more complex and more comprehensive than the other questions, as they test your ability to take all the knowledge you have gained from reading the chapter and apply it to complicated, real-world situations.

Some Pointers

Once you've finished reading this book, set aside some time to do a thorough review. You might want to return to the book several times and make use of all the methods it offers for reviewing the material:

- **Reread all the Two-Minute Drills or have someone quiz you.** You also can use the drills as a way to do a quick cram before the exam. You might want to make some flash cards out of 3 × 5 index cards that have the Two-Minute Drill material on them.

- **Reread all the Exam Watch notes.** Remember that these notes are based on the OCP exam that I took and passed. I've tried to draw your attention to what you should expect—and what you should be on the lookout for.

- **Retake the Self Tests.** It is a good idea to take the test right after you've read the chapter because the questions help reinforce what you've just learned. However, it's an even better idea to go back later and do all the questions in the book in one sitting. Pretend that you're taking the live exam. (When you go through the questions the first time, you should mark your answers on a separate piece of paper. That way, you can run through the questions as many times as you need to until you feel comfortable with the material.)

I personally wouldn't recommend taking the actual test until you're able to answer upwards of 95 percent of the Self Test questions correctly.

■ **Complete the Exercises.** Did you do the chapter Exercises and the Lab Questions when you read each chapter? If not, do them! These exercises are designed to cover exam topics, and there's no better way to get to know this material than by practicing. Be sure you understand why you are performing each step in each exercise. If there is something you are not completely clear about, reread that section in the chapter.

Test Structure

Because the exam for which I designed this book is an upgrade exam, all of the test takers will be OCP certification holders; you shouldn't dread the OCP test by any means. The new test follows on the lines of the old tests, and there are no changes to the style or format of the certification test. As in the older OCP tests, you'll have multiple choice questions only, with several questions having multiple correct answers.

The exam has 85 multiple-choice questions (time allowed is 105 minutes), and you need to answer at least 61 percent of the answers correctly to pass the test. The passing percentage translates to answering 52 out of the 85 questions correctly.

If you work your way through all eight chapters of this book, diligently completing the exercises and paying close attention to the Exam Watches and Inside the Exam sections, you shouldn't have any problem passing the exam with flying colors.

A word of caution regarding questions for which there are several correct choices. If you pick only part of the correct answers, you won't get credit for the answer, even if your pick is among the correct alternatives. Please be very careful that you picked all the possible choices when there are multiple correct choices.

How to Prepare for the Exam

You are holding in your hands the only tool you'll need to pass the OCP upgrade exam. You should read the chapters, preferably from the beginning to the end, and you must answer the end-of-chapter review questions correctly. However, most chapters can be read in any particular order. So if, for example, you are interested in RMAN new features, start with Chapter 7. Cover all eight chapters, in any order you wish, and that will ensure you're covering all the OCP official objectives.

I've covered every OCP certification objective carefully in this book. However, this is a test guide; therefore, I'm limited as to the length of discussion of any particular topic. I strongly recommend that you refer to the pertinent Oracle topics in Oracle's voluminous manuals (available at http://technet.oracle.com) for in-depth discussion of all the new topics.

OCP tests are rigorous, and you can't expect to certify by merely "brushing up" on the new features. You must really understand the new concepts, both from a theoretical standpoint and a practical one. OCP exam questions typically are divided into questions that test your knowledge of syntax and new commands, on the one hand, and those that test in-depth your understanding of how a particular new feature works in practice, on the other. Your basic strategy for questions that test your knowledge of Oracle syntax is simply to learn and remember the new commands and syntax. However, when it comes to preparing for the significant number of questions (often called *scenario-based* questions) that test your grip on *how* things work, there is no substitute to actually working out the Exercises and Lab Questions in this book. In addition, you should try practicing all the relevant commands shown in Oracle Corporation's manuals.

Use the Exam Readiness Checklist to guide you in your preparation for the exam. Check off each exam topic after you really understand how the command or feature works. You're ready to take the exam when you check off all the objectives on the checklist!

Good luck and have fun!

Exam IZ0-050 Readiness Checklist

OCP Official Objective	Certification Objective	Chapter	Page
Installation and Upgrade Enhancements			
Install Oracle Database 11g	Installing Oracle Database 11g	1	3
Upgrade your database to Oracle Database 11g	Upgrading to Oracle Database 11g	1	19
Oracle Direct NFS	Direct NFS Client	8	473
Use online patching	Hot Patching	8	462
Storage Enhancements			
Set up ASM fast mirror resync	ASM Fast Mirror Resync	5	265
Understand scalability and performance enhancements	ASM Scalability and Performance Enhancements	5	272
Set up ASM disk group attributes	Changing ASM Disk Group Attributes	5	279
Use various new manageability options	New Manageability Options for Commands	5	280
Use the md_backup, md_restore, and ASMCMD extensions	Enhancements in ASMCMD	5	283
Intelligent Infrastructure Enhancements			
Creating and using AWR baselines	Enhancements in AWR Baselines	3	148
Setting AWR baseline metric thresholds	Enhancements in AWR Baselines	3	148
Control automated maintenance tasks	Controlling Automated Maintenance Tasks	3	158
Using Database Resource Manager new features	Database Resource Manager New Features	3	167
Using new Scheduler features	Using New Oracle Scheduler Features	3	173
Performance Enhancements			
ADDM enhancements	ADDM Enhancements	6	322
Set up automatic memory management	Automatic Memory Management	6	328
Enhancements in statistics collection	Enhancements in Optimizer Statistics Collection	6	334
Partitioning and Storage-Related Enhancements			
Implement the new partitioning methods	Partitioning Enhancements	5	289
Employ data compression	OLTP Table Compression	8	472
SQL Access Advisor overview	SQL Access Advisor Enhancements	4	240

Exam 1Z0-050 Readiness Checklist

OCP Official Objective	Certification Objective	Chapter	Page
Create SQL Access Advisor analysis session using PL/SQL	SQL Access Advisor Enhancements	4	240
Using RMAN Enhancements			
Managing archive logs	Archived Redo Log Deletion Policy	7	403
Duplicating a database	Active (Network-Based) Database Duplication	7	384
Back up large files in multiple sections	Parallel Backup and Restore of Large Files	7	392
Perform archival backups	Archival (Long-Term) Backups	7	394
Using Flashback and LogMiner			
Overview of Flashback Data Archive	Flashback Data Archive	7	413
Manage Flashback Data Archive	Flashback Data Archive	7	413
Back-out transactions using Flashback Transaction	Flashback Transaction Backout	7	427
Working with LogMiner	Using LogMiner	8	476
Diagnosability Enhancements			
Set up automatic diagnostic repository	Automatic Diagnostic Repository	2	80
Use Support Workbench	Support Workbench	2	96
Run health checks	Health Monitor	2	105
Use SQL Repair Advisor	SQL Repair Advisor	2	110
Database Replay			
Overview of workload capture and replay	Database Replay	1	33
Using workload capture and replay	Database Replay	1	33
Using the Data Recovery Advisor			
Overview of Data Recovery Advisor	Data Recovery Advisor	2	115
Repairing data failures using Data Recovery Advisor	Using RMAN to Manage the Data Recovery Advisor	2	119
Perform proactive health check of the database	Running a Health Check	2	106
Security: New Features			
Configure the password file to use case-sensitive passwords	Security Enhancements	3	185

Exam 1Z0-050 Readiness Checklist

OCP Official Objective	Certification Objective	Chapter	Page
Encrypting a tablespace	Encrypting Tablespaces	3	194
Configure fine-grained access to network services	Security Enhancements	3	185
Oracle SecureFiles			
Use Secure File LOBs to store documents with compression, encryption, deduplication, caching	Creating SecureFiles	8	454
Use SQL and PL/SQL APIs to access Securefile LOBs	Oracle SecureFiles	8	450
Miscellaneous New Features			
Describe and use the enhanced online table redefinition	Minimal Invalidation of Dependent Objects	8	460
Enhanced finer-grained dependency management	Minimal Invalidation of Dependent Objects	8	460
Use enhanced DDL; apply the improved table lock mechanism	Locking Enhancements	8	458
Create invisible indexes	Invisible Indexes	8	463
Use Query Result Cache and PL/SQL Result Cache	Result Cache	6	347
Adaptive cursor sharing	Adaptive Cursor Sharing	6	362
Temporary tablespace enhancements	Shrinking Temporary Tablespaces	8	465
SQL Performance Analyzer			
Overview of SQL Performance Analyzer	The SQL Performance Analyzer	1	51
Using SQL Performance Analyzer	The SQL Performance Analyzer	1	51
SQL Plan Management			
SQL plan baseline architecture	SQL Plan Management	4	225
Set up SQL plan baseline	SQL Plan Management	4	225
Using SQL plan baseline	SQL Plan Management	4	225
Automatic SQL Tuning			
Set up and modify automatic SQL tuning	Automatic SQL Tuning Advisor	4	214
Interpret reports generated by Automatic SQL Tuning	Automatic SQL Tuning Advisor	4	214

1

Installing, Upgrading, and Change Management

CERTIFICATION OBJECTIVES

1.01   Installing Oracle Database 11g

1.02   New Features in Database Creation

1.03   Upgrading to Oracle Database 11g

1.04   Real Application Testing

✓   Two-Minute Drill

Q&A   Self Test

This chapter reviews the new installation features of the Oracle server software for Oracle Database 11g Release 1 (11.1). Although the installation process is essentially the same as in the previous release, I review the important enhancements. Several components are automatically installed now that were optional installations previously, and I'll review these components. The chapter then looks at changes in the database upgrade process. The new installation features include changes in the server install options, new installable components, and an enhanced optimal flexible architecture (OFA) for the flash recovery area and the datafiles. Some old components aren't available, and there are several new components that you can install with the database server software.

Of course, one of the most important things you may be planning to do is to upgrade your present database to the Oracle Database 11g release. This chapter will describe changes in the manual upgrade method as well as in the Database Upgrade Assistant (DBUA).

System changes, database version changes, and application upgrades often cause a considerable amount of uncertainty in organizations. Oracle has made effective change management a hallmark of the Oracle Database 11g release. Oracle provides an exciting new feature called Real Application Testing, which contains two powerful solutions, Database Replay and SQL Performance Analyzer. Together they can solve most of your change management problems by letting you test database performance and SQL query performance after a system change, including a database upgrade or an upgrade to a new release of the database.

Following are the topics I discuss in this chapter:

■ Installing Oracle Database 11g
■ New features in database creation
■ Database upgrade new features
■ Real Application Testing

Please refer to the Oracle Database 11g documentation for complete details on a particular feature. The main purpose of this book is to help you upgrade your OCP certification from Oracle Database 10g to Oracle Database 11g. (The complete name of the test required for upgrading your certification is "Oracle Database 11g: New Features for Administrators (Exam 1Z0-050).") Unless a database feature is completely new to Oracle Database 11g, I don't attempt to fully explain it in this book.

CERTIFICATION OBJECTIVE 1.01

Installing Oracle Database 11g

In this section, let's review the important changes in the installation of the Oracle Database 11g server software. These changes include changes in the optimal flexible architecture (OFA), changes in the installation options, new database components available during installation, and role and privilege changes. I'll also take you through an actual Oracle Database 11g server installation, to highlight the changes in the installation procedures in the new release.

Changes in the Optimal Flexible Architecture

Oracle Database 11g includes changes in how you specify important Oracle environmental variables such as the Oracle home and Oracle base, as well as the location of the flash recovery area. Oracle Database 11g introduces the new automatic diagnostic repository (ADR), which consolidates all database diagnostic data. You must create a separate directory for the ADR. You'll find a description of the ADR later in this chapter, and Chapter 2 contains a thorough discussion of the ADR as well as the new diagnostic framework introduced in this release.

In summary, the major changes made to the Oracle base to make it comply with OFA are as follows:

- ORACLE_BASE is a recommended environment variable and will be mandatory in future releases.
- You must *not* create an Oracle Clusterware home under the Oracle base. During an Oracle Clusterware installation, the Oracle base and the Oracle Clusterware home are at the same directory level.
- Oracle recommends creating the flash recovery area and the datafiles under the Oracle base.
- Oracle recommends that you keep the flash recovery area and the datafiles on separate disks.

Oracle Base Location   The Oracle Installer now provides a list box for you to select or edit the recommended Oracle base location. The Oracle base directory is the starting point for the installation of Oracle software. The recommended path for the Oracle base is /*mount_point*/app/*oracle_software_owner*. If the mount point is /u01 and the Oracle software owner is oracle, for example, the recommended Oracle base location will be /u01/app/oracle.

The Oracle base environmental variable is only a recommended and not a mandatory variable, but Oracle might make it a mandatory variable in a future release. The Oracle home directory is where you install the Oracle binaries. The Oracle Universal Installer will derive the Oracle home location from the Oracle base location you choose.

on the job

Oracle recommends that you use the same Oracle base for multiple Oracle homes created by a user.

Oracle logs the Oracle base location you provide during the installation in its inventory. You can share a single Oracle base location among all the Oracle homes you create on a server. If you don't set an Oracle base location, you'll see warnings in the alert log.

Datafile and Flash Recovery Area Locations   In Oracle Database 10g, by default, the flash recovery area and the datafiles were placed one level above the Oracle home directory. Depending on your storage and backup strategies, this posed some problems in some installations. In Oracle Database 11g, the starting point for both the flash recovery area and the datafiles is the Oracle base. Oracle recommends that you place the flash recovery area on different disks from those you assign to the datafiles. Assuming your Oracle base location is /u01/app/oracle, the datafiles and the flash recovery area would have the following locations:

```
/u01/app/oracle/oradata
/u01/app/oracle/flash_recovery_area
```

on the job

In Oracle Database 11g, the Oracle Universal Installer tries to install its inventory one level beneath the Oracle base ($ORACLE_BASE/..). You must, therefore, ensure that the $ORACLE_BASE/.. directory is writable by the user installing the Oracle software. Of course, if you have installed Oracle software from an earlier release, the installer will use the pre-existing Oracle inventory.

You'll receive a warning from the Oracle Universal Installer if you try to place the datafiles and the flash recovery area in the same location.

Automatic Diagnostic Repository

Oracle Database 11g offers a new automatic diagnostic repository (ADR), which provides a single directory location for all the diagnostic data needed for diagnosing and repairing database problems. The ADR uses standard methods to store diagnostic data for the database as well as other Oracle products. Various automatic diagnostic tools then use this diagnostic data to quickly diagnose and resolve problems. The ADR also provides a consolidated location for the collection of all diagnostic data you want to send to Oracle Support for diagnosing and resolving problems.

You specify the ADR directory location by providing the directory location as the value for the `diagnostic_dest` initialization parameter. Using the ADR isn't mandatory, and specifying the `diagnostic_dest` parameter means that the traditional diagnostic directories such as bdump, cdump, and udump are redundant.

The ADR contains several subdirectories such as alert and cdump, where the traditional diagnostic data as well as new types of diagnostic data are stored. You have two versions of the alert log in Oracle Database 11g, one a regular text file and the other an XML-formatted file. You can read the alert log using a normal text editor, the Enterprise Manager, or the new ADRCI tool, which lets you perform a variety of tasks pertaining to problem diagnosis.

You must provide the Oracle Universal Installer a directory location for the ADR base if you want to use the ADR. The ADR base is the root directory for the ADR, under which various "ADR homes" live. Oracle recommends that you choose the same ADR base for all Oracle products in order to consolidate diagnostic data.

The Oracle Universal Installer will set the ADR's base directory to the Oracle base location by default. You can set an alternate location for the ADR base directory by setting a value for the `diagnostic_dest` initialization parameter. The default ADR base directory is then of the form $ORACLE_BASE. Under this directory, there is a directory named rdbms, which contains all diagnostic files for Oracle databases on that server. In the rdbms directory, the diagnostic files for each database are organized by the database name and instance name. For example, if the Oracle base is /u01/app/oracle and the database name and the instance name are both orcl2, the subdirectories such as alert and trace are located in the following directory:

```
/u01/app/oracle/diag/rdbms/orcl2/orcl2
```

Chapter 2 discusses the new fault diagnosability infrastructure in detail.

exam

Watch *Understand the changes made with regard to the ORACLE_BASE environment variable to make it compliant with the Oracle Flexible Architecture.*

Changes in the Installation Options

Following are the important changes in the server installation options in Oracle Database 11g.

- The Oracle Configuration Manager, which gathers software configuration information, is integrated with the Oracle Universal Installer as an optional component. The Oracle Configuration Manager was previously called the Customer Configuration Repository (CCR).
- The Oracle Data Mining option is chosen by default when you install the Enterprise Edition; the catproc.sql script that you run after creating a new database will automatically install this option.
- The Oracle XML DB option isn't an optional component in the new release. The Database Configuration Assistant will install and configure this option for you. If you're creating a database manually, the catproc.sql script will create the XML DB automatically.
- Oracle Database Vault is an optional component when you select the Custom Installation option.

The following components aren't part of the Oracle Database 11g installation (but were part of the Oracle Database 10g release 2):

- iSQL*Plus
- Oracle Workflow
- Oracle Enterprise Manager Java Console
- Oracle Data Mining Scoring Engine
- Raw storage support for datafiles (installer only)

The following features are deprecated, although they are retained for backward compatibility:

- Oracle Ultra Search
- Java Development Kit (JDK) 1.4
- CTXXPATH index

Oracle recommends that you migrate from the components listed here. For the JDK, Oracle recommends using JDK 5.0. Instead of CTXXPATH index, Oracle recommends using XMLIndex.

New Database Components

You have the following new components in Oracle Database 11g server installation, some of which are optional; the others are automatically installed by the Oracle Universal Installer:

- **Oracle Application Express (APEX)**   Oracle's browser-based rapid application development tool, known earlier as Oracle HTML DB, now contains prepackaged applications for blogs, storefronts, and discussion forums, in addition to new reporting capabilities and support for drag-and-drop forms layout. APEX is now installed with Oracle database 11g as part of the base Oracle installation CD instead of the companion CD.

- **Oracle SQL Developer**   Oracle's free database development productivity tool, SQL Developer, is installed automatically when you choose a template-based database installation by selecting an installation option such as General Purpose/Transaction Processing and Data Warehousing. SQL Developer contains new tuning enhancements such as database activity reporting and expanded support for version control and visual query building.

- **Oracle Real Application Testing**   This new component, which consists of two new features—Database Replay and SQL Performance Analyzer—is automatically installed when you select the Enterprise Edition installation option.

- **Oracle Configuration Manager (OCM)**   This is an optional component. The OCM gathers software configuration information and uploads it to the Oracle configuration repository.

- **Oracle Warehouse Builder**   This tool is installed as part of the Oracle Database server software.

- **Oracle Database Vault**   This tool is now installed with the Oracle Database 11g, *but* as an optional component, instead of as a component of the companion CD. The Oracle Database Vault installation provides a baseline security policy for the database. When you install the Oracle Database Vault, all security-related initialization parameters are assigned default values.

Role and Privilege Changes

Oracle Database 11g seeks to demarcate database administration and ASM administration. Oracle now recommends that you create an optional operating system–level group for the users who'll manage automatic storage management

(ASM). You can do this during the installation or later on. Oracle also recommends that you assign a new ASM-related system privilege for ASM administrators. Even if you are performing both regular DBA chores as well as the ASM tasks in your organization, it may be a good idea to formally separate the two types of tasks, so it's easy to remember which environment you're operating in.

Oracle Database 11g introduces the new operating system OS group named OSASM, exclusively for users who'll manage ASM. Oracle recommends that you grant ASM access only to users who are members of the OSASM group.

There is also a new ASM-related system privilege called SYSASM, which Oracle recommends that you grant to those users who perform ASM administrative tasks. For example, a user who needs to create an ASM instance must have the SYSASM privilege. This means that you must not assign the SYSDBA privileges for users who perform only ASM-related tasks and not general database administration.

The OSASM operating system group and the SYSASM system privilege are purely optional in this release. However, Oracle may make them mandatory in a future release by requiring that users not belonging to the OSASM group be denied access to ASM and by requiring ASM administrators to have the SYSASM system privilege.

An Oracle Database 11g Installation

There are no major innovations in the installation process itself in Oracle Database 11g, although there are a few changes during the installation, which I'll point out in this section. Whether you're installing from the DVD or from the downloaded Oracle software files, you'll start the installation by executing the runInstaller script as usual. To start the installation, invoke the Oracle Universal Installer by moving to the directory where the runInstaller script is located and typing in the following:

```
$ ./runInstaller
```

If you're installing from a DVD, invoke the Oracle Universal Installer by supplying the full path for the database directory:

```
$ /<directory_path>/runInstaller
```

You're ready to start the installation of the Oracle software once the Oracle Universal Installer confirms that the server passes all the requirements regarding space, operating system patches, and so on. Here are the steps in the installation of Oracle Database 11g:

1. On the Select Installation Method page, Select Advanced Installation and click Next.

2. On the Select Installation Type page, choose Enterprise Edition and click Next.

3. On the Install Location page, specify the path for the Oracle base and Oracle home locations and click Next.

4. On the Product-Specific Prerequisite Checks page, the Oracle Universal Installer verifies that your system meets the minimum requirements for installation. Click Next.

5. On the Select Configuration Option page, choose Install Software Only and click Next.

6. On the Privileged Operating System Groups page, which is new in Oracle Database 11g, Oracle prompts you to create the optional new system privilege called SYSASM for managing ASM and the new UNIX/Linux group called OSASM for ASM administrators. Figure 1-1 shows the Privileged Operating System Groups page.

FIGURE 1-1   The Privileged Operating System Groups page

Privileged Operating System Groups

SYSDBA and SYSOPER privileges are required to create a database using operating system (OS) authentication. SYSASM privileges are required to create an Automatic Storage Management (ASM) instance or cluster using OS authentication. These are granted through membership in the UNIX groups OSDBA, OSOPER and OSASM respectively. The 'dba', 'oper', and 'asmadmin' groups are usually used for this purpose. If you would like another group used, select the name of the UNIX group of which you are a member, to be used for OSDBA, OSOPER and OSASM.

Database Administrator (OSDBA) Group: `dba`

Database Operator (OSOPER) Group: `oper`

ASM administrator (OSASM) Group: `oinstall`

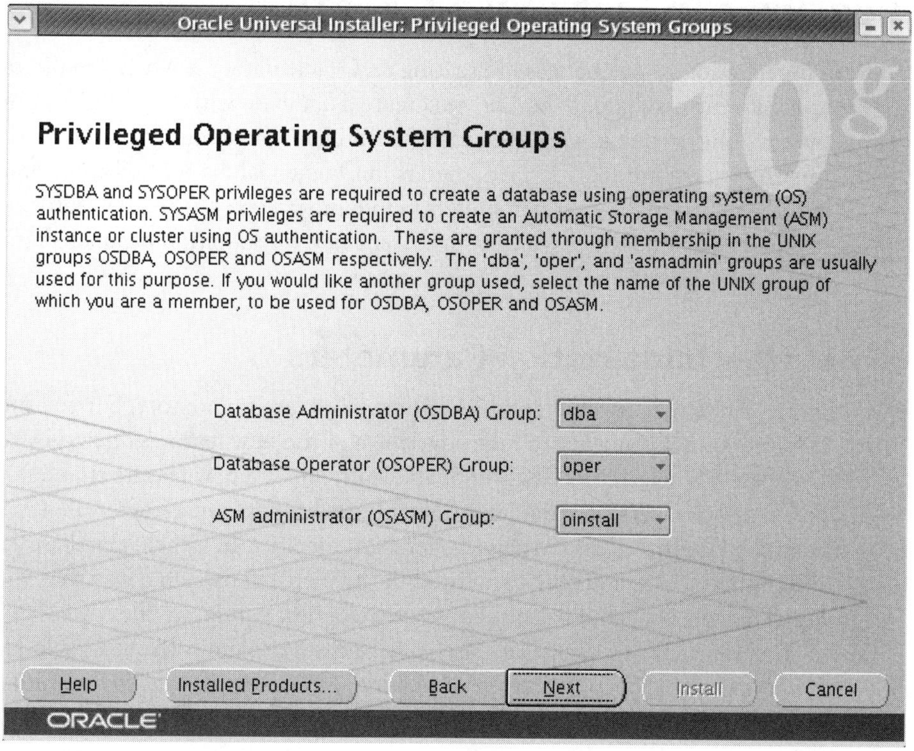

7. On the Summary page, click Next after reviewing the summary.

8. On the Install page, once the installation completes successfully, exit the Oracle Universal Installer by first clicking Exit and then clicking Yes.

If you choose to create a new database during installation itself by choosing the Create a Database option in Step 5, you can select new Oracle Database 11g features such as automatic memory management. You'll also get to configure the Oracle Configuration Manager if you choose to create a starter database during the installation. Oracle Configuration Manager gathers configuration information so you can link your Oracle Support service requests in MetaLink with the configuration information. Chapter 2 shows how the Configuration Manager can facilitate the transmission of configuration information to Oracle Support.

CERTIFICATION OBJECTIVE 1.02

New Features in Database Creation

There are some key changes in creating an Oracle database when you use the DBCA to create the database. Whether you create a database with the DBCA or manually by using the `create database` SQL statement, you must be aware of the important new initialization parameters in Oracle Database 11g. I thus summarize the key new initialization parameters before moving on to the new features in database creation. I discuss all the important new initialization parameters in more detail subsequently, in the relevant chapters.

Summary of New Initialization Parameters

None of the new parameters that I discuss here are mandatory, but you must use most of them if you want to take advantage of the new features offered by the Oracle Database 11g release. In Chapter 8, you learn about a new feature that lets you create an initialization parameter file (init.ora) or server parameter file (SPFILE) from the current values of the parameters in memory. In Oracle Database 11g, the initialization parameters are listed in the alert log in such a way that you can conveniently copy and paste them to create a new parameter file.

Your Oracle9i or Oracle Database 10g databases can run with the Oracle 11g software (after upgrading, of course) without making significant changes to the initialization parameters. You must set the value of the initialization parameter `compatible` to at least 10.0.0 before the upgrade to the new oracle Database 11g release. The default value for the compatible parameter is 11.1.0 and the maximum value is 11.1.0.n.n. The following review of the important initialization parameters provides a quick overview, and I discuss these in the relevant portions of the book in greater detail:

- Two new memory-related parameters—memory_target and memory_max_target—provide support for the new automatic memory management feature, discussed in Chapter 6.

- The plsql_code_type parameter lets you turn on PL/SQL native compilation, as explained in Chapter 8.

- The diagnostic_dest parameter lets you set the ADR base directory. This parameter replaces the traditional background_dump_dest, user_dump_dest, and core_dump_dest parameters. The diagnostic_dest parameter's value defaults to $ORACLE_BASE. The diagnostic_dest parameter is recommended but not mandatory. If you do set this parameter, the database will ignore any *_dump_dest parameters you may have set.

- The result_cache_mode parameter supports result caching, a major new feature. In addition to the result_cache_mode parameter, you have other result cache–related initialization parameters, such as the result_cache_max_result, result_cache_max_size, and result_cache_remote_expiration parameters. The new parameters client_result_cache_size and client_result_cache_lag support the new client-side result caching feature. Both server-side and client-side result caching are discussed in Chapter 4.

- The ddl_time_lockout parameter enables you to control the duration for which a DDL statement will wait for a DML lock. Chapter 8 describes the new capability to control the length of time a DDL statement will wait for a necessary DML lock.

- The db_securefile parameter enables you to specify whether to treat a LOB file as a traditional Oracle LOB or the new Oracle SecureFiles format. Oracle SecureFiles is a new Oracle Database 11g feature that offers a more efficient approach to storing file content such as images, audio, video, PDFs, and spreadsheets. Chapter 8 discusses the Oracle SecureFiles feature.

- The db_ultra_safe parameter enables you to control three corruption-checking parameters—db_block_checking, db_block_checksum, and db_lost_write_protect.

- The `sec_case_sensitive_logon` parameter lets you manage the enabling and disabling of password case sensitivity in the database. By default, Oracle Database 11g enforces password case sensitivity.

- The parameter `sec_max_failed_login_attempts` enables you to specify the maximum number of times a client can make a connection attempt. Chapter 3 explains how to use the `sec_max_failed_login_attempts` parameter.

- The parameters `optimizer_capture_sql_plan_baselines` and `optimizer_use_sql_baselines` support the SQL Plan Management feature, which replaces the stored outlines feature. The parameter `optimizer_use_private_statistics` enables you to create private optimizer statistics. Another optimizer-related new initialization parameter, `optimizer_use_invisible_indexes`, enables you to manage invisible indexes, as discussed in Chapter 8.

- The new parameter `control_management_pack_access` determines which Server Manageability Pack can be active in the database. You can choose to activate either or both of these management packs:

  - Diagnostic pack, which includes the AWR, ADDM, and other diagnostic tools.
  - Tuning pack, which includes the SQL Tuning Advisor, the SQL Access Advisor, and related tools.

You must have a license for the diagnostic pack in order to use the tuning pack. The possible values for the `control_management_pack_access` parameter are NONE, DIAGNOSTIC, and DIAGNOSTIC+TUNING. The last value is the default value for this parameter.

DBCA Enhancements

The Database Configuration Assistant (DBCA) includes several enhancements in Oracle Database 11g. I summarize the main changes to the DBCA in the following sections.

New Database Configuration Options

Oracle Database 11g contains quite a few changes in configuring databases through the DBCA. These include the configuration of the new automatic memory management feature, secure database configuration by default, and others. Following is a review of the important database configuration options in the new release.

Automatic Memory Management The DBCA doesn't specify values for the memory-related initialization parameters `sga_target` and `pga_aggregate_target` by default. Instead, it uses the `memory_target` parameter, which allows you to configure the new automatic memory management feature. You select automatic memory management in the Memory Management page, as you'll see later in the DBCA database creation example.

Automatic Secure Configuration The DBCA will configure a secure database by default in Oracle Database 11g. If you want, you can even configure this later on, but Oracle recommends that you opt for automatic secure configuration when you create the database.

Automatic switching to Grid Control In previous releases, it took quite a bit of work to reconfigure a database from Database Control to Grid Control. In Oracle Database 11g, you can use the Enterprise Manager plug-in provided by the DBCA to automate the switching of a database from Database Control to Grid Control.

Configuration of Oracle Base and Diagnostic Destination

DBCA now uses the values for the Oracle base directory, stored in the Oracle home inventory, to derive the default locations for datafiles and the `diagnostic_dest` initialization parameter, which is the ADR base directory.

on the
job

The initialization parameter `diagnostic_dest` replaces the traditional parameters used for setting the background dump, user dump, and core dump destinations.

Using the DBCA to Create a Database

There are a couple of new features to be aware of when using the DBCA to create an Oracle Database 11g release database. The changes concern security settings and the new automatic memory management feature.

Here are the steps to follow in order to create a new database with the DBCA. I'll emphasize the changes in the database creation process. First, invoke the DBCA by typing in *dbca* after setting your environment variables to point to the Oracle Database 11g binaries.

1. On the DBCA Operations page, select the Create a Database option.
2. On the Database Templates page, select one of the following database types: Data Warehouse, General Purpose, or Transaction Processing.

3. On the Database Identification page, select the database name and the system identifier (SID).

4. On the Management Options page, select Database Control.

5. On the Database Credential page, specify passwords for database accounts such as SYS and SYSTEM.

6. On the Security Settings page (shown in Figure 1-2), you must choose the security settings for the database you'll be creating. In Oracle Database 11g, the DBCA provides secure database configuration by default. You have the option of turning off this default security configuration if you want. The secure database configuration applies to the following entities:

   - Audit settings
   - Password profiles
   - Revoking grants to the public role

FIGURE 1-2   DBCA's Security Settings page

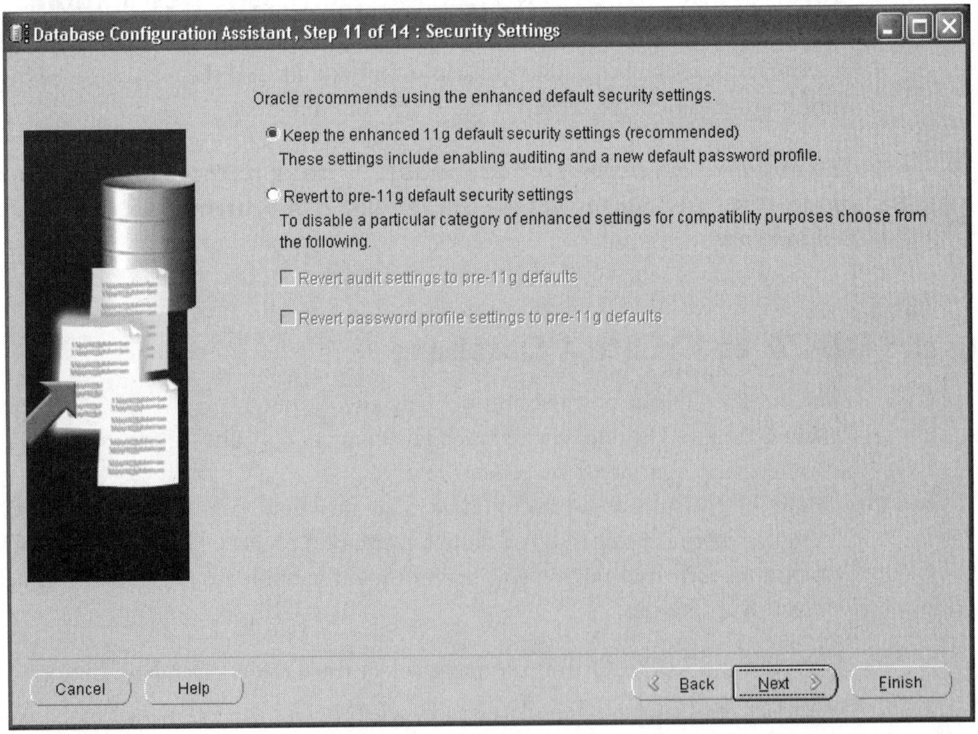

7. On the Network Configuration page, you are offered a choice of listeners for the new database. Select the listener or listeners for which you want to register the database. This is also new in Oracle Database 11g. Figure 1-3 shows the new Network Configuration page.

8. On the Storage options page, select the storage mechanism you want to use for the new database, such as automatic storage management or file system–based storage.

9. On the Database File Locations page, specify the Oracle software home and the directory for the database files. You can also select the Oracle-Managed Files (OMF) option.

10. On the Recovery Configuration page, choose archivelog or noarchivelog mode as well as the flash recovery area location.

FIGURE 1-3   DBCA's new Network Configuration page

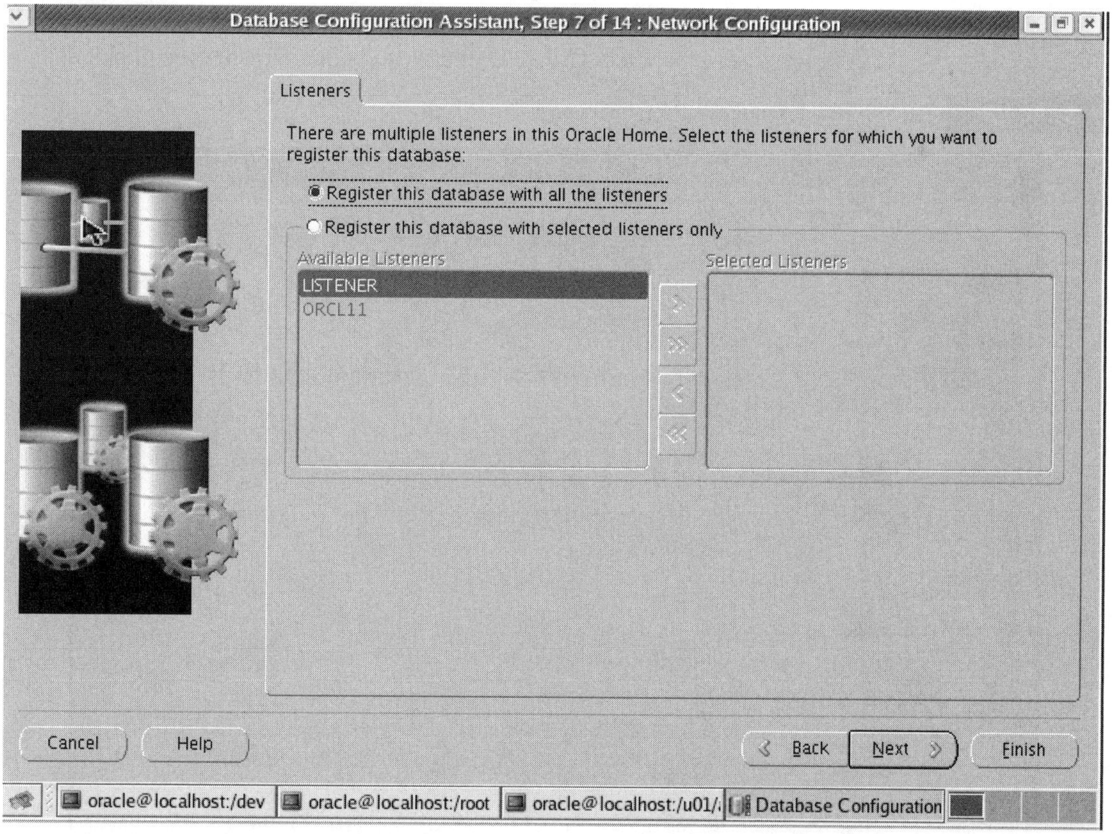

11. On the Database Content page, specify the sample schemas and custom scripts you want the DBCA to run after database creation.

12. On the Initialization Parameters page (shown in Figure 1-4), you can either accept the default settings for various initialization parameters such as memory and character sets, or provide different values for the parameters. You have a choice of three types of memory allocation—automatic memory management (new in Oracle Database 11g), automatic shared memory management, or manual memory management. Note that automatic memory management is a new feature introduced in Oracle Database 11g, so this page in DBCA is different from the one from previous releases. (This option has been modified in Oracle Database 11g.)

13. On the Database Storage page, make changes in the storage structure of the database.

14. On the Database Creation Options page, you can choose from three options: Create Database, Save As a Database Template, or Generate Database Creation Scripts. Select Create Database and click Finish; then click OK.

FIGURE 1-4	DBCA's new Initialization Parameters page

When you're on the Security Setting page (Step 6), you don't have to choose the new Secure Configure option during the creation of the database, but Oracle strongly recommends that you do so. Choosing the Secure Configure option at this point means you choose to use the new default enhanced security settings for the newly created database. If you disable the default security settings by checking the Disable Security Settings box, you can always configure the Secure Configuration option later on by using the DBCA again. If you disable the default enhanced security settings, DBCA will create the database with the default security options for Oracle Database 10g Release 2.

During the creation of a new database, Oracle recommends that you enable the default security settings offered through the Security Settings window. These default security settings mainly affect two areas of security: password and auditing. Let's examine how the default security settings regarding password management and auditing work.

A profile, as you are aware, is a set of parameters that specifies a limit on a user's use of various types of resources in the database. A key resource in a user's profile is the password resource, and here are the password-specific default security settings you can enable when you're creating a new Oracle database, by configuring the password settings in the default profile:

- **FAILED_LOGIN_ATTEMPTS** Specifies the maximum number of times a user can try to log in. The default value for this parameter is 10, which is the same as in the previous release.

- **PASSWORD_GRACE_TIME** Specifies the number of days within which users must change their password before it expires. The default value for this setting is 7 days, whereas it was unlimited before.

- **PASSWORD_LIFE_TIME** Sets the duration for which users can use the same password. This is set to 180 days by default, whereas it was unlimited before.

- **PASSWORD_LOCK_TIME** Sets the number of days for which an account will remain locked after a set number of failed attempts to log in. The default value is 1, compared to unlimited in the previous release.

- **PASSWORD_REUSE_MAX** Sets the number of days that must pass before you can reuse a password after it expires. The default value is set to unlimited, the same value as before.

- **PASSWORD_REUSE_TIME** Sets the number of new passwords you must use before you are permitted to reuse the current password. By default, there is no limit on the number of times you can reuse a password.

on the **Job**

If you don't enable the default password-specific settings when you create the database, you can always enable or modify the settings later on by using the `create profile` ***or*** `alter profile` ***SQL statement.***

Note that in Oracle Database 11g, the following resources are much more restricted:

■ PASSWORD_GRACE_TIME is now 7 days by default, instead of being unlimited.

■ PASSWORD_LIFE_TIME is set by default to 180 days, instead of being unlimited.

■ PASSWORD_LOCK_TIME is 1 day, instead of being set to the value of DEFAULT as in the Oracle Database 10g release.

on the **Job**

If you install Oracle Database Vault, you can't change the Secure Configuration option using DBCA.

If you choose to accept the default security settings, Oracle will set the `audit_trail` initialization parameter to `db` and automatically audit security-relevant SQL statements and privileges. The database will audit all privileges and statements `by access` in a SQL statement. Here are some of the privileges the database will audit by default when you choose the default security settings:

■ alter any procedure, alter any table, alter database

■ create any procedure, create any job, create external job, create public database link, create user, create session

■ drop any table, drop user, drop any procedure

■ alter system, alter user, audit system, audit system by access, audit role by access

■ grant any privilege, grant any role

Oracle strongly supports auditing by default, for security reasons as well to comply with requirements specified by laws such as the Sarbanes-Oxley Act. Depending on the types of applications your database supports, the audit-related default security settings may not be appropriate for you. If this is true, simply choose the Oracle 10g Release 10.2 settings for auditing, which will disable the default auditing. Because the default audit settings may impose a server performance overhead in some organizations, you may have to decide if the default security settings are appropriate for you.

When you're on the Initialization Parameters page, you can choose the type of memory management for the new database you're creating. The choice of *Typical* means you don't have to configure anything really. The DBCA will create a database with minimal configuration or use the amounts of memory you input on this page. Oracle believes that for the less experienced DBA, this option is plenty. If the DBA enters a value in the PERCENTAGE field, Oracle will allocate the most efficient amount of memory based as a percentage of the total available system memory.

Choosing the Custom option means you have to provide configuration values for memory, but this also means that you can exert more control over how the database uses the system memory. By selecting the *Typical* option, you can let Oracle automatically tune both SCA and PGA with the new Oracle Database 11g memory allocation method called `automatic memory management`. Oracle also determines the memory to be allocated to the new instance, based on the amount of memory available with the operating system.

Choosing the *Custom* option means that you get to select both the amount of memory to allocate to the new instance, as well as the type of memory allocation, which can be one of the following:

- Automatic memory management (new in Oracle Database 11g)
- Automatic shared memory management
- Manual shared memory management

In order to choose automatic memory management, you must first select the *Typical* option and then select the Use Automatic Memory Management option. You can change the amount of memory allocated to Oracle later on by specifying the new initialization parameters `memory_target` and `memory_max_target`.

CERTIFICATION OBJECTIVE 1.03

Upgrading to Oracle Database 11g

There are a few changes in the database upgrade process in Oracle Database 11g, which I summarize in the following sections.

Moving Data as Part of the Upgrade

You can now move datafiles to ASM, OFS, SAN, and NAS during the upgrade to the 11g release. You can not only avoid downtime, but also rebalance disks and move datafiles to more efficient storage devices.

New Privileges for Storage Management

Oracle Database 11g introduces a new system privilege called SYSASM, for performing ASM administration tasks. Although you can still perform these tasks using the SYSDBA system privilege, Oracle recommends that you use the new SYSASM privilege instead for performing ASM-related tasks. Although using the SYSASM privilege is optional, Oracle wants to separate database administration and ASM administration, and intends to require the use of the SYSASM privilege in future releases. The SYSASM privilege enables you to separate the SYSDBA database administration privilege from the ASM storage administration privilege.

Oracle Database 11g also introduces a new optional operating system group called OSASM, for the ASM administrators. You create the OSASM group in addition to the normal dba and oper operating system groups before installing Oracle. Again, creating and using the OSASM group is purely optional, but the OSASM group will most likely be mandatory in a future release. You can grant a user access to the SYSASM privilege by granting the user membership in the new OSASM operating system group. When you install ASM, you can divide system privileges so that DBAs, storage administrators, and database operators each have a distinct operating system privilege group. The following are the different operating system authentication groups for ASM and the privileges that the members of each group are granted:

- **OSASM**   SYSASM privilege, which provides full administrative privileges for administering an ASM instance.
- **OSDBA for ASM**   SYSDBA privilege on the ASM instance. The privilege grants access to data stored on ASM as well as the SYSASM administrative privileges.
- **OSOPER for ASM**   SYSOPER privilege on the ASM instance.

Regardless of whether you create separate operating system groups or provide operating system authentication for all system privilege through a single group, you must use the SYSASM privilege to manage an ASM instance. If you use the SYSDBA privilege for managing an ASM instance, Oracle will place warnings in the alert log. In future releases, Oracle plans to remove the ability to administer an ASM instance with the SYSDBA privilege.

Upgrading to Oracle Database 11g

Oracle Database 11g uses similar pre-upgrade and post-upgrade scripts as the Oracle Database 10g release. However, the pre-upgrade checks are more refined and there is also simpler error management. The database upgrade process is, on the whole, faster than in Oracle Database 10*g*.

Enhancements in the Upgrade Process

Oracle Database 11*g* provides the following enhancements to the database upgrade process.

- There are improvements to the Pre-Upgrade Information Tool in statistics gathering, space estimation, initialization parameters, and warnings.
- For both major releases and patch upgrades, use the catupgrd.sql script for the upgrades and the catdwdgrd.sql script for downgrades.
- The Post-Upgrade Status Tool collects and displays errors for each component as it is being upgraded.
- The DBUA automatically performs parallel object recompilation for multi-CPU systems.

The Compatibility Factor

One of the things you must pay close attention to before upgrading your pre–Oracle Database 11*g* databases is the database compatibility issue. If you don't set a value for the initialization parameter `compatible`, it defaults to 11.1.0. However, Oracle recommends that you set the value of the `compatible` parameter to 10.0.0, which is the minimum allowable for upgrading to Oracle Database 11*g*. The reason for doing this is that in the unlikely event that your upgrade process is messed up, your database still remains compatible with the previous release. Of course, you must change the compatibility setting to 11.1 after the upgrade process completes successfully, so you can take advantage of all the nice new features in the Oracle Database 11*g* release. Once you set the compatibility level to 11.1 and restart the database, you must be aware that you can't downgrade to the older release. You must restore the backups of the pre-upgrade database instead.

After you complete upgrading a database to the Oracle Database 11*g* release and are thinking about changing the compatibility level to 11.1 (`compatible=11.1.0`, for example), first back up the database. Then, make the following change to the current SPFILE:

```
SQL> alter system set compatible ='11.1.0' scope=spfile;
```

Once you change the compatible parameter's value to 11.1 or higher and restart the database, you can't go back to the older release without restoring the pre-upgrade backup of the database.

The Upgrade Path to Oracle 11g

Depending on your current database release, you may or may not be able to directly upgrade to the Oracle Database 11g Release 1 (11.1) version. You can directly upgrade to Oracle Database Release 1 if your current database is based on an Oracle 9.2.0.4 or newer release. For Oracle database releases older than Oracle 9.2.0.4, you have to migrate via one or two intermediate releases, as shown by the following upgrade paths:

- 7.3.3 (or lower) => 7.3.4 => 9.2.0.8 => 11.1
- 8.0.5 (or lower) => 8.0.6 => 9.2.0.8 => 11.1
- 8.1.7 (or lower) => 8.1.7.4 => 9.2.0.8 => 11.1
- 9.0.1.3 (or lower) => 9.0.1.4 => 9.2.0.8 => 11.1
- 9.2.0.3 (or lower) => 9.2.0.8 => 11.1

For example, if you want to upgrade a database from the 8.1.6 release, the following would be your game plan: upgrade release 8.1.6 to 8.1.7; upgrade 8.1.7 to release 9.2.0.8; upgrade release 9.2.0.8 to release 11.1

Upgrading to Oracle Database 11g

You can upgrade to Oracle Database 11g with the Oracle-provided upgrade scripts or with the help of the DBUA. Of course, for smaller databases, you can also use the Data Pump export and import utilities to migrate the database to the new release. As far as the Oracle clients are concerned, you can upgrade an Oracle 8i, Oracle 9i, or Oracle Database 10g client to the Oracle 11.1 release. You can use the Oracle 11.1 client to access an Oracle 8i, Oracle 9i, Oracle Database 10g, and Oracle Database 11g (11.1) database.

Let's first look at the manual upgrade process using Oracle-supplied upgrade scripts. Then, we'll review the upgrade process using the DBUA.

Upgrading Using the Manual Method   You use Oracle-supplied pre- and post-upgrade scripts to upgrade to Oracle Database 11g. You can find all these scripts in the $ORACLE_HOME/rdbms/admin directory. There is a different set of upgrade scripts you must use, depending on the release number of the database you're upgrading from. In this example, I'm upgrading from an Oracle Database 10g release database to Oracle Database 11g and would need to use the scripts utlu111i.sql, catupgrd.sql,utlu111s.sql, catuppst.sql, and utlrp.sql to perform the manual upgrade. Following is a summary of the functions performed by each of the upgrade scripts:

- **utlu111i.sql**   This script, also known as the Pre-Upgrade Information Tool, gathers information from the database and analyzes it to make sure that it meets all the upgrade requirements, such as whether the database already contains the SYSAUX tablespace or not. As you know, a pre–Oracle Database 10*g* database doesn't have a SYSAUX tablespace; therefore, the Pre-Upgrade Information Tool would recommend that you create the SYSAUX tablespace to meet the requirements for the upgrade. The Pre-Upgrade Information Tool will issue warnings about potential upgrade issues such as database version and compatibility, redo log size, initialization parameters, and tablespace size estimates, and generates warnings if your database doesn't satisfy the requirements for upgrading to Oracle Database 11*g*.

- **catupgrd.sql** This is the script that performs the actual upgrading of the database to the Oracle Database 11*g* release and it now supports parallel upgrades of the database.

- **utlu111s.sql** This is the Upgrade Status Utility script which lets you check the status of the upgrade—that is, whether the upgraded database's components have a valid status.

- **catuppst.sql** This is the script you run to perform post-upgrade actions. This is new in Oracle Database 11*g* Release 1.

- **utlrp.sql** This script recompiles and revalidates any remaining application objects.

Because our pre-upgrade database is newer than the Oracle 9.2.0.4 release, you can directly upgrade to the Oracle Database release. Before you start the upgrade itself, run the Pre-Upgrade Information Tool by executing the Oracle supplied script utlu111i.sql. Copy the utlu111.i sql file from the $ORACLE_HOME/rdbms/admin directory to a staging directory such as /u01/app/oracle/upgrade. Log in as the owner of the Oracle home directory of the older release and run the utlu111.i sql script (from the /u01/app/oracle/upgrade directory). Spool the results so you can review the output. Here's an example showing the output of an execution of the utlu111i.sql script on my system:

```
SQL> spool upgrade.log
SQL> @utlu111i.sql
Oracle Database 11.1 Pre-Upgrade Information Tool
01-30-2008 05:33:22
**********************************************************
Database:
**********************************************************
--> name:          ORCL10
--> version:       10.2.0.1.0
--> compatible:    10.2.0.1.0
--> blocksize:     8192
--> platform:      Linux IA (32-bit)
```

```
--> timezone file: V2
.
.
**********************************************************
Tablespaces: [make adjustments in the current environment]
***********************************************************
--> SYSTEM tablespace is adequate for the upgrade.
.... minimum required size: 723 MB
.... AUTOEXTEND additional space required: 243 MB
--> UNDOTBS1 tablespace is adequate for the upgrade.
.... minimum required size: 471 MB
.... AUTOEXTEND additional space required: 441 MB
--> SYSAUX tablespace is adequate for the upgrade.
.... minimum required size: 412 MB
.:.. AUTOEXTEND additional space required: 182 MB
--> TEMP tablespace is adequate for the upgrade.
.... minimum required size: 61 MB
.... AUTOEXTEND additional space required: 41 MB
--> EXAMPLE tablespace is adequate for the upgrade.
.... minimum required size: 69 MB
.
.
***********************************************************
Update Parameters: [Update Oracle Database 11.1
init.ora or spfile]
***********************************************************
WARNING: --> "sga_target" needs to be increased to at
least 336 MB
.
.
***********************************************************
Renamed Parameters: [Update Oracle Database 11.1
 init.ora or spfile]
***********************************************************
-- No renamed parameters found. No changes are required.
.
.
***********************************************************
Obsolete/Deprecated Parameters: [Update Oracle Database
 11.1 init.ora or spfile]
***********************************************************
--> "background_dump_dest" replaced by  "diagnostic_dest"
--> "user_dump_dest" replaced by  "diagnostic_dest"
--> "core_dump_dest" replaced by  "diagnostic_dest"
.
.
***********************************************************
Components: [The following database components will be
 upgraded or installed]
***********************************************************
--> Oracle Catalog Views          [upgrade]  VALID
--> Oracle Packages and Types      [upgrade]  VALID
```

```
--> JServer JAVA Virtual Machine [upgrade]  VALID
--> Oracle XDK for Java          [upgrade]  VALID
--> Oracle Workspace Manager     [upgrade]  VALID
--> OLAP Analytic Workspace      [upgrade]  VALID
--> OLAP Catalog                 [upgrade]  VALID
--> EM Repository                [upgrade]  VALID
--> Oracle Text                  [upgrade]  VALID
--> Oracle XML Database          [upgrade]  VALID
--> Oracle Java Packages         [upgrade]  VALID
--> Oracle interMedia            [upgrade]  VALID
--> Spatial                      [upgrade]  VALID
--> Data Mining                  [upgrade]  VALID
--> Expression Filter            [upgrade]  VALID
--> Rule Manager                 [upgrade]  VALID
--> Oracle OLAP API              [upgrade]  VALID
.
******************************************************
Miscellaneous Warnings
******************************************************
WARNING: --> Database is using an old timezone file version.
.... Patch the 10.2.0.1.0 database to timezone file version 4
.... BEFORE upgrading the database.  Re-run utlu111i.sql after
.... patching the database to record the new timezone file
version.
WARNING: --> Database contains stale optimizer statistics.
.... Refer to the 11g Upgrade Guide for instructions to update
.... statistics prior to upgrading the database.
.... Component Schemas with stale statistics:
....    SYS
....    OLAPSYS
....    SYSMAN
....    CTXSYS
....    XDB
WARNING: --> Database contains schemas with objects dependent
 on network packages.
.... Refer to the 11g Upgrade Guide for instructions to
 configure Network ACLs.
.... USER SYSMAN has dependent objects.
WARNING: --> EM Database Control Repository exists in the
database.
.... Direct downgrade of EM Database Control is not supported.
 Refer to the
.... 11g Upgrade Guide for instructions to save
 the EM data prior to upgrade.

PL/SQL procedure successfully completed.
SQL> spool off
```

Make sure you have enough free space in the SYSTEM and SYSAUX tablespaces, as these are likely to run out of space during the upgrade. In my case, the Upgrade Information Utility shows that no changes are necessary before I can upgrade to the Oracle Database 11g release. You may have to adjust the size of a tablespace or the redo log files.

The Upgrade Information Utility may recommend the following:

- Removing obsolete initialization parameters
- Adjusting the values of some initialization parameters
- Adding space to tablespaces such as SYSTEM and SYSAUX

Here are the prerequisite steps you must follow before upgrading a database to Oracle Database 11g.

1. Make sure you have enough free space in the SYSTEM and SYSAUX tablespaces as these are two tablespaces that are likely to fill up during an upgrade process. In this case, the Upgrade Information Utility didn't raise any red flags or issue any recommendations to fix things, so we merrily move to the next step.

2. Shut down the Oracle Database 10g release database (`tenner` in this example) by issuing the `shutdown immediate` command. On a Windows system, make sure you stop the Oracle Service either from the Control Panel or by using the `net stop` command. Then, delete this service by invoking the oradim utility. You must then create a brand-new Oracle Database 11g instance (`eleven` in this example), again by using the oradim utility from the new Oracle home for Oracle Database 11g.

3. Back up the Oracle Database 10g release database, so you can revert to it if things don't go right during the upgrade.

4. Make sure you set the value of the `compatible` initialization parameter to 10.0, the minimum allowable compatibility level.

5. If you're using a password file for the pre–Oracle Database 11g release database, copy it to the new Oracle Database 11g directory.

6. Point all relevant Oracle environment variables such as ORACLE_HOME, PATH, and LD_LIBRARY_PATH to the new Oracle Database 11g release 1 (11.1) directories. Set the value of the ORACLE_SID variable to the new database name (*eleven*).

And here are the actual upgrade steps:

1. Log in as the Oracle software owner (oracle in this example) and start SQL*Plus from the 11g $ORACLE_HOME/rdbms/admin directory, as the user sys.

2. Start the new database in the upgrade mode as shown here:

   ```
   SQL> startup upgrade
   ```

   The `startup upgrade` command lets you start a database based on an older Oracle Database release and automatically handles the setting of system parameters that may potentially cause problems during the upgrade. The command disables all system triggers and prepares the environment for the database upgrade.

   If you're upgrading from the Oracle 9.2 release, you must create a SYSAUX tablespace at this point. Since I'm upgrading from a more recent release, I already have the SYSAUX tablespace in the database that's being upgraded.

3. Start a spool file so you can review the upgrade process later:

   ```
   SQL> spool upgrade.log
   ```

   You can review the spool file later on to find out details about any errors during the upgrade.

4. Start the upgrade process by executing the catupgrd.sql script, as shown here:

   ```
   SQL> @catupgrd.sql
   ```

5. The catupgrd.sql script upgrades the database to the Oracle Database 11g release and shuts down the upgraded database once the upgrade is completed. Restart the database in the normal mode.

   ```
   SQL> startup
   ```

   The starting of the upgraded database ensures that the database is consistent after the upgrade.

6. Once the upgrade is completed, run the utlu111s.sql script, also known as the Post-Upgrade Status Tool, to confirm the validity of the upgrade.

   ```
   SQL> @utlu111s.sql

   Oracle Database 11.1 Upgrade Status Utility
   01-30-2008  22:05:04
   Component                            Status   Version   HH:MM:SS
   ```

```
Oracle Server                      VALID   11.1.0.1.0   00:14:01
JServer JAVA Virtual Machine       VALID   11.1.0.1.0   00:11:08
Oracle Workspace Manager           VALID   11.1.0.1.0   00:00:40
OLAP Analytic Workspace            VALID   11.1.0.0.0   00:00:25
OLAP Catalog .                     VALID   11.1.0.1.0   00:00:50
Oracle OLAP API                    VALID   11.1.0.1.0   00:00:31
Oracle Enterprise Manager          VALID   11.1.0.1.0   00:08:06
Oracle XDK                         VALID   11.1.0.1.0   00:00:58
Oracle Text                        VALID   11.1.0.1.0   00:00:45
Oracle XML Database                VALID   11.1.0.1.0   00:09:29
Oracle Database Java Packages      VALID   11.1.0.1.0   00:01:00
Oracle interMedia                  VALID   11.1.0.1.0   00:16:11
Spatial                            VALID   11.1.0.1.0   00:04:43
Oracle Expression Filter           VALID   11.1.0.1.0   00:00:13
Oracle Rules Manager               VALID   11.1.0.1.0   00:00:11
.

Total Upgrade Time: 01:13:55
PL/SQL procedure successfully completed.
SQL>
```

The utlu111s.sql script (Post-Upgrade Status Tool) shows that all database components have been successfully upgraded, as indicated by a status of VALID for each of the database components. If you see the status INVALID for one or more components, the next step, where you run the utlrp.sql script, may fix the problem. If that doesn't work, rerun the catupgrd.sql script. You can rerun the catupgrd.sql script multiple times if you see problems in the Post-Upgrade Status Tool's output.

7. Run the post-upgrade actions, by executing the following script:

```
SQL> @catuppst.sql
```

The catuppst.sql script is new in Oracle Database 11g. This is a post-upgrade script that performs the remaining upgrade actions that don't require the database to be open in the upgrade mode. You can run it simultaneously with the utlrp.sql, which I describe in the next upgrade step.

8. Execute the utlrp.sql script to recompile the stored PL/SQL and Java code:

```
SQL> @utlrp.sql
```

The utlrp.sql script is a wrapper that's based on the UTL_RECOMP package supplied by Oracle, which provides a more general recompilation interface. By default, this script database invokes the utlrp.sql script with 0 degrees of parallelism for the recompilation. The UTL_RECOMP package determines the degree of parallelism for the utlrp.sql script based on the cpu_count and the `parallel_threads_per_cpu` initialization parameters. Thus, In Oracle Database 11g, the utlrp.sql script can take advantage of multiple CPUs to speed up the recompilation of PL/SQL and Java code. This is an enhancement provided in the Oracle Database 11g release.

9. Verify that there aren't any invalid objects in the upgraded database:

```
SQL> select count(*) from dba_invalid_objects;
```

You've now upgraded your Oracle database to the Oracle Database 11g release. If you encounter problems during the upgrade process that you can't overcome by rerunning the catupgrd.sql script, you must revert to the pre-upgrade release by restoring the backup of the database that you made earlier. To rerun the upgrade, shut down the database and restart the database by issuing the `startup upgrade` command. All the steps after this remain the same as the ones shown earlier.

Oracle Database 11g offers a new password case-sensitivity feature, which is explained in detail in Chapter 3. In order to take advantage of this feature, you'll have to manually reset all user passwords upon upgrading to Oracle Database 11g.

You can check the current status of the user passwords by querying the DBA_USERS view, as shown here:

```
SQL> select username, password, password_versions
     from dba_users;

USERNAME                       PASSWORD         PASSWORD
------------------------------ ---------------- --------
MGMT_VIEW                                       10G 11G
SYS                                             10G 11G
SYSTEM                                          10G 11G
DBSNMP                                          10G 11G
RMAN                                            10G 11G
. . .
```

Note the new column PASSWORD_VERSIONS in the DBA_USERS view, which denotes the case sensitivity of the password. The value `10G 11G` for the PASSWORD_VERSIONS column means that the user has been upgraded from an Oracle Database 10g version database or is a new user created in an Oracle Database 11g version database. In addition, notice that the PASSWORD column isn't populated, unlike in the previous releases. Of course, the passwords do exist, but not even the encrypted versions are displayed any longer in the DBA_USERS view. If you need to use the encrypted version of a user's password, say to log in as a particular user, you can get the encrypted password from the PASSWORD column in the USER$ view.

You can also check if any users in the upgraded database are using default passwords, which creates a security loophole. Use the new view DBA_USERS_WITH_DEFPWD to identify the users with default passwords. The view has a single column, USERNAME:

```
SQL> desc dba_users_with_defpwd
 Name                Null?        Type
 ------------        ---------    -------------
 USERNAME            NOT NULL     VARCHAR2(30)
```

The following query in the DBA_USERS_WITH_DEFPWD view shows that there are several users with default passwords in the upgraded database:

```
SQL> select * from dba_users_with_defpwd;

USERNAME
---------
DIP
MDSYS
RMAN
HR
SCOTT
...
SQL>
```

You must change the passwords of all the usernames that appear in the output of the query shown here. Ideally, the query must return no rows.

Downgrading a Database   You can easily downgrade a database back to the release from which you upgraded it to the Oracle Database 11*g* release. Here are the steps:

1. Shut down the database and start it up in the downgrade mode.

   ```
   SQL> startup downgrade
   ```

2. Spool the results of the downgrade script.

   ```
   SQL> spool downgrade.log
   ```

3. Execute the downgrade script, called catdwgrd.sql.

   ```
   SQL> @catdwgrd.sql
   ```

4. After the catdwgrd.sql script finished executing, shut down the database cleanly.

   ```
   SQL> shutdown immediate
   ```

5. Start up the database in the upgrade mode, from the pre-upgrade ORACLE_
   HOME environment.

   ```
   SQL> startup upgrade
   ```

6. Reload the old PL/SQL packages and data dictionary views.

   ```
   SQL> @catrelod.sql
   ```

7. After the reloading of the old packages and views, shut down the database
   and restart it.

   ```
   SQL> shutdown immediate
   SQL> startup
   ```

8. Run the utlrp.sql script to recompile any packages, procedures, and types that
   became invalid during the downgrading of the database.

   ```
   SQL> @utlrp.sql
   ```

This completes the downgrading process. You can run the utlrp.sql script multiple
times if necessary.

Upgrading with the DBUA   The DBUA is essentially unchanged from the
Oracle Database 10*g* release. There are a couple of important changes which you'll
see when we go through a manual upgrade process. You'll have an additional screen
during the upgrade process, which asks you to specify a location for the diagnostic
directory. The DBA automatically starts when you choose to upgrade your database
during the installation of the Oracle Database 11*g* server software. Note that when
you use the manual upgrade method, you must upgrade an ASM instance separately,
whereas the DBUA lets you perform the ASM upgrade along with the upgrade of
the database instance.

EXERCISE 1-1

Scripts to Run for Upgrading a Database

Upgrade an Oracle Database 10*g* release database to the Oracle Database 11*g* release
using the Oracle-supplied scripts for upgrading a database.

The following are the steps you use in upgrading a database to the Oracle
Database 11*g* release:

- ■ **utlu111i.sql**   The Pre-Upgrade Information tool

■ **catupgd.sql**   The script that performs the actual upgrade process

■ **utlu111s.sql**   The Post-Upgrade Status tool

■ **catuppst.sql**   The post-upgrade actions script

■ **utlrp.sql**   The script you run at the end of the upgrade process, to recompile all objects that were invalidated during the upgrade

While the DBUA offers less control over the individual upgrade steps when compared to a manual upgrade process, it provides significant benefits by automating the entire upgrade process. DBUA supports RAC installations and can automatically fix the upgrade prerequisites. It reports errors found in the spooled upgrade log and provides a complete HTML report of the upgrade process. You can also run the DBUA from the command line (silent mode), which enables the automation of the upgrade process across your organization.

CERTIFICATION OBJECTIVE 1.04

Real Application Testing

The Real Application testing feature, which consists of two separate tools, Database Replay and the SQL Performance Analyzer, is arguably the most significant new feature in the Oracle Database 11.1 release. The two new features address significant unmet needs regarding change management. Organizations often find that upgrading operating system or database server software or making major application changes is fraught with considerable risk. There simply is no way to predict how a production system is going to perform pursuant to major changes. Real Application Testing addresses this need by letting you quickly and exhaustively test changes using Oracle's own tools instead of your having to resort to third-party tools that may not be able to capture all the required changes.

A *snapshot standby database* is a database that you activate from a physical standby database. You could create a snapshot standby databases in the previous release, but the setting up of a snapshot standby database is simpler in Oracle Database 11g. You can temporarily open a physical standby database for reporting and testing. In the snapshot standby mode, a physical standby database continues to receive redo data from the primary database. You can use the snapshot standby database for writes for application testing and discard the writes after the testing completes. You can then reconcile the standby database with the primary database by applying the necessary redo logs. Because the standby database continues to receive redo logs from the primary database, it provides data protection. Thus, the snapshot standby database can function as the primary database as far as testing goes and act as a physical standby database by continuing to receive the redo logs from the primary database. You thus will need only a single copy of the database to provide both testing and disaster recovery functions. Using a snapshot standby database facilitates the use of both Database Replay and SQL Performance Analyzer.

The new Oracle-supplied packages DBMS_WORKLOAD_CAPTURE and DBMS_WORKLOAD_REPLAY provide the APIs for the Database Replay feature. The DBMS_SQLPA package supports the SQL Performance Analyzer feature. The following sections first look at the Database Replay feature and then the SQL Performance Analyzer.

Database Replay

System changes such as a database upgrade require substantial testing and validation before you can actually migrate the changes to a production system. The trick is to simulate a real production workload on a test system. The Database Replay feature enables you to perform real-life testing of major changes by letting you capture the actual database workload on the production system and replay it on a test system. Thus, you essentially re-create the production workload effortlessly on a test system. Database Replay performs a sophisticated replay of the production workload by adhering to the original concurrency and timing characteristics. Once you complete the testing, you can analyze and review the reports produced by Database Replay to see if there was a performance divergence between the two runs and also if there were any errors. Finally, you can choose to implement the recommendations made by Database Replay to fix any problems it encountered during the replay of the production workload.

Currently, the main problem in using third-party software to test systems and application changes is the inability of those tools to test real-world production workloads, thus causing many issues to go undetected during testing. Database Replay changes the entire ballgame in terms of the implementation and testing of system changes by making real workload testing a reality. Database Replay enables you to capture production workload with true load, timing, and concurrency characteristics. You move the workload that you capture to a test system before making the changes you're planning to the test system. You then replay the captured workload with the exact production load, timing, and concurrency characteristics. The production data is captured over an illustrative period such as a peak period. The goal is to use a workload on the test system that's indistinguishable from the production workload.

The drive to add the Database Replay functionality to the Oracle database came from Oracle customers, who evinced keen interest in having change-assurance functionality within the database itself instead of relying on trial-and-error methods and inadequate third-party tools. Database Replay lets you quickly, and with great confidence, test and implement system changes, with a much lower risk than ever before. Database Replay is especially useful when you're evaluating a move from a single-instance system to an Oracle RAC (real application clusters) environment. You can first capture the single instance workload and replay it on a test RAC system to compare database performance. Another use for Database Replay is debugging applications. You can record and replay sessions to make it easier to reproduce bugs. Database Replay is also ideal to test manageability feature testing. You can test the effectiveness and stability for control strategies through multiple replay iterations.

The Database Replay tool first records all workload that's directed at the RDBMS. It then exercises the RDBMS code during the replay in a way that's similar to the way the workload was exercised during the data capture phase. You achieve this by re-creating all the external client requests to the RDBMS. The ultimate objective is to replay the exact production workload as seen by the RDBMS, in the form of requests made by various external clients.

You can employ Database Replay to test significant system changes such as the following:

- Operating system and database upgrades and migrations
- Configuration changes such as moving to an oracle RAC environment
- Storage changes

Database Replay captures all external requests made while the production database is running, including SQL queries, PL/SQL blocks, limited PL/SQL remote procedure calls, logins and logoffs, session switches, DML and DDL statements, and OCI calls. It doesn't capture background jobs and requests made by internal clients such as the Enterprise Manager, for example. To be precise, Database Replay doesn't capture the following types of client requests:

- SQL*Loader direct path load of data
- Oracle Streams
- Data Pump Import and Export
- Advanced replication streams
- Non–PL/SQL-based Advanced Queuing (AQ)
- Flashback Database and Flashback queries

- Distributed transactions and remote describe/commit operations
- Shared server
- Non–SQL-based object access

In an RAC environment, during the workload capture, the captured data is written in each instance's file system. The data is then consolidated into a single directory for the preprocessing and replay stages.

Following are the steps you must follow to use Database replay to analyze significant changes in your system:

1. Capture the production workload.
2. Preprocess the captured workload.
3. Replay the workload.
4. Analyze the replayed workload and create a report.

In the following sections, let's review the key steps in using the Database Replay feature. Oracle recommends that you use Enterprise Manager to work with the Database Replay feature, but in this chapter, I show you how to use Oracle APIs to perform a replay of a production workload.

Capturing the Production Workload

Database Replay captures all requests made to the database by external clients in binary files called *capture files*. You can transport these capture files to another system for testing after the workload is completed. The capture files contain key information regarding client requests such as SQL queries, bind values, and transaction details. Note that background activities and work performed by database scheduler jobs aren't part of the captured database workload. The workload that Database Replay captures pertains strictly to calls made to the database by the external clients. While the capture process imposes minimal performance overhead, you must allocate the necessary space to store the workload recording.

You use procedures from the DBMS_WORKLOAD_CAPTURE package to capture workload data. Before you can capture the workload, you must follow the steps shown in the sections that follow.

Restart the Database   Restarting the database, while not mandatory, ensures that you won't have needless data divergences as a result of in-progress or uncommitted transactions when you start the workload capture. To avoid partial capture of transactions and errors due to dependent transactions in the workload, restart the production database and start clean. This also ensures an authentic replay of the workload later on as well as minimizes the chances for errors and data divergence since the application data at the start of the capture and replay processes will match. You can restore this database for the database replay later by using a physical restore method to perform a point-in-time recovery, a logical restore of the application data, or even a flashback or snapshot standby technique.

Restart the database in the restricted mode using the `startup restrict` command, in order to prevent users from connecting and starting transactions before you start the workload capture. Once you start the workload capture, the instance automatically switches to the unrestricted mode, allowing normal user connections to the database. If you're dealing with an Oracle RAC environment, you must first shut down all instances and restart one of the instances in the restricted mode and start the workload capture. You can then restart the other instances after the workload capture starts.

Define Workload Filters   You can use optional workload filters to restrict the workload capture to only a part of the actual production workload. For example, you can use an exclusion filter to exclude Enterprise Manager sessions. You can use inclusion filters to capture subsets of the actual production workload by specifying user sessions to capture in the workload. All other activity will be ignored by Database replay as a result. Note that you can use either an inclusion filter or an exclusion filter during any workload capture, but not both.

The following example shows how to add a workload filter using the ADD_FILTER procedure:

```
SQL> begin
        dbms_workload_capture.add_filter (
                        fname      => 'user_salapati',
                        fattribute => 'USER',
                        fvalue     => 'salapati'
     end;
     /
```

In the ADD_FILTER procedure, the various parameters are defined as follows:

- `fname` specifies the filter name.
- `fattribute` specifies the filter attributes such as `program`, `module`, `action`, `service`, `instance_number`, and `user`.
- `fvalue` specifies the value of the attribute corresponding to the `fattribute` parameter you choose. In my example, I chose `user` as the `fattribute` parameter's value. The `fvalue` attribute specifies the particular username of the user (salapati) whose actions will be captured.

The ADD_FILTER procedure example shown here restricts the workload capture to external calls made by a single user, salapati. Everything else that happens in the database is completely ignored by Database Replay. You can remove a filter by using the DELETE_FILTER procedure, as shown here:

```
SQL> begin
       dbms_workload_capture.delete_filter (fname =>
       'user_salapati');
     end;
```

Note that there is only a single required parameter for the DELETE_FILTER procedure, fname, which provides the name of the filter. Use the DBA_WORKLOAD_FILTERS view to see all the workload filters defined in a database.

Set Up a Capture Directory   Make sure you set up a directory on your file system that's large enough to hold the results of the workload capture process. You don't have to create a new directory specifically for the workload capture because you can use a preexisting directory path. Of course, the workload capture will stop if there isn't sufficient free space in the directory you allocate for the data capture. For an Oracle RAC environment, you can use a shared file system or a separate physical directory for each of the instances, but it's easier to use the shared file system.

Capturing the Production Workload   You can select the workload capture period based on a representative peak period. Use the AWR (automatic workload repository) or ASH tools to select the appropriate period based on the workload history of the production database. Note that although you don't have to restart the database before beginning the workload capture, you increase the potential for data divergence during the replay phase because of the possible existence of in-flight transactions. To minimize data divergences, restart the database before you start the data capture.

on the !Job

Because your goal is to collect the production workload during a time of heavy usage, the additional overhead imposed by the workload capture process would be minimal.

Start the workload capture by using the START_CAPTURE procedure, as shown here:

```
SQL>begin
      dbms_workload_capture.start_capture (name     => '2008Jan',
                                           dir      => 'jan08',
                                           duration => 1200);
    end;
```

The three parameters of the START_CAPTURE procedure stand for the following:

- `name` stands for the name of the workload capture.
- `dir` specifies the directory object pointing to the workload capture directory.
- `duration` specifies the number of seconds for which the workload will be captured.

Of the three parameters shown here, only the DIR parameter is mandatory. If you don't specify the DURATION parameter, the workload capture will continue indefinitely, until you stop it with the FINISH_CAPTURE procedure, as shown here:

```
begin
    dbms_workload.capture.finish_capture ();
end;
/
```

Once the time specified by the `duration` parameter is reached, or when you execute the FINISH_CAPTURE procedure, the workload capture is completed. When you execute the FINISH_CAPTURE procedure, the workload capture stops and the database closes the open workload datafiles. Use the DBA_WORKLOAD_CAPTURES view to see all the workload captures performed by the database.

Preprocessing the Workload

Before you can replay the captured workload, you must first preprocess the captured data. Preprocessing involves creating replay files that you can use to replay the workload on a test system. However, you need to preprocess the captured workload only once, no matter how many times you replay the workload. Any files that were created by the database aren't modified when you run the preprocessing step multiple times. The database will create new files but not modify the older files. Thus, if you run into any errors, you can run the preprocess step multiple times without any problem.

on the
Job

You can preprocess the captured workload on the production system, a test system, or even a different system as long as the database versions are the same.

In order to preprocess the captured workload data, first move the captured workload datafiles to the test system where you're planning to preprocess it. You can perform the resource-intensive step of preprocessing on the test server where you plan to replay the workload or on a different server.

Use the PROCESS_CAPTURE procedure to preprocess the captured workload, as shown here:

```
begin
dbms_workload_replay.process_capture (capture_dir => 2008jan');
end;
```

The `capture_dir` parameter refers to the directory where the database has stored the captured workload. Preprocessing the data will produce the metadata for the captured workload and transform the captured workload datafiles into replay streams called *replay files* that you can now replay on the test system.

Making the System Change

Once you move the captured workload to the test system, it's time to make the system change, such as an upgrade to a new version of the database. After making the system change you are interested in testing, you'll replay the workload on the test system to see what changes the upgrade has made to the performance and other characteristics of the workload.

As mentioned earlier, the system change can be a database or server upgrade, schema changes or hardware changes, or a migration to an Oracle RAC environment from a single instance setup.

Replaying the Captured Workload

You replay the captured workload on a test system, which must be a duplicate of the production system. You must ensure that the state of the application data on the replay system is the same as the production system. You can do this by creating a duplicate database on the test server, or use Data Pump import and export to re-create the production database. You can also use a snapshot standby database for this purpose

After preprocessing the data as shown in the previous section, there are several steps you must follow in order to replay the captured workload on the test system. Of course, performing these steps is a whole lot easier if you use the Enterprise Manager instead of the Oracle APIs. In my example, I show how to do this using the APIs to present the underlying process clearly.

Setting up the Test System   Prepare the test database by first restoring it from the backups that you made of the production system, so it reflects the same application state as the production system. As mentioned earlier, you may choose to use a point-in-time recovery, flashback, or import and export to restore the application data. Oracle also recommends that you reset the system time on the test system to the time when you started the workload capture in order to avoid encountering invalid data when processing time-sensitive data, as well as to avoid a potential failure of any scheduled jobs. The key to a successful replay is to have the application transactions access an identical version of the application data as that on the system where you captured the initial workload.

Set up the replay directory where you'll copy the captured production workload. You must make sure there's a directory object for the directory when you want to store the captured workload. Start the test database in the restricted mode to prevent an accidental modification of data during the workload replay. The following sections describe the steps involved in replaying the captured workload.

Resolving External References   Before the replay, resolve all external references from the databases such as database links. If these links exist in the captured workload, you must fully disable or reconfigure them so they are fully functional in the test system. In addition to database links, external references include objects such as directory objects, URLs, and external tables that point to production systems. You're likely to encounter unexpected problems if you replay a workload with unresolved external references. Also, resolving the external references would ensure that replaying the production workload won't cause any harm to your production environment. For example, an external reference such as a database link may be referencing a production database, and you don't want to do this during the workload replay.

Set up the Replay Clients   The *replay driver* is a special application that consumes the captured workload by sending replay requests to the test database. The replay driver consists of one or more replay clients that connect to the test system and send requests to execute the captured workload. The replay driver thus replaces the multiple external clients that interact with the production system with a single external client in charge of all interaction with the RDBMS. The replay client in essence simulates the production system on the test database by sending appropriate requests that make the test system behave as if those requests came from the external clients during the workload capture. The replay driver distributes the replay workload streams among the multiple replay clients based on network bandwidth, CPU, and memory capabilities.

on the job
The replay client is a multi-threaded client, capable of driving multiple workload sessions. The program is included in both the standard Oracle Client as well as the Oracle Instant Client.

Ideally, you should install multiple replay clients on non-production servers. You must ensure that each of the replay clients can access the directory that contains the replay files,

Before starting the workload replay, the database will wait for the replay clients to connect to it (the database). Each of the workload clients, which you start with the `wrc` executable from the command line, submits a session's workload. It's the replay client that actually connects to the database and drives the replay. First make sure you've moved the preprocessed workload files to the replay directory and that the replay clients can access that directory. Also check to ensure that the replay user has the correct credentials to connect to the database. Once you make these checks, you're ready to start the replay clients.

The `wrc` executable, which you execute from the command line, has the following syntax.

```
$ wrc [user/password[$server]] mode=[value] [keyword=[value]]
```

The `server` parameter refers to the server where you installed the `wrc` executable. The `mode` parameter specifies the mode in which you run the `wrc` executable. You can run the `wrc` executable in three modes: REPLAY, CALIBRATE, and LIST_HOSTS. The parameter `keyword` enables you to specify options for the execution, depending on the mode you select. You can display all the keywords and their possible values by typing in **wrc** at the operating system level, as shown here:

```
$ wrc
Workload Replay Client: Release 11.1.0.6.0 - Production on Sat
Feb 09 1:45:01 2008
Copyright (c) 1982, 2007, Oracle.  All rights reserved.
FORMAT:
=======
 wrc [user/password[@server]] [MODE=mode-value] KEYWORD=value
Example:
========
   wrc   REPLAYDIR=.
   wrc   scott/tiger@myserver REPLAYDIR=.
   wrc   MODE=calibrate REPLAYDIR=./capture
 The default privileged user is: SYSTEM

Mode:
=====
wrc can work in different modes to provide additional
functionalities.
The default MODE is REPLAY.
```

```
Mode         Description
------------------------------------------------------------------
REPLAY       Default mode that replays the workload in REPLAYDIR
CALIBRATE    Estimate the number of replay clients and CPUs
             needed to replay the workload in REPLAYDIR.
LIST_HOSTS   List all the hosts that participated in the capture
             or replay.

Options (listed by mode):
=========================
MODE=REPLAY (default)
---------------------

Keyword      Description
------------------------------------------------------------------
USERID       username (Default: SYSTEM)
PASSWORD     password (Default: default password of SYSTEM)
SERVER       server connection identifier (Default: empty string)
REPLAYDIR    replay directory (Default:.)
WORKDIR      work directory (Default:.)
DEBUG        FILES, STDOUT, NONE  (Default: NONE)
             FILES  (write debug data to files at WORKDIR)
             STDOUT (print debug data to stdout)
             BOTH   (print to both files and stdout)
             NONE   (no debug data)
CONNECTION_OVERRIDE  TRUE, FALSE (Default: FALSE)
             TRUE   All replay threads connect using SERVER,
                    settings in DBA_WORKLOAD_CONNECTION_MAP
                    will be ignored!
             FALSE  Use settings from DBA_WORKLOAD_CONNECTION_MAP
SERIALIZE_CONNECTS  TRUE, FALSE (Default: FALSE)
             TRUE   All the replay threads will connect to
                    the database in a serial fashion one after
                    another. This setting is recommended when
                    the replay clients use the bequeath protocol
                    to communicate to the database server.
             FALSE  Replay threads will connect to the database
                    in a concurrent fashion mimicking the
                    original capture behavior.
MODE=CALIBRATE
'''
MODE=LIST_HOSTS
...
$
```

By default, the wrc executable mode is set to run in the REPLAY mode, but it's better to run it first in the CALIBRATE mode to get an estimate of the number of replay clients and hosts you'll need to replay the captured workload on the test system. The number of replay clients you'll need will depend on the number of user sessions you need to replay in the captured workload. If you need multiple hosts because of a large number of usr sessions, you must install the `wrc` executable on each of the hosts.

You must open a new terminal window to start the `wrc` replay clients. You can start multiple clients if you want, each of which will initiate one or more replay threads with the database. Each of these replay threads represents a single stream from the workload capture. Here's the general syntax for starting the `wrc` replay clients:

```
$ wrc userid=<user id> password=<password>
server=<server connection string>
Replaydir=<replay directory>
Workdir=<client work directory>
```

Before you can start the replay client, you must ensure that the replay client software is installed on the hosts, and the client can access the replay directory where you've stored the workload replay files. The replay user must be able to use the workload replay.

Running the `wrc` executable in the LIST_HOSTS mode displays the hosts that are part of the workload capture and workload replay, as shown in this example:

```
$ wrc mode=list_hosts replay_dir=./replay
```

Note that the host or hosts involved in capturing the workload as well as the hosts involved in the replay of the workload are displayed.

The following example shows how to start the `wrc` executable in the CALIBRATE mode:

```
$ wrc system/<system_passwordd> mode=calibrate
     replay_dir=./test_dir
```

In the example shown here, only the `mode` and the `replay_dir` parameters are specified. The `mode` parameter is the only required parameter. If you don't specify the `replay_dir` parameter, the replay directory will default to the current directory. In addition to these parameters, you can also specify the following optional parameters:

- `process_per_cpu` specifies the maximum number for client processes per CPU and its default value is 4.
- The `threads_per_process` parameter specifies the maximum number of threads in a single `wrc` client process and its default value is 50.

After the CALIBRATE mode execution enables you to determine the number of hosts and `wrc` clients necessary for the replay, execute the `wrc` in the REPLAY mode, as shown here:

```
$ wrc system/<system_password> mode=replay replay_dir=./test_dir
```

When you execute the `wrc` in the REPLAY mode, you can specify the following parameters:

- `userid` and `password` are optional parameters used to specify the credentials of the replay user for the replay client. The default values for this parameter are the credentials of the user SYSTEM.
- `server` specifies the connection string to connect to the replay system; it defaults to an empty string.
- `replay_dir` specifies the directory containing the preprocessed workload; it defaults to the current directory.
- `work_dir` specifies the directory where the replay client logs are stored; it defaults to the current directory.
- `debug` is an optional parameter, with a default value of `none`. Possible values are `files`, `stdout`, and `both` (debug data written to both files and stdout).
- `connection_override` specifies whether `wrc` must override the connection mapping stored in the DBA_WORKLOAD_CONNECTION_MAP view. The default value of this parameter is `FALSE`, meaning all replay threads will use the connection mappings in the DBA_WORKLOAD_CONNECTION_MAP view to connect.

on the **job** *The database version of the system where you replay the workload must match the version of the database where you captured the workload.*

The following steps show how to initialize the replay data, remap external connections used in the workload capture process, and start and stop a workload replay, all by using the new DBMS_WORKLOAD_REPLAY package.

Initializing the Replay Data   Use the INITIALIZE_REPLAY procedure to initialize the data, which loads the metadata into tables required by the workload replay process.

```
SQL> exec dbms_workload_replay.initialize_replay(replay_name =>
     'test_replay',replay_dir => 'test_dir');
```

The `replay_name` parameter specifies the replay name, and the `replay_dir` parameter specifies the directory containing the captured workload. Among other things, the initialization process will load captured connection strings so they can be remapped for the database replay.

Remapping External Connections   You can use the DBA_WORKLOAD_ CONNECTION_MAP view to check the external connection mappings made by database users during the workload capture. You must remap the external connections so the individual user sessions can connect to all the external databases. Use the REMAP_CONNECTION procedure to remap external connections. On a single-instance system, the capture and replay system connection strings are mapped one-to-one.

The following example shows how to remap external connections:

```
SQL> exec dbms_workload_replay.remap_connection (connection_id =>
     111, replay_connection => 'prod1:1522/testdb');
```

In the REMAP_CONNECTION procedure, the `connection_id` parameter shows the connection from the workload capture, and the optional `replay_ connection` parameter specifies the new connection string you want to use during the workload replay. If the `replay_connection` parameter's value is set to its default value of `null`, all replay sessions will connect to the default host. When dealing with an Oracle RAC environment, you can map all the connection strings to a single load balancing connection string.

Setting Workload Options   After initializing the replay data and remapping necessary external connections, you must set various workload replay options. You can specify the following four options while replaying the production workload.

■   `synchronization`   By default, the value for this parameter is TRUE, meaning that the commit order of the captured workload will be preserved during the workload replay. Replay actions execute only after all the dependent commit actions are completed successfully. This leads to the elimination of data divergence that results when commit order is not followed correctly among dependent transactions. If the captured workload consists primarily of independent transactions, you can set the value of the `synchronization` parameter to FALSE because you aren't worried about data divergence in this case. Synchronized commit-based replay ensures minimal data divergence when compared with unsynchronized replay. Unsynchronized replay is useful for load or stress testing where you don't have to adhere to the original commit ordering. Unsynchronized replay leads to high data divergence.

on the **Job** *Synchronized replay, which is commit-based, ensures minimal data divergence.*

- `connect_time_scale` This is an optional parameter. Use the `connect_time_scale` parameter to calibrate the time between the beginning of the workload capture and the time when a session connects with the specified value. This parameter enables you to adjust the number of concurrent users during the workload replay. The default value for this parameter is 100.

- `think_time_scale` An optional parameter that lets you calibrate the speed at which you send user calls to the database. The parameter scales the elapsed time between user calls from the same session. The default value for this parameter is 100. If you set this value to 0, you'll send client requests to the database in the fastest time possible.

on the **Job** *Note the difference between how elapsed time is computed during a workload capture and a workload replay. During a workload capture, elapsed time is the sum of two components: user time and user think time. User time is the time it takes to make a user call to the database, and user think time is the time the user waits between calls. Workload replay includes three components: user time, user think time, and synchronization time.*

- `think_time_auto_correct` Also an optional parameter that automatically corrects the think time set by the `think_time_scale` parameter. By default, this parameter is set to FALSE, meaning there's no automatic adjustment of the think time. When you set it to TRUE, the database will automatically reduce the value set for the `think_time_scale` parameter if the replay is progressing slower than the data capture. If the replay is going faster than the data capture, it'll automatically increase the think time.

Preparing the Workload for Replay To prepare the workload to replay the test system, first prepare the workload by executing the PREPARE_REPLAY procedure, as shown here:

```
SQL> dbms_workload_replay.prepare_replay (replay_name =>
     'replay1', replay_dir => 'test_dir',
     synchronization= FALSE);
```

In this example, the `synchronization` parameter is set to FALSE (default value is TRUE). This means that the commit order of transactions in the captured workload may not be preserved during the workload replay. This is a good strategy if you believe that the workload is composed mostly of independent transactions, which means the commit order need not be preserved by setting the synchronization parameter to TRUE.

EXERCISE 1-2

Procedure for Capturing and Replaying a Database Workload

Summarize the steps involved in capturing and replaying a database workload when you're using the Database Replay feature.

Following is the sequence of steps you must follow when using Database Replay to capture and replay a database workload:

1. Start the workload capture using the DBMS_WORKLOAD_REPLAY. START_CAPTURE procedure.

2. Process the captured workload using the DBMS_WORKLOAD_REPLAY. PROCESS_CAPTURE procedure.

3. Prepare the workload for replay using the DBMS_WORKLOAD_REPLAY. PREPARE_REPLAY procedure.

4. Remap the captured external connections using the DBMS_WORKLOAD_ REPLAY.REMAP_CONNECTIONS procedure.

5. Start the database reply using the DBMS_WORKLOAD_REPLAY.START_ REPLAY procedure.

Starting the Workload Replay   After initializing the preprocessed data and setting up the replay clients, you are finally ready to replay the captured workload on the test system. You must start a minimum of one wrc client before you can start the workload replay. Use the START_REPLAY procedure to begin the workload replay on the test system:

```
SQL> exec dbms_workload_replay.start_replay();
```

Use the CANCEL_REPLAY procedure to stop the workload replay, as shown here:

```
SQL> exec dbms_workload_replay.cancel_replay();
```

Executing the CANCEL_REPLAY procedure results in a direction to the wrc clients to stop submitting new workload for replay.

The database automatically exports all AWR snapshots corresponding to the replay period at the end of the workload replay process. You can also manually export them by executing the EXPORT_AWR procedure if the automatic export of the AWR fails for some reason. Once you export the AWR snapshots to the replay system, you must import them into the AWR schema by executing the IMPORT_AWR procedure.

Analyzing Workload Capture and Replay

After the workload replay process is completed, you must analyze the data replay by creating a workload replay report. This will enable you to check the data and performance differences between the captured workload and the replayed workload. In addition, you can examine any errors that were generated during the workload replay process. Use the REPORT function to generate a workload replay report.

```
declare
     cap_id      number;
     rep_id      number;
     rep_rpt     clob;
begin
    cap_id  :=  dbms_workload_replay.get_replay_info (dir =>
              'testdir');
    select max(id) into rep_id
     from dba_workload_replays
     where capture_id = cap_id;
    rep_rpt   :=  dbms_workload_replay.report(replay_id
                => rep_id,
                format => dbms_workload_replay.type_text);
end;
/
```

The GET_REPLAY_INFO function provides a history of the workload capture in the specified replay directory (testdir). The REPORT function generates a workload replay report. The DBA_WORKLOAD_REPLAYS view will contain the history of the replays as well. You can specify text, HTML, or XML as the value for the REPLAY_TYPE parameter. Here's a typical report produced by the REPORT function:

```
Error Data
(% of total captured actions)
New errors:
 12.3%
Not reproduced old errors: 1.0%
Mutated errors:
```

```
 2.0%
Data Divergence

Percentage of row count diffs:
 7.0%
Average magnitude of difference (% of captured):
4.0%
Percentage of diffs because of error (% of diffs):
20.0%
Result checksums were generated for 10% of all
actions(% of checksums)
Percentage of failed checksums:
0.0%
Percentage of failed checksums on same row count:
0.0%
Replay Specific Performance Metrics
Total time deficit (-)/speed up (+):
-32 min
Total time of synchronization:
44 min
Average elapsed time difference of calls:
0.1 sec
Total synchronization events:
3675119064
```

Following are the key types of information you must focus on in order to judge the performance on the test system:

- Pay special attention to the divergence of the replay from the captured workload performance. If an online divergence reveals serious divergence, you can stop the replay. Alternatively, you can use offline divergence reporting at the end of the replay to determine how successful the replay was. Your goal is to minimize all types of negative record-and-replay divergence. Data divergence is shown by the differences in the number of rows returned by queries in response to identical SQL statements. Data divergences merit your utmost scrutiny. Data divergences can be any one of the following:
  - Smaller or larger results sets
  - Updates to a database state
  - A return code or an error code
- Errors generated during the workload replay.
- Performance deviations between workload capture and workload replay. You can see how long the replay took to perform the same amount of work as

the captured workload. If the workload replay takes longer than workload capture, it's a cause for concern and you must investigate this further.

■ Performance statistics captured by AWR reports. You can also use ADDM to measure the performance difference between the workload capture system and the replay system.

You must investigate any of the data divergences listed in order to reduce the divergence between recording and replaying the database workload. Any of the following workload characteristics will increase data or error divergence between capture and replay of the workload:

■ Implicit session dependencies due to things such as the use of the DBMS_ PIPE package

■ Multiple commits within PL/SQL

■ User locks

■ Using non-repeatable functions

■ Any external interaction with URLs or database links

In addition to data divergences, you can also have time divergences between the capture and replay systems.

The following data dictionary views help you manage the Database Replay feature:

■ **DBA_WORKLOAD_CAPTURES** shows all workload captures you performed in a database.

■ **DBA_WORKLOAD_FILTERS** shows all workload filters you defined in a database.

■ **DBA_WORKLOAD_REPLAYS** shows all workload replays you performed in a database.

■ **DBA_WORKLOAD_REPLAY_DIVERGENCE** helps monitor workload divergence.

■ **DBA_WORKLOAD_THREAD** helps monitor the status of external replay clients.

■ **DBA_WORKLOAD_CONNECTION_MAP** shows all connection strings used by workload replays.

In addition to the data dictionary views listed here, the dynamic view V$WORKLOAD_REPLAY_THREAD enables you to monitor the status of all external replay clients.

One of the biggest advantages of Database Replay is that it can test virtually 100 percent of an actual Oracle database workload, as compared to a third-party tool such as LoadRunner, which can only simulate workload that's about 10 percent of the actual workload. Database Replay, since it's engineered to work as an integral part of the Oracle database, executes much faster, completing its analysis long before the other tools can.

The SQL Performance Analyzer

The Database Replay feature provides the capability to test the performance of the workload in a database. Although you can use filters to restrict the workload, you can't use Database Replay to focus on SQL performance changes. SQL Performance Analyzer, which, along with the Database Replay constitutes the Total Replay feature, lets you test the impact of potential changes such as a server or database upgrade on SQL workload response time. The SQL Performance Analyzer focuses on comparing the performance of a specific SQL workload before and after a major system change. The analyzer does this by building two versions of the SQL workload performance, which includes both the SQL execution plans as well as their execution statistics. After analyzing SQL performance both before and after you make a major change, the SQL Performance Analyzer provides suggestions to prevent potential performance degradation of SQL statements. This is especially handy when you're planning an upgrade of your database to a newer release of the Oracle database. The SQL Performance Analyzer, by enabling you to compare SQL performance on two systems running on different versions of the Oracle database, lets you know ahead of the upgrade which of the SQL statements may show a deterioration in performance. Thus, you can reengineer those statements prior to the actual upgrade.

on the
Ⓙob
The SQL Performance Analyzer executes SQL in a serial fashion and ignores concurrency.

If the analysis of the SQL Performance Analyzer shows a potential performance degradation following a system change such as a database upgrade, you can arrange to preserve the original SQL execution plans using the SQL Plan Management feature or by using the SQL Tuning Advisor to tune the regressed SQL statements.

You can use the SQL Performance Analyzer to predict performance changes resulting from the following system changes:

- Database and application upgrades
- Hardware upgrades
- Operating system upgrades

■ Initialization parameter changes

■ SQL tuning actions such as the creation of SQL profiles

■ Statistics gathering

■ Schema changes

For example, to test an initialization parameter change, you create a SQL Performance Analyzer task and perform an initial trial run with the initialization parameter set to the original value. You execute the SQL Performance Analyzer task a second time with the parameter set to the new value. You then compare the results of the two runs to compare the performance. You can run the SQL Performance Analyzer on the production system whose performance you're analyzing, or use a test system. If you're using a test system, make sure it's configured in a similar way as your production system, with an identical database version and initialization parameters. It's probably a good idea to use a test system to avoid additional overhead on your production database. Once you capture the SQL workload on the production system, you can import it to the test system and run the SQL Performance Analyzer on the test system—to compare a pre- and post-upgrade performance, for example.

In the following example, you learn how to predict SQL performance changes following an upgrade from the Oracle Database 10.2 release to the Oracle Database 11.1 release, with the help of the SQL Performance Analyzer. Although Oracle recommends that you use the Enterprise Manager to run the SQL Performance Analyzer, I show you how to run the tool using the new Oracle-supplied PL/SQL package, called DBMS_SQLPA, which offers a task-oriented interface for using the SQL Performance Analyzer. Using the DBMS_SQLPA package, you can build and compare two versions of workload performance—one before the change and one after the change—and compare the differences between the two versions and easily trap the SQL statements that are adversely affected by the system change.

In addition to the new DBMS_SQLPA package, you can also use several procedures in the DBMS_SQLTUNE package to create the SQL Tuning Set that you need to capture the SQL workload and conduct a performance analysis.

on the
Ü o b *Running the SQL Performance Analyzer on the production database requires additional resource usage but gives you the most representative results. However, if performance is a concern, use a test system to run the analysis.*

You use a SQL Tuning Set (STS) to capture the SQL workload on the production system. The STS includes the SQL text, bind variables, as well as information relating to the execution environment, execution plans, and execution statistics of one or more SQL statements. You export the STS from the production system to the test system to provide the SQL workload input to the SQL Performance Analyzer. Because the STS is a persistent database object, you can modify the STS as you want and even select data from the STS as you would from a table. You can use an STS's filtering capability to weed out any undesirable SQL.

You can use one of the following sources to load statements into an STS:

- Automatic workload repository (AWR) snapshots
- AWR baselines
- A cursor cache
- Another STS

You can either collect all the SQL statements at once or over a period of time. The SQL Performance Analyzer, which is primarily designed to predict the impact of major system changes on the SQL workload response time, does the following things when analyzing the SQL workload performance:

- Builds different versions of SQL workload performance
- Executes SQL serially without respecting concurrency characteristics
- Analyzes performance differences including the response time of the before- and after-change SQL workloads
- Uses the SQL Tuning Advisor to tune regressed SQL statements

Following is the workflow involved in using the SQL Performance Analyzer:

1. *Capture the pre-change SQL workload performance.* Use the SQL Performance Analyzer to capture the SQL workload in an STS that you create beforehand. You may also use the AWR instead to capture the top SQL statements in order to provide a complete SQL workload capture. You transport the SQL workload to a test system for analysis.

2. *Analyze the pre-change SQL workload performance.* The performance data includes execution plans and execution statistics for metrics such as elapsed time and disk reads.

3. *Make the system changes.* Once you capture the pre-change SQL workload from the production system, make the necessary changes on the test system. For example, if you want to test the impact of an upgrade to a new version of the database, install the new Oracle release software on the test system and upgrade a copy of the production database to the new release.

4. *Capture the post-change SQL workload performance.* Use the SQL Performance Analyzer to capture the workload, this time on the post-change test system.

5. *Analyze the post-change SQL workload performance.* Examine the execution plans and execution statistics for the same metrics you examined before you made the system change.

6. *Compare and analyze the SQL performance.* Use the SQL Performance Analyzer to compare the SQL performance in the production system and the post-change test system in order to identify changes in SQL execution plans. You can also compare statistics relating to user-specified metrics such as execution time, buffer gets, disk reads, and others. You can then calculate the impact of the change on both individual SQL statements and on the SQL workload as a whole. This enables you to foresee whether the change would lead to an improvement or regression in SQL performance or whether it would have no net impact on the SQL workload. The SQL Performance Analyzer may recommend running the SQL Tuning Advisor to tune any SQL statements that lead to a performance regression. You can also use the results of the analysis to seed SQL Plan Management (SPM) baselines. SQL Plan baselines let you prevent performance regressions, instead of using the SQL Tuning Advisor to tune the statements. If the performance of a SQL statement prior to the change is better than its post-change performance, you can "freeze the performance" by using the SQL Plan baselines. I explain the SQL Plan baselines feature in Chapter 4. Oracle recommends that you implement changes piecemeal, one feature at a time, and retest.

In the following sections, let's examine the workflow of the SQL Performance Analyzer.

Capturing the Production SQL Workload

The SQL workload you must capture from the production system must be from a representative peak period. The SQL workload contains environmental information such as bind variables, execution frequency of statements, along with the actual SQL text of the statements. In the following example, I show you how to use an STS to capture the production SQL workload.

Create the SQL Tuning Set   In order to capture the production workload, you must first create an STS using the CREATE_SQLSET procedure of the DBMS_ SQLTUNE package, as shown here:

```
SQL> exec dbms_sqltune.create_sqlset(sqlset_name => 'test_set',
          description  => '11g upgrade workload';
```

The new STS *test_set* is an empty STS that is used to store the captured SQL workload on the production system.

Load the SQL Tuning Set   The next step is to load the production system SQL workload into the empty STS *test_set* that you created in the previous step, using the SELECT_CURSOR_CACHE procedure of the DBMS_SQLTUNE package.

```
declare
  mycur dbms_sqltune.sqlset_cursor;
begin
  open  mycur for
    select value (P)
    from table (dbms_sqltune.select_cursor_cache(
      'parsing_schema_name <> ''SYS'' AND elapsed_time >
      2500000',null,null,null,null,1,null,
      'ALL')) P;
    dbms_sqltune.load_sqlset(sqlset_name => 'test_set',
                             populate_cursor => mycur);
end;
/

PL/SQL procedure successfully completed.
SQL>
```

The database uses an incremental capture method to populate the STS from the cursor cache over a period of time. During the populating of the STS, the database filters out any undesirable SQL.

The next step is to export the captured SQL workload in the form of the STS to the test system so you can invoke the SQL Performance Analyzer there.

Transport the SQL Tuning Set   Before you can transport the SQL tuning set, you must first create a staging table using the CREATE_STGTAB_SQLSET procedure, so you can use this table to export the STS that contains the production SQL workload to the test system. After you export the STS, you must import it into the test database.

```
SQL> exec dbms_sqltune.create_stgtab_sqlset (table_name =>
     'stagetab');
```

The CREATE_SQLTAB_SQLSET procedure creates a staging table named STAGETAB. Export the production STS into the staging table STAGETAB that you just created, using the PACK_STGTAB_SQLSET procedure:

```
SQL> exec dbms_sqltune.pack_stgtab_sqlset (sqlset_name =>
     'test_sts',
     staging_table_name => 'stagetab');
```

Now you must import the STS into the test system where you'll be running the SQL Performance Analyzer to compare the SQL workload performance.

Import the STS into the Test System Use the Data Pump import utility to import the staging table STAGETAB from the production system to the test system. Once you import the staging table, run the UNPACK_STGTAB_SQLSET procedure to import the STS into the test database where you'll replay the SQL workload.

```
SQL> exec dbms_sqltune.unpack_stgtab_sqlset (sqlset_name = '%',
          replace => true, staging_table_name => ('stagetab');
```

You're now ready to create your SQL Performance Analyzer task.

Create the SQL Performance Analyzer Task Create a SQL Performance Analyzer task using the DBMS_SQLPA package. Use the CREATE_ANALYSIS_TASK procedure to create the tuning task:

```
SQL> exec dbms_sqlpa.create_analysis_task(sqlset_name => 'sts1',
          task_name => 'spa_task1');
```

The CREATE_ANALYSIS_TASK procedure enables you to create an analysis task for one or more SQL statements. Once you create the SQL Performance Analyzer task, you must perform three different analyses of the captured SQL workload that you imported to the test system in the form of an STS. The three analyses pertain to:

- The pre-change SQL workload
- The post-change SQL workload
- Comparison of the pre- and post-change SQL workload

on the
job

The STS includes both SQL execution plans and execution statistics.

Analyze the Pre-Change SQL Workload In this example showing how to use the SQL Performance Analyzer, your goal is to compare the performance of an identical SQL workload on the production system running an Oracle Database 10g database and the test system, which is running an Oracle Database 11g Release 1 (11.1) database. First, set the `optimizer_features_enable` initialization parameter on the test system to the exact value of that parameter on the production system:

```
optimizer_features_enable=10.2.0
```

You can now analyze the pre-upgrade SQL performance data using the EXECUTE_ANALYSIS_TASK procedure of the DBMS_SQLPA package, as shown here:

```
SQL> exec dbms_sqlpa.execute_analysis_task (task_name =>
       'spa_task1',
       execution_type => 'test_execute',
       execution_name= 'before_change');
```

The EXECUTE_ANALYSIS_TASK procedure executes an analysis task that you've already created. The `execution_type` parameter of the EXECUTE_ANALYSIS_TASK procedure can take one of the following three values:

- `TEST_EXECUTE` Executes all SQL statements in the captured SQL workload. The database only executes the query portion of the DML statements, in order to avoid adversely impacting user data or the database itself. The database generates both execution plans and execution statistics (for example, disk reads and buffer gets).
- `COMPARE_PERFORMANCE` Compares performance between two executions of the workload performance analysis.
- `EXPLAIN PLAN` Lets you generate SQL plans only, without actually executing them.

The EXECUTE_ANALYSIS_TASK procedure executes all DML statements but ignores any DDL statements to avoid unduly affecting the test data. You can view the before-change version of the SQL performance as the SQL workload performance baseline.

You can specify execution parameters by using the `execution_params` parameter that you can specify as `DBMS_ADVISOR.arglist((name,value,...)`. Use the `time_limit` parameter to specify a global time limit for processing all statements in the STS. Use the `local_time_limit` parameter to specify the time limit to process a single statement in the STS.

Once you create the SQL Performance Analyzer pre-change task and execute it, you can retrieve a report of the task execution by executing the REPORT_ANALYSIS_TASK function, as shown here:

```
SQL> select dbms_sqlpa.report_analysis_task (task_name =>
     'spa_task1',
     type => 'text', section=> 'summary') from dual;
```

The previous step captures system performance consisting of both execution plans and execution statistics such as elapsed time, buffer gets, disk reads, and the number of rows processed. You can use the performance as a baseline to compare SQL performance after you make the changes to the database.

Analyze the Post-Upgrade SQL Workload   Our goal is to compare the performance of an identical SQL workload on an Oracle 10.2 release database and an Oracle Database 11g release database. To test the impact of upgrading to Oracle Database 11g, change the value of the initialization parameter `optimizer_features_enable` to match the Oracle Database 11g version:

```
optimizer_features_enable=11.1
```

Run the EXECUTE_ANALYSIS_TASK procedure again, with identical parameter values as in the previous execution except for the parameters TASK_NAME and EXECUTION_NAME in order to distinguish the task name and execution name from the pre-change execution that you performed earlier.

```
SQL> exec dbms_sqlpa.execute_analysis_task (task_name   =>
        'spa_task2',
        execution_type => 'test_execute',
        execution_name => 'after_change')
```

Once again, get a report of the task execution by executing the REPORT_ANALYSIS_TASK function, as shown here.

```
SQL> select dbms_sqlpa.report_analysis_task (task_name =>
     'spa_task2,
     type => 'text', section=> 'summary') from dual;
```

You can use the contents of this report to review the performance after you made the changes.

Compare the SQL Performance   You have executed the EXECUTE_ANALYSIS_TASK procedure twice thus far, once for the pre-change analysis and the other for the post-change analysis, using `test_execute` as the value for the `execute_type` parameter both times. To compare the SQL performance before and after upgrading to Oracle Database 11g, you must execute the EXECUTE_ANALYSIS_TASK procedure a third time, but with the value `compare performance` for the `execution_type` parameter. This will let the SQL Performance Analyzer analyze and compare the SQL performance data from the two previous runs.

```
SQL> exec dbms_sqltune.execute_analysis_task (task_name =>
        'spa_task3',
        execution_type => 'compare performance',
        execution_params =>
        dbms_advisor.arglist('execution_name1','before_change',
        execution_name2','after_change''comparision_metric',
        'disk_reads',);
```

The comparison metric I chose to compare in this case is DISK_READS, but you can also use ELAPSED_TIME, OPTIMIZER_COST, DIRECT_WRITE, PARSE_TIME, or BUFFER_GETS as a comparison metric, in order to compare the pre- and post-change SQL performance.

Generating the SQL Performance Analyzer Report   You can get a report of the SQL performance comparison by executing the REPORT_ANALYSIS_TASK function, as shown here:

```
var report clob;
exec :report := dbms_sqlpa.report_analysis_task('spa_task3',
            'text',
            'typical','summary');
set long 100000 longchunksize 100000 linesize 120
print :report
```

The REPORT_ANALYSIS_TASK function shows the results of an SQLPA analysis task. The REPORT_EXECUTE_ANALYSIS_TASK function shown here will print a text report. You can also choose to print an HTML or XML formatted report if you want. The value of `summary` for the report format means that the procedure will result in the printing of a summary report.

You can do the following during the compare and analysis phase:

- Calculate the impact of the change on specific SQL statements.
- Calculate the impact of the change on the SQL workload as a whole.
- Assign weights to important SQL in the workload.
- Detect performance regression and improvements.
- Detect changes in the execution plans of the SQL statements.

■ Recommend the running of the SQL Tuning Advisor to tune regressed SQL statements. After using the advisor, you can create a new after-change version of the SQL workload performance to ensure that you have acceptable performance.

You can use the following views when working with the SQL Performance Analyzer:

■ **DBA_ADVISOR_TASKS** shows details about the analysis task.

■ **DBA_ADVISOR_FINDINGS** shows analysis findings, which are classified as performance regression, symptoms, informative messages, and errors.

■ **DBA_ADVISOR_EXECUTIONS** shows metadata information for task executions.

■ **DBA_ADVISOR_SQLPLANS** shows a list of SQL execution plans.

■ **DBA_ADVISOR_SQLSTATS** shows a list of SQL compilation and execution statistics.

Analyzing the Performance Report   The SQL Performance Analyzer report consists of three main sections:

■ General information

■ Result summary

■ Result details

The Result Summary section shows at a glance whether the system change you're putting in place will result in an improvement or a deterioration of the SQL workload performance. You also get detailed execution statistics for all the SQL statements in the STS you offered as input to the SQL Performance Analyzer. If the report shows deterioration in SQL workload performance, it also performs a root cause analysis and provides recommendations to improve the execution plans of the affected SQL statements, which will help you easily tune the SQL statements that have regressed following the system change.

As with the Data Replay tool, the SPA offers the unique advantage in that it's integrated with the Oracle database. This lets you take advantage of other tools such as the SQL Tuning Advisor and features such as the SQL Plan Management to avoid SQL performance deterioration. When you use Enterprise Manager to perform the

SQL Performance Analyzer tasks, you can invoke the SQL tuning Advisor directly from the SQL Performance Analyzer Task result page. You can easily run a new SQL tuning task that analyzes all the regressing SQL statements found by the SQL Performance Analyzer. Alternately, you can prevent SQL regressions by using SQL plan baselines, as I explain in Chapter 4, which discusses SQL Plan Management with the help of SQL baselines.

EXERCISE 1-3

Testing SQL Performance Following a Database Upgrade

How would you test whether a database upgrade will affect the performance of the SQL statements used in your database?

Use the SQL Performance Analyzer to test the changes in SQL performance following a system change such as a database upgrade. Here are the steps:

1. Capture the production SQL workload by first creating an STS to capture the production workload.

2. Load the STS.

3. Transport the STS from the production database to a test database.

4. Create a SQL Performance Analyzer task.

5. Analyze the SQL performance before the upgrade by executing the EXECUTE_ANALYSIS_TASK procedure. Use `test_execute` as the value for the `execution_type` parameter.

6. Upgrade the database to the new release.

7. Analyze the SQL performance by executing the EXECUTE_ANALYSIS_ TASK procedure. Use `test_execute` as the value for the `execution_ type` parameter.

8. Analyze the post-upgrade SQL workload.

9. Compare the SQL performance by executing the EXECUTE_ANALYSIS_ TASK procedure. Use `compare_performance` as the value for the `execution_type` parameter.

INSIDE THE EXAM

The exam will test you about the setting of the ORACLE_BASE environmental variable. You must understand the modifications made to the ORACLE_BASE environment variable to bring it into conformity with Oracle Flexible Architecture guidelines. While the variable isn't mandatory, it will be in a future release. The exam is likely to test your understanding of the `startup upgrade` command.

The exam will test your understanding of the SQL Performance Analyzer's testing characteristics. You must understand concepts such as the serial execution of SQL statements and the disregarding of transac-tion concurrency. Expect to be tested on the different values of the `execution_type` parameter in the EXECUTE_ANALYSIS_TASK procedure.

In the Database Replay feature, you probably will see questions on the various replay options such as `synchronization`, `think_time_scale`, `think_time_auto_connect`, and `connect_time_scale`. For example, what do you have to do if the users are taking longer to complete their transactions during the replay than during the capture phase? Remembering the correct sequence of steps for replaying a workload can also be helpful on the exam.

CERTIFICATION SUMMARY

This chapter explained the most important new features in the installation of Oracle Database 11g. You learned about the changes in the way the Oracle base location is set, as well as the requirements for the datafile and flash recovery area locations.

This chapter introduced you to the automatic diagnostic repository and how to use the `diagnostic_dest` initialization parameter. You learned about the changes in the installation options and the new database components. This chapter also explained the new OSASM operating system group and the SYSASM privilege for ASM administrators. You also learned about the new initialization parameters in Oracle Database 11g that are most relevant to DBAs.

As part of the review of the changes in the DBCA, I introduced both automatic secure configuration and automatic memory management features. The section on upgrading the database explained the compatibility factor when upgrading, as well as the upgrade path to Oracle Database 11g. The chapter showed an actual database upgrade to the new release.

The final part of the chapter explained two revolutionary new features—Database Replay and SQL Performance Analyzer, which, together make change management a much easier affair, without recourse to third-party tools.

✓ # TWO-MINUTE DRILL

Installing Oracle Database 11g

❏ The Oracle Installer provides a list box to select or edit the recommended Oracle base location.

❏ The recommended Oracle base location is /mount_point/app/oracle_software_owner.

❏ The Oracle Universal Installer derives the location of the Oracle home from the Oracle base location you provide.

❏ The default location for both datafiles and the flash recovery area is one level below the Oracle base.

❏ Oracle recommends that you place the datafiles and flash recovery area on different disks.

❏ The ADR provides a single consolidated location for diagnostic data.

❏ Using the ADR is not mandatory.

❏ You use the `diagnostic_dest` initialization parameter to specify a non-default location for the ADR.

❏ The ADR base is the root directory for the ADR.

❏ The default ADR base directory is $ORACLE_BASE/diag.

❏ Each Oracle product under the ADR base has a separate home.

❏ The Oracle Configuration Manager is integrated with the Oracle Universal Installer as an optional component.

❏ Oracle Real Application testing option is automatically installed when you select the Enterprise Edition installation option.

❏ The new OS group OSASM is designed for the exclusive use of users who manage ASM.

❏ The new ASM-related system privilege, SYSASM, is recommended for users who perform ASM administrative tasks.

❏ The OSASM operating system group and the SYSASM system privilege are optional in the Oracle Database 11g release.

New Features in Database Creation

❏ The initialization parameters are listed in the alert log in a format that makes it easy for you to copy and paste them to create a new parameter file.

❑ The minimum value for the `compatible` initialization parameter is 10.0.0.

❑ The default value for the `compatible` parameter is 11.1.0.

❑ The maximum value for the `compatible` parameter is 11.1.0.n.n.

❑ The DBCA lets you select automatic memory management during database creation.

❑ You can use the Enterprise Manager plug-in to automatically switch from Database Control to Grid Control.

❑ DBCA uses the value set for the Oracle base directory to derive the default location for datafiles and the `diagnostic_dest` initialization parameter.

❑ You don't have to set the bdump, cdump, and udump directories in the parameter file if you provide a value for the `diagnostic_dest` initialization parameter.

❑ In Oracle Database 11g, the DBCA provides secure database configuration by default.

❑ You're offered a choice of listeners for a new database when you create one through the DBCA.

❑ You are offered the choice of automatic memory management when using the DBCA to create a new database.

❑ If you disable the default security settings when using the DBCA to create a new database, you can configure the Secure Configuration Option later on.

Upgrading to Oracle Database 11g

❑ You can directly upgrade to Oracle Database 11g Release 1 if your current database is using an Oracle 9.2.0.4 or newer release.

❑ If you're using 9.2.0.3 or older releases, you must go through intermediate upgrades.

❑ The utlu111i.sql script serves as the Pre-Upgrade Information Tool.

❑ The utlu111s.sql script is the Post-Upgrade Status Tool.

❑ The catupgrd.sql script is the script that performs the actual upgrade of the database.

❑ You can run the catupgrd.sql script multiple times if necessary.

❑ The utlrp.sql script recompiles stored PL/SQL and Java code.

❑ The DBUA lets you upgrade both the database instance and the ASM instance simultaneously.

❑ If you're using the manual method to upgrade the database, you must upgrade the ASM instance separately from the database instance.

Real Application Testing

❑ Database Replay is part of Real Application Testing, which allows you to perform real-world workload testing.

❑ The workload capture process captures all external requests made to the database, such as SQL queries, logins and logoffs, remote procedural calls, and OCI calls.

❑ The workload capture doesn't include background jobs and requests made by internal clients.

❑ Database Replay doesn't capture flashback queries, Oracle Streams data, distributed transactions, and other types of data.

❑ Capture files are binary files that contain the captured external requests made to the database.

❑ Use the DBMS_WORKLOAD_CAPTURE package to capture the database workload.

❑ Oracle recommends that you restart the production database before starting the workload capture, although it isn't mandatory to do so.

❑ After you start the database in the restricted mode, the database automatically switches to an unrestricted mode after you start the workload capture.

❑ You can use inclusion and exclusion workload filters to restrict the captured workload to a subset of the actual workload.

❑ The ADD_FILTER and DELETE_FILTER procedures enable you to add and delete a workload filter.

❑ Oracle recommends that you capture the workload during a representative peak period.

❑ Only the DIR parameter in the START_CAPTURE procedure is mandatory.

❑ You can either specify a value for the duration parameter in the START_CAPTURE procedure, or execute the FINISH_CAPTURE procedure, to end a workload capture.

❑ Preprocessing the workload data re-creates the replay files.

❑ Before replaying the captured workload on the test system, you must resolve external references such as database links, directory objects, external tables, and URLs.

❑ The wrc is a special client application that acts as the replay driver.

❑ The replay driver consists of one or more replay clients that actually connect to the test system and act as the external clients to the database.

❑ The replay driver allocates replay workload among multiple replay clients.

❑ You can run the wrc in the REPLAY, CALIBRATE, or LIST_HOSTS mode.

❑ The default mode of the wrc executable is REPLAY.

❑ The CALIBRATE mode lets the wrc estimate the number of replay clients and CPUs necessary to replay the captured workload.

❑ The INITIALIZE_REPLAY procedure loads the metadata about the captured workload into the tables required by the workload replay process.

❑ In the REMAP_CONNECTION procedure, if you set the replay_connection parameter's value to null, all replay sessions will connect to the default host.

❑ A synchronized replay (synchronization=TRUE) will lead to minimal data divergence.

❑ Synchronization preserves the commit order during the workload replay.

❑ Unsynchronized replay is useful for load testing and is faster. It doesn't follow the original commit ordering.

❑ Unsynchronized replay leads to a high data divergence.

❑ The connect_time_scale parameter lets you adjust the number of concurrent users during the workload replay.

❑ The think_time_scale parameter lets you adjust the speed of user calls to the database.

❑ The think_time_auto_correct parameter automatically corrects the think time set by the think_time_scale parameter.

❑ By default, there's no automatic adjustment of think time.

❑ The database automatically exports all AWR snapshots corresponding to the replay period, after the completion of the workload replay.

❑ The replay_type parameter in the GET_REPLAY_INFO procedure can take the values text, HTML, or XML.

❑ A data divergence can be desirable or undesirable.

❑ Multiple commits within PL/SQL can lead to increased data or error divergence between capture and replay of the workload.

❑ User locks can also lead to increased data or error divergence between capture and replay of the workload.

❑ The SQL Performance Analyzer focuses only on the effect of a system change on SQL performance.

❑ You can run the SPA on the production system or on a test system.

❑ The DBMS_SQLPA package is a task-oriented interface for implementing the SPA.

❑ The SPA analyzes SQL performance differences before and after a system change.

❑ You use an STS to capture the production SQL workload.

SELF TEST

The following questions will help you measure your understanding of the material presented in this chapter. Read all the choices carefully because there might be more than one correct answer. Choose all correct answers for each question.

Installing Oracle Database 11g

1. What does a DBA need to do for Oracle to perform the automatic pre-installation requirements check when you are beginning the installation of Oracle software?
   - A. Run the Upgrade Information Tool.
   - B. Do nothing—Oracle automatically performs the pre-installation checks.
   - C. Use the `upgrade database` command first, to open the database.
   - D. Execute the `utlu111s.sql` script.

2. The Oracle Configuration Manager
   - A. Is installed automatically.
   - B. Is an optional component.
   - C. Can be installed during the installation only.
   - D. Can be installed during the installation or later.

3. Which of the following is true?
   - A. The OSASM OS group and the SYSASM privilege are both mandatory in Oracle Database 11g.
   - B. The OSASM OS group and the SYSASM privilege are both optional in Oracle Database 11g.
   - C. The OSASM OS group is mandatory and the SYSASM privilege is optional in Oracle Database 11g.
   - D. The OSASM OS group is optional and the SYSASM privilege is mandatory in Oracle Database 11g.

4. The Real Application testing feature is
   - A. Automatically installed when you choose the custom installation method.
   - B. Installed only if you license it separately.
   - C. Installed from a separate CD as the server.
   - D. Automatically installed when you select the Enterprise Edition installation option.

New Features in Database Creation

5. Which of the following is a new initialization parameter in Oracle Database 11g?

   A. `plsql_code_type`

   B. `sga_max_target`

   C. `result_cache`

   D. `memory_max`

6. Oracle Database 11g release 1 (11.1)

   A. Doesn't enforce password case sensitivity.

   B. Doesn't enforce password case sensitivity by default.

   C. Enforces password case sensitivity by default.

   D. Doesn't use any initialization parameters to enforce password case sensitivity.

7. Secure database configuration is

   A. Installed by default with the Oracle database server.

   B. Provided by DBCA by default.

   C. Something you can configure only after completing the creation of a new database.

   D. Not provided by the DBCA.

8. The minimum value of the compatible initialization parameter is

   A. 10.0.0

   B. 11.2.0

   C. 11.1.0.n.n

   D. 11.1

Upgrading to Oracle Database 11g

9. Which of the following Oracle database versions can you *not* use to upgrade directly to Oracle Database 11g Release 1 (11.1)?

   A. 9.2.0.3

   B. 9.2.0.4

   C. 10.1.0.0

   D. 8.1.7.1

10. The Upgrade Information Tool provides information about which of the following?

   A. Optimal SQL allocation to various components of the SGA such as the shared pool.

   B. Optimal performance features of Oracle Database 11g.

   C. Recommendations for additional space for tablespaces.

   D. A time estimate for the upgrade.

11. What is the name of the Oracle-supplied script that runs the pre-upgrade requirements checks?

   A.   utlu111s.sql

   B.   utlui111i.sql

   C.   utlu111x.sql

   D.   utlu111p.sql

12. Which of the following scripts performs the post-upgrade validation when you upgrade to Oracle Database 11g?

   A.   utlu111s.sql

   B.   utlu11x.sql

   C.   utlu111i.sql

   D.   utlu111p.sql

Real Application Testing

13. Which of the following external references must be resolved before you can replay a workload with Database Replay?

   A.   Database links

   B.   Directory objects

   C.   External tables

   D.   URLs

14. To estimate the number of replay clients that need to be started to replay a particular workload, you must run the `wrc` executable in which mode?

   A.   REPLAY

   B.   CALIBRATE

   C.   PROCESS

   D.   OVERRIDE

15. What happens if you don't set a time for finishing a workload capture with database replay?

   A.   The workload capture will run forever.

   B.   The workload capture will not start.

   C.   The workload capture will run until it runs out of space in the directory where it stores the workload files.

   D.   There is a default maximum time limit for each workload capture process.

16. What can you use the `think_time_auto_correct` parameter for when setting workload options for Database Replay?

   A.   To automatically correct the think time set by the `think_time_scale` parameter.

B. To automatically correct the think time set by the `connection_time_scale` parameter.

C. To manually correct the think time set by the `think_time_scale` parameter.

D. To manually correct the think time set by the `connection_time_scale` parameter.

17. Which one of the following can you *not* use as a source to load statements into an STS?

A. AWR baselines

B. A cursor cache

C. AWR snapshots

D. A user-created file with SQL statements stored in the file system

18. What are the modes in which you can execute the EXECUTE_ANALYSIS_TASK procedure?

A. TEST EXECUTE, SPEED OF PERFORMANCE

B. SIMULATE, SYNCHRONIZE, and COMPARE PERFORMANCE

C. TEST EXECUTE, COMPARE PERFORMANCE, and EXPLAIN PLAN

D. EXECUTE, PERFORMANCE, and EXPLAIN

19. Which of the following parameters doesn't change during the three executions of the EXECUTE_ANALYSIS_TASK procedure?

A. task_name

B. task type

C. execution_type

D. execution_params

20. Which of the following changes can the SQL performance *not* compare?

A. Changing the application code

B. Database upgrade

C. Increase in the number of users

D. Changes in the initialization parameter values

LAB QUESTION

You want to use the Database Replay feature to test your database workload before and after an upgrade to Oracle Database 11*g*. Show how to prepare a database for a replay of a workload. You notice two things during the data capture stage: long time periods elapse between the user logins, and quite a bit of time is spent between the time users issue a call and the time the calls are completed by the database. You want to increase the number of concurrent users during the workload replay and also finish the workload replay in a shorter time than the time it took to capture the workload.

SELF TEST ANSWERS

Installing Oracle Database 11g

1. ☑ **B** is correct because the Oracle Universal Installer automatically makes the pre-installation check of the requirements.
   ☒ **A** is incorrect because you run the Upgrade Information Tool to check the prerequisites for upgrading the database, not for installing the server software. **C** is incorrect because you don't start the database before installing the software—there may not be a database yet. **D** is incorrect because you use the utl111s.sql script for a post-upgrade status check.

2. ☑ **B** and **D** are correct. **B** is correct because the Oracle Configuration Manager is an optional component during installation. **D** is correct because you can install the Oracle Configuration Manager during the installation or later on.
   ☒ **A** is incorrect because the Oracle Configuration isn't installed automatically. **C** is incorrect because you can install the Oracle Configuration Manager after the installation.

3. ☑ **B** is correct because both the SYSASM privilege and the OSASM group are optional.
   ☒ **A** is incorrect because the SYSASM privilege and the OSASM group aren't mandatory in Oracle Database 11g. **C** and **D** are incorrect because both the SYSASM privilege and the OSASM group aren't mandatory in Oracle Database 11g.

4. ☑ **D** is correct because the Oracle Real Application Testing feature is automatically installed when you select the Enterprise Edition installation option.
   ☒ **A** is incorrect because the feature isn't installed as part of the custom installation method, unless you choose the Enterprise edition Installation. **B** is incorrect because you don't need a separate license for using the Real Application Testing feature. **C** is incorrect because the Real Application testing feature is installed from the same CD as the server software.

New Features in Database Creation

5. ☑ **A** is correct because the `plsql_code_type` initialization parameter is new in Oracle Database 11g.
   ☒ **B** is incorrect because this parameter has been available from the Oracle 9i release. **C** and **D** are incorrect because there are no such initialization parameters.

6. ☑ **C** is correct because Oracle Database 11g enforces password case sensitivity by default.
   ☒ **A** is incorrect because Oracle Database 11g enforces password case sensitivity by default. **B** is incorrect because Oracle Database 11g enforces password case sensitivity by default. **D** is

incorrect because you do have to use a new initialization parameter to enforce password case sensitivity.

7. ☑ **B** is correct because the DBCA provides secure database configuration by default.

☒ **A** is incorrect because secure database configuration is done during database creation and not during server installation. **C** is incorrect because you can adopt secure database configuration at database creation time or at a later time. **D** is incorrect because the DBCA does offer secure database configuration.

8. ☑ **A** is correct because the minimum value for the `compatible` initialization parameter is 10.0.0.

☒ **B, C,** and **D** are incorrect because they refer to incorrect values for the `compatible` parameter.

Database Upgrade New Features

9. ☑ **A** and **D** are correct because you can only directly upgrade from an Oracle 9.2.0.4 or newer release.

☒ **B** and **C** are correct because they satisfy the direct upgrade requirement.

10. ☑ **C** is correct because the Upgrade Information Tool makes recommendations for adding space to key tablespaces such as the SYSTEM and SYSAUX tablespaces.

☒ **A, B,** and **D** are incorrect because the Upgrade Information Tool doesn't provide information regarding any of these.

11. ☑ **B** is correct because the utlu111i.sql script is the Upgrade Information Tool.

☒ **A** is incorrect because the utlu111s.sql script is the Upgrade Status Tool. **C** and **D** are incorrect because they refer to nonexistent upgrade scripts.

12. ☑ **A** is correct because the utlu111s.sql script performs the post-upgrade checks.

☒ **B** is incorrect because there is no such script. **C** is incorrect because the utlu111i.sql script runs the pre-upgrade checks. **D** is incorrect because it refers to a nonexistent script.

Database Replay

13. ☑ **A, B, C,** and **D** are all correct. All of them are external references that must be resolved before you can replay a workload.

14. ☑ **B** is correct because you must run the `wrc` executable in the CALIBRATE mode to estimate the number of replay clients that you must start.

☒ **A** is incorrect because you use the replay mode when you're actually replaying the workload. **C** and **D** are incorrect because those modes actually don't exist.

15. ☑ **C** is correct because the workload will run until there is no longer room for storing the workload files.

☒ **A** is incorrect because the workload can't run forever because eventually the workload capture will run out of room to store the workload files. **B** is incorrect because the workload capture process will start even if you don't specify a time limit for the workload capture. **D** is incorrect because there isn't an automatic maximum time limit for the workload capture process.

16. ☑ **A** is correct because you can use the `think_time_auto_correct` parameter to automatically correct the think time set by the `think_time_scale` parameter.

☒ **B** is incorrect because you can't affect the `connection_time_scale` parameter by setting the `think_time_auto_correct` parameter. **C** and **D** are incorrect because you use the `think_time_auto_correct` parameter to automatically correct the think time set by the `think_time_scale` parameter.

SQL Performance Analyzer

17. ☑ **D** is correct because you can't load SQL statements into an STS from a user created file.
☒ **A, B,** and **C** are incorrect because all of them are valid sources to load statements into an STS.

18. ☑ **C** is correct because it correctly lists the three possible modes in which you can execute the EXECUTE_ANALYSIS_TASK procedure.

☒ **A, B,** and **D** are incorrect because all of them contain one or more invalid execution modes.

19. ☑ **A** is correct because the task_name parameter remains the same in each of the three executions of the EXECUTE_ANALYSIS_TASK procedure.

☒ **B, C,** and **D** are incorrect because you need to change all of these parameters during each execution of the EXECUTE_ANALYSIS_TASK procedure.

20. ☑ **C** is correct because the SQL Performance Analyzer isn't really meant to test the effect of a change in the system load.

☒ **A, B** and **D** are incorrect because you can compare the effects of all of these changes by using the SQL Performance Analyzer.

LAB ANSWER

Use the DBMS_WORKLOAD_PREPARE_REPLAY procedure to prepare a database for a database replay. The following are all the parameters you can specify and their default values:

```
DBMS_WORKLOAD_REPLAY.PREPARE_REPLAY (
    synchronization          IN BOOLEAN   DEFAULT TRUE,
    connect_time_scale       IN NUMBER    DEFAULT 100,
    think_time_scale         IN NUMBER    DEFAULT 100,
    think_time_auto_correct  IN BOOLEAN   DEFAULT TRUE);
```

And here is what you must do to increase the number of concurrent users during the workload replay:

■ Change the value of the `connect_time_scale` attribute to less than its default value of 100. The lower the value, the faster a session can connect to the database.

■ Change the value of the `think_time_scale` attribute to decrease the time that elapses between successive calls from the same session. This will also potentially increase the number of concurrent users in the database during the replay, in addition to letting you complete the workload replay in a shorter time span than it took to capture the workload.

■ Keep the `think_time_auto_correct` parameter at its default value of TRUE, which ensures that the database automatically reduces think time if the data replay is progressing slower than the data capture.

2
Diagnosing and Resolving Problems

CERTIFICATION OBJECTIVES

2.01   Automatic Diagnostic Repository

2.02   Incidents and Problems

2.03   Support Workbench

2.04   Health Monitor

2.05   SQL Repair Advisor

2.06   Data Recovery Advisor

✓   Two-Minute Drill

Q&A   Self Test

O ne of the key new features of the Oracle Database 11g release concerns fault management. An entire new fault management infrastructure is introduced in this release to further the goals of both preventing and resolving problems caused by critical errors such as data corruption, code bugs, and missing or renamed datafiles. This chapter discusses the following important topics pertaining to fault management:

- The Automatic Diagnostic repository
- Incidents and problems
- The Support Workbench
- The Health Monitor
- The SQL Repair Advisor
- The Data Recovery Advisor

Following are the goals of the new fault diagnosability infrastructure:

- Preventing problems
- Proactive detection of problems
- Limiting the damage caused by database problems
- Reducing the time it takes to diagnose problems
- Reducing the time it takes to resolve problems
- Easier interaction with Oracle Support

The fault diagnosability infrastructure contains the following components:

- **Automatic diagnostic repository** The automatic diagnostic repository (ADR) is a special storage facility that is located outside the database (in the file system), which you can access with a command-line utility or with Enterprise Manager. The key to the new fault diagnosability feature is the timely capturing of critical error information following a database failure. You can use this information to create incident packages that you can send to Oracle Support Services. A memory-based trace system collects diagnostic data proactively and stores it in the ADR. The ADR contains the traditional diagnostic files such as the alert log, trace files, dump files, and core files as well as new content such as Health Monitor reports.

- **Health Monitor** The Health Monitor is a new database framework that runs diagnostic checks automatically following a critical error in the database. The results of these health checks are merged with the diagnostic data collected for an error. You can also run health checks manually as and when you need.

- **Incident packaging service**   The incident packaging service lets you easily collect diagnostic data pertaining to a critical error in the form of trace files and health check reports pertaining to a critical error and package it into a Zip file for transmission to Oracle Support.
- **The ADR Command Interpreter**   The ADR Command Interpreter (ADRCI) is a command-line tool that lets you view diagnostic data stored in the ADR and package diagnostic information into Zip files that you can then transmit to Oracle Support.
- **The Support Workbench**   This new Enterprise Manager wizard lets you view problem and incident details, run manual health checks, collect diagnostic data, and upload incident packages to Oracle Support.
- **Data Recovery Advisor**   This new advisor is integrated with both the Health Monitor and RMAN, and lets you automate the repair process to fix database problems. You can view database failures and recommendations to fix those problems as well as implement repairs for the problems through the Data Recovery Advisor.
- **SQL Repair Advisor**   The SQL Repair Advisor is a new tool that lets you fix SQL statement failures by providing patches or workarounds for the failed SQL statements that you can then implement in the database.
- **SQL Test Case Builder**   Automates the gathering of information about a SQL-related problem, including the environment in which the SQL statement(s) executed, so Oracle Support Services can easily re-create and test the problem.

A new in-memory diagnostic tracing facility captures relevant diagnostic data upon the appearance of a critical database error. This information is automatically stored in the ADR and forms the nucleus of the incident packages that you can then send to Oracle Support Services for problem resolution. The workflow for a diagnostic session following an error in the database is as follows:

- The database raises an alert following an incident.
- You can view the alert in the Enterprise Manager on the EM Home page.
- You can then drill down to the incident details level:
- You can request EM to create an incident package for you and transmit that automatically to Oracle Support Services, using your MetaLink credentials. You can also add ancillary information such as trace files or scrub the diagnostic data to remove proprietary data before sending the incident package to Oracle Support Services (referred to simply as Oracle Support from here on).

Let's review the main components of the new fault diagnosability infrastructure in the following sections.

CERTIFICATION OBJECTIVE 2.01

Automatic Diagnostic Repository

The automatic diagnostic repository tracks all problems and incidents that occur in the database. The ADR is a file-based repository that you create for storing traditional diagnostic data such as the alert log and trace file, as well as new types of diagnostic data such as the Health Monitor reports. Not only the database, but the ASM, CRS, and other Oracle products and components store all their diagnostic data in the ADR. It's important to understand that each instance of an Oracle product has its own separate ADR home directory within the ADR. Thus, each database instance stores its diagnostic data in a separate directory in the ADR. For example, in an environment with RAC and ASM storage, each of the database instances and the ASM instances have their own home directory under the ADR. The interesting thing is that the ADR uses a consistent diagnostic data format across all Oracle products and all instances, thus making it easier for users and Oracle Support to correlate diagnostic data from multiple instances.

Note that the ADR replaces the traditional diagnostic directories such as the bdump and cdump directories we have been using for years. The traditional *_ dump_dest initialization parameters such as bdump still exist, but the database will ignore them in the new release. You use the new initialization parameter diagnostic_dest to set the location of the ADR base directory, which is the root of the ADR structure.

Because the ADR is located in an operating system directory and not within the database tables, you can always access it, even when you can't access the database instance itself. Consequently, the ADR has been likened to the black box used in airplanes, which records all vital activity of the plane, so officials can diagnose what led to a plane crash. Of course, you had access to the alert log and other dump and trace files at all times in the older releases; however, the addition of additional powerful diagnostic files, incident reports, and the like and the fact

e x a m

ᗯatch *You can have multiple ADR homes within the ADR base.*

that all diagnostic information is centralized, makes the ADR stand apart from the diagnostic framework in previous releases.

The Structure of the ADR

Use the new initialization parameter `diagnostic_dest` to set the location of the ADR base. The `diagnostic_dest` parameter is optional, not mandatory, but does let you pick your own choice for the location of the ADR. If you don't specify a value for the `diagnostic_dest` parameter, the database itself will set a value for the parameter upon database startup. Here's how Oracle determines the default location of the ADR base:

- If you set the ORACLE_BASE environment variable, the database sets the `diagnostic_dest` parameter value to that of the $ORACLE_BASE environment variable.

- If you haven't set the ORACLE_BASE environment variable, the database sets the `diagnostic_dest` parameter value to $ORACLE_HOME/log.

It's important to distinguish between the ADR base, which is the common root directory for the ADR and an ADR home. The former is the location you set with the help of the `diagnostic_dest` parameter. An ADR home represents the path of the ADR home for the current database instance. An ADR base can contain multiple ADR homes, each of them serving as the root directory for a specific instance of a particular Oracle component or product. Each ADR home has the following path, starting from the ADR base:

```
diag/product_type/product_id/instance_id
```

For example, for a database with the identical SID and database name of orcl2 and the ADR base being /u05/app/oracle, the ADR home would be the following:

```
/u05/app/oracle/diag/rdbms/orcl2/orcl2
```

on the **job** *Diagnostic data includes alert log contents, trace files, incident- and problem-related data, and Health Monitor reports.*

exam

watch *The XML-formatted alert log is located in the ALERT directory of* *each ADR home. The text-formatted alert log is located in the TRACE directory.*

ADR Home Subdirectories

Each database instance stores its diagnostic data in various subdirectories, the most important of which are the following:

- **alert** Oracle stores an alert log in the XML format in this directory.
- **hm** Contains the checker run reports, which are generated by the new Health Monitor facility.
- **incident** Contains incident reports for the instance.
- **trace** Contains the text-based alert log, similar to the traditional alert log file.

Note that the alert directory contains an XML–formatted alert log. Oracle Database 11g provides two identical alert logs in different formats for each instance. Besides the XML-formatted alert log, there is also a regular text-based alert log in the trace directory. Later on, I show you how to use the new command-line diagnostic tool ADRCI to strip the XML tags from the XML-formatted alert log file.

on the **job**

In an Oracle RAC environment, you can create an ADR base on each of the nodes or set a central ADR base on shared storage. Setting up a central ADR base on shared storage enables you to view aggregated diagnostics from all instances in the RAC in addition to letting you use the powerful Data Recovery Advisor to diagnose and repair data failures. You can't use the Data Recovery Advisor if you don't use shared storage.

Viewing the ADR Locations

Use the V$DIAG_INFO view to see all the ADR locations for your Oracle database instance, as shown here:

```
SQL> select * from v$diag_info;
INST_ID  NAME             VALUE
-------  --------------   --------------------------------
1        Diag Enabled     TRUE
1        ADR Base         /u01/app/oracle
1        Diag Trace       /u01/app/oracle/diag/rdbms/orcl2/
                            orcl2/trace
1        Diag Alert       /u01/app/oracle/diag/rdbms/orcl2/
                            orcl2/alert
1        Diag Incident    /u01/app/oracle/diag/rdbms/orcl2/
                            orcl2/incident
1        Diag Cdump       /u01/app/oracle/diag/rdbms/orcl2/
```

```
                               orcl2/cdump
1            Health Monitor    /u01/app/oracle/diag/rdbms/orcl2/
                               orcl2/hm1
1            Def Trace File    /u01/app/oracle/diag/rdbms/orcl2/
                               orcl2/trace
                               /orcl2_ora_4813.trc
1            Active Problem    Count                    2
1            Active Incident   Count                    4

11 rows selected.
SQL>
```

The following is a list of the important ADR locations:

- **ADR Base**   Directory path for the ADR base.
- **ADR Home**   Directory path for the ADR home for a specific database instance.
- **Diag Trace**   The text-based alert file is stored here in addition to trace files. This directory corresponds to the old bdump directory.
- **Diag Alert**   The XML-version alert log is found here.
- **Diag incident**   Location for the incident packages.
- **Diag Cdump**   Core dump directory corresponding to cdump.
- **Default trace file**   Path to the session trace files (SQL trace files).

Note that there really is no environment variable named $ADR_HOME to enable the setting of the ADR home. You set the ADR home by using the `set homepath` command after starting the ADRCI tool.

ADRCI

The ADR Command Interpreter (ADRCI) is a brand-new command-line tool that is a key component of the new fault diagnosability infrastructure. The ADRCI tool enables you to interact with the ADR from the command line. You can do the following with the help of the ADRCI:

- View ADR diagnostic data
- Package together incident and problem data for transmission to Oracle Support using the Incident Packaging Service (IPS)
- View Health Monitor reports

All ADRCI commands work with data in the current ADR home and you can have multiple ADR homes current at any given time. Some ADR commands work with multiple ADR homes but other commands require a single ADR home to be current in order for those commands to work. The key here is the ADR homepath, which points to the directory under the ADR base. By default, the value of the homepath is null when you start ADRCI, meaning that all ADR homes under the ADR base are current. If you want to make a single ADR home the current ADR home, you must set the homepath.

Starting ADRCI

You don't need to log into ADRCI because the ADRCI data isn't considered secure data and is, therefore, merely secured by operating system permissions on the ADR directories. Simply enter *adrci* at the command line to use the ADRCI in an interactive mode, as shown here:

```
$ adrci

ADRCI: Release 11.1.0.6.0 - Beta on Thu Sep 27 16:59:27 2007
Copyright (c) 1982, 2007, Oracle.  All rights reserved.

ADR base = "/u01/app/oracle"
adrci>
```

Once you start up the ADRCI utility, you can enter various ADR interactive commands at the ADRCI prompt, and when you are done, leave the interpreter by typing in **exit** or **quit**.

To view a list of all ADRCI commands, enter **help** at the ADRCI prompt:

```
adrci> help
```

To get detailed help on a specific command, enter the keyword **help** followed by the name of the command you want help with. Here's an example:

```
adrci> help ips create package
   Usage:   IPS CREATE PACKAGE
               [INCIDENT <incid> | PROBLEM <prob_id> |
                PROBLEMKEY <prob_key> |
                SECONDS <seconds> |
                TIME <start_time> TO <end_time>]
               [CORRELATE BASIC | TYPICAL | ALL]

   Purpose: Create a package, and optionally select contents
```

```
            for the package.

Arguments:
<incid>:   ID of incident to use for selecting package contents.
<prob_id> :ID of problem to use for selecting package contents.
<prob_key> Problem key to use for selecting package contents.
<seconds> :Number of seconds before now for selecting
           package contents.
<start_time>:Start of time range to look for incidents in.
<end_time>: End of time range to look for incidents in.
    Example:
    ips create package incident 861

adrci>
```

The help command shown here displays information about the ips create package command, which lets you create incident packages to send to Oracle Support.

Setting the ADR Homepath

As mentioned earlier, by default, the ADR homepath is set to null when you first start up ADRCI. This means that all ADR homes for all the instances or components you have under the ADR base are current. Here's an example that shows this:

```
adrci> show homes
ADR Homes:
diag/rdbms/orcl/orcl
diag/rdbms/orcl2/orcl2
diag/rdbms/eleven/eleven
diag/rdbms/nina/nina
adrci>
```

The ADR homepath points to multiple ADR homes. Note that the ADR homepath is shown relative to the ADR base. This means that if the ADR base is /u01/app/oracle, the absolute homepath of the database and instance which are both named orcl2, for example, would be the following:

```
/u01/app/oracle/diag/rdbms/orcl2/orcl2
```

If I want only the single ADR home for the orcl2 instance to be current, I must set the ADR homepath in the following way, by using the set homepath command.

```
adrci> set homepath diag/rdbms/orcl2/orcl2
```

Confirm the setting of the single ADR home with the following command:

```
adrci> show homes
ADR Homes:
diag/rdbms/orcl2/orcl2
adrci>
```

By setting the homepath to diag/rdbms/orcl2/orcl2, only the ADR home for the instance with the SID orcl2 would be current. This means that when you execute the various commands from ADRCI now, the ADRCI will access diagnostic data from this ADR home, which pertains to just the orl2 instance.

on the **Job**

As soon as you start ADRCI, set the homepath for the instance you want to work with.

There are four types of ADRCI commands:

- Commands that don't need a current ADR home
- Commands that work only with a single current ADR home and error out if there are multiple current homes
- Commands that prompt you to select a single ADR home if there are multiple current ADR homes
- Commands that work with one or more current ADR homes

To summarize, all ADRCI commands work with a single current ADR home, but some commands won't work with multiple current ADR homes.

Using ADRCI in Batch Mode

Thus far, you've seen how to use the ADRCI tool by invoking it from the operating system command line. However, you can also use the ADRCI tool from the batch mode, just as you do the SQL*Loader tool, for example, thus allowing you to incorporate ADRCI commands in shell scripts and Windows batch files.

Two command line parameters—`exec` and `script`—help you perform batch operations with ADRCI commands. The `exec` parameter enables you to submit ADRCI commands in the batch mode, shown by the following general syntax:

```
adrci exec="command [; command]..."
```

For example, to run the `show homes` command from the command line (in batch mode), you enter the following command:

```
adrci exec="show homes"
```

The other command-line parameter, `script`, helps you run ADRCI scripts. Here's the general syntax for using the script parameter:

```
adrci script =file_name
```

A script file can consist of any number of ADRCI commands, each separated by a semicolon or a line break. For example, the ADRCI script adrci.txt consists of the following commands:

```
set homepath diag/rdbms/orcl2/orcl2
show alert
```

In order to run the script file adrci.txt, enter the following command at the operating system command prompt:

```
adrci script=adrci.txt
```

The script shown here will run the `show homes` and `show incident` commands.

Viewing Alert Log Contents with ADRCI

As explained earlier, there are two alert logs for each database instance in an Oracle Database 11g Release 1 database, one in the trace directory and the other in the alert directory under the ADR base. You can use the ADRCI utility to view the alert log, as shown in the following example. First, set the ADR homepath to the database instance you're interested in and issue the command `show alert` or `show alert -tail`. The `show alert -tail` command shows the last few lines of the alert log and continuously appends new messages as they arrive, thus letting you perform a live monitoring of the alert log.

```
adrci> show alert -tail
2007-10-17 16:49:50.579000 -04:00
****************************************************************
2007-10-17 16:49:58.405000 -04:00
Starting background process FBDA
Starting background process SMCO
SMCO started with pid=24, OS id=3841
FBDA started with pid=23, OS id=3839
replication_dependency_tracking turned off (no async multimaster
 replication found)
2007-10-17 16:50:03.386000 -04:00
Starting background process QMNC
QMNC started with pid=26, OS id=3849
2007-10-17 16:51:21.040000 -04:00
Completed: ALTER DATABASE OPEN
adrci>
```

You can return to the ADRCI command prompt after issuing the `show alert -tail` command line by pressing CTL-C. You can also specify the number of lines to be shown and also spool the results of the command, just as you can in SQL*Plus.

CERTIFICATION OBJECTIVE 2.02

Incidents and Problems

Oracle introduces two new diagnostic concepts in Oracle Database 11g: problems and incidents. These concepts are crucial to the understanding of the new fault diagnosability infrastructure:

- Any critical error in the database is called a *problem*—for example, a critical error such as the one manifested by the Oracle error ORA-4031 (unable to allocate more bytes of shared memory). A problem is identified by a problem key and includes Oracle error codes.
- A single occurrence of a problem is called an *incident*. Multiple occurrences of the same problem lead to multiple incidents. An incident is identified by a unique incident ID.

The ADR tracks both problems and incidents in the database. When the database encounters a critical error, it displays an incident alert in the Database Home page of the Enterprise Manager. You then use either the Enterprise Manager or the command-line utility ADRCI to view the incidents and the associated problem.

Following an incident, the database adds information about the incident to the alert log and collects diagnostic data about the incident and attaches an incident ID to this data before storing it in a subdirectory it creates for this incident in the ADR. Each incident is tagged with a problem key that relates the incident to a problem. ADR automatically creates a problem when the first incident of that problem key occurs. It removes the problem metadata after the last incident with that problem key is removed from the ADR.

on the *Job*

The MMON background process is in charge of automatically purging expired ADR data.

ADR uses what it refers to as a flood-controlled incident system, whereby it allows only a certain number of incidents under a problem to log diagnostic data.

By default, ADR allows 5 diagnostic data dumps per hour for a single problem. If an incident occurs 20 times but all the incidents are connected to the same problem, you have to report to Oracle Support only one incident. Flood-controlled incident reporting ensures that numerous incidents pertaining to the same problem don't overwhelm the ADR by taking up an inordinate amount of space.

The set of diagnostic data pertaining to an incident or incidents relating to a problem (or problems) is called an *incident package*. When you ask for help from Oracle Support, it's this incident package that they will expect. You can add other files, delete files, or scrub data from the incident package before sending it to Oracle Support. As a DBA, you'll most likely be dealing with problems instead of single incidents, and you'll package the problem data through the IPS to send to Oracle Support.

By default, the database automatically creates incidents upon the occurrence of a critical error. You can also create incidents yourself through the new Enterprise Manager Support Workbench when you want to report problems to Oracle Support that haven't been raising any critical errors in the database.

ADR follows a retention policy so it can limit the amount of diagnostic data it must store. The retention policy actually includes two different settings, one for metadata retention and the other for incident files and dumps retention, as explained here:

■ The incident metadata retention policy, which has a default setting of one year, determines how long ADR retains the incident metadata.

■ The incident files and dumps retention policy, with a default setting of one month, determines how long ADR retains the dump files generated for critical errors.

You can change either of the different policies pertaining to the ADR incidents by using the Incident Package configuration link on the Support Workbench page in Enterprise Manager.

The background process MMON (memory monitor) is in charge of removing expired ADR data.

on the job **You can't disable automatic incident creation for critical errors.**

An incident can be in any one of the following states at a given point in time:

■ **Collecting**   A newly created incident is currently collecting diagnostic data.

■ **Ready**   The incident's data collection phase is complete, and you can package the incident to send to Oracle Support.

■ **Tracking**   The incident must be kept in the ADR indefinitely because the DBA is currently working on it. You must manually set the incident status to this value.

■ **Closed**   The incident is resolved and the ADR will purge it once the incident passes its retention period.

■ **Data-Purged**   The incident metadata is still valid but the associated files have been detached from the incident.

on the
job

If an incident remains in the collecting or ready state for a period that's twice as long as its retention period, it automatically is moved to a closed state.

To check an incident's current status, use either the Support Workbench or issue the following ADRCI command:

```
adrci> show incident -mode detail
```

You can issue just the plain `show incident` command to get basic details about all incidents currently considered open.

Incident Packaging Service

In previous releases of the Oracle database, you had to manually gather diagnostic data from multiple sources to submit to Oracle Support when you notified them of a problem. Oracle Database 11g provides a new feature called the *incident packaging service* (IPS), which lets you automatically gather all diagnostic data pertaining to a critical error such as the trace files and dump files that you're familiar with, as well as the new health check reports, SQL test cases, and related information, and package the data into a Zip file for sending to Oracle Support. The IPS uses a critical error's incident number to automatically identify and gather all relevant diagnostic files and adds them to the incident package. The IPS uses rules to package all dumps and traces for a given problem and lets you package them easily for sending to Oracle Support. You can use rules to gather files generated around a time period, or related to a particular client or a specific error code, for example.

You are allowed the latitude to add, delete, or remove diagnostic files before finalizing an incident package and sending it to Oracle Support. Here are some things you need to know about incident packages:

- An incident package is a logical construct that represents one or more problems. By default, the first and the last three incidents for a problem are included in an incident package. It contains just the metadata for a problem,

- The package you need to send in the form of a Zip file to Oracle Support is a physical package (Zip file) that contains all the files referenced by the metadata in the logical incident package.

- You must finalize a package before the ADRCI can generate a physical package from the initial logical package. During the "finalizing" stage, you can add other diagnostic information in the form of alert log entries, trace files, SQL test cases, and configuration information. You can finalize a package manually through the ADRCI utility and can remove any files you want after reviewing the finalized package.

- You can generate complete and incremental Zip files.

- Oracle employs an incident flood control mechanism, as explained earlier, to limit the amount of diagnostic data that a problem generates in the ADR. Flood control in this context means that ADRCI lets only a certain number of incidents under a given problem be dumped during a given time interval. Once a certain threshold is reached, a flood controlled incident merely generates an alert log entry but not any incident dumps. You can't change the preset threshold levels for incident flood control. Here's how the thresholds are determined:

  - After 5 incidents relating to a certain problem in one hour, further incidents are flood controlled for that hour.

  - After 25 incidents occur for any problem during one day, further incidents for that problem key are flood controlled for that day.

You manage the IPS through either the new Support Workbench, which you can access from the Enterprise Manager, or through the ADRCI tool. You can create packages and upload them to Oracle Support through either means, although the Support Workbench is more intuitive. The ADRCI tool, however, makes up by providing more capabilities to manage incidents and problems in the database. Let's first learn how to manage incidents through the ADRCI tool and then learn how to do the same thing using the Support Workbench. You can set the IPS rules by using the command `ips set configuration`.

Viewing Incidents with the ADRCI

You can display information about all incidents by using the show incident command, as illustrated here:

```
adrci> show incident

ADR Home = /u01/app/oracle/diag/rdbms/orcl2/orcl2:
*********************************************************************

INCIDENT_ID     PROBLEM_KEY          CREATE_TIME
------------    ---------------      ---------------------------------
17060           ORA 1578             2007-09-25 17:00:18.019731 -04:00
14721           ORA 1578             2007-09-08 06:06:33.703485 -04:00
14658           ORA 600              2007-09-09 07:01:31.874206 -04:00
14657           ORA 600              2007-09-09 07:01:21.395179 -04:00

4 rows fetched

adrci>
```

The show incident command lists all incidents, including both open and closed incidents, associated with the current ADR home. You can use the command show incident -mode detail... to get more information about any incident, including trace file names and other information. Here's an example:

```
adrci> show incident -mode DETAIL -p "incident_id=1234"
```

The previous command uses the INCIDENT_ID attribute to identify a specific incident. In this case, the command will show a detailed view for incident 1234.

Packaging Incidents with ADRCI

You use an incident package to transmit incident information to Oracle Support. You can create and submit incident packages easily using the Support Workbench. However, you can also create packages from the command line with the ADRCI tool, as I explain in this section.

Creating a Logical Package   Before you can create a physical incident package and transmit it to Oracle Support, you must create a logical package, which the ADR stores as metadata.

You can create a logical package as an empty package and add diagnostic information later on. Or, you can create a logical package based on an incident number, problem number, problem key, or a time interval. When you create a non-empty logical package, diagnostic information is automatically added to the logical package.

You create a logical package with the `ips create package` command. To create an empty package, use this command:

```
adrci> ips create package
Created package 4 without any contents,
correlation level typical
```

The package just created (Package 4) is an empty logical package. To create a nonempty logical package with diagnostic information about an incident, use the following command.

```
adrci> ips create package incident 17060
Created package 5 based on incident id 17060,
correlation level typical
adrci>
```

You can also create a logical package covering all incidents between two time periods, as shown here:

```
adrci> ips create package time '2007-09-20 00:00:00 -12:00' to
       '2007-09-30 00:00:00 -12:00'
```

The previous command will create a logical package that includes diagnostic information for all incidents that occurred between September 20 and September 30 of 2007. If you want, you can also use the following variations of the `create package` command:

- ■ `ips create package problem`   Create a package based on a problem ID.
- ■ `ips create package problemkey`   Create a package based on a problem key.
- ■ `ips create problem seconds`   Create a package that includes all incidents generated from the specified number of seconds in the past until the present time.

Adding Logical Information to a Logical Package   If you create a logical package by using the `ips create package` command without specifying an incident ID, problem ID, or time range, the package will be empty and you must then add diagnostic information to the existing logical package. Here's how you add diagnostic information for an incident to an empty logical package:

```
adrci> ips add incident 17060 package 4
Added incident 17060 to package 4
adrci>
```

You can add files to an existing package by using the following command:

```
adrci> ips add file <file_name> package <package_number>
```

Note that you can add only those files that are located in the ADR directory hierarchy (under the ADR base).

Generating a Physical Incident Package   Once you load the logical package with diagnostic data, it's time to create the physical package so you can send it to Oracle Support. Here's how you create a physical incident package:

```
adrci> ips generate package 4 in /u01/app/oracle/diag
Generated package 4 in file
/u01/app/oracle/diag/IPSPKG_20070929163401_COM_1.zip,
mode complete
adrci>
```

The previous command generates a physical package in the directory /u01/app/oracle/support from the logical package 4 that you created earlier. Note that the physical file has the COM_1 suffix in its filename, indicating it's a complete incident file. You can create an incremental physical incident package by specifying the keyword incremental, as shown here:

```
adrci> ips generate package 4 in /u01/app/oracle/diag
       incremental
Generated package 4 in file
/u01/app/oracle/diag/IPSPKG_20070929163401_INC_2.zip,
mode incremental
adrci>
```

Once you've incorporated all the diagnostic data and are ready to transmit the physical package to Oracle Support, you can finalize the incident package using the following command:

```
adrci> ips finalize package 4
Finalized package 4
adrci>
```

You're now ready to upload the physical package you've just created to Oracle Support. Note that you still have to send the file the old-fashioned way, by uploading it manually. If you use the Support Workbench to package incidents, you can automate the transmission of the package. We now turn to a review of the Support Workbench.

EXERCISE 2-1

Creating an Incident Package with ADRCI

Create an incident package using the ADRCI tool. Create an empty package first, and then add information about an incident or incidents to the package. Also show how you'd generate a package and add an incident file to the already generated incident package.

Following are the steps you must follow to create an incident package and add incidents and files to that package:

1. Create an empty package using the following command:

   ```
   adrci> ips create package;
   ```

2. Once you create the empty package with the command shown in Step 1, add information about an incident by using the following command:

   ```
   adrci> ips add incident 17060 package 4
   ```

   In the `ips add incident` command, you must provide the incident number and the package number. You can get the package number from the output of the `ips create package` command.

3. Issue the following command to generate a physical package from the logical package you have now.

   ```
   adrci> ips generate package 4 in /u01/app/oracle/support
   ```

   Note that you must provide both the logical package number and a location to store the physical package.

4. To add additional diagnostic files to the physical package created by the previous command, issue the following command:

   ```
   adrci> ips add file /u01/app/oracle/diag/orcl2/orcl2/
          trace/123456.trc package 4
   ```

5. Finalize the package with the following command:

   ```
   adrci> ips finalize package 4
   ```

Now you have a physical package that you can transmit to Oracle Support Services.

CERTIFICATION OBJECTIVE 2.03

Support Workbench

The Support Workbench is an Enterprise Manager wizard that enables you to easily manage incidents and problems in the database caused by critical errors. You can completely automate the process of viewing incidents, creating and submitting incident packages, filing Service Requests with Oracle Support, and tracing the Service Requests with the Support Workbench. The Support Workbench helps you perform the following incident management–related tasks:

- View problems and incident details.
- Generate additional diagnostic data for a problem.
- Run advisors to fix the problems.
- Collect diagnostic data for an incident, create the incident package, and transmit it to Oracle Support.
- Close the problem upon its resolution.

In addition to these incident management features, you can also use the Support Workbench to run health checks and for other purposes, as I explain later in this chapter.

The Support Workbench Wizard enables you to upload IPS incident files to Metalink, but you must first install and configure the Oracle configuration manager to use this feature. During the installation of Oracle Database 11g, you are given the opportunity to enable the Oracle Configuration Manager, as shown in Figure 2-1.

If you don't configure the Oracle Configuration Manager, you must upload the incident packages to MetaLink the old-fashioned way, by manually sending them. For details about the configuration of the Oracle Configuration Manager, please refer to the Oracle manual titled *Oracle Configuration Manager Installation and Administration Guide*.

In the following sections, let's look at how you can use the Support Workbench to investigate and resolve problems in your database.

Viewing Critical Error Alerts

You can investigate any outstanding problems in the database by directly going to the Support Workbench homepage. However, the best way to access the Support

FIGURE 2-1   The Oracle Configuration Manager registration screen

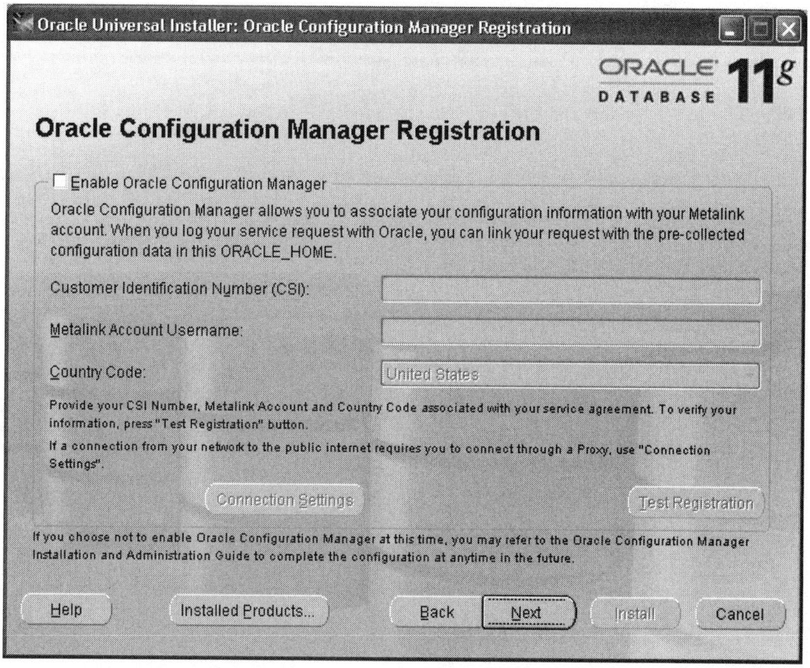

Workbench is to first check if there are any outstanding critical alerts in the database. To do this, go to the Database Home page in Enterprise Manager and scroll down to the Diagnostic Summary section, where you'll see the Active Incidents link. You'll see a circle with a red X inside it if there are any active incidents in the database. You can also click on the Critical Alert link in the Alerts section if you want, to go to the Support Workbench. In addition to these methods of access, you can invoke the Support Workbench by first clicking the Software and Support link and then clicking Support Workbench under the Support section.

In this case, let's access the Support Workbench by first clicking the Software and Support link on the Database Home page. Click Support Workbench in the Support section. On the Support Workbench home page that appears, select All from the View list to view all problems. Figure 2-2 shows the Support Workbench page.

Note that you can also examine problems by reviewing the table of the Alerts section at the bottom of the Database Home page. A critical error is denoted by a red X under the Severity column, and the Message column describes the problem.

FIGURE 2-2 The Support Workbench page

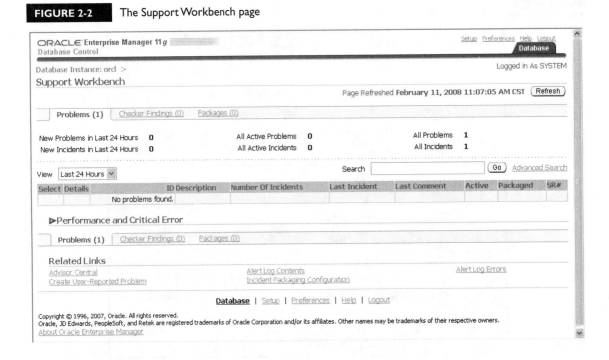

Examining Problem Details

In order to view details about a problem, click View Incident Details on the Incident page. The Problem Details page comes up, as in Figure 2-3, which shows the Incidents subpage. Select an incident and click View to examine the incident details. On the Incident Details page, click the Checkers Findings link to get to the Support Workbench page. In order to examine the problem details from the Support Workbench, click on a finding in the description column. The Support Workbench page will now display details about the alert it showed you. Figure 2-3 shows the Incident Details page of the Support Workbench.

In our case, the problem details show one outstanding problem.

Collecting Additional Diagnostic Data

The database always automatically gathers diagnostic data based on the health check it ran upon the detection of critical alerts. You can have the database collect additional diagnostics by doing one or both of the following:

■ Invoke a health check.

■ Invoke the SQL Test case Builder.

I explain both of these later in this chapter.

Creating a Service Request

Your first step when seeking help from Oracle Support is to create a service request. Follow these steps to create the service request:

1. Go to Metalink by clicking the Go to Metalink button in the Investigate and Resolve section of the Problem Details page.

2. Log in to MetaLink using your normal MetaLink credentials and create a service request.

3. Click the Edit button in the Summary section and enter the service request number in the window that opens. Click OK.

FIGURE 2-3   The Support Workbench page showing incident details

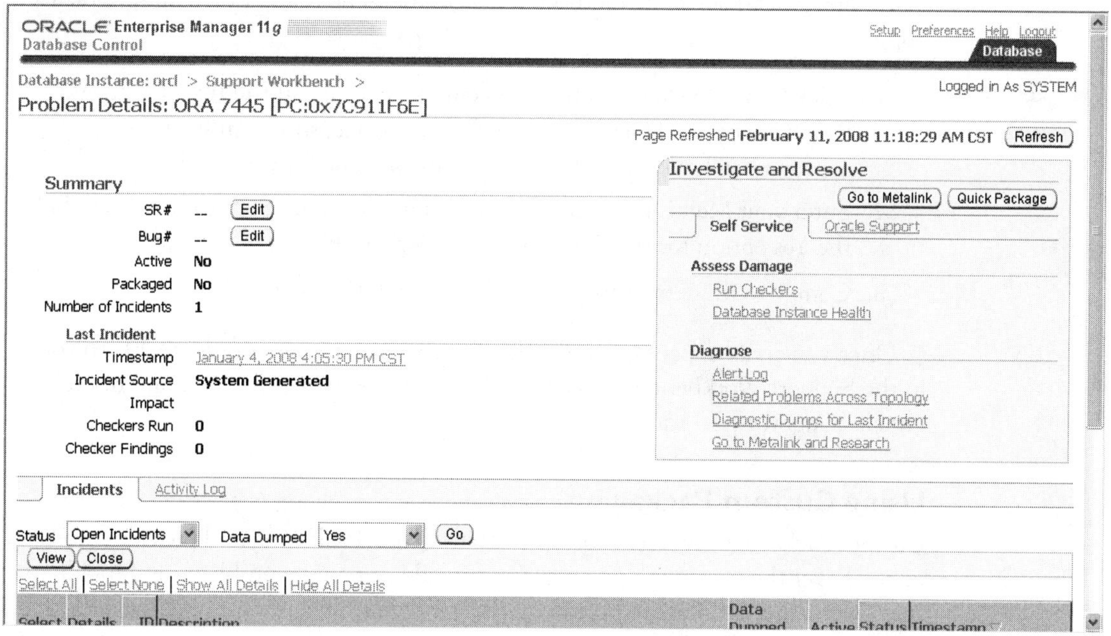

Following the steps enumerated here, you can create your service request with MetaLink. If you want, you can go back to the Problem Details page and record the Service Request number in that page for future reference.

Packaging and Uploading Diagnostic Data

There are two methods for creating and submitting incident packages through the Support Workbench: the Quick Packaging method and the Custom Packaging method. The Quick Packaging method offers you a simple way to package and update diagnostic data. However, you can't edit or customize the diagnostic data you upload to Oracle Support generated in the Quick Packaging method. The Custom Packaging method involves more steps but it enables you to edit and remove diagnostic data and customize the incident package in other ways.

Let's review how to create a package using both of these methods.

Using Quick Packaging

The Quick Packaging Wizard in the Enterprise Manager Support Workbench lets you quickly package and transmit incidents to Oracle Support. Here are the steps to use the Quick Packaging method to collect and send diagnostic data to Oracle Support.

1. Click Quick Package on the Problem Details page in the Investigate and Resolve section. The Create New Package page, shown in Figure 2-4, appears. You have the option of entering a name for your package.

2. Enter your MetaLink credentials and your Customer Service Identifier. Select the Yes option for the Send to Oracle Support button. Click Next.

3. Complete the remaining pages of the Quick Packaging Wizard.

Once you create a package and upload it, the package remains available to you in the Support Workbench. You can update and modify this package and resend to Oracle Support if you want.

Using Custom Packaging

Custom Packaging involves more steps than Quick Packaging and provides more control over the packaging process. You can add or remove problems and incidents, trace files, external files, and other diagnostic data from a new or updated package, using the Custom Packaging method.

FIGURE 2-4   The Create New Package page in Support Workbench

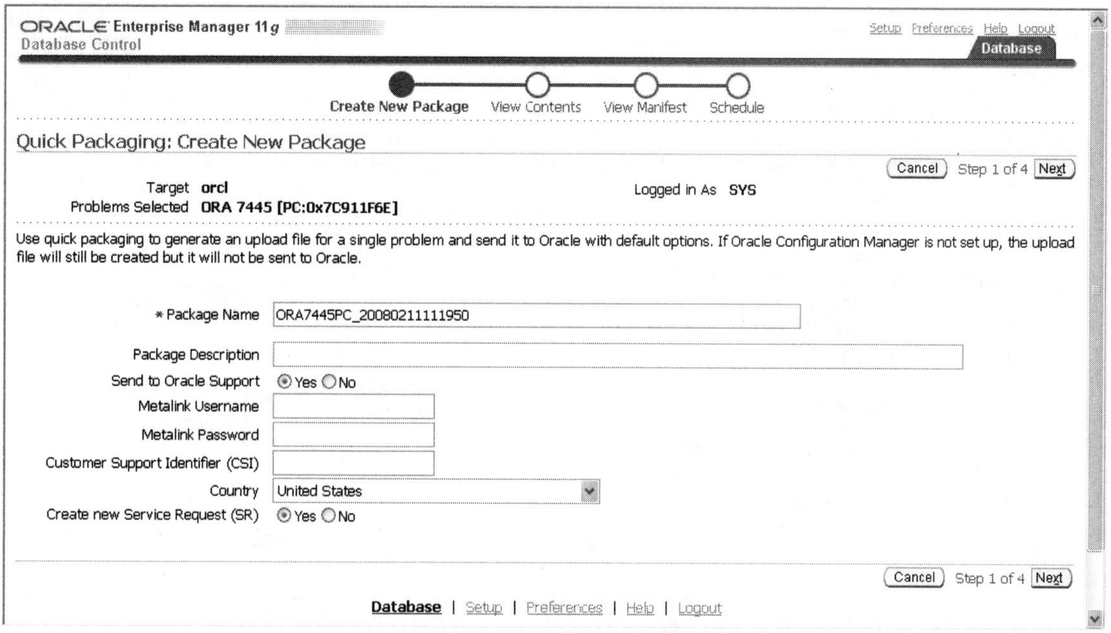

Follow these steps to choose Custom Packaging:

I. Click the Package link on the Incident Details page.

2. On the Select Packaging Mode page, select Custom Packaging and click OK.

3. On the Select Package page, you can select from existing packages or create a new package. In this case, select the Create new Package option, enter a package name, and click OK.

4. The Customize Package page appears, with a confirmation that your new package was successfully created. Figure 2-5 shows the Customize Package page.

5. At this point, the package is created, but not finalized yet. You can perform other tasks listed in the Packaging Tasks section on the Customize Package page, such as editing the package contents, adding diagnostic data, or scrubbing user data.

6. In the Packaging Tasks section (Customize Package page), under the Send to Oracle Support section, click Finish Contents Preparation to finalize the package.

FIGURE 2-5   The Customize Package page

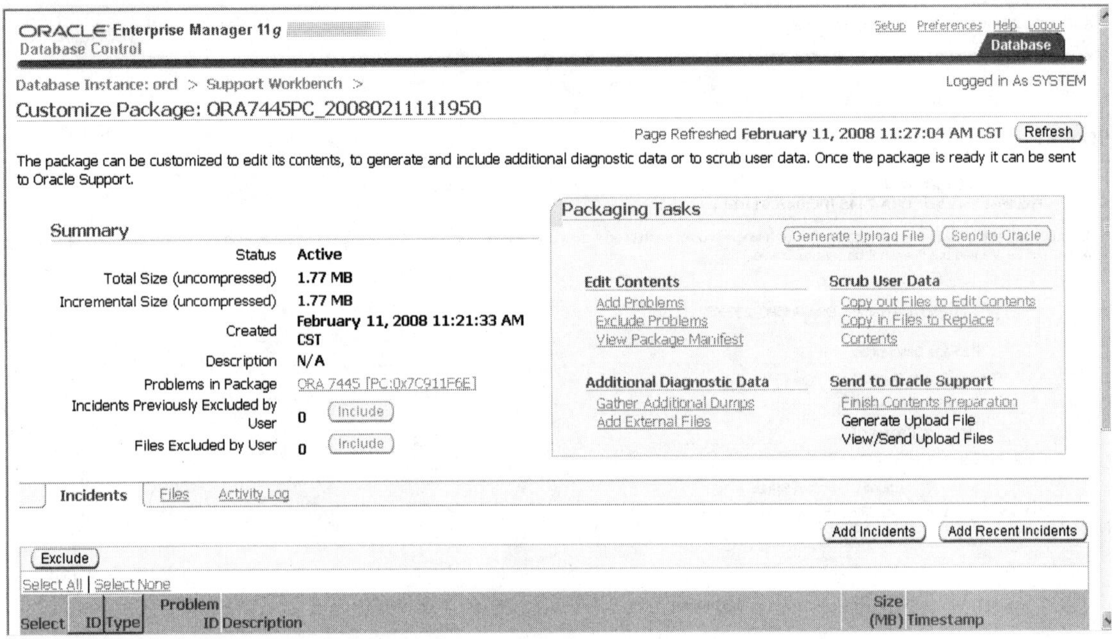

7. Click Generate Upload File to generate the upload file. Select Full or Incremental to generate a full or an incremental Zip file for the incident package. Click either Immediately or Later and then click Submit to schedule the submission of the package to Oracle Support.

8. After processing the Zip file and confirming it, the Customize Package page returns. Click Send to Oracle. The View/Send Upload Files page appears, with a list of Zip files, too. After selecting the Zip files to upload, click Send to Oracle. Fill the MetaLink required information and select whether to create a new service request. Click Submit after selecting either an immediate or a scheduled upload.

Tracking the Service Request

Once you submit an incident package to Oracle Support, you can perform the following additional activities to track your service request and implement repairs:

- Add comments to the problem activity log so all the DBAs in your organization have the latest information on the service request's progress.
- Add new incidents to the package and resend it to Oracle Support.

Implementing Repairs

You can use the Support Workbench to implement any recommendations made that involve the use of an Oracle advisor. You can run the Data Recovery Advisor and/or the SQL Repair Advisor to repair data corruption or SQL failures respectively, if they are recommended. I discuss both of these new Oracle advisors later in this chapter.

Closing Incidents

Once a particular incident is resolved to your satisfaction, you can close the incident from the Support Workbench home page. By default, Oracle purges all incidents after 30 days, unless you disable the purging of an incident.

Generating a User-Created Problem

The database automatically adds critical errors (system-generated problems) to the ADR and tracks them in the Support Workbench. You can use the Support Workbench to add additional diagnostic data to these problems and upload the diagnostic data to Oracle Support. However, there may be times when you want Oracle Support to diagnose a problem that wasn't trapped as a critical error by the database. You can generate what's known as a *user-reported problem* by using the following steps:

1. Go to the Support Workbench from the Software and Support tab on the Database Control (or Enterprise Manager) Home page.

2. Click Create User-Reported Problems under Related Links. Figure 2-6 shows the Create User-Reported Problem page that appears.

3. Select the issue type, such as System Performance or Resource Usage, and click Run Recommended Advisor. If you need further help or if you didn't run the recommended advisor, you can do one of the following:

   - Select the issue type and click Continue with Creation of Problem.
   - Select the issue type None of the Above, enter the problem description, and click Continue with Creation of Problem.

4. In the Problem Details page, follow the instructions to finish reporting the problem.

FIGURE 2-6 The Create User-Reported Problem page in the Support Workbench

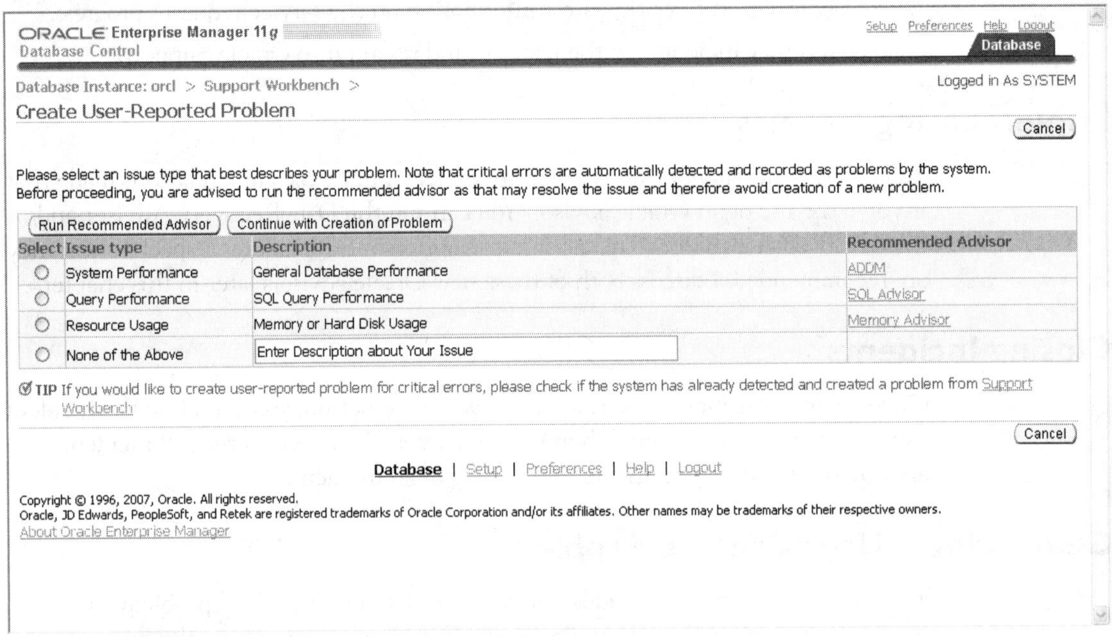

Viewing the Alert Log

As mentioned earlier, in Oracle Database 11g, there are two alert logs for each instance, one a text-based file and the other an XML-formatted file. You can view the alert log for an instance in several ways:

- Use a text editor to view the text editor, whose location you can find by looking at the path given for the Diag Trace entry in the V$DIAG_INFO query results.
- You can view the XML-formatted alert log after finding out its location from the Diag Alert entry in the V$DIAG_INFO query results.
- You can view the alert log by clicking Alert Log Contents in the Database Home page in Enterprise Manager (under Related Links).
- You can use the ADRCI utility to view the XML-formatted alert log after stripping the XML tags.

Health Monitor

Oracle Database 11g includes a new framework called the Health Monitor, which runs diagnostic checks in the database. The data base automatically runs Health Monitor checks in response to critical errors. The checks examine database components such as memory, process usage, and transaction integrity. You can also run your own health checks by using either Enterprise Manager or the new DBMS_HM package. Each time a health check runs, it generates a report of its execution, which includes information such as the health check's findings graded accorded to priority (high, critical, or low) and execution statistics.

You can run the Health Monitor checks in two ways:

- **Reactive** checks are run automatically by the database.
- **Manual** checks are run by the DBA.

You can query the V$HM_CHECK view to get a list of the possible health checks that can be run, as shown here:

```
SQL> select name, description from v$hm_check;

NAME                                    DESCRIPTION
--------------------                    --------------------------
HM Test Check                           Check for HM Functionality
DB Structure Integrity Check            Checks integrity of all
                                        Database files
Data Block Integrity Check              Checks integrity of a
                                        datafile block
Redo Integrity Check                    Checks integrity of redo
                                        log content
Logical Block Check                     Checks logical content of
                                        a block
Transaction Integrity Check             Checks a transaction for
                                        corruptions
Undo Segment Integrity Check            Checks integrity of an
                                        undo segment
All Control Files Check                 Checks all control files
                                        in the database
CF Member Check                         Checks a multiplexed copy
                                        of the control file
```

```
All Datafiles Check                    Check for all datafiles
                                       in the database
Single Datafile Check                  Checks a datafile
Log Group Check                        Checks all members of a
                                       log group
Log Group Member Check                 Checks a particular member
                                       of a log group
Archived Log Check                     Checks an archived log
Redo Revalidation Check                Checks redo log content
IO Revalidation Check                  Checks file accessibility
Block IO Revalidation Check            Checks file accessibility
Txn Revalidation Check                 Revalidate corrupted txn
Failure Simulation Check               Creates dummy failures
Dictionary Integrity Check             Checks dictionary
                                       integrity

21 rows selected.
SQL>
```

At any given time, the database may be running only some of the checks listed in the V$HM_CHECK view. The V$HM_RUN view shows details about the actual checks performed by the Health Monitor, both automatic as well as the ones that were run by the DBA.

There are two types of health checks: DB-online and DB-offline. The online checks can be run when the database is in the open or mount mode. The offline checks can also be run in the nomount mode. All checks are online except the Redo Check and Data Crosscheck, which are offline checks.

Running a Health Check

You can run a health check from Enterprise Manager's Health Monitor interface or by using the DBMS_HM package. You can access the Health Monitor interface in Enterprise Manager by clicking the Checkers tab on the Advisor Central page. From this page, you can run checks (also called checkers) and view the findings of those checks.

You can use the RUN_CHECK procedure of the DBMS_HM package to run any check that's listed in the V$HM_CHECK view. The RUN_CHECK procedure can take the following four parameters:

- **check_name** Provides the name of the check you want to invoke. Use the following query to get the list of checks that you can manually run:

```
SQL> select name from v$hm_check where internal_check='N';
```

■ run_name A user-generated name for identifying a check's run. If you pass a NULL value, the Health Monitor creates a unique name for the check run.

■ timeout Provides a time limit for the checker run. If you pass a NULL value for this parameter, there won't be a time limit for the checker run.

■ input_params Lets you specify name/value pairs de-limited by a special character (;), as shown in the following example in the case of a Data Block Integrity Check.

```
BLC_DF_NUM=1;BLC_BL_NUM=23456
```

EXERCISE 2-2

Running a Health Check with Input Parameters

You can use input parameters for most health checks. Some of the input parameters are optional and the others are mandatory. The following exercise shows how to pass an input parameter for a transaction integrity check. First, use the following query on the V$HM_CHECK_VIEW to find out the parameter values for different health checks.

```
SQL> select c.name check_name, p.name parameter_name,
     p.type,p.default_value, p.description
     from v$hm_check_param p, v$hm_check c
     where p.check_id = c.id and c.internal_check = 'N'
     order by c.name;
```

To pass input parameters to a specific health check, use the name/value pair notation, with the name and value separated by a semicolon (;). Here's an example:

```
begin
dbms_hm run_check (
   check_name   => 'Transaction Integrity Check',
   run_name     => 'testrun1',
   input_params => 'TXN_ID=9.44.1');
end;
```

The example shows how to pass a value for the transaction id parameter, with the check name being Transaction Integrity Check.

Every check has its own specially defined set of inputs. You can view the input parameters for each of the checks you can run by querying the V$HM_CHECK_PARAM view.

The following example shows how to run a health check using the RUN_CHECK procedure.

```
SQL> exec dbms_hm.run_check ('Dictionary Integrity
     Check','TestCheck1',0);

PL/SQL procedure successfully completed.
SQL>
```

The RUN_CHECK procedure in the example runs a dictionary integrity check. You can provide a name for the check you're running. In this example, the check name is TestCheck1.

The Health Monitor stores its reports in the ADR. You can query the VHM_RUN, VHM_FINDING, and V$HM_RECOMMENDATION views to get the findings and recommendations made by the check you ran. Alternatively, you can view the report of the check you just ran, with the help of the GET_RUN_REPORT function, as shown here:

```
SQl> set long 100000

SQL> select dbms_hm.get_run_report('TestCheck1') from dual;

      DBMS_HM.GET_RUN_REPORT('TESTCHECK1')
--------------------------------------------------------------
Basic Run Information
 Run Name                    : TestCheck1
 Run Id                      : 42721
 Check Name                  : Dictionary Integrity Check
 Mode                        : MANUAL
 Status                      : COMPLETED
 Start Time                  : 2007-10-03 16:40:47.464989 -04:00
 End Time                    : 2007-10-03 16:41:23.068746 -04:00
 Error Encountered           : 0
 Source Incident Id          : 0
 Number of Incidents Created : 0
Input Parameters for the Run
 TABLE_NAME=ALL_CORE_TABLES
 CHECK_MASK=ALL

Run Findings And Recommendations
 Finding
 Finding Name : Dictionary Inconsistency
 Finding ID   : 42722
```

```
Type           :FAILURE
Status         : OPEN
Priority       : CRITICAL
Message        : SQL dictionary health check:
dependency$.dobj# fk 126 on object DEPENDENCY$ failed
Message        : Damaged rowid is AAAABnAABAAAOiHABI -
description: No further damage description available

SQL>
```

The GET_RUN_REPORT procedure relies on the HM_* views listed earlier to provide you the findings and recommendations based on the check. The GET_RUN_REPORT procedure can take three values: run_name, type, and level. Of these, only the run_name parameter is mandatory. The default report type is text and the other possible values are html and xml. The level parameter determines the details shown in the report and the possible values are basic and detail, although currently only the basic level of detail is supported.

You can also use the ADRCI utility to view the reports of Health Monitor checks. After setting the homepath to point to the current database instance, issue the show hm_run command first, as shown here:

```
adrci> show hm_run

*****************************************************************
HM RUN RECORD 2131
*****************************************************************
    RUN_ID                       42721
    RUN_NAME                     TestCheck1
    CHECK_NAME                   Dictionary Integrity Check
    NAME_ID                      24
    MODE                         0
    START_TIME                   2007-10-03 16:40:47.4649 -04:00
    RESUME_TIME                  <NULL>
    END_TIME                     2007-10-03 16:41:23.0687 -04:00
    MODIFIED_TIME                2007-10-03 16:41:59.7867 -04:00
    TIMEOUT                      0
    FLAGS                        0
    STATUS                       5
    SRC_INCIDENT_ID              0
    NUM_INCIDENTS                0
    ERR_NUMBER                   0
    REPORT_FILE
    /u01/app/oracle/diag/rdbms/orcl2/orcl2/hm/HMREPORT_TestCheck1
2131 rows fetched

adrci>
```

The `show hm_run` command shows all test runs that were run in the database. Here, I'm showing only the single HM run we're interested in, called TestCheck1. In my example, the output of the `show hm_run` command shows the filename of the report under the `report_file` column. This means the report for this particular check has already been generated. If the `report_file` column shows a NULL value, you must first generate the report using the create `report hm_run` command, as shown here:

```
adrci> create report hm_run TestCheck1
```

You can view a report by issuing the `show report hm_run` command, as shown here:

```
adrci> show report hm_run TestCheck1
```

Note that you pass the check name as a parameter to both the `create report hm_run` and the `show report hm_run` commands.

Viewing the Health Monitor Reports

The Health Monitor stores its checker reports in the ADR, and you can view the reports through the Enterprise Manager, the ADRCI, the DBMS_HM package, and the V$HM_RUN view.

CERTIFICATION OBJECTIVE 2.05

SQL Repair Advisor

When a SQL statement failure results in a critical error, the new SQL Repair Advisor analyzes the statement and in many cases recommends a patch to fix the failed statement. The fix is usually in the form of a recommendation to apply a SQL patch to bypass the failure, without changing the SQL statement itself. Applying the recommended patch leads the query optimizer to select an alternate execution plan for the problem statement. If the SQL Repair Advisor fails to provide a patch, you can, of course, use the Support Workbench to package the incident files and send the diagnostic data to Oracle Support for help.

The SQL Repair Advisor tries to recommend a SQL patch when it's unable to find a fix for the problem SQL statement(s). A SQL patch is very similar to a SQL profile, but it's used mostly as a workaround to fix a failing SQL statement.

There are two ways you can invoke the SQL Repair Advisor. The first way is to use the Support Workbench to launch the SQL Repair Advisor. You can also use the new DBMS_SQLDIAG package to invoke the SQL Repair Advisor. First, let's learn how to invoke the advisor from the Support Workbench.

Using the Support Workbench

Here are the steps to invoke the SQL Repair Advisor from the Support Workbench home page:

1. From the Support Workbench home page, go to the Problem Details page by clicking on the ID of the problem you're investigating.
2. Click the specific problem message resulting from the failed SQL statement.
3. Click SQL Repair Advisor in the Investigate and Resolve section on the Self Service tab.
4. Enter the appropriate options to run the advisor immediately or at a scheduled time later.
5. Click Submit.
6. On the SQL Repair Results page, click View to examine the Report Recommendations page.
7. Click Implement to carry out the SQL Repair Advisor's recommendations.
8. The implementation is completed when the SQL Repair Results page shows you a confirmation message.

You can disable or remove the patches installed through the SQL Repair Advisor by going to the Database Control home page and navigating to Server | SQL Plan Control | SQL Patch | Disable (or Drop). You may want to do this when you migrate to a new version of the database.

Using the DBMS_SQLDIAG Package

Although using the Enterprise Manager is the most straightforward way to invoke the SQL Repair Advisor, you can also use the new DBMS_SQLDIAG package to invoke the advisor. In the following example, I first create a SQL Repair Advisor task and then apply and test the SQL patch offered by it:

1. Identify the problem SQL statement, as shown in the following example, which results in an error:

```
SQL> delete from t t1 where t1.a = 'a'
       and rowid <> (select max(rowid)
       from t t2 where t1.a= t2.a and t1.b = t2.b and t1.d=t2.d);
```

You can fix the error resulting from executing the SQL statement by using the SQL Repair Advisor.

2. Create a SQL Repair Advisor diagnostic task by passing the offending SQL query as the value for the `sql_text` attribute:

```
SQL> declare
  2    report_out clob;
  3    task_id   varchar2(50);
  4    begin
  5    task_id := dbms_sqldiag.create_diagnosis_task(
  6    sql_text=>' delete from t t1 where t1.a = 'a'
                   and rowid <> (select max(rowid) from t t2
                   where t1.a= t2.a and t1.b = t2.b
                   and t1.d=t2.d)',
  8    task_name   =>'test_task1',
  9    problem_type=>dbms_sqldiag.problem_type_compilation
                   _error);
 10* end;
SQL> /

PL/SQL procedure successfully completed.
SQL>
```

The previous code specifies the SQL statement you want the SQL Repair Advisor to analyze. In addition, it specifies the task name and the problem type. I chose `problem_type_compilation_error` as the value for the `problem_type` parameter in this example. The other possible value for the `problem_type` parameter is `problem_type_execution_type`.

3. Once you create the new task, you can provide the new task parameters by executing the `set_tuning_task_parameter` procedure, as shown here:

```
SQL> exec dbms_sqltune.set_tuning_task_parameter('task_id,
'-SQLDIAG_FINDING_MODE', dbms_sqldiag.SQLDIAG_FINDING_
FILTER_PLANS);
```

You are now ready to execute the task, as shown in the next step.

4. Execute the diagnostic task you created earlier, by passing the task name as a parameter to the EXECUTE_DIAGNOSTIC_TASK procedure:

```
SQL> exec dbms_sqldiag.execute_diagnosis_task('test_task1');

PL/SQL procedure successfully completed.

SQL>
```

The EXECUTE_DIAGNOSTIC_TASK procedure has only a single parameter, `task_name`.

5. Use the REPORT_DIAGNOSTIC_TASK procedure to get an analysis of the diagnostic task you executed:

```
SQL> declare rep_out clob;
  2 begin
  3  rep_out := dbms_sqldiag.report_diagnosis_task
  4              ('test_task1',dbms_sqldiag.type_text);
  5  dbms_output.put_line ('Report : ' || rep_out);
  6*end;
SQL> /

Report             : GENERAL INFORMATION
SECTION
-------------------------------------------------
Tuning Task Name        : test_task1
Tuning Task Owner       : SYS
Tuning Task ID          : 3219
Workload Type           : Single SQL Statement
Execution Count         : 1
Current Execution       : EXEC_3219
Execution Type          : SQL DIAGNOSIS
Scope                   : COMPREHENSIVE
Time Limit(seconds)     : 1800
Completion Status       : COMPLETED
Started at              : 10/20/2007 06:33:42
Completed at            : 10/20/2007 06:36:45
Schema Name             : SYS
SQL ID                  : 44wx3x03jx01v
SQL Text                : delete from t t1 where t1.a = 'a'
                          and rowid <> (select max(rowid)
                          from t t2 where t1.a= t2.a
                          and t1.b = t2.b and t1.d=t2.d)
...
PL/SQL procedure successfully completed.

SQL>
```

6. If the SQL Repair Advisor recommends a patch, you can accept the patch by executing the ACCEPT_SQL_PATCH procedure, as shown here:

```
SQL> exec dbms_sqldiag.accept_sql_patch (task_name=>
    'test_task1',task_owner=> 'SYS')
```

You can now execute the problem SQL statement to ensure that the workaround patch did fix the problem. Check the explain plan output for the SQL statement to make sure it shows use of the SQL patch. The DBA_SQL_PATCHES view contains the names of all the patches recommended by the SQL Repair Advisor.

If you want to drop the SQL patch for any reason, you can do so by using the DROP_SQL_PATCH procedure. You can remove the SQL patch, for example, if you receive an official patch from Oracle to fix the problem. You can also drop the SQL patches when you upgrade your database to the next patch set or Oracle release.

You can export a SQL patch into another database by using a staging table. Inserting a patch is called *packing* the staging table and creating patches using the staging table is called *unpacking*. The following exercise shows how to export a SQL Patch.

EXERCISE 2-3

Exporting a SQL Patch to Another Database

1. Create a staging table by executing the CREATE_STGTB_SQLPATCH procedure:

```
SQL> exec dbms_sqldiag.create_stgtab_sqlpatch (
    table_name  => 'mystagetab1',
    schema_name =>  'hr');
```

In the next step, you'll use this table to store the SQL patch information.

2. Execute the PACK_STGTAB_SQLPATCH procedure to write SQL patch information to the staged table you created in Step 1.

```
SQL> exec dbms_sqldiag.pack_stgtab_sqlpatch (
    staging_table_name => 'mystagetab1');
```

This will copy all SQL patches in the DEFAULT category to the staging table mystgtab1. You can now move the staging table to the new database using the Data Pump Export and Import utilities.

3. Use the UNPACK_STGTAB_SQLPATCH procedure to create SQL patches on the new system using the patches in the staging table.

```
SQL> exec dbms_sqldiag.unpack_stgtab_sqlpatch
     (staging_table_name => 'mystgtab1');
```

By default, Oracle will unpack all patches in the staging table and apply those patches to the target database.

In addition to the SQL Repair Advisor, Oracle Database 11g also provides the new SQL Test Case Builder tool, to help you create test cases so Oracle Support Services can reproduce and test a problem. The new tool simplifies the effort and reduces the time involved in gathering information about SQL-related problems. The SQL Test Case Builder tool gathers information about the following things: the query that was being executed, table and index definitions, procedures, functions and packages, initialization parameter settings, and optimizer statistics.

The following are the steps to access the SQL Test Case Builder from the Support Workbench page:

1. Click the Problem ID you are interested in to get to the problem details page.
2. Click the Oracle Support tab.
3. Click "Generate Additional Dumps and Test Cases."
4. On the "Additional Dumps and test Cases" page, click the icon in the Go to Task column to start the SQL Test Case Builder analysis.

The SQL Test Case Builder produces a SQL script with the commands necessary to re-create the necessary database objects in an identical environment. You can also execute the DBMS_SQLDIAG.EXPORT_SQL_TESTCASE_DIR_BY_INC function to manually invoke the SQL Test Case Builder.

CERTIFICATION OBJECTIVE 2.06

Data Recovery Advisor

The Data Recovery Advisor (DRA) is a new tool that automatically diagnoses failures in the database, determines the repair options and, optionally, executes the repairs if you want. A database *failure* could be a corruption or loss of data, including the loss of datafiles. You can access DRA through the RMAN client or Enterprise Manager.

The DRA uses Oracle Database 11g's new diagnosability infrastructure and the new diagnostic concepts such as problems, incidents, and failures to automatically diagnose data failures. The DRA can help you fix problems such as lost datafiles, data block corruption, I/O failures, and a crashed database. Here are the main goals of the DRA:

- Early detection of data failures, which limits damage
- Automatic detection of failures, along with recommendations and even repair of the failures
- Reduced database downtime

The Data Recovery Advisor can diagnose and help fix problems such as the following:

- Inaccessible datafiles and control files
- Physical data corruption such as invalid block header field values
- Inconsistencies such as one datafile being older than others
- I/O failures such as hardware errors

A checker or check is a specific diagnostic procedure registered with the Health Monitor. You can proactively invoke these checkers, known as data integrity checks, yourself, and they are also run reactively by the database itself. The Health Monitor automatically runs a data integrity check whenever it finds an error in the database. The data integrity check searches the database for any failures that caused the errors. A failure is defined as a problem such as data corruption that is diagnosed by the database. All diagnosed failures are stored in the ADR.

You can use the DRA to fix the data failures that caused the errors, but you can only do so after the failure diagnostics are stored in the ADR. You can use the Data Recovery Advisor to diagnose a failure and in most cases, fix it, either through a manual course of action or through an automated repair strategy. The failure data is stored outside the database. Consequently, you can view failures and fix them even when the database is in the nomount state.

All findings in the DRA are organized into groups pertaining to a specific failure. The DRA also assigns severity levels such as *critical* and *high* to each database failure it captures. Once the DBA requests the DRA for repair advice, the DRA provides all the automatic and manual repair choices available to you, along with its advice. You can choose to fix the problem yourself using the manual methods or to have the DRA perform the repairs.

Note that the DRA consolidates related failures into a single failure. If 100 data blocks are corrupted in a datafile, the DRA will show a single failure. You can drill down to the level of an individual sub-failure.

The DRA doesn't automatically tag a database error that is logged in the alert log file, such as an ORA-600 error, as a failure. To be considered a failure, a problem must be diagnosed by a check (or checker) registered with the Health Monitor. So, the chain of causation is this: an error leads to a Health Monitor data integrity check, which investigates the failures related to the error. If the database finds related failures, it lodges the information about the failure in the ADR. It is at this point that you can call on the DRA to generate repair advice.

The preceding chain of causation relates to a reactive data integrity check, but the logic is the same when you launch your own proactive data integrity checks. A failure that your check reveals will be treated just as a failure that's detected by a Health Monitor data integrity check. Also, any `validate` or `backup` commands you issue through RMAN will invoke an automatic data integrity check.

Failures

You must be aware of three failure characteristics: *status, priority* and *grouping*:

- **Failure status**   When the database first reports a failure, the failure has a status of `open`. Once the failure is repaired, the status changes to `closed`. When you run the `list failure` command, it automatically closes all failures that have been resolved. If, for some reason, the database doesn't set the status of a fixed failure to `closed`, you can do so by using the `change failure ... closed` command. But remember that if you try to set the status of an unresolved failure to `closed`, the Data Recovery Advisor will re-create the failure with a different ID following the next data integrity check, when the check encounters the unresolved failure.

- **Failure priority**   A failure can be assigned three levels of priority: `critical`, `high`, or `low`. A `high` priority level, such as the one assigned to a missing current control file, could bring the database down. Events such as a missing archived red log are assigned the `high` level of priority. The DRA, however, assigns only the `critical` or `high` level of priority to a failure, and the `list failure` command shows you only the failures with these two levels of priority. If, in your opinion, a failure with a `high` priority isn't really a big deal and can wait for fixing, you can manually change the priority level of that failure to `low`, thus keeping that failure from appearing in the `list failure` output. You can't, however, change the priority level of a failure from `critical` to `low`.

- **Failure grouping** The DRA always groups related failures together under a single parent failure. You can, however, use the detail option in the list failure command to view details about the individual failures in a group.

Repair Options

The DRA offers you two types of repair options in some cases, manual and automatic. It's your responsibility to perform the manual repair actions, whereas the DRA performs the automatic repair actions itself. The DRA first checks to see if it can perform the automatic repair before offering the repair choice to you. For example, in the case of a failure repair that involves restoring and recovering a datafile, the DRA will offer to automatically perform this repair only after first verifying that the necessary datafile backups and archived redo logs do exist and that RMAN can access them. It may further divide the manual repair actions into mandatory or optional actions. If a manual option is easier to perform than undertaking a more drastic repair in the way of restoring and recovering datafiles, for example, the Data Recovery Advisor presents both the manual and the automatic repair choices. If the Data Recovery Advisor knows that a problem can't be fixed with an automatic repair, the DRA will state that the manual repair action is mandatory. If a repair action can be performed either manually or automatically, such as restoring and replacing a missing datafile, the DRA will offer both options.

Whenever the DRA offers an automatic repair option, it shows you the directory location where the repair script it's going to use is stored. You can then edit and execute this file yourself, if you so desire.

Wherever it's possible to do so, the DRA tries to consolidate its repairs for multiple failures into a single repair consisting of several individual steps. If it can't repair a failure that results from, say, a missing controlfile, it'll report that information to you and suggest that you first fix those other problems. In this case, you may create a new control file and issue the list failure, advise failure, and repair failure commands once again, so the DRA can fix the failure for you.

Oracle does inform you that a DRA failure repair sometimes may not do the trick because the DRA doesn't check every single byte in a backup file or an archived redo log. This leaves room for the possibility that a corrupt block in either a backup file or an archived redo log may still keep you from fixing the database failure.

In Oracle Database 11g Release 1, the Data Recovery Advisor supports only a single instance and not Oracle RAC databases. If all the instances of an Oracle RAC setup crash, you can mount the database in the single instance mode and use the DRA to fix certain problems as well as invoke data recovery checks. You can't, however, use the DRA to detect failures such as an inaccessible datafile, which is local to another instance in the Oracle RAC configuration.

You can invoke the DRA through RMAN as well as through Enterprise Manager. In Enterprise Manager, the DRA is integrated with both the Support Workbench and the Health Monitor. Let's first examine how to use the DRA through an RMAN client.

Using RMAN to Manage the Data Recovery Advisor

You can use the RMAN interface to invoke the Data Recovery Advisor and manage and resolve various types of data failures. Before you actually walk through a data failure repair with RMAN, it's important to review the key RMAN commands pertaining to the DRA.

Viewing Failures

Use the `list failure` command to view a list of database failures that were caught by invoking an automatic or manual database check prompted by an error in the database. Here's an example:

```
RMAN> list failure;
```

The V$IR_FAILURE view stores the results of all the `list failure` commands you issue.

on the
Öob

The `list failure` command lists a failure only if the database has diagnosed a failure. The `list failure` command doesn't initiate a data integrity check by itself—it merely reports an already diagnosed failure.

You can view individual sub-failures by issuing the `list failure...detail` command. Because the Data Recovery Advisor consolidates failures wherever possible, you use the `detail` option to list individual failures. You can provide options such as `critical`, `high`, `low`, or `closed` to limit the `list failure` command's output to only those failures that belong to a specific priority level. By default, the `list failure` command shows all failures with a priority level of `critical` or `high`. Here are some `list failure` command variations:

```
RMAN> list failure critical;
RMAN> list failure open;
RMAN> list failure closed;
```

The first command shows only those failures with a priority level of `critical`, and the second, only those failures that are currently `open`. The failure status remains `open` until you invoke a repair action; after the failure is repaired manually or automatically by the DRA, its status will be `closed`. You can exclude some failures from the `list failure` output by adding the `exclude failure` option, as shown here:

```
RMAN> list failure exclude failure 12345;
```

Once a failure is repaired, the Data Recovery Advisor will remove that failure from the `list failure` output.

exam
watch *You must understand the implications of using various Data Recovery Advisor commands. For example,* *you must know that the `advise failure` command implicitly closes all open failures that are already fixed.*

Dealing with Failures

Use the `change failure` command to change the priority level of a database failure. This command is useful when you want to close a failure that's really trivial. Note that you can change a priority of `high` to `low` and vice versa, but you can't change a `critical` priority level. The default output list of the `list failure` command shows all high-priority failures. If there are too many high-priority failures that you're already aware of, you may want to change a failure's status from `high` to `low` to avoid seeing those failures in the output of the list failure command.

The following example shows how to change the priority level of a command from `high` to `low`:

```
RMAN> change failure 1 priority low;
```

You can change a problem's status to `closed` any time you want, even if the failure wasn't really fixed. However, if the DRA gets new checker data pertaining to that problem, it will re-create the failure with a different ID.

Getting Repair Advice

Use the `advise failure` command to get advice on a failure. The command prints a summary of the failure. It also implicitly closes all open problems that have been fixed. By default, the command reports on all `critical` and `high` priority repairs. The command lists all failures that have a critical or high level of priority. The command shows a summary of the repair options as well as a single repair option for each failure. The repair options can be manual as well as automated. The two repair options are a *no-data-loss* and a *data-loss* repair.

Manual repair options can be mandatory or optional. Often, a manual repair option may be the best option, as it avoids more extreme measures such as restoring and recovering entire datafiles, as in the automatic repair option. For this reason, Oracle recommends that you try the manual repair options first before considering the automatic repair options suggested by the `advise failure` command.

After showing the available repair options, RMAN generates a repair script to implement the repair option it recommends. You can then use this script, also called a *manual checklist*, after making any necessary changes to it, to repair the failure.

Using the RMAN-generated repair script may often help you fix a problem quicker than letting RMAN perform the repair. For example, it's far easier to manually restore a lost table from another database rather than to let RMAN perform a laborious restore and recover operation to fix the problem.

Once you issue the `advise failure` command, you can query the V$IR_MANUAL_CHECKLIST view to examine the recommended repair, as shown here:

```
SQL> select advise_id, rank, message from v$ir_manual_checklist;

ADVISE_ID    RANK    MESSAGE
------       ------  ------------------------------------------
21           0       if file /u01/app/oracle/nick/users01.dbf
                     was unintentionally renamed or moved,
                     restore it
21           0       if file /u01/app/oracle/nick/example01.dbf
                     was unintentionally renamed or moved,
                     restore it

SQL>
```

In the V$IR_MANUAL_CHECKLIST view, the MESSAGE column shows a summary of the repair advice offered by the DRA. Note that the DRA always tries to consolidate the repair actions so multiple failures can be fixed with a single repair job.

The repair script generated by RMAN shows the commands RMAN will use to fix the failure. Here's an example showing how RMAN might fix a failure involving a missing datafile:

```
# restore and recover datafile
restore check readonly datafile 1;
recover datafile 1;
```

You can choose to execute this repair script yourself, or fix the problem using a less time-consuming option, such as the importing of a table or tables, instead of letting the DRA automatically execute the repair script.

Repairing Failures

Once the `advise failure` command reports its repair recommendations, you can either manually repair the failures or choose the automatic repair option. If you want the Data Recovery Advisor to automatically fix the failures, simply issue the `repair failure` command so RMAN can fix the failure. Sometimes, the `advise failure` command may ask you to perform some manual repairs first before executing the `repair failure` command. Here's the basic `repair failure` command:

```
RMAN> repair failure;
```

You must issue the `advise failure` command before you can fix problems with the `repair failure` command. Otherwise, you'll get an error, as shown in this example:

```
RMAN> repair failure;
using target database control file instead of recovery catalog
RMAN-00571: =========================
RMAN-00569: =============== ERROR MESSAGE STACK FOLLOWS ========
RMAN-00571:
=================================================================
RMAN-03002: failure of repair command at 10/21/2007 12:15:24
RMAN-06954: REPAIR command must be preceded by ADVISE command in
 same session
RMAN>
```

By default, the `repair failure` command will implement the single repair recommendation shown in the output for the `advise failure` command. You can also choose to merely view RMAN's repair procedure without actually repairing the failure by using the preview option with the `repair failure` command:

```
RMAN> repair failure preview;
```

The `repair failure preview` command is helpful in ascertaining the actual steps of the RMAN repair procedure, without embarking on the repair process.

The V$IR_REPAIR view shows the results of the `repair failure` command. Here's the structure of the V$IR_REPAIR view:

```
SQL> desc v$ir_repair
 Name                          Null?     Type
 ----------------------        ------    ---------------
 REPAIR_ID                               NUMBER
 ADVISE_ID                               NUMBER
 SUMMARY                                 VARCHAR2(32)
```

```
RANK                              NUMBER
TIME_DETECTED                     DATE
EXECUTED                          DATE
ESTIMATED_DATA_LOSS               VARCHAR2(20)
DETAILED_DESCRIPTION              VARCHAR2(1024)
REPAIR_SCRIPT                     VARCHAR2(512)
ESTIMATED_REPAIR_TIME             NUMBER
ACTUAL_REPAIR_TIMENUMBER
STATUS                            VARCHAR2(7)
```

The following query on the V$IR_REPAIR view shows details about the current repairs:

```
SQL> select repair_id,advise_id,summary,rank
     from v$ir_repair;

REPAIR_ID   ADVISE_ID   SUMMARY                 RANK
----------- ---------   --------------------    --------
    23         21       NO DATA LOSS OPTION       1
    69         67       NO DATA LOSS OPTION       1
    82         80       NO DATA LOSS OPTION       1
SQL>
```

The NO DATA LOSS option under the summary column means that the failure can be fixed without losing any data.

In addition to the V$IR_REPAIR view, there are also the following new views that help you investigate database errors:

- **V$IR_MANUAL_CHECKLIST**   Lists the manual repair advice produced by the `advise failure` command.
- **V$IR_FAILURE**   Lists all failures that result from the `list failure` command and includes closed failures. For example, the following command shows all failures detected on February 10, 2008:

```
SQL> select * from v$ir_failure
     where trunc(time_detected) = '10-FEB-2008';
```

- **V$IR_FAILURE_SET**   Is a cross-reference of failure and advice identifiers.

Using the DRA to Restore a Missing Datafile

In the following example, the database fails to start up because a datafile is missing:

```
SQL> startup
ORACLE instance started.
Total System Global Area  615055360 bytes
```

```
Fixed Size                  1324864 bytes
Variable Size             239757504 bytes
Database Buffers          369098752 bytes
Redo Buffers                4874240 bytes
Database mounted.
ORA-01157: cannot identify/lock data file 4 - see
DBWR trace file
ORA-01110: data file 4: 'C:\ORACLE\PRODUCT\10.2.0\ORADATA\NICK
\USERS01.DBF'
SQL>
```

You can fix this problem by using the Data Recovery Advisor as follows:

1. Start RMAN and issue the `list failure` command:

```
RMAN> list failure;

List of Database Failures
Failure ID Priority Status   Time Detected Summary
---------- -------- ------- ------------- ---------------
4          HIGH     OPEN     20-OCT-07    multiple datafiles
                                          are missing

RMAN>
```

You can get more details about the failure by issuing the `list failure` command with the keyword `detail` and by passing the unique identifier for the specific failure, as shown here:

```
RMAN> list failure 4 detail;
```

The previous command shows all sub-failures under the failure identified by the unique identifier 4.

2. Issue the `advise failure` command to get recommendations from the DRA to fix the missing datafiles problem.

```
RMAN> advise failure;

List of Database Failures
Failure ID Priority Status    Time Detected Summary
---------- -------- --------- --------- ---------------
4          HIGH     OPEN      20-OCT-07  multiple datafiles
                                         are missing

analyzing automatic repair options; this may take some time
allocated channel: ORA_DISK_1
```

```
channel ORA_DISK_1: SID=152 device type=DISK

analyzing automatic repair options complete

Manual Checklist
==============================================================
if file C:\ORACLE\PRODUCT\10.2.0\ORADATA\NICK\USERS01.DBF
was unintentionally renamed or moved, restore it

if file C:\ORACLE\PRODUCT\10.2.0\ORADATA\NICK\EXAMPLE01.DBF
was unintentionally renamed or moved, restore it

Automated Repair Options
==============================================================
Option Strategy Repair Description
------ -------- ------------------
               no data loss restore and recover datafile 4,
               Restore and recover datafile
    Repair script: C:\ORCL11\APP\ORACLE\NICK\DIAG\diag\
    rdbms\nick\nick\hm\reco_1139896242.hm

RMAN>
```

Note that RMAN provides you a manual set of options as well as an automated repair options list. The manual options call for you to replace the two missing datafiles. The automated repair option asks you to run an RMAN repair script, which will do the same job as the manual repair actions.

3. The following is an optional step, where you can examine RMAN's plans to repair the problem:

```
RMAN> repair failure preview;

Strategy          Repair script
-----------       -------------------------------------
no data loss C:\ORCL11\APP\ORACLE\NICK\DIAG\diag\
rdbms\nick\nick\hm\reco_1139896242.hm

contents of repair script:
   # restore and recover datafile
   restore check readonly datafile 4, 5;
   recover datafile 4, 5;

RMAN>
```

The repair failure preview command shows that RMAN plans to restore and recover datafiles 4 and 5 and that this is a "no data loss" strategy.

4. Once you've ascertained that the repair strategy is safe, issue the `repair failure` command to let RMAN repair the missing datafile problem:

```
RMAN> repair failure;

Strategy      Repair script
-----------  -------------------------------------------------
no data loss
C:\ORCL11\APP\ORACLE\NICK\DIAG\diag\rdbms\nick\
nick\hm\reco_8213224112.hm

contents of repair script:
   # restore and recover datafile
   restore check readonly datafile 4, 5;
   recover datafile 4, 5;

Do you really want to execute the above repair
(enter YES or NO)? yes
executing repair script

Starting restore at 23-OCT-07
using channel ORA_DISK_1

channel ORA_DISK_1: starting datafile backup set restore
channel ORA_DISK_1: specifying datafile(s) to restore
from backup set
Finished restore at 23-OCT-07

Starting recover at 23-OCT-07
starting media recovery
RMAN-08187:WARNING:media recovery until SCN 3212445 complete

Finished recover at 23-OCT-07
repair failure complete
Do you want to open the database (enter YES or NO)? yes

RMAN>
```

By selecting the *Yes* option, you let RMAN automatically open the database after completing the recovery.

Proactive Checks

Although the database runs reactive checks on its own, Oracle recommends that your run proactive database health checks on a regular basis. It's also best to run a proactive check to dig deeper into a problem when a reactive check indicates there is a database component failure. You can run these proactive checks through either the Health Monitor or by executing the new validate database command.

The new validate database command in Oracle Database 11*g* lets you invoke a proactive health check for the database and its components. The validate database command is similar to the old validate backupset command, but is more sophisticated. Any time the validate database command detects a database failure, it initiates a failure assessment and logs the failure in the ADR. You can view these failure findings when you issue the list failure command. Here's an example showing how to use the command:

```
RMAN> validate database;

Starting validate at 16-OCT-07
using target database control file instead of recovery catalog
allocated channel: ORA_DISK_1
channel ORA_DISK_1: SID=109 device type=DISK
RMAN-06169: could not read file header for datafile 7 error
 reason 7
RMAN-00571: ===========================================================
RMAN-00569: =============== ERROR MESSAGE STACK FOLLOWS =======
RMAN-00571: ===========================================================
RMAN-03002: failure of validate command at 10/16/2007 12:25:33
RMAN-06056: could not access datafile 7

RMAN>
```

You can employ the validate database command to validate at a fine level of granularity because you can validate individual backup sets or even individual data blocks now with the command. By default, the command checks for physical and not logical database corruption. However, you can make the command check for logical corruption by specifying the CHECK LOGICAL option. Of the two types of block corruption, intrablock and interblock, the validate database command checks for intrablock corruption only.

Issue the list failure command to review the failure:

```
RMAN> list failure;
List of Database Failures
=========================
Failure ID Priority Status Time Detected Summary
---------- -------- ------ ------------- -------
73427      HIGH     OPEN   16-OCT-07     One or more
                                         non-system
                                         datafiles are corrupt
```

Next, issue the `advise failure` command:

```
RMAN> advise failure;
List of Database Failures
==========================
Failure ID Priority Status  Time Detected Summary
---------- -------- ------- ------------- -------
73427      HIGH     OPEN    16-OCT-07     One or more
                                          non-system
                                          datafiles are corrupt

analyzing automatic repair options; this may take some time
using channel ORA_DISK_1
analyzing automatic repair options complete

Mandatory Manual Actions
========================
Optional Manual Actions
========================
no manual actions available
Automated Repair Options
========================
Option Repair Description
------ ------------------
1      Restore and recover datafile 7


  Strategy: The repair includes complete media recovery with
  no data loss
  Repair script:
/u01/app/oracle/diag/rdbms/orcl2/orcl2/hm/reco_1899054268.hm
RMAN>
```

The `advise repair` command shows that you can fix the data corruption without any data loss by automatically restoring and recovering the corrupted datafile 7.

Although RMAN helped us in this case by providing a repair option and easily let us fix the problem, the Data Recovery Advisor can't fix every failure that occurs in your database. Here's an example:

```
RMAN> list failure;

using target database control file instead of recovery catalog
List of Database Failures
==========================
```

```
Failure ID Priority Status     Time Detected Summary
---------- -------- ---------- ------------- --------------------
42725      CRITICAL OPEN        03-OCT-07     SQL dictionary
 health check:
dependency$.dobj# fk 126 on object DEPENDENCY$ failed
42722      CRITICAL OPEN        03-OCT-07     SQL dictionary
                                              health check:
dependency$.dobj# fk 126 on object DEPENDENCY$ failed
```

Issue the advise failure command, to view the repair options for the failures:

```
RMAN> advise failure;

List of Database Failures
===========================

Failure ID Priority Status     Time Detected Summary
---------- -------- ---------- ------------- -------
42725      CRITICAL OPEN        03-OCT-07     SQL dictionary
                                              health check:
dependency$.dobj# fk 126 on object DEPENDENCY$ failed
42722      CRITICAL OPEN        03-OCT-07     SQL dictionary
                                              health check:
dependency$.dobj# fk 126 on object DEPENDENCY$ failed

Mandatory Manual Actions
==========================
1. Please contact Oracle Support Services to resolve
failure 42725: SQLdictionary health check:
dependency$.dobj# fk 126 on object DEPENDENCY$
failed
2. Please contact Oracle Support Services to resolve failure
42722: SQLdictionary health check: dependency$.
dobj# fk 126 on object DEPENDENCY$failed

Optional Manual Actions
========================
no manual actions available

Automated Repair Options
=========================
no automatic repair options available

RMAN>
```

The Data Recovery Advisor doesn't provide either a manual or an automated repair option in this case. Instead, it asks you to contact Oracle Support Services to resolve the failure reported by the SQL dictionary health check.

Managing the DRA with Database Control

Although using RMAN to access the Data Recovery Advisor is simple enough, Oracle recommends that you use Database Control to fix database failures. Suppose a health check invoked by the database in response to an error results in an error diagnosis, which you see in the Health Monitor on the Database Home page. You can see from the Alerts section on the same page that a physical block corruption caused the database failure. Here are the steps in the Oracle advised recovery strategy:

1. Click Availability on the Database Home page.

2. On the Availability page, click Perform Recovery under the Manage section.

3. The Perform Recovery page appears, as shown in Figure 2-7. Based on the failures listed in the Oracle Advised Recovery section, you can follow the next steps.

FIGURE 2-7 The Perform Recovery page

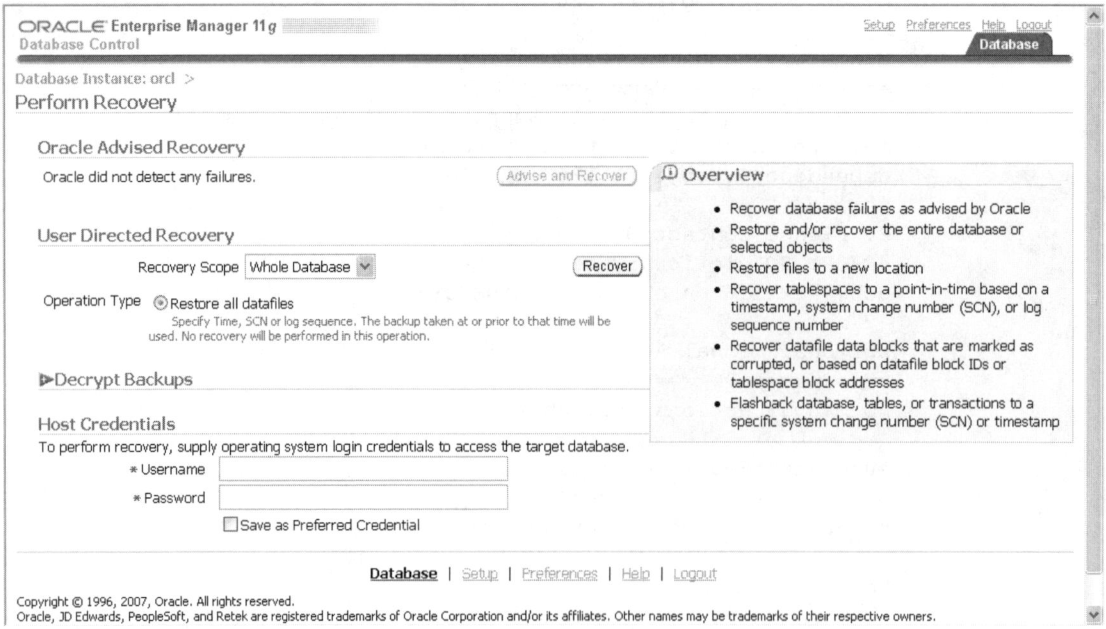

4. Click Advise and Recover.

5. Click the number next to the failure status.

6. In the View and Manage Failures page, click All in the Priority list and click Go.

7. Select Data Failures from the navigation tree.

8. Select the failure you're interested in and click Advise.

9. Click Continue. You'll see the Review page next, which summarizes the proposed data recovery actions.

Note that the Perform Recovery page has two sections titled Oracle Advised Recovery and User Directed Recovery. To access the Data Recovery Advisor, go to the new Oracle Advised Recovery section. In the Oracle Advised Recovery section, the Advise and Recover button is grayed out if the Data Recovery Advisor hasn't trapped any failures. However, when the DRA detects a failure, you can click the Advise and Recover button.

Oracle recommends that when dealing with data corruption or other data failures, to access the Data Recovery Advisor through the Support Workbench. From the Support Workbench, you can access the Data Recovery Advisor in either of these ways:

- From the Checker findings subpage on the Support Workbench home page
- From the Problem Details page

New Parameter to Detect Database Corruption

Oracle database 11g introduces a new initialization parameter called `db_ultra_safe`, to help you manage the other corruption detection–related initialization parameters. The value you set for the `db_ultra_safe` parameter affects the default values of the parameters `db_block_checking`, `db_block_checksum`, and the new parameter `db_lost_write_protect`. Here's what the different corruption detection–related parameters stand for:

e x a m

ⓦatch *By setting the `db_ultra_` safe parameter, you can affect the default values of the three corruption-detecting* *initialization parameters—`db_block_checking`, `db_block_checksum`, and `db_lost_write_protect`.*

- `db_block_checking` Checks database blocks to prevent memory and data corruption. The default value is `false`, and Oracle recommends the value `full`.

- `db_block_checksum` Specifies the writing of checksums in the header of every data block when writing to disk to detect corruption caused by the storage system. The default value is `typical`, which is the same as the recommended value.

- `db_lost_write_protect` This is a new initialization parameter, which initiates checking for any data block *lost writes* that may occur on a physical standby database when the I/O subsystem signals block write completion before it's completely written to disk. The default value for this parameter is `typical`, same as the value Oracle recommends that you use.

- You can set values of the three corruption detection–related parameters explicitly. However, you can control the values of this parameter by simply setting a value for the `db_ultra_safe` parameter. The `db_ultra_safe` parameter sets the default values for the three initialization parameters that control protection levels. The `db_ultra_safe` parameter's value implicitly changes the values of the three parameters. The `db_ultra_safe` parameter can take the following values: `off`, `data_only`, and `data_and_index`. The `data_and_index` value means a more intensive form of corruption checking than that specified by the `data_only` value. The value of the three corruption detection parameters depends on the value you set for the `db_ultra_safe` parameter. If the value of the `db_ultra_safe` parameter value is `off`, the value of the `db_block_checking` parameter is `off` (or `false`), the value of the `db_block_checksum` parameter is `typical`, and the value of the `db_lost_write_protect` parameter is `typical`. In brief, if you set any of the three parameters explicitly, no changes are made to those values.

- If the value of the `db_ultra_safe` parameter value is `data_only`, the value of the `db_block_checking` parameter is `medium`, the value of the `db_block_checksum` parameter is `full`, and the value of the `db_lost_write_protect` parameter is `typical`. When the value of the `db_block_checking` parameter is set to `medium`, the database will check for logical corruption in the data blocks. Any time a block's contents change, say because of an `update` or `insert` operation, the database performs block header checks, including semantic block checking, for all data blocks.

- If the value of the `db_ultra_safe` parameter value is `data_and_index`, the value of the `db_block_checking` parameter is `full` (or `true`), the value of the `db_block_checksum` parameter is `full`, and the value of the `db_lost_write_protect` parameter is `typical`. When the value of the `db_block_checking` parameter is set to `full`, the database will check for logical corruption in the data blocks as well as the index blocks. Any time a block's contents change, say because of an `update` or `insert` operation, the database performs block header checks, including semantic block checking, for both data and index blocks.

As you can see, you can calibrate the level of block checking by setting appropriate values for the `db_ultra_safe` parameter. You can set the most stringent level of checking by setting the value `data_and_index` for this parameter. Of course, if you set the value `off` for this parameter, the database will enforce the least rigorous form of block checking.

INSIDE THE EXAM

The exam is likely to have a question or two regarding the new `diagnostic_dest` initialization parameter. If you don't explicitly set this parameter, what does it default to? What is the relationship between the ADR base and an ADR home? You must also know where the alert log files are stored in the new release.

You must understand the steps involved in creating an incident package. What do you have to do first in order to upload Zip files automatically to MetaLink? (You need to configure the Oracle Configuration Manager.) You must be familiar with the Incident Packaging Service (IPS) commands to gather diagnostic data and package the data into Zip files for transmission to Oracle Support. You may encounter a question dealing with Support Workbench. What are the two methods to create and upload an Incident package? (Be prepared to explain the Quick Packaging method and the Custom Packaging method.)

You can expect the exam to contain a question about the SQL Repair Advisor.

How does the advisor fix a SQL statement failure? Expect questions about the different Data Recovery Advisor commands such as `change failure`, `advise failure`, and `list failure`. For example, how does the `advise failure` command affect open failures that are fixed? How does the `list failure` command deal with new failures between multiple executions of the command?

Expect to be tested on your understanding of the new `validate database` command, which helps in performing proactive health checks. Does the `validate` command help in checking physical or logical corruption? What about intrablock and interblock corruption checking with the `validate` command? You must also review the new parameter to detect corruption, paying special attention to how setting the `db_ultra_safe` parameter affects the three corruption-detecting initialization parameters.

CERTIFICATION SUMMARY

This chapter started with a discussion of the automatic diagnostic repository, which the new diagnostic framework introduced in Oracle Database 11g. You learned how to use the `diagnostic_dest` parameter to set the ADR base. You learned how to use the V$DIAG_INFO view to find out all the ADR locations for a database. The chapter explained the ADRCI command-line tool, which helps you view the diagnostic data, in addition to helping you package incidents and view Health Monitor reports. The chapter showed how to set the ADR homepath and how to use ADRCI in batch mode. You also learned how to view the alert log contents using ADRCI.

This chapter introduced the classification of incidents and problems, which is one of the key concepts of the new diagnostic framework in Oracle Database 11g. You learned about the incident packaging service and how to create logical and physical packages and to finalize a package using ADRCI commands. The chapter showed you how to use the Support Workbench to view critical errors. You learned how to create incident reports through the Quick Packaging and the Custom Packaging methods, how to upload incidents reports to Oracle Support through the Support Workbench, and how to track and close incidents using the Support Workbench.

You can use the new Health Monitor to run both reactive and manual health checks. You can use the `show hm_run` command to view all health checks performed by the database. Use the DBMS_HM package to run health checks and to get the findings and recommendations of those checks.

You can use the SQL Repair Advisor to fix SQL statement failures. The SQL Repair advisor fixes the SQL statements by offering recommendations for a SQL patch to bypass the problem SQL statement. You can use either the Support Workbench or the DBMS_SQLDIAG package to access the SQL Repair Advisor. The chapter also showed you how to use the new SQL Test Case Builder to enable Oracle Support Services to easily re-create and test a problem.

The Data Repair Advisor diagnoses failures and determines repair options, and can even automatically make the repairs. The three key failure characteristics are status, priority, and grouping. You have both manual and automatic repair options when using the Data Repair Advisor. You can use RMAN for accessing the Data Recovery Advisor. RMAN offers commands such as `list failure`, `advise failure`, and `repair failure` to fix database failures. You can also manage the Data Recovery Advisor through Database Control, by choosing the Oracle Advised Recovery option.

✓ TWO-MINUTE DRILL

Automatic Diagnostic Repository

❑ The ADR tracks all problems and incidents that occur in the database.

❑ The ADR is a file-based repository for storing all diagnostic data for the database and other Oracle products and components.

❑ Each instance of an Oracle product has its own ADR home directory within the ADR.

❑ The `diagnostic_dest` parameter sets the location of the ADR home directory.

❑ The `diagnostic_dest` parameter is an optional parameter.

❑ There can be multiple ADR homes under an ADR base.

❑ There is both an XML-formatted and a text-based alert log file in an Oracle Database 11g database.

❑ The V$DIAG_INFO view shows you all the ADR locations for an instance.

❑ The ADRCI is a command-line tool that helps you work with the ADR.

❑ You can have multiple ADR homes current at a given time.

❑ All ADRCI commands work with the current ADR home.

❑ By default, the value of the ADR homepath is `null`.

❑ Use the `set homepath` command to set an ADR home.

❑ The command-line parameters `exec` and `script` let you perform batch operations with ADRCI commands.

Incidents and Problems

❑ A critical database error is called a *problem*.

❑ A single occurrence of a problem is termed an *incident*.

❑ The database automatically collects diagnostic data about all incidents.

❑ You can't disable the creation of automatic incidents for critical errors.

❑ An incident package is the set of diagnostic data pertaining to an incident or incidents.

❑ ADR uses a retention policy to determine how long it retains diagnostic data for incidents.

❑ An incident can be in any one of four states at a given point in time.

❑ The IPS automatically gathers and packages the diagnostic data to send to Oracle Support.

❑ You must first finalize a package before generating a physical package.

❑ You can create complete and incremental Zip files.

❑ Oracle uses a flood controlled incident system to limit the logging of diagnostic data for similar incidents.

❑ You can manage IPS through the ADRCI or the Support Workbench.

❑ A logical package contains just the metadata about the incidents.

❑ A physical package is the actual package that you upload to Oracle Support.

Support Workbench

❑ You can upload incident packages to Oracle Support directly from the Support Workbench, provided you've installed the Oracle Configuration Manager.

❑ Quick Packaging lets you easily create and upload incident packages, but doesn't let you edit the packages.

❑ Custom Packaging enables you to edit the incident packages, but involves more steps than the Quick Packaging method.

❑ The database automatically generates diagnostic data for critical errors, but you can create your own "user-reported" problems.

Health Monitor

❑ A check or checker is a specific diagnostic procedure registered with the Health Monitor.

❑ The Health Monitor runs diagnostic checks in the database automatically in response to critical errors.

❑ You can run manual health checks.

❑ The V$HM_CHECK view shows all the possible health checks you can run in the database.

❑ The V$HM_RUN view shows details and status of all reactive and manual database Health Monitor checks.

❑ You can run health checks from the Enterprise Manager Health Monitor interface or through executing procedures from the DBMS_HM package.

❑ Use the RUN_CHECK procedure to run a health check.

❑ The GET_RUN_REPORT function gets the report for a specified checker run.

❑ The show hm_run command shows all Health Monitor checks.

❑ The Health Monitor stores all its reports in the ADR.

SQL Repair Advisor

❑ Use the SQL Repair Advisor to fix SQL statement failures.

❑ The SQL Repair Advisor doesn't recommend changing the failed SQL statement.

❑ The SQL Repair Advisor recommends implementing a SQL patch as a workaround for the failed SQL statement when it's unable to find a fix for the problem.

❑ You can access the SQL Repair Advisor through the Support Workbench or through the DBMS_SQLDIAG package.

❑ The adoption of the SQL patch recommended by the SQL Repair Advisor will change the execution plan of the SQL statement.

❑ You can drop the SQL Patch or export it into another database.

Data Recovery Advisor

❑ The DRA automatically diagnoses failures, determines the repair options, and optionally, executes the repairs.

❑ The Health Monitor runs an automatic diagnostic check when it detects an error in the database.

❑ The DRA consolidates related failures into a single failure.

❑ In order for a database error to be considered a failure, it must be first diagnosed by a check registered with the Health Monitor.

❑ A `validate` or `backup` command issued through RMAN will initiate an automatic data integrity check.

❑ The three important characteristics for a failure are status, priority, and grouping.

❑ If the database doesn't automatically close a fixed failure, you can do so by issuing the `change failure ... closed` command.

❑ The three levels of failure priority are: critical, high, and low.

❑ The DRA offers you both manual and automatic repair options.

❑ DRA doesn't support Oracle RAC installations.

❑ The `list failure` command lets you view the failures in the database.

❑ You must issue the `advise failure` command before issuing the `repair failure` command.

SELF TEST

The following questions will help you measure your understanding of the material presented in this chapter. Read all the choices carefully because there might be more than one correct answer. Choose all correct answers for each question.

Automatic Diagnostic Repository

1. How does the database determine the default location of the ADR base?
    A. If you set the ORACLE_BASE environment variable, the database sets the `diagnostic_dest` parameter value to the $ORACLE_BASE directory.
    B. If you haven't set the ORACLE_HOME environment variable, the database sets the `diagnostic_dest` parameter value to $ORACLE_HOME/log.
    C. If you set the ORACLE_BASE environment variable, the database sets the `diagnostic_dest` parameter value to $ORACLE_HOME/log.
    D. If you haven't set the ORACLE_BASE environment variable, the database sets the `diagnostic_dest` parameter value to $ORACLE_HOME/diag.

2. The diagnostic_dest initialization parameter sets the location of
    A. The ADR home.
    B. The ADR base.
    C. The ADR home and ADR base.
    D. Neither the ADR home nor the ADR base.

3. All ADRCI commands will work with
    A. The current single ADR home.
    B. All ADR homes that are current at a given time.
    C. All ADR homes, whether they are current or not.
    D. The Support Workbench.

4. By default,
    A. No ADR homes under the ADR base are current.
    B. The homepath is null.
    C. All ADR homes under the ADR base are current.
    D. All ADR homes under the ADR base are null.

Incidents and Problems

5. When a critical error occurs, the database

A. Automatically creates an incident report, but doesn't send it to Oracle Support.

B. Automatically creates and sends an incident report to Oracle Support.

C. Automatically creates an incident.

D. Does nothing—you must initiate the incident creation process manually.

6. Which of the following statements is correct?

A. If an incident remains in the closed state for a period that's twice as long as its retention period, it automatically is moved to an expired state.

B. If an incident remains in the collection or ready state for a period that's as long as its retention period, it automatically is moved to a closed state.

C. If an incident remains in the data_purged state for a period that's twice as long as its retention period, it automatically is moved to a closed state.

D. If an incident remains in the collection or ready state for a period that's twice as long as its retention period, it automatically is moved to a closed state.

7. Which of the following is the correct sequence of steps in creating and sending an incident report to Oracle Support?

A. Create the logical package, finalize the package, and generate the physical package.

B. Create the physical package, finalize the package, and generate the logical package.

C. Create an empty physical package, finalize the package, and generate the physical package.

D. Create the logical package, generate the physical package, and finalize the package.

8. Which of the following commands lets you add diagnostic information to a package?

A. `ips generate package 4 in /u01/app/oracle/diag`

B. `ips add incident 17060 package 4`

C. `ips generate package 4 in /u01/app/oracle/diag incremental`

D. `ips create package`

Support Workbench

9. The Support Workbench can

A. Collect only diagnostic data for an incident and transmit the incident package to Oracle Support

B. Only create the incident package and transmit the package to Oracle Support

C. Only transmit an incident package to Oracle Support

D. Collect diagnostic data for an incident, create the incident package, and transmit the incident package to Oracle Support

10. You must manually upload an incident package to Oracle Support
   A. Only if you haven't installed the Oracle Configuration Manager
   B. Whether you have installed the Oracle Configuration Manager or not
   C. Only if you have installed the Oracle Configuration Manager during installation of the server
   D. Only if you've installed the Oracle Configuration Manager separately, after completing the installation of the server

11. Which of the following statements is true?
   A. You cannot edit the diagnostic data you're sending to Oracle Support when you use the Quick Packaging method, but you can customize the data.
   B. You cannot edit the diagnostic data you're sending to Oracle Support when you use the Custom Packaging method, but you can customize the data.
   C. You cannot edit or customize the diagnostic data you're sending to Oracle Support when you use the Quick Packaging method.
   D. You cannot edit or customize the diagnostic data you're sending to Oracle Support when you use the Custom Packaging method.

12. Oracle purges all incidents automatically after a period of
   A. 30 days
   B. 7 days
   C. 90 days
   D. Oracle will never automatically purge an incident.

Health Monitor

13. Which of the following views provides you a list of all the health checks you can run in a database?
   A. V$HM_CHECK
   B. V$HM_RUN
   C. V$CHECKERS
   D. V$HM

14. You can view the Health Monitor checker reports
   A. Only through the DBMS_HM package or the V$HM_RUN view
   B. Through the Enterprise Manager, the ADRCI, the DBMS_HM package, and the V$HM_RUN view
   C. Only through the Enterprise Manager or the ADRCI
   D. Only through the DBMS_HM package and the ADRCI

15. Which of the following ADRCI commands will show you the recommendations of a database health check?

A. `show report hm`

B. `show hm_run <check_name>`

C. `show hm_run`

D. `show report hm_run <check_name>`

16. Which of the following parameters are mandatory when you execute the GET_RUN_REPORT procedure to get the findings of a database health check?

A. `run_name, type, and level`

B. `type and level`

C. `check_name, run_name, and type`

D. `run_name`

SQL Repair Advisor

17. You can invoke the SQL Repair Advisor

A. Only from the Support Workbench

B. From the Support Workbench or through the DBMS_SQLDIAG package

C. From the Support Workbench or through the DBMS_DIAG package

D. Only by using the DBMS_SQLDIAG package

18. The SQL Repair Advisor fixes a problem SQL statement

A. By providing a patch as a workaround

B. By providing a new SQL profile to fix the problem

C. By rewriting the problem SQL statement completely

D. By creating a new explain plan for the statement directly

19. By accepting the SQL Advisor's recommendation, you ensure that

A. The optimizer reuses the same execution plan.

B. The optimizer will never use the failed SQL statement again.

C. The optimizer collects new statistics for the objects referenced by the failed SQL statement.

D. The optimizer use an alternate explain plan.

20. Once you apply a SQL patch,

A. You can never remove the patch.

B. You can drop the patch any time by using the REMOVE_SQL_PATCH procedure.

C. You can drop the patch any time by using the DROP_SQL_PATCH procedure.

D. You must obtain an official patch from Oracle to fix the error.

Data Recovery Advisor

21. You can access the Data Recovery Advisor through the

    A. Enterprise Manager and SQL Workbench

    B. Enterprise Manager and ADRCI

    C. Enterprise Manager and RMAN

    D. SQL Workbench and ADRCI

22. When you use the Data Recovery Advisor through RMAN, you can perform

    A. Only manual repair

    B. Manual and automatic repair

    C. Only automatic repair

    D. You can't repair problems through RMAN.

23. When do you use the `failure...closed` command when dealing with the Data Recovery Advisor?

    A. If the database doesn't set the status of a fixed failure to `closed`, you can do so by using the change `failure...closed` command.

    B. If the database doesn't set the status of an open failure to `closed`, you can do so by using the change `failure...closed` command.

    C. After the database fixes any problem, you must close the problem by running the `failure...closed` command.

    D. Only if you manually fix a problem must you use the `failure...closed` command.

24. Which of the following is the correct sequence of commands when you use the Data Recovery Advisor to fix failures?

    A. `advise failure, list failure, fix failure`

    B. `list failure, repair failure, advise failure`

    C. `advise failure, list failure, repair failure`

    D. `list failure, advise failure, repair failure`

LAB QUESTION

You receive an Oracle error ORA-01578, indicating that one more Oracle data blocks are corrupted. How would you go about fixing the database corruption using the Data Recovery Advisor?

SELF TEST ANSWERS

Automatic Diagnostic Repository

1. ☑ **A** is correct because the default location of the ADR base is the value you assign to the $ORACLE_BASE environment variable.

☒ **B, C,** and **D** are incorrect because they point to the wrong directory for the ADR base location.

2. ☑ **B** is correct because the diagnostic_dest parameter sets the location of the ADR base.

☒ **A, C,** and **D** are incorrect because the diagnostic_dest parameter has nothing to do with the setting of the ADR home.

3. ☑ **A** is correct because all ADRCI commands will work with the current ADR home.

☒ **B** and **C** are incorrect because some ADRCI commands don't work with all ADR homes. **D** is incorrect because you can't use ADRCI commands from the Support Workbench. The ADRCI is a command-line utility whereas the Support Workbench is a GUI.

4. ☑ **B** and **C** are correct. **B** is correct because, by default, the ADR homepath is null. **C** is correct because all ADR homes under an ADR base are current if you don't specify a single database using the set homepath command.

☒ **A** is incorrect because all ADR homes are current by default. **D** is incorrect because all ADR homes are current by default, rather than all of them being null.

Incidents and Problems

5. ☑ **C** is correct because the database will only create an incident following a critical error. It's up to you to generate the incident report, using either the ADRCI tool or the Support Workbench.

☒ **A** and **B** are incorrect because the database doesn't create an incident report automatically on its own. **D** is incorrect because you don't have to initiate the incident creation process—the database does that automatically.

6. ☑ **D** is correct because the database will automatically move an incident to the closed status if that incident is in the collection or ready state for a period that's twice as long as its retention period.

☒ **A** is incorrect because there is no such thing as an expired state. **B** is incorrect because an incident is moved to the closed state after it's in the collection or ready state for twice as long, not merely as long as the retention period. **C** is incorrect because an incident isn't moved from the data_purged state to the closed state.

7. ☑ **A** is correct because it shows the correct sequence of steps in the incident reporting process.

☒ **B, C,** and **D** are incorrect because they don't show the correct sequence of steps.

8. ☑ **B** is correct because the `add incident` command adds diagnostic information pertaining to a specific incident to a previously created incident package.
   ☒ **A** is incorrect because the `generate package...` command generates a physical package from a logical package. **C** is incorrect because this command will create an incremental package. **D** is incorrect because the `create package` command just creates a logical package with no diagnostic information in it.

Support Workbench

9. ☑ **D** is correct because Support Workbench can collect data, create an incident package, and transmit the package to Oracle Support directly, provided you've installed and configured the Oracle Configuration Manager.
   ☒ **A**, **B**, and **C** are incorrect because they specify only some of the tasks performed by the Support Workbench.

10. ☑ **A** is correct because you'll have to perform a manual upload of the incident package only if you haven't installed the Oracle Configuration Manager.
    ☒ **B** is incorrect because you don't have to perform a manual upload if you install the Oracle Configuration Manager. **C** and **D** are incorrect because it doesn't matter when you install the Oracle Configuration Manager, as long as you've installed and configured it.

11. ☑ **C** is correct because you neither edit nor customize the diagnostic data when you use the Quick Packaging method.
    ☒ **A** and **B** are incorrect because you can't edit the data or customize it when you use the Quick Packaging method. **D** is incorrect because you can edit or customize data when you choose the Custom Packaging method.

12. ☑ **A** is correct because Oracle purges all incidents automatically 30 days after an incident is created.
    ☒ **B** and **C** are incorrect because they specify the wrong duration for automatic purges of incidents. **D** is incorrect because Oracle will automatically purge an incident, unless you explicitly specify that it not do so.

Health Monitor

13. ☑ **A** is correct because the V$HM_CHECK shows all the health checks you can run in the database.
    ☒ **B** is incorrect because the V$HM_RUN shows only the various Health Monitor runs, but doesn't show the types of database checks you can run. **C** and **D** are incorrect because they refer to nonexistent views.

14. ☑ B is correct because you can view the Health Monitor reports through all of those methods.
☒ A, C, and D are incorrect because they list only two of the four ways you can view the reports.

15. ☑ D is correct. The show report hm_run command will show you the recommendations of a database health check.
☒ A and B are syntactically incorrect. C is incorrect because the show hm_run command shows only the various Health Monitor runs, but doesn't report on the recommendations made by the health checks.

16. ☑ D is correct because only the run_name parameter is mandatory when you execute the GET_RUN_REPORT procedure.
☒ A, B, and C are incorrect because only the run_name parameter is a required parameter.

SQL Repair Advisor

17. ☑ B is correct because you can invoke the SQL Repair Advisor from the Support Workbench or by using the DBMS_SQLDIAG package.
☒ A and D are incorrect because they refer to only one of the two ways in which you can access the SQL Repair Advisor. C is incorrect because there is no DBMS_DIAG package.

18. ☑ A is correct because the SQL Repair Advisor fixes problems by providing a patch as a workaround.
☒ B is incorrect because the SQL Repair Advisor doesn't provide new SQL profiles. C is incorrect because the SQL Repair Advisor doesn't rewrite the problem SQL statement. D is incorrect because the SQL Repair Advisor doesn't create the explain plan for the statement.

19. ☑ D is correct because accepting the SQL Repair Advisor's recommendation leads to the application of a patch for the problem SQL statements and, therefore, the use of a new explain plan by the optimizer.
☒ A is incorrect because once you accept the recommendations of the SQL Repair Advisor, the optimizer will use a new execution plan. B is incorrect because the SQL Repair Advisor will always use the same SQL statement, but applies a patch to it. C is incorrect because the SQL Repair Advisor doesn't require the database to collect new optimizer statistics.

20. ☑ C is correct because you use the DROP_SQL_PATCH procedure to remove a SQL patch.
☒ A is incorrect because you can remove any patch that you apply. B is incorrect because there is no procedure called REMOVE_SQL_PATCH. D is incorrect because you don't have to get an official patch from Oracle after you apply a SQL patch recommended by the SQL Repair Advisor.

Data Recovery Advisor

21. ☑ **C** is correct because you can access the Data recovery Advisor through either the Enterprise Manager or RMAN.

☒ **A** is incorrect because you can't access the Data Recovery Advisor through the SQL Workbench. **B** and **D** are incorrect because you can't access the Data Recovery Advisor by using the ADRCI command-line tool.

22. ☑ **B** is correct because RMAN lets you perform both manual and automatic repairs.

☒ **A** and **C** are incorrect because you can perform both types of repairs through RMAN. **D** is incorrect because you can repair problems through RMAN.

23. ☑ **A** is correct because you use the `failure . . . closed` command if the database doesn't set the status of a fixed failure to a `closed` status.

☒ **B** is incorrect because it is the fixed failures that must be set to a `closed` status, not the open problems. **C** is incorrect because the database normally changes the status of all fixed problems to a `closed` status by itself. **D** is incorrect because you don't have to change the status of a problem to `closed` after manually fixing a problem.

24. ☑ **D** is correct because it shows the correct sequence of commands.

☒ **A**, **B**, and **C** are incorrect because they all show an incorrect sequence of commands.

LAB ANSWER

Follow these steps to resolve the problem.

1. Confirm the data block corruption by running the following command from RMAN:

   ```
   RMAN> validate database;
   ```

2. Issue the `list failure` command to review the failure:

   ```
   RMAN> list failure
   ```

3. Issue the `advise failure` command to review RMAN's repair recommendations:

   ```
   RMAN> advise failure
   ```

4. Issue the following command to preview the repair actions:

   ```
   RMAN> repair failure preview;
   ```

5. If the repair actions are simple, use the manual repair advice to fix the problem. If the repair actions involve the restoring and recovering of a datafile, follow the automatic repair advice and let RMAN do the repair. Issue the `repair failure` command to fix the failure:

   ```
   RMAN> repair failure;
   ```

   The `repair failure` command repairs the specified failure and closes it. By default, RMAN asks you to confirm the command execution.

3

Intelligent Infrastructure and Database Security

CERTIFICATION OBJECTIVES

3.01	Enhancements in AWR Baselines		3.04	Using New Oracle Scheduler Features
3.02	Controlling Automated Maintenance Tasks		3.05	Security Enhancements
			✓	Two-Minute Drill
3.03	Database Resource Manager New Features		Q&A	Self Test

W e start the chapter with a discussion of the enhancements in the AWR baselines. In Oracle Database 11g, the various concepts of baselines are consolidated into the single concept of the Automatic Workload Repository (AWR) baselines. You can create dynamic and future baselines and easily manage performance data for comparing database performance between two periods.

CERTIFICATION OBJECTIVE 3.01

Enhancements in AWR Baselines

A baseline is any set of snapshots taken over a period of time. The snapshots are selected such that they yield a set of baselines that change during the period of time that you're collecting data. The baseline captures the time-based variations for a set of baseline statistics and alerts you when the current values differ significantly from the baseline values. An AWR baseline contains a set of AWR snapshots collected over a period of time that provides a frame of reference for a known "good period," which you can then use as a reference period to compare performance during another time period of interest. The snapshots in an AWR baseline are grouped to provide a set of baseline values that change over time. For example, the I/O rate is highest during the peak usage times in the database. One of the most difficult problems you have in setting alert thresholds is setting those thresholds to the correct levels for appropriate alerts. Arbitrary alerts that remain identical throughout are not optimal because they will likely miss the natural peaks and valleys in the workload of a real production database. Baselines, on the other hand, are ideal for setting time-dependent alert thresholds because the baselines let the database compare apples with apples and oranges with oranges, by enabling the comparison of present performance with baseline data from a similar time period.

When a performance problem occurs, you can perform comparative performance analysis with the help of AWR baselines. Oracle excludes the snapshots that are part of an AWR baseline from the normal baseline purging process.

Oracle Database 11g enables you to collect two types of baselines: static baselines and moving window baselines. A static baseline can be a single baseline collected over a single fixed time period (for example, from Jan 1, 2008 at 10:00 A.M. to Jan 1, 2008 at 12:00 P.M.) or a repeating baseline collected over a repeating time period (for example, every first Monday in a month from 10:00 A.M. to 12:00 P.M. for the year 2008). The moving window baseline captures data over a window that keeps moving over time. Oracle Database 11g creates a system-defined moving window baseline by default. This default moving window corresponds to the AWR data captured during the AWR retention period, which is now eight days, rather than seven days, as it was in the Oracle Database 10g release.

Baselines help you set alert thresholds, monitor performance, and compare advisor reports. This is a definite improvement over the Oracle Database 10g release, where all you can really do with an AWR baseline is to just create and drop static single baselines. Oracle Database 11g provides several enhancements to the AWR baselines feature, including the following:

- Baseline templates to schedule the creation of a baseline
- Moving window baselines from which you can specify adaptive thresholds
- AWR Baseline Metric Thresholds

In addition, you can now rename AWR baselines and also set an expiration period for them.

on the Job

If you set the `statistics_level` parameter to typical or all, AWR baselines are enabled by default.

In order to support the new functionality of AWR baselines, Oracle has added several new procedures to the DBMS_WORKLOAD package:

- `CREATE_BASELINE_TEMPLATE` Lets you create both one-time and repeating baseline templates that you can use as the basis for creating new baselines.
- `RENAME_BASELINE` Enables you to rename an AWR baseline.
- `MODIFY_BASELINE_WINDOW_SIZE` Lets you modify the size of the `system_moving_window`.
- `DROP_BASELINE_TEMPLATE` Lets you drop an AWR baseline.

There is also a new function named SELECT_BASELINE_METRICS, which displays the metric thresholds corresponding to an AWR baseline. Let's briefly review how Oracle Database 11g enhances the AWR baselines.

Managing Baseline Templates

In Oracle Database 10g, you could create an AWR baseline only on those snapshots that already existed in the database. New in Oracle Database 11g is the concept of a *baseline template*. A baseline template helps you to automatically create baselines to capture specified time periods in the future. That is, you can use a set of snapshots for capturing performance data during a specified period in the future. This means that you don't have to explicitly use the CREATE_BASELINE procedure to create a baseline for a set of two snapshots. Instead, you can schedule the creation of an AWR baseline using a baseline template. If you want to capture the baseline for a future time period that you know will be useful, use baseline templates to schedule the baseline creation.

The time period spanned by a baseline template can lie in the future or it can encompass a past timeline. No matter which timeframe you choose, the manageability infrastructure automatically generates a task and creates a baseline right away. Each night, the MMON (Memory Monitor background process) task checks to see whether the end time has passed for any baseline templates you created. If it discovers that a template for baseline generation contains a completed time range, it will create the baseline for the period specified by the baseline template.

You can create two types of baseline templates—a *single* baseline template or a *repeating* baseline template. Let's examine the two types of baseline templates in the following sections.

Single AWR Baseline Template

You can schedule the creation of an AWR baseline for a contiguous future time period such as a known heavy usage period. Using the single AWR baseline template, you can then automatically capture a baseline of the performance during the period you specify. The following example shows how to create a single baseline template using the CREATE_BASELINE_TEMPLATE procedure:

```
SQL> begin
  2  dbms_workload_repository.create_baseline_template (
  3  start_time => '2008-03-02 22:00:00 CST',
  4  end_time => '2008-03-02 08:00:00 CST',
  5  baseline_name => 'test_baseline1',
  6  template_name => 'test_template1',
  7* expiration => 30);
     end;
SQL> /
```

The optional `expiration` parameter specifies that this baseline will expire in 30 days. The value you set for the `expiration` parameter specifies the length of time for which the database will maintain a baseline. If you don't specify an expiration time period (NULL), the baseline will never expire. The `baseline_name` and `template_name` parameters are self-explanatory. The `start_time` and `end_time` parameters specify the beginning and ending snapshot time periods. You can also specify a DBID parameter, but its value defaults to NULL if you omit it, as in this case.

e x a m

ⓦ a t c h *Pay particular attention to the CREATE_BASELINE_TEMPLATE procedure and its parameters. How do you automatically remove a baseline after a specific time period?*

The database will capture the performance data during a fixed time interval in the future. In this example, the template will generate an AWR baseline that is captured between 10 P.M. on March 1, 2008 through 8:00 A.M. on March 2, 2008. Note that because you're using a time-based template definition, you don't have to specify start and snapshot identifiers when creating the baseline template.

Creating a Repeating Baseline Template

You can create a repeating baseline template to schedule the creation of an AWR baseline for a known period such as around 3:00 P.M. every Friday evening for an entire year. The database will automatically create a new baseline every Friday and you can have the database also automatically remove older baselines after a specified expiration time. Here's how you create a repeating baseline template using the CREATE_BASELINE_TEMPLATE procedure again:

```
begin
dbms_workload_repository.create_baseline_template(
day_of_week            => 'Friday',
hour_in_day            =>  15,
duration               => 4,
expiration             => 30,
start_time             => '2008-10-01 22:00:00 PST'.
end_time               => '2007812-31   22:00:00 PST',
baseline_name_prefix   => 'Friday_Baseline',
template_name          => Friday_Template',
dbid                   => 1234567899);
end;
/
```

The following is a brief explanation of the values of the various parameters in the CREATE_BASELINE_TEMPLATE procedure:

- **DAY_OF_THE_WEEK**   Specifies the day of the week the baseline will repeat and can be any of the seven days in a week.
- **HOUR_IN_DAY**   Allows you to specify a value between 0 and 23 to determine when the baseline will start.
- **DURATION**   The number of hours for which the baseline should last.
- **START_TIME**   Time to start generating the baseline, determined by converting to the nearest snapshot ID.
- **END_TIME**   Time to stop generating the baseline, determined by converting to the nearest snapshot ID.
- **BASELINE_NAME_PREFIX**   Specifies the baseline prefix, which will be appended to the date information.

- **TEMPLATE_NAME**   Specifies the name of the repeating baseline template.
- **EXPIRATION**   The number of days for which the database will maintain the baseline. Default value is NULL, meaning the database will always maintain the baseline and never drop it.
- **DBID**   The database identifier. Defaults to NULL.

Dropping a Baseline Template

When you don't need a baseline template, you can save space by removing the template, using the DROP_BASELINE_TEMPLATE procedure as shown here:

```
SQL> begin
        dbms_workload_repository.drop_baseline_template (
        template_name => 'mytemplate1',
        dbid          => 22233344455);
        end;
        /
```

Only the `template_name` parameter is mandatory. If you don't specify a DBID parameter, by default, the procedure uses the local database identifier.

Renaming a Baseline

You can now rename existing baselines, using the RENAME_BASELINE procedure. Use the DBA_HIST_BASELINE view first, to find out the baselines you want to rename. Here's how you rename a baseline:

```
SQL> begin
        dbms_workload_repository.rename_baseline (
        old_baseline_name => 'mybaseline1',
        new_baseline_name => 'mynewbaseline1')
      end;
       /
```

There is also a third parameter, DBID, which is optional.

Setting AWR Baseline Metric Thresholds

Sometimes, you want to examine the metric threshold settings for the time period spanned by a baseline. Using the AWR data contained in the baseline, you can compute the metric threshold values. Use the SELECT_BASELINE_METRICS function to display the metric value statistics during the period covered by a baseline.

```
SQL> begin
        dbms_workload_repository.select_baseline_metrics (
```

```
     baseline_name => 'peak_baseline',);
  end;
```

The previous code will display the metric thresholds for the baseline named peak_baseline.

Oracle Database 11g provides a built-in alert infrastructure that warns you about potential problems in the database. The default alerts include alerts pertaining to tablespace usage, recovery area space problem, suspended resumable sessions, and the "snapshot too old" error. However, you can also specify a custom performance alert based on performance-related metric thresholds. For example, a `blocked_user` threshold issues an alert when the number of users blocked by any one session exceeds the metric threshold you set.

Performance alert thresholds can be difficult to determine because the expected metric values do vary by the type and amount of the workload. Using baselines, you can capture metric value statistics. If the baseline is static, you can manually compute the metric value statistics over the baseline. If you're using a system moving window, the database can automatically compute the metric value statistics over the moving window. You can then use the baseline metric statistics to define the alert thresholds specific to the baseline.

Baselines capture metric values, which the database will then compare against current performance metrics to judge how current performance measures up against performance during a known good period. If there's a serious discrepancy—that is, if the expected values are very different from the actual present statistics—the database will issue a performance alert. Whether you use a manually computed static baseline or a baseline automatically computed over the system moving window, the baseline values are compared to present statistics to see if an alert is justified. Adaptive thresholds are so named because the thresholds aren't fixed, but vary according to the conditions in the database—they adapt to the type and amount of the workload.

on the
Üob
The database computes statistics from the system moving window according to the BSLN_MAINTAIN_STATS_SCHED schedule.

The database always compares the baseline statistics to the current database performance. The metric statistics that you capture over a baseline enable you to set thresholds for comparing baseline statistics to current activity. You can use three different threshold types, as explained here:

■ **Significance level** Thresholds based on significance level use statistical significance to determine whether the current levels observed are unusual compared to baseline values, thus meriting an alert. For example, if you set the significance level to 0.99 for a metric, the alert threshold will be set where 1 percent of the observed metric values are outside the value set for the metric. The database will thus issue an alert when 1 percent of the metric values are different from the expected metric value. Note that the higher the significance level, the fewer the number of alerts that will be issued by the database. For example, a significance level of 0.9999 would cause fewer alerts to be raised than a significance level of 0.99.

exam

ⓦatch *You must understand the configuration of adaptive thresholds, including the setting of the various attributes such as the significance level. What does the significance level that you select imply regarding the number of alerts?*

- **Percentage of maximum** An alert is generated if the observed metric is at or above a percentage of the maximum that you specified. For example, if you specify 120 as the percentage of maximum where the maximum value captured by the baseline is 1000, the database will issue an alert when the observed metric crosses 1200, which is 120 percent of the maximum (1000).

- **Fixed values** Fixed values are standard Enterprise Manager fixed thresholds, which the database compares with the actual metrics. The DBA sets the fixed values, without the need for any AWR baselines.

Oracle Database 11g fully integrates the selection of adaptive thresholds for performance metrics with the AWR baselines, with the baselines serving as the source of the metrics. The database determines the alert thresholds by examining the metric statistics captured over the baseline time period. Thus, the database sets the thresholds based on data provided by the database itself, and you don't have to know any system-specific metrics. The database sets the thresholds based on system data itself and some metadata provided by you. Using the Enterprise Manager, you can choose a starter set of thresholds based on either the OLTP or the Data Warehouse workload profile. Once you select the appropriate workload profile, the database will automatically configure and maintain the adaptive thresholds based on the default SYSTEM_MOVING_WINDOW baseline. The adaptive thresholds will cover all metrics suitable for the chosen workload profile.

Once you configure the adaptive thresholds, you can edit the thresholds levels. When you're editing the threshold levels, Oracle recommends that you set the initial significance level thresholds conservatively in the beginning because a very high significance level will keep the number of alerts low.

It's very easy to configure baseline metric thresholds from the Enterprise Manager. On the Database home page, click the Adaptive Metric Thresholds link in the Related Links section. The Baseline Metric Thresholds window appears, as shown in Figure 3-1. You can configure thresholds from this page by selecting one of the three threshold types: Significance Level, Percentage Of Maximum, or Fixed Values.

Moving Window AWR Baselines

Oracle Database 11g offers you a choice between a static baseline and a moving window baseline. It also allows you to create both a single static baseline and a repeating static baseline. You can create a moving window AWR baseline instead of a mere fixed baseline corresponding to a fixed, contiguous past period in time. Oracle creates and maintains a system-defined moving window baseline by default. A moving window baseline encompasses AWR data during the AWR retention period, which is, by default, eight days. (In Oracle Database 11g, the default retention period has been increased to eight days from the previous retention period of seven days.) This default moving window baseline is called the system_moving_window.

FIGURE 3-1   The Baseline Metric Thresholds page

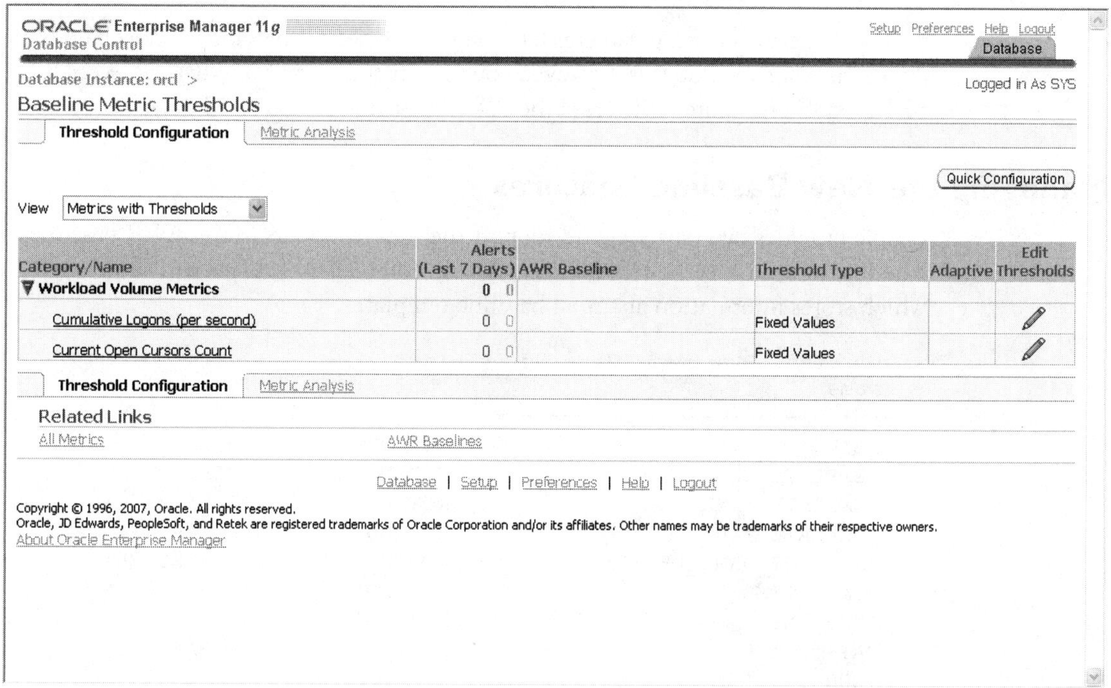

Oracle schedules the statistics collection for this window every Sunday at midnight. The setting for days is always null for this baseline, thereby making the window size exactly match the duration of the AWR retention setting. Enterprise Manager uses the system-defined baseline as the default to compare performance with the current database performance.

Moving window baselines are especially useful when you're using adaptive thresholds because you can then utilize the data from the entire AWR retention period to compute the values for the metric thresholds you've selected. By default, the adaptive thresholds feature uses statistics on the default moving window baseline (SYSTEM_MOVING_WINDOW baseline). However, Oracle advises you to use a larger moving window such as 30 days rather than the default AWR retention period of 8 days, if you're considering using adaptive thresholds. Because a moving window baseline depends on the AWR data, it can range over the length of the AWR retention period or a shorter time span. If you want to increase the size of the moving window, make sure that you first increase the size of the AWR retention period. Use the MODIFY_BASELINE_WINDOW_SIZE procedure to resize the default moving window baseline size of 8 days. Here's an example that sets the moving window baseline size to 30 days:

```
SQL> exec dbms_workload_repository.modify_baseline_window_size(
        window_size => 30);
```

The `window_size` parameter lets you size the default moving window baseline duration. Before you do this, however, you must first use the MODIFY_SNAPSHOT_ SETTINGS procedure to increase the AWR retention period to 30 days.

Managing the New Baseline Features

Oracle provides two new views to support the improvements in the AWR baselines. The first new view is the DBA_HIST_BASELINE_TEMPLATE view, shown here, which stores information about all baseline templates.

```
SQL> desc dba_hist_baseline_template
 Name                                Null?       Type
 ----------------------------------- ----------- ----------------
 DBID                                NOT NULL    NUMBER
 TEMPLATE_ID                         NOT NULL    NUMBER
 TEMPLATE_NAME                       NOT NULL    VARCHAR2(30)
 TEMPLATE_TYPE                       NOT NULL    VARCHAR2(9)
 BASELINE_NAME_PREFIX                NOT NULL    VARCHAR2(30)
 START_TIME                          NOT NULL    DATE
 END_TIME                            NOT NULL    DATE
 DAY_OF_WEEK                                     VARCHAR2 (9)
 HOUR_IN_DAY                                     NUMBER
```

```
DURATION                                    NUMBER
EXPIRATION                                  NUMBER
REPEAT_INTERVAL                             VARCHAR2 (128)
LAST_GENERATED                              DATE

SQL>
```

The database (actually the background process MMON) utilizes the information in this view to determine which baselines it must create or delete. In the DBA_HIST_BASELINE_TEMPLATE view, the following columns bear explanation:

- **TEMPLATE_TYPE** Can take the values SINGLE or REPEATED.
- **EXPIRATION** Number of days the database must retain the baseline.
- **REPEAT_INTERVAL** Takes a string representing the interval timings in the same format as that used by the DBMS_SCHEDULER package.

The DBA_HIST_BASELINE_DETAILS view shows details about all AWR baselines.

```
SQL> desc dba_hist_baseline_details
 Name                                Null?      Type
 ----------------------------------- --------   -------------
 DBID                                           NUMBER
 INSTANCE_NUMBER                                NUMBER
 BASELINE_ID                                    NUMBER
 BASELINE_NAME                                  VARCHAR2(64)
 BASELINE_TYPE                                  VARCHAR2(13)
 START_SNAP_ID                                  NUMBER
 START_SNAP_TIME                                TIMESTAMP(3)
 END_SNAP_ID                                    NUMBER
 END_SNAP_TIME                                  TIMESTAMP(3)
 SHUTDOWN                                       VARCHAR2(3)
 ERROR_COUNT                                    NUMBER
 PCT_TOTAL_TIME                                 NUMBER
 LAST_TIME_COMPUTED                             DATE
 MOVING_WINDOW_SIZE                             NUMBER
 CREATION_TIME                                  DATE
 EXPIRATION                                     NUMBER
 TEMPLATE_NAME                                  VARCHAR2(64)
SQL>
```

Following are the key new columns in this view:

- **SHUTDOWN** Indicates whether the database was shut down during this time period. The possible values are YES, NO, and NULL.

■ **PCT_TOTAL_TIME** The amount of time spanned by the snapshots divided by the total possible time for the baseline.

■ **ERROR_COUNT** Number of errors in the snapshots in the baseline snapshot range.

The DBA_HIST_BASELINE view has the following new columns in Oracle Database 11g:

■ **BASELINE_TYPE** The possible values are STATIC, MOVING_WINDOW, and GENERATED. Static windows are other ones that you manually created. The start and end snapshot IDs are dynamic for a moving window baseline. The generated baselines are the ones automatically created by the database based on a template.

■ **MOVING_WINDOW_SIZE** The value of this attribute depends on the value of the BASELINE_TYPE attribute. If BASELINE_TYPE is NULL, the moving window size is the same as the value of the AWR retention period. If the BASELINE_TYPE is MOVING_WINDOW, then the value of the MOVING_WINDOW_SIZE attribute is the same number of days as the moving window.

■ **CREATION_TIME** The time when the database created the baseline.

■ **EXPIRATION** How long the database must keep the baseline. NULL means the database will never drop the baseline.

■ **TEMPLATE_NAME** Name of the template used to create this baseline, if any.

■ **LAST_COMPUTED** Shows the last time the database computed statistics for a baseline.

CERTIFICATION OBJECTIVE 3.02

Controlling Automated Maintenance Tasks

You're familiar with the concept of automated maintenance tasks from the Oracle Database 10g release. These are jobs that are run automatically by the database to perform maintenance operations. In Oracle Database 10g, you had two automatic maintenance tasks: the Automatic Optimizer Statistics collection and the Automatic Segment Advisor. In Oracle Database 11g, there is a third automatic maintenance task named Automatic SQL Tuning Advisor. The Automatic SQL Tuning Advisor reviews all high resource consuming SQL statements in the database and provides recommendations to tune them. If you want, you can configure the database so it automatically implements some types of recommendations, such as SQL profiles.

The Automatic SQL Tuning Advisor runs during the default system maintenance window on a nightly basis, just as the other two automated maintenance tasks do. A maintenance window is an Oracle Scheduler window that's part of the MAINTENANCE_WINDOW_GROUP. You choose low system load time interval periods for the maintenance windows. A Scheduler resource plan specifies how the database will allocate resources during the duration of a window. When a Scheduler window opens, the database automatically enables the resource plan associated with that window.

Please see Chapter 4 for a detailed discussion of the new Automatic SQL Tuning Advisor feature.

Predefined Maintenance Windows

In Oracle Database 10g, you had two maintenance windows: `weeknight_window` and `weekend_window`. In Oracle Database 11g, there are seven predefined *daily maintenance windows*, one for each day of the week. Here are the predefined maintenance windows and their descriptions:

```
MONDAY_WINDOW           Starts 10 P.M. on Monday ends at 2 A.M.
TUESDAY_WINDOW          Starts 10 P.M. on Tuesday ends at 2 A.M.
WEDNESDAY_WINDOW        Starts 10 P.M. on Wednesday ends at 2 A.M.
THURSDAY_WINDOW         Starts 10 P.M. on Thursday ends at 2 A.M.
FRIDAY_WINDOW           Starts 10 P.M. on Friday ends at 2 A.M.
SATURDAY_WINDOW         Starts 6 A.M on Saturday ends at 2.A.M
SUNDAY_WINDOW           Starts 6 A.M. on Sunday ends at 2 A.M.
```

Note that the first five windows that run during the weekdays are open for 4 hours and the two weekend maintenance windows are open for 20 hours. By default, all seven daily windows belong to the MAINTENANCE_WINDOW_GROUP group. You can change the time and duration of the daily maintenance windows, create new maintenance windows, or disable or remove the default maintenance windows.

Managing the Automatic Maintenance Tasks

In Oracle Database 10g, you had to use the DBMS_SCHEDULER package to enable and disable the automatic maintenance tasks. The ENABLE procedure lets you enable an automatic maintenance job such as the automatic statistics collection job, and the DISABLE procedure lets you disable it, if you wanted to manually collect the optimizer statistics. In Oracle Database 11g, use the new DBMS_AUTO_TASK_ADMIN package to manage the automatic maintenance tasks. You can also use the Enterprise Manager to access the controls for the automatic maintenance tasks. The DBMS_AUTO_TASK_ADMIN package provides a more fine-grained management capability to control the operation of the automatic maintenance tasks. For example, the DBMS_SCHEDULER package only lets you enable or disable an automatic task. With the new DBMS_AUTO_TASK_ADMIN package, you can now disable a task only in selected maintenance windows instead of completely disabling the entire task.

Before you start looking into the management of the automatic maintenance tasks, it's a good idea to get familiar with two new views that provide information you might need to manage the tasks: the DBA_AUTOTASK_CLIENT view and the DBA_AUTOTASK_OPERATION view. The two views contain several identical columns. The DBA_AUTOTASK_CLIENT view shows data for all three automated tasks over a 1-day and a 30-day period. The following query shows details about the automatic maintenance tasks:

```
SQL> select client_name, status,
  2  attributes, window_group,service_name
  3  from dba_autotask_client;

CLIENT_NAME                STATUS     ATTRIBUTES
-------------------        --------   ---------------------------
auto optimizer             ENABLED    ON BY DEFAULT, VOLATILE,
statistics collection                 SAFE TO KILL
auto space advisor         ENABLED    ON BY DEFAULT, VOLATILE,
                                      SAFE TO KILL
sql tuning advisor         ENABLED    ONCE PER WINDOW,ON BY DEFAULT,
                                      VOLATILE, SAFE TO KILL

SQL>
```

You can see that all three of the automatic maintenance tasks are enabled. When the maintenance window opens, Oracle Scheduler automatically creates the automatic maintenance jobs and runs them. If the maintenance window is long, Oracle restarts the automatic optimizer statistics collection and the automatic segment advisor jobs every four hours. However, the automatic SQL advisor job runs only once per maintenance window, as evidenced by the ONCE PER WINDOW attribute for that job. The attributes column shows only ON BY DEFAULT as the value for the other two automated maintenance tasks.

Each of the automatic maintenance tasks is called a *client* and is given a client name. The actual Scheduler job associated with each of the three clients is called an

operation and is given an operation name. The following query on the DBA_AUTO
TASK_OPERATION view shows the operation names:

```
SQL> select client_name, operation_name from
dba_autotask_operation;
CLIENT_NAME                   OPERATION_NAME
--------------------          -------------------------
auto optimizer                auto optimizer stats job
stats collection
auto space advisor            auto space advisor job
sql tuning advisor            automatic sql tuning task
SQL>
```

The DBA_AUTO TASK_OPERATION view shows all automatic task
operations for each of the clients.

Enabling a Maintenance task

Use the DBMS_AUTO_ADMIN.ENABLE procedure to enable a client, operation,
target type, or individual target that you previously disabled. Before you can do this,
you must first query the DBA_AUTOTASK_CLIENT and the DBA_AUTOTASK_
OPERATION views to find the values for the client_name and operation_
name attributes of the procedure.

```
SQL> begin
  2  dbms_auto_task_admin.enable
  3  (client_name    => 'sql tuning advisor',
  4  operation       => 'automatic sql tuning task',
  5  window_name     => 'monday_window');
  6* end;
SQL> /
PL/SQL procedure successfully completed.
SQL>
```

If the default maintenance windows aren't long enough to cover one of your
automated maintenance tasks, you can reconfigure the maintenance windows to
suit your needs.

Disabling a Maintenance Task

By default, all three maintenance jobs will run in every maintenance window. You
can use the DBMS_AUTO_ADMIN.DISABLE procedure to disable a client or
operation for a specific window, as shown here:

```
SQL> begin
  2  dbms_auto_task_admin.disable
```

```
   3  (client_name   => 'sql tuning advisor',
   4  operation      => 'automatic sql tuning task',
   5  window_name    => 'monday_window');
   6* end;
SQL> /
PL/SQL procedure successfully completed.
SQL>
```

In this example, the SQL tuning advisor task is disabled only during the `monday_window`, but continues to run during all other defined maintenance windows. You can enable and disable any maintenance task in one or all maintenance windows.

You can also use the Enterprise Manager, shown in Figure 3-2, to effortlessly configure and manage the three automated maintenance tasks. You can enable or disable the three automated maintenance tasks, and you can select some or all of the seven available maintenance windows for running the three automated maintenance tasks.

FIGURE 3-2   Automated Maintenance Tasks Configuration

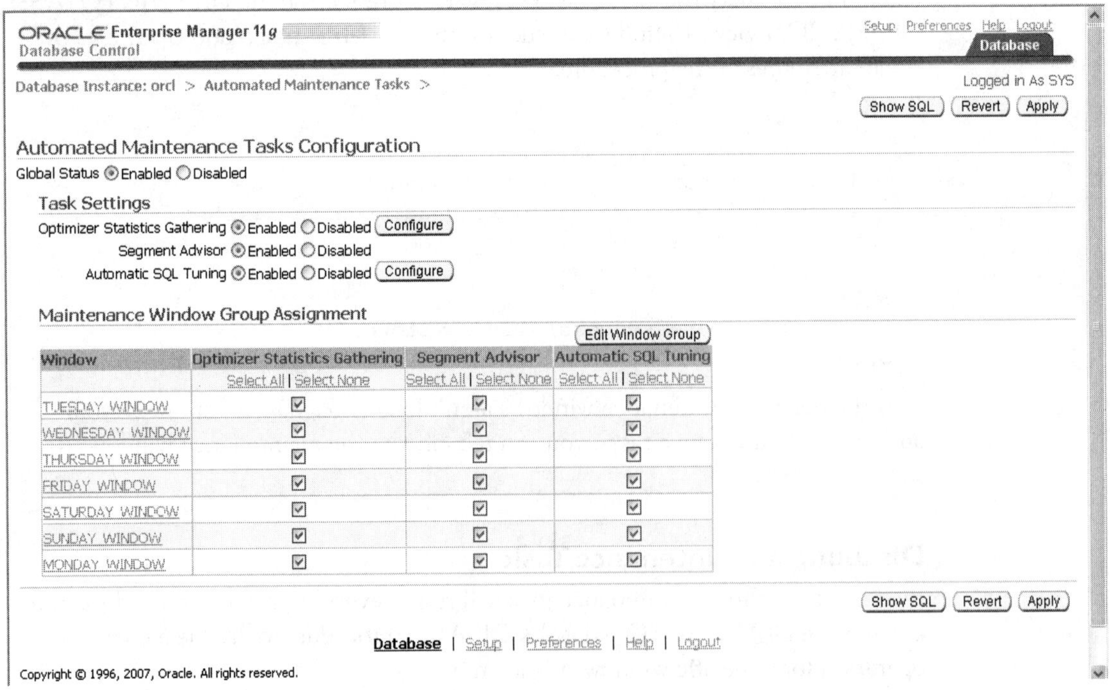

Implementing Automatic Maintenance Tasks

The database doesn't assign any permanent Scheduler jobs to the three automated maintenance tasks. You therefore can't manage the jobs with the usual DBMS_ SCHEDULER package. Use the new DBMS_AUTO_TASK_ADMIN package instead to manage the automated maintenance tasks. The new background process, Autotask Background Process (ABP), implements the automated maintenance tasks. The ABP maintains a history of all automated maintenance task executions in the repository that it maintains in the SYSAUX tablespace. Another background process, MMON, spawns (usually when a maintenance window opens), monitors, and restarts the ABP process.

The ABP is in charge of converting tasks into Scheduler jobs. The ABP creates a task list for each maintenance job and assigns them a priority. There are three levels of job priorities: urgent, high, and medium. The ABP creates the urgent priority jobs first, after which it creates the high priority and the medium priority jobs. Various Scheduler job classes are also created, in order to map a task's priority consumer group to the corresponding job class. The ABP is in charge of assigning the jobs to the job classes. The job classes map the individual jobs to a consumer group, based on the job priority.

The ABP stores its data in the SYSAUX tablespace. You can view the ABP repository by querying the DBA_AUTOTASK_TASK view.

Configuring Resource Allocation for Automatic Tasks

You can control the percentage of resources allocated to the maintenance tasks during a given maintenance window. The default resource plan for each predefined maintenance window is the DEFAULT_MAINTENANCE_PLAN. When a maintenance window opens, the DEFAULT_MAINTENANCE_PLAN is activated to control the amount of CPU used by the various automatic maintenance tasks. The three default maintenance tasks run under the ORA$AUTOTASK_SUB_PLAN, which is a subplan of the DEFAULT_MAINTENANCE_PLAN, with all three plans sharing the resources equally. ORA$AUTOTASK_SUB_PLAN gets 25 percent of the resources at the priority level 2. The consumer group SYS_GROUP takes priority in the DEFAULT_MAINTENANCE_PLAN resource plan, getting 100 percent of the level 1 resources in the DEFAULT_MAINTENANCE_PLAN. If you want to change the resource allocation for the automatic tasks in a specific window, you must change the resource allocation to the subplan ORA$AUTOTASK_SUB_PLAN in the resource plan for that window.

Priorities for the various tasks that run during the maintenance window (three tasks altogether) are determined by assigning different consumer groups to the DEFAULT_ MAINTENANCE_PLAN. For example, the new Automatic SQL Tuning task is assigned to the ORA$AUTOTASK_SQL_GROUP consumer group. The Optimizer Statistics Gathering task is part of the ORA$AUTOTASK_STATS_GROUP, and the Segment Advisor task belongs to the ORA$AUTOTASK_SPACE_GROUP.

I/O Calibration

Oracle Database 11g introduces an I/O Calibration mechanism, whereby you can run I/O calibration tests either through the Enterprise Manager Performance page or a PL/SQL package. Oracle's I/O calibration is a variation on the Clarion tool. In an Oracle database, the I/O workload is of two basic types—small random I/O and large sequential I/O. OLTP applications usually experience the small random I/O workload, where the speed with which small I/O requests are serviced is paramount. Thus, disk spinning and seeking times are of critical importance. OLAP applications, on the other hand, employ the large sequential I/O in general. For these types of applications, the critical factor is the capacity of the I/O channel. The larger the I/O channels between the database server and the storage system, the larger the I/O throughput. Oracle uses the following two metrics, each measuring the efficacy of one type of I/O workload:

- **IOPS (I/O per second)** The IOPS rate is the number of small random I/Os the system can perform in a second and depends on the spin speed of disks. You can increase the IOPS rate by increasing the number of disks in the storage array or by using faster disk drives, which have a high RPM and lower seek time.

- **MBPS (megabytes per second)** This metric measures the data transfer rate between the server and the storage array and depends on the capacity of the I/O channel between the two systems. A larger I/O channel means a higher MBPS rate.

EXERCISE 3-1

Calibrating I/O Resources

The following exercise shows how to find out the capabilities of your I/O sub-system. You can then monitor your I/O load in relation to its I/O capacity.

1. On the Database control Home page, click the Performance tab.

2. Click the I/O tab on the Performance page.

3. Click the I/O Calibration button.

4. If the Calibration page shows that `filesystemio_options` isn't set, you'll have to set the following initialization parameter and restart the instance.

   ```
   filesystemio_options = asynch
   ```

5. Check the kernel parameters by viewing them in the /proc file system. If the `aio-nr` (current number of asynch IO requests in the database) is equal to the `aio-max-nr` (maximum asynch IO request that the database can make), you must increase the value of `aio-max-nr`. You do this by adding a line such as the following to the sysctl.conf file:

   ```
   fs.aio-max-nr = 131072
   ```

6. Apply the new parameter to the kernel by executing the following command as the root user:

   ```
   # sysctl -p
   ```

Two important terms need clarification in this discussion: *throughput* and *latency*. The throughput of a system determines how fast it can transfer data and is measured by the MBPS metric. The channel capacity determines the overall throughput of the system, and it thus puts the ceiling on the amount of data transfer. Latency refers to the lag between the time an I/O request is made and when the request is serviced by the storage system. High latency indicates a system that's overloaded and you can reduce latency by striping data across multiple spindles, so different disks can service the same I/O request in parallel.

Oracle recommends that you use the new I/O Calibration tool to determine I/O metrics in a database. It takes about 10 minutes to run the tools and you should pick a time when the database workload is light to avoid overstressing the storage system. You can run only a single calibration task at a time. If you perform the task in an RAC environment, the workload is generated simultaneously from all instances in the system. You can either run the tool with Enterprise Manager or through PL/SQL.

Calibrating I/O through Enterprise Manager

The easiest way to run the I/O calibration tool is through the Enterprise Manager. Here are the steps:

1. Click the Performance tab on the Home page of Database Control.

2. Click the I/O calibration button.

3. You'll be in the I/O Calibration page now. Specify the number of physical disks and the maximum tolerable latency for a single-block I/O request. Specify when to execute the calibration task in the Scheduler section. Click Submit to create a Scheduler job.

4. On the Scheduler jobs page, you can find out the length of time for which the calibration job will run.

5. Once the Calibration task completes, you can view results of the calibration task concerning the following metrics on the I/O Calibration page:

   ■ Maximum I/O per second

   ■ Maximum megabytes per second

   ■ Average latency metrics

Calibrating I/O Using PL/SQL

You can also use the new procedure CALIBRATE_IO from the DBMS_RESOURCE_MANAGER package to run the I/O Calibration task. Here is an example:

```
begin
  exec dbms_resource_manager.calibrate_io(-
  num_disks        => 1,    -
  max_latency      => 10, -
  max_iops         => :max_iops, -
  max_mbps         => :max_mbps, -
  actual_latency   => :actual_latency);
 end;
 /
```

In the CALIBRATE_IO procedure, the following are the key parameters:

■ num_disks   Approximate number of disks in the storage array.

■ max_latency   Maximum tolerable latency (in milliseconds) for an I/O request.

■ max_ios   Maximum number of random DB block-sized read requests that can be serviced.

■ max_mbps   Maximum number of randomly distributed 1MB reads that can be serviced (in megabytes per second).

■ actual_latency   Average latency of DB block-sized I/O requests at max_iops rate (in milliseconds).

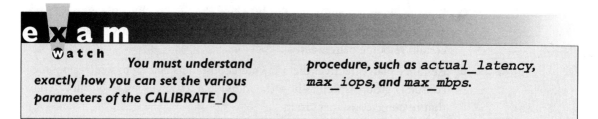

ⓦatch

You must understand exactly how you can set the various parameters of the CALIBRATE_IO *procedure, such as `actual_latency`, `max_iops`, and `max_mbps`.*

Once you execute the CALIBRATE_IO procedure, you can query the V$IO_CALIBRATION_STATUS and the DBA_RSRC_IO_CALIBRATE views to check the results. Here's a sample query:

```
SQL> select max_iops, max_mbps, max_pmbps, latency
     from dba_rsrc_io_calibrate;

MAX_IOPS       MAX_MBPS       MAX_PMBPS      LATENCY
----------     ------------   ------------   ----------
133            12             6              64
SQL>
```

Oracle Database 11g collects I/O statistics in three different dimensions to provide a consistent set of statistics for I/O calls. These dimensions are

- RDBMS components grouped into 12 functional groups. The V$IOSTAT_FUNCTION view provides the details.
- I/O statistics are collected for each consumer group that's part of the currently enabled resource plan. The V$IOSTAT_CONSUMER_GROUP view has the details.
- Individual file level I/O statistics are collected and stored in the V$IOSTAT_FILE view for details.

CERTIFICATION OBJECTIVE 3.03

Database Resource Manager New Features

You're familiar with the Database Resource Manager (Resource Manager) from the earlier release. You use the Database Resource Manager to efficiently allocate resources among competing database sessions. Here are the key elements of the Resource Manager:

- Resource Consumer Group is a group of sessions that share similar resource requirements. The Resource Manager allocates resources directly to the resource consumer groups instead of the individual sessions.

- Resource Plan is a container for directives that dictate how the resources are to spread about among the resource consumer groups. At any given time, a certain resource plan is active.
- Resource plan directives dictate which consumers belong to which resource consumer group as well as how the individual resources are to be allocated to that resource consumer group.

There are Database Resource Manager–related enhancements in the following areas:

- Per Session I/O Limits
- New mixed workload resource plan

on the Job

The *CPU_Pn* *parameters of the* **CREATE_PLAN_DIRECTIVE** *procedure are deprecated now. Instead, use the new* *MGMT_Pn* *parameters. Also, in the same procedure, use the new* *switch_call* *parameter instead of the* *switch_ time_in_call* *parameter.*

I discuss each of these major innovations in detail in the following sections.

Per Session I/O Limits

The Resource Manager provides both manual as well as automatic methods to switch a user's session to a different resource consumer group. However, whether you change a current resource consumer group manually or automatically, the changes don't persist and the user's default resource consumer group remains the same when the user logs in again. In Oracle Database 10g, automatic switching of a session to another resource consumer group could be triggered by a change in a session attribute. The change in session attributes could cause new session-to-consumer group mapping rules to take effect that directed the Resource Manager to move the session to another, typically lower, priority group, based on the dynamic change in the session attribute(s).

on the Job

The session limits examine the resource usage during a call to the database. A top call is an entire PL/SQL block, which the database considers an individual SQL statement.

Oracle Database 11g provides a second way to automatically switch a user's session from one consumer group to another. Now, automatic session switching can also occur when a session exceeds a CPU or an I/O consumption limit set by the consumer group to which that session is originally assigned. So, you can now specify automatic resource consumer group switching with mapping rules as in the previous release, and also by setting resource limits. If a user is using an excessive amount of CPU, you don't have to kill that user's session; you can set up automatic resource group switching so the user is automatically assigned to a resource group with a lower CPU allocation.

Specifying Automatic Switching by Setting Resource Limits

You can now specify limits for CPU and I/O consumption for all sessions in a consumer group when you're creating a resource plan directive for that consumer group. More specifically, you can dictate what the database can do when a single database call within a session exceeds a CPU or I/O limit. You can choose one of the following actions when a session exceeds a specific resource limit:

- Switch the session to another resource consumer group with a lower resource allocation. In order for this to happen, you must first grant the session owner the "switch" privileges on the new resource consumer group.
- The database can terminate the session.
- The database can abort the SQL statement issuing the call.

The database allows only those sessions that are actually consuming resources to dynamically switch their resource consumer group. A session that's waiting either for a user's input or waiting on CPU doesn't qualify for switching its resource consumer group under the automatic switching feature.

Automatic session switching involves the use of the following resource plan directive parameters, which you specify in the CREATE_RESOURCE_PLAN procedure. The examples in the following section illustrate how to use the various parameters.

- `switch_group` The consumer group a session is switched to automatically when a switching criterion is satisfied. Here are some things to note about this parameter:
  - The default value is NULL.
  - If the group name is CANCEL_SQL, the database cancels the current database call.
  - If the group name is KILL_SESSION, the session is terminated.
- `switch_time` Specifies the duration for which a call can execute before the database switches the session to that specified by the `switch_group` parameter. The default value is UNLIMITED.

- `switch_estimate`   If you set this parameter to TRUE, the database will estimate the execution time of each call before the call begins. If the estimated execution time for a call is greater than the limit specified by the `switch_time` parameter, the database switches the session to the specified group (specified by the `switch_group` parameter). The default value is FALSE.

- `switch_io_megabytes`   Specifies the maximum I/O (in megabytes) that a session can transfer in the form of read and write operations before the database takes action. Default is NULL, which means it is unlimited.

- `switch_io_reqs`   Specifies the maximum number of I/O requests a session can execute before the database takes the action specified by the SWITCH_GROUP parameter. Default is NULL, which means it is unlimited.

- `switch_for_call`   By setting this parameter to TRUE, you tell the database to return a session that was automatically switched to a different consumer group to its original consumer group, once the top level call is completed. The default value is NULL. This parameter comes in handy for three-tier applications where the middle tier is employing session pooling.

Note that the `switch_io_megabytes` and the `switch_io_reqs` parameters enable you to specify I/O resource limits when creating a Resource Plan directive. When the database dynamically switches a session's resource consumer group, the consumer group is allowed to run more sessions than permitted by its active session pool.

Examples of Automatic Session Switching

Use the CREATE_PLAN_DIRECTIVE procedure to create resource plan directives. When you want to specify automatic resource usage–based session switching, you specify values for the relevant parameters such as `switch_io_megabytes` and `switch_io_reqs` . Here are three examples of automatic session switching based on a session exceeding its resource limits.

Switching to a Different Resource Group Based on CPU Usage   In order to prevent a single session from consuming a disproportionate amount of resources, you can specify that a session will switch automatically to a low-priority consumer group (LOW_GROUP) if a single call in a session uses the CPU beyond a preset limit. Here's an example:

```
SQL> begin
    dbms_resource_manager.create_plan_directive (
```

```
        plan               => 'peaktime',
        group_or_subplan => 'oltp',
        mgmt_p1            => 75,
        switch_group       => 'low_Group',
        switch_time        => 10);
end;
```

In this example, the session is automatically switched to the LOW_GROUP, which is a resource group with a low amount of resource allocation. It's common to assign a lower priority resource group as the switch group for sessions that exceed resource limits. This allows the session to continue while allowing more critical sessions to have an adequate chance to use the existing resources.

Switching to a Different Resource Group Based on I/O Limits   The following example shows how to automatically switch a session from one group to another when it exceeds a certain number of I/O requests (switch_io_reqs) or after it transfers more than a set amount of data (switch_io_megabytes).

```
SQL> begin
        dbms_resource_manager.create_plan_directive (
        plan                   => 'peaktime',
        group_or_subplan       => 'oltp',
        mgmt_p1                => 75,
        switch_group           => 'low_group',
        switch_io_reqs         =>  5000,
        switch_io_megabytes    =>  1000,
        switch_for_call        => true);
     end;
```

Note that once the session completes the high resource using call, it goes back to its original resource group.

Terminating a Session Based on CPU Usage   You can also create a resource plan directive that lets the database terminate a session that exceeds a specified length of time during which it can use the CPU resource, as shown in this example:

```
SQL> begin
        dbms_resource_manager.create_plan_directive (
        plan                   => 'peaktime',
        group_or_subplan => 'oltp',
        mgmt_p1            =>    75,
        switch_group       => 'kill_session',
        switch_time        =>    60);
     end;
```

When a user exceeds 60 seconds of CPU usage time, the database automatically kills the session by moving the session to the kill_session group specified by the switch_group parameter.

Pre-Created Mixed Workload Resource Plan

Oracle Database 11g provides a new predefined resource plan named MIXED_WORKLOAD_PLAN. This Oracle-supplied plan gives priority to interactive operations over batch jobs. The plan is disabled by default, and you must enable it in order to assign this plan to user sessions. The MIXED_WORKLOAD_PLAN resource plan consists of the following groups or subplans:

- *interactive_group*, primarily intended for short online transactions
- *batch_group*, primarily intended for long batch operations

Following is the way Oracle allocates CPU to the different resource consumer groups in the MIXED_WORKLOAD_PLAN:

- The sys_group gets 100 percent of the CPU at level 1.
- The interactive_group gets preference over the batch_group because its CPU resource allocation is 85 percent of the Level 2 allocation. The other 15 percent of the level 2 CPU allocation is equally distributed among the following subplan and groups:
  - ORA$AUTOTASK_SUB_PLAN
  - ORA$DIAGNOSTICS
  - OTHER_GROUPS
- The batch_group gets only Level 3 allocation of CPU, although it's 100 percent. If a session that is mapped to the interactive_group goes over 60 seconds of execution time, the database automatically switches it to the batch_group. For the interactive_group then, the following automatic consumer resource group switching parameter values hold:
  - `switch_group`: batch-group
  - `switch_time`: 60 seconds
  - `switch_for_call`: true

You can take advantage of the pre-built resource plans by mapping your online application users to the interactive_group consumer group and the batch applications to the batch_group consumer group. You can modify the CPU resource allocations to the batch_group and the interactive_group to suit the needs of your workload.

CERTIFICATION OBJECTIVE 3.04

Using New Oracle Scheduler Features

The following are important new features related to the Oracle Scheduler in Oracle Database 11g:

- Lightweight jobs
- Remote external jobs
- Application to a Data Guard environment

I discuss the three major new Oracle Scheduler features in the following sections.

Lightweight Jobs

In Oracle Database 10g, there was only a single type of Scheduler job. In Oracle Database 11g, you can also create what's called a lightweight job (also referred to as a persistent lightweight job), which derives its privileges, and in some cases, its job metadata, from a job template. Regular jobs, which are fully self-contained unlike the lightweight jobs, are still the more flexible type of jobs, but you incur overhead each time you create one. In a situation in which the database may have to create and delete thousands of jobs, it may be smarter to use a lightweight job instead. If you're going to use a small number of infrequent jobs, you are better off sticking to the traditional regular jobs.

Lightweight jobs aren't schema objects, as regular Scheduler jobs are. Thus, the overhead in creating and dropping a lightweight job is much smaller when compared with a regular job. Lightweight jobs are also faster to create and take up space only for the job metadata and runtime data. Lightweight jobs help make recovery and load balancing easier in an RAC environment because they have a smaller physical footprint and require less redo because of the minimal amount of metadata that's created for the jobs. The overall goal is to reduce the time it takes to create jobs and to lower the overhead involved in the job creation process.

Unlike a regular Scheduler job, you must use a *job template* when creating a lightweight job. The job template is a new type of database object that provides the metadata for a lightweight job, in addition to providing privileges that the lightweight jobs will inherit. Either a stored procedure or a Scheduler program can serve as a template for lightweight job. The lightweight jobs thus inherit their privileges from the parent job template. You must create and drop a database object when you create and drop a regular job. Because they are not full fledged database objects, lightweight jobs are much faster to create and run because they don't require the same overhead as regular jobs. Although they offer superior overhead cost, lightweight jobs have the following disadvantages when compared to a regular job:

■ You can't create a fully self-contained lightweight job. Instead, you must use a template. You can use either a stored procedure or a Scheduler program as a template for a lightweight job.

■ You can't set the privileges on a per job basis because the lightweight jobs inherit privileges from the parent job template.

■ Only a limited set of job attributes are applicable to lightweight jobs, whereas a regular job offers more choices.

To summarize, then, lightweight jobs are a special type of Scheduler jobs that you can use instead of traditional jobs if your database has to quickly create a large number of jobs.

Creating a Job Template

You can create a job template, which is mandatory for lightweight jobs, by using the CREATE_PROGRAM procedure from the DBMS_SCHEDULER package. Here's an example showing how to create a simple job template, with a Scheduler program serving as the template.

```
begin
dbms_scheduler.create_program(
program_name => 'test_prog',
program_action =>
  'declare current_time   date;
    begin
      select
      sysdate into current_time from dual;
    end;',
program_type => 'plsql_block',
enabled=> true);
end;
/
```

In the CREATE_PROGRAM procedure, the `program_action` attribute can be an actual anonymous PL/SQL code block or a named procedure. In the example, I used an anonymous PL/SQL code block. The Scheduler passes the following for execution to the PL/SQL engine: `DECLARE ... BEGIN job_action END;`.

If you want to use a named stored procedure instead of an anonymous PL/SQL code block, you can do so by specifying the name of the procedure as the value for the `program_action` attribute.

The `program_type` attribute lets you specify the type of program you are creating. For a lightweight job, you can use either `plsql_block` or `stored_procedure` as the value for the program_type attribute. You specify the `plsql_block` value for an anonymous PL/SQL block, which is the case in this example. You specify the value `stored_procedure` for a program that's a PL/SQL or Java stored procedure or an external C subprogram.

Creating a Single Lightweight Job

You create a lightweight job using the CREATE_JOB procedure of the DBMS_SCHEDULER package, just as you do for a regular Scheduler job. However, for a lightweight job, you must use the new job parameter `job_style` and assign it a value of `LIGHTWEIGHT`. You can create a lightweight job by specifying the time and frequency directly within the CREATE_JOB procedure, or use a schedule to set the timing and frequency attributes for the job. You can specify only a few parameters for a lightweight job. These are the job parameters and the schedule parameter. The lightweight jobs inherit the other metadata for running the job, as well as its privileges, from the parent job template. Here's an example that shows how to create a lightweight Scheduler job by specifying the time and frequency attributes directly in the CREATE_JOB procedure.

```
begin
dbms_scheduler.create_job (
job_name          => 'test_ltwtjob1',
program_name      => 'test_prog',
repeat_interval   => 'freq=daily,by_hour=10',
end_time          => '31-DEC-08 06:00:00 AM Australia/Sydney',
job_style         => 'lightweight',
comments          => 'A lightweight job based on a program');
end;
/
```

Note that a lightweight job always needs a job template, which is based on a procedure or a Scheduler program. Unlike a regular job, you can't inline a lightweight job, but must always use a named program. The program test_prog in our example serves as the template for this lightweight job.

You can also create a lightweight job based on a named program (which acts as the template) and a preexisting schedule, as shown in this example:

```
begin
dbms_scheduler.create_job (
job_name           => 'test_ltwtjob2',
program_name       => 'test_prog',
schedule_name      => 'test_sched',
job_style_         => 'lightweight',
comments           => 'A job based on a program and a schedule');
end;
/
```

The new lightweight job you create depends on the program test_prog and the schedule test_sched, which already exist. Note that providing a named program and schedule means that you don't have to use the repeat_interval or the end_time attributes when creating the new lightweight job.

Creating an Array of Lightweight Jobs

Oracle Database 11g offers you a way to create a set of jobs through the creation of a *job array*. When you need to create a fairly large number of Scheduler jobs (regular or lightweight), it's far more efficient to create a job array and submit it once, instead of submitting a large number of single job creation requests to the database. You can use the concept of a job array for both regular jobs and the new lightweight jobs. In the following example, I make use of a job array to create a set of lightweight jobs.

1. Declare two variables, one to hold the job definition and the other to hold the job array:

```
declare
testjob sys.job;
testjobarr sys.job_array;
```

2. Initialize the job array using the sys.job_array constructor:

```
begin
testjobarr := sys.job_array();
```

The array testjobarr is an array of JOB object types. The initialization of the job array creates a slot for one job in the job array named testjobarr.

3. Set the size of the new job array to the number of lightweight jobs you expect to create in your database:

```
testjobarr.extend(500);
```

Now the database allocates sufficient space in the array to hold information on about 500 jobs.

4. Create the jobs and place them in the job array:

```
for I in 1...500 loop
testjob := sys.job(job_name => 'TESTJOB'||TO_CHAR(I),
job_style    => 'LIGHTWEIGHT',
job_template => 'TEST_PROG',
enabled      => TRUE);
testjobarr(i) := TESTJOB;
end loop;
```

The code within the loop will create 500 jobs at once, using the `job_template` TEST_PROG<>. The `I in 1...500 loop` adds the definitions for the jobs. The assignment `testjobarr(i) := testjob` adds jobs to the array. The jobs are scheduled to run immediately because the `start_time` parameter defaults to null when you omit it.

Submit the job array as a single transaction, using the CREATE_JOBS procedure:

```
dbms_scheduler.create_jobs (testjobarr, 'transactional');
```

The CREATE_JOBS procedure treats the `testjobarr` array as a single transaction and creates all 500 lightweight jobs.

EXERCISE 3-2

Creating an Array of Regular Scheduler Jobs

In Oracle Database 11g, you can create an array of jobs at once, instead of creating a single job at a time. The following example shows how to create a set of 1,000 regular Scheduler jobs.

```
declare
testjob sys.job;
testjobarr sys.job_array;
begin
testjobarr := sys.job_array();
testjobarr.extend(1000);
for I in 1...1000 loop
```

```
testjob := sys.job(job_name => 'TESTJOB'||TO_CHAR(I),
job_template => 'TEST_PROG',
enabled => TRUE);
testjobarr(i) := TESTJOB;
end loop;
dbms_scheduler.create_jobs (testjobarr, 'transactional');
```

Because there is no `job_style` parameter, by default, Oracle creates regular instead of lightweight jobs.

Monitoring Lightweight Jobs

Use the same views that you use for regular jobs to view information about lightweight jobs. For example, you can query the DBA_SCHEDULER_JOBS view to find out details about lightweight jobs, as shown here:

```
SQL> select job_name, program_name from dba_scheduler_jobs
    where job_style='LIGHTWEIGHT';
JOB_NAME               PROGRAM_NAME
-----------            -------------
TEST_JOB1              TEST_PROG1
```

Note that you can't view any lightweight jobs in the DBA_OBJECTS view because, unlike a regular Scheduler job, lightweight jobs aren't database objects.

Remote External Jobs

An external job is a job that you can execute outside the database. Usually it's an operating system executable that you execute through the Oracle database, but runs entirely outside the database. You specify the `job_type` parameter for an external job as `executable`. You may also use a named Scheduler program for an external job, in which case you must specify the `job_type` parameter as `executable`. The `job_action` parameter (or `program_action` parameter if you're using a Scheduler program instead) points to the full path of the directory where the operating system executable is stored. An external job can be an operating system–based job or a database job. External jobs were available in the previous release. What's new in Oracle Database 11g are *remote external jobs*. The traditional external jobs are now referred to as *local external jobs* and they run only on the server on which the scheduling Oracle database runs. Remote external jobs can run on any host, not just the server hosting the Oracle database that's scheduling the external job. You can thus administer operating system or Oracle database jobs across your entire network from a centralized location.

The remote host on which you run a remote external job doesn't need you to install an Oracle database. You merely need to install a Scheduler agent so an Oracle database can communicate with the agent to run external jobs on that remote host. The agent listens to incoming job requests from the Oracle database issuing the job requests and executes those requests on the target server. The agent is also responsible for returning the job execution results to the database originating the external job.

on the **Job**   ***You must install Oracle XML DB on the source database from where you're originating the job requests.***

Running local external jobs is pretty straightforward. You may have to set the credentials for the user account on which the OracleJobScheduler service runs on a Windows system, to enable local external jobs. Running remote external jobs involves the installation of the scheduler agent on all remote hosts where you want to run an external job. In addition, you must also perform other tasks such as setting the credentials for executing an external job. The following sections explain how to set up remote external jobs.

Setting up the Database

Before you can run an external remote job, you must first set up the database from which you want to originate the external job request, which involves the following steps:

1. Check that the Oracle XML DB option is installed on your database host. This option is installed by default and you can confirm that it has been successfully installed by issuing the following `describe` command to examine the contents of the RESOURCE_VIEW view.

```
SQL> desc resource_view
 Name                     Null?      Type
 ----------------         -----      ------------------------------
 RES
 XMLTYPE                             (XMLSchema "http://xm
                                     lns.oracle.com/xdb/XDBResour
                                     ce.xsd" Element "Resource")
 ANY_PATH                           VARCHAR2(4000)
 RESID                              RAW(16)

SQL>
```

The results of the query show that Oracle XML DB is indeed installed on the database host. If the Oracle XML DB wasn't installed, you'd have to install it before proceeding further.

2. Run the Oracle script prvtrsch.plb as the user SYS, as shown here:

```
SQL> connect sys/sammyy1 as sysdba
SQL> @$ORACLE_HOME/rdbms/admin/prvtrsch.plb
PL/SQL procedure successfully completed.
...
PL/SQL procedure successfully completed.
no rows selected
Package created.
Package body created.
No errors.
...
User altered.

SQL>
```

3. Your final step in preparing the scheduling database is to set a registration password for the Scheduler agent. The Scheduler agent will use this password to register with the database.

```
SQL> exec dbms_scheduler.set_agent_registration_pass(
registration_password => 'sammyy1'.-
expiration_date       => systimestamp + interval '7' day,-
max_uses              => 25)
PL/SQL procedure successfully completed.

SQL>
```

The previous example sets the Scheduler agent registration password for the database host to sammyy1. The `expiration_date` and the `max_uses` parameter set an expiration time for the credential and limit the number of times a credential can be invoked, respectively. In this case, the `max_uses` parameter is set to 25, meaning that the credential is allowed to be used a maximum of 25 times within a period of 7 days. Both the `expiration_date` and the `max_uses` parameters are optional, serving to limit the usage of the password to a short time, as recommended by Oracle.

Installing and Configuring the Scheduler Agent

To run a remote external job, you must install the Scheduler agent on all remote hosts where you want to run a scheduled external job. The Scheduler agent isn't installed as part of the database server installation. You must install it either from the installation media for the Oracle Database Gateway (included in the Database CD pack) or download it from the Oracle web site.

The following are the steps to install the Scheduler agent on a remote host:

1. On a UNIX/Linux system, log in as the owner of the Oracle software (user Oracle, usually).

2. Start the Oracle Installer from the directory where the Oracle Database Gateway installation files are located.

   ```
   $ /oracle11g/gateways/runInstaller
   ```

3. On the Welcome screen, click Next.

4. On the Select a Product page, select Oracle Scheduler Agent 11.1.0.6.0 and click Next.

5. On the Specify Home Details page, select a name and provide the directory path for the Oracle Scheduler Agent home. Click Next.

6. On the Oracle Scheduler Agent page, provide the host name where you are installing the agent, as well as the port number you want the agent to use for communicating with the database making the remote external job requests. Click Next.

7. On the Summary page, review the selections you made and click Install.

on the
job

If you have a large number of remote sites, you can simplify the installation of the agent by automating the procedure (silent install). This means that you must include the database registration password in the installer file.

8. The installer prompts you to log in as the root user and execute the root.sh script. Once you execute the root.sh script, click OK.

9. The End of Installation page appears, indicating that the installation of the Scheduler agent was successful. Click Exit to leave the Oracle Universal Installer.

The schagent.conf text file, located in the Scheduler Agent home, contains the configuration parameters for the agent. Use the `schagent` executable to invoke the Scheduler agent. Your first task is to register the Scheduler agent with all databases that will run a remote external job on the host where you installed the agent. Use the following command to register the agent with each database:

```
$ schagent -registerdatabase localhost  1522
```

In this example, local host and 1522 are the database host and the port number for the Scheduler agent. The Scheduler agent will then prompt you for the agent registration password that you set earlier:

```
$./schagent -registerdatabase localhost.localdomain 1522
Agent Registration Password ?  ******
$
```

You must repeat the previous step for each database from which you want to run remote external jobs.

Finally, start the Scheduler agent by using the following command:

```
$./schagent -start
Scheduler agent started
$
```

You can stop the Scheduler agent by using the following command:

```
$./schagent -stop
Scheduler agent stopped
$
```

On a Windows server, you must install and start the OracleSchedulerExec utionAgent service. You can install the service by using the following command:

```
$ schagent -installagentservice
```

Note that the service you create with the schagent command is different from the regular Oracle service.

Creating and Enabling a Remote External Job

There is more involved in creating a remote external job than in creating a local external job. The big difference is that you must create a *credential* so the remote jobs can be executed. A credential is a schema object that contains a username/password pair of values. The credential_name attribute of an external job specifies the credential to be used for that job. Only a job whose owner has execute privileges on a credential can use that credential. Use the following steps to create a remote external job:

1. Create a credential using the CREATE_CREDENTIAL procedure.

   ```
   SQL> exec dbms_scheduler.create_credential('hrcredential,
        'hr','sammyy1');
   ```

2. Once you create a credential, you must grant privileges on that credential so a user can use those credentials.

```
SQL> grant execute on system.hrcrdential to sam;
```

The DBA_SCHEDULER_CREDENTIALS view shows all credentials created in a database.

3. Create a remote external job named *removelogs*, as shown here:

```
SQL> begin
  2  dbms_scheduler.create_job(
  3  job_name => 'remove_logs',
  4  job_type => 'executable',
  5  job_action => '/u01/app/oracle/logs/removelogs',
  6  repeat_interval => 'freq=daily; byhour=23',
  7  enabled => false);
  8* end;
SQL> /

PL/SQL procedure successfully completed.

SQL>
```

4. Use the SET_ATTRIBUTE procedure to set the `credential_name` attribute of the remote job.

```
SQL> exec dbms_scheduler.set_attribute('remove_logs',
     'credential_name','hrcredential');
PL/SQL procedure successfully completed.
SQL>
```

5. Using the SET_ATTRIBUTE procedure again, set the `destination` attribute of the remote job,

```
SQL> exec dbms_scheduler.set_attribute('remove_logs',
     'destination', 'remotehost.remotedomain:1522');

PL/SQL procedure successfully completed.
SQL>
```

Note that you must use the host and port numbers of the Scheduler agent in order to specify the destination host or database.

6. Enable the remote external job:

```
SQL> exec dbms_scheduler.enable('remove_logs');

PL/SQL procedure successfully completed.
SQL>
```

The remote external job you created is now enabled on the remote host.

Disabling Remote External Jobs

You can disable the capability of a database to run remote external jobs by dropping the user remote_scheduler_agent using the following command:

```
SQL> drop user remote_scheduler_agent cascade;
```

Once you drop the user remote_scheduler_agent, you can't register new scheduler agents or execute any remote external jobs. In order for the database to regain the ability to run remote external jobs, you must re-execute the prvtrsch.plb script.

Scheduler Support for Data Guard

Oracle Database 11g provides support for the Scheduler in an Oracle Data Guard setup. You can now set up Scheduler jobs to run based on the particular role that the database is playing at a given time. That is, you can specify that a certain job run only when the database is in the primary role and not in the logical standby role and vice versa.

You use the new DATABASE_ROLE attribute in the DBMS_SCHEDULER package's SET_ATTRIBUTE procedure to denote the role of the database to the Scheduler. The new functionality means that you can run a Scheduler job in the following two ways:

- Run a job only when the database is in one of the two roles, primary or logical standby.
- Run the job when the database is in both primary and logical standby roles. In order to make the same job run in both roles, you must make a copy of the job and assign each of the copies a separate role—primary and logical standby.

The following example shows how to create a Scheduler job so it can run based on the role the database is in:

1. Create a regular Scheduler job on the primary database.

```
begin
 dbms_scheduler.create_job (
 job_name       => 'primary_job',
 program_name  => 'test_prog',
 schedule_name => 'test_sched');
end;
/
```

The job named primary_job will run automatically in the primary database because it was created when the database was in the primary database role.

The primary_job is also enabled to run because all Scheduler jobs are enabled upon their creation.

2. Make a copy of the job you created in the previous step, as shown here:

```
SQL> exec dbms_scheduler.copy_job ('primary_job',
     'standby_job');
```

The copy you made of the original job is disabled by default.

3. Set the database role of the copied job to logical standby, using the database_role attribute.

```
SQL> exec dbms_scheduler.set_attribute('standby_job',
     'database_role', 'logical standby');
```

4. Enable the copied job, using the enable procedure:

```
SQL> exec dbms_scheduler.enable (name=> 'standby_job');
```

You can confirm that you've correctly copied the original job to run when the database is in the logical standby role, by issuing the following query:

```
SQL> select job_name,database_role
     from dba_scheduler_job_roles;
JOB_NAME                          DATABASE_ROLE
-------------------               -----------------
PRIMARY_JOB                       PRIMARY
STANDBY_JOB                       LOGICAL STANDBY
```

You can see that your original job now will run when it's in the primary database role or the logical standby database role. Upon a switchover or a failover, the jobs specific to the role (primary/logical standby) will be run automatically by the Scheduler.

CERTIFICATION OBJECTIVE 3.05

Security Enhancements

There are several new security-related features in Oracle Database 11g, but for the purpose of the certification test, you must focus on the following new security-related enhancements.

- Secure password support
- Configuring fine-grained access to network services
- Encrypting a tablespace

In the following sections, I describe the three major security-related new features in Oracle Database 11g.

Secure Password Support

Oracle Database 11g provides several new ways to make database passwords more secure. Among these are the following new password-related features:

- Case-sensitive passwords make databases more secure. I discuss this feature in the following sections.
- You can include multibyte characters in a password without enclosing them in quotation marks.
- All passwords entered by users are passed through the string hash algorithm (SHA-1, which uses a 160-bit key) and compared with the stored credential for that user.
- Passwords always use *salt*, which is a random unique value added to the passwords to ensure a unique output credential.

Configuring Case-Sensitive Passwords

In Oracle Database 11g, for the first time, database passwords are case-sensitive by default. That is, when you create or modify a user account, the passwords are automatically case sensitive. You can control case sensitivity in the database by setting the new initialization parameter sec_case_sensitive_logon. Because, by default, the database now enforces password case sensitivity, the default value of this parameter is set to TRUE.

Although Oracle recommends that you adhere to the new default of case-sensitive passwords, there may be times when you have to disable case sensitivity in order to be compatible with some applications that, say, use hard-coded, case-insensitive passwords. In such a case, you may reinstate the old-fashioned case insensitivity if you want, by changing the value for this parameter to FALSE.

```
$ alter system set sec_case_sensitive_logon = false scope=pfile;
```

Case Sensitivity and Upgrading

When you upgrade from Oracle Database 10g or an older release of the database to Oracle Database 11g, the passwords remain case insensitive. You must change the passwords for the users in order to make the passwords case sensitive. Use the following query on the DBA_USERS view to find out which of your users have case-sensitive passwords, as shown here:

```
SQL> select username, password,
password_versions from dba_users;

USERNAME                          PASSWORD          PASSWORD
------------------                ----------------  -----------------
MGMT_VIEW                                           10G       11G
SYS                                                 10G       11G
SYSTEM                                              10G       11G
DBSNMP                                              10G       11G
SYSMAN                                              10G       11G
RMAN                                                10G       11G
SH                                                  10G       11G
...
39 rows selected.
SQL>
```

In the preceding query, the new Oracle Database 11g column PASSWORD_
VERSIONS shows the database release in which that password was originally
created or changed. In this case, it shows that all passwords were either created
in Oracle Database 10g (or earlier releases) and changed in Oracle Database
11g, or were created in Oracle Database 11g. When you upgrade from the Oracle
Database 10g release to the Oracle Database 11g release, all passwords remain case
insensitive. You must make the passwords case sensitive by using the alter user
<username> identified by <new_password> command. If you create a
new Oracle Database 11g database, on the other hand, the user accounts you create
will have case-sensitive passwords by default.

e x a m
ⓦatch
Is password sensitivity
automatically enforced upon upgrading
to Oracle Database 11g from Oracle
Database 10g? How about when you create
a database in Oracle Database 11g?

Note that unlike in the previous releases, the PASSWORD column is blank. In
the older releases, Oracle showed you the encrypted passwords. In Oracle Database
11g, you can't see the encrypted passwords by querying the DBA_USERS view.
The encrypted passwords, of course, are still stored—in the USER$ view. In Oracle
Database 11g, user passwords are stored as a user credential after first passing them
through a hash algorithm. Whenever you log in, the database hashes the password
you enter and compares it with the stored credential. In Oracle Database 11g, when
a user tries to connect with a wrong password, the database will delay subsequent

login attempts after the third failed attempt. The database will gradually increase the delay between consecutive attempts, up to a maximum of about ten seconds.

Case Sensitivity and Password Files

You are familiar with password files, which you use to specify passwords for users with the SYSDBA and SYSOPER privileges. In Oracle Database 11g, there is a new optional parameter you may specify when creating a new password file. The parameter, named `ignorecase`, determines whether the passwords in the password file are case sensitive or not. By default, the value of the `ignorecase` parameter is set to `no (n)`, meaning that all passwords inside a password file will be automatically case sensitive. Here's an example that shows how you specify the `ignorecase` parameter:

```
$ orapwd file=orapw entries=30 ignorecase=y
Enter password for SYS:
$
```

In the preceding example, the value of the `ignorecase` parameter is set to `y`, meaning the database will ignore the case in which you enter the password when logging into the database. When you import users from an older database release, the passwords of any users with the SYSDBA or SYSOPER privilege will be imported into your current password file. These passwords will be case insensitive by default and Oracle recommends that you have the users change their passwords. If you enable case sensitivity (setting the `sec_case_sensitive_logon` parameter to `TRUE`), when these users change their passwords they automatically become case sensitive.

By the by, in addition to the new `ignorecase` parameter, the `orapwd` command has other modifications in this release, as shown here:

```
$ orapwd
Usage: orapwd file=<fname> password=<password> entries=<users>
              force=<y/n> ignorecase=<y/n> nosysdba=<y/n>
   where
     file - name of password file (required),
     password - password for SYS (optional),
     entries - maximum number of distinct DBA (required),
     force - whether to overwrite existing file (optional),
     ignorecase - passwords are case-insensitive (optional),
     nosysdba - whether to shut out the SYSDBA logon (optional
     Database Vault only).
       There must be no spaces around the equal-to (=) character.
$
```

Oracle Database 11g comes with a new version of the Oracle PL/SQL script utlpwdmg.sql, which provides you a simple password verification function. You can customize this function.

Note the following differences in the usage of the `orapwd` command:

- The `password` parameter is optional now, whereas it was required before.
- The `ignorecase` parameter is new, as explained earlier.
- The `nosysdba` parameter is also new, but is relevant only if you've installed Oracle Database Vault.

New Password Management Function

Oracle provides a script named utlpwdmg.sql (stored in the $ORACLE_HOME/rdbms/admin directory) to let you implement several password management features such as the setting of the default password resource limits. The script contains code for creating a password verification function named `verify_function_11g`, for checking password complexity. The function checks only for minimal password complexity and you can customize it to satisfy more complex password checks.

Oracle offers both the old `verify_function` creation code and the code to create an updated Oracle Database 11g version of the function (`verify_function_11g`). The new version of the function includes the following *additional* password protection features:

- Ensures that the password is at least eight characters long. In the previous release, the minimum length of the password was only four characters.
- Checks if the password is the same as the username reversed.
- Checks if the password is the same or similar to the server name.

The following `alter profile` statement in the utlpwdmg.sql script will first create the new 11g version of the `verify_function` and then alter the DEFAULT profile.

```
alter profile default limit
password_life_time 180
password_grace_time 7
password_reuse_time_unlimited
password_reuse_max_unlimited
failed_login_attempts 10
password_lock_time 1
password_verify_function verify_function_11g;
```

As you are aware from earlier releases, the database assigns the DEFAULT profile to all new users in the database who haven't been assigned a specific profile. It's the default profile inherited by all users in the database. Note the last part of the SQL statement (`password_verify_function verify_function_11g`). This means that if you create the password verify function in your database as recommended by Oracle, any time a user (including the DBA) attempts to create a new password or to change an existing password, the database will execute the `verify_function_11g` function to ensure that the new password meets all the requirements specified by that function.

New Security-Related Initialization Parameters

You've learned about the new parameter `sec_case_sensitive_logon`, which allows you to control the case sensitivity of user passwords, thus reducing your vulnerability to brute force attacks. In addition, there are also these new parameters that affect security:

- `sec_protocol_error_further_action`   Specifies what action the database must take when it receives bad packets from a client, the presumption being that the client is acting with a malicious intent. The possible actions you can specify are: continue, drop the connection, or delay the acceptance of requests from the client.

- `sec_protocol_error_trace_action`   Specifies a monitoring action such as none, trace, log, or alert.

- `sec_max_failed_login_attempts`   Drops a connection after a specified number of failed login attempts. This policy remains enabled even if you don't enable a password profile.

- `ldap_directory_sysauth`   Specifies whether the database uses strong authentication for database administrators. You must set the value of this parameter to `yes` if you want to implement strong authentication such as Kerberos tickets or certificates over a Secure Socket Layer (SSL). You disable strong authentication when you specify the value `no` for this parameter.

Configuring Fine-Grained Access to Network Services

It's quite common for users to connect to external network hosts using PL/SQL network–related packages such as UTL_TCP, UTL_SMTP, UTL_MAIL, UTL_HTTP, and UTL_INADDR. Because all the PL/SQL utility packages, including the ones listed here, are created with the `execute` privilege granted to the user PUBLIC, there is an inherent security hole in the database. Once an unauthorized user breaks into the database, it's a simple hop, skip, and jump from there to the network. At least, it was. Oracle Database 11*g* offers you fine-grained access control capability so you can control the access of users to external network services from within the Oracle database. Fine-grained access means that you can now choose which host computers a user can connect to from the Oracle database when using the previously listed PL/SQL Oracle utility packages, by granting explicit privileges to do only that and nothing else.

Oracle provides new packages—DBMS_NETWORK_ACL_ADMIN and DBMS_NETWORK_ACL_UTILITY—to create and maintain access control lists (ACLs) for database users. You can also create access control lists through Oracle XML DB.

Creating an Access Control List

An access control list is simply a list of users and their privileges. The database stores the XML document containing the usernames and privileges in the /sys/acl folder in Oracle XML DB. The following example demonstrates how to use the DBMS_NETWORK_ACL_ADMIN.CREATE_ACL procedure to create an ACL:

```
SQL> begin
        dbms_network_acl_admin.create_acl (
        acl           =>  'test_xml',
        description   => 'Permissions for my network',
        principal     => 'APPOWNER',
        is_grant      => 'TRUE',
        privilege     =>  'connect');
     end;
```

Here are the key things to note in the CREATE_ACL procedure:

■ The `acl` parameter specifies the name of the XML file holding the usernames and privileges in the ACL.

■ `principal` indicates the username and must match the username of the session.

■ `is_grant` shows whether a privilege is granted or denied.

■ `privilege` specifies the network privilege you want to grant or deny. The two possible values for this parameter are `connect` and `resolve`. A user will need the `connect` privilege to a network host if the user is connecting through any one of the UTL_TCP, UTL_HTTP, UTL_SMTP, or UTL_MAIL packages. The `resolve` privilege is necessary to resolve a host name that was given the host IP address instead, or an IP address that was given the host name instead, with the UTL_INADDR package.

You can also add multiple hosts in the same ACL and you can add more users to the same ACL after you create an ACL. To add more users and privileges to the ACL you just created, use the ADD_PRIVILEGE procedure, as shown here:

```
SQL> begin
        dbms_network_acl_admin.add_privilege (
        acl             => 'test.xml',
        principal       => 'test_users',
        is_grant        => true,
        privilege       => 'connect')
     end;
```

You can use the ADD_PRIVILEGE procedure to grant or deny network access to users. If the ACL doesn't already exist in the database, the procedure will create it.

Assigning the Access Control List to a Host

Use the ASSIGN_ACL procedure to associate the ACL with a network host. Optionally, you can also associate the ACL with a range of ports. Here's an example:

```
SQL> begin
        dbms_network_acl_admin.assign_acl (
        acl             => 'test.xml',
        host            => '*.us.mycompany.com',
        lower_port      => 80,
        upper_port      => null);
     end;
```

exam

watch *Understand exactly how you can set up fine-grained access to external network services through an ACL. You must know how to set up values for* *the various parameters such as* `lower_port` *and* `upper_port` *when executing the* **DBMS_NETWORK.ASSIGN_ACL** *procedure.*

You can use the ASSIGN_ACL procedure to assign an ACL to a host, domain, or IP subnet. You can optionally also specify the TCP port range. Here are some things to note about using the ASSIGN_ACL procedure:

- ■ You can assign only one ACL per host, domain, or IP subnet (or TCP port range, if you specify it).

- If you assign a new ACL to a network target, Oracle unassigns the previous ACL list assigned to that target, but doesn't drop it. You can drop the ACL with the DROP_ACL procedure.

- If you assign a TCP port range, make sure that both `lower_port` and `upper_port` aren't NULL. In addition, the `upper_port` value must be at least as large as the port number you assign for the `lower_port` parameter. You must take care that the port range must not overlap other port ranges you may have already assigned for this host.

- You can unassign an ACL by using the UNASSIGN_ACL procedure.

Precedence Order for a Host Computer

In the previous example, I used a wild card character (*) for the host name. This means that the ACL is assigned to all the hosts in the domain specified there. Here's the order of precedence for the evaluation of host names in an ACL:

- Fully qualified host names with ports are evaluated before hosts with ports.
- Full qualified host names are evaluated before partially qualified host names.
- Subdomains under a domain name are evaluated before the top-level domain name.

For example, if your host name is www.us.mycompany.com, the following would be the order of precedence, in decreasing order:

```
www.us.mycompany.com
*.us.mycompany.com
*. mycompany.com
*.com
*
```

Similarly, ACLs assigned to individual IP addresses take the highest precedence, followed by ACLs assigned to subnets, followed by the ACL assigned to smaller subnets. If, for example, the IP address for a host is 192.168.0.100, the following is the precedence, in decreasing order:

```
192.168.0.100
192.168.0.*
192.168.*
192.*
*
```

As you can see, individual IP addresses get the highest precedence.

Checking the Privileges and Host Assignments

You can use the CHECK_PRIVILEGE function to check the privileges granted to or denied to a user in an ACL, as shown here.

```
SQL> select decode (dbms_network_acl_admin.check_privilege (
     test.xml', 'hr','resolve'),
     1, 'granted', 0, 'denied', null) privilege
     from dual;
```

The CHECK_PRIVILEGE function will return 1 if a privilege is granted and 0 if the privilege is denied. If a privilege is neither granted nor denied, it returns NULL.

Encrypting Tablespaces

Oracle has been gradually improving its encryption capabilities over the years. In Oracle 8*i*, Oracle introduced the DBMS_OBFUSCATION_TOOLKIT, and the Oracle 10.1 release introduced the DBMS_CRYPTO package to facilitate encryption. Both the toolkit and the DBMS_CRYPTO package required that the application manage the encryption keys and call the APIs to perform necessary encryption/decryption operations.

In Oracle Database 10g, Oracle introduced the new Transparent Data Encryption (TDE) feature, which let you easily encrypt a column's data in a table. The encryption is called transparent because the Oracle database takes care of all the encryption and decryption details, with no need for you to manage any tables or triggers to decrypt data. Now, in Oracle Database 11g, you can encrypt an entire tablespace by simply using a pair of special clauses during tablespace creation.

The tablespace creation statement for an encrypted tablespace has the following syntax:

```
create tablespace <tbsp_name>
encryption
default storage(encrypt)
```

The `encryption` clause in line 2 doesn't actually encrypt the tablespace. You provide the encryption properties by setting values for the keyword `encryption`. You may additionally specify the `using` clause along with the `encryption` clause (`encryption using ...`) to specify the name of the encryption algorithm you want to use, such as 3DES168, AES128, AES192, and AES256. If you want to use the default algorithm of AES128, you can omit the `using` clause altogether. It is the `encrypt` keyword passed to the `storage` clause in line 3 that encrypts the tablespace.

In the following sections, let's review how to encrypt a tablespace. But before I actually encrypt a tablespace, let me show you how to create an Oracle wallet, because you'll need the wallet when you encrypt a tablespace.

Creating the Oracle Wallet

An Oracle Wallet is a container to store authentication and signing credentials. The tablespace encryption feature uses the wallet to protect the master key used in the encryption. There are two kinds of Oracle wallets—*encryption wallets* and *auto-open wallets*. You must manually open an encryption wallet after database startup, whereas the auto-open wallet automatically opens upon database startup. The encryption wallet is commonly recommended for tablespace encryption, unless you're dealing with unattended Data Guard environments, in which case the automatic opening of the wallet comes in handy.

In order to use Oracle Wallet, you must create the wallet itself and then add a master key to it. You can create a wallet in a couple of ways. You can create the Oracle Wallet by:

- Using the `mkstore` command from the operating system command line
- Invoking the Oracle Wallet Manager either through a GUI interface or by issuing the command `owm` at the command line
- Executing the `alter system` statement from SQL*Plus

Here is the syntax to create a wallet from the OS:

```
$ mkstore -wrl $ORACLE_BASE/admin/$ORACLE_SID/wallet -create
Enter password:
Enter password again:
```

However, the simplest way to create the wallet is to simply use the following command in SQL*Plus:

```
SQL> alter system set encryption key identified by "password"
```

This command both creates the wallet if it doesn't already exist and adds a master key to it.

Oracle stores the encryption keys outside the database, in a file called an Oracle Wallet. By default, this file is named ewallet.p12 under both Windows and UNIX/Linux-based systems. The location where Oracle stores this file is operating system–specific. However, you can specify a different location by using the parameter `encryption_wallet_location` in the sqlnet.ora file.

```
ENCRYPTION_WALLET_LOCATION =
  (SOURCE=
     (METHOD=file)
     (METHOD_DATA=
        (DIRECTORY=/apps/oracle/general/wallet)    )  )
```

You must have the `alter system` privilege as well as a password for an Oracle Wallet. If you don't have an Oracle Wallet, you must create one. You can create a new Oracle Wallet using the Oracle Wallet Manager (OWM) or by using special SQL statements. In the following example, we show you how to create and open an Oracle Wallet using a SQL statement.

Before you create the Oracle Wallet, you must first create a directory named *wallet* under the directory $ORACLE_BASE/admin/$ORACLE_SID. If you don't do this, you'll get the error *ORA-28368: cannot auto-create wallet*. After you create the directory named *wallet*, issue the following statement from SQL*Plus:

```
SQL> alter system set encryption key identified by "sammyy11";
System altered.
SQL>
```

The `alter system` statement you issued in the previous example works in the following way:

- If you already have an Oracle Wallet, it opens that wallet and creates (or re-creates) the master encryption key.
- If you don't have an Oracle Wallet already, it creates a new wallet, opens the wallet, and creates a new master encryption key.

Now that you've successfully created the Oracle Wallet and ensured it is open, you're ready to encrypt tablespaces using the new tablespace encryption feature.

Creating an Encrypted Tablespace

Once you create the Oracle Wallet, creating an encrypted tablespace is a breeze. The following is an example showing how to create a simple encrypted tablespace that uses the default DES128 encryption. Because you don't have to specify the default encryption level, you don't specify the `using` clause for the encryption clause in line 3.

```
SQL> create tablespace encrypt1
  2  datafile 'c:\orcl11\app\oracle\oradata\eleven\
  3  encrypt_01.dbf' size 100m
  4  encryption
  5* default storage (encrypt);

Tablespace created.
SQL>
```

The storage parameter `encrypt` ensures that the tablespace is encrypted. The `encryption` clause determines the tablespace encryption properties. In this example, I use the `encryption` clause by itself, without specifying a particular encryption algorithm for the tablespace. The database will use the default AES128 encryption algorithm to encrypt the tablespace. You can also specify the optional `using <algorithm>` clause along with the `encryption` clause, as shown in the following example, to specify the exact encryption algorithm you want.

```
SQL> create tablespace encrypt1
  2  datafile 'c:\orcl11\app\oracle\oradata\eleven\
  3  encrypt_01.dbf' size 100m
  4  encryption using '3des168'
  5* default storage (encrypt);

Tablespace created.
SQL>
```

The previous example shows how to specify a particular encryption algorithm, 3DES168, instead of the default AES128 algorithm.

The new column ENCRYPTED in the DBA_TABLESPACES view lets you check the encryption status of a tablespace:

```
SQL> select tablespace_name, encrypted
  2  from dba_tablespaces;

TABLESPACE_NAME            ENC
---------------            ----
SYSTEM                     NO
SYSAUX                     NO
UNDOTBS1                   NO
TEMP                       NO
USERS                      NO
ENCRYPT1                   YES
6 rows selected.
SQL>
```

Oracle encrypts the data in the tablespace upon writing it and decrypts it upon reading the data. There is no additional memory requirement because the tablespace encryption and decryption aren't performed in memory, but there is an encryption overhead on I/O. The encrypted data will remain encrypted in both the undo segments as well as the redo logs, in addition to being encrypted in temporary tablespaces during typical operations such as sort and join operations that make use of a temporary tablespace.

on the *Job*

If you want to change the key for an encrypted tablespace, the only method in the present release is to create a new tablespace and move all the objects in the encrypted tablespace to the new tablespace. You can then encrypt the new tablespace.

Restrictions on Tablespace Encryption

When you encrypt a column(s) for a table, there are limitations on certain queries. By encrypting the entire tablespace, some of these restrictions are removed. For example, in Oracle Database 10g, if the column is part of a foreign key or used in another Database Constraint, it cannot be encrypted. By encrypting the entire tablespace instead of just a table or tables, this restriction is lifted. Note the following restrictions on tablespace encryption. You

- Can transport an encrypted tablespace only if the two operating system platforms have the same endianness and the same wallet.
- Can't change the key for an encrypted tablespace.
- Can't encrypt temporary and undo tablespaces.
- Can't encrypt bfiles and external tables.

INSIDE THE EXAM

The exam will probe your understanding of AWR baselines. You must know how to create a static and a moving window baseline, as well as a single and repeating window baseline template. One of the questions might relate to the expiration attribute in the CREATE_BASELINE_TEMPLATE procedure. How does the setting of the expiration attribute affect the removal of a baseline? The exam will review your understanding of the system moving window and the adaptive threshold's functionality. How do baseline metric statistics determine alert thresholds? You must know how to use significance level, percentage of maximum, and threshold values methods to compare baseline metric statistics to current database activity.

You must be familiar with both the new set of maintenance windows in this new release and how the default maintenance plan works,

as well as the role of the Autotask Background Process (ABP) in scheduling the automated maintenance tasks. The exam will test your understanding of the new I/O calibration tool. You must know the DBMS_RESOURCE_MANAGER.CALIBRATE_IO procedure thoroughly. Pay special attention to the parameters of the CALIBRATE_IO procedure, such as `actual_latency` and `max_latency`, and how to set their values. The exam will test your understanding of the I/O resource limit thresholds, and using parameters such as `switch_io_megabytes`. You must know the difference between a workload consisting of small random I/O and large sequential I/O. You must know the meaning of I/O metrics such as IOPS (I/O per second) and MBPS (megabytes per second). Which metrics can you use to measure throughput and I/O latency?

Expect a question about the new lightweight Scheduler jobs. How do you create a lightweight job? What are the key differences between a lightweight job and a regular Scheduler job? Review the use of the CREATE_JOB procedure in creating a lightweight job. What are the advantages in creating a lightweight job?

The exam is likely to include a question about the new automatic secure configuration feature. You must know how to use the new `sec_case_sensitive_logon` and other security-related new initialization parameters. Review the new password case-sensitivity feature and how it is different in the case of an upgrade and after creating a database. You must also be familiar with the tablespace encryption feature. Review the new initialization parameters `ldap_directory_sysauth` and `ldap_directory_access` and the role they play in setting up directory authentication for administrative users. The exam will certainly ask you about the setting up of an ACL. What do the `connect` and `resolve` privileges imply? How do you add new users and privileges to an ACL?

CERTIFICATION SUMMARY

Oracle Database 11g offers several enhancements to the AWR baselines. These enhancements include the ability to create baseline templates and moving window baselines. You can also rename baselines now and create a single or repeating baseline. There is also an integration of the selection of adaptive thresholds for performance metrics with the AWR baselines. The database automatically configures and maintains the adaptive thresholds, based on the system moving window baseline.

Oracle Database 11g offers seven pre-defined maintenance windows, one for each day of the week. You must use the new package DBMS_AUTO_TASK_ADMIN to manage the automated maintenance tasks. There is a new automated maintenance task known as the Automatic SQL Tuning Advisor. You can now perform an I/O calibration test either through Enterprise Manager or through the new CALIBRATE_IO procedure, belonging to the DBMS_RESOURCE_MANAGER package. I/O calibration testing enables you to measure the efficacy of different types of I/O workload.

Enhancements in the Database Resource Manager include the capability to automatically switch heavy resource usage sessions based on per-session I/O limits and a new default mixed workload resource plan. Oracle Scheduler now lets you create a new type of small footprint job called a lightweight job. You must use a template to create a lightweight job. You can also create remote external jobs in Oracle Database 11g by installing a Scheduler agent on the remote server to handle job requests. You can also create arrays of both regular and lightweight jobs in Oracle Database 11g. The Oracle Scheduler also supports Data Guard installations in this release.

For the first time, database passwords are case sensitive. You can use the new password management function to make passwords more complex than before. You can also configure fine-grained network access through creating ACLs, to keep unauthorized users from accessing the network through various UTL_* packages. In Oracle Database 11g, you can encrypt an entire tablespace when you create a tablespace.

✓ TWO-MINUTE DRILL

Enhancements in AWR Baselines

❏ An AWR baseline contains representative performance data from a known period.

❏ An AWR baseline consists of a set of AWR snapshots.

❏ The snapshots that are part of an AWR baseline are excluded from the routine snapshot purging process.

❏ A baseline template helps in the automatic creation of baselines for time periods in the future.

❏ You can create both a single baseline template and a repeating baseline template.

❏ The expiration parameter in the CREATE_BASELINE_TEMPLATE procedure specifies how long the database will retain a baseline.

❏ By default, the database will maintain baselines forever.

❏ In Oracle Database 11g, you can rename an AWR baseline.

❏ If you use a system moving window, the database automatically computes metric statistics over the moving window.

❏ The three threshold types you can specify are: significance, percentage of maximum, and fixed values.

❏ A moving window baseline encompasses AWR data during the AWR retention period.

❏ Oracle maintains a system-defined moving window baseline by default.

❏ The default moving window size is the same as the AWR retention period.

Controlling Automated Maintenance Tasks

❏ There are three automated maintenance tasks in Oracle Database 11g.

❏ The Automatic SQL Tuning Advisor is the new automated maintenance task in Oracle Database 11g.

❏ There are seven redefined maintenance windows in Oracle Database 11g.

❏ The new package DBMS_AUTO_TASK_ADMIN helps manage automated maintenance tasks.

❑ Oracle restarts the automatic optimizer collection task and the automatic segment advisor task every four hours if the maintenance window is long.

❑ The DBA_AUTOTASK_OPERATION view shows all automatic task operations for all clients.

❑ The new Oracle background process Autotask Background Process (ABP) converts automated tasks into Scheduler jobs.

❑ The default resource plan for the maintenance windows is the DEFAULT_MAINTENANCE_PLAN.

Database Resource Manager New Features

❑ In Oracle Database 11g, the database can automatically switch sessions to other resource consumer groups based on resource usage by the sessions.

❑ switch_time is the time allowed for a session before it's switched to a different consumer group.

❑ switch_estimate directs the database to estimate the execution time for database calls before the calls begin.

❑ switch_for_call lets you specify that the database return a session to its original consumer group.

❑ You can have the database automatically switch sessions based on CPU and I/O usage.

❑ Oracle Database 11g provides a new predefined resource plan named MIXED_WORKLOAD_PLAN.

❑ You can take advantage of the pre-built resource plan by mapping users to different predefined consumer groups.

Using New Oracle Scheduler Features

❑ Lightweight jobs have a small physical footprint and are faster to create.

❑ You must use a job template in order to create a lightweight job.

❑ You can't set privileges on a per job basis for lightweight jobs.

❑ You specify lightweight as the value for the job_style parameter in the CREATE_JOB procedure in order to create a lightweight job.

❑ Oracle Database 11g enables you to create a job array.

❑ Oracle Database 11g enables you to execute remote external jobs.

❑ The remote database doesn't need to have Oracle installed on it.

❑ You must install Oracle XML DB on the external job originating database.

❑ You must run the prvtsch.plb script on the job originating database.

❑ The Scheduler agent is responsible for communicating with the job originating database and handling the external job requests.

❑ The schagent.conf file contains the configuration parameters for the Scheduler agent.

❑ The `schagent` command lets you manage the Scheduler agent.

❑ A credential is a schema object that holds username/password information.

❑ You can run a Scheduler job when the database is in either the primary or the logical standby role.

Security Enhancements

❑ In Oracle Database 11g, passwords are case sensitive by default.

❑ You can control password case sensitivity by setting the initialization parameter `sec_case_sensitive_logon`.

❑ When you upgrade to Oracle Database 11g, all passwords remain case insensitive.

❑ When you create a new Oracle Database 11g database, the passwords will be case sensitive by default.

❑ The default value of the `ignorecase` parameter in the `orapwd` command is no (n).

❑ You can use the utlpwdmg.sql script to enforce password verification.

❑ Fine-grained network access controls show how users connect to the network from the Oracle database when using the UTL_* network-related packages.

❑ An access control list is a list of users and their privileges.

❑ Fully qualified host names are evaluated before hosts with ports.

❑ ACLs assigned to individual IP addresses take the highest precedence.

❑ The encryption clause in a `create tablespace` command provides the encryption properties.

❑ The keyword `encrypt` in the `storage` clause encrypts the tablespace.

❑ The two types of Oracle wallets are encryption wallets and auto-open wallets.

❑ Oracle stores the encryption keys in the Oracle wallet.

SELF TEST

The following questions will help you measure your understanding of the material presented in this chapter. Read all the choices carefully because there might be more than one correct answer. Choose all correct answers for each question.

Enhancements in AWR Baselines

1. An AWR baseline template allows you to
   A. Capture specific time periods in the past only
   B. Capture specific time periods in both the past and in the future
   C. Capture specific time periods in the future only
   D. Schedule the creation of AWR baselines

2. What happens if you don't specify a value for the expiration parameter when executing the CREATE_BASELINE_TEMPLATE procedure?
   A. The database will never drop the baseline.
   B. You can never drop the template manually.
   C. You'll have to maintain the template yourself.
   D. The database will not create any new baselines using this template

3. How does a database determine the alert thresholds when it uses the new adaptive metric thresholds?
   A. The database configures the adaptive thresholds based on the SYSTEM_MOVING_ WINDOW baseline.
   B. You have to set the adaptive thresholds manually.
   C. The adaptive thresholds are already configured when you create the database.
   D. The database configures the adaptive thresholds based on the MAINTENANCE_WINDOW baseline.

4. What must you do before increasing the size of the AWR moving window?
   A. Set the WINDOW_SIZE parameter to its default value.
   B. Increase the size of the AWR retention period to match the size of the moving window.
   C. Decrease the size of the AWR retention period to match the size of the moving window.
   D. You can't change the size of the AWR moving window.

Controlling Automated Maintenance Tasks

5. What is the duration of the predefined AWR maintenance windows?
  A. Weekday windows are 4 hours long and weekend windows are 24 hours long.
  B. Weekday windows are 12 hours long and weekend windows are also 12 hours long.
  C. Weekday windows are 4 hours long and weekend windows are also 4 hours long.
  D. Weekday windows are 4 hours long and weekend windows are 20 hours long.

6. Which automatic maintenance task runs only once per maintenance window?
  A. SQL Tuning Advisor
  B. Auto Optimizer
  C. Auto Segment Advisor
  D. SQL Access Advisor

7. If you want to change the resource allocation for the automatic tasks in a specific Scheduler window, you must
  A. Change the resources allocation to the DEFAULT_MAINTENANCE_PLAN.
  B. Change the resource allocation to the sub-plan ORA$AUTOTASK_SUB_PLAN.
  C. Change the resources allocation to the DEFAULT_MAINTENANCE_WINDOW.
  D. Change the resources allocation to the ORA$AUTOTASK_SQL_GROUP resource consumer group.

8. Which of the following statements is true?
  A. Oracle Scheduler assigns permanent Scheduler jobs for the automated maintenance tasks.
  B. The MMON background process assigns Scheduler jobs for the automated maintenance tasks.
  C. You must manually assign Scheduler jobs for the automated maintenance tasks.
  D. The Autotask background process converts the automated maintenance tasks into Scheduler jobs.

Database Resource Manager New Features

9. You can enable automatic switching of resource-intensive active sessions to a lower priority group by
  A. Specifying automatic resource consumer group switching with session-to-consumer group mapping rules
  B. Setting resource limits for a top call in a session
  C. Using the default value for the `switch_time` parameter
  D. Manually changing the session attributes while the session is active

10. The `switch_estimate` parameter in the CREATE_PLAN_DIRECTIVE procedure
    A. Lets the database estimate the execution time of a call before the call begins
    B. Lets the database estimate the group to which it will switch a session to a different resource consumer group
    C. Specifies the duration for which a call can execute before the database automatically switches the session to a different resource consumer group
    D. Is true by default

11. The Oracle supplied resource plan named MIXED_WORKLOAD_PLAN
    A. Gives priority to batch jobs over interactive jobs
    B. Gives equal priority to batch and interactive jobs
    C. Gives priority to mixed workload jobs
    D. Gives priority to interactive jobs over batch jobs

12. Which of the following resource allocations are correct?
    A. The interactive_group gets 85% of the level 2 allocation.
    B. The interactive_group gets 15% of the level 2 allocation.
    C. The batch_group gets 85% of the level 1 allocation.
    D. The batch_group gets 100% of the level 2 allocation.

13. If you specify the `switch_group` value as `cancel_sql`, Oracle
    A. Cancels the session
    B. Kills the active session
    C. Cancels the current database call issued by the session
    D. Cancels resource allocation to the session immediately

Using New Oracle Scheduler Features

14. A lightweight Scheduler job
    A. Inherits its privileges from similar lightweight jobs
    B. Inherits its privileges from a similar regular job
    C. Inherits its privileges from a Scheduler program
    D. Inherits its privileges from the parent job template

15. You can create a lightweight job by using
    A. A job array
    B. A named program
    C. A schedule
    D. The CREATE_JOB procedure

16. You must install Oracle XML DB on the
    A. Database from which you issue a remote external job request
    B. Database that executes the remote external job
    C. On the database issuing the external job request and the database fulfilling the request
    D. On neither the database issuing the external job request nor the database fulfilling the request

17. When you use the SET_AGENT_REGISTRATION_PASS procedure, which of the following sets of parameters are optional?
    A. `registration_password` and `max_uses`
    B. `expiration_date` and `max_uses`
    C. `registration_password` and `expiration_date`
    D. `credential` and `expiration_date`

Security Enhancements

18. Which of the following statements is true?
    A. By default, passwords are case insensitive in Oracle Database 11g.
    B. By default, passwords are case sensitive in Oracle Database 11g.
    C. When you upgrade from the 10.2 release to the 11.1 release, all the passwords remain case insensitive.
    D. When you upgrade from the 10.2 release to the 11.1 release, all the passwords are made case sensitive.

19. Which of the following statements are true, when you are using the ASSIGN_ACL procedure?
    A. You can assign multiple ACLs to a host.
    B. You can assign only one ACL to a host.
    C. If you assign a new ACL to a network target, Oracle drops the old ACL.
    D. If you're assigning TCP port range, you must ensure that at least one of the two ports (`lower_port` and `upper_port`) isn't NULL.

20. Which of the following clauses can be used in encrypting a tablespace?
    A. `encryption using '3des168'`
    B. `encryption using default`
    C. `default storage (encrypt '3des168')`
    D. `default '3des168'`

LAB QUESTION

What is the best way to create multiple privileges for multiple users and assign those privileges to multiple host computers?

SELF TEST ANSWERS

Enhancements in AWR Baselines

1. ☑ **C** and **D** are correct. **C** is correct because an AWR baseline template helps you capture data for specific time periods in the past. **D** is correct because you can use baseline templates to schedule the creation of AWR baselines, both for a single time period as well as for a recurring time period
   ☒ **A** and **B** are incorrect because you can't use the AWR baselines to capture data for past time periods.

2. ☑ **A** is correct because the database retains the baseline forever if you omit the expiration parameter.
   ☒ **B** is incorrect because you can always drop a baseline template manually. **C** is incorrect because you don't have to maintain the AWR baselines—the database manages them. **D** is incorrect because the expiration parameter has nothing to do with the creation of new baselines. It has to do with the retention of a baseline template.

3. ☑ **A** is correct because when a database uses adaptive metric thresholds, it configures the thresholds based on the SYSTEM_MOVING_WINDOW baseline.
   ☒ **B** is incorrect because you don't manually set the adaptive metric thresholds. **C** is incorrect because adaptive thresholds aren't preconfigured when you create the database. The database configures the adaptive thresholds based on the activity in the database. **D** is incorrect because the adaptive thresholds are based on the SYSTEM_MOVING_WINDOW baseline.

4. ☑ **B** is correct. You must match the AWR retention period to the size of the AWR moving window.
   ☒ **A** is incorrect because you don't have to set the window_size parameter default value. **C** is incorrect because you must increase, not decrease, the size of the AWR retention period, assuming that you want to create an AWR moving window that's larger than its default value. **D** is incorrect because you can change the size of the AWR moving window.

Controlling Automated Maintenance Tasks

5. ☑ **D** is correct. The default weekday maintenance window duration is 4 hours, and the duration of the two weekend windows is 20 hours.
   ☒ **A**, **B**, and **C** are incorrect because they offer the wrong window duration.

6. ☑ **A** is correct. The SQL Tuning Advisor runs only once during a maintenance window.
   ☒ **B** and **C** are incorrect because the database will rerun both of these tasks if the maintenance window is long. **D** is incorrect because the SQL Access Advisor isn't one of the three automated maintenance tasks.

7. ☑ **A** is correct. You change resource allocation for automatic tasks by changing the resources you allocate for the DEFAULT_MAINTENANCE_PLAN.
☒ **B** is incorrect because you must change the resource allocation to the DEFAULT_ MAINTENANCE_PLAN plan. **C** is incorrect because you don't allocate resources to a Resource Manager window. **D** is incorrect because you don't directly allocate resources to a resource consumer group.

8. ☑ **D** is correct. The new Autotask background process is in charge of converting the automated maintenance tasks into Scheduler jobs.
☒ **A** is incorrect because the Oracle Scheduler doesn't assign permanent Scheduler jobs for automated maintenance tasks. **B** is incorrect because the MMON process doesn't assign Scheduler jobs to the automated maintenance tasks. **C** is incorrect because you don't assign the Scheduler jobs manually to the automated maintenance tasks.

Database Resource Manager New Features

9. ☑ **A** and **B** are correct. **A** is correct because you can specify consumer group switching by sessions based on the session-to-consumer group mapping. **B** is correct because Oracle Database 11g introduces the capability whereby the database can automatically switch sessions among resource groups based on the resource limits you specify for the top call in an active session.
☒ **C** is incorrect because the default value of the `switch_time` parameter is `unlimited`, which means that a database will never switch a session automatically. **D** is incorrect because manually changing the session attributes doesn't fall under automatic switching of active sessions by the database.

10. ☑ **A** is correct. The `switch_estimate` parameter lets the database figure out how long a call will take to execute, before the call starts.
☒ **B** is incorrect because the `switch_estimate` parameter tells you the estimated time to complete a call, not the group to which the session will be switched. **C** is incorrect because the `switch_estimate` parameter doesn't have anything to do with the duration for which a call can execute before it's automatically switched to another consumer group. **D** is incorrect because the `switch_estimate` parameter is `FALSE` by default.

11. ☑ **D** is correct. The Oracle-supplied resource plan MIXED_WORKLOAD_PLAN gives priority to interactive jobs over batch jobs.
☒ **A**, **B**, and **C** are incorrect because interactive jobs get a higher priority than batch jobs.

12. ☑ **A** is correct. The `interactive_group` gets 85% of the level 2 allocation.
☒ **B**, **C**, and **D** are incorrect because they all show the wrong allocation of resources. The `interactive_group` gets 85% of the level 2 allocation and the `batch_job` gets 100% of the level 3 allocation. Neither gets any allocation at level 1.

13. ☑ **C** is correct. If the `switch_group` parameter has the value `cancel_sql`, Oracle cancels the currently executing database call made by the session once the session exceeds a resource limit.

☒ **A** is incorrect because Oracle doesn't terminate the session. **B** is incorrect because Oracle doesn't terminate the session. **D** is incorrect because the database doesn't alter the resource allocation to the session—it simply cancels the currently running database call.

Using New Oracle Scheduler Features

14. ☑ **D** is correct. You must use a template for creating a lightweight job and the job will inherit all its privileges from the parent job template.
☒ **A**, **B**, and **C** are incorrect because a lightweight job inherits its privileges from the parent job template.

15. ☑ **A**, **B**, **C**, and **D** are correct. You can create a lightweight job with a job array, a named program, a schedule, and with the CREATE_JOB procedure, so all alternatives are correct.

16. ☑ **A** is correct. You must install Oracle XML DB on the database originating the remote external job.
☒ **B** is incorrect because you don't need the Oracle database to be installed on the job executing host. You just need to install the Scheduler agent on that host. **C** is incorrect because you need the Oracle database to be installed only on the job originating database. **D** is incorrect because you do need to install Oracle on the job originating database.

17. ☑ **B** is correct. Both the `expiration_date` and `max_uses` parameters are optional, although Oracle recommends that you specify both parameters in order to tightly control network access.
☒ **A** and **C** are incorrect because the `registration_password` parameter is mandatory. **D** is incorrect because there is no credential parameter in the SET_AGENT_REGISTRATION_ PASS procedure.

Security Enhancements

18. ☑ **B** and **C** are correct. **B** is correct because, by default, passwords are case sensitive in Oracle Database 11*g*. **C** is correct because the password remains case insensitive when you upgrade to Oracle Database 11*g* from an older release database.
☒ **A** is incorrect because passwords are case sensitive by default in Oracle Database 11*g*. **D** is incorrect because when you upgrade to the 11.1 release, passwords continue to remain case insensitive. You can make all the passwords casesensitive by using the `alter user...` statement.

19. ☑ **B** is correct. When you use the ASSIGN_ACL procedure to assign ACLs to a host, you can assign only one ACL per host.
☒ **A** is incorrect because you can't assign multiple ACLs to a host. **C** is incorrect because Oracle doesn't drop an ACL when you assign a new ACL to a network target. If you assign a new ACL

to a network target, Oracle unassigns the previous ACL list assigned to that target. **D** is incorrect because you must ensure that *both* the `lower_port` and the `upper_port` aren't NULL.

20. ☑ **A** is correct. The `encryption using '3des168'` clause is syntactically correct. It specifies the encryption algorithm to use for the tablespace you're encrypting.

☒ **B, C,** and **D** are incorrect because they aren't syntactically correct.

LAB ANSWER

You can specify multiple role privileges in a single ACL creation statement. You can assign the privileges to multiple host computers in a single execution of the ASSIGN_ACL procedure. In the following example, I create the ACL first and then assign privileges.

Create the access control list by executing the CREATE_ACL procedure, as shown here:

```
begin
  DBMS_NETWORK_ACL_ADMIN.CREATE_ACL (
    acl           => 'test.xml',
    description   => 'Network connection permission for -
                     SUPERVISOR and CLERK',
    principal     => 'SUPERVISOR',
    is_grant      => TRUE,
    privilege     => 'resolve');
  DBMS_NETWORK_ACL_ADMIN.ADD_PRIVILEGE (acl => 'test.xml',
    principal     => 'CLERK',
    is_grant      => TRUE,
    privilege     => 'connect',
    position      => null);
end;
```

The CREATE_ACL procedure creates the first procedure and grants the `resolve` privilege to the first user (`principal`), who is named SUPERVISOR. The ADD_PRIVILEGE procedure adds the second user (`clerk`) and grants the `connect` privilege to that user.

Assign the access control list to multiple hosts by executing the ASSIGN_ACL procedure.

```
begin
  DBMS_NETWORK_ACL_ADMIN.ASSIGN_ACL (
    host          => '*.mycompany.com');
  DBMS_NETWORK_ACL_ADMIN.ASSIGN_ACL (
    acl           => 'test.xml',
    host          => '*.us.mycompany.com',
    lower_port    => 80,
    upper_port    => 99);
end;
```

The first invocation of the ASSIGN_ACL procedure creates the first target host, and the second invocation creates the second target host.

4
Automatic SQL Tuning and SQL Plan Management

CERTIFICATION OBJECTIVES

4.01   Automatic SQL Tuning Advisor

4.02   SQL Plan Management

4.03   SQL Access Advisor Enhancements

✓   Two-Minute Drill

Q&A   Self Test

Some of the most important enhancements in Oracle Database 11g pertain to the SQL tuning process. The database can run the SQL Tuning Advisor automatically to tune high-load SQL statements. SQL Plan Management is a brand feature that automatically controls SQL plan evolution by maintaining what are called SQL plan baselines. Unlike stored outlines, SQL Plan Management is a preventative mechanism that helps stabilize the performance of the database by avoiding plan regressions. There are significant enhancements in the SQL Access Advisor, including the ability to make partitioning recommendations for tables, indexes, and materialized views. I'll start the chapter with a review of the Automatic SQL Tuning Advisor.

CERTIFICATION OBJECTIVE 4.01

Automatic SQL Tuning Advisor

In Oracle Database 10g, Oracle introduced the Automatic Tuning Optimizer, which is the name given to the optimizer when it is running in the tuning mode instead of in the normal mode. In the normal mode, the optimizer creates an execution plan under strict time constraints. In the tuning mode, the optimizer is given more latitude to produce a better execution plan. The output of the optimizer isn't an execution plan but recommendations for improvements along with a summary of the benefits you might expect by implementing those recommendations. Oracle offered the Automatic Tuning Optimizer for complex and high-load SQL statements. The advisor's goal is to target poorly written SQL statements as well as SQL statements that perform poorly because the optimizer generates a poor execution plan due to the lack of up-to-date statistics. A good way to find these types of statements is to use the Automatic Database Diagnostic Monitor (ADDM). The Automatic Tuning Optimizer performs the following types of analysis for high-load SQL statements:

- Statistics analysis
- SQL profiling
- Access path analysis
- SQL structure analysis

The ADDM identifies high-load SQL statements and you can use the SQL Tuning Advisor to fix these SQL statements. The SQL Tuning Advisor invokes the Automatic Tuning Optimizer to tune the SQL statements it offers the Optimizer. However, this still leaves the responsibility for reviewing the ADDM reports and running the SQL Tuning Advisor in the hands of the Oracle DBAs, as the SQL Tuning Advisor only makes recommendations and doesn't automatically tune the statements in any way.

In Oracle Database 11*g*, by default, the Automatic Tuning Optimizer runs regularly during the Oracle Scheduler maintenance window, as the new automated maintenance task called the SQL Tuning Advisor task. You can also customize the maintenance window by changing attributes such as the days of the week, the frequency, and the start and end time. The database can automatically tune problem SQL statements by implementing the recommendations made by the SQL Tuning Advisor during the nightly maintenance window. The Automatic SQL Tuning Advisor is essentially the same as the Automatic Tuning Optimizer introduced in Oracle Database 10*g*. The automatic part of the SQL Tuning Advisor is what's new in Oracle Database 11*g*. During its run each night, the Automatic SQL Tuning Advisor picks the high-load SQL statements from the AWR and offers tuning recommendations. The Automatic SQL Tuning Advisor can also automatically implement any SQL profile recommendations without your intervention.

The Automatic SQL Tuning Advisor chooses the tuning candidates from the AWR. When you manually run the SQL Tuning Advisor, you have to provide the advisor the SQL queries you want it to analyze. You normally use SQL Tuning Sets to provide the SQL statements to the optimizer. In automatic SQL tuning, the SQL workload is automatically chosen by the Advisor, without the need for the DBA to create and load any SQL tuning sets. The advisor also automatically tests SQL profiles and can automatically implement them if you want. The advisor also automatically retunes any SQL statements whose performance is found to deteriorate over time.

The SQL Tuning Advisor still takes into account the same four things that it did in Oracle Database 10*g*:

- **Statistical analysis**   Gathering missing or stale statistics
- **SQL profiling**   Creating new SQL profiles
- **Access path analysis**   Adding indexes
- **SQL structure analysis**   Modifying SQL statements to make them efficient.

Automatic SQL Tuning targets SQL statements for automatic tuning based on the Automatic Workload Repository (AWR) Top SQL identification. The SQL statements are identified if they are at the top of the list in four distinct time periods: any hour in the past week, any day in the past week, the past week, or single response time. When the Automatic SQL Tuning task executes during the maintenance window, the candidate SQL statements identified by the AWR are automatically tuned by it. The advisor will create any SQL profiles that are necessary to improve the performance of the candidate SQL statements. Before implementing the SQL profiles, the advisor tests the profiles first. You can request a report of the tuning analysis and check the tuned SQL statements to determine if you want to retain the new SQL profiles implemented by the tuning advisor or remove them.

SQL Profiles

Because of the limited nature of its run, often the cost optimizer's estimates of important things such as cardinality and selectivity and cost aren't accurate, leading the optimizer to pick less than optimal execution plans. When you run the SQL Tuning Advisor with the comprehensive scope, it invokes the cost optimizer in the tuning mode, requiring the optimizer to collect additional statistics beyond what it usually collects by using partial execution and sampling techniques. A SQL profile contains these additional statistics. SQL Profiles, since they don't require changing of the SQL statement itself, are ideal for use in packaged applications where you can't easily change the code.

Once a SQL profile is generated, the optimizer uses its normal statistics that it gathers, along with the additional information collected in the SQL profile, to turn out more accurate execution plans. The Automatic SQL Tuning Advisor may recommend SQL profiles as part of its overall recommendations and you can choose to have these SQL profiles automatically implemented as well.

The auxiliary information contained in a SQL profile includes the following:

■ Customized optimizer settings based on past execution history for statements

■ Adjustments to compensate for missing or stale optimizer statistics

■ Adjustment for estimation errors in optimizer statistics resulting from factors such as a skewed data distribution

The Automatic Tuning Optimizer (ATO) uses the additional time at its disposal to gather the auxiliary information, which it stores in a SQL profile and makes a recommendation for the acceptance of the SQL profile. Once you implement a SQL profile, the query optimizer will make use of that profile to generate a more accurate and efficient execution plan for a SQL statement.

Limitations

Automatic SQL tuning doesn't tune the following types of SQL statements:

- Recursive SQL statements.
- Ad hoc or rarely repeated SQL statements. If a SQL statement isn't repeatedly run, or if a SQL statement isn't repeated at least once a week, it is deemed ad hoc.
- Parallel queries.
- A query that continues to show a long execution time even after SQL profiling, thus making it impractical to test-execute those queries. The advisor ignores such queries. As long as a new SQL profile makes a long running query finish much faster, the advisor can accept them because it can test-execute them.
- SQL statements using the `insert` and `delete` statements.
- Statements using DDL statements such as the `create table as select` statement.

The interesting thing is that with the exception of the ad hoc statements, you can tune all the other types of statements by running the SQL Tuning Advisor yourself!

The Automatic SQL Tuning Process

Automatic SQL tuning consists of first identifying candidates for the tuning process, tuning the SQL statements, making recommendations, and automatically implementing any SQL profile recommendations. In the following sections, I describe the steps in the automatic SQL tuning process.

Identification of SQL Tuning Candidates

Using the sum of the CPU time and the I/O time as metrics, the database orders SQL statements as candidates for tuning. Only those statements that offer a high potential for improvement are accepted as candidates. The automatic SQL tuning process bases the candidates on the top SQL identified by the AWR. The AWR prepares a candidate list by putting the top queries in the past week into the following four "buckets":

- Top for the week
- Top for any day in the week
- Top for any hour during the week
- Highest average single execution

Each of the buckets can have a maximum of 150 SQL statements in it. The SQL tuning advisor combines the four buckets into a single group, by assigning weights to each of the buckets. The advisor then ranks the candidate SQL statements based on the impact they'll have on performance. The advisor figures the performance impact of each SQL statement by combining the CPU time and the I/O time statistics captured by the AWR for the statement.

Tuning and Making Recommendations

The SQL Tuning Advisor tunes each of the candidate SQL statements in the order of their performance impact. If a SQL profile is found for a statement, the advisor verifies that the base optimizer statistics are current for the SQL profile. If not—that is, if the advisor finds stale or missing statistics—it passes along this information to the GATHER_STATS_JOB job, which gathers statistics. The advisor makes different types of recommendations and reports them, but it can automatically implement only those recommendations that involve the creation of SQL profiles. In order for the advisor to automatically implement SQL profiles, you must set the `accept_sql_profiles` task parameter to `true` when executing the DBMS_SQLTUNE.SET_TUNING_TASK_PARAMETER procedure. The other types of recommendations (besides SQL profiles) include the creation of new indexes, refreshing stale statistics, and restructuring SQL statements.

Testing the Recommendations for New SQL Profiles

For each SQL profile it recommends, the automatic SQL Tuning Advisor will run the problem statement with and without the SQL profile and compare the performance. The database will accept a new SQL profile only if it offers a potential performance improvement of at least threefold. The advisor creates all SQL profiles in the standard EXACT mode. The SQL Tuning Advisor will have to consider implementing a new SQL profile only if the profile results in a new explain plan for a SQL statement. The advisor will implement a new SQL profile after tests reveal that it will result in at least a threefold improvement in performance. The benefit is computed by summing the CPU and I/O time savings that result from the adoption of the new SQL profile. The advisor will not only look for a threefold improvement in the sum of the CPU and I/O usage, but it also stipulates that neither statistic must become worse as a result of implementing the new SQL profile. Thus, the adoption of a new SQL profile by the advisor will ensure that the SQL statement in question will run much faster.

on the Job *The benefit percentage for each recommendation uses the formula benefit%=(time_old – time_new)/(time_old).*

Implementing the SQL Profiles That Meet the Criteria

Besides the threefold improvement in performance, a new SQL profile may have to satisfy other requirements as well, such as the objects involved in the query having recent optimizer statistics.

on the
ǒob

You must set the `statistics_level` *initialization parameter to at least typical in order for automatic SQL tuning to work. If you set the value of the parameter to* `basic`, *automatic SQL tuning will be disabled because this setting will also disable the functioning of the AWR, which is the source of the SQL statements.*

Use the DBA_SQL_PROFILES view to determine which SQL profiles have been automatically implemented by the database. The value of the TYPE column in this view will be set to AUTO for all automatically implemented SQL profiles.

Configuring Automatic SQL Tuning

The DBMS_SQLTUNE package provides several procedures to control various aspects of the Automatic SQL Tuning task (SY_AUTO_SQL_TUNING_TASK). Use the SET_TUNING_TASK_PARAMETERS procedure to configure automatic SQL tuning in your database. You must log in as the user SYS to configure automatic SQL tuning because SYS owns the automatic SQL tuning task. The following are the various parameters you can specify for an automatic SQL tuning task, using the SET_TUNING_TASK_PARAMETERS procedure:

- `accept_sql_profiles` determines whether the database must automatically accept a SQL profile.
- `replace_user_sql_profiles` determines whether the task should replace the SQL profiles created by the user.
- `max_sql_profiles_per_exec` specifies the maximum number of SQL profiles that can be accepted for a single automatic SQL tuning task.
- `max_auto_sql_profiles` determines the total number of SQL profiles that are accepted by the database.
- `execution_days_to_expire` specifies the maximum number of days for which the database saves the task history. Default is 30 days.

on the
ǒob

The five parameters shown here are applicable only to the automatic tuning task and not to the manual SQL tuning tasks.

The database implements Automatic SQL Tuning as an automated maintenance task some time after the start of the maintenance window. The job's name is SYS_AUTO_SQL_TUNING_TASK. The job first sorts the candidate SQL statements that it gets from the AWR. The job then tunes each statement according to its performance rank. If it creates a SQL profile recommendation for any candidate statement, it tests that profile before moving on to the tuning of the next SQL statement. By default, the automatic SQL Tuning Advisor runs for a maximum of one hour but you can change this by specifying a higher value for the time_limit parameter in the SET_TUNING_TASK_PARAMETERS procedure, as shown in this example:

```
SQL> exec dbms_sqltune.set_tuning_task_parameters
     ('SYS_AUTO_SQL_TUNING_TASK', 'TIME_LIMIT', 14400);
```

In the example, the TIME_LIMIT parameter has a value of 14400 seconds, which means that the Automatic SQL Tuning task will run for 4 hours (14400 seconds) during a maintenance window.

on the **Job**

Automatic SQL Tuning will be disabled if you set the `statistics_level`
***initialization parameter to BASIC, turn off the AWR snapshots, or set the AWR
retention period to less than seven days.***

You can control the SYS_AUTO_TUNING_TASK, which runs the Automatic SQL Tuning Advisor job, by using the following procedures from the DBMS_SQLTUNE package:

- SET_TUNING_TASK_PARAMETERS   You've already seen how you can use the special task parameters such as max_sql_profiles_per_exec to control the automatic tuning task.
- EXECUTE_TUNING_TASK   Use this to manually run the turning task in the foreground.
- REPORT_TUNING_TASK   Lets you produce a text report of the task execution.

You can disable and re-enable the Automatic SQL Tuning Advisor job by using the DBMS_AUTO_TASK_ADMIN package.

Managing Automatic SQL Tuning

The Automatic SQL Tuning process runs as part of a single automated maintenance task on a single instance, during the maintenance window. Use the new PL/SQL package DBMS_AUTO_TASK_ADMIN to manage all automated maintenance tasks including the automatic SQL tuning task. For example, you can enable the automatic SQL tuning advisor task using the ENABLE procedure, as shown here:

```
begin
 dbms_auto_task_admin.enable (
 client_name => 'sql tuning advisor',
 operation => 'NULL',
 window_name='NULL');
end;
```

In the previous example, the `window_name` parameter has a value of NULL, meaning that the task is enabled in all maintenance windows. You can specify a window name instead, to enable the task only in a specific maintenance window, as shown in the following example:

```
begin
 dbms_auto_task_admin.enable (
 client_name => 'sql tuning advisor',
 operation => 'NULL',
 window_name='monday_night_window');
end;
```

The Automatic SQL Tuning Advisor task (SYS_AUTO_SQL_TUNING_TASK), which runs nightly as part of the automated maintenance tasks infrastructure, generates a list of candidate SQL statements for tuning from the AWR data and tunes the statements in order of importance, one SQL statement at a time. After it tests each recommendation successfully, it accepts the recommendation and moves on to the next SQL statement in the candidate list. To disable the automatic SQL tuning advisor task, just replace the ENABLE procedure with the DISABLE procedure, as shown here:

```
begin
 dbms_auto_task_admin.disable (
 client_name => 'sql tuning advisor',
 operation => 'NULL',
 window_name='NULL');
end;
```

Because I specified NULL as the value for the `window_name` attribute, that task is disabled in all maintenance windows. As in the case of enabling the task, you can disable the task only in a specific maintenance window by providing the window name as the value for the `window_name` attribute.

Here's an example that shows how to configure an automatic SQL tuning task to automatically accept SQL profiles recommendations made by the SQL Tuning Advisor:

```
SQL> begin
  2  dbms_sqltune.set_tuning_task_parameters(
```

```
   3  task_name => 'SYS_AUTO_SQL_TUNING_PROG',
   4  parameter => 'accept_sql_profiles', value => 'true');
   5* end;
SQL> /
```

By setting the value of the `accept_sql_profiles` parameter to `true`, you ensure that the task will accept SQL profiles automatically. Similarly, you can specify the maximum number of automatic SQL profiles allowed by setting a value for the `max_auto_sql_profiles parameter` and the maximum number of SQL profiles that the database can automatically implement per execution a task by setting a value for the `max_sql_profiles_per_exec` parameter.

Note that the `accept_sql_profiles, max_sql_profiles_per_exec,` and the `max_auto_sql_profiles` parameters apply exclusively to the Automatic SQL Tuning task.

on the
ⓘob   *You can run the SQL Tuning Advisor in the test-execute mode to save time. The test-execute mode will use just the costs of executing a plan to test performance. You can run the advisor in the test-execute mode by using the `test_execute` parameter when you execute the SET_TUNING_TASK_ PARAMETERS procedure.*

You can configure various Automatic SQL Tuning task parameters easily by using the Enterprise Manager. To configure using Database Control, you use the Automatic SQL Tuning Settings page, which you can access by clicking the Configure button on the Automated Maintenance tasks page. This takes you to the Automated Maintenance Tasks Configuration page, where you'll see all the predefined maintenance windows. SQL Tuning Advisor will run in all these predefined maintenance windows by default, but you can disable it from any window you like. You can click the Edit Window Group button to edit the windows.

You can specify all the Automatic SQL Tuning parameters just discussed on the Automatic SQL Tuning Settings page. Note that by default, automatic implementation of SQL profiles is deactivated.

EXERCISE 4-1

Using Enterprise Manager to Access the SQL Tuning Advisor

The following exercise shows how to use the SQL Tuning Advisor to get recommendations for fixing a SQL statement to improve its performance. In this example, use the ADDM finding with the highest impact as the source of the SQL statement that you want the SQL Tuning Advisor to tune. Here are the steps:

1. On the Database Home page, click the finding with the highest impact on database time.
2. The SQL Details page appears. Click Schedule SQL Tuning Advisor.
3. Click Submit on the Scheduler Advisor page that appears.
4. When the advisor task is completed, the database displays the recommendations. Click Implement if you want to adopt the recommendations.
5. Click Yes on the Confirmation page. This will create a new SQL profile to improve the performance of the statement that the advisor is tuning.
6. Once you implement the SQL Profile that the advisor recommends, access the Performance page after the database executes the tuned SQL statement the next time, to view the benefits of the tuning.

You can view information about the recent runs of the Automatic SQL Tuning task by going to the Automated Maintenance Tasks page. On the Database Control home page, click the Server tab. Under the Tasks section in the Server page, click the Automated Maintenance Tasks link. You'll see all predefined tasks on the Automated Maintenance Tasks page. Click either the Automatic SQL Tuning task or the most recent execution icon to get to the Automatic SQL Tuning Result Summary page.

Interpreting Automatic SQL Tuning Reports

Execute the REPORT_AUTO_TUNING_TASK function from the DBMS_SQLTUNE package to get the automatic SQL tuning reports. The report you get contains all SQL statements analyzed in the most recent execution of the Automatic SQL Tuning task. The report includes recommendations that were implemented as well as those that weren't.

```
SQL> begin
  2   :test_report :=dbms_sqltune.report_auto_tuning_task (
  3   type         => 'text',
  4   level        => 'typical',
  5   section      => 'all');
  6* end;
SQL> /
```

```
PL/SQL procedure successfully completed.
SQL>
print :test_report
```

The text report produced by the REPORT_AUTO_TUNING_TASK procedure contains all SQL statements that the Automatic SQL Tuning Advisor analyzed in its last execution, including both the implemented as well as the unimplemented recommendations made by it. The text report contains the following sections:

- General information section describes the task and the inputs for the report and the number of SQL profiles created.
- Summary section lists the tuned SQL statements, the estimated benefits for each SQL profile, and the test execution statistics for the SQL statements after incorporating the SQL profiles.
- Tuning Findings section shows all findings and information as to whether the profiles were accepted or not.
- Explain Plans section shows explain plans for the SQL statements both before and after tuning.
- Errors section lists all errors produced during the tuning task.

Data Dictionary Views

The following views provide information on automatic SQL tuning job executions:

- DBA_ADVISOR_EXECUTIONS   Shows metadata information for each task.
- DBA_ADVISOR_SQLSTATS   Shows a list of all SQL compilation and execution statistics.
- DBA_ADVISOR_SQLPLANS   Shows a list of all SQL execution plans.

For example, you can use the following statement to get a list of all the SQL Tuning Advisor task executions:

```
SQL> select execution_)name, status, execution_start,
     execution_end
     from dba_advisor_executions
     where task_name='SYS_AUTO_SQL_TUNING_TASK';
```

Note that the SYS_AUTO_SQL_TUNING_TASK is the name given to the automated maintenance task that runs the SQL Tuning Advisor.

SQL Plan Management

Once the cost optimizer provides an efficient execution plan for a SQL statement, you can't assume that the optimizer will always use that execution plan. There may be any number of changes in the database, ranging from changes such as the addition or deletion of an index, changes in the composition of data that affects factors such as selectivity and cardinality, to the obvious changes such as a database or server upgrade. In previous releases, Oracle provided the stored outlines feature to preserve SQL execution plans to prevent unexpected performance deterioration caused by a major system change such as a database upgrade. In Oracle Database 11g, Oracle provides a brand-new feature called SQL Plan Management (SPM), to preserve SQL performance across major system changes. You can use SPM to preserve SQL performance when you encounter the following types of system changes:

- Database upgrades
- New optimizer versions
- Changes in optimizer parameters
- Changes in system settings
- Changes in schema and metadata definitions
- Deployment of new application modules

Although the SQL Tuning Advisor does provide you SQL profiles to improve SQL performance of high-load statements, that's done only after the database identifies the SQL statements as poor performing. If the poor performance resulted from an execution plan change brought about by one of the large sets of factors that influence the explain plan, you still have to wait for the ADDM to capture the bad SQL statements and for the Automatic SQL Tuning Advisor to tune that statement. This, in other words, is a reactive mechanism at best, to cope with poorly performing SQL statements. Using stored outlines is a practical alternative, but also requires manual intervention. Oracle intends SPM as a *preventative mechanism* from the outset. The database automatically controls SQL plan evolution with the help of what are called SQL plan baselines. SPM's job is to capture and evaluate the execution plans over time and build SQL plan baselines containing only efficient execution plans. A new execution plan will be allowed to be part of the SQL plan baseline for a specified SQL statement only if the new plan doesn't cause performance regression. During the execution of any SQL statement, only a plan that's a part of that SQL statement's SQL plan baseline can be selected for execution. The database uses these SQL plan baselines to preserve the SQL statement performance in the face of system changes such as the ones listed previously. The goal is to avoid plan regressions, while minimizing the time that you have to spend tracking down and analyzing SQL performance regressions and fixing them.

The SQL plan verification is managed by the new automated maintenance task, Automatic SQL Tuning Advisor, discussed earlier in this chapter. Because SQL plan baselines are at the heart of the new SQL Plan Management feature, I review those next.

SQL Plan Baselines

A SQL plan baseline is a set of all accepted plans in the *plan history* that the database maintains for each repeatable SQL statement that the database executes. The plan history contains all the SQL Plans generated for a particular SQL statement over time by the optimizer, but only some of those plans may be *accepted plans*. The database maintains a plan history for only repeatable SQL statements, but not for ad-hoc statements. This plan history thus contains all the plans generated for a specific SQL statement over time and is the key to determining whether a plan has been changing over time and if newer versions are better than the previous plan versions stored in the plan history. The plan history includes all information used by the optimizer when figuring out an optimal execution plan, including information regarding the SQL text, bind variables, and the environment in which the SQL statement is being compiled.

Earlier, I said that the SQL plan baseline consists of the set of *accepted plans* for a SQL statement. The database defines a plan as acceptable when it verifies that the plan doesn't lead to a performance regression when compared to the other plans in the plan history. Note that the very first execution plan the database generates for a SQL statement is always considered acceptable by the optimizer and becomes the original SQL plan baseline as well as the plan history for that statement. Later execution plans for that statement will automatically become part of the plan history but not the SQL plan baseline initially. The database will include them in the SQL plan baseline only if it verifies that they don't lead to a performance regression.

The database verifies SQL plans as part of the Automatic SQL Tuning task that runs as one of the automated tasks in the maintenance windows. You don't have to configure this automatic verification of SQL plans by the database. The Automatic SQL Tuning aims strictly at high load SQL statements and automatically converts a successfully verified plan into an accepted plan.

Using SQL plan baselines helps minimize potential performance regressions and stabilize SQL performance over time. Oracle Database 11g provides the new package DBMS_SPM to support the SQL Plan Management feature. Of course, you can also use the Enterprise Manager to manage SPM. I explain both methods of managing the SPM in the following sections.

Capturing SQL Plan Baselines

You capture SQL plan baselines by either having the database automatically capture SQL plans or you can manually load them yourself. Let's look at both methods in the following sections.

Automatic Plan Capture

Set the new initialization parameter `optimizer_capture_sql_plan_ baselines` to `true` to let the datable automatically create and maintain a SQL plan history. By default, this parameter is set to a value of `false`. Because the parameter is dynamic, you can enable automatic SQL plan capturing on-the-fly, with the following statement:

```
SQL> alter system set
    optimizer_capture_sql_plan_baselines=true scope=pfile;
```

Once you set the `optimizer_capture_sql_plan_baselines` parameter to `true`, as shown here, the database will automatically recognize all repeatable SQL statements and capture the SQL plans for those SQL queries for each SQL statement. Setting the parameter to `true` will also generate SQL plan baselines for the repeatable SQL statements. The database will automatically create a plan history for each repeatable SQL statement when you set the `optimizer_ capture_sql_plan_baselines` parameter to `true`. Of course, as explained earlier, the very first SQL plan that the database generates for any SQL statement is automatically integrated into the corresponding SQL plan baseline. You can use the automatic SQL plan capturing mechanism to retain good execution plans for use after a database upgrade. Once you complete the upgrade to Oracle Database 11g, for example, leave the `optimizer_features_enable` parameter set to 10.2 (or whatever release you upgraded from, as long as it's at least equal to 10.0.0, which is the minimum level you can set the `compatible` parameter to). The SQL Plan Management feature will collect the pre-Oracle Database 11g execution plans and store them as SQL plan baselines in the upgraded database. Once you're sure that the database has had a chance to capture all the necessary SQL plan baselines, you can set the `optimizer_features_enable` parameter to 11.1, to take advantage of the new features offered by Oracle Database 11g. You can thus have your cake and eat it too, because you'll be taking advantage of the new features without suffering a possible performance regression of the SQL statements.

When you turn automatic SQL plan capture on, the database recognizes repeatable SQL statements and automatically retains a plan history for those statements. The first SQL plan that the optimizer generates will be part of the original SQL plan baseline for any given statement. Obviously, if there is but a single execution plan for a SQL statement it has nothing to compare against. You can also use the SQL Performance Analyzer that you learned about in Chapter 1 to help you seed a newly upgraded database with known SQL plans that don't cause a performance regression upon upgrading to a new release of the Oracle database. For example, you can use the SQL Performance Analyzer to find out which SQL statements are likely to regress following an upgrade to Oracle Database 11g Release 1 from Oracle Database 10g Release 2. You can then capture all the execution plans for the likely-to-regress SQL statements from the 10.2 release database and load them manually into the SQL Management Base in the 11g release database.

Manual Plan Loading

You can use manual plan loading instead of, or together with, automatic plan capture. There is a major difference between manual plan loading and automatic loading of plans. When you load plans manually, the database doesn't verify them for performance. It immediately adds the plans you manually load as accepted plans to the SQL plan baseline.

One of the biggest worries when upgrading to a new release of the Oracle database is the possibility of SQL plan regressions following the use of the new optimizer. You can now cross this hurdle either by capturing the current SQL plans manually and exporting them to the target database after the upgrade or by first capturing your SQL workload into SQL tuning sets before upgrading the database. Once the database upgrade is completed, you can bulk load the SQL plans into the SQL plan baselines. Note that even though you start off with manual bulk loading of the SQL execution plans, you can still have the database automatically capture SQL plans from that point on.

There are two basic ways you can manually load SQL plans to create SQL plan baselines—using a SQL Tuning Set (STS) and AWR snapshots and loading from the database cursor cache. In both cases, you make use of the DBMS_SPM package to manually manage the SQL plan baselines.

Loading SQL Plans from a SQL Tuning Set
In order to load plans from an STS, use the LOAD_PLANS_FROM_SQLSET function of the DBMS_SPM package, as shown in the following set of steps:

1. Create an empty SQL Tuning Set, as shown here:

```
begin
dbmns_sqltune.create_sqlset(
sqlset_name => 'testset1',
description => 'Test STS to capture AWR Data');
end;
/
```

You can now use the STS you just created to load selected SQL statements from the AWR. If you're loading plans from a remote database, you can load the plans into the STS first and then export and import the STS into the target database where you want to load the SQL plans.

2. Use the LOAD_SQLSET procedure to populate the empty STS with SQL statements from the AWR snapshots. In this example, I load the STS from the AWR baseline peak baseline. The STS will include the top 20 statements from the AWR peak baseline, based on the elapsed time attribute.

```
declare
test_cursor1 dbms_sqltune.sqlset_cursor;
begin
open baseline_cursor for
select value(p) from table (dbms_sqltune.
select_workload_repository(
'peak baseline',null,null,'elapsed_time',null,null,null,20)) p;
dbms_sqlset.load_sqlset (
sqlset_name  => 'testset1',
populate_cursor => test_cursor1);
end;
/
```

Before you can load the top 20 SQL statements into the STS, you must first select them from the AWR baseline using a ref cursor and a predefined table function to select the columns you need. The STS testset1 now contains the top 20 SQL statements in the AWR, ordered by elapsed time.

3. In order to load the SQL plans from the STS as SQL plan baselines, use the LOAD_PLANS_FROM_SQLSET function of the DBMS_SPM package:

```
declare
test_plans pls_integer;
begin
 test_plans := dbms_spm.load_plans_from_sqlset(
 sqlset_name => 'testset1');
end;
/
```

The previous three steps showed how to load SQL plans from an STS. In the next section, I show you how to load SQL plans from the cursor cache instead.

Loading SQL Plans from the Cursor Cache   Instead of using an STS to load SQL plans, you can use the cursor cache to directly load the plans or the SQL statements stored in the cache. Here's the syntax of the LOAD_PLANS_FROM_CURSOR_CACHE function:

```
dbms_spm.load_plans_from_cursor_cache (
sql_id in varchar2,
plan_hash_value in number := null,
sql_text in clob,
fixed in varchar2 :='no',
enabled in varchar2 := 'yes')
return pls_integer;
```

Note that the LOAD_PLANS_FROM_CURSOR_CACHE function is overloaded. You can use the SQL_ID, PLAN_HASH_VALUE, or the ATTRIBUTE_NAME and ATTRIBUTE_VALUE pair in the function. Here's what the key parameters of the LOAD_PLANS_FROM_CURSOR_CACHE function mean:

- `sql_id` represents the SQL statement ID used to identify a statement in the cursor cache.
- `plan_hash_value` identifies the plan. A value of `null` (default) for this parameter means the database must capture all execution plans for the SQL statements with a particular SQL ID that are in the current cache.
- The `sql_text` parameter helps identify the SQL plan baseline into which you are loading the plans from the cursor cache.
- `sql_handle` identifies the SQL plan baseline into which you're loading the plans from the cursor cache.
- `fixed` means that the optimizer will consider only those plans and not others. If you assign the value of `yes` for the `fixed` parameter, the plans you load will be treated as fixed plans and the database will not evolve the SQL plan baseline. The default is `yes`.
- `attribute_name` can take the following values:
  - SQL_TEXT
  - PARSING_SCHEMA_NAME
  - MODULE
  - ACTION
- `attribute_value` helps specify a selection filter if it is being used as a search pattern of a `like` predicate. If not, it's used as an equality search value.

■ The default value for `enabled` is `yes`, which means that all loaded plans are usable by the optimizer.

Here's an example that shows how to load SQL plans from the cursor cache, using the LOAD_PLANS_FROM_CURSOR_CACHE function:

```
declare
test_plans pls_integer;
begin
 test_plans := dbms_spm.load_plans_from_cursor_cache (
 sql_id => '123456789999')
 return pls_integer;
end;
/
```

In this example, I used a make-believe value for the `sql_id` parameter. In a real-life situation, you must provide the actual `sql_id` for the SQL statement whose plans you want to load from the cursor cache.

Selecting SQL Plan Baselines

Once you collect the SQL plans either from the AWR or from the cursor cache, the next step is to enable use of the SQL plan baselines. To do this, you must set the `optimizer_use_sql_plan_baselines` initialization parameter to `true`. The parameter is set to `false` by default, meaning SQL plan baselines aren't enabled by default. When the optimizer compiles any SQL statements, it follows a conservative explain plan selection strategy when you use SQL plan baselines, which I summarize here.

exam

ⓦatch

Know the role played by the two initialization parameters optimizer_capture_sql_plan_ baselines and optimizer_use_ sql_plan_baselines in the SQL Plan Management feature.

■ When the database recognizes a new SQL statement as a repeatable statement for the first time, it adds the lowest cost plan for that statement to the SQL plan baseline for that statement. The database will then use this SQL plan baseline to execute the SQL statement.

■ When the initialization parameter `optimizer_use_sql_plan_ baselines` is set to its default value of `true`, it enables the use of the SQL plan baselines stored by the database in the SQL Management Base (SMB). The optimizer will look for a SQL plan baseline for the SQL statement the database is compiling. If a SQL plan baseline exists for that SQL statement, the database uses a comparative plan selection policy—that is, the optimizer will figure out the cost of each of the baseline plans and pick the one with the lowest cost. The optimizer will create a best cost plan and try to match it to a plan in the SQL plan baseline. If it finds a match, it goes ahead and executes the statement using the best cost plan. If the database fails to match the best cost plan with any plan in the SQL plan baseline, it will add the new plan to the plan history as a non-accepted plan first. It then chooses the lowest cost plan from the set of accepted plans in the SQL plan baseline and executes the statement using that plan for the statement after comparing it with all the accepted plans in the SQL plan baseline. If it matches a plan in the baseline, it will go ahead and use that plan. In reality, only the outline for each plan is stored in the SMB. Therefore, the optimizer will reproduce the actual execution plan from the stored outline of the selected plan and execute the statement using that plan.

■ If the database can't reproduce any of the accepted plans in the baseline, say because you dropped an index, then the optimizer uses the lowest cost plan for a newly compiled SQL statement.

on the
job

You can view the execution plan for the specified SQL_HANDLE of a plan baseline by executing the DBMS_XPLAIN.DISPLAY_SQL_PLAN_BASELINE function.

■ The end result is that the optimizer will always produce a plan that's either the best cost plan or a baseline plan. You can query the OTHER_XML column in the PLAN_TABLE after running an explain plan on a SQL statement, to find out exactly what strategy the optimizer has adopted in a specific case.

Evolving SQL Plan Baselines

The database routinely evaluates new plan performance with a view to integrating plans with superior performance into the SQL plan baseline for the corresponding SQL statement. Evolving SQL plan baselines is the critical phase when the database changes a non-accepted plan in the plan history to an accepted plan and makes it part of the SQL plan baseline. In order to deem a plan in the history an accepted plan, its performance must be better than already accepted plans that are in the SQL plan baseline. To successfully verify a non-accepted plan, the database compares the plan's performance to that of a plan it selects from the SQL plan baseline and ensures that the former delivers superior performance.

You need to formally evolve a SQL plan baseline only if you're using automatic plan capture. If you're using the manual capture process through an STS or a cursor cache, the moment you load a new plan into a SQL plan baseline, they are considered accepted plans and thus don't have to go through the evolution process described here. You must, however, formally evolve all SQL plans that the database captures automatically.

You can evolve SQL plan baselines in two ways: with the EVOLVE_SQL_PLAN_ BASELINE function or the SQL Tuning Advisor. I describe both methods in the following sections.

Using the **EVOLVE_SQL_PLAN_BASELINE** Function   The EVOLVE_ SQL_PLAN_BASELINE function determines whether a new plan added to the plan history performs better than a plan from the corresponding SQL plan baseline. If so, it adds the new plan to the SQL plan baseline as an accepted plan. Here's an example:

```
SQL> exec dbms_spm.evolve_sql_plan_baseline (sql_handle =>
     '123456789999');
```

In this example, I used the `sql_handle` attribute to evolve a plan for a particular SQL statement. However, you can also provide a list of plans or simply provide no value for the `sql_handle` attribute. In this case, the database will evolve all non-accepted plans that are in the SQL Management Base.

Let's look at the EVOLVE_SQL_PLAN_BASELINE procedure in more detail. Here's the syntax of the function:

```
dbms_spm.evolve_sql_plan_baseline (
sql_handle       in    varchar2  :=null,
plan_name        in    varchar2  :=null,
time_limit       in    integer   :=dbms_spm.auto_limit,
verify           in    varchar2  := 'YES',
commit           in    varchar2  := 'YES')
return clob;
```

There is also a second form of the EVOLVE_SQL_PLAN_BASELINE function, where you can use a PLAN_LIST attribute instead of the SQL_HANDLE and the PLAN_NAME attributes.

Here are the different parameters of the EVOLVE_SQL_PLAN_BASELINE function:

- `sql_handle` identifies the SQL statement. If you don't specify a `plan_name`, a null value for this parameter requests the database to evaluate all non-accepted plans.

- `plan_name` is the plan identifier. If this is `null` (the default) and the `sql_handle` parameter is `null` as well, the database evaluates all SQL statements. If the `plan_name` parameter is `null` but the `sql_handle` parameter isn't, the database evaluates all non-accepted explain plans for the specified SQL statement.

- `plan_list` provides a list of plan names.

- The `time_limit` parameter specifies the time limit for the evolution of the SQL plans. The default is `dbms_spm.auto_limit`, which means the database will select the time limit based on the number of plan verifications it has to perform. You can use the `dbms_spm.no_limit` value for the `time_limit` parameter to remove a time limit for the plan verification process.

- The `verify` parameter can take a value of `yes` (default) or `no`. The `yes` value means that the database will verify a non-accepted plan to make sure it does yield better performance than a plan chosen from the SQL plan baseline for the relevant statement. If you pass the value `no` for the `verify` parameter, the database will change non-accepted plans into accepted plans without any plan execution and performance comparison.

- The `commit` parameter specifies whether the database should update the accepted status of non-accepted plans to `yes`. The default is `yes`, meaning the status of qualifying non-accepted plans is updated. A value of `no` for the `commit` parameter means the database will not update the accepted status of non-accepted plans.

- The `return` parameter is a CLOB that contains a text report showing all non-accepted plans, with the changes in their accepted status. If you specify `yes` as the value for the `verify` parameter, the text report will also contain the result of the performance verification of plans.

on the
job *You can export SQL baseline plans from the SQL Management Base into a staging table and then import the baselines from the staging table into the SQL Management Base in a different database.*

Evolving SQL Plans with the SQL Tuning Advisor   You can also evolve SQL plan baselines by running the SQL Tuning Advisor. This applies to both manual and automatic executions of the SQL Tuning Advisor task. When the SQL Tuning Advisor recommends accepting a SQL profile, it does so because the explain plan with the SQL profile is better than the original explain plan for the untuned statement. Once you accept the SQL profile recommendation and implement it, the advisor automatically adds the plan to the SQL plan baseline for that SQL statement.

Fixed SQL Plan Baselines

If a SQL plan baseline contains one or more enabled plans for which the `fixed` attribute value is set to `yes`, the baseline is considered fixed. You can set the `fixed` attribute to YES for any plan you want, thereby limiting the set of possible plans for a given SQL statement. You usually fix one plan per baseline and, because the optimizer will give preference to the fixed plans over the nonfixed plans in the SQL plan baseline, it will use the fixed plan. Remember that this will make the optimizer pick the fixed plan even if some of the nonfixed plans are actually cheaper, with a lower cost of execution.

The database doesn't evolve a fixed SQL plan baseline because the optimizer doesn't add any new execution plans to a fixed SQL plan baseline. You may, however, evolve even a fixed SQL plan baseline by manually loading a new plan either from the cursor cache or a SQL Tuning Set.

SQL Plan Baseline Attributes

A SQL plan baseline has several attributes that you can change in order to fine-tune the SQL Plan Management feature. The DBA_SQL_PLAN_BASELINES view provides detailed information about all the SQL plan baselines stored in the SMB. Here's a query that shows how to find out key information about the SQL plan baselines in your database:

```
SQL> select sql_handle, sql_text, plan_name,
     origin, enabled, accepted, fixed, autopurge
     from dba_sql_plan_baselines;
```

```
SQL_HANDLE    SQL_TEXT     PLAN_NAME ORIGIN ENA ACC  IX AUT
----------    -----------  -------- ------ --- ---- --- ---
SQL_TEXT
SYS_SQL_02a   delete from... SYS_SQL_PL AUTO  YES YES   NO  YES

SYS_SQL_a6f   SELECT...      SYS_SQL_PL  AUTO YES YES   NO  YES

SQL>
```

on the ! job

If you're using a fixed plan, the explain plan for that statement will indicate at the end that the plan is a fixed plan.

The following is a brief explanation of the key attributes of a SQL plan baseline:

- SQL_HANDLE, SQL_TEXT, and PLAN_NAME identify the SQL statement.
- The ORIGIN attribute denotes whether the plan was loaded manually (MANUAL-LOAD) and tuned by you (MANUAL-SQLTUNE), or if the database automatically captured the load (AUTO-CAPTURE) and tuned it (AUTO-SQLTUNE).
- enabled specifies whether the baseline plan is enabled by the optimizer for use.
- accepted shows whether the plan has been verified and found not to lead to a performance regression.
- fixed indicates whether this plan is one of the "fixed" cases. If any of the plans in a baseline are fixed, the database will consider the best plan among the fixed plans only. All other plans are ignored in preference to the fixed plans.
- auto_purge shows whether the plan is automatically purged by the database.

Note that any plans that you load manually will always have the accepted status because they are deemed to be verified plans. The database can also automatically change the status of a plan to accepted after its verification. In addition, you can manually set the status of any SQL plan to accepted through the ALTER_SQL_PLAN_BASELINE procedure, as shown here:

```
SQL> exec dbms_spm.alter_sql_plan_baselines(
     sql_handle => SYS_SQL_122222222',
     plan_name  => 'SYS_SQL_PLAN_b5429522ee05ab0e',
     attribute_name => 'accepted-status',
     attribute_value => 'YES');
```

You can also disable an accepted plan by removing the enabled setting through the ALTER_SQL_PLAN_BASELINE view. Here's an example:

```
declare
   ctr binary_integer;
```

```
begin
   ctr                := dbms_spm.alter_sql_plan_baseline (
   sql_handle        => 'SYS_SQL_e0b19f65b5429522',
   plan_name         => 'SYS_SQL_PLAN_b5429522ee05ab0e',
   attribute_name    => 'ENABLED',
   attribute_value   => 'NO'
   );
end;
```

on the
job

A job must have the enabled and the accepted status in order for the optimizer to consider its use.

Once you disable a plan, the optimizer won't consider that plan any longer. When you re-enable the plan, the optimizer starts taking the plan into account again.

Managing SQL Plan Baselines

You can view the SQL plans stored in the SQL plan baseline for a specific SQL statement, using the DISPLAY_SQL_PLAN_BASELINE function of the DBMS_XPLAN package, as shown the following example:

```
SQL> set serveroutput on
SQL> set long 100000
SQL> select * from table(
  2  dbms_xplan.display_sql_plan_baseline(
  3  sql_handle => 'SYS_SQL_ba5e12ccae97040f',
  4* format => 'basic'));
PLAN_TABLE_OUTPUT
----------------------------------------------------------------------

----------------------------------------------------------------------
SQL handle: SYS_SQL_ba5e12ccae97040f
SQL text: select t.week_ending_day, p.prod_subcategory, sum(s.
          amount_sold) as dollars, s.channel_id,s.promo_id
          from sales s,times t, products p where   s.time_id =
          t.time_id and s.prod_id = p.prod_id and
          s.prod_id > 10 and s.prod_id <50 group by
          t.week_ending_day, p.prod_subcategory,
PLAN_TABLE_OUTPUT
----------------------------------------------------------------------
       s.channel_id,s.promo_id
----------------------------------------------------------------------
----------------------------------------------------------------------
Plan name: SYS_SQL_PLAN_ae97040f6b60c209
Enabled: YES  Fixed: NO  Accepted: YES  Origin: AUTO-CAPTURE
----------------------------------------------------------------------
```

```
Plan hash value: 1944768804
---------------------------------------------------------------
PLAN_TABLE_OUTPUT
---------------------------------------------------------------
| Id  | Operation                      | Name         |        |
---------------------------------------------------------------
|   0 | SELECT STATEMENT               |              |        |
|   1 |  HASH GROUP BY                 |              |        |
|   2 |   HASH JOIN                    |              |        |
|   3 |    TABLE ACCESS FULL           | TIMES        |        |
|   4 |    HASH JOIN                   |              |        |
|   5 |     TABLE ACCESS BY INDEX ROWID| PRODUCTS     |        |
|   6 |      INDEX RANGE SCAN          | PRODUCTS_PK  |        |
|   7 |     TABLE ACCESS FULL          | SALES        |        |
---------------------------------------------------------------

29 rows selected.
SQL>
```

The output of the DISPLAY_PLAN_BASELINE function shows the following information:

- The plan was captured automatically.
- The plan is enabled and accepted.
- The plan is not fixed.

on the
Job
If the SQL Tuning Advisor finds an execution plan to be superior to a plan in the statement's SQL plan baseline, it will recommend that you accept a SQL profile. If you accept the SQL profile, the Tuning Advisor automatically adds the tuned plan to the SQL plan baseline of the SQL statement.

The SQL Management Base

The database stores all SPM related information, such as statement logs, plan histories, and SQL profiles as well as the SQL plan baselines, in a new component of the data dictionary called the SQL Management Base (SMB). The database stores the SMB in the SYSAUX tablespace. You must, therefore, ensure that the SYSAUX tablespace is online because SPM will be disabled if it can't access the SYSAUX tablespace.

Configuring the SQL Management Base

You configure the SQL Management Base by setting values for two parameters, space_budget_percent and plan_retention_weeks. You can view the current values of these two parameters by querying the DBA_SQL_MANAGEMENT_CONFIG view, as shown here:

```
SQL> select parameter_name, parameter_value from
     dba_sql_management_config;

PARAMETER_NAME              PARAMETER_VALUE
----------------------     ----------------
SPACE_BUDGET_PERCENT        30
PLAN_RETENTION_WEEKS        105
SQL>
```

The `space_budget_percent` parameter determines the percentage of space the SMB can take up in the SYSAUX tablespace. You can select a value between 1 and 50 percent for this parameter. The default space limit is 10 percent of the size of the SYSAUX tablespace. A new Oracle background process will generate daily warnings that it writes to the alert log when the SMB exceeds its allocated space limit. You can do one of the following to make the alert warnings go away:

- Increase the size of the SYSAUX tablespace
- Increase the SMB space limit
- Purge outdated SQL plan baselines or SQL profiles to clear up space in the SMB

You can modify the value of the `space_budget_percent` parameter by executing the DBMS_SPM.CONFIGURE procedure, as shown here:

```
SQL> exec dbms_spm.configure ('space_budget_percent', 40);
```

The previous procedure will increase the space allocation of the SMB in the SYSAUX tablespace to 40 percent.

Purging Policies

A weekly purging task that's part of the automated tasks that run during the maintenance windows takes care of removing older unused baselines, to conserve space in the SQL Management Base. By default, the database purges all SQL plans that the database hasn't used in over a year (53 weeks, to be precise). You can, however, change this setting by adjusting the value of the `plan_retention_weeks` parameter to a value between 5 weeks and 523 weeks. The following example shows how to change the plan retention period to 2 years:

```
SQL> exec dbms_spm.configure ('plan_retention_weeks', 105);
```

In addition to the automatic purging of unused SQL baselines, you can manually purge the plan baseline for a specific statement by using the PURGE_SQL_PLAN_BASELINE procedure, as shown here:

```
SQL> exec dbms_spm.purge_sql_plan_baseline(
     ''SYS_SQL_PLAN_b5429522ee05ab0e');
```

A query on the DBA_SQL_MANAGEMENT_CONFIG view shows the current configuration settings for the SQL Management Base.

Managing SPM with the Enterprise Manager

Instead of using the DBMS_SPM package, you can simply use the Enterprise Manager to perform SQL Plan Management tasks. Use the SQL Plan Management page to manage both SQL profiles and SQL plan baselines. You can get to the SQL Plan Management page by going to Home page | Server | SQL Plan Control (under the Query Optimizer section).

CERTIFICATION OBJECTIVE 4.03

SQL Access Advisor Enhancements

Oracle introduced the SQL Access Advisor in the Oracle database 10g Release to help you create efficient access structures to optimize SQL queries. The advisor accepted either an actual workload as input (from the cursor cache or an STS from the automatic workload repository) or used a hypothetical workload created by you to recommend which indexes, materialized views, or materialized view logs to create and drop to improve SQL performance. In Oracle Database 11g, there are several enhancements to the SQL Access Advisor:

- New procedures.
- In addition to its usual table, index, materialized view, and materialized view log recommendations, the advisor now also recommends *partitioning* of tables, indexes, and materialized views.
- Reporting of intermediate results at publish points.

I explain the enhancements in more detail in the followings sections.

New Procedures

Although you can use other sources for the workload, in Oracle Database 11g, Oracle seems to suggest using a SQL Tuning Set (STS) as the source for the SQL Access Advisor. An STS has the benefit of being a separate identity and can be shared by various Advisor tasks, not just the Advisor that creates it. Once an Advisor task references an STS, that STS can't be deleted or changed until all Advisor tasks remove their dependency on it. An STS also lets you capture and store different types of SQL workload together as a persistent object in the database. As in Oracle Database 10g, you use the DBMS_SQLTUNE package to create the initial empty STS.

In Oracle Database 10g, you used a SQL Workload object to capture the workload, which you can create by using the CREATE_SQLWKLOAD procedure. Because the SQL Workload is independent, you used the ADD_SQLWKLD_REF procedure to link the SQL Workload object to a SQL Advisor task to protect the workload from being removed or modified. Finally, you used the DELETE_SQLWKLD_REF procedure to remove the workload reference manually from the Advisor task (you could also drop the Advisor task to make the SQL Workload go away).

on the *When using the SQL Access Advisor, you can choose your workload from one*
Job *of the following sources: Current and Recent SQL Activity, an existing STS, or a hypothetical workload.*

In Oracle Database 11g, you make use of two new procedures that are part of the DBMS_ADVISOR package: ADD_STS_REF and DELETE_STS_REF, to link and unlink SQL Access Advisor tasks and SQL Tuning Sets, which contain the workload for the advisor.

The ADD_STS_REF Procedure

The ADD_STS_REF procedure, shown here, links the current SQL Access Advisor task and a SQL tuning set.

```
DBMS_ADVISOR.ADD_STS_REF(
   task_name   IN VARCHAR2 NOT NULL,
   sts_owner   IN VARCHAR2,
   sts_name    IN VARCHAR2 NOT NULL);
```

Oracle recommends using the ADD_STS_REF procedure for any advisor runs that use a SQL tuning set.

The DELETE_STS_REF Procedure

The DELETE_STS_REF procedure is the counterpart of the ADD_STS_REF procedure. You use it to remove the link between the current SQL Access Advisor task and a SQL tuning set.

```
DBMS_ADVISOR.DELETE_STS_REF (
   task_name   IN VARCHAR2 NOT NULL,
   sts_owner   IN VARCHAR2,
   sts_name    IN VARCHAR2 NOT NULL);
```

Oracle recommends using the DELETE_STS_REF procedure for any advisor runs that use a SQL tuning set. Don't confuse the DELETE_STS_REF procedure with the DELETE_TASK procedure, which you use to remove an advisor task from the repository.

Partitioning Recommendations

In addition to its usual table, index, and materialized view recommendations, the SQL Access Advisor makes the following recommendations in Oracle Database 11g.

- **Partition a table** The partitioning methods are range, interval, list, hash, range-hash, and range-list.
- **Partition an index** The partitioning methods are local, range, and hash.
- **Partition materialized view** The partitioning schemes are range, interval, list, hash, range-hash, and range-list.

The SQL Access Advisor invokes the DBMS_REDEFINITION package to implement its partition recommendations online. The SQL Access Advisor can make partitioning recommendations both under the limited tuning option and the comprehensive tuning option. The comprehensive tuning option uses SQL profiles and also allows you to specify a time limit for the tuning task, which is 30 minutes, by default. Partitioning is usually a more time-consuming and complex task when compared to, say, the creation of a simple index. Follow these guidelines when using the SQL Access Advisor in Oracle Database 11g, if you want to get good partitioning recommendations:

- The tables must be large, with a minimum of 10,000 rows.
- If the base tables have a bitmap index defined on them, you must remove them before running the advisor recommendation script because you can't migrate the bitmap indexes correctly. After the advisor creates a partitioned table from an unpartitioned table, you can re-create the dropped bitmap index.
- The advisor will generate partitioning recommendations for only columns of type DATE and NUMBER. If a SQL statement in the workload doesn't use a predicate or join with these types of columns, the database won't make any partitioning recommendations.
- Interval is the default partitioning mode. Hash partitioning is offered only to facilitate partition-wise joins.
- You must ensure that you have enough space to hold the original table and a copy of it because the DBMS_REDEFINITION packages make a temporary copy of the source table.

■ If the recommendations include a partitioning recommendation along with other types of recommendations such as creating a new index, it's not a good idea to decide to only create the index and leave the table as is, without partitioning it. If you can't partition the table for some reason, you must run the SQL Access Advisor again, this time with the partitioning option disabled. The reason for this is that the index recommendation in this case was predicated on the existence of a partitioned table. Therefore, skipping the partitioning recommendation but accepting the indexing recommendations isn't a correct choice.

Back up your database before starting the advisor session because that's probably the quickest and easiest way to undo a major table partitioning task.

Publish Points

Previously, once the SQL Access Advisor started its recommendation analysis, the only way to access the results was to wait until the processing was completed or to interrupt the task. In Oracle Database 11g, you can access the results even *before* the advisor task is completed. This offers you the potential to save considerable time in implementing key advisor recommendations because you can interrupt a long running task and glean an idea about the recommendations. You can break down a large workload into smaller chunks using your own criteria and have the advisor analyze each chunk of the workload and report its intermediate results at the publish points.

Once you interrupt a task, the advisor will mark the task as INTERRRUPTED, and you can view the intermediate results and generate the recommendation scripts. You also have the choice to tell the advisor to resume the task that you interrupted. A word of caution, however: in order to make any base table partitioning recommendations, the SQL Access Advisor needs to analyze almost the entire workload. If you interrupt a task early, you probably won't see any type of partition-related recommendations. However, a late stage intermediate result may quite possibly yield partition recommendations if the advisor figures out it's beneficial to do so.

Running a SQL Access Advisor Job Using PL/SQL

In this section, I show you how to run the SQL Access Advisor using procedures and functions from the DBMS_ADVISOR and DBMS_SQLTUNE packages.

Creating the SQL Access Advisor Task

You can create an advisor task by using the CREATE_TASK procedure and specifying the various attributes of the task or creating your task from a template. If you specify a template at task creation time, the SQL Access Advisor will copy the parameter settings from the template to the new task. You may also specify an already existing task as the template. Here's an example that shows you how to use the CREATE_TASK procedure to create a new SQL Access Advisor task:

```
SQL> exec dbms_advisor.create_task(
    advisor_name => 'SQL Access Advisor',
    task_name => 'test_task1')
```

The previous code creates a new advisor task named test_task1.

Creating a SQL Tuning Set

First, create an empty STS to hold the SQL workload that you want to pass to the SQL Access Advisor task as input for its analysis:

```
SQL> exec dbms_sqltune.create_sqlset (-
    sqlset_name => 'test_sts1', -
    description => 'Test STS for Access Advisor');
```

In this case, we created a new empty STS named teststs1. If you wish to transfer existing SQL objects to a SQL Tuning Set, use the COPY_SQLWKLD_TO_STS procedure to copy the workload to an STS. Here's an example:

```
SQL> exec dbms_advisor.copy_sqlwkld_to_sts('test_workload',
    'test_sts1','new');
```

Loading the SQL Tuning Set

In this step, I show you how to load the STS with a set of SQL statements. By default, the LOAD_SQLSET procedure will load only new statements to the STS, but you can also update existing statements in the STS if you want.

```
SQL> declare
  2  mycursor dbms_sqltune.sqlset_cursor;
  3  begin
  4    open mycursoror
  5    select value(p)
  6    from table (
  7    dbms_sqltune.select_cursor_cache(
  8    'parsing_schema_NAME <>  ''SYS''',NULL,NULL,NULL,NULL,1,
       NULL,'ALL')) p;
  9    dbms_sqltune.load_sqlset(sqlset_name => 'test_sts1',
       populate_cursor => mycursor);
 10* end;
```

```
SQL> /
PL/SQL procedure successfully completed.
SQL>
```

Note that the LOAD_SQLSET procedure uses a cursor reference with which to populate the STS. In this case, I use the SELECT_CURSOR_CACHE function to collect the SQL statements from the SQL cursor cache. The function returns a `sqlset_row` per SQL_ID and PLAN_HASH_VALUE combination it finds in the cursor cache. The LOAD_SQLSET procedure is called after first opening the cursor *mycursor* and selecting all statements in the cursor cache with the exclusion of those that were parsed by the user SYS.

In this example, I showed how to load SQL statements from the SQL cursor cache. You can also use the SELECT_WORKLOAD_REPOSITORY function to select SQL statements from the automatic workload repository instead.

Linking the Advisor Task and the Workload

Now you have both the SQL Access Advisor task and a SQL Tuning Set with the SQL statements you want the advisor to analyze. Your next task is to link the task to the STS, by using the new ADD_STS_REF procedure, as shown here:

```
SQL> exec dbms_advisor.add_sts_ref (
     task_name      => 'test_task1',
     sts_owner      => 'SH',
     sts_name       =>'test_sts1');
```

You can create as many links to SQL Tuning Sets as you like.

on the **Job** *Oracle advises that you use the ADD_STS_REF procedure instead of the older procedure, ADD_SQLWKLD_REF, which is supported only for backward compatibility.*

Setting the Task Parameters

Use the SET_TASK_PARAMETER procedure to set the task parameters. There are a large number of parameters you can set, but if you don't explicitly set any of these parameters, the database will use default values for them. Execute the SET_TASK_PARAMETER procedure as many times as you have parameters to set. Here are some examples:

```
SQL> exec dbms_advisor.set_task_parameter ('test_task1',
     'valid_table_list','SH.SALES,SH.CUSTOMERS);'
SQL> exec dbms_advisor.set_task_parameter ('test_task1',
     'mode', 'comprehensive');
SQL> exec dbms_advisor.set_task_parameter ('test_task1',
     'journaling',4);
```

```
SQL> exec dbms_advisor.set_task_parameter ('test_task1',
     'analysis_scope','all');
```

The first example (the valid_task_list parameter) filters out all SQL queries that don't reference the sales and customers tables in the SH schema. The second example (the mode parameter) sets the tuning mode to comprehensive rather than limited. The third example (the journaling parameter) shows how to set the journaling attribute, which controls the logging of messages to the journal, which you can view by querying the DBA_ADVISOR_JOURNAL view. The higher the setting for this parameter, the more detailed will be the messages. The final example (the analysis_scope parameter) shows how to set the analysis_scope attribute to all, which will generate recommendations for indexes, materialized views, and partitions.

If you want only to get partition recommendations, you can do so by specifying the option `partition` along with the index, table, or mview (materialized view) options. You may also use the `def_partition_tablespace` attribute to specify the default tablespace for the partitioned tables. If you don't specify this attribute, the partitioning recommendations in the script will not contain a tablespace name for the partitioned table. One other useful attribute is `max_number_partitions`, which specifies the maximum number of partitions for a table, index, or materialized view. This attribute can range from 1 to 4294967295 and the default value is `advisor_unlimited`.

Execute the Task

Execute the task by issuing the following command:

```
SQL> exec dbms_advisor.execute_task (task_name => 'test_task1');
```

Once the SQL Access Advisor task finishes executing, you can view the recommendations made by the advisor.

Viewing the Recommendations

The SQL Access Advisor links each of its recommendations to a specific SQL statement from the workload. You can use the GET_TASK_REPORT function to view a report, as shown here:

```
SQL> exec DBMS_ADVISOR.GET_TASK_REPORT (
    task_name       IN VARCHAR2,
    type            IN VARCHAR2 := 'TEXT',
    level           IN VARCHAR2 := 'TYPICAL',
    section         IN VARCHAR2 := 'ALL',
    owner_name      IN VARCHAR2 := NULL,
    execution_name  IN VARCHAR2 := NULL,
    object_id       IN NUMBER   := NULL)
RETURN CLOB;
```

The function creates the task report and presents it to you.

You can stop the task anytime using the CANCEL_TASK procedure, but you won't be able to see any recommendations. Use the INTERRUPT_TASK procedure to terminate an advisor task before it reaches its end. You can still get any recommendation that has been created up to that point. The following example shows how to interrupt a task:

```
SQL> exec dbms_advisor.interrupt_task ('test_task1');
```

One you interrupt a task midway, you can't restart it.

Generating SQL Scripts

You can view the SQL script that the advisor creates to implement its recommendations by executing the GET_TASK_REPORT procedure, which will save the script containing the executable SQL statements in a file. Note that you must first create a directory with the `create directory` statement before you execute the previous code. Here's how you create the directory:

```
SQL> create directory access_adv_rslts as
     '/u01/app/oracle/access';
Directory Created.
```

Once you create the directory, execute the CREATE_FILE procedure to generate the SQL script in that directory, as shown here:

```
SQL> execute dbms_advior.create_file (
        dbms_advisor.get_task_script ('test_task1'),
        'access_adv_rslts', 'testscript1.sql');
```

Review the SQL script before you execute it. Here's the SQL script showing the SQL Access Advisor recommendations for the example task:

```
Rem SQL Access Advisor: Version 11.1.0.6.0 - Production
Rem Username: SH
Rem Task: SQLACCESS9252895
Rem Execution date:
Rem Repartitioning table "SH"."SALES"
SET SERVEROUTPUT ON
SET ECHO ON
Rem Creating new partitioned table
CREATE TABLE "SH"."SALES1"
(    "PROD_ID" NUMBER,
     "CUST_ID" NUMBER,
     "TIME_ID" DATE,
     "CHANNEL_ID" NUMBER,
     "PROMO_ID" NUMBER,
     "QUANTITY_SOLD" NUMBER(10,2),
```

```
     "AMOUNT_SOLD" NUMBER(10,2)
) PCTFREE 10 PCTUSED 40 INITRANS 1 MAXTRANS 255
NOCOMPRESS LOGGING
TABLESPACE "USERS"
PARTITION BY HASH ("PROD_ID") PARTITIONS 32;
Rem Copying constraints to new partitioned table
ALTER TABLE "SH"."SALES1" MODIFY ("PROD_ID" NOT NULL ENABLE);
Rem Copying indexes to new partitioned table
Rem
CREATE UNIQUE INDEX "SH"."PRODUCTS_PK1" ON "SH"."SALES1"
("PROD_ID")
PCTFREE 10 INITRANS 2 MAXTRANS 255 NOLOGGING COMPUTE STATISTICS
TABLESPACE "EXAMPLE";
Rem Populating \partitioned table with data from original table
INSERT /*+ APPEND */ INTO "SH"."SALES1"
SELECT * FROM "SH"."SALES";
COMMIT;
begin
dbms_stats.gather_table_stats('"SH"', '"SALES1"', NULL, dbms_
stats.auto_sample_size);
end;
/
Rem Renaming tables to give new partitioned table the original
 table name
ALTER TABLE "SH"."SALES" RENAME TO "SALES1";
ALTER TABLE "SH"."SALES1" RENAME TO "SALES";
Rem Revalidating materialized views for use with new
partitioned table
BEGIN DBMS_MVIEW.REFRESH('"SH"."FWEEK_PSCAT_SALES_MV"',
'C',atomic_refresh => FALSE); END;
/
BEGIN DBMS_MVIEW.REFRESH('"SH"."CAL_MONTH_SALES_MV"',
'C',atomic_refresh => FALSE); END;
/
```

The script shows what the SQL Access Advisor will do to partition a table if you choose to accept its partition recommendations:

- Create a new partitioned table named sales1.

- Copy the constraints on the table sales to the new empty table sales1.

- Copy the indexes (in this case, a single index) on the table sales to the new empty table sales1.

- Load data into the new table sales1 from the original sales table.

- Execute the DBMS_STATS.GATHER_TABLE_STATS procedure to collect statistics on table sales1.

- Rename the old table sales to sales1 and the new table sales1 to sales.
- Execute the DBMS_MVIEW.REFRESH procedure to revalidate the materialized views on the partitioned sales table.

Using Enterprise Manager

Although I explained how to utilize the SQL Access Advisor through the execution of PL/SQL procedures, Oracle recommends that you use the Oracle Enterprise Manager (Database Control/Grid Control) to manage the SQL Access Advisor. Here are the steps you must follow to get recommendations from the SQL Access Advisor.

1. In the Database Home page, click the Advisor Central link at the bottom of the page, under Related Links.
2. In the Advisor central page, click SQL Advisors under the Advisors section.
3. In the SQL Advisors page, click SQL Access Advisor.
4. In the Initial Options page, select Recommend new access structures. The other option will merely verify the use of existing access structures such as indexes, but doesn't recommend new access structures. Click Next.
5. In the Workload Source page, select Current and Recent SQL Activity. This means that the advisor will select the SQL statements to analyze from the SQL cache. Click Next.
6. In the Recommendations Options page, shown in Figure 4-1, select all three access structures: indexes, materialized views, and the new partitioning recommendation option. Click Next.

    You can customize the task name and description and the scheduling of the task on the Schedule page. By default, the SQL Access Advisor runs the job immediately. Click Next.
7. The Review page shows the options you selected for the SQL Access Advisor task. Click Submit after verifying the options.
8. The Confirmation page appears, indicating that your job was submitted successfully.
9. Once the STATUS column shows that the access advisor job is completed, click View Result after selecting the task first. You can view the potential for improvement in a graphical form. The Workload I/O Cost chart shows

FIGURE 4-1 The SQL Access Advisor Recommendation Options page

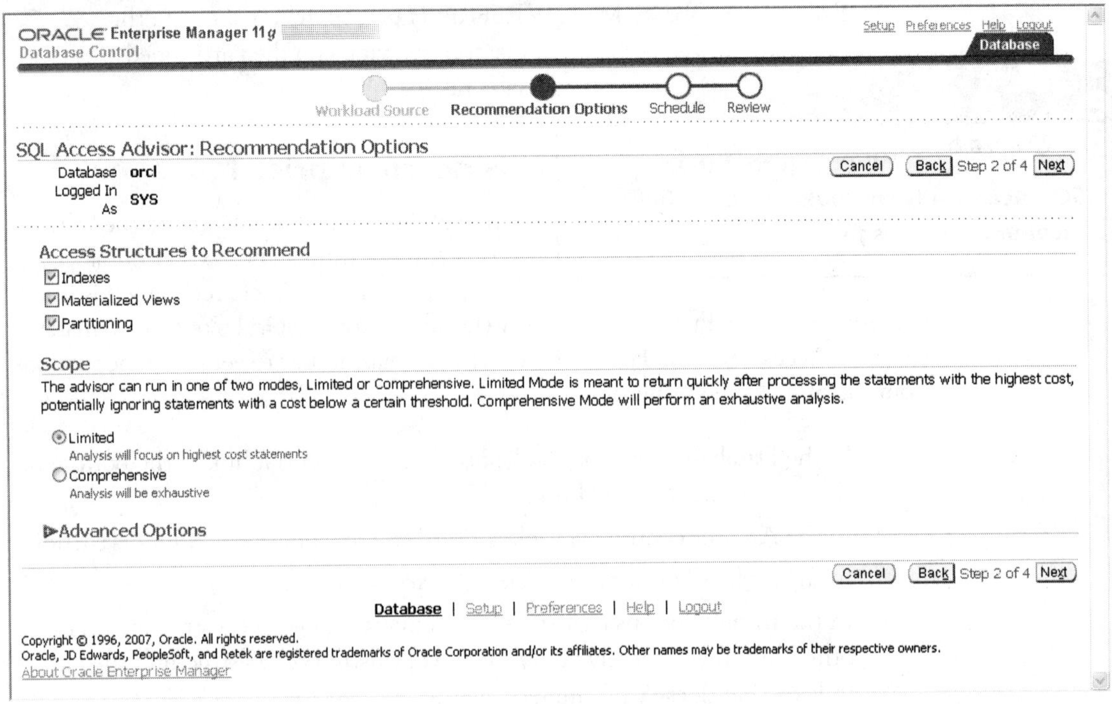

the new cost (69591) and the old cost (144178). The Query Execution Time Improvement chart shows that the Query Improvement factor is about 2. You can view the next page, the Results For Task page, where the advisor presents a chart of the potential benefits from adopting the various recommendations. You can also review a table that shows each recommendation and the cost improvement that you can gain by adopting that recommendation. Figure 4-2 shows the Results For Task page.

10. Click Schedule Implementation if you want to accept the recommendations. If you want to modify the recommendations, click SQL to view the actual SQL statements to implement the recommendations, which can consist of new indexes, new materialized views, new materialized view logs, or recommendations to partition existing base tables.

FIGURE 4-2   The Results For Task page

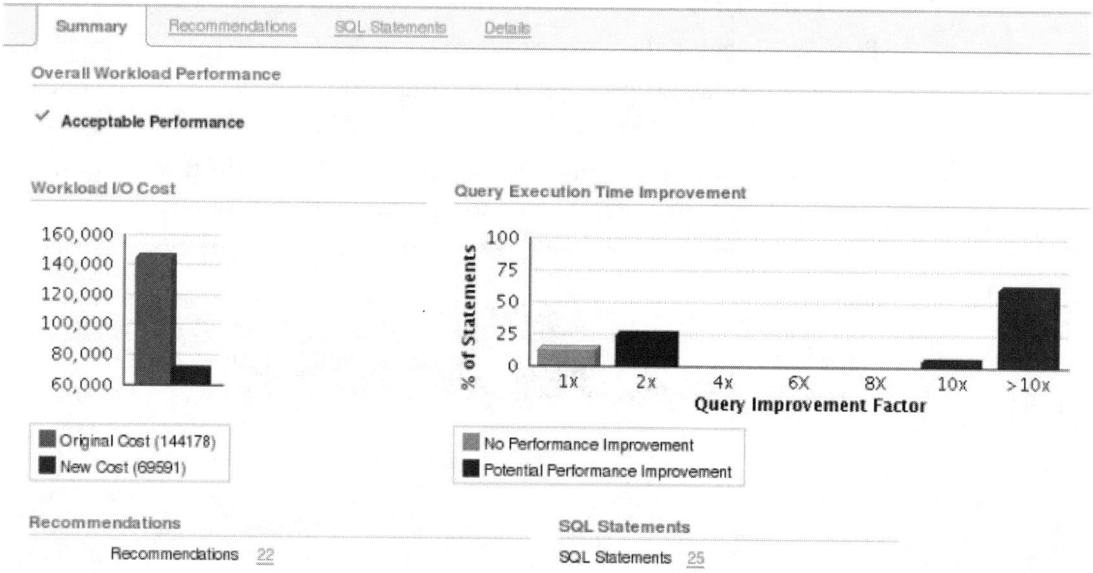

EXERCISE 4-2

Using the Cursor Cache to Get SQL Access Advisor Recommendations

The following exercise shows how to use statements from the SQL Cache to obtain recommendations from the SQL Access Advisor. Here are the steps:

1. On the bottom of the Database Home page, click Advisor Central under Related Links.

2. Click the SQL Advisors link.

3. Click the SQL Access Advisor link.

4. Select Recommend new access structures. Click Continue.

5. Make sure that the Current and Recent SQL Activity shows up in the box. Expand Filter Options and select Filer Workload Based on these Options. In the Users field, select the name of the user who is the owner of the structures. Click Next.

6. Select indexes, materialized views, and partitioning, and then click Next.

7. Enter the task name and, under Scheduling Options, select Standard as the schedule type.

8. Click Submit in the Review page.

9. The Confirmation page appears, showing that your SQL Access Advisor job was submitted successfully.

10. Monitor the task to ensure it's completed and click on the task name on the SQL Access Advisor main page to view the recommendations.

INSIDE THE EXAM

The exam will review your understanding of the new Automatic SQL Tuning Advisor. You must know how to configure an automatic SQL tuning task and how to enable and disable the feature. Under what circumstances will the SQL Tuning Advisor implement a SQL profile? Review the `accept_sql_profiles` task parameter and how it determines the acceptance of SQL profiles. You must also be familiar with the SET_TUNING_TASK_PARAMETER procedure and the use of various attributes such as `accept_sql_profiles` and `max_auto_sql_profiles`, for example.

In terms of the SQL Plan Management feature, you can expect the exam to test your understanding of how the optimizer maintains SQL plan baselines. What's the difference between a verified and an unverified plan? When does a plan become an accepted plan? What is a SQL plan baseline? Understand what the `fixed` attribute implies for a plan in the SQL plan baseline. The exam is likely to ask you about the SQL plan baseline attributes such as `enabled` and `accepted`. Can you manually change the status of a plan to `accepted`?

You must know how to manage the SQL Management Base. How does the plan retention period work? The exam will probably query your understanding of the new initialization parameters, `optimizer_capture_sql_plan_baselines` and `optimizer_use_sql_plan_baselines`. You must also understand how to use the DBMS_SPM package to load SQL plan baselines. How does the database purge the SMB to make more room for new SQL plan baselines? What type of objects does the SMB store besides SQL Plan baselines?

The exam will contain at least one question about the new capabilities of the SQL Access Advisor, such as its ability to make table, materialized view, and index partitioning recommendations.

CERTIFICATION SUMMARY

In Oracle Database 11g, the database runs a new automated maintenance task named the Automatic SQL Tuning Advisor during the maintenance window. The advisor makes recommendations to improve heavy load SQL statements that it picks from the AWR. It can also automatically implement SQL profiles for those statements. You can configure automatic SQL tuning by using the SET_TUNING_TASK_PARAMETER procedure in the DBMS_SQLTUNE package.

SQL Plan Management replaces stored outlines as the way to maintain plan stability when your system is undergoing changes such as a database upgrade. The database now maintains SQL plan baselines, which consist of all accepted plans in the plan history of each repeatable SQL statement. You can capture SQL plans yourself or let the database automatically capture them by specifying the value `true` for the initialization parameter `optimizer_capture_sql_plan_baselines`. To enable the use of the SQL plan baselines, you must set the parameter `optimizer_use_sql_plan_baselines` to `true`. In order for a non-accepted plan to become an accepted plan, the database must evolve the SQL plan baseline. You can do this by running the SQL Tuning Advisor or by executing the EVOLVE_SQL_PLAN_BASELINE function. The optimizer always prefers a fixed plan baseline over all other accepted plans. You use the new package DBMS_SPM to manage the SQL Management Base, which is the repository for the SQL plan baselines.

In Oracle Database 11g, the SQL Access Advisor can also make partitioning recommendations for tables, indexes, and materialized views. You can also get intermediate results from a SQL Access Advisor run.

✓ TWO-MINUTE DRILL

Automatic SQL Tuning Advisor

❑ The Automatic SQL Tuning Advisor runs automatically during the maintenance window as part of the automated maintenance tasks feature.

❑ Automatic SQL Tuning Advisor chooses the tuning candidates from the AWR.

❑ Automatic SQL Tuning Advisor takes into account statistical analysis, SQL profiling, access path analysis, and SQL structure analysis.

❑ A SQL profile contains auxiliary information such as customized optimizer settings, adjustments for missing or stale statistics, and adjustments for errors in optimizer statistics.

❑ You can't use the Automatic SQL Tuning Advisor for recursive statements, ad-hoc statements, parallel queries, and queries using certain DDL statements.

❑ The database orders SQL statements as candidates for tuning, based on the sum of the CPU time and the I/O time usage.

❑ The Automatic SQL Tuning Advisor can automatically implement only recommendations that involve the creation of SQL profiles.

❑ The Automatic SQL Tuning Advisor will accept a new SQL profile for implementation only if the profile offers a threefold improvement in performance.

❑ Use the SET_TUNING_TASK_PARAMETER procedure to configure automatic SQL tuning.

❑ You can enable and disable the Automatic SQL Tuning Advisor by using the DBMS_AUTO_TASK_ADMIN package.

❑ The actual name of the Automatic SQL Tuning Advisor task is SYS__AUTO_SQL_TUNING.

SQL Plan Management

❑ SQL Performance Management lets you preserve SQL performance across major system changes such as an upgrade of the database to a new release.

❑ SQL Performance Management is intended as a preventative mechanism to control SQL plan evolution with little manual effort from the DBA.

❑ A SQL plan baseline is a set of accepted plans in the plan history the database maintains for each distinct repeatable SQL statement.

❑ Not all plans in the plan history for a statement are accepted plans.

❑ A plan becomes an accepted plan only if the plan doesn't lead to a performance regression when compared to other plans in the plan history of a SQL statement.

❑ The DBMS_SPM package supports the SQL Plan Management feature.

❑ In order for the database to automatically capture and maintain SQL plans, set the parameter `optimizer_capture_sql_plan_baselines` to `true`.

❑ The very first SQL plan that's captured for a repeatable statement is part of the SQL plan baseline for that statement.

❑ When you load a plan manually, it automatically is regarded as an accepted plan.

❑ You can manually load plans from a SQL Tuning Set or from the SQL cursor cache.

❑ In order to enable the use of SQL plan baselines, you must set the `optimizer_use_sql_plan_baselines` parameter to `true`.

❑ Evolving a SQL plan baseline entails making a non-accepted plan an accepted plan and integrating it with the SQL plan baseline for a SQL statement.

❑ You must formally evolve all automatically captured plans.

❑ You can use the EVOLVE_SQL_PLAN_BASELINE procedure or the SQL Tuning Advisor to evolve SQL plan baselines.

❑ By changing the status of a SQL plan baseline to `fixed`, you limit the set of possible plans for SQL statement.

❑ The database can't evolve a fixed plan baseline, but you can manually do it by loading a new plan into the SQL plan baseline for a statement.

❑ In order for the optimizer to consider using a specific plan, its status must have both the enabled and accepted status.

❑ The database stores all SPM-related information in the SQL Management Base.

❑ The `space_budget_percent` parameter determines the percentage of space allocated to the SQL Management Base in the SYSAUX tablespace.

❑ The `plan_retention_weeks` parameter specifies how long the database retains unused SQL plans in the SQL Management Base.

SQL Access Advisor Enhancements

❑ The SQL Access Advisor in Oracle Database 11g can also recommend the partitioning of tables, indexes, and materialized views.

❑ You can interrupt a SQL Access Advisor execution to get intermediate results at "publish points."

❑ The new ADD_STS_REF and the DELETE_STS_REF procedures in the DBMS_ADVISOR package enable you to link and unlink a SQL Access Advisor task and a SQL tuning set, respectively.

❑ The SQL Access Advisor recommends partitioning only those tables with columns of type DATE and NUMBER.

❑ The default partitioning mode for a table is interval. You can also use range, hash, range-hash, and range-list partitioning schemes.

❑ Use the SET_TASK_PARAMETERS procedure in the DBMS_ADVISOR package to set task parameters.

SELF TEST

The following questions will help you measure your understanding of the material presented in this chapter. Read all the choices carefully because there might be more than one correct answer. Choose all correct answers for each question.

Automatic SQL Tuning Advisor

1. The Automatic SQL Tuning Advisor tunes only one of the following types of SQL statements:
   A. Recursive SQL statements
   B. Parallel queries
   C. Queries involving the `select` statement
   D. Queries involving the insert or delete statement

2. The SET_TUNING_TASK procedure in the DBMS_SQLTUNE package enables you to do the following:
   A. Specify whether the database must automatically accept a SQL profile
   B. Specify the total number of SQL profiles that can be accepted by the database
   C. Specify whether the SQL Tuning Task must be manual or automatic
   D. Specify the format of the report of the test execution

3. The actual name of the Automatic SQL Tuning Advisor task is
   A. AUTO_SQL_TUNING_TASK
   B. <username>_AUTO_SQL_TUNING_TASK
   C. SQL_AUTO_TUNING_TASK
   D. SYS_AUTO_SQL_TUNING_TASK

4. If you leave the `window_name` parameter in the DBMS_AUTO_TASK_ADMIN.ENABLE procedure as NULL
   A. The task is disabled in all windows.
   B. The task is enabled in all windows.
   C. The task can't be run automatically by the database.
   D. You'll receive an error.

SQL Plan Management

5. The plan history for a SQL statement includes
   A. Only the accepted plans for an ad-hoc statement
   B. Both accepted and non-accepted plans for an ad-hoc statement
   C. Both accepted and non-accepted plans for a repeatable statement
   D. Only the non-accepted plans for a repeatable statement

6. If you assign the value `yes` for the `fixed` parameter in the LOAD_PLANS_FROM_ CURSOR_CACHE procedure, Oracle will
   - A. Treat the plans you load as fixed plans and continue to evolve the SQL plan baseline
   - B. Treat the plans you load as fixed plans and stop evolving the SQL plan baseline
   - C. Drop that plan from the SQL plan baseline
   - D. Prevent you from manually loading further plans for that SQL statement

7. If the best cost plan the optimizer evolves doesn't match any of the accepted plans in a SQL plan baseline, what will the optimizer do?
   - A. It will first add the new plan to the plan history and select the accepted plan with the least cost.
   - B. It will first add the new plan to the SQL plan baseline and select the accepted plan with the least cost.
   - C. It won't add the new plan to the plan history for that SQL statement.
   - D. It will use the new best cost plan it just evolved.

8. What are three ways to make alert warnings about the SMB exceeding its allocated space limit go away?
   - A. Decrease the percentage of space allocated to the SMB in the SYSAUX tablespace.
   - B. Increase the percentage of space allocated to the SMB in the SYSAUX tablespace.
   - C. Increase the size of the SYSAUX tablespace.
   - D. Purge outdated SQL plan baselines.

SQL Access Advisor Enhancements

9. The SQL Access Advisor will make partitioning recommendations for only those tables with the following data types:
   - A. Date
   - B. Integer
   - C. Varchar2
   - D. Number

10. What does the SET_TASK_PARAMETER procedure in the DBMS_ADVISOR package specify when you use the `valid_table_list` attribute?
    - A. It includes all SQL queries that reference valid tables.
    - B. It includes only those SQL queries that refer to the tables passed as arguments for the `valid_table_list` attribute.
    - C. It makes partitioning recommendations only for the tables specified as arguments for the `valid_table_list` attribute.

    D. It ensures that only SQL statements in the VALID_TABLE_LIST table are used in making recommendations.

11. Which of the following statements about the SQL Access Advisor are true?

    A. Once you interrupt a task, you can't restart it.

    B. You can always restart an interrupted task by manually restarting the SQL Access Advisor.

    C. You can sometimes get intermediate recommendations after interrupting a task.

    D. You can always get intermediate recommendations after interrupting a task.

12. When you adopt the SQL Access Advisor recommendations concerning partitioning a table, the recommendations script will

    A. Copy the constraints from the old table to the partitioned table

    B. Copy the indexes from the old table to the partitioned table

    C. Load the data from the old table to the partitioned table

    D. Analyze the data in the newly partitioned table

LAB QUESTION

How can you use the SQL Performance Analyzer and the SQL plan baselines features together during a database upgrade in order to prevent SQL performance regression?

SELF TEST ANSWERS

Automatic SQL Tuning Advisor

1. ☑ **C** is correct. The Automatic SQL Tuning Advisor always tunes SQL select statements.
   ☒ **A, B,** and **D** are incorrect because the Automatic SQL Tuning Advisor doesn't tune any of these types of statements.

2. ☑ **A** and **B** are correct. A is correct because you can use the accept_sql_profiles parameter in the SET_TUNING_TASK_PARAMETER procedure to specify whether the database can automatically accept a SQL profile. B is correct because you can specify the max_auto_sql_profiles parameter in the SET_TUNING_TASK procedure to determine the total number of profiles that the database can accept.
   ☒ **C** is incorrect because the SET_TUNING_TASK_PARAMETERS procedure helps you to set the task parameters for an advisor run. It doesn't specify whether the task must be automatic or manual. **D** is incorrect because you use the `report_auto_tuning_task` parameter to specify the format of the Automatic SQL Tuning Advisor.

3. ☑ **D** is correct. The actual name of the Automatic SQL Tuning Advisor task is SYS_AUTO_SQL_TUNING_TASK.
   ☒ **A, B,** and **C** are incorrect because they provide the wrong name for the task.

4. ☑ **B** is correct. If you omit the `window_name` parameter in the DBMS_AUTO_TASK-ADMIN.ENABLE procedure, the task is enabled in all windows.
   ☒ **A** is incorrect because the task is enabled in all windows, not disabled. **C** is incorrect because the task will be run automatically by the advisor in all windows. **D** is incorrect because you can leave the `window_name` parameter out if you want, to let the task run in all windows.

SQL Plan Management

5. ☑ **C** is correct. The plan history for a SQL statement includes both accepted and non-accepted execution plans for a repeatable statement.
   ☒ **A** and **D** are incorrect because both accepted and non-accepted execution plans become part of the plan history for a SQL statement. **B** is incorrect because only exaction plans for repeatable statements are stored, but not those for ad-hoc statements.

6. ☑ **B** is correct. When you specify a plan as fixed when you load it, Oracle will treat the plan as a fixed plan and stops evolving the SQL plan baseline for that SQL statement.

☒ **A** is incorrect because when you specify a plan as fixed, Oracle will stop evolving the SQL plan baseline for that statement. **C** is incorrect because the database doesn't drop a plan from the SQL plan baseline because you specify it as a fixed plan. Rather, it prefers to use the fixed plan over all other plans. **D** is incorrect because you can continue to load new plans, even after specifying a plan as fixed.

7. ☑ **A** is correct. The optimizer will first add the new plan to the plan history and select the accepted plan with the least cost to execute the statement.
☒ **B** is incorrect because the optimizer adds the new plan first to the plan history, not the SQL plan baseline. Only accepted plans are added to the SQL plan baseline. **C** is incorrect because the optimizer adds the new plan to the plan history. **D** is incorrect because it won't necessarily use the new best cost plan it has evolved.

8. ☑ **B**, **C**, and **D** are correct. By taking any of the steps indicated in these three alternatives, you could potentially make the space alerts stop.
☒ **A** is incorrect because decreasing the space allocation to the SMB actually could make matters worse regarding the availability of space in the SMB.

SQL Access Advisor Enhancements

9. ☑ **A** and **D** are correct. The SQL Access Advisor will make partitioning recommendations for only those tables with the DATE and NUMBER data types.
☒ **B** and **C** are incorrect because the advisor doesn't make any partitioning recommendations for tables with these two data types.

10. ☑ **C** is correct. You can use the `valid_table_list` attribute to limit the partitioning recommendations to only those SQL queries that refer to a specified table or tables.
☒ **A** is incorrect because the `valid_table_list` parameter has nothing to do with a table being valid. **B** is incorrect because the `valid_table_list` attribute limits only the partitioning recommendations. **D** is incorrect because the tables specified by the `valid_table_list` parameter don't contain any SQL statements.

11. ☑ **A** and **C** are correct. **A** is correct because once you interrupt a SQL Access Advisor task, you can't restart it. **C** is correct because you can get intermediate advisor recommendations after interrupting a task, provided the advisor has run long enough to provide recommendations. If you interrupt too soon, you may not get any intermediate recommendations.
☒ **B** is incorrect because you can't restart an interrupted task. **D** is incorrect because you are not guaranteed intermediate results when you interrupt a task.

12. ☑ **A**, **B**, **C**, and **D** are correct. The SQL Access Advisor scripts for implementing its partitioning recommendations include the code for performing all four of the tasks.

LAB ANSWER

Let's assume that you are upgrading from the Oracle Database Release 2 to Oracle Database 11g Release 1. You can seed the SQL Management Base in the upgraded database with known execution plans that guarantee that there won't be a performance regression by using the SQL Performance Analyzer and the SQL plan baselines in the following sequence:

1. Capture the pre-upgrade SQL plans in an STS.

2. Upgrade your database on a test server.

3. Change the `optimizer_features_enable` parameter to 10.2.

4. Import the captured SQL workload to the upgraded database.

5. Run the SQL Performance Analyzer, using the imported STS as the source for the SQL workload.

5

Automatic Storage
Management
and Partitioning
Enhancements

CERTIFICATION OBJECTIVES

5.01   Automatic Storage Management New
Features

5.02   Partitioning Enhancements

✓   Two-Minute Drill

Q&A   Self Test

O racle Database 11g introduces several enhancements in the Automatic Storage Management (ASM) area. The new features in ASM enhance performance while making it easier to manage the storage system. Oracle has had the table partitioning capability since Oracle 8. In this release, several new and exciting partitioning schemes have been introduced. I'll start with a review of the new features in ASM and then discuss the partitioning innovations.

CERTIFICATION OBJECTIVE 5.01

Automatic Storage Management New Features

Oracle Database 11g contains several important enhancements to Automatic Storage Management. These changes include the following:

- Fast mirror resync feature
- Preferred mirror read feature
- ASM compatibility–related enhancements
- The SYSASM privilege for managing ASM

I discuss the main new ASM features in the following sections after a quick review of the ASM architecture.

ASM Architecture

Before we delve into the ASM enhancements in Oracle Database 11g, let's quickly review the main features where Oracle has provided enhancements.

- An ASM *disk group* is the fundamental unit of storage management in ASM, and contains a set of disks. ASM assigns all files from the disk groups and not directly from the disks. An ASM disk group can contain files from multiple Oracle databases and, conversely, a single Oracle database can use files from multiple disk groups.
- ASM disks are the actual physical storage devices that are assigned to disk groups. An ASM disk could be a disk from storage array, an entire disk or partition of a disk, a logical volume, or a network-attached file system (NFS).
- ASM spreads files evenly across all the disks that are in the disk groups to ensure I/O load balancing among the disks.

The database divides each ASM disk into an *allocation unit* (AU), which is the basic unit of allocation in a disk group. An ASM file consists of one or more file extents and a file extent consists of one or more allocation units. Each extent resides on a single disk.

A *failure group* is a set of ASM disks that share a common failure mechanism, such as a set of SCSI disks that share a common SCSI Controller. ASM uses separate failure groups to store redundant copies of data when you specify two-way or three-way mirroring for a file. You can create failure groups only if you use normal or high redundancy disk groups.

When you add a new disk or remove disks from a disk group, ASM automatically redistributes evenly across all disks of a disk group while the database is online. This feature is known as *automatic rebalancing*. Thus, when a disk fails, ASM automatically rebalances data to maintain the full redundancy for all files with extents on the failed disk. Similarly, when you replace a failed disk with another disk, ASM rebalances data to include the new disk.

ASM uses striping to spread data evenly across disks in a disk group, thus balancing load and also lowering I/O latency. ASM uses coarse-grained striping for load balancing and fine-grained striping for reducing I/O latency. ASM separates files into stripes, thus spreading the data across all disks in the disk group. The fine-grained striping size is 128KB and the coarse-grained striping size is equal to the size of the allocation unit.

ASM Fast Mirror Resync

In Oracle Database 10g, when an ASM disk failure occurs, say, because of a bad cable or controller, ASM won't be able to complete the writing of an extent to the failed disk if it's in the middle of doing so. This is true, of course, only if you're using ASM redundancy. ASM will then take the failed disk offline. Once it re-creates the failed disk's extents on the other disks in the disk group using redundant extent copies, ASM drops the failed disk. ASM doesn't read from the offline disk any longer because it assumes that the disk contains only stale data. You'd have to manually add the failed disk back after the failure is fixed, by migrating all its extents back onto it. Or, you must add a new disk to the disk group to take the place of the dropped disk. In either case, the two-step process of writing and rewriting of the failed disk's extents takes time and resources. Even when a disk failure is transient, caused by a failure of cables, controllers, or disk power supply interruptions, you'll still have to go through this time-consuming process to take care of a failed disk by fixing the transient failure, adding the dropped disk back to its disk group, and incurring the cost of migrating the extents back to the fixed disk after that.

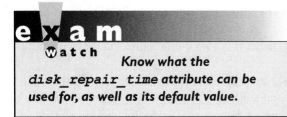

In Oracle Database 11g, the ASM *fast mirror resync feature* lowers the overhead involved in resynchronizing disk groups following a transient disk failure. Following a temporary failure, ASM tracks the extents that were changed during the failure and after the failure is fixed, resynchronizes only the changed extents. Thus, the database has to rewrite only a miniscule portion of the contents of the failed disk. The database fixes only the damaged portions of the affected disk and doesn't have to copy the contents of the entire disk when you take a disk offline and bring it back online after repairing it. Of course, the feature works under the assumption that the offline disk's contents haven't been damaged or modified. When you enable this feature, the database will merely take the affected disk offline but won't drop it.

The ASM fast mirror resync feature works only in cases where there is no actual disk damage or any modification in the disk's contents. For the ASM disk to be taken offline but not dropped following a transient failure, you must have set the disk_repair_time attribute for the disk group to which the offline disk belongs. The length of time specified by the disk_repair_time attribute determines how long ASM will wait for you to complete the repair and still be able to resynchronize the disk.

Note that the fast mirror resync feature is applicable to only those cases where you are forced to take a disk offline for issues unrelated to the data on the disk. The fast mirror resync feature dramatically lowers the time it takes to bring a disk online after you take it offline and drop it from the disk group to fix the problem. The reason for this is that, without this feature, once you take a disk offline and fix the problem, you must wipe off the disk first with the dd command before adding it back to the disk group. The dd command is a popular UNIX/Linux command used to make a copy of a file system. (dd is especially useful for copying regions of raw device files and reading fixed amounts of data from special files such as /dev/zero.)

In Oracle Database 10g, you have to follow these steps to offline, drop, and add a disk back to a disk group.

1. First take the disk offline and then specify the drop after clause. By setting the disk repair time to 0, the after disk group command instructs the database not to wait to drop the database.

   ```
   SQL> alter disk group dgroup1 disk data_00001 drop after 0 h;
   ```

   When you drop the offline disk as shown here, ASM rebalances the list mirrored extents that were on the disk across the remaining disks in the disk group.

2. Wipe the dropped disk before adding it back to the disk group:

```
$ dd if=/dev/zero of=asm_disk1 bs=1024k count=100
```

You must log in as root to perform the preceding operation.

3. Add the repaired disk back to the disk group using the `alter diskgroup` command.

```
SQL> alter diskgroup dgroup1 add disk '/dev/raw/raw1'
        size 100 M;
```

Once you add the disk back, ASM will perform a rebalance operation so the new disk has approximately the same amount of data as the rest of the disks in the disk group.

In Oracle Database 11g, you don't have to wipe off the dropped disk. When you're ready to add it back to the disk group, just add the disk without wiping off the contents. ASM will add the disk back immediately without the long rebalance operation it used to perform without the fast mirror resync feature.

Setting Up ASM Fast Mirror Resync

You enable the fast mirror resync capability by specifying the `disk_repair_time` attribute for a disk group, after you create the disk group. That is, you must use the `alter diskgroup` command to enable fast mirror resync. The `disk_repair_time` attribute accepts time as a value, which it then uses to determine the length of time after a disk failure for which ASM can ensure it will resynchronize the disk. That is, the setting of this parameter determines the duration for which ASM can tolerate a disk outage and still be able to resynchronize the contents of the disk after you repair the disk failure. Here's an example that shows how to specify ASM fast mirror resync for a disk group:

```
SQL> alter diskgroup dgroupA
        set attribute 'disk_repair_time'='2h';
```

The value of the `disk_repair_time` attribute in this example is set to 6h, which means two hours. Let's say the disk group dgroupA has two disks, DISK1 and DISK2. If you have to take DISK1 offline because a few blocks went bad, ASM will wait for two hours before dropping the disk. You can fix DISK1 and bring it back online within two hours. If you do that, ASM will copy the extents on the bad blocks from DISK2, which mirrors the data in DISK1. This process of resynchronizing the damaged extents by copying the few blocks that were damaged is much shorter than copying the entire disk's contents.

The default value for the `disk_repair_time` attribute is 3.6 hours. You can also enable fast mirror resync by setting more complex time duration, as shown here:

```
SQL> alter diskgroup dgroupA
    set attribute 'disk_repair_time'="2D6H30M";
```

The previous example shows how to set the duration to two days, six hours, and 30 minutes.

Once you repair a disk, you bring it online using the following command:

```
SQL> alter diskgroup dgroupA online;
```

Once you issue the `diskgroup <diskgroup_name> online` command, the database starts copying all extents on the redundant copies of the disk that are marked stale. Initially, the disk is brought online only for write operations while the database synchronizes the stale data with the current data. Once the resynchronization process is complete, the database brings the disk online for read operations as well.

on the Job

You can always bring a disk offline for maintenance reasons. Once you finish the disk maintenance, you can use the `alter diskgroup <diskgroup_name> online` statement to bring the disk back online.

You can override the time defined at the disk group level by specifying the `drop after` clause in an `alter diskgroup <diskgroup_name> offline...` command, as shown here:

```
SQL> alter diskgroup dgroupA
    offline disks in failuregroup controller1
    drop after 4h;
```

The previous command uses the `drop after` clause to specify that the database take the disk group dgroupA offline only after waiting for four hours. You can similarly require the database to wait for a specific period before bringing a disk online by specifying the `wait` option, as shown in this example:

```
SQL> alter diskgroup dgroupA
    online disks in failuregroup controller1 power 2 wait;
```

This command requires the database to wait for two hours before bringing the disk group dgroupA online again.

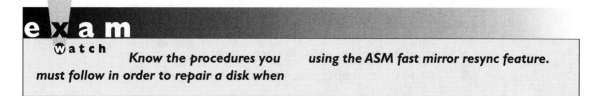

If you can't repair an offline disk group, you can use the `force` option to drop the disk group, as shown here:

```
SQL> alter diskgroup dgroupA
     drop disks in failuregroup controller1 force;
```

ASM reconstructs the data that was stored on the dropped disk from the redundant copies of the data it stores on other disks in the same disk group.

Using Enterprise Manager

You can also use Enterprise Manager to perform an ASM fast mirror resync operation. Once you offline the selected disk or disk, the ASM instance waits for the time period you specify with the `disk_repair_time` attribute and then drops the disk (or disks). You can repair the disk and place it online during the interval specified by the `disk_repair_time` attribute. Once you successfully place a disk online, ASM cancels the pending disk drop operation and starts the data resynchronization process.

o n   t h e

Ⓘ o b   *When you change the value of the `disk_repair_time` attribute, it doesn't affect the disks you've previously taken offline.*

Monitoring

You can monitor the fast mirror resync process using the V$ASM_DISK and the V$ASM_DISK_IOSTAT views. The V$ASM_OPERATION view also shows a row corresponding to each disk resync operation, with the OPERATION column set to the value of `sync`.

ASM Preferred Mirror Read

Mirroring is an ASM feature that protects the integrity of data by storing copies of data on multiple disks. ASM offers you different levels of mirroring, ranging from less stringent to more stringent mirroring strategies. You can specify different disk group types to assign each disk group to a different level of mirroring strategy. You can specify an ASM disk group based on the following three redundancy levels:

- For 2-way mirroring, choose a normal type.
- For 3-way mirroring, choose a high disk group type.
- If you don't want to use ASM mirroring and prefer to configure hardware RAID for redundancy, choose external redundancy.

The disk group type you specify then determines the mirroring level for a file in a disk group. The redundancy level determines how many disk failures the database can tolerate before losing data or having to drop a disk. ASM uses a failure group to place the mirrored copies of a disk, storing different copies of the data in a different failure group. For a normal redundancy file, when ASM allocates a new extent, it allocates a primary copy and a secondary copy, storing the secondary copy in a different failure group than the primary group. A normal redundancy disk group requires a minimum of two disk groups for 2-way mirroring. A high redundancy disk group, because it requires 3-way mirroring, requires at least three failure groups. Because a disk group with external redundancy doesn't use ASM mirroring, it doesn't require any failure groups at all.

In Oracle Database 10g, ASM always reads the primary copy of a mirrored extent whenever you configured an ASM failure group for normal or high redundancy disk groups. That is, ASM only read from the primary failure group and not the secondary failure group, unless the primary failure group wasn't available. This was true even in cases where it is more efficient to read from a secondary failure group extent that's closer to the node. In Oracle Database 11g, the database can read from a list of preferred group names that you provide. That is, you can configure a node to read from a specific failgroup instead of automatically reading from the primary failgroup. Thus, if reading from a local copy of an extent is more efficient, the database will do so. Once you configure a preferred mirror read, every node can read from its local disks. This is called the ASM *preferred mirror read* feature. In order for the ASM instance to read from specific fail groups, you create a preferred read group for the disk groups. The preferred mirror read feature proves very efficient when it comes to reads that involve stretch clusters, which are clusters in which the nodes are spread out far in terms of distance.

Setting Up ASM Preferred Mirror Read

You can configure the preferred mirror read feature by using the new initialization parameter, `asm_preferred_read_failure_groups`. Using this parameter, you can specify the list of preferred mirrored read failure group names. The database

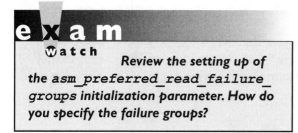

e x a m

ⓦatch

Review the setting up of the asm_preferred_read_failure_ groups *initialization parameter. How do you specify the failure groups?*

will, from then on, prefer to read from disks in the failure groups you specify in the list. The ultimate effect of setting up the ASM preferred read feature is that every node will always read from its local extents, thus improving performance and decreasing network activity.

Here's an example that shows how to set up ASM preferred mirror read by using the initialization parameter asm_preferred_read_failure_groups:

```
asm_preferred_read_failure_groups=data.locationA,data.locationB
```

The asm_preferred_read_failure_groups initialization parameter contains a string that you can use to list multiple failure groups, with each name separated by a comma (asm_preferred_read_failure_groups = <diskgroup_name>.<failure_group_name>,...). You must prefix each failure group with its disk group name and a dot or period (.) character. ASM treats the disks in the failure groups that you specify as the preferred read disks. You can specify only disks that are local to the corresponding instance. The asm_ preferred_read_failure_groups parameter is dynamic so you can change it using the alter system statement, as shown here:

```
SQL> alter system set asm_preferred_read_failure_groups =
     'DGRP1.DGRP1_0000','DGRP2.DGRP2_0000'
```

The alter system statement shown here makes the database prefer the failure groups DGRP1_0000 and DGRP2_0000 in the disk groups DGRP1 and DGRP2, respectively.

You can see which disks are in a preferred read failure group, by issuing the following command:

```
SQL> select preferred_read from v$asm_disk;
```

If a disk belongs to a disk group that is a preferred read failure group, the value of the PREFERRED_READ column will be Y.

Using Enterprise Manager

You can use Enterprise Manager to specify a set of disks as preferred disks for each ASM instance. The ASM configuration page in Oracle Database 11g contains the new Preferred Read Failures Group field. The values shown in this field show the failure groups you specified as values for the asm_preferred_read_failure_groups initialization parameter. The asm_preferred_read_failure_groups initialization parameter takes effect when ASM mounts a disk group or when you create a disk group.

If you haven't already migrated your instances to ASM, you can do so easily using the Enterprise Manager. Figure 5-1 shows the Migrate Database to ASM: ASM Instance page in Database Control. You can configure and start up your ASM instance from this page.

Configuration Best Practices

Following are some best practices to configure the ASM preferred mirror read feature to achieve the best performance and availability in a two-site stretch cluster.

- If you use normal redundancy, you must use only two failure groups and all local disks must belong to the same failure group.

- Each instance can specify only one failure group as its preferred read failure group. If you specify more than one failure group, ASM may not be able to mirror a virtual extent across both groups in the two sites.

- If you create a high redundancy failure group, you can have a maximum of two failure groups on each site with its local disks. You can specify both local failure groups as preferred read failure groups for the ASM instance.

In a three-site stretch cluster, you must use a high redundancy disk group with three failure groups so that ASM can ensure that each virtual extent has a local mirror copy. In addition, this protects the database in the event of a disaster in any one of the three sites.

ASM Scalability and Performance Enhancements

An AU is the basic unit of allocation within an ASM disk group. In Oracle Database 10g, each AU had a single extent, which created problems with memory usage. If you have a large database with numerous default-sized allocation units, the database would need a very large amount of memory in the shared pool. The default AU size is only 1MB. File extents contain a minimum of one AU and an ASM file consists of at least one extent. You can set variable size extents with extents of size 1, 4, 16, 32, and 64 megabytes. The ability to set variable-size ASM extents means that ASM can now support larger file size extents while using less memory. ASM sets thresholds for each file and, as a file grows, ASM will increase the extent size based on the file size thresholds. Thus, a file can start with 1MB extents, with ASM increasing the extent

The Migrate Database to ASM: ASM Instance page in Enterprise Manager

size to 4, 16, 32, or 64 megabytes as the file size grows. Note that the size of an extent can vary among files as well as within a file. As a result of the variable extents feature, the database needs fewer extent pointers to describe an ASM file and less memory to manage the extent maps in the shared pool, thus making it easier to implement large ASM configurations.

Variable size extents raise the maximum possible ASM file size and also reduce shared pool memory requirements. You can periodically rebalance a disk group to avoid external fragmentation, which may occur because of allocating and freeing up of small data extents. However, the database will also automatically perform defragmentation when it has a problem finding the right size extent during extent allocation.

ASM is also more scalable in Oracle Database 11g as compared to Oracle Database 10g. The maximum ASM file size for external redundancy is now 140 petabytes, instead of 35 terabytes in Oracle Database 11g. Variable extent sizes enable you to configure ASM installations that are several hundred terabytes or even several petabytes in size.

You can set the `au_size` attribute easily in Oracle Database 11g, by using the new `attribute` clause in the `create diskgroup` command, as shown here:

```
create diskgroup dg6
external redundancy
disk
'/dev/raw/raw1'
attribute 'au_size' = '8M'
```

You can also specify the `au_size` in bytes instead of megabytes. You can set an `au_size` of 1, 2, 4, 8, 16, 32, or 64 megabytes.

You can find out the allocation unit sizes for all disk groups by executing the following query on the V$ASM_DISKGROUP view:

```
SQL> select name, allocation_unit_size
     from v$asm_diskgroup;
NAME                ALLOCATION_UNIT_SIZE
-------             --------------------
DGROUP1             1048576
DGROUP3             1048576
DGGROUP4            1048576
DGGROUP2            1048576
```

The variable extent sizes feature means that you can tailor the allocation unit sizes to meet the needs of your system.

New SYSASM Privilege

Oracle Database 11g introduces a new system privilege called SYSASM to enable you to separate the SYSDBA database administration privilege from the ASM storage administration privilege. To improve security, Oracle recommends that you use the new privilege called SYSASM when performing ASM-related administrative tasks. The SYSASM privilege is quite similar to the SYSDBA and SYSOPER privileges, which are system privileges given to users that perform administrative tasks in the database.

on the **Job**

Oracle recommends that you use the SYSASM privilege rather than the SYSDBA privilege to administer an ASM instance.

Although the default installation group for the users with the SYASM privilege is the dba group, Oracle intends to require the creation of a separate OS group for ASM administrators in future releases. In this release, Oracle recommends that you create a new operating system group called the OSASM group, and grant the SYSASM privilege only to members of this group. ASM users will then be limited to ASM instances and won't be able to use the SYSDBA privilege for the main database. The key behind the creation of the new SYSASM privilege is to provide distinct operating system privileges for database administrators, storage administrators, and database operators.

exam

ⓦatch *How do you grant the new SYSASM privilege to a user?*

In Oracle Database 11g, the default operating system group for SYSASM is the same group as that for the SYSDBA users—the dba group. If a user is a member of the dba group, the user can connect to the ASM instance using the following command:

```
SQL> connect / as sysasm
```

You can execute the `grant` SQL statement to grant the SYSASM privilege to a user, as shown here:

```
SQL> grant sysasm to salapati;
```

The V$PWFILE_USERS view includes a new column called SYSASM, which shows whether a user can connect with the SYSASM privilege or not. You can revoke the SYSASM privilege from a user by using the `revoke sysasm` SQL statement.

You can still log into an ASM instance as a user with the SYSDBA privilege, but the database will issue a warning that's recorded in the alert log for the database.

ASM Compatibility

ASM in Oracle Database 11g can support databases from both the 11g release as well as the 10g release. The ASM version must be the higher version or at least the same as the RDBMS version for ASM to support that database.

exam

ⓦatch *The* `compatible.asm` *and* `compatible.rdbms` *attributes enable environments with disk groups from Oracle Database 10g Release 1 (10.1), Oracle Database 10g Release 2 (10.2), and*

Oracle Database 11g Release 1 (11.1) to work together. Both attributes are set to 10.1 by default, and you must advance the two attributes to take advantage of the enhancements offered by the new releases.

ASM's disk group compatibility feature lets an Oracle Database 10g client use disk groups created under Oracle Database 11g. You can advance the Oracle database and the ASM disk group compatibility settings across software versions. There are two attributes that determine compatibility settings for each disk group—compatible.asm and compatible.rdbms. The compatible. asm attribute specifies the minimum software version required to use a disk group for ASM. The compatible.rdbms attribute enables you to specify the minimum software version required to use an ASM disk group for a database. The compatible.asm attribute determines the ASM compatibility and controls the ASM metadata on disk structures. The compatible.rdbms setting determines the RDBMS compatibility and controls the minimum client level. I explain the two compatibility-related attributes further here:

- compatible.rdbms indicates the minimum Oracle Database version for the RDBMS instance. This parameter controls the minimum client level and indicates the minimum compatible version of the RDBMS instance that would let the instance mount the ASM disk group. For example, if the RDBMS compatibility is set to 10.1, the Oracle Database client version must be at least 10.1. An ASM instance can support different RDBMS clients running at different compatibility settings. The compatible.rdbms setting specifies the minimum compatible RDBMS version for the ASM instance to mount the disk groups. Each instance supported by ASM must have a database compatible version setting that's at least equal to or greater than the RDBMS compatibility of all disk groups used by that instance. The database compatible initialization parameter setting for each of the instances must be at least equal to the compatible.rdbms setting. Thus, the compatible parameter setting for each instance and the compatible. rdbms setting together determine if an instance can mount a disk group.

- The compatible.asm setting controls the format of data structures for ASM metadata on disks that are part of the ASM disk groups. For example, if you set the compatible.asm attribute to 11.1, the ASM software version must be at least 11.1. The ASM compatibility level must be at least equal to the RDBMS compatibility for that disk group. Remember that the ASM compatibility is concerned with just the format of the ASM metadata while the format of the actual file contents is determined by the compatibility of the database instance. Let's say the compatible.asm setting is 11.0 and the compatible.rdbms setting is 10.1. This means that ASM can manage the disk group only if the ASM software version is 11.0 or higher.

At the same time, a database client needs to have a software version at least at 10.1 to use that disk group.

The default for both the compatible.asm and compatible.rdbms attributes is 10.1. As with the database compatibility feature where you use the initialization parameter compatible in the spfile to set the compatibility level of the database, higher disk group RDBMS and ASM compatibility settings enable you to take advantage of the new ASM-related features in Oracle Database 11g. Once you advance the compatible.rdbms attribute, you can't revert to the old setting. If you want to go back to the previous value, you must create a new disk group with the previous compatibility setting and restore all the database files that were part of the disk group.

on the Job

If you've made backups with the md_backup command before updating the disk group compatibility settings, the backup is useless once you update the disk group. However, you can use an older backup to revert to the previous compatibility setting.

Specifying the Compatibility Settings

You can specify both the compatible.rdbms and the compatible.asm attributes in a create diskgroup SQL statement. The following example shows how to create a normal redundancy disk group with the ASM compatibility set to 11.1:

```
SQL> create diskgroup dgroup1 disk '/dev/raw*'
     attribute 'compatible.asm' = '11.1';
```

The compatible.rdbms setting would be set to the default value of 10.1 in this case.

The following example shows how to create a normal redundancy disk group and set both the ASM and the RDBMS compatibility to 11.1:

```
SQL> create diskgroup dgroup1 disk '/dev/raw*'
     attribute 'compatible.asm' = '11.1';
     attribute 'rdbms.asm' = '11.1';
```

You can also use the alter diskgroup statement to change the compatible attribute settings for a disk group. When you are advancing the disk compatibility you must first advance the compatible.asm attribute before advancing the compatible.rdbms attribute. In the following example, the alter diskgroup statement advances the compatible.asm setting to 11.1:

```
SQL> alter diskgroup dgrp2 set attribute
     'compatible.asm' = '11.1';
```

Once you execute the previous `alter diskgroup` statement, you can then advance the RDMBS compatibility of the disk group to 11.1 with the following statement:

```
SQL> alter diskgroup dgrp2 set attribute
     'compatible.rdbms' = '11.1';
```

e x a m

ⓦatch *Know the relationship between ASM compatibility and RDBMS compatibility, including their differences.*

Note that the fact that you set the compatibility at the disk group level rather than at the ASM instance level means that the same ASM instance can support multiple database versions.

You can view the current compatibility setting by querying the V$ASM_ATTRIBUTE or the V$ASM_DISKGROUP views. Here's an example:

```
SQL> select compatibility, database_compatibility
  2  from  v$asm_diskgroup
  3  where name = 'DGRP1';

COMPATIBILITY            DATABASE_COMPATIBILITY
-----------------        -----------------------
10.1.0.0.0               10.1.0.0.0
```

The column COMPATIBILITY shows the ASM compatibility, which is set to 10.1.0.0.0. This means that the disk group DGRP1 supports only the 10.1 ASM structures. The column DATABASE_COMPATIBILITY shows the RDBMS compatibility setting, which is also 10.1.0.0.0. This means that databases from the 10.1 release and higher can use the disk group DGRP1.

Compatibility Considerations

Here are some things to note regarding the compatibility settings:

- You can't change the compatibility settings during a rolling upgrade.
- You can only advance compatibility settings. That is, you can't reverse a compatibility setting that you have advanced.
- Various new disk group features are enabled only if you use a valid combination of the `compatible.asm` and `compatible.rdbms` settings.

Changing ASM Disk Group Attributes

You can use the new `attribute` clause—either when creating a disk group or when altering a disk group—to specify or change several types of attributes for that disk group. The following sections offer a brief explanation of the new ASM attributes you can control with the `attribute` clause.

Allocation Unit Size

As you learned earlier in this chapter, in Oracle Database 11g, ASM lets you specify multiple allocation unit (AU) sizes when you create a disk group. The allocation units can be any of the following sizes: 1, 2, 4, 8, 16, 32, or 64 megabytes.

RDBMS Compatibility

Use the `compatible.rdbms` parameter to specify the RDBMS compatibility level, as I explained earlier in this chapter.

ASM Compatibility

Use the `compatible.asm` parameter to specify the ASM compatibility level, as I explained earlier in this chapter.

Disk Repair Time

The default value for the `disk_repair_time` attribute, which controls the length of time the database waits before dropping an offlined disk, is 3.6 hours. You can issue the `alter diskgroup...disk offline` statement to specify a different value for the `disk_repair_time` attribute, in units of minutes, hours, or days.

Template Redundancy

You can use the `template.tname.redundancy` attribute to set the redundancy of a template. You can choose among the values `unprotect`, `mirror`, and `high`.

Template Striping

You can use the `template.tname.striping` attribute to specify the striping attribute of a template. The possible values for this attribute are `coarse` and `fine`.

Here's an example showing how to use the `attribute` clause in a `create diskgroup` statement to set a value for the `compatible.asm` attribute.

```
SQL> create diskgroup data normal redundancy
     disk '/dev/raw/raw1', '/dev/raw/raw2'
     attribute 'compatible.asm'='11.1';
```

As you learned earlier in this chapter, the default ASM and database compatibility for a pre-11g ASM instance is 10.1. For an 11g ASM instance, the default ASM compatibility is 11.1 and the default database compatibility is 10.1.

New Manageability Options for Commands

Oracle Database 11g enhances several management options for ASM, including the `check` command, mounting and dropping disk groups, and the ASMCMD command-line utility. The following sections describe these enhancements.

Changes in the check Command

The `check` command lets you verify if the ASM disk group metadata is consistent. If there are any inconsistencies, the command shows you a summary of the errors and records the details in the alert log. In Oracle Database 10g, you could specify the following values with the `check` command:

- `all`
- `disk`
- `disks in failgroup`
- `file`

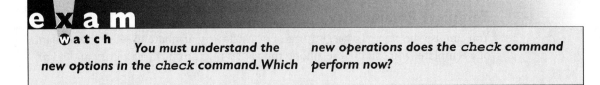

In Oracle Database 11g, the `check` command syntax is much simpler and checks all metadata directories by default. The `check` command performs the following checks in Oracle Database 11g:

- The `file` and `disk` options will perform the same checks as the `all` option in the previous release.

- Checks disk consistency, acting as an equivalent command to the `check disk` and `check disks in failgroup` clauses in the Oracle Database 10*g* release.
- Cross checks all file extent maps and allocation tables, which is equivalent to what the `check file` command did in Oracle Database 10*g*.
- Checks to ensure that the alias metadata directory and the file directory are correctly linked.
- Checks that the alias directory tree is correctly linked.
- Checks to ensure that the ASM metadata directories don't contain any allocated blocks that are unreachable.

You can specify the `repair/norepair` clause to tell ASM whether you want it to attempt to repair any errors found during the disk group checks. The default value is `repair`, meaning ASM will attempt to automatically fix any inconsistencies it finds during its disk group checks.

The New restricted Mount Mode

ASM automatically mounts the disk groups that you specify in the `asm_diskgroups` initialization parameter so they are available to the database instances. Similarly, when you shut down the ASM instance, the disk groups are automatically dismounted.

In addition to the automatic mounting and dismounting described here, you can also manually mount or dismount a disk group any time. You use the `alter diskgroup ... mount` command to mount a disk group and the `alter diskgroup ... dismount` statement to dismount a disk group.

Oracle Database 11*g* introduces a new mount mode for disk groups, called the *restrict* mode. Whenever you add a disk to a disk group, ASM immediately starts a rebalance operation, which requires an elaborate system of locks to ensure that the correct blocks are accessed and changed. Mounting a disk group in the restricted mode improves the performance of a rebalance operation because the ASM instance doesn't have to message the database client for locking and unlocking extent maps, thus reducing the locking overhead during rebalancing of disks. Once you finish all maintenance operations in the restrict mode, you must dismount the disk group and mount it again in the normal mode so database clients can use the disk group.

Here's how you can mount a disk group in the restrict mode:

1. Dismount the mode before mounting it again in the restrict mode.

```
SQL> alter diskgroup test dismount;
```

2. Mount the disk group in the restricted mode with the following statement:

```
SQL> alter diskgroup test mount restrict;
```

The ASM clients won't be able to access the disk group test now.

3. Perform your maintenance tasks such as adding and removing disks.

4. Dismount the disk group once you finished your maintenance tasks, as shown here:

```
SQL> alter diskgroup test dismount;
```

5. Mount the disk group in the normal unrestricted mode so users can access it once again:

```
SQL> alter diskgroup test mount;
```

Note the following when you mount a disk group in the mount mode:

- You can mount a disk group only on a single instance in the mount mode.
- Database clients can't have access to the disk group.
- A rebalancing operation won't have any locking overhead when you mount a disk group in the restricted mode.

The previous example showed how to manually mount a single disk group in the restricted mode. Mounting a disk group in the restricted mode tells ASM that it doesn't need to use extensive locking that slows down the rebalance operation because there are no other users in the system that are accessing the disks. If you want to perform maintenance operations on several or all of the disk groups, you can simply use the `startup restrict` command when starting the ASM instance. This will mount all the disk groups that you defined in the `asm_diskgroups` initialization parameter in the restricted mode.

The FORCE option in the DROP DISKGROUP Command

In Oracle Database 10g, Oracle mounts a disk group even when there are potentially missing or damaged failure groups. That is, a command to mount an incomplete group will succeed as long as there are enough failure groups to mount the disk group. If ASM finds at least one complete set of extents in the disk group, it will mount the disk group. The problem with this approach is that ASM is liable to drop a missing ASM disk, which means you have to add them back after repairing them and perform an expensive rebalancing operation.

In Oracle Database 11g, ASM won't mount an incomplete disk group automatically. Rather, you must specify the `force` option when mounting a disk group, for the operation to succeed. This means that if there are any errors, in say, the `asm_diskstring` parameter or if there are any connectivity issues, you can correct them before mounting the disk group.

By default, the `mount diskgroup` operation uses a `noforce` option. Under this option, the database will mount a disk group only if all the disks belonging to that disk group are available. Use the `force` option when you know beforehand that some of the disks are unavailable. ASM will then mount the disk group, even when some disks are unavailable, as long as it finds enough disks to form a quorum. When you mount a disk group with the `force` option, if one or more disks aren't available at mounting time, the disks can be offlined. You must restore those devices before the duration set by the `disk_repair_time` attribute expires to avoid a costly rebalancing operation to restore redundancy for all files in the disk group.

drop disk group force Command

In Oracle Database 10g, you'd sometimes run into a problem when dealing with a badly damaged disk or lost disk. Because of the problem with the damaged or lost disk, you may want to drop the entire disk group or rearrange the disks in the disk group in other disk groups. If a disk is missing, you can't mount the disk group, however. The only alternative you have is to use the `dd` command to wipe the disk headers off, as shown here:

```
$ dd if=/dev/zero of=asm_disk1 bs=1024k count=100
```

The example shown here would use the `dd` command to wipe off the disk asm_disk1.

In Oracle Database 11g, it's much easier to drop disk groups that you can't mount. You can use the new `drop disk group force` command to drop disk groups that can't be mounted by an ASM instance, as shown here:

```
SQL> drop diskgroup dgroup1 force including contents;
```

Note that you must specify the `including contents` clause when executing the `drop diskgroup` command with the `force` option. The command will fail if the disk group you're dropping is being used by the ASM instance anywhere in the subsystem. If the disk group is in the same cluster or on the same node and is in use, the command fails. However, if the disk group is on another cluster, the command fails if ASM verifies that the disk group is in use. Once the drop `diskgroup ... force` command succeeds, it results in the marking of the headers of the disks in the disk group that wasn't mounted as FORMER.

Enhancements in ASMCMD

The ASMCMD utility is a command-line tool that helps you view and manage files and directories within an ASM disk group. You can list the contents of disk groups, perform a search, and create and remove directories with the help of the ASMCMD utility. In Oracle Database 11g, there are new options you can use with the ASMCMD utility to help you perform ASM metadata backup and recovery operations. In Oracle Database 10g, you could use RMAN to restore lost files when an ASM disk group was lost, but this required you to re-create the ASM disk group as well as any user directories or templates. In Oracle Database 11g, the new md_ backup and md_restore options let you re-create an ASM disk group with an identical template and alias directory structure.

The new ASM metadata backup and restore (AMBR) functionality works in the backup and restore modes. In the backup mode, AMBR gathers information about disk groups and failure group configuration, templates, and alias directory structures, and stores this metadata in a text file. In the restore mode, AMBR reconstructs the disk group from the information it saves to the text file. In addition to the md_backup and md_restore options, ASMCMD also has the new cp, lsdsk, and remap commands. You look at each of these new options in detail in the following sections.

cp   The cp command helps copy one or more files to another destination. For example, you can use this command to copy files between ASM disk groups on a local instance and a remote instance. The destination is of the form target/connect_identifier, where connect_identifier can be a HOSTNAME, HOSTNAME.SID, or HOSTNAME.[PORT.]SID (where PORT is an optional attribute). You can use the cp command to copy an ASM file to the operating system. With the cp command, you can:

- Copy a file locally:

  ```
  cp +DATA/ORCL/DATAFILE/TBSFV.256.123456789  +DATA/ORCL/tbsjfv.bak
  ```

- Copy an ASM file to the operating system:

  ```
  cp +DATA/ORCL/DATAFILE/TBSFV.256.123456789
  /home/oracle/tbsjfv.dbf
  ```

- Copy an operating system file to an ASM directory:

  ```
  cp /home/oracle/tbsjfv.dbf  +data/jfv
  ```

- Copy an ASM file from a local ASM instance to a remote ASM instance:

  ```
  cp +DATA/orcl/datafile/tbsjfv.256.123456789
  \sys@mydb . +ASM2 : +D2/jfv/tbsjfv.dbf
  ```

lsdsk   The lsdsk command lists ASM-visible disks. You can restrict the output to only those disks that match a pattern, which can include wildcard characters and slashes. You can run this command in either the connected mode or the non-connected mode. In the connected mode, the command retrieves disk information from the V$ and the GV$ tables. In the non-connected mode, the command scans disk headers to retrieve the disk information. Unless you specify the -i flag, the lsdsk command runs in the connected mode when you are connected to an ASM instance.

Here is an example of the lsdsk command.

```
ASMCMD> lsdsk
/dev/raw/raw1
/dev/raw/raw3
. . .
```

You can also specify the following flags with the lsdsk command:

- The -k flag provides a detailed set of information about disks, including their total size and free sizes, failgroups, and their paths.
- The -s flag shows I/O statistics relating to the disks.
- The -p flag provides the status of the disks.
- The -t flag provides repair related information.

The -d flag along with another flag such as -t, limits the output to a specific disk group, as shown here:

```
ASMCMD> lsdsk -t -d dgrp1
```

on the
() o b

*Use the **help lsdsk** command to get information about all the options of the **lsdsk** command.*

You can also attach the -l flag to any other flag to make ASM retrieve the information directly from the file headers instead of the V$ views. For example:

```
ASMCMD> lsdsk -lk
```

The preceding command gets detailed disk information from the disk headers. If the ASM instance isn't available for some reason, you can still get the information you need by letting ASM extract the information from the file headers.

You can get information for a specific disk group by using the -d flag with any of the other flags, as shown here:

```
ASMCMD> lsdsk -t -d dgrp1
```

The previous lsdsk command gets detailed information about the disks in disk group dgrp1.

remap The `remap` command lets you remap a range of unreadable bad disk sectors. It can't, however, remap blocks with incorrect content, whether they are readable or not. Here's an example showing how to use the `remap` command:

```
ASMCMD> remap DATA DATA_0001 5000-7500
```

md_backup As you are aware, an ASM instance doesn't store data. It merely maintains the storage metadata such as the names of the disk groups, directories, and so on and stores this metadata in the disk headers. This means that if there is a disk crash and you lose the disk headers, you're in trouble. You can use RMAN to restore a backup for the database itself, but you'll have to first re-create the ASM disk groups and directories. If you haven't kept careful records, you're in trouble again. Even if you have the records, you must still take the time to re-create the necessary ASM metadata.

In Oracle Database 11g, the ASMCMD utility is extended to provide ASM metadata backup and restore functionality through the `md_backup` and `md_restore` commands. This functionality is known as the ASM *metadata backup and restore* (AMBR). The goal is to enable you to easily re-create an ASM disk group with an identical template and alias directory structure, using the backup of the ASM metadata. This eliminates the need for manually re-creating the disk groups and the necessary directories or templates following the loss of an ASM disk group.

The new `md_backup` option in Oracle Database 11g lets you perform an ASM metadata backup for a disk group. The command will back up into a backup text file, disk group metadata including fail groups, disks, attributes, aliases, and templates. Here's the syntax of the `md_backup` command:

```
md_backup  [-b <backup_file>]
           [-g '<diskgroup_name>,<diskgroup_name>,...']
```

- The −b option lets you specify the backup file to store the information. By default, the filename is ambr_backup_intermediate_file.
- The −g option lets you specify the disk groups to back up. The command backs up all disk groups by default.

Here's an example showing how to use the `md_backup` command to back up a single disk group named admdsk1.

```
ASMCMD> md_backup -b /tmp/asmbkp1 -g admdsk1
```

The `md_backup` command shown here uses the −g option to create a backup of the disk group admdsk1 and saves it in the /tmp/dgbackup07022 file. The −b option specifies that the backup information containing the ASM metadata be recorded in the file named asmblp1 instead of in the default file named ambr_backup_intermediate_file.

md_restore   The md_restore command is the counterpart of the md_backup command and helps you restore the ASM metadata for a disk group. Before you can restore data files in a disk group, you must first restore the disk group using this command. The md_restore command has the following syntax:

```
md_restore -b <backup_file> [-li]
           [-t (full)|nodg|newdg] [-f <sql_script_file>]
           [-g '<diskgroup_name>,<diskgroup_name>,...']
           [-o '<old_diskgroup_name>:<new_diskgroup_name>,...']
```

The following lists the various flags and their meanings:

- **-b** Read metadata information from <backup_file>.
- **-l** Print messages to a file (Not implemented).
- **-i** Ignore errors. Normally, if md_restore encounters an error, it will stop. When you specify the -i flag, errors are ignored.
- **-t** Specify diskgroup creation.
    - **full** Create disk group and restore metadata.
    - **nodg** Restore metadata only.
    - **newdg** Create disk group with a different name and restore metadata.
- **-f** Write SQL commands to <sql_script_file> instead of executing them.
- **-g** Select the disk groups to be restored. If no disk groups are defined, all of them will be restored.
- **-o** Rename disk group <old_diskgroup_name> to <new_diskgroup_name>.

You can initiate the creation of a disk group as well as restore its metadata by executing the md_restore command. The following examples show how to use this command in various scenarios:

- Restoring a disk group from the backup script and creating a copy:

    ```
    ASMCMD> md_restore -t full -g asmdsk1 -i backup_file
    ```

- Restoring an existing disk group's metadata:

    ```
    ASMCMD> md_restore -t nodg - asmdsk1 -i backup_file
    ```

- Restoring a disk group and creating a new disk group:

    ```
    ASMCMD> md_restore -t newdg -o 'DGNAME=asmdsk1:asmdsk2'
            -i backup_file
    ```

The md_restore command restores the disk groups, creates the attributes such as disk_repair_time, modifies the templates, and creates the directories. It's important to understand that any data in the disk groups will be lost, however. The md_restore command creates a disk group and the directories without any data. The md_restore uses the backup file created by the md_backup command, which backs up just the ASM metadata. You must use your RMAN database backups to restore the information on the re-created disk groups.

The following md_restore command example specifies the −f flag to create a text file with the commands to create the disk groups, directories, and so on.

```
ASMCMD> md_restore -b dgroup1.backup -t full -f create_dgroup1.sql
```

You can execute the md_restore command with the −f option on a regular basis to maintain a record of the ASM metadata.

EXERCISE 5-1

Using the md_backup and md_restore Commands

This exercise shows you how to use the new ASM commands md_backup and md_restore to quickly restore lost data in an ASM instance.

1. Take an RMAN backup of the USERS tablespace:

```
RMAN> backup tablespace users;
```

2. Create a new directory called abc in the disk group dgroup1. Once you create the directory, create an alias called +DGROUP1/abc/users.f. This alias will point to the ASM datafile in which the USERS tablespace is stored:

```
ASMCMD> mkdir +DGROUP1/abc
ASMCMD> mkalias TBSJFV.254.434252532        +DGROUP1/abc/users.f
```

3. Back up the ASM metadata for the DGROUP1 disk group:

```
ASMCMD> md_backup -g dgroup1
```

The md_backup command produces the restore script, named ambr_ backup_intermediate_file, in the current directory. You'll need this file to perform the restore operation later on.

4. Drop the disk group DGROUP1 to simulate the failure. You can use the dismount force clause to dismount the disk group and then force drop it.

```
SQL> alter diskgroup dgroup1 dismount force;
SQL> drop diskgroup dgroup1 force including contents;
```

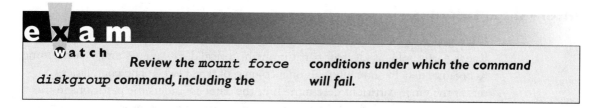

Review the *mount force diskgroup* command, including the conditions under which the command will fail.

5. Edit the ambr_backup_intermediate_file to remove the `au_size` entry. Once you make the change and save the restore file, run the `md_restore` command to restore the ASM metadata for the dropped disk group.

```
ASMCMD> md_restore -b ambr_backup_intermediate_file
          -t full -g data
```

6. Once you restore the ASM metadata for the disk group, you must restore the USERS tablespace that was in the dropped disk group. You use the backup you made earlier of the USERS tablespace for this.

```
RMAN> restore tablespace users;
```

Once RMAN competes restoring the tablespace, exit from RMAN.

CERTIFICATION OBJECTIVE 5.02

Partitioning Enhancements

Oracle partitioning lets you manage large tables, allowing scalability and performance when dealing with data warehouses and other large databases. Partitioning is well known to provide super fast access to data. Oracle Database 11g has made significant enhancements in partitioning tables and indexes, which include the following new partitioning schemes:

- Interval partitioning
- System partitioning
- Virtual column–based partitioning
- Reference partitioning
- Enhancements to composite partitioning

In the following sections, I describe each of the partitioning enhancements.

Interval Partitioning

Interval partitioning is an extension of the familiar range partitioning scheme. Range partitioning is ideal for partitioning historical data. You use range partitioning to organize data by time intervals on a column of type DATE. The boundaries you set for the range partitions determine how the database orders the partitions in the table or indexes. Let's first briefly review range partitioning, as interval partitioning is an extension of the range partitioning scheme.

Range partitioning is Oracle's most common partitioning scheme and you use it mostly with data involving dates. For example, if your query is something like: "Select data from a period that is 18 months in the past," you can employ interval partitioning to cut back drastically on the amount of data the database needs to scan. If you divide your table into partitions representing data for a single month, the database has to scan only a small fraction of the table's data. This method of limiting the data to be scanned by the database is an optimization method called *partition pruning*.

Under range partitioning, you map data to different partitions in a table based on a range of values for each partition. You set the range of values by specifying a partition key for each partition. For example, when you use the DATE column as the partitioning key for a table, the December-2008 partition will include all rows where the date column has values ranging from 01-DEC-2008 to 31-DEC-2008. Each of the partitions will have a `value less than` clause that specifies a (non-inclusive) upper bound for the date column values. Any rows with a date column value higher than this upper bound value are added to the next partition. Thus, the partitions will contain successively higher values of the date column. Under range partitioning, you can also define a `maxvalue` literal for the highest partition. The `maxvalue` is a virtual infinite value that is larger than any possible value for the partitioning key.

Think of interval partitioning as the old range partitioning, with the partitions defined by an interval after a set point, although the table or index starts off as a range partitioned table. Under range partitioning, you had to explicitly define the range of values for each partition. As the number of partitions grows, explicitly defining the partition bounds is not an easy task. This is especially so in the case of range partitions covering small ranges, such as adding a new partition every day. If a user enters a row with the partition key value greater than the highest or most recent partition, the database issues an error and the insert operation fails. Interval partitioning takes the management of partitions completely out of the DBA's hands, by creating partitions on demand as the data is added to the table. The new internal partitioning automates the creation of range partitions. Interval partitioning tells the database to create partitions of the interval that you specify when new data exceeds all the range partitions.

In order to use interval partitioning, you must specify a minimum of one range partition. When you set up interval partitioning, the database will create range partitions for all the ranges you specified. The high value of the range partitions, called the *transition point*, determines when interval partitioning kicks in. In other words, the database will start off by creating one or more range partitions. Once the data reaches a value that's beyond the transition point, the database will start creating interval partitions. The following example makes this point clear:

```
SQL> create table interval_sales
     ( prod_id          number(6)
     , cust_id          number
     , time_id          date
     , channel_id       char(1)
     , promo_id         number(6)
     , quantity_sold    number(3)
     , amount_sold      number(10,2)
     )
   partition by range (time_id)
   interval(numtoyminterval(1, 'month'))
      (partition p0 values less than
      (to_date('1-1-2005', 'DD-MM-YYYY')),
       partition p1 values less than
      (to_date('1-1-2006', 'DD-MM-YYYY')),
       partition p2 values less than
      (to_date('1-7-2006', 'DD-MM-YYYY')),
       partition p3 values less than
      (to_date('1-1-2007', 'DD-MM-YYYY')) );
```

Note that in the `create table` statement, while the `partition` clause creates the mandatory range partition(s), it's the `interval` clause that sets up the interval partitions. The single argument to the `interval` clause, `numtoyminterval`, is a constant of the `interval` type. The `interval` clause instructs the database to create monthly partitions. In the example, the database will create four range partitions, with different widths for the partitions. The first four partitions, p0, p1, p2, and p3, are range partitioned, each with a width of one year. Once the transition point, which is the high value 1-1-2007 contained in partition p3 is reached, the database will start creating interval partitions, all with a width of one month. The new partition Pi1 is automatically created when a row with a `TIME_ID` value corresponding to January 2007 is inserted into the INTERVAL_SALES table.

on the Job

You can use the optional `store in` clause to instruct the database to store the interval partitions in multiple tablespaces, as shown here:

```
interval (numtoyminterval(1, 'MONTH'))
store in (TS1,TS2,TS3)
```

Remember that interval partitioning extends range partitioning by automating the creation of the range partitions. Instead of your having to add new range partitions daily, the database will automatically create new partitions as the data is inserted into the table. Each time the new data exceeds a range partition value, the database will automatically create a new partition with a width of one month.

Initially, before you insert any data, the INTERVAL_SALES table will show the following partitions.

```
SQL> select partition_name, partitioning_type, high_value
     dba_tab_partitions
     where table_name ='INTERVAL_SALES'
     order by partition_position;


PARTITION_NAME PARTITIONING_TYPE HIGH_VALUE
-------------- ----------------- -----------------------------
P0             RANGE             TO_DATE('2005-01-01 00:00:00')
P1             RANGE             TO_DATE('2006-01-01 00:00:00')
P2             RANGE             TO_DATE('2005-07-01 00:00:00')
P1             RANGE             TO_DATE('2007-01-01 00:00:00')

4 rows selected.
SQL>
```

As you can see, initially there are only range partitions. This table in the example has four range partitions, but only a minimum of one range partition is required. Whether you choose to create the minimum necessary single range partition or more range partitions initially, the highest bound of the most recent range partition will be the transition point. In the example, the transition point is the high bound of the partition p3, which is 1-1-2007. Let's see what happens when I insert new data into the INTERVAL_SALES table whose ORDER_ID column values fall beyond 1-1-2007. When I insert the new data into the INTERVAL_SALES table, the insertion forces the creation of new partitions to accommodate the rows. These new partitions are interval partitions, created by the clause `interval(numtoyminterval(1, 'month'))` in the table creation statement. When I query the DBA_TAB_PARTITIONS views, this is what I see:

```
SQL> select partition_name, partitioning_type, high_value
     dba_tab_partitions
     where table_name ='INTERVAL_SALES'
     order by partition_position;


PARTITION_NAME PARTITIONING_TYPE  HIGH_VALUE
-------------- -----------------  -------------
P0             RANGE              TO_DATE('2005-01-01 00:00:00')
P1             RANGE              TO_DATE('2006-01-01 00:00:00')
```

```
P2              RANGE           TO_DATE('2005-07-01 00:00:00')
P1              RANGE           TO_DATE('2007-01-01 00:00:00')
SYS_P01         INTERVAL        TO_DATE('2007-02-01 00:00:00')
SYS_P02         INTERVAL        TO_DATE('2007-03-01 00:00:00')...
SQL>
```

When new data that has an ORDER_DATE column value higher than the maxvalue of the last range partition is inserted into the table, the database creates interval partitions to store the new data. The new interval partitions are created for monthly intervals. The database assigns system-generated names to the new interval partitions.

Note the following when you're considering interval partitioning:

- You can only specify a single partitioning key column, of the type NUMBER or DATE.
- You can perform interval partitioning on an index-organized table.
- You can't create domain indexes on an interval-partitioned table.

Moving the Transition Point

You can use Oracle's partition merging capability to merge any two adjacent interval partitions. You can even merge the very first interval partition with the highest range partition. When you merge any two adjacent partitions, the new partition you create will have as its upper bound the higher of the upper bounds of the merged partitions.

When you merge two adjacent interval partitions, the transition point automatically moves to the higher of the two upper bounds. Remember that the transition point is defined as the high value of the range partitions. Thus, whenever you merge any two interval partitions, the range partition component of the interval-partitioned table will move up to the higher bound of the two merged partitions. If you have any interval partitions with boundaries below this new merged partition, the database will automatically convert them into range partitions. Let's use the following example to make this automatic conversion of interval partitions clearer. The create table statement in the example creates the one mandatory range partition and a single interval partition.

```
SQL> create table transactions
     (id                 NUMBER
     , transaction_date DATE
     , value             NUMBER
     )
   partition by range (transaction_date)
   interval (numtodsinterval(1,'DAY'))
   (partition p_before_2008 values less than
   (to_date('01-JAN-2008','dd-MON-yyyy')));
```

Now let's insert some data into this table. The single range partition will accept all rows with a `transaction_date` value of 01-JAN-2008 or earlier. If you insert any rows with a date higher than 01-JAN-2008, the database will automatically create new interval partitions and insert the rows into those partitions. Because the `interval` clause specifies 1 day as the interval, the database will create a separate interval for each day after January 1, 2008. The following three `insert` statements insert data into three newly created adjacent partitions. The database will create the two partitions, give them a system-generated name, and place the three new rows in the three new partitions, all adjacent to one another.

```
insert into transactions values
(1,TO_DATE('15-JAN-2008','dd-MON-yyyy'),100);
insert into transactions values
(2,TO_DATE('16-JAN-2008','dd-MON-yyyy'),600);
insert into transactions values
(3,TO_DATE('30-JAN-2008','dd-MON-yyyy'),200);
```

Because you can merge any two adjacent interval partitions into a single partition, let's now merge the first two new partitions. You don't have to provide the names of the partitions because Oracle will automatically figure out the names of the partitions in the `merge partitions` clause by looking up their values and seeing which partitions they fall into. Here's the `alter table` statement to merge two partitions:

```
alter table transactions
merge partitions for(to_date('15-JAN-2008','dd-MON-yyyy'))
, for(to_date('16-JAN-2008','dd-MON-yyyy'));
```

The `alter table...merge` statement will do the following:

- Move the transition point for the table to January 17, 2008, which is the non-inclusive high value of the two merged partitions.

- Create a new range partition, combining the values of the partition key in the two merged partitions as the value for its own partition key. The partition key for this new range partition is January 17, 2008.

Where the database will place a newly inserted row will depend on the value of the TIME_ID column in that row:

- If the value of the TIME_ID column is less than 01-JAN-2008, the data goes into the first range partition.

- If the value of the TIME_ID column is between 01-JAN-2008 and 16-JAN-2008, both values inclusive, it will go into the newly created range partition.

■ If the value of the TIME_ID column is greater than JAN-17-2008, it will be placed in an interval partition.

Note that in Oracle Database 11g, the partition syntax is extended so that you can use it to refer to a partition without specifying a name for the partition. If you use a value that represents a possible value for the partition, the database will know which partition the value belongs to. You can use this new syntax for all partition management operations such as a `drop`, `truncate`, `merge`, and `split partition`. You can use the syntax not just for the new interval partitioning scheme, but also to existing range, list, and hash partitioning schemas. Here is an example of the new syntax:

```
SQL> select * from sales_data partition
     for (to_date('01-JUN-2008','dd-MON-yyyy'));
```

You use the new `for` clause to specify a value with which to directly reference a partition, instead of providing a partition name. In cases such as interval partitioning, where the database provides system-generated partitions, you may not even know the name of the partition you're interested in. The new syntax of addressing a partition indirectly by the values contained in it rather than by its name is of great help in cases like this.

When to Use Interval Partitioning

Because interval partitioning is an extension of range partitioning, if range partitioning is ideal for a situation, interval partitioning is ideal as well. Use interval partitioning in the following situations:

■ When your SQL statements that access a large table use a range predicate on a partitioning column such as ORDER_DATE, using interval partitioning helps you reap the benefits of partition pruning.

■ If you constantly load new data and purge old data to maintain a rolling window of data, interval partitioning is ideal because it lets the database automatically create new interval partitions as the data is inserted.

■ If you want to cut up a large table into smaller logical pieces to complete administrative operations in short maintenance windows, once again, interval partitioning is the way to go.

System Partitioning

System partitioning is quite different from all other types of data partitioning. System partitioning is meant to enable application controlled table partitioning. Just for starters, there aren't any partitioning keys when you use system partitioning. Under system partitioning the database lets you break a table down into meaningless partitions and you don't control the partitioning ranges for the actual data placement. The application controls the partitioning and actual data placement.

Because a system-partitioned table doesn't use partitioning keys, you can't direct the mapping of the rows to a particular partition. Instead, the application must specify the actual partition in which the database must place a row. Thus, `insert` statements must use the partition information explicitly. It's important to remind yourself that system partitioning doesn't use any partitioning method and thus can't distribute table rows to partitions. It's the application's job to do the data distribution to the partitions.

System partitioning provides the benefit of easier manageability that comes with equipartitioning a table. You can, for example, create a nested table as a system-partitioned table with the same partitions as the base table. System partitioning doesn't support the normal partition pruning and partition-wise joins like the other types of partitioned tables. You thus lose the performance benefits inherent in partitioning a table.

A System Partitioning Example

Use the `partition by system` clause to create a system-partitioned table. The following example shows you how to create a system-partitioned table:

```
SQL> create table test (c1 integer, c2 integer)
     partition by system
     (
     partition p1 tablespace tbs_1,
     partition p2 tablespace tbs_2,
     partition p3 tablespace tbs_3,
     partition p4 tablespace tbs_4
     );
```

The `partition by system` clause specifies system partitioning.

The big difference between a system-partitioned table and the other types of partitioned tables is seen during the insertion of data into the partitioned table. Unlike the traditional partitioned tables, when inserting data into a system-partitioned table, you must specify the specific partition into which you want to insert the new data. If you use the normal `insert` statement for other types of partitioned tables, it will fail, as shown here:

```
SQL> insert into test values (1,999);
insert into test values (1,999)
            *
ERROR at line 1:
ORA-14701: partition-extended name or bind variable must be
```

```
used for DMLs on tables partitioned by the System method
SQL>
```

Because there is no partitioning key under system partitioning, the database doesn't know into which partitions it should insert the new data. Thus, it issues an `error` when you issue an `insert` statement without any partition information. Because the partition bounds are unknown, you must provide that information using the new partitioning syntax that I explained earlier in this chapter. You'll recall that this new syntax lets you refer to a specific partition based on the values you cite for a column in the partitioned table. The following example shows you how to insert a row into our new system-partitioned table named TEST, using the new partitioning syntax:

```
SQL> insert into test partition (p1) values (1,999);
```

Note that it is mandatory to use the `partition` clause when inserting data into a system-partitioned table. The `insert` statement uses the partition-enhanced syntax (the `partition` clause) to tell the database into which partition it must insert the new row. In this case, the `insert` statement tells the database to insert the row in partition p1, but you could have chosen any of the four partitions that you created in the table TEST.

In addition to the `insert` statement, the `merge` statement also requires that you specify the partition-extended syntax to identify the partition into which you want the database to place the merged partition rows. Here's an example:

```
SQL> alter table test merge
       partitions p1,p2 into partition p1;
```

The previous statement specifies that the database must merge the partitions p1 and p2 into the partition p1. You don't have to specify the partition for a `delete` or `update` operation. However, Oracle recommends that you use the partitioned enhanced syntax as in the case of an `insert` statement. If you omit the `partition` clause during a `delete` or `update` statement, the statement will work fine. However, the database will have to scan the entire table because a system-partitioned table can't avail itself of the partition pruning capability, which reduces search time for data in other types of partitioning.

You can perform the following operations with a system-partitioned table:

- Partition maintenance operations
- All DML and DDL operations
- Creation of local indexes, as long as they are not unique
- Creation of local bitmapped indexes
- Creation of global indexes

Restrictions on System Partitioning

You can't use system partitioning for the `create table as select` (CTAS) operation. Because system partitioning can't distribute the rows to the partitions, your only alternative is to create a new table and insert the data from the source table, providing the partition names in the statement. For a similar reason, you can't employ system partitioning when using the `insert into table_name as` statement. However, you can use an `insert as select` operation with the partition extended syntax, as shown here:

```
SQL> insert into table_name
     partition (
     PartitionName)
     dataobj_to_partition(base_table, :physical_partid))
     as SubQuery...
```

You also can't use the `alter table split partition` and the `alter index split` partition operations with a system-partitioned table.

Virtual Column-Based Partitioning

Oracle Database 11g lets you include a virtual column in a table. Unlike normal columns, a virtual column's values aren't inserted directly into a table. The column's values are derived on-the-fly by computing a function or an expression. Once you create a table with one or more virtual columns, you can then employ the new virtual column-based partitioning scheme to partition that table. Before I provide a virtual column-based partitioning example, let me first explain virtual columns in more detail.

The virtual column you specify is always based on computing an expression or a function based on one or more other columns in the same table. Once you create a virtual column, you can query it just as you do any other column.

Virtual columns have the following important features:

- You can index a virtual column.
- You can use a virtual column in all types of DDL and DML statements.
- The database doesn't store the values of the virtual column on disk because these values are only computed on-the-fly when you reference the virtual column.
- The datatype for a virtual column is optional. If you don't explicitly specify the datatype, the virtual column will inherit the same datatype as the underlying expression.
- You can collect optimizer statistics on a virtual column.
- You can partition a table or an index on a virtual column.

Creating a Table with a Virtual Column

You can create a virtual column either when you create a table, or later on, by using the `alter table` statement. There are two ways to create a virtual column. The first method, shown here, is to create the virtual column when you create the table:

```
SQL> create table hr.admin_emp (
        empno       NUMBER(5) PRIMARY KEY,
        ename       VARCHAR2(15) NOT NULL,
        ssn         NUMBER(9) ENCRYPT,
        job         VARCHAR2(10),
        mgr         NUMBER(5),
        hiredate    DATE DEFAULT (sysdate),
        photo       BLOB,
        sal         NUMBER(7,2),
        hrly_rate   NUMBER(7,2) GENERATED ALWAYS
                    AS (sal/2080),
        comm        NUMBER(7,2),
        deptno      NUMBER(3) NOT NULL
     );
```

The column HRLY_RATE is a virtual column. You must specify the `generated always as` clause when you create a virtual column. Actually, the `generated always` part of this clause is optional. The `generated always` clause tells us that the database doesn't store the column values on disk, but rather, generates them only when a SQL statement refers to this virtual column. The last part of the clause (`as`) shows the expression the database uses to compute the values for the virtual column. In this example, the values of the HRLY_RATE column are generated from the SAL column, by computing the expression sal/2080. Because the SAL column provides the annual salary, the expression sal/2080 gives you the hourly salary for an employee.

The following restrictions apply to the creation of a virtual column:

- You create a virtual column only on a heap table, which is the normal Oracle table. You can't create a virtual column on an index-organized, temporary, external, object, or cluster table.
- A virtual column can't refer to another virtual column.
- A virtual column can be built only on the columns from the same table as the virtual column is in.
- The output of the virtual column must always be a scalar value.
- The virtual column can't be an Oracle-supplied datatype or a user-defined type, LOB, or `LONG RAW` type.

Note that you can't directly update a virtual column. That is, the following statement would fail if we assume that HRLY_RATE is a virtual column:

```
SQL> update table employees
     set hrly_rate ...
```

You can, however, specify a virtual column in the `where` clause of an `update` statement. Similarly, you can specify a virtual column in the `where` clause of a `delete` statement.

The second way to create a virtual column is to do so after table creation, by using the `alter table` statement, as shown here:

```
SQL> alter table employees add (income AS
     (salary + (salary*commission_pct)));
```

All the restrictions that apply in the case of creating a virtual column through a `create table` statement apply in this case as well.

Now that you have learned how to create a virtual column and what you can and can't do with a virtual column, let's turn to the partitioning of a table based on a virtual column.

Partitioning a Table on a Virtual Column

Sometimes, a business requirement to logically partition a table may not match any of the existing columns in the table. In cases such as these, you can devise a partitioning strategy based on one or more virtual columns, thus enabling a better match between business requirements and data. When you partition on a virtual column of a table, you can think of the virtual column as any other column. You can use all the available partitioning methods, including composite partitioning methods, with a virtual column.

on the
job

Make sure that the virtual column you want to use for partitioning doesn't use calls to a PL/SQL function. These types of columns are ineligible for partitioning.

Following is an example that shows how to partition a table using a range-range composite partitioning scheme on a virtual column. The example uses the virtual column for the subpartitioning key. The virtual column TOTAL_AMOUNT calculates the total value of sales using an expression that multiplies the AMOUNT_SOLD and the QUANTITY_SOLD columns.

```
SQL> create table sales
     ( prod_id       NUMBER(6) NOT NULL
     , cust_id       NUMBER NOT NULL
```

```
        , time_id        DATE NOT NULL
        , channel_id     CHAR(1) NOT NULL
        , promo_id       NUMBER(6) NOT NULL
        , quantity_sold  NUMBER(3) NOT NULL
        , amount_sold    NUMBER(10,2) NOT NULL
        , total_amount AS (quantity_sold * amount_sold)
        )
    partition by range (time_id)
    interval (numtoyminterval(1,'month'))
    subpartition by range(total_amount)
    subpartition template
        (subpartition p_small values less than (1000)
        , subpartition p_medium values less than (5000)
        , subpartition p_large values less than (10000)
        , subpartition p_extreme values less than (maxvalue)
        )
    (partition sales_before_2008 values less than
            (to_date('01-JAN-2008','dd-MON-yyyy'))
    )
    enable row movement;
```

This example shows a range-range partitioning scheme (this is a new composite partitioning scheme in Oracle Database 11g, and I explain this in detail later in this chapter). The original range partitioning is on the TIME_ID column. The subpartitioning is also range partitioning, on the virtual column named TOTAL_AMOUNT. What you must remember is that the values for the TOTAL_AMOUNT column are never directly inserted into the table. Because it is a virtual column, the TOTAL_AMOUNT column's values are generated dynamically based on the values inserted for the columns QUANTITY_SOLD and AMOUNT_SOLD, which are used to generate the TOTAL_AMOUNT column. The last line of the code in the example shows that you can specify row movement when partitioning on a virtual column. When you enable row movement, if the virtual column's value belongs to another partition, a row migrates to the appropriate partition from its current partition.

Reference Partitioning

Reference partitioning is a new partitioning scheme in Oracle Database 11g that lets you partition a table on the basis of the partitioning scheme of the table that its reference constraint refers to. Reference partitioning is probably the hardest new partitioning scheme to grasp. The partitioning key is determined through the parent-child relationship between the tables, as enforced by the active primary key or foreign key constraints. Reference partitioning thus lets you logically equipartition a table inheriting the partitioning the key from its parent table. You thus don't have to duplicate the key columns. Partition maintenance operations are no problem because the database automatically maintains the logical dependency between the two tables during those operations.

Let's walk through a reference partitioning example by looking at two tables, ORDERS and ORDER_ITEMS, which are related by a referential constraint. The referential constraint is named orderid.refconstraint. This constraint reflects the fact that the ORDER_ITEMS table's column ORDER_ID references the ORDER_ID column in the ORDERS table. Figure 5-2 shows that the foreign key references the ORDER_ID column in the ORDERS table. Let's say you partition the ORDERS table by range on the ORDER_DATE column. If you then use reference partitioning on the orderid.refconstraint for ORDER_ITEMS, it will create a partitioned table that is equipartitioned with respect to the ORDERS table.

If you used a non-reference partitioning scheme to partition the ORDERS and ORDER_ITEMS table to equipartition on the ORDER_DATE column, both tables must define the ORDER_DATE column, of course. Because we know there is a primary key/foreign key relationship between the two tables, however, it is redundant to define the ORDER_DATE column in the ORDER_ITEMS table as

FIGURE 5-2 The ORDER_ITEMS table's columns and its constraints

le: OE.ORDER_ITEMS

Actions Create Like [ ] (Go) (Edit) (OK)

Name **ORDER_ITEMS**
Schema **OE**
Tablespace **EXAMPLE**
Organization **Standard (Heap Organized)**

s

Name	Data Type	Size	Scale	Not NULL	Default Value	Encrypted
ORDER_ID	NUMBER	12		☑		☐
LINE_ITEM_ID	NUMBER	3		☑		☐
PRODUCT_ID	NUMBER	6		☑		☐
UNIT_PRICE	NUMBER	8	2	☐		☐
QUANTITY	NUMBER	8		☐		☐

es a Primary Key column
es a Unique Key column
ates a Secure File LOB column

ints

⊚ Previous **1-5 of**

	Type	Table Columns	Disabled	Deferrable	Initially Deferred	Validate	RELY	Check Condition	Referenced Schema	Referenced Table	Referenced Table Columns
TEMS_ORDER_ID_FK	FOREIGN	ORDER_ID	NO	NO	NO	NO	NO		OE	ORDERS	ORDER_ID
TEMS_PK	PRIMARY	ORDER_ID, LINE_ITEM_ID	NO	NO	NO	YES	NO				
TEMS_PRODUCT_ID_FK	FOREIGN	PRODUCT_ID	NO	NO	NO	YES	NO		OE	PRODUCT_INFORMATION	PRODUCT_II

well. Reference partitioning lets you define the ORDER_ITEMS column only in the ORDERS table. The ORDER_ITEMS table will then inherit its partition key from the existing primary key/foreign key relationship. You thus take advantage of the relationship between the two tables to avoid duplicating the key columns, which entails unnecessary storage and maintenance overhead.

on the job

You can't use interval partitioning with reference partitioning.

Unlike in Oracle Database 10g, where partition-wise joins would work only if the partitioning and predicates were identical, reference partitioning has no such limitation. That is, a partition-wise join will work even when query predicates are different. For example, you can partition on the ORDER_DATE column and issue a query on ORDER_ITEMS.

A Reference Partitioning Example

The first thing you must do is ensure that the referential constraint between the two tables is created, enabled, and enforced. You create a reference-partitioned table by specifying the clause `partition by reference`. You must specify the name of the referential constraint in this clause when you create the reference-partitioned table. It is this referential constraint that will be the basis for the reference partitioning and used as the partitioning referential constraint.

The following example shows you how to create a reference-partitioned table.

```
SQL> CREATE TABLE ORDERS
       ( order_id              NUMBER(12),
         order_date            TIMESTAMP WITH LOCAL TIME ZONE,
         order_mode            VARCHAR2(8),
         customer_id           NUMBER(6),
         order_status          NUMBER(2),
         order_total           NUMBER(8,2),
         sales_rep_id          NUMBER(6),
         promotion_id          NUMBER(6),
         CONSTRAINT orders_pk PRIMARY KEY(order_id)
       )
     PARTITION BY RANGE(order_date)
       ( PARTITION Q1_2008 VALUES LESS THAN
       (TO_DATE('01-APR-2008','DD-MON-YYYY')),
         PARTITION Q2_2008 VALUES LESS THAN
       (TO_DATE('01-JUL-2008','DD-MON-YYYY')),
         PARTITION Q3_2008 VALUES LESS THAN
       (TO_DATE('01-OCT-2008','DD-MON-YYYY')),
         PARTITION Q4_2008 VALUES LESS THAN
       (TO_DATE('01-JAN-2009','DD-MON-YYYY'))
       );
```

The previous `create table` statement creates the parent table ORDERS, which is range-partitioned on the ORDER_DATE column. There are four partitions in the ORDERS table, based on the ORDER_DATE partitioning key.

Because you know that the ORDER_ITEMS table is a child table of the parent table ORDERS, you can use reference partitioning to partition the ORDER_ITEMS table, as shown here:

```
CREATE TABLE ORDER_ITEMS
    ( order_id            NUMBER(12) NOT NULL,
      line_item_id        NUMBER(3)  NOT NULL,
      product_id          NUMBER(6)  NOT NULL,
      unit_price          NUMBER(8,2),
      quantity            NUMBER(8),
      CONSTRAINT ORDER_ITEMS_fk
      FOREIGN KEY(order_id) REFERENCES orders(order_id)
    )
    PARTITION BY REFERENCE(ORDER_ITEMS_fk);
```

on the **ⓘob**

You must ensure that the foreign key relationship between the master and the reference table is enabled and enforced in order to use reference partitioning.

The ORDER_DATE column appears only in the parent table ORDERS and isn't repeated in the child table ORDER_ITEMS. The clause `partition by reference` in the reference-partitioned child table simply inherits the partitioning key from the parent table ORDERS to perform the partitioning of the table. Thus, we don't duplicate the ORDER_DATE column in the child table. The child table ORDER_ITEMS is also created with the same four partitions as the parent table— Q1_2008, Q2_2008, Q3_2008, and Q4_2008. Each of these four partitions contains the same ORDER_ITEMS rows as the corresponding partition in the parent table ORDERS.

The new table will have one partition for each partition in the parent table. If the parent table is subpartitioned, the new partitioned table will have one partition for each subpartition in the parent table. Note the following:

- If you don't specify a tablespace for the new table, the database creates its partitions in the same tablespace as the corresponding partition of the parent table. In a partitioned table in an Oracle database, by default, the database creates the partitions in the same tablespace as that of the parent table.

- You can't specify partition bounds for the partitions of a reference-partitioned table.

- You can name the partitions of a reference-partitioned table as long as there's no conflict with any inherited names. In the case of a conflict, the database will assign the partition a system-generated name.

- You can't disable the foreign key constraint of a reference-partitioned table.
- You can't directly perform a partition management operation such as adding or dropping a partition belonging to a reference partitioned table. However, when you perform a partition maintenance operation on the parent table, the operation automatically cascades to the child table.

You don't see a high value for the partitions in the child table ORDER_ITEMS, as shown by the following query.

```
SQL> select partition_name, high_value
     from dba_tab_partitions
     where table_name = 'ORDER_ITEMS'';

PARTITION_NAME   HIGH_VALUE
--------------   ----------
P1
P2
SQL>
```

You don't see a high value because the child table derives the partition boundaries from the parent table. You can use the following query to view information about the reference partitioned table ORDER_ITEMS:

```
SQL> select table_name,partitioning_type,
     ref_ptn_constraint_name
     from dba_part_tables
     where table_name in ('ORDERS','ORDER_ITEMS');
```

TABLE_NAME	PARTITION	REF_PTN_CONSTRAINT_NAME
ORDERS	RANGE	
ORDER_ITEMS	REFERENCE	ORDER_ITEMS_ORDERS_FK

```
2 rows selected.
SQL>
```

The partitions for the child table are named the same as the parent table's partitions. The PARTITION column shows the type of partitioning and it shows RANGE for the parent table ORDERS, and REFERENCE for the partitioned table ORDER_ITEMS. The REF_PTN_CONSTRAINT_NAME column shows the name of the foreign key constraints used to partition the child table.

The following query shows how the ORDERS and ORDER_ITEMS tables share the same partitions:

```
SQL> select table_name,partition_name,high_value
     from dba_tab_partitions
     where table_name in ('ORDERS','ORDER_ITEMS')
     order by partition_position,table_name;
```

```
TABLE_NAME    PARTITION_NAME   HIGH_VALUE
-----------   --------------   -----------------------------
ORDERS        P_2006_JAN       TO_DATE ('2006-02-01 00:00:00')
ORDER_ITEMS   P_2006_JAN
SQL>
```

You manage a reference partitioned table just as you would a normal partitioned table. Whenever you add a partition to the ORDERS table, the ORDER_ITEMS table automatically inherits that partition. The following example shows this:

```
SQL> alter table orders
     add partition p2007_01
     values less than (to_date('01-feb-2007','dd-mon-yyyy'))
     tablespace test

Table altered.
SQL>
```

You can issue the following query next, to see how the parent and child table partitions are co-located:

```
SQL> select table_name, partition_name,
     tablespace_name,high_value
     from dba_tab_partitions
     where table_name in ('ORDERS','ORDER_ITEMS')
     order by partition_position,table_name;
```

TABLE_NAME	PARTITION_NAME	TABLESPACE	HIGH_VALUE
ORDERS	P2007_01	TEST	TO_DATE ('2007-02-01 00:00')
ORDER_ITEMS	P2007_01	TEST	

When to Use Reference Partitioning

You can benefit from reference partitioning in the following types of situations:

- Whenever you are thinking of duplicating a column in a child table to get partition pruning benefits, you might want to consider reference partitioning instead. For example, you might want to duplicate a column such as ORDER_DATE that's already in the parent table ORDERS, in the child table ORDER_ITEMS, so the ORDER_ITEMS table can utilize partition pruning. With reference partitioning, you can avoid this duplication of data. When a query joins the ORDERS and ORDER_ITEMS tables and uses a predicate on the ORDER_ITEMS column, it automatically takes advantage of the partition pruning for both tables.

■ In cases where you frequently join two large tables that aren't partitioned on the join key, you can use reference partitioning to take advantage of partition-wise joins. This is because reference partitioning implicitly enables the use of full partition-wise joins.

■ Reference partitioning helps manage tables that share the same life cycle, by automatically cascading partition operations on the master table to its descendants.

Composite Partitioning Enhancements

In previous releases, you could use only range partitioning as the top-level partitioning method. Thus, the only composite partitioning methods that you could use were the range-list and range-hash partitioning schemes. In Oracle Database 11g, you can also use the list partitioning and the new interval partitioning method as top-level partitioning methods. You can thus use the following composite partitioning methods:

■ Range-list

■ Range-hash

■ List-list

■ List-hash

■ List-range

■ Range-range

■ Interval-range

■ Interval-list

■ Interval-hash

Creating a Composite Interval-Range Partitioned Table

You must use subpartition templates to define range subpartitions for future interval partitions. Without a subpartition template, you will be able to create only range subpartition with a `maxvalue` upper boundary for every interval partition.

The following example shows you how to create a composite interval-list partitioned table (as is the case for all interval-partitioned tables, you start with at least one range partition). I use daily intervals on the TIME_ID column for the interval partitioning and the CHANNEL_ID column for the list subpartitioning.

I use a partition template to subpartition the table, with CHANNEL_ID as the partitioning key.

```
SQL> CREATE TABLE sales
     (prod_id        NUMBER(6)
     , cust_id       NUMBER
     , time_id       DATE
     , channel_id    CHAR(1)
     , promo_id      NUMBER(6)
     , quantity_sold NUMBER(3)
     , amount_sold   NUMBER(10,2)
     )
  PARTITION BY RANGE (time_id)
  INTERVAL (NUMTODSINTERVAL(1,'DAY'))
  SUBPARTITION BY LIST (channel_id)
    SUBPARTITION TEMPLATE
    (SUBPARTITION p_catalog VALUES ('C')
     SUBPARTITION p_internet VALUES ('I')
     SUBPARTITION p_partners VALUES ('P')
     SUBPARTITION p_direct_sales VALUES ('S')
     SUBPARTITION p_tele_sales VALUES ('T')
    )
  (PARTITION before_2000 VALUES LESS THAN (
   TO_DATE('01-JAN-2000','dd-MON-yyyy')))
  PARALLEL;
```

Because I use a template in this example, all the partitions will have an equal number of subpartitions, with identical bounds specified by the template. If you don't specify a partition template, the database creates a single default partition, with a maxvalue upper bound for the range partition or the default value for the list partition. This example illustrates the interval-list composite partitioning technique. The other new composite partitioning methods use a similar syntax. In addition, all the new composite methods support partition pruning for all queries on the subpartitioning key.

Creating a Composite Range-Range Partitioned Table

Here's an example that shows how to use range-range partitioning to logically partition a table along two dimensions. Composite range-range partitioning enables you to partition a table in tune with your business needs. The original range partitioning is on the ORDER_DATE column and the subpartitioning, which is also a range partition, is on the SHIP_DATE column.

```
SQL> create table shipments
(order_id number not null,
order_date date not null,
ship_date date not null,
customer_id number not null,
sales_amount number not null)
partition by range (order_date)
subpartition by range (ship_date)
( partition p_2008_jul values
less than (to_date('01-AUG-2008','dd-MON-yyyy'))
( subpartition p_2008_jul_early values
less than (to_date('15-AUG-2008','dd-MON-yyyy')),
subpartition p_2008_jul_agreed values
less than to_date('01-SEP-2008','dd-MON-yyyy')),
subpartition p_2008_jul_late values less than (maxvalue)
),
( partition p_2008_aug values
less than (to_date('01-SEP-2008','dd-MON-yyyy'))
( subpartition p_2008_aug_early values
less than (to_date('15-SEP-2008','dd-MON-yyyy')),
subpartition p_2008_aug_agreed values
less than to_date('01-OCT-2008','dd-MON-yyyy')),
subpartition p_2008_jul_late values less than (maxvalue)
),
( partition p_2008_sep values
less than (to_date('01-OCT-2008','dd-MON-yyyy'))
( subpartition p_2008_sep_early values
less than (to_date('15-OCT-2008','dd-MON-yyyy')),
subpartition p_2008_sep_agreed values
less than to_date('01-NOV-2008','dd-MON-yyyy')),
subpartition p_2008_jul_late values less than (maxvalue)
));
Table created.
SQL>
```

The example first creates range partitions for each month based on the ORDER_DATE column. Each of these monthly partitions is then subpartitioned by range in the SHIP_DATE column, into two partitions. The example shows how to take each month's orders and put them into three different partitions, the first one storing the orders that were delivered before the promised delivery date, the second partition storing orders delivered in the agreed upon time frame, and the last partition storing deliveries that were made after the promised delivery date.

INSIDE THE EXAM

Review the important new ASM features such as fast mirror resync, preferred mirror read, and variable extents. You must understand how to set up the ASM fast mirror resync feature, including things such as when to take disks offline and online. Expect questions on using the `disk_repair_time` attribute of the `alter diskgroup` command. What is the default value for this attribute?

The exam will test your understanding of the ASM compatibility and the RDBMS compatibility levels. You must know whether a disk group can be managed by ASM software from a certain release based on the ASM and RDBMS compatibility levels.

Understand how the enhanced disk group checks work. For example, what are the additional checks performed in the new release? How do the different clauses of the `check` command (such as `repair` and `norepair`) work? The exam will test your understanding of the new restricted mode of mounting a disk group as well as the `mount force` option and the `drop diskgroup...force`

command. You must understand the way the `lsdsk` command works, including how it works in the connected and nonconnected modes.

Expect a question or two on the `md_backup` and `md_restore` commands. Review the various flags you can specify for both commands and their meanings.

In terms of the new partitioning methods, there will be questions on the new interval partitioning method. You must know how interval partitioning relates to the old range partitioning. Expect a question on the role a transition point plays in creating an interval partitioned table. How do you move a transition point? Similarly, you can expect to be queried about the new system and reference partitioning methods. Pay particular attention to how system partitioning is different from all other types of Oracle partitioning methods in that it doesn't use a partitioning key and how reference partitioning relies on an existing referential constraint. Understand how a virtual column works and how you can partition a table on a virtual column.

CERTIFICATION SUMMARY

ASM's fast mirror resync feature lowers the overhead involved in resynchronizing the disk system following a transient disk failure. You can use the `disk_repair_time` attribute to specify how long ASM can wait for you to complete a disk repair. The default value for the `disk_repair_time` attribute is 3.6 hours. The ASM preferred mirror read feature lets ASM read from a local copy of an extent in cases when it is efficient to do so. You use the initialization parameter `asm_preferred_read_failure_groups` to specify the list of preferred mirrored read failure group names.

ASM scalability and performance enhancements include the new variable size extents feature, which raises the maximum ASM file size while reducing the memory requirements. The new SYSASM privilege is meant to separate the management of ASM and the database. The new `compatible.asm` attribute determines ASM compatibility, and the `compatible.rdbms attribute` determines the RDBMS compatibility.

There are improvements in several ASM commands such as the `check` command. The `check` command in Oracle Database 11g is simpler and checks all metadata directories by default. The new restricted mount mode lets you perform maintenance tasks without incurring an overhead. The new `force` option when mounting a disk group is necessary to automatically mount an incomplete disk group. You can use the new `drop disk group force` command to drop a disk group that can't be mounted by an ASM instance. There are also enhancements in the `cp` and `lsdsk` commands. The new ASM metadata backup and restore feature enables you to back up and restore ASM metadata easily by using the `md_backup` and `md_restore` commands.

Interval partitioning is an extension of the range partitioning scheme and lets the database automatically create interval partitions as new data is inserted into a table. System partitioning enables application-controlled table partitioning. You don't use any partitioning keys under system partitioning, with the application controlling the partitioning and actual data placement. Virtual column–based partitioning enables you to create partitions based on a virtual column. Reference partitioning enables you to partition a table on the basis of the partitioning scheme of another table that the first table's reference constraint points to. Reference partitioning lets you avoid storing the same data in two different tables, if the two tables are related to each other.

✓ TWO-MINUTE DRILL

Automatic Storage Management New Features

❑ The ASM fast mirror resync feature lowers the overhead involved in resynchronizing a failed disk.

❑ ASM tracks the changed extents on a disk during a temporary failure and uses these extents to resynchronize just the changed extents.

❑ When you enable the fast mirror resync feature, the database takes a failed disk offline but doesn't drop it.

❑ You enable the fast mirror resync capability by setting the `disk_repair_time` attribute for a disk group. When you bring a disk online, initially the database allows only write operations to the disk. After it resynchronizes the disk, it allows read operations.

❑ You can specify the `drop after` clause in an `alter diskgroup` statement to override the time you specify with the `disk_repair_time` attribute.

❑ You can specify the `force` option to drop a disk group that you are unable to repair.

❑ The ASM preferred mirror read capability lets you specify a list of preferred mirror read names.

❑ By setting up preferred mirror read capability, each node will read from its local extents, leading to a better performance.

❑ Use the initialization parameter `asm_preferred_read_failure_groups` to configure the preferred mirror read capability.

❑ In a two-site stretch cluster, with normal redundancy, each instance can specify, at most, one failure group as its preferred read failure group.

❑ In a two-site stretch cluster, with high redundancy, you can specify both local failure groups as preferred read failure groups.

❑ In a three-site stretch cluster, you must use a high redundancy disk group with three failure groups.

❑ You can set variable size extents for extents of size 1, 4, 16, 32, and 64 megabytes.

❑ Oracle recommends that you use the new SYSASM system privilege to administer an ASM instance.

❑ The disk group compatibility feature lets an Oracle Database 10g client use a disk group created under Oracle Database 11g.

❑ The `compatible.asm` attribute determines ASM compatibility and controls ASM metadata on disk structures.

❑ The `compatible.rdbms` attribute determines the RDBMS client and controls the minimum Oracle Database version for the RDBMS instance.

❑ The value for the `compatible.asm` attribute must be at least equal to the value of the `compatible.rdbms` attribute.

❑ The default value for both the `compatible.asm` and the `compatible.rdbms` attributes is 10.1.

❑ You can't revert to the older RDBMS version once you advance the `compatible.rdbms` attribute.

❑ You must first advance the `compatible.asm` attribute before advancing the `compatible.rdbms` attribute.

❑ You can use the new `attribute` clause to change the AU size, RDBMS and ASM compatibility, disk repair time, template redundancy, and template striping for a disk group.

❑ The `check` command in Oracle Database 11g has been enhanced to perform additional checks such as testing for disk consistency, and checking the file extents maps, the alias metadata directory, and so on.

❑ You can use the new restrict mode to mount a disk group when you want to perform maintenance operations on a disk group.

❑ Issue the `startup restrict` command to start an entire ASM instance in the restricted mode.

❑ You must specify the `force` option for the database to automatically mount an incomplete disk group.

❑ Use the `drop disk group force` command to drop a disk group that an ASM instance can't mount.

❑ The new command `md_backup` lets you back up ASM metadata for a disk group.

❑ The `md_restore` command lets you restore the ASM metadata for a disk group.

❑ The `full` option for the `md_backup` command creates the disk group and restores the metadata, whereas the `nodg` option just restores the data.

❑ The `newdg` option creates a disk group but with a different name and also restores the metadata.

Partitioning Enhancements

❑ Interval partitioning is an extension of the range partitioning scheme.

❑ Interval partitioning automates the creation of range partitions.

❑ You must specify at least one range partition when using the interval partitioning scheme.

❑ The high value for the range partitions in an interval-partitioned table is called the transition point because the table transitions into interval partitioning at this point.

❑ When you merge two interval partitions, the transition point automatically moves to the higher of the two upper bounds for the partitions.

❑ The partition syntax is extended so you can refer to a partition by specifying a value that falls into that partition, without providing a name for the partition.

❑ In system partitioning, it's the application and not the DBA that controls the partitioning and actual data placement.

❑ System partitioning doesn't use partitioning keys and therefore you can't map rows to partitions.

❑ In system partitioning, you must specify the partition information when using an `insert` statement.

❑ System partitioning hurts performance because it doesn't provide the normal partition pruning and partition wise joins.

❑ Reference partitioning enables you to partition a child table according to the partitioning scheme of the table that the child table references.

❑ Reference partitioning lets you avoid duplicating data into two related tables.

❑ You can't use interval partitioning with reference partitioning.

❑ Reference partitioning automatically cascades partitioning operations on the master table to the descendant tables.

❑ You have more composite partitioning schemes available in Oracle Database 11g because you can use the list and interval partitioning schemes as top-level partitioning methods now.

SELF TEST

Automatic Storage Management New Features

1. When you enable the ASM fast mirror resync feature, the database
   A. Will take an affected disk offline and never drop it.
   B. Will take an affected disk offline first and then drop it.
   C. Will never take an affected disk offline.
   D. Will drop the disk online, without taking it offline.

2. How many failure groups can you configure in a preferred read failure group, when using normal redundancy in a two-site stretch cluster?
   A. At least two
   B. Only one
   C. One or two
   D. Only two

3. When you're advancing disk compatibility in ASM, you
   A. Must first advance the `compatible.rdbms` attribute before the `compatible.asm` attribute
   B. Must advance the `compatible.asm` and the `compatible.rdbms` attributes at the same time
   C. Can only advance the `compatible.asm` attribute because you can't change the setting of the `compatible.rdbms` attribute
   D. Must first advance the `compatible.asm` attribute before the `compatible.rdbms` attribute.

4. Which of the following statements(s) is (are) correct?
   A. By default, the `mount diskgroup` operation uses a `noforce` option.
   B. By default, the `mount diskgroup` operation uses a `force` option.
   C. In Oracle Database 11*g*, ASM will automatically mount an incomplete disk group.
   D. In Oracle Database 11*g*, ASM will not automatically mount an incomplete disk group.

5. What do the `newdg` and the `nodg` flags stand for in the `md_restore` command?
   A. `newdg` stands for "create new group with the same name" and `nodg` stands for "don't create a disk group."
   B. `newdg` stands for "create new group with a new name" and `nodg` stands for "don't restore metadata for the disk group."
   C. `newdg` stands for "create new group with a new name" and `nodg` stands for "don't create a disk group."
   D. `newdg` stands for "create new group with a new name" and `nodg` stands for "restore metadata and create a disk group."

Partitioning Enhancements

6. There are no partitioning keys in

    A. Interval-range partitioning

    B. Interval partitioning

    C. Range-interval partitioning

    D. System partitioning

7. You can't name the partitions of a

    A. Reference-partitioned table

    B. System-partitioned table

    C. Interval-partitioned table

    D. Range-partitioned table

8. What are the three top-level partitioning methods when you are considering composite partitioning in Oracle Database 11*g*?

    A. Range, list, hash

    B. List, range, system

    C. Range, list, interval

    D. Range, list, reference

9. Which of the following is true when you're using interval partitioning?

    A. You must have at least one range partition before the database can create any interval partitions.

    B. The first partition is always an interval partition.

    C. The high value of the interval partitions is called the transition point.

    D. The high value of the range partitions is called the transition point.

10. If your database constantly gets new data and purges old data to maintain a rolling window of data, which of the following partitioning methods is ideal for it?

    A. System

    B. Reference

    C. Interval

    D. List

LAB QUESTION

You have a non-data issue in one of the disks that belongs to the ASM storage. You want to fix the problem and replace the disk through Database Control, by performing an ASM Fast Mirror Resync operation. What are the steps you must follow for this operation?

SELF TEST ANSWERS

Automatic Storage Management New Features

1. ☑ **B** is correct. When you enable the fast mirror resync feature, the database always takes the affected disk offline first. It then waits for the interval you specify with the `disk_repair_time` attribute and then drops the disks if you don't bring it online before the interval is up.
☒ **A** is incorrect because ASM will drop the disk after the time you specify with the `disk_repair_time` attribute. **C** is incorrect because the database does take the affected disk offline. **D** is incorrect because ASM doesn't drop a disk while it's still online.

2. ☑ **B** is correct because you can specify a maximum of one failure group in a preferred read failure group configuration for a two-site stretch cluster.
☒ **A, C,** and **D** are incorrect because you must specify only one failure group in a two-site stretch cluster.

3. ☑ **A** is correct because you must first advance the `compatible.asm` attribute before you can advance the `compatible.asm` attribute.
☒ **B, C,** and **D** are incorrect because you must first advance the `compatible.asm` attribute.

4. ☑ **A** and **D** are correct. **A** is correct because the `mount diskgroup` operation uses the `noforce` option, by default. ASM will mount a disk group only if the entire set of disks belonging to the disk group is available. **D** is correct because in Oracle Database 11g, ASM won't automatically mount an incomplete disk group.
☒ **B** is incorrect because the database uses the `noforce` option, not the `force` option, by default. **C** is incorrect because ASM will not automatically mount an incomplete disk in Oracle Database 11g.

5. ☑ **C** is correct because the `newdg` option specifies that ASM must create a new disk group with a new name, and the `nodg` option specifies that ASM must restore only the metadata.
☒ **A, B,** and **D** are incorrect because they specify either an incorrect or nonexistent value for the two flags.

Partitioning Enhancements

6. ☑ **D** is correct because there are no partitioning keys under system partitioning. The database creates arbitrary partitions instead of using a specific partitioning key as in the other partitioning methods.

⊠ **A, B,** and **C** are incorrect because all partitioning methods except system partitioning employ a partitioning key.

7. ☑ **B** and **C** are correct. **B** is correct because under system partitioning, the database creates arbitrary partitions into which it places the table data. **C** is correct because under interval partitioning, the database creates new interval-based partitions based on the values of the newly inserted data and the interval you specify with the `interval` clause in the `create table` statement. The database assigns system-generated names to the interval partitions it creates.
⊠ **A** and **D** are incorrect because you can name the partitions under each of these partitioning methods.

8. ☑ **A** is correct because the range, list, and hash partitioning methods are the only three top-level partitioning methods.
⊠ **B, C,** and **D** are incorrect because they all contain a partitioning method that you can't use as a top-level partitioning method in Oracle Database 11g.

9. ☑ **A** and **D** are correct. **A** is correct because you must always start off with a range partition before the database can create interval partitions. You can have as many range partitions as you like, but the minimum is one. **D** is correct because the max value of the range partitions is called the transition point. It is at this value that interval partitioning kicks in.
⊠ **B** is incorrect because under interval partitioning, the first partition must be a range partition. **C** is incorrect because it is the highest value of the range partitions that is called the transition point.

10. ☑ **C** is correct because interval partitioning is ideal for databases where new data is being constantly loaded and old data is being purged as well to maintain a rolling window of data. Interval partitioning allows the database to automatically create the new partitions as the new data is inserted into the partitioned table.
⊠ **A** is incorrect because system partitioning is ideal for cases where the developers want to maintain control over data placement instead of letting the database do it. **B** is incorrect because reference partitioning is ideal for related tables where you don't want to unnecessarily duplicate a column in a child table if the parent table that it references is already partitioned on that column. **D** is incorrect because list partitioning is ideal for data that contains discrete column values.

LAB ANSWER

Here are the steps you must follow to perform an ASM Fast Mirror Resync operation using Database Control.

1. Your first task is to take the affected disk offline. You do this by going to the Disk Group: DATA General page, selecting the affected disk, and clicking *offline*.

2. Change the Disk Repair Time on the Confirmation page to 0 from its default value of 3.6 hours. Click return.

3. At the Confirmation page, click Yes.

4. On the Disk Group: DATA General page, refresh the browser page until the offlined disk stops showing up.

5. Log in as the root user to wipe off the dropped disk, so you can add it back. Here's the dd command that will accomplish this:

```
$ dd if=/dev/zero of=asm_disk1 bs=1024k count=100
```

6. In this example, I'm using asm_disk1 as the name for the affected disk.

7. On the Disk Group: DATA General page, click Add.

8. On the Add Disk page, select the device for the disk you want to add—for example, /dev/raw/raw1 from the Member Disks table.

9. On the Add Disks page, click OK.

10. On the Disk Group: DATA General page, refresh the browser until the rebalance activity completes.

6
Performance Enhancements

CERTIFICATION OBJECTIVES

6.01   ADDM Enhancements

6.02   Automatic Memory Management

6.03   Enhancements in Optimizer Statistics
       Collection

6.04   Result Cache

6.05   Adaptive Cursor Sharing

✓   Two-Minute Drill

Q&A   Self Test

Oracle Database 11g introduces several powerful performance-related features, besides enhancing existing features such as the Automatic Database Diagnostic Monitor (ADDM). Among the most important of the new performance-related features is the server-side result cache, which stores the results of both SQL queries as well as PL/SQL functions. You can also use a new client-side caching feature in this release to improve performance and reduce the load on the server. Adaptive cursor sharing is a brand-new feature that seeks to resolve the tradeoffs of cursor sharing with the help of bind variables and query optimization.

The new release improves cost optimizer statistics collection by providing for the gathering of statistics for expressions and related columns. You can now run the ADDM in different modes. You can run it at the instance level as before, and you can also run it at the cluster level in an Oracle RAC environment. This chapter begins by reviewing the ADDM new features in Oracle 11g.

CERTIFICATION OBJECTIVE 6.01

ADDM Enhancements

The Automatic Database Diagnostic Monitor, which Oracle introduced in Oracle Database 10g, analyzes the AWR data, diagnoses the root causes for performance problems, and makes recommendations for fixing those problems. The database performs an ADDM analysis on a pair of AWR snapshots, which determine the time period for the ADDM analysis. In Oracle Database 11g, the ADDM has the following new features:

- ADDM for Real Application Clusters
- New DBMS_ADDM package
- Naming Advisor Findings and Directives
- New ADDM views

In the following sections, I explain the main ADDM enhancements in Oracle Database 11g.

ADDM for Real Application Clusters

In Oracle Database 11g, you can deploy the ADDM to perform a cluster-wide performance analysis. In addition to analyzing a single instance, you can now use the ADDM to analyze an entire Oracle Real Application Cluster (RAC). The traditional single instance–wide analysis you're familiar with from Oracle Database 10*g* is called *Instance ADDM* and the cluster-wide mode is called *Database ADDM*. The cluster-wide mode is a special mode of the ADDM, in which the tool reports on the performance of the entire cluster in addition to the individual instances in the cluster. When operating in an Oracle RAC environment, you can deploy ADDM in the following three analysis modes.

- **Database ADDM**   Analyze all instances of the RAC
- **Instance ADDM**   Analyzes a particular instance (equivalent to the Oracle Database 10*g* ADDM analysis)
- **Partial ADDM**   Analyzes a subset of the instances in the RAC

Of course, if you're not using a RAC environment, you have only one mode available—the *instance* mode.

Run the ADDM in the Database analysis mode if you're using an Oracle RAC system, to analyze performance of all instances in the database. The Database ADDM accesses the AWR data of all instances in the system and identifies critical performance problems for an entire RAC cluster. As with the single-instance ADDM that you're familiar with from Oracle Database 10*g*, Database ADDM runs automatically by default when a new AWR snapshot is taken by the database. In this mode, the ADDM will add the DB time for all instances in the RAC to come up with the DB time for the database. The Database analysis mode presents the problems and recommendations for each instance in a single report, instead of your having to peruse multiple reports for the same information.

In the Database mode (Database ADDM), the ADDM accesses the AWR data generated by all the instances in a RAC system to analyze the throughput performance of the entire cluster instead of any single instance in the cluster. Database ADDM performs an analysis of the following entries:

- Global resources such as global locks and global I/O usage
- High-load SQL
- Contention across the instances
- Global cache interconnect traffic
- Network latency issues
- Skew in instance response times

You can utilize Database ADDM's reports to analyze the entire RAC performance.

The ADDM will aggregate any findings across instances if they affect the entire database. If a finding pertains to a global resource such as I/O, that finding will be deemed as a global finding affecting multiple resources. On the other hand, if a finding pertains to a local resource such as a CPU-bound instance, it results in just a local finding for a single instance.

By default, Database ADDM analysis is performed automatically after each AWR snapshot. If you want, you can run the ADDM in the `partial` analysis mode by having the ADDM analyze only a subset of the instances in the cluster. Database ADDM is mainly targeted for use by DBAs so they can test the cluster performance as a whole, whereas Instance ADDM is more useful for application development to test application or system changes.

Automatic database diagnostic monitoring is enabled by default. You can control automatic database diagnostic monitoring by setting the `control_management_pack_access` parameter, which has the default value `diagnostic+tuning`. You must specify either the value `diagnostic` or the value `diagnostic+tuning` (default value) to enable the ADDM. If you set the value to `none`, you disable the ADDM. Of course, you must also ensure that the initialization parameter `statistics_level` is set to either `typical` or `all` (but not `basic`) to enable automatic database diagnostic monitoring.

New DBMS_ADDM Package

Oracle Database 11g introduces the DBMS_ADDM package to facilitate the managing of the ADDM. You can use the DBMS_ADDM package to create an ADDM task and view the results. The following list offers a brief description of the important procedures and functions of the DBMS_ADDM package:

- **ANALYZE_DB**   Creates a global ADDM task
- **ANALYZE_INST**   Creates an instance ADDM task
- **ANALYZE_PARTIAL**   Creates an ADDM task to analyze a set of instances
- **DELETE**   Deletes an ADDM task
- **GET_REPORT**   Gets a text report of an ADDM task

The following example shows how to create and execute a database ADDM task for an Oracle RAC configuration:

```
SQL> begin
  2   :tname := 'Test ADDM Run1';
  3   dbms_addm.analyze_db(:tname,1664,1665);
  4* end;
SQL> /
```

```
PL/SQL procedure successfully completed.
SQL>
```

In the example, I use the ANALYZE_DB procedure to create a global ADDM task that pertains to all instances in an Oracle RAC configuration. The numbers 1664 and 1665 are specified as values for the `begin_snapshot` and `end_snapshot` parameters for the ADDM analysis. You use the ANALYZE_INST procedure to run the ADDM in the Instance mode, to analyze a particular instance of a database. You execute the ANALYZE_PARTIAL procedure to run the ADDM in a Partial analysis mode, which analyzes a subset of all instances in the RAC system.

To get the ADDM report, use the DBMS_ADDM.GET_REPORT function, as shown here:

```
SET LONG 100000
SET PAGESIZE 50000
  1* select dbms_addm.get_report(:tname) from dual;
DBMS_ADDM.GET_REPORT(:TNAME)
-----------------------------------------------------------------
         ADDM Report for Task 'Test ADDM Run3'
         -----------------------------------
AWR snapshot range from 1664 to 1665.
Time period starts at 10-NOV-07 03.00.04 PM
Time period ends at 10-NOV-07 04.00.12 PM
Analysis Target
---------------
Database 'ORCL2' with DB ID 611115374.
Database version 11.1.0.6.0.
ADDM performed an analysis of instance orcl2,
numbered 1 and hosted at localhost.localdomain.
...
SQL>
```

Naming Advisor Findings and Directives

Oracle Database 11g classifies and names all ADDM advisor findings. The database stores the ADDM findings in the DBA_ADVISOR_FINDINGS and the USER_ADVISOR_FINDINGS views. The classification of ADDM findings enables you to query the DBA_ADVISOR_FINDINGS view to find which findings occur most frequently in the database. You can query the new DBA_ADVISOR_FINDING_NAMES view to see all the finding names, as shown here:

```
SQL> select finding_name from dba_advisor_finding_names;

FINDING_NAME
-----------------------------
normal, successful completion
```

```
"Administrative" Wait Class
"Application" Wait Class
"Cluster" Wait Class
"Concurrency" Wait Class
"
...80 rows selected.
SQL>
```

In Oracle Database 11g, you can create an ADDM task by inserting a *finding directive* to limit or filter the findings. The DBMS_ADDM package contains several "directive" procedures to add specific directives to create directives of various kinds. For example, the following code shows how to use the INSERT_FINDING_ DIRECTIVE procedure to stipulate that the ADDM report show an "Undersized SGA" finding only if it meets two specific conditions: The first condition specifies that the finding must be responsible for at least two average active sessions during the analysis period (MIN_ACTIVE_SESSIONS), and the second condition specifies that the finding must cover at least 10 percent of the total database time during the same period (MIN_PERC_IMPACT).

```
SQL> var tname varch2(60);
SQL> begin
     dbms_addm.insert_finding_directive(NULL,
     'SGA Directive',
     Undersized SGA',
     2,
     10);
     :tname := 'Test ADDM Task';
     dbms_addm.analyze_inst(:tname,1634,1635);
     end;
     /
```

The previous directive specifies that an undersized SGA finding be reported only if:

■ The finding is responsible for at least two average active sessions (MIN_ ACTIVE_SESSIONS) during the period of the ADDM analysis.

■ The finding constitutes at least 10 percent (MIN_PERC_IMPACT) of the total DB time during the period of the ADDM analysis.

In addition to the INSERT_FINDING_DIRECTIVE illustrated here, which helps you create a directive to limit the reporting of a specific finding type, you can also use the following ADDM directives:

■ **INSERT_SQL_DIRECTIVE**   Creates a directive to limit reporting of actions on specific SQL statements

■ **INSERT_SEGMENT_DIRECTIVE**   Creates a directive to prevent the ADDM from creating actions to run the Segment Advisor on certain segments

■ **INSERT_PARAMETER_DIRECTIVE**   Creates a directive to prevent the ADDM from creating actions that alter the value of a specific system parameter

You can delete any of the four INSERT_* procedures by replacing the `INSERT` with `DELETE` at the beginning of the procedure name. For example, you can execute the DELETE_FINDING_DIRECTIVE procedure to delete a finding directive you created through the INSERT_FINDING_DIRECTIVE procedure.

New ADDM Views

Oracle Database 11g introduces the following new ADDM views:

■ **DBA_ADDM_TASKS**   Shows all executed ADDM tasks

■ **DBA_ADDM_INSTANCES**   Shows instance-level information for all completed ADDM tasks

■ **DBA_ADDM_FINDINGS**   An extension of the corresponding advisor view

■ **DBA_ADVISOR_FINDING_NAMES**   Provides a list of all registered finding names

Each of the four views shown here also has a corresponding USER_* view associated with it. In addition, the DBA_ADVISOR_FINDINGS, DBA_ADVISOR_RECOMMENDATIONS, and DBA_ADVISOR_ACTIONS views have a new column named FILTERED, which shows if a row in the view was filtered out by a directive. If the FILTERED column shows a value of Y, it means that row was filtered out by a directive or directives. A value of N means the row wasn't filtered.

CERTIFICATION OBJECTIVE 6.02

Automatic Memory Management

Oracle database 10g offered you both automatic shared memory management and automatic PGA management. You could set two memory-related parameters, `sga_target` and `sga_max_target`, to control memory allocation to the SGA. You could use the `pga_aggregate_target` to enable the database to automatically manage the PGA memory available to the instance. Oracle Database 11g automates memory management even further, by introducing the *automatic memory management* feature. With automatic memory management, you set only a pair of new memory-related parameters—`memory_target` and `max_memory_target`, to manage both SGA and PGA. The database transfers memory between the SGA and PGA as necessary and automates the sizing of these two components according to the database workload. For the first time, Oracle unifies the SGA and PGA memory management and maximizes memory utilization by automatically adapting to workload changes, besides helping prevent out-of-memory errors. The operating system frees up the shared memory that's not being used by Oracle and allocates it to other components that request it.

on the **Job**

The automatic memory management feature is currently implemented on the Linux, Solaris, HP-UX, AIX, and Windows platforms.

The `memory_target` parameter is also known as the target memory size initialization parameter and the `memory_max_target` parameter, the maximum memory size initialization parameter. In order to convert to the new, automatic method of memory management, use the `memory_target` initialization parameter, as shown here:

```
SQL> alter system set memory_target=900M scope spfile;
```

If you've set the `sga_target` and the `pga_target` parameters previously, you must also use the following statements to set those two components to zero:

```
SQL> alter system set sga_target=0 scope=spfile;
SQL> alter system set pga_target=0 scope=spfile;
```

Once you execute the `alter system` statements, restart the instance for automatic memory management to take effect. You can also set a `memory_max_target` parameter in your parameter file to specify the upper bound of the `memory_target` parameter. Note that setting the `memory_target` parameter automates the sizing of both the SGA and the PGA. The `memory_target` parameter is dynamic, so you can change it while the instance is running. If you want, you can still set lower bound values for the individual components of the SGA, such as the shared pool and the database cache. If you decide to do so, these lower bounds will act as the minimum values below which the database can't size these caches. The database won't let you set the `memory_target` parameter below a specific level in order to enable adequate memory for certain SGA components that require a minimum size or that can't be easily shrunk.

Once you set automatic memory management, you can confirm the choice by using the `show parameter target` command, as shown here:

```
SQL> show parameter target
NAME                              TYPE          VALUE
--------------------              -----------   -------
archive_lag_target                integer            0
db_flashback_retention_target     integer         1440
fast_start_io_target              integer            0
fast_start_mttr_target            integer            0
memory_max_target                 big integer     252M
memory_target                     big integer     252M
pga_aggregate_target              big integer        0
sga_target                        big integer        0
SQL>
```

The two automatic memory related initialization parameters show positive values, which means that automatic memory management is enabled for this instance. Note that the values of the `memory_target` and `memory_max_target` parameters are identical. If you set the `memory_target` parameter but don't set the `memory_max_target` parameter, the value of the latter parameter defaults to the value you specify for the `memory_target` parameter. The `sga_target` and the `pga_target` parameters are `zero`, which means that manual or automatic shared memory management techniques are not in use. In addition, it also means that there are no DBA-set minimum levels for the SGA or the PGA.

SGA, PGA, and the MEMORY_TARGET Parameter

If you set the `memory_target` parameter to a positive value for an instance, the following is true:

■ If you don't set the `sga_target` and the `pga_aggregate_target` parameters, then the database will set the sizes for these two components and calibrate them according to the database workload. There are no minimum or default values for either the SGA or the PGA. The usual policy is to give 60 percent of the initial `memory_target` size to the SGA and 40 percent to the PGA component.

- If you also set the `sga_target` and the `pga_aggregate_target` parameters, the database will consider them the minimum values for the SGA and PGA allocations of memory. The `memory_target` parameter can take a value anywhere between the sum of SGA and PGA to the high value set by the `memory_max_target` parameter.

- If you set the SGA but not the PGA, the database will automatically tune both parameters and set the initial size of the PGA to the value of the `memory_target` parameter minus the value of the SGA (`memory_target` – SGA).

- If you set the PGA but not the SGA, the database will automatically tune both parameters and set the initial size of the SGA to the value of the minimum of the following two entities: value of the `memory_target` parameter minus the PGA and the `sga_max_target` parameter value, if you've set it.

on the
Job

If you exclude the `memory_max_target` parameter but use automatic memory management by setting the `memory_target` parameter, the database sets the `memory_max_target` parameter to the value of the `memory_target` parameter.

The default value of the `memory_target` parameter is zero. If you don't set the `memory_target` parameter or explicitly set it to zero, the following would be true:

- If you set neither the `pga_aggregate_target` nor the `sga_target` parameters, SGA is not automatically tuned, but the PGA is.

e x a m

watch
Review the relationships among the various memory-related initialization parameters such as `memory_target`, `memory_max_target`, `sga_target`, and `sga_max_size`. Can you set just one of the `memory_target` and `memory_max_target` parameters? What are the implications?

- If only the `sga_target` parameter is set, the database automatically tunes only the subcomponents of the SGA. PGA is auto-tuned whether you set it or not.

■ If you set the `memory_max_target` parameter in an initialization parameter file (init.ora) but not the `memory_target` parameter, the database will set the `memory_target` parameter's size to its default value of zero. That is, automatic memory management will be disabled.

If you set the `memory_target` parameter in the initialization parameter file but leave out the `memory_max_size` parameter, the database sets the `memory_max_size` parameter's value to that of the `memory_target_size` parameter.

EXERCISE 6-1

Using Automatic Memory Management

The following example shows how to set up automatic memory management and monitor how the database allocates memory to the various components of Oracle's memory allocation.

1. Set up automatic memory management by issuing the following statements

   ```
   SQL> alter system set pga_aggregate_target = 0    scope=spfile
   SQL> alter system set sga_target = 0    scope=spfile
   SQL> alter system set memory_target = 280M    scope=spfile
   SQL> alter system set memory_max_target = 900M    scope=spfile
   ```

2. Restart the database:

   ```
   SQL> shutdown immediate;
   SQL> startup
   ```

3. Confirm that the database is now using automatic memory management:

   ```
   SQL> show parameter target
   ```

   If the `memory_target` parameter shows a positive value, it means that the instance is set up for automatic memory management.

4. Check the current allocation of memory to the various components by issuing this query:

   ```
   SQL> select component, current_size, user_specified_size
      2  from v$memory_dynamic_components
      3* where current_size!=0;
   ```

   Make a note of the current allocations to the SGA, PGA, and the Large Pool components.

5. Execute a few SQL statements that use a lot of SGA memory, such as an expensive parallel query, for example, or an expensive PL/SQL code block that consumes a lot of PGA memory. Issue the following command:

```
SQL> select component, current_size, user_specified_size
  2  from v$memory_dynamic_components
  3* where current_size!=0;
```

You'll see the Large Pool grow at the expense of the buffer cache in the first case. In the second case (PL/SQL block execution), the database automatically raises the PGA component and shrinks the SGA component. When you use automatic memory management, the database automatically shrinks and grows the component that requires less or more memory based on the instance workload.

Monitoring Automatic Memory Management

Use the V$MEMORY_DYNAMIC_COMPONENTS view to monitor the current sizes of all dynamically tuned memory components, as shown here:

```
SQL> select component, current_size, user_specified_size
  2  from v$memory_dynamic_components
  3* where current_size!=0;
COMPONENT               CURRENT_SIZE      USER_SPECIFIED_SIZE
-------------------     -------------     -------------------
shared pool             109051904         0
large pool              4194304           0
java pool               12582912          0
SGA Target              134217728         0
DEFAULT buffer cache    4194304           0
PGA Target              130023424         0
6 rows selected.
SQL>
```

As you can see, the query also shows the current total size of the SGA and the PGA components. The V$MEMORY_RESIZE_OPS view contains a circular buffer of the 800 most recent completed memory resizing operations. You can find the current memory resize operations that are in progress by querying the V$MEMORY_CURRENT_RESIZE_OPS view. You can use the Enterprise Manager to easily monitor how the database is allocating memory between the SGA and the PGA components, as well as the Large Pool and other components. Figure 6-1 shows the Memory Advisors page in Database Control, which shows a history of the memory allocation between the SGA and the PGA over time.

FIGURE 6-1 Allocation history under Automatic Memory Management

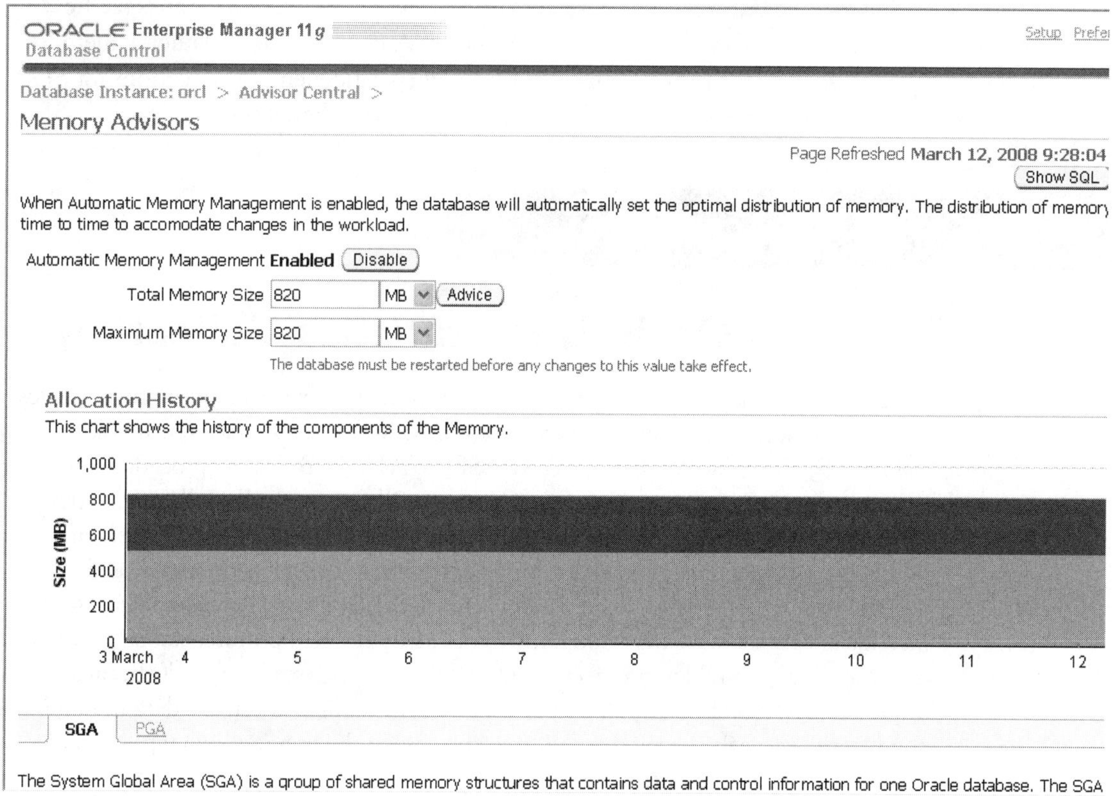
ORACLE Enterprise Manager 11g
Database Control
Setup Prefe
Database Instance: orcl > Advisor Central >
Memory Advisors
Page Refreshed March 12, 2008 9:28:04
Show SQL
When Automatic Memory Management is enabled, the database will automatically set the optimal distribution of memory. The distribution of memory
time to time to accomodate changes in the workload.
Automatic Memory Management Enabled Disable
Total Memory Size 820 MB Advice
Maximum Memory Size 820 MB
The database must be restarted before any changes to this value take effect.
Allocation History
This chart shows the history of the components of the Memory.
Size (MB)
1,000
800
600
400
200
0
3 March 2008
4
5
6
7
8
9
10
11
12
SGA
PGA
The System Global Area (SGA) is a group of shared memory structures that contains data and control information for one Oracle database. The SGA

DBCA and Automatic Memory Management

When you upgrade to Oracle Database 11*g* using the DBUA (Database Upgrade Assistant), by default, the `memory_target` parameter is set to zero, meaning automatic memory management is disabled by default. However, when you create a new database using the DBCA (Database Creation Assistant), you can specify automatic memory management. You specify your choice in the Initialization Parameters page by clicking the Memory tab on that page. Following are two options offered on that page:

- The Typical option lets you configure memory for a new database with minimal input and is ideal for most environments. Just enter a value in the Memory Size field and check the Use Automatic Memory Management option in the Typical section of the page to institute automatic memory management for the new database.

■ The Custom option provides you more control over the allocation of memory to the database. You can select the Automatic option to allocate specific amounts of memory to the SGA and PGA components of database memory. You can select the Manual option to set specific memory allocations for SGA subcomponents such as the buffer pool and the shared pool.

CERTIFICATION OBJECTIVE 6.03

Enhancements in Optimizer Statistics Collection

Oracle recommends that you let the database automatically gather optimizer statistics. The automatic optimizer statistics collection process collects statistics by invoking the DBMS_STATS.GATHER_DATABASE_STATS_JOB_PROC procedure during the nightly maintenance window. The database will automatically collect statistics on all objects that have either no statistics or have stale statistics because a significant number of a table's rows have changed. To ensure that it collects the most needed statistics before the maintenance window closes, the database processes objects that most need new statistics first. You need to manually collect optimizer statistics only in the case of volatile tables or objects that are loaded with large bulk loads. Because the optimizer statistics collection job runs only during the night when the data in table changes significantly during the day, as in the case of the previous two types of tables, manual loading of statistics is warranted.

There are two major innovations in optimizer statistic collection in the Oracle Database 11g release: pending statistics and extended statistics. In addition, the Statistics Preferences feature has been enhanced so you can easily change statistics collection settings that are different from the database default settings for specific objects. Let's examine the optimizer statistics collection improvements in the following sections.

Statistics Preferences

Although automatic statistics gathering takes the burden of collecting statistics off the DBA, it isn't perfect. Often, you have to manually collect statistics or provide non-default options for subsets of database objects for which the default statistics collection options aren't appropriate. For example, you'd have to specify your own sample size for tables with a heavily skewed data distribution, instead of letting the database automatically determine the sample size by using the AUTO_SAMPLE_SIZE value for the `estimate_percent` attribute. The Statistics Preference feature enables automatic statistics gathering to function better, by allowing you to easily customize statistics collection settings for specific objects that need special treatment. Under the Statistics Preferences feature, when you execute any of the GATHER_*_STATS procedures or the database runs the automatic Optimizer Statistics Gathering task, you can override the default behavior of the procedure and the task at the object or schema level.

You can view the current settings for statistics preferences by querying the DBA_TAB_STAT_PREFS view, which has the following structure:

```
SQL> desc dba_tab_stat_prefs
 Name                                      Null?        Type
 ----------------------------------------- ------------ --------------
 OWNER                                     NOT NULL     VARCHAR2(30)
 TABLE_NAME                                NOT NULL     VARCHAR2(30)
 PREFERENCE_NAME                                        VARCHAR2(30)
 PREFERENCE_VALUE                                       VARCHAR2(1000)
SQL>
```

You can set preferences at the table, schema, database, and global level. A preference set at the database level applies to all tables in the database, whereas the global preferences apply to all tables for which you don't set any preferences. Preferences you set at a lower granularity level override preferences at a higher level. That is, the preferences are in decreasing order of priority in this list: table level, schema level, database level, global level. A table level preference setting, for example, overrides a database level preference setting.

You could set preferences such as `estimate_percent`, `degree`, and `method_opt` in Oracle Database 10g. In Oracle Database 11g, you can set the following three new options:

- `publish`   Determines whether the database should make the statistics it collects public by storing them in the data dictionary. This is called publishing the statistics, and it was the only option when the database gathered statistics for any object in Oracle Database 10g. In Oracle Database 11g, if you choose not to automatically make the new statistics public, but rather wait until you confirm that the new statistics are conducive to better performance, the database treats the statistics as *pending statistics*. I explain pending statistics in detail later in this chapter. You can set the values of `TRUE` or `FALSE` for the publish preference.

- `stale_percent`   Lets you specify the threshold level for classifying an object's statistics as stale. The parameter uses a percentage of the rows that were modified since the database collected statistics. If, for example, the default is 10 percent for a table, you can change it to 20 percent if you want.

- incremental   Lets the database incrementally collect global statistics on partitioned tables. The two possible values for this parameter are TRUE and FALSE. I explain incremental statistics collection in the following section.

You can use either the SET_PREFS procedure of the DBMS_STATS package or the Enterprise Manager to set preferences at various levels. You can also use Enterprise Manager to easily modify preferences for various attributes. Figure 6-2 shows the Add Table Preferences page, which enables you to configure various table level preferences, including the three new preferences: stale_ percent, incremental, and publish.

FIGURE 6-2	The Add Table Preferences page

Query the DBA_TAB_STATS_PREFS view to find out all the current statistics preference settings for any table in the database.

Partitioned Tables and Incremental Statistics

For a partitioned table, the optimizer maintains statistics both at the global level for the entire table as well as partition-level statistics for each partition. However, in most types of partitioned tables, the data remains the same in most of the older partitions, and DML changes are made only to the data in the new or more recent partitions. In Oracle Database 11g, the database collects statistics only for those partitions that show a significant change in data. The default value of the threshold for significant change is 10 percent of the rows in a partition. Traditionally, the database had to scan the entire table for global statistics. In Oracle Database 11g, the database maintains global statistics incrementally, by scanning only those partitions that have undergone significant changes and using the old statistics for all partitions that remain unchanged since the last statistics collection job. The end result is that you can now collect global statistics much faster on large partitioned tables because the database doesn't have to scan the entire table to collect the statistics.

on the
job
The incremental statistics feature for partitioned tables doesn't incrementally maintain histograms.

Use the DBMS_STAT package to specify the granularity on a partitioned table.

You can specify a granularity level of `auto`, `global`, `global and partition`, `all`, `partition`, or `subpartition`. The database collects global statistics on an incremental basis if you specify the granularity level as `global` and mark the table as `incremental`. The database will also automatically collect statistics for the changed partitions of the table.

If you want the database to update global table statistics by scanning only the changed partitions instead if the entire table, you must satisfy the following conditions:

- Set the `incremental` value for the table to TRUE.
- Se the `publish` value for the table to TRUE.
- Specify the `auto_sample_size` value for the `estimate_percent` attribute and the `auto` value for the `granularity` attribute when executing the GATHER_TABLE_STATS procedure to collect the statistics.

New Sampling Technique

Selectivity of the data in a table is of critical importance when the optimizer is figuring out an execution plan. The optimizer normally uses the number of distinct values in a column to figure out the selectivity of a predicate using a column. In Oracle Database 10g, you had to choose a sample size when gathering table statistics. It's well known that you could complete the statistic gathering task faster by choosing a small sample size, but the results were of dubious value, especially when dealing with a skewed data distribution. On the other hand, using a very large sample or even a full table scan gives you more accurate results but at the expense of a longer execution time for the statistics collection job. DBAs often had a tough time meddling with the sample size factor, alternately trying to lower it if the statistic gathering job took too long to finish, and raising the sample size if the job finished quickly but was yielding bad results.

Oracle Database 11g provides the best of both the worlds, by providing a row-sampling technique that uses a small sample such as 1 or 5 percent of the data but provides results that are as accurate as those from a full table scan. Simply let the `estimate_percent` option remain at its default value of `auto_sample_size`. Oracle recommends this option when collecting statistics.

Deferred Statistics Publishing

By default, the database automatically allows the optimizer to immediately make use of the statistics that it collects. In other words, by default, once the statistics gathering is complete for the database, table, or schema, the database automatically publishes the new optimizer statistics into the dictionary tables. Oracle Database 11g introduces the concept of *pending statistics*, wherein you have the option to save new statistics as pending until you validate those statistics. You have the option now of publishing only those statistics that you consider are satisfactory, but not all statistics. This means that as a DBA, you can test the new statistics before publishing them for use by the optimizer. This also means that you can have two types of statistics in your database, based on their publication status: *current statistics* (published statistics) and *pending statistics*. Current or published statistics are for public use by the optimizer, and pending statistics are private statistics that you may or may not choose to make public.

In addition to permitting testing by the DBA before allowing the optimizer to use the new statistics, the concept of pending statistics provides another significant benefit. In the prior release of Oracle Database, the database could end up with inconsistent statistics when a table's statistics were published before the statistics for its index or partition. This could occur because the statistics gathering job failed midway through its execution. In Oracle Database 11g, the entire statistics gathering job is treated as one atomic transaction. The database publishes the statistics for all of a schema's objects at the same time. Thus, you can ensure that the statistics viewed by the optimizer are always consistent. If a statistics gathering job fails, you can resume it with the RESUME_GATHER_STATS procedure and publish the entire schema's statistics at a single point in time after you've verified and tested the statistics.

Determining the Status of the Statistics

The DBMS_STATS package's GET_PREFS function tells you whether the database will automatically publish optimizer statistics or not. The GET_PREFS function is new in Oracle Database 11g. The function returns the default values of various preferences, including `estimate_percent`, `stale_percent`, and others. The preference that is of interest to us with regard to publishing statistics is the preference named `publish`. Here's the query to determine whether new statistics will be published automatically or not:

```
SQL> select dbms_stats.get_prefs('PUBLISH') publish from dual;

PUBLISH
--------
TRUE
```

The query returns a value of TRUE, meaning the database will automatically publish the new statistics once the statistics gathering process completes. If the query returns a value of FALSE, it means that the database will keep the new statistics in the pending status until you decide to publish them. By default, the database publishes all statistics automatically, so the default value for the previous query is TRUE. You can determine the publishing mode for a single table by executing the `get_prefs` function with the table parameters, as shown in the example here:

```
SQL> select dbms_stats.get_prefs('PUBLISH','stats','test_table')
     from dual;
```

The database stores the published statistics in the DBA_TAB_STATS and the DBA_IND_STATS views. The database stores the pending statistics in the DBA_TAB_PENDING_STATS and the DBA_IND_PENDING_STATS views.

Changing the Status of Statistics

In order to change the default behavior of automatically publishing all newly gathered statistics, use the SET_TABLE_PREFS procedure or the SET_SCHEMA_PREFS procedure. You can change the publishing setting at the table or the schema level. By default, the database publishes the statistics for all objects immediately upon the gathering of the statistics. In order to change the publishing setting of the EMPLOYEES table in the HR schema from the default value of TRUE to FALSE, execute the SET_TABLE_PREFS procedure, as shown here:

```
SQL> exec dbms_stats.set_table_prefs ('HR','EMPLOYEES',
     'PUBLISH','FALSE');
```

Once you execute the previous statement, the current statistics for the EMPLOYEES table continue to be available for use by the optimizer. However, the next time the database collects statistics for the EMPLOYEES table, those statistics will not be published. Instead of storing the newly collected statistics with the other published statistics in the DBA_TAB_STATS view, the database will store them in the new DBA_TAB_PENDING_STATS view.

Making Pending Statistics Public

Once you decide to keep some statistics in the pending status, you can test them against a workload to see how the unpublished statistics affect performance. If the statistics seem like they are helping performance, you can publish the statistics. If not, you can drop the statistics. In order to make pending statistics available to the optimizer, set the new initialization parameter `optimizer_use_pending_statistics` to TRUE. The default value of this parameter is FALSE, meaning the optimizer doesn't use pending statistics by default, as shown here:

```
SQL> show parameter optimizer_use_pending_statistics
NAME                                     TYPE      VALUE
--------------------------------------   -------   ------
optimizer_use_pending_statistics         boolean   FALSE
SQL>
```

The setting shown for the `optimizer_use_pending_statistics` parameter (FALSE) means that the database will parse SQL statements in your session by using the current optimizer statistics that the database had previously collected and stored in the data dictionary. In order for the session to switch to using the new pending statistics, you issue the following `alter session` statement:

```
SQL> alter session set optimizer_use_pending_statistics=TRUE
```

Once you execute the `alter session` command shown here, when the optimizer compiles a SQL statement that refers to objects with pending statistics, it will make use of the new pending statistics.

If your tests show that the new statistics that you just enabled for public use in the session with the `alter session` statement shown in the example aren't satisfactory, you don't want to make these statistics public in the production database. If, however, your tests show that the new statistics enhance performance, you can then change the status of these statistics to current statistics in the production database. You can change the status of all pending statistics in the database to current statistics, by executing the PUBLISH_PENDING_STATS procedure, as shown here:

```
SQL> exec dbms_stats.publish_pending_stats (NULL,NULL);
```

You can also publish the pending statistics for only a single table in the following manner:

```
SQL> exec dbms_stats.publish_pending_stats('HR','EMPLOYEES');
```

If, after testing a workload that includes a table with pending statistics, you decide you're better off with the older statistics, delete the pending statistics by executing the DELETE_PENDING_STATS procedure, as shown here:

```
SQL> exec dbms_stats.delete_pending_stats('HR','EMPLOYEES');
```

The DELETE_PENDING_STATS procedure helps you delete any pending statistics that you haven't published. You can also test the new pending statistics against a workload in a test database by exporting the pending statistics to another database with the EXPORT_PENDING_STATS procedure, as shown here:

```
SQL> exec dbms_stats.export_pending_stats('HR', 'EMPLOYEES');
```

The EXPORT_PENDING_STATS procedure exports any statistics that the database has gathered and kept as pending statistics.

Extended Statistics

In this release, Oracle has introduced major new capabilities in statistics gathering, which are referred to as *extended statistics*, to make the optimizer statistics reflect the true selectivity of the data. There are two types of extended statistics: *multicolumn statistics*, which involve collecting statistics for column groups, and *expression statistics*. Extended statistics include the statistics collected for both column groups and expressions and use the following new procedures:

- CREATE_EXTENDED_STATS function
- DROP_EXTENDED_STATS procedure
- SHOW_EXTENDED_STATS_NAME function

In the following sections, you learn how to use the new functions and procedure.

Multicolumn Statistics (Column groups)

The selectivity of a column is a crucial optimizer statistic, playing a key role in the execution plan that the cost optimizer creates for a SQL statement. Currently, Oracle collects statistics by computing the selectivity of each of a table's columns separately, and ignores the relationship between the columns. However, the relationship between certain columns may be so strong that it can affect the combined selectivity of the two columns. In most cases, the optimizer assumes that the values of the different columns in a complex predicate are independent. Based on this assumption, the optimizer simply multiplies the selectivity of individual predicates to arrive at the selectivity of a conjunctive predicate, which usually leads to an underestimation of the selectivity.

In Oracle Database 10g, when figuring out the selectivity of multiple predicates, the query optimizer took into account the correlation between related columns only under a limited set of circumstances, as I summarize here:

- The optimizer used the number of distinct keys in an index to estimate selectivity provided all columns of a conjunctive predicate match all columns of a concatenated index key. In addition, the predicates must be equalities used in equijoins.

- If you set DYNAMIC_SAMPLING to level 4, the optimizer used dynamic sampling to estimate the selectivity of predicates involving multiple columns from a table. Because the sampling size is quite small, the results are dubious in most cases.

With the exception of the two cases presented here, the optimizer always assumed that the values of all columns in a table that were used in a complex predicate were independent of each other. Based on this naïve assumption, the optimizer simply multiplied single column selectivity estimates to arrive at the selectivity of a conjunctive predicate involving multiple columns. The end result of this strategy was a severe underestimation of the real selectivity of those types of predicates in a SQL statement. Oracle Database 11g attempts to alleviate this major problem by letting you collect the following types of statistics on multiple columns in a table, which it refers to as a group of columns:

- Number of distinct values
- Density
- Number of nulls
- Frequency histograms

The idea behind the capturing of statistics for a group of columns as a single entity is to capture the underlying functional dependency between related columns in a table.

The database collects the number of distinct values, the number of null values, frequency histograms, and density for groups of columns.

Let's use an example from the CUSTOMERS table in the SH schema to drive home this point. In this table, the two columns CUST_STATE_PROVINCE and COUNTRY_ID are strongly correlated. The CUST_STATE_PROVINCE column determines the value of the COUNTRY_ID column for a customer. The following query using California as the value for the CUST_STATE_PROVINCE column shows this:

```
SQL> select count(*)
     from sh.customers
     where cust_state_province = 'CA';

COUNT(*)
----------
    3341
```

The query returns the value 3341. That is, there are a total of 3341 customers in the customers table who are from the state of California. Of course, if you issue the following query, which asks how many customers are from the state of California and the U.S. (`country_id=52790`), you get the same result as before:

```
SQL> select count(*)
     from customers
     where cust_state_province = 'CA'
     and country_id=52790;

COUNT(*)
----------
    3341
```

But it is clear that if you repeat this query for any COUNTRY_ID other than the U.S., the result would be, in all likelihood, zero because California is a state in the U.S. but not in the other countries. In cases such as these, it makes sense for the optimizer to rely not merely on the selectivity of the individual columns, but on the selectivity for the group of related columns as well. Oracle Database 11*g* lets you do precisely that—you can now gather statistics on related columns as a group, called a column group. The optimizer uses the statistics on column groups to account for the correlation between two columns. If, for example, your query has the predicates c1=1 and c2=1 and if you collect statistics on (c1, c2) as a single group, the optimizer will use the column group statistics for estimating the combined selectivity of the two predicates.

Oracle creates column groups for related columns based on its analysis of the database workload. You can, however, create a column group yourself using the DBMS_STATS package. You can execute the CREATE_EXTENDED_STATS function to create a column group, as shown in the following section.

Creating Column Groups Use the CREATE_EXTENDED_STATS function to create a new column group. The function returns a system-generated name for the column group. Here's the structure of the CREATE_EXTENDED_STATS function:

```
DBMS_STATS.CREATE_EXTENDED_STATS (
    ownname     VARCHAR2,
    tabname     VARCHAR2,
    extension   VARCHAR2)
  RETURN VARCHAR2;
```

The function creates a column statistics entry for the column group you're creating. When the database next collects statistics for a table, it also collects statistics for the column group you create. To create the column group for the COUNTRY_ID and CUST_STATE_PROVINCE columns, execute the CREATE_EXTENDED_STATS function, as shown here:

```
declare
  cg_name varchar2(30);
begin
  cg_name := dbms_stats.create_extended_stats(null,'customers',
  '(cust_state_province',country_id)');
end;
/
```

The CREATE_EXTENDED_STATS function returns a system-generated virtual column name, which you can see in the next query. You can verify that you've successfully created the extension by issuing the following query on the DBA_STAT_EXTENSIONS view:

```
SQL> select extension_name, extension
     from dba_stat_extensions
     where table_name='CUSTOMERS';


EXTENSION_NAME                        EXTENSION
------------------------------        ------------------------------------
SYS_STU#S#WF25Z#QAHIHE#MOFFMM_  ("CUST_STATE_PROVINCE","COUNTRY_ID")
```

To view the name of the column group for a pair of columns in a table, you can also use the SHOW_EXTENDED_STATS_NAME function, as shown in this example:

```
SQL> select
     sys.dbms_stats.show_extended_stats_name ('sh','customers',
     '(cust_state_province,country_id)') col_group_name
     from dual;

COL_GROUP_NAME
------------------------------
SYS_STU#S#WF25Z#QAHIHE#MOFFMM
```

The SHOW_EXTENDED_STATS_NAME function returns the name of the statistics entry that the database creates for a user-specified extension. You can drop a column group from a table by using the DROP_EXTENDED_STATS procedure:

```
SQL> exec dbms_stats.drop_extended_stats('sh','customers','
     (cust_state_province, country_id)');
```

The DROP_EXTENDED_STATS function helps you drop the statistics entry that the database created for a user-specified extension.

Collecting Statistics for Column Groups   Use the `method_opt` argument of the DBMS_STATS.GATHER_TABLE_STATS procedure to have the database collect optimizer statistics on column groups. If you set the `method_opt` argument to the value `for all columns`, the optimizer will collect statistics for all column groups in the database.

You can also have the database create a new column group automatically as part of its statistics gathering process, by using the `for columns` clause when executing the DBMS_STATS package, as shown here:

```
SQL> exec dbms_stats.gather_table_stats (null,
     'customers',method_opt =>
     'for all columns size skewonly
     for columns (cust_state_province,country_id) skewonly');
```

Executing the GATHER_TABLE_STATS procedure as shown here results in the creation of a new column group as well as the collection of statistics for that column group.

Expression Statistics

When you apply a function to a column inside a query, the value of the column in the resulting output would, of course, change as a result. Here's a simple example:

```
SQL> select count(*)
     from customers
     where lower(cust_state_province)='ca';
```

The `lower` function in the example returns a string in lowercase. The optimizer, however, has only the original column statistics and not the estimates of the actual values of the column or columns after they are transformed by the `lower` function. The application of the function will affect the selectivity of the column, but the optimizer has no way of knowing this. For computing statistics on predicates that use expressions on a column, the optimizer used to simply assume a fixed selectivity value of 1 percent, which led it to arrive at suboptimal plans for such predicates in many occasions.

In Oracle Database 10g, the optimizer can collect expression statistics on some types of expressions on columns, thus deriving more accurate selectivity estimates. This functionality applies only to certain special cases where a function preserves the data distribution characteristics of the original column, as is the case when you use an expression such as TO_NUMBER. In addition, the database in the previous release used dynamic sampling to get better estimates of built-in functions on columns. In Oracle Database 11g, the database uses expression statistics that include user-defined functions as well as function-based indexes. The new feature relies on the virtual column infrastructure to create expression statistics, that is, statistics on predicates involving expressions on columns.

As with multicolumn statistics (column groups), you can use the CREATE_EXTENDED_STATS function to create statistics on a column expression, as shown in this example:

```
SQL> select
     dbms_stats.create_extended_stats(null,'customers',
     '(lower(cust_state_province))')
     from dual;
```

You can also create expression statistics by using the `for columns` clause in the GATHER_TABLE_STATS procedure, as shown here:

```
SQL> exec dbms_stats.gather_table_stats(null,'customers',
     method_opt =>'for all columns size skewonly
     for columns (lower(cust_state_province)) skewonly');
```

You can view the DBA_STAT_EXTENSIONS view to make sure your expression statistics have been created successfully, as shown here:

```
SQL> select extension_name, extension
     from DBA_STAT_EXTENSIONS
     where table_name='CUSTOMERS';


EXTENSION_NAME                          EXTENSION
------------------------------------    ------------------------------
SYS_STUBPHJSBRKOIK9O2YV3W8HOUE          (LOWER("CUST_STATE_PROVINCE"))
```

The DBA_STAT_EXTENSIONS view shows information about all statistics extensions in the database.

Result Cache

The shared pool component of the SGA, as you are aware, stores the parsed and compiled versions of SQL queries, which lets the database quickly execute frequently run SQL statements and PL/SQL functions. In Oracle Database 11g, the database uses the *result cache*, a new component of the SGA, to store the results of both SQL queries and PL/SQL functions, thus letting it quickly return query and function results without having to re-execute the code. Once a session executes a query, it retrieves the results and stores them in the SQL query result cache. A second session that executes the same query will retrieve the result directly from the cache instead of from the disk. Obviously, this leads to tremendous improvements in database performance. You don't have to develop your own cache-management policies, letting the database automatically cache the results for you. You can turn on result caching only on a database-wide level. When any of the objects in the cached results are modified, the database automatically invalidates the cached results that reference the modified objects. Good candidates for caching are queries that access many rows and return only a few rows, which is quite common in data warehousing applications.

The result cache consists of two components: the SQL Query Result Cache and the PL/SQL Function Result Cache, both sharing the same infrastructure. In addition, there is also a new client result cache, which caches results on the client side. In the following sections, I discuss the different types of result caches.

Result Cache Memory Pool

The result cache component of the SGA is formally called the *Result Cache Memory* pool and it contains the results of both SQL queries as well as PL/SQL function results. Within the Result Cache Memory pool, the SQL Query Result Cache component stores the results of SQL queries and the PL/SQL Function Result Cache component stores the values returned by PL/SQL functions. The default value of the Result Cache Memory pool is based on the size of the initialization parameter memory_target if you have set that parameter, or based on the sga_target parameter or the shared_pool_size parameter if you have set one or both of those instead.

Managing the Result Cache

Three new initialization parameters—`result_cache_max_size`, `result_cache_max_result`, and `result_cache_remote_expiration`—help you manage the result cache. The result cache draws its share of the memory from the shared pool component of the SGA. You set the size of the result cache by specifying a value for the initialization parameter `result_cache_max_size`. The value of the `result_cache_max_size` parameter sets the high limit to the memory allocated to the result cache from the SGA. As mentioned in the previous section, by default, the database derives the size of the result cache from the values of the `shared_pool_size`, `sga_target`, and `memory_target` initialization parameters, depending on which of these parameters you have set. The value for the `result_cache_max_size` parameter can range from 0 to a system-dependent maximum.

By default, the result cache is always set to a positive number, which automatically enables the result cache. You can disable the result cache by setting the `result_cache_max_size` parameter to zero through an `alter system` statement, as shown here:

```
SQL> alter system set result_cache_max_size=0;
```

Of course, if the result cache is disabled, the database can't use the SQL Result Cache or the PL/SQL Function Result Cache. The default value of the `result_cache_max_size` parameter is dependent on other memory settings set through initialization parameters such as `memory_target` and `sga_target`. The minimum is 0.25 percent of the `memory_target` parameter, 0.5 percent of the `sga_target` parameter, and 1 percent of the shared pool, depending on the memory management system you choose for the instance. However, the cache can't be greater than 75 percent of the shared pool.

Use the `result_cache_max_result` parameter to specify the maximum percentage of the result cache that a single cached result can use. The default value is 5 percent and you can specify a value between 1 percent and 100 percent.

The `result_cache_remote_expiration` parameter specifies the length of time for which a result that depends on remote objects will remain valid. The default value for this parameter is 0, which implies that you mustn't use remote objects. Setting a positive value could lead to invalid results because it gives time for the remote objects to be modified.

Caching SQL Results with a Result_Cache Hint

Let me use a simple example to show how to make the database cache the results of a SQL query in the result cache. If the `result_cache_mode` initialization parameter is set to `manual`, you must specify the ResultCache operator in the SQL statement to cache the query results. In the following example, I specify a `result_cache` hint to direct the database to cache the query results in the result cache:

```
SQL> select /*+ result_cache +*/
  2   department_id, avg(salary)
  3   from hr.employees
  4*  group by department_id;
SQL>
```

The `result_cache` hint in Line 1 tells the database to cache this query's results. The hint will introduce the ResultCache operator into the execution plan for this query. You can get an explain plan for this statement to verify that the database caches the results for the query.

```
SQL> explain plan for select /*+ result_cache +*/
  2   department_id,avg(salary)
  3   from hr.employees
  4*  group by department_id
SQL> /
Explained.
SQL>
```

You can view the explain plan for the query by using the DBMS_XPLAN. DISPLAY procedure, as shown here:

```
SQL> select plan_table_output from table(DBMS_XPLAN.DISPLAY());
PLAN_TABLE_OUTPUT
-------------------------------------------------------------------
Plan hash value: 1192169904
-------------------------------------------------------------------
| Id  | Operation          | Name         | Rows  | Bytes | Cost |
(%CPU)| Time               |
PLAN_TABLE_OUTPUT
-------------------------------------------------------------------
|   0 | SELECT STATEMENT   |              |    11 |    77 |    4 |
  (25)| 00:00:01           |
|   1 | RESULT CACHE       | 8nk7a7rfhymzy0s0b89ksn9bfz |  |  |
|   2 | HASH GROUP BY      |              |    11 |    77 |    4 |
  (25)| 00:00:01 |
|   3 | TABLE ACCESS FULL  | EMPLOYEES    |   107 |   749 |    3 |
   (0)| 00:00:01 |
PLAN_TABLE_OUTPUT
-------------------------------------------------------------------

-------------------------------------------------------------------
Result Cache Information (identified by operation id):
-------------------------------------------------------------------
   1 - column-count=2; dependencies=(HR.EMPLOYEES);
name="select /*+ result_cache +*/
```

```
department_id,avg(salary)
from hr.employees
group by department_id"

15 rows selected.
SQL>
```

The ResultCache operator would lead the database to check the result cache every time you execute the previous query to see if the results for this query are in the cache from a previous execution of the query. If so, the database retrieves the results from the result cache. Otherwise, the database executes the query and returns the results, as well as stores the results in the result cache. The explain plan for the statement shows that the optimizer will use the ResultCache operator when you execute this query.

The previous example showed how to override the `manual` setting of the `result_cache_mode` parameter, under which the database will cache a query's results only if you specify the `result_cache` hint in a SQL query. If the `result_cache_mode` parameter is set to `force`, the database will cache query results wherever it can. However, you can still force the database to bypass the result cache by specifying the `no_result_cache` hint. The `result_cache` and the `no_result_cache` hints always take precedence over the setting of the `result_cache_mode` initialization parameter.

Using the DBMS_RESULT_CACHE Package

The new Oracle-supplied PL/SQL package DBMS_RESULT_CACHE contains various procedures and functions that help you manage the portion of the shared pool that the database allocates to the result cache, which is used by both the SQL result cache and the PL/SQL function result cache. You can use the DBMS_RESULT_CACHE package to perform operations such a checking whether the result cache is open or closed, retrieving statistics on the result cache usage, and flushing the result cache.

e x a m

ⓦ a t c h   *You must be able to explain   DBMS_RESULT_CACHE package enable*
how the different procedures of the   you to manage the result cache.

Execute the MEMORY_REPORT function to view the current result cache memory allocation, as shown here:

```
SQL> set serveroutput on
SQL> exec dbms_result_cache.memory_report
R e s u l t   C a c h e   M e m o r y   R e p o r t
[Parameters]
Block Size        = 1K bytes
Maximum Cache Size = 672K bytes (672 blocks)
Maximum Result Size = 33K bytes (33 blocks)
[Memory]
Total Memory = 5132 bytes [0.005% of the Shared Pool]
... Fixed Memory = 5132 bytes [0.005% of the Shared Pool]
... Dynamic Memory = 0 bytes [0.000% of the Shared Pool]

PL/SQL procedure successfully completed.
SQL>
```

The MEMORY_REPORT function shows the default allocation of memory to the result cache. When you turn off result caching for the entire instance by setting the `result_cache_max_size` initialization parameter to zero, executing the MEMORY_REPORT procedure will show you this:

```
SQL> set serveroutput on
SQL> exec dbms_result_cache.memory_report
R e s u l t   C a c h e   M e m o r y   R e p o r t
Cache is disabled.

PL/SQL procedure successfully completed.
SQL>
```

You can see that the result cache is disabled because you set the initialization parameter `max_result_cache_size` to zero. Because the parameter is static, you'll have to restart the instance after making the change in the initialization parameter file.

Here's how to use the DBMS_RESULT_CACHE.STATUS function to ascertain whether the result cache is enabled:

```
SQL> SELECT dbms_result_cache.status() FROM dual;

DBMS_RESULT_CACHE.STATUS()
--------------------------
ENABLED
SQL>
```

The DBMS_RESULT_CACHE.STATUS function tells you whether the cache is available for use or not. In a RAC environment, it also shows if the cache is available but synchronizing with the RAC nodes. Use the FLUSH procedure to remove the contents of the result cache, as shown here:

```
SQL> begin
  2   dbms_result_cache.flush;
  3   end;
  4   /
PL/SQL procedure successfully completed.
SQL>
```

The DBMS_RESULT_CACHE package contains both a procedure as well as a function named FLUSH. By default, both the procedure and the function will clear the cache of existing results and return the freed memory to the system. In addition, the DBMS_RESULT_CACHE.FLUSH function will return the value TRUE if it is successful in removing all the objects from the result cache.

on the **job**

The Result Cache doesn't automatically release memory that you allocate to it. The cache will grow until it reaches its maximum size limit. You use the DBMS_RESULT_CACHE.FLUSH procedure to purge the Result Cache.

The DBMS_RESULT_CACHE.FLUSH procedure comes in handy when you load a new version of a function or a package that contains a function that includes the `result_cache` hint. When you replace the function, the database doesn't automatically flush the contents of the result cache, which includes the results from the earlier version of the function. In a case like this, first flush the contents of the result cache after putting the result cache in the bypass mode, as shown here:

```
SQL> begin
  2   dbms_result_cache.bypass(TRUE);
  3   dbms_result_cache.flush;
  4   end;
  5   /
PL/SQL procedure successfully completed.
SQL>
```

on the **job**

Because both the SQL result cache and the PL/SQL function result cache use the same result cache, the BYPASS procedure will affect both caches. Similarly, executing the FLUSH procedure removes the cached results for both SQL queries and PL/SQL functions.

on the **Job**

The result cache doesn't automatically release memory; it grows until it reaches its maximum size. You can use the DBMS_RESULT_CACHE.FLUSH procedure to purge the result cache. Make sure you disable the cache before executing the DBMS_RESULT_CACHE.FLUSH procedure.

Once you put the result cache in the bypass mode, the database bypasses the result cache and results aren't cached any longer. Once you flush the contents of the result cache, replace the function or the package with the `result_cache` hint with new code that doesn't use the hint. You can then execute the BYPASS procedure with the value `FALSE` to turn off the bypassing of the result cache, as shown here:

```
SQL> begin
  2  dbms_result_cache.bypass(FALSE);
  3  end;
  4  /
PL/SQL procedure successfully completed.
SQL>
```

Once you run the DBMS_RESULT_CACHE.BYPASS procedure, the result cache is active again and when the database executes the new version of the function, it'll cache the function results once again and use them for subsequent executions of that function. The database immediately stops using the cached results when you turn the bypass mode on. It also stops saving new results in the result cache. The result cache resumes its normal operation when you turn off the bypass mode.

Using Dynamic Performance Views

Use the following views to manage the query result cache:

- **V$RESULT_CACHE_STATISTICS**   Lists cache settings and memory usage statistics
- **V$RESULT_CACHE_OBJECTS**   Lists all cached objects and their attributes
- **V$RESULT_CACHE_DEPENDENCY**   Shows the dependency information between the cached results and dependencies
- **V$RESULT_CACHE_MEMORY**   Shows all memory blocks and their statistics

In the V$RESULT_CACHE_OBJECTS view, the STATUS column can take the following values.

- `new` The cached result is still being built
- `published` The cached result is available for use by other queries
- `bypass` Other queries will bypass the cached result
- `expired` The cached result has crossed the expiration time limit
- `invalid` The cached result is unavailable for use by other queries

You can find out information about the objects currently in the result cache by using the following query:

```
SQL> select type,status,name from v$result_cache_objects;
TYPE             STATUS       NAME
------------     ----------   ------------------------------------
Dependency       Published    HR.COUNT_EMP
Result           Published    select  /* + result_cache
                              query name(q1) */
                              last_name, salary from hr.employees
                              order by salary

SQL>
```

The output of the previous query shows that there are two cached results in the result cache.

The SQL Query Result Cache

You can ask the database to cache the results of a SQL query or a PL/SQL function. The database caches the SQL query results in the SQL Query Result Cache component of the Result Cache. You control the use of the SQL query result cache by setting the `result_cache_mode` initialization parameter. This parameter specifies when the optimizer will include the ResultCache operator inside a query's execution plan. Once you turn query result caching on, the database will cache all SQL query results from that point on. The database uses a least recently–used algorithm to age out the cached results, thus making room for fresh query results.

Whether the database caches a SQL query's results in the Result Cache depends on the setting of the `result_cache_mode`

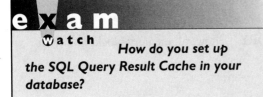

How do you set up the SQL Query Result Cache in your database?

initialization parameter. Following is an explanation of how the values you specify for the `result_cache_mode` parameter determine the caching behavior for SQL results.

The `result_cache_mode` parameter has two possible values—`manual` and `force`. The default value is `manual`. It's a dynamic parameter that you can modify with the `alter session` and the `alter system` statements. If you set the value to `manual` (`result_cache_mode=manual`), the database won't automatically cache SQL query results. You must use the `result_cache` hint in a query to make the database cache the query results. The optimizer adds the ResultCache operator only if you annotate the query by adding a hint to it. Once you specify the `result_cache` hint, the database executes the query once and will serve the results to subsequent executions of that statement. As mentioned earlier, the `result_cache_mode` parameter is set to `manual` by default, as shown here:

```
SQL> show parameter result_cache_mode

NAME                     TYPE        VALUE
-----------------        -------     -------
result_cache_mode        string      MANUAL
SQL>
```

If you set the value of the parameter to `force` (`result_cache_mode=force`), the database caches the results of all SQL queries, as long as it's valid to do so, subject to the availability of space in the cache. You can change the default value of `manual` for the `result_cache_mode` parameter by specifying the value `force` in the initialization parameter file. You can also dynamically change the setting at the session level by executing the following `alter session` statement:

```
SQL> alter session set result_cache_mode=force;
```

Even if you set the `result_cache_mode` parameter to `force`, you can still specify the `no_result_cache` hint in a SQL query to tell the database to bypass the cache, as shown in this example:

```
SQL> select /*+ no_result_cache */ department_id, avg(salary)
     from employees
     group by department_id;
```

The `no_result_cache` hint takes precedence over the `force` setting for the `result_cache_mode` initialization parameter, thus preventing the caching of this SQL query's results in the result cache.

The ResultCache Operator

As I mentioned earlier, when you set the `result_cache_mode` parameter to `manual`, you can make the database use the result cache only by specifying the `result_cache` hint in the query, as shown here:

```
SQL> select /*+ result_cache */ deptno, avg(sal)
     from emp
     group by deptno;
```

When you use the `result_cache` hint as shown in the example, the database uses the ResultCache operator in the execution plan for the query. The ResultCache operator will search the result cache when you execute the query. If the result exists in the cache, the operator fetches the result from there. If the result doesn't exist in the cache, the operator executes the query and stores the result in the result cache.

Restrictions on Using the SQL Query Result Cache

You can't use the SQL Query Result Cache for the following objects or SQL functions.

- Temporary tables
- Dictionary tables
- Non-deterministic PL/SQL functions
- The `currval` and `nextval` pseudo functions
- The `sysdate`, `sys_timestamp`, `current_date`, `current_timestamp`, `local_timestamp`, `userenv`, `sys_context` and `sys_quid` functions

If you're trying to cache a user-written function used in a function-based index, ensure that the function is declared with the *deterministic* keyword, meaning the function will always return an identical output for a given set of input values. The database won't cache a query result that is based on a read-consistent snapshot of data that's older than the most recently committed version of the data. The database also won't cache a result involving any tables that are undergoing modifications in an ongoing transaction during the current session. The database can cache flashback queries, however.

You can't cache subqueries, but you can use a `result_cache` hint inside an inline view. Doing this will disable certain optimizations between the outer query and the inline view, such as view merging, predicate push-down, and column projection. This means that the initial execution of the query takes a longer time in order to maximize the reusability of the cached result. Here's an example:

```
SQL> select prod_subcategory, revenue
    from (select /*+ result_cache */
    p.prod_category,p.prod_subcategory,
    sum(s.amount_sold) revenue
    from products p, sales s
    where s.prod_id = p.prod_id and
    s.time_id between to_date('01-JAN-2008','dd-MON-yyyy')
    and
    to_date(('01-DEC-2008','dd-MON-yyyy')
    group by rollup (p.prod_category, p.prod_subcategory))
    where prod_category = 'Men');
```

Once you execute this query, all subsequent executions of the query will run much faster because the database stores the results of the query in the result cache. Note that even queries with a different predicate value for PROD_CATEGORY in the last line will execute much faster.

The PL/SQL Function Result Cache

The PL/SQL function result cache uses the same infrastructure as the SQL query result cache, and caches the results of the PL/SQL functions in the result cache component of the SGA. Ideal candidates for caching are functions that the database invokes frequently but which depend on information that changes infrequently or never. If you invoke a function with different combinations of parameter values, the database will cache one result for every unique combination of parameter values. The database uses the input parameters of the function as the lookup key. As with the SQL result cache, the database employs a least recently used algorithm to age out cached results. You can optionally specify the database objects that the cached result depends on, and the database will invalidate the cached results when those database objects change.

Creating a Cacheable Function

To make the database cache the results of a PL/SQL function, simply include the result_cache clause in the function definition. You can optionally specify the relies_on clause to make the database invalidate the cache when the database modifies any of the listed tables or views. The following example shows how to create a function that specifies that the database cache its results:

```
SQL> create or replace function
    get_dept_info (dept_id number) return dept_info_record
    result_cache relies_on (employees)
    is
    rec dept_info_record;
    begin
```

```
         select avg(salary), count(*) into rec
         from employees
         where department_id = dept_id;
         return rec;
      end get_dept_info;
   /
```

The GET_DEPT_INFO function fetches the number of employees and their average salary from a department that you specify. The `result_cache` clause ensures that the database saves the results of the function's execution in the result cache. The optional `relies_on` clause specifies that the database must invalidate the cached results of this function whenever the EMPLOYEES table changes.

How the PL/SQL Function Cache Works

The very first time you execute the body of a result-cached PL/SQL function with a set of parameter values, the function will execute. The function will re-execute under the following circumstances:

■ When the cached result for the parameter values is invalid because an object specified in the `relies_on` clause has changed

■ When the function bypasses the result cache

■ When the cached result for the set of parameter values has aged out because the system needs memory

Restrictions

In order for the database to cache its results, a function must satisfy *all* of these criteria:

■ It can't be a pipelined table function.

■ It can't have any `out` or `in out` parameters.

■ It is not defined in an anonymous block; it must be a named function.

■ It isn't defined in a module that has invoker's rights.

■ It can't have any `in` parameters belong to the LOB type, ref cursor, and collection, object, or record types.

In addition, the function must not have any side effects or depend on session-specific settings or session-specific application contexts.

The Client Query Result cache

In addition to the SQL result cache and the PL/SQL function result cache, which are server-side caches, Oracle Database 11g also provides a new Oracle Call Interface (OCI) result cache to enable client-side caching of SQL result sets. All OCI applications and drivers, such as JDBC-OCI, ODP.NET, OCCI, Pro*C/C++, Pro*COBOL, and ODBC, can take advantage of the client result cache. The OCI result cache, which is transparent to OCI applications, keeps the result data set consistent with any changes in the session attributes or in the database itself. OCI client caching leads to a tremendous improvement in query performance for frequently repeated statements because the results are cached on the client itself, thus avoiding the expensive round trip to the server. Because you use fewer server resources as a result, this feature also enhances server scalability. In addition to a lower server CPU usage, client result caching also relieves the server of additional I/O burden to process frequently repeated queries.

The OCI result cache, which is on a per-process basis among multiple client sessions, can use the same cached result sets. The database automatically refreshes the result sets in the cache and manages memory allocation to the cache. If, during the round trips the OCI process makes to the server, any database changes affect the result set, the database automatically invalidates the cached result sets. That is, the database keeps the client result set transparently consistent with changes on the server.

The big difference between the server-side result cache and the OCI client result cache, of course, is that the OCI result cache is located on the client and, therefore, doesn't make any use of the server SGA. While the server result cache is enabled by default, the client result cache is not. The server result cache and the client result cache work independent of each other. You can enable the client result cache even if you decide to disable the server result cache. Note that while the client result cache caches only the results of top-level SQL queries, the server result cache can also cache query fragments.

Client result caching is especially useful when applications produce repeatable or small result sets, which tend to be static over time. Frequently executed queries are also candidates for caching on the client. Lookup tables are particularly attractive candidates for client caching.

Enabling and Disabling the Client Result Cache

As with the server-side result cache, you set the `result_cache_mode` initialization parameter to control whether the database caches the query results on the client.

Here's how the `result_cache_mode` initialization parameter settings affect client-side result caching:

- If you set the `result_cache_mode` parameter to `manual`, you must annotate a query with the `result_cache` hint for the database to store it in the client cache, as shown here:

```
SQL> select /*+ result_cache */ deptno, avg(sal)
     from emp
     group by deptno;
```

- If you set the `result_cache_mode` parameter to `force`, the database will store all SQL query results in the client cache whenever it's possible to do so. If you don't want the database to use the client cache for a query, you must specify the /*+ `no_result_cache` */ hint in the query, as shown here:

```
SQL> select /*+ no_result_cache */ deptno, avg(sal)
     from emp
     group by deptno;
```

on the
Job

You can set the `result_cache_mode` parameter with the `alter system` or `alter session` statement.

As mentioned earlier, the `no_result_cache` hint overrides the `force` setting of the `result_cache_mode` parameter, which would cause result caching behavior without the hint.

How Client Result Caching Works

As I explained earlier, if you set the `result_cache_mode` initialization parameter to `force`, the database automatically caches all query results on the client side, and you don't have to do anything to cache results on the client. You can, however, explicitly specify that the database not cache the results by using the /*+ `no_result_cache` */ hint in a query. And if you set the parameter to a value of `manual`, you must include the /* `result_cache` */ hint in a query for the database to cache the result on the client.

When you specify either the `result_cache` or the `no result_cache` hint, you must add the hint to the SQL text you pass to the `OCIStmtPrepare()` and the `OCIStmtPrepare2()` calls.

Managing the Client Result Cache

You manage the client result cache by setting the following initialization parameters:

- `client_result_cache_size` This parameter determines the maximum size of the client per-process result set cache (in bytes). The setting of the parameter also determines if the cache is enabled. By setting this parameter to its default value of zero, you can disable the client result cache. By default, the database allocates every OCI client process the maximum size specified by this parameter. As I explain later, you can override this parameter with the server-side configuration parameter `oci_result_ cache_max_size`. If you disable client result caching on the server itself, the client result cache will remain disabled, even if you set the `client_ result_cache_size` parameter to a positive value on the client. The following query shows the current value of the `client_result_ cache_size` parameter:

```
SQL> show parameter client_result_cache_size

NAME                         TYPE          VALUE
---------------------------  -----------   -----
client_result_cache_size     big integer     0
SQL>
```

  As this parameter is static, you must restart the database to affect a change in the maximum size of the client result cache.

- `client_result_cache_lag` This parameter determines the lag time for the client result cache. If you set a low value for this parameter, it results in more round trips to the database from the OCI client library to keep the client result cache in sync with the database. If your OCI application accesses the database only infrequently, you can set this parameter to a low value.

You can also use a client configuration file, which overrides the parameters you set in the server initialization parameter file. You can use the sqlnet.ora file to specify the parameter values on the client side. When you use the client configuration file, you can specify the following three parameters:

- `oci_result_cache_max_size` enables you to set the maximum size of the query cache for a process (in bytes). This parameter overrides the value you set for the `client_result_cache_lag_size` initialization parameter on the server.
- `oci_result_cache_max_rset_size` enables you to set the maximum size (in bytes) of a single query result in the query cache for a process.
- `oci_result_cache_max_rset_rows` enables you to set the maximum size of a query result set (in rows) for a process.

You can specify the `result_cache` and the `no_result_cache` hints in OCI applications, as with the SQL statements for the SQL query cache. However, the `OCIStmtExecute()` mode settings override the SQL hints.

Monitoring the Client Result Cache

The CLIENT_RESULT_CACHE_STATS$ view shows the client result cache settings and the cache usage statistics. The view includes information such as the number of results cached on the client, the number of cache hits, and the number of invalidated result sets.

Restrictions

You can't cache queries that include the following objects on the OCI client, even though you may cache them in the server-side result cache:

- Views
- Remote objects
- Complex types in the select list
- Flashback queries
- Queries that include PL/SQL functions
- Queries that reference VPD polices on the tables

CERTIFICATION OBJECTIVE 6.05

Adaptive Cursor Sharing

You use the `cursor_sharing` initialization parameter to specify whether only identical SQL statements or statements that differ in some literals can share a cursor. It is well known that using bind variables improves both performance and scalability because they reduce parse time and memory usage, especially in databases with heavy concurrent usage. However, what is not as well known is the fact that using literal values instead of bind variables leads to better execution plans because the optimizer has better information when dealing with literal values. Thus, forced cursor sharing (by specifying `cursor_sharing=exact` or `similar`) can lead to suboptimal execution plans for some statements because of the specific values of the bind variables in a SQL query.

Oracle uses the *bind peeking* technique, which allows the optimizer to peek at or to examine the bind values when you first execute a SQL statement. Based on the values it sees, the optimizer will formulate execution plans for subsequent executions of the same statement. The database performs bind peeking when it first hard parses a statement. If the data is heavily skewed, you run into a major problem with this bind peeking technique. The optimizer will base its execution plans on the initial values it sees during bind peeking. If, based on the values it observes, it decides that the plan needs to use an index, it will continue to include the index, even if the majority of values of the bind variable may indicate that using a full scan is actually a better strategy.

Under bind peeking, when you first execute a query, the optimizer hard-parses the statement and peeks at the bind variable in the process to glean an idea about the variable's actual values. The optimizer creates an explain plan based on the values it observed during its peeking and uses the same plan for subsequent executions of the query. If, during bind peeking, the optimizer sees representative values for the bind variable, everything is fine because that means the variable has a uniform selectivity. If the table is heavily skewed, on the other hand, the initial values the optimizer gleans during the bind peeking stage are critical. The skewed distribution means the optimizer's execution plan for the statement is likely to be correct only for those executions that use the same values for the bind variable as those observed by the optimizer during the initial "peeking." For other values of the bind variables, the execution plan could be way off. Traditionally, you avoided this problem by abandoning the use of bind variables altogether and using hard-coded values for the variables instead.

Oracle Database 11*g* introduces an adaptive cursor sharing feature to resolve the conflict between cursor sharing, which is supposed to increase efficiency, and query optimization. Under adaptive cursor sharing, when the database thinks that the cost of generating a new execution plan for a SQL statement is low enough that it outweighs the benefits of using the same cursor, it will generate new child cursors. The database still tries to keep the number of child cursors it generates to a minimum so the database can take advantage of cursor sharing, while avoiding automatically sharing the same cursor, as was the behavior in the previous release.

on the
‖
(j)o b

Adaptive cursor sharing is an automatic feature of Oracle Database 11g, and you can't turn it off. You don't have to configure any initialization parameters to avail yourself of this feature.

How Adaptive Cursor Sharing Works

Oracle Database 11g uses two key concepts—bind sensitivity of a cursor and a bind-aware cursor—to implement the new adaptive cursor sharing feature. A bind-sensitive cursor is one where caching the values of the bind variable could potentially lead to different execution plans. The database observes the different values passed to the bind variable before deciding whether to change the execution plan or to keep it the same. If the database estimates that the values are so different that it must work out a new execution plan, it marks the cursors as bind sensitive. If the database marks a cursor for bind-sensitive cursor sharing, the cursor is termed *bind-aware*. Adaptive cursor sharing works independent of the cursor sharing feature. Whether a user provides the bindings or the database replaces the literal values of a variable with system-generated bind variables doesn't matter.

Let's consider an example to demonstrate how adaptive cursor sharing works. The database executes the following query multiple times:

```
SQL> select * from hr.employees where salary = :1
     and department_id = :2;
```

The statement shown here uses two bind variables, one for the SALARY column and the other for the DEPARTMENT_ID column.

The very first time the database executes the SQL statement, it hard parses the statement and marks the cursor as a bind-sensitive cursor if it peeks at the bind values and uses histograms to compute the selectivity of the predicate with the two bind variables. The database stores the selectivity information, such as (0.15, 0.0025), in a selectivity cube. The database associates each plan with a selectivity cube. The selectivity cube provides a selectivity range for an execution plan. If the new bind values fall in the cube—that is, if the values lie in the selectivity range—the database will use the same plan. Otherwise, the optimizer generates a new execution plan for the statement. The database then monitors the execution of the statement to decide whether it should treat the cursor as a bind-aware cursor for each subsequent execution. The database soft parses the statement and compares the execution statistics to those of the first execution.

If the database determines that a cursor is bind-aware, it uses bind-aware cursor matching during the next execution of the query. Using the selectivity estimates that it stored in the selectivity cubes, the database performs a cursor check for the query. If the new bind values fall in the selectivity cube, the database will use the same plan. Otherwise, the database assumes that a matching child cursor hasn't been found and performs a hard parse to generate a new child cursor with a different execution plan. If the new hard parse produces an identical execution plan, it merges the child cursors. This means that when the bind values are approximately the same, SQL statements will share an execution plan.

If you're using SQL Plan Management by setting the parameter `optimizer_capture_sql_plan_baselines` to `TRUE`, the very first plan that the database captures for a SQL statement with bind variables is marked as the SQL plan baseline for that statement. If new plans are found later on, they are added to the plan history for that SQL statement and marked for verification, but aren't used. Only the first generated plan based on the first set of bind values is used, even though the adaptive cursor sharing feature comes up with new plans based on a new set of bind values. Under SQL Plan Management, the database doesn't use the other plans until it has verified them not to cause performance deterioration. The workaround is to disable the SQL Plan Management feature to begin with, by setting the `optimizer_capture_sql_plan_baselines` parameter to `FALSE`. Run your application and once the database populates the cursor cache with several plans with different bind values, manually load the entire plan from the cursor cache in the SQL plan baseline for that SQL statement. Now, by default the database marks all the plans for a statement as SQL plan baselines.

Monitoring Adaptive Cursor Sharing

You can monitor adaptive cursor sharing by using the new IS_BIND_SENSITIVE and IS_BIND_AWARE columns in the V$SQL view. The IS_BIND_SENSITIVE column indicates whether a cursor is bind sensitive. The IS_BIND_AWARE column indicates whether the database has marked a cursor to use bind-aware cursor sharing. Here's a query that uses the two columns described here:

```
SQL> select sql_id, executions, is_bind_sensitive, is_bind_aware
     from v$sql;
SQL_ID              EXECUTIONS      I      I
--------------      ----------      ---    ---
57pfs5p8xc07w       21              Y      N
1gfaj4z5hn1kf       4               Y      N
1gfaj4z5hn1kf       4               N      N
...
294 rows selected.
SQL>
```

The IS_BIND_SENSITIVE column shows whether the optimizer will generate multiple execution plans based on the bind variable values. In the example, the columns show `Y` as the value, meaning the database considers the cursor bind sensitive.

exam **watch** *Explain the difference between the IS_BIND_SENSITIVE and IS_BIND_AWARE columns in the V$SQL view.*

If, during its observation of the initial values of the bind variable, the database figures that the various values for the variables could potentially result in a different execution plan, it marks the cursor as bind sensitive, storing a value of Y in the IS_BIND_SENSITIVE column. Thus, a cursor marked as bind sensitive is a potential candidate for a change in its execution plan. The database waits for some more executions of the statement to find out more about the cursors, and either changes the execution plan or decides to keep it intact. If it changes the execution plan for a statement, it marks the cursor as bind aware and stores the value of Y in the IS_BIND_AWARE column. Cursors marked as bind aware are cursors for which the database has actually changed the execution plans based on its observation of the bind variable values.

If the IS_BIND_AWARE column shows a value of Y, the optimizer is planning to use multiple execution plans, depending on the value of the bind variable. This means that the optimizer knows that the bind variable values result in different data patterns and thus the statement may need hard parsing when the database executes it again.

In addition to the new columns in the V$SQL view, there are three new views to support the adaptive cursor sharing feature, as shown here:

- **V$SQL_CS_HISTOGRAM**   Shows the distribution of the execution count across the execution history histogram.
- **V$SQL_CS_SELECTIVITY**   Shows the selectivity cubes or ranges stored in cursors for predicates with bind variables.
- **V$SQL_CS_STATISTICS**   Contains the execution statistics of a cursor using different bind sets gathered by the database to decide on whether it should use bind-aware cursor sharing. The view contains execution statistics such as buffer gets and CPU time.

INSIDE THE EXAM

The exam will definitely query your understanding of the new ADDM features. You must be aware of the new global mode and the instance mode of the ADDM. Pay particular attention to the procedures that add directives to the ADDM, such as INSERT_SQL_DIRECTIVE and INSERT_ SEGMENT_DIRECTIVE. How does the execution of the INSERT_SEGMENT_ DIRECTIVE procedure constrain ADDM?

In terms of the new automatic memory management feature, you can expect to be questioned about the setting of the new initialization parameters memory_target and `memory_max_target`. What happens if you omit the `memory_target` parameter but set the `memory_max_target` parameter?

The exam will review the optimizer statistics collection new features such as extended statistics. The exam is likely to contain a question about the new multicolumn statistics enhancement. You must know how to use the DBMS_STATS.CREATE_EXTENDED_STATS function. What kind of column name does this function return? You must know how to set the appropriate attributes (`granularity=incremental`) for efficiently gathering global statistics. The exam will likely contain a question or two on the new pending statistics feature. Review the process of publishing pending statistics with the help of the DBMS_STATS.PUBLISH-PENDING_STATS procedure. You must know how to set the new initialization parameter `result_cache_`

mode and the values it can take. In terms of the SQL Query Result Cache, you should understand how to use the new parameters `result_cache_max_size`, `result_cache_max_result`, and `result_cache_max_expiration`. How do you use the DBMS_RESULT_CACHE package to manage memory allocation for the result cache and to view the status of the cache? Regarding the new client-side query cache, you must know how to set the initialization parameters `client_result_cache_size` and `client_result_cache_lag`.

You should understand how the adaptive cursor sharing feature works. Under what circumstances does the optimizer create new plans and when does it reuse an existing plan? What are bind-aware and bind-sensitive cursors?

CERTIFICATION SUMMARY

In Oracle Database 11g, you can use the ADDM in a special database mode to analyze the performance of an entire RAC system. You can also use DDM in a partial mode to analyze a subset of the instances in a cluster. You could also use several new finding directives to limit or filter the ADDM advisor findings.

The initialization parameters `memory_target` and `memory_max_target` let you enable automatic memory management. Under automatic memory management, the instance automatically calibrates the sizes of the SGA and the PGA based on the database workload.

You can set preferences such as `publish`, `stale_percent`, and `incremental` at the table, schema, database, and global level to override the default behavior of the GATHER_STATS procedure and automatic statistics gathering job. You can now collect global statistics for a partitioned table on an incremental basis, which is much faster than collecting statistics for the whole table. The deferred statistics publishing feature lets you test new statistics before publishing them. Until you publish the new statistics, they remain as pending statistics in a pending area.

You can use the multicolumn statistics feature to collect statistics for related column groups, thus improving the selectivity estimates. Expression statistics enable you to collect statistics of some types of expressions on columns, enhancing the accuracy of the selectivity estimates.

The result cache is a special area in the database where the database stores the results of frequently executed SQL statements and PL/SQL functions. Performance is significantly better when the database uses the result cache because the database simply retrieves the results for these statements and functions from memory instead of re-executing the code. The client query result cache operates on the client side to cache the results of frequently executed queries, saving resources and reducing network usage in the process. The Adaptive Cursor sharing feature is an attempt to resolve the inherent conflict between query optimization and efficient processing of queries.

✓ TWO-MINUTE DRILL

ADDM Enhancements

❑ You can use the ADDM to analyze an entire RAC system.

❑ You can deploy the ADDM in Database, Instance, and Partial analysis modes.

❑ The Database analysis mode analyzes performance of all instances.

❑ The Instance mode analyzes a particular instance.

❑ The Partial mode analyzes a subset of the instances in an Oracle RAC.

❑ Use the SET_DEFAULT_TASK_PARAMETER procedure to specify the mode in which you want to run the ADDM.

❑ Use the new package DBMS_ADDM to manage the ADDM.

❑ Oracle Database 11g classifies and names the ADDM advisor findings.

❑ The new DBA_ADVISOR_FINDINGS view shows which findings occur most frequently in the database.

❑ You can use an ADDM finding directive to limit or filter the ADDM findings.

❑ You can create directives to limit findings reports of a specific finding type, a specific SQL statement, or a segment or a set of segments.

❑ The FILTERED column in the DBA_ADVISOR_ACTIONS view shows if a row was filtered out by a directive.

Automatic Memory Management

❑ Under automatic memory management, the database moves memory between the SGA and the PGA as necessary based on the workload.

❑ You set up automatic memory management by using the initialization parameters `memory_target` and `memory_max_target`.

❑ If you set the `sga_target` and `pga_target` parameters along with the `memory_target` parameter, the database will consider them the minimum values for the SGA and PGA.

❑ By default, the `memory_max_target` parameter's value is set to that of the `memory_target` parameter.

❑ The default value of the `memory_target` parameter is zero, which means that automatic memory management is disabled by default.

❑ If you set the `memory_max_target` parameter but leave out the `memory_target` parameter, automatic memory management will be disabled.

❑ You can specify automatic memory management when you create a database using the DBCA.

Enhancements in Optimizer Statistics Collection

❑ The Statistics Preference feature allows you to easily modify statistics collection settings for specific database objects by overriding default behavior of procedures in the DBMS_STATS package.

❑ The DBA_TAB_STATS_PREFS view shows current settings for statistics preferences.

❑ You can set preferences at the table, schema, database, and global level.

❑ Preferences you set at the table level override database and global-level preferences.

❑ The three new statistics preferences you can set in Oracle Database 11g are `publish`, `stale_percent`, and `incremental`.

❑ You can use the SET_PREFS procedure of the DBMS_STATS package to set preferences at various levels.

❑ In Oracle Database 11g, the database maintains global statistics incrementally, by scanning only the changed partitions and using the old statistics for the unchanged partitions.

❑ You must specify the granularity level as `global` and mark a table as `incremental`, to collect global statistics on an incremental basis.

❑ Oracle recommends that you let the `estimate_percent` attribute remain at the default value of `auto_sample_size` to take advantage of a new row sampling technique that offers very accurate results with small sample sizes.

❑ Pending statistics are private statistics that aren't yet made available to the optimizer.

❑ The GET_PREFS procedure can tell you whether the database will automatically publish new optimizer statistics.

❑ Use the SET_TABLE_PREFS and the SET_SCHEMA_PREFS procedures to change the publishing setting for statistics.

❑ Set the initialization parameter `optimizer_pending_statistics` to TRUE, to make all pending statistics available to the optimizer.

❑ You can also use the PUBLISH_PENDING_STATS procedure to make all pending statistics public.

❑ Using statistics for a column group enables you to estimate the combined selectivity of related columns in a table.

❑ You use the CREATE_EXTENDED_STATS function to create a new column group.

❑ You can have the database collect statistics for column groups by using the METHOD_OPT parameter of the GATHER_TABLE_STATS procedure.

❑ The optimizer can now collect expression statistics that include user-defined functions as well as function-based indexes.

❑ You can execute either the CREATE_EXTENDED_STATS function or the GATHER_TABLE_STATS procedure to collect extension statistics.

Result Cache

❑ The result cache is a component of the shared pool, and the database uses it to store the results of both SQL queries and PL/SQL functions.

❑ Good candidates for result caching are queries that access many rows and return only a few rows.

❑ Both components of the server-side result cache—the SQL query result cache and the PL/SQL function cache—share the same infrastructure.

❑ The database automatically determines the size of the Result Cache Memory pool.

❑ You set the size of the result cache by using the `result_cache_max_size` parameter.

❑ You can disable the result cache by setting the `result_cache_max_size` parameter to zero.

❑ The `result_cache_max_result` parameter specifies the maximum percentage of the result cache that can be used by a single cached result.

❑ The `result_cache_remote_expiration` period determines the length of time for which a result that uses remote objects will remain valid.

❑ There are several procedures in the DBMS_RESULT_CACHE procedure that help you manage the result cache.

❑ If you set the `result_cache_mode` parameter to `manual`, the database won't cache any results unless you use a `result_cache` hint in a query.

❑ If you set the `result_cache_mode` parameter to `force`, the database caches all results, unless you specify the `no_result_cache` hint in a query.

❑ When you use the `result_cache` hint in a query, the database uses the ResultCache operator in the execution plan for that query.

❑ The `relies_on` clause inside a PL/SQL function specifies that the database invalidate the cached results of the function when the tables listed under this clause are modified.

❑ The OCI result cache enables client-side caching of SQL result sets.

❑ The server result cache and the client result cache work independent of each other.

❑ As with the server-side result cache, you use the `result_cache_mode` initialization parameter to manage the client-side result caching.

❑ You set the `client_result_cache_size` parameter to a positive value to enable client-side result caching.

❑ The `client_result_cache_lag` parameter determines the lag time for the client result cache. You can use a client configuration file to set parameters that will override the parameters affecting the client result cache that you set in the server initialization parameter file.

Adaptive Cursor Sharing

❑ Bind peeking by the optimizer can lead to inefficient execution plans, because of skewed data distributions.

❑ Adaptive cursor sharing attempts to resolve the inherent conflict between the efficiency brought about by using bind variables and query optimization.

❑ Adaptive cursor sharing is automatic in Oracle Database 11g.

❑ If the optimizer generates multiple execution plans based on the bind variable values, the database considers the cursor bind sensitive.

❑ If the optimizer knows that the bind variable values result in different data patterns, the database considers the SQL statement bind aware.

SELF TEST

ADDM Enhancements

1. In the Partial mode of analysis, ADDM analyzes performance for
   A. Part of the day
   B. Part of the database
   C. Part of all tables in a database
   D. A subset of instances in the RAC

2. In the following example, what do the numbers 5 and 50 mean?

```
SQL> begin
        dbms_addm.insert_finding_directive(NULL,
        'SGA Directive',
        Undersized SGA',
        5,
        50);
    :   tname := 'Test ADDM Task';
        dbms_addm.analyze_inst(:tname,1634,1635);
end;
```

   A. The number of average active sessions and the percent of the total database time
   B. Total number of sessions and the percent of the total database time
   C. The number of average active sessions and the total database time
   D. The number of average active sessions and the time for which the ADDM analysis must run

3. What does the `insert_sql_directive` do when you are executing an ADDM job?
   A. Inserts SQL statements that the directive must test
   B. Inserts SQL statements that the ADDM must test
   C. Creates a directive to limit a reporting on specific SQL statements
   D. Inserts a directive to limit a reporting on specific SQL statements

Automatic Memory Management

4. If you set the `memory_target` parameter, which of the following would be true?
   A. If you set the `sga_target` and the `pga_aggregate_target` parameters, then the database will override your settings for these two components.
   B. If you also set the `sga_target` and the `pga_aggregate_target` parameters, they will be considered the minimum values for the SGA and PGA allocations of memory.
   C. If you set the SGA but not the PGA, the database will not automatically tune SGA.
   D. If you set the PGA but not the SGA, the database will not automatically tune PGA.

5. If you don't set the `memory_target` initialization parameter or explicitly set it to zero, the following would be true:
   A. If you set neither the `pga_aggregate_target` nor the `sga_target` parameters, SGA is not automatically tuned, but the PGA is.
   B. The database will not automatically tune the SGA or the PGA.
   C. The database will always automatically tune the SGA.
   D. Automatic memory management will be disabled.

6. What happens if you exclude the `memory_max_target` parameter when you use automatic memory management?
   A. The database will have no maximum memory usage setting.
   B. The `memory_max_target` parameter will be set to the value of the `memory_target` parameter.
   C. The database can only manage the SGA automatically, but not the PGA.
   D. If you set the `memory_max_target` initialization parameter but not the `memory_target` parameter, the `memory_target` parameter's value will be the same as the value of the `memory_max_target` parameter.

Enhancements in Optimizer Statistics Collection

7. What does the database do when collecting statistics if you specify the granularity level as `global` and mark a table as `incremental`?
   A. The database collects global statistics on an incremental basis.
   B. The database collects partition statistics on an incremental basis.
   C. The database won't collect any statistics at all.
   D. The database collects incremental statistics on a global basis.

8. Which of the following statements or commands will let the optimizer make use of pending statistics for its execution plans?
   A. `exec dbms_stats.export_pending_stats('hr','employees');`
   B. `exec dbms_stats.import_pending_stats('hr','employees');`
   C. `exec dbms_stats.publish_pending_stats(null, null);`
   D. `exec dbms_stats.delete_pending_stats('hr','employees');`

9. What argument in the DBMS_STATS package do you use to make the database collect optimizer statistics on column groups?
   A. `method_opt` argument of the GATHER_TABLE_STATS procedure
   B. `estimate_only` argument of the GATHER_TABLE_STATS procedure
   C. `method_opt` argument of the CREATE_EXTENDED_STATS function
   D. `method_opt` argument of the CREATE_PREFS procedure

Result Cache

10. What does the `result_cache_max_result` parameter do?
  A. It sets the maximum time for which a result will remain valid in the result cache.
  B. It sets the maximum number of times the database can reuse a result in the result cache.
  C. It specifies the maximum percentage of the result cache that a single cached result can use.
  D. It specifies the maximum number of cached results in the result cache at any given time.

11. When the result cache grows until it reaches its maximum size,
  A. The result cache automatically releases the memory.
  B. You must use the BYPASS procedure to bypass the result cache.
  C. You must restart the result cache.
  D. You must use the FLUSH procedure to purge the result cache.

12. If you set the `result_cache_mode` parameter to the value `force` in order to make the database cache SQL query results,
  A. The database determines which queries to cache.
  B. You can override the default behavior by specifying the `result_cache` hint in a query.
  C. You can override the default behavior by specifying the `no_result_cache` hint in a query.
  D. The database will cache only the results with the `result_cache` hint in a query.

Adaptive Cursor Sharing

13. A bind-sensitive SQL query is one where
  A. During its observation of the initial values of the bind variable, Oracle comes to the conclusion that the various values could potentially result in a different execution plan, so it marks the cursor as bind sensitive.
  B. Caching the bind variable values leads to only a single execution plan.
  C. A query's results depend on the bind variable values.
  D. The database determines that changing the execution plan will lead to inefficient results.

14. If you're using SQL Plan Management,
  A. The very first plan captured for a statement is the only plan that the database can ever use.
  B. If new plans are found, they automatically become a part of the SQL plan baseline for that statement.
  C. If new plans are found, they are added to the plan history for that statement, verified, and used automatically.
  D. If new plans are found, they are added to the plan history for that statement and marked for verification, but they aren't automatically used.

15. When you use adaptive cursor sharing, if new values for a bind variable are within the selectivity cube of bind values for that cursor,

   A. The database will use a different execution plan.

   B. The database will use the same execution plan and perform a hard parse.

   C. The database will use the same execution plan and doesn't perform a hard parse.

   D. The database doesn't use an explain plan for that SQL statement.

LAB QUESTION

Show you can use the deferred statistics publishing feature to test the statistics the optimizer collects before publishing them. Use the HR schema and the EMPLOYEES table to demonstrate how you'd implement the feature.

SELF TEST ANSWERS

ADDM Enhancements

1. ☑ **D** is correct because you use this mode of analysis to let the ADDM analyze a subset of the instances in a RAC system.

   ☒ **A** is incorrect because the partial mode has to with a subset of instances in the RAC system, not the length of time for which the ADDM analysis task runs. **B** is incorrect because you can't use the ADDM to analyze only a part of the database. **C** is incorrect because the ADDM analyzes all the tables in a database under all three modes in which you can run it.

2. ☑ **A** is correct because the first name refers to the number of average active sessions and the second number, the percent of total database time.

   ☒ **B, C,** and **D** are incorrect because they refer to the wrong parameters.

3. ☑ **C** is correct because you use the `insert_sql` directive to limit the ADDM findings on specific SQL statements.

   ☒ **A** is incorrect because the `insert_sql` directive doesn't insert SQL statements for the directive to test. **B** is incorrect because you can't use this directive to specify any SQL statements for the ADDM to test. The ADDM can only use the SQL statements it finds in the Automatic Workload Repository. **D** is incorrect because the `insert_sql` directive doesn't insert a directive, but creates a directive.

Automatic Memory Management

4. ☑ **B** is correct. If you set the `memory_target` parameter, the database will treat any values you assign that you set for the `sga_target` and the `pga_aggregate_target` parameters as the minimum values for the SGA and the PGA, respectively.

   ☒ **A** is incorrect because the database doesn't ignore the values you set for the `sga_target` and the `pga_aggregate_target` parameters under automatic memory management. Rather, the database considers the values you set for these two parameters as the minimum values for the SGA and the PGA, respectively. **C** is incorrect because the database will automatically tune the SGA. **D** is incorrect because the database will always tune the PGA.

5. ☑ **A** and **D** are correct. **A** is correct because if you don't set the `pga_aggregate_target` and the `sga_target` parameters, the database won't automatically tune the SGA component. The database always automatically tunes the PGA. **D** is correct because setting the `memory_target` parameter to zero disables automatic memory management.

   ☒ **B** is incorrect because even if you don't institute automatic memory management, the database always automatically tunes the PGA. **C** is incorrect because if you don't set the `memory_target` parameter or set it to zero, the database doesn't automatically tune the SGA. You must specify the `sga_target` parameter to set your own value for this parameter.

6. ☑ **D** is correct. If you don't set the `memory_max_target` parameter, it defaults to the value you set for the `memory_target` parameter.

☒ **A** is incorrect because the database will have a maximum memory usage setting, which will be the same as the value for the `memory_target` parameter. **B** is incorrect because the instance will have a maximum memory setting, the value being that set by the `memory_max_target` parameter. **C** is incorrect because the database automatically manages both SGA and PGA when you set the `memory_target` parameter. The fact that you didn't set a value for the `memory_max_target` has no bearing on whether the database automatically manages the SGA or the PGA.

Enhancements in Optimizer Statistics Collection

7. ☑ **A** is correct because the database will collect global statistics for the partitioned table on an incremental basis. The database will look at only the changed contents of the table instead of scanning the entire table when it collects statistics.

☒ **B** is incorrect because the database collects global statistics on incremental basis, not partition statistics on an incremental basis. **C** is incorrect because the database does collect global incremental statistics. **D** is incorrect because the database collects global statistics on an incremental basis.

8. ☑ **C** is correct. The PUBLISH_PENDING_STATS procedure allows the optimizer to make use of the pending statistics for a table.

☒ **A** is incorrect because the EXPORT_PENDING_STATS procedure only allows you to export the pending statistics on objects to a test database, where you can test their impact. **B** is incorrect because the IMPORT_PENDING_STATS procedure enables you to import pending statistics from one database to another for testing purposes, but won't help you publish the statistics. **D** is incorrect because the DELETE_PENDING_STATS procedure lets you delete the pending statistics on an object if they don't prove useful after testing.

9. ☑ **A** is correct. You use the `method_opt` argument of the GATHER_TABLE_STATS procedure to let the database collect optimizer statistics on a column group.

☒ **B, C,** and **D** are incorrect because they either refer to a wrong or nonexistent argument of a function or procedure.

Result Cache

10. ☑ **C** is correct. The `result_cache_max_result` parameter lets you specify the maximum percentage of the result cache that any single cached result can use.

☒ **A** is incorrect because the parameter has nothing to do with the amount of time a result will remain valid. A result will remain valid as long as the underlying objects don't change and there is enough free memory in the result cache. **B** is incorrect because there is no limit on the number of times the database can reuse a result stored in the result cache. **D** is incorrect because you can't specify the number of cached results that the database can store in the result cache. The number of results in the cache depends on the memory the database allocates to the result cache.

11. ☑ **A** is correct because the result cache automatically releases the memory being used by stored results when the result cache reaches its maximum size. The results are removed on the basis of a least recently used (LRU) algorithm.

☒ **B** is incorrect because if you use the BYPASS procedure, you won't be able to take advantage of the result cache any longer. You can free up space by executing the FLUSH procedure instead to purge the result cache. **C** is incorrect because you don't have to resort to disabling and enabling the result cache to free up space for new results. While this will provide room for storing new results, the fact that the result cache has reached its maximum size implies that there are several results already cached there. By disabling and then enabling the result cache, which has the effect of restarting the result cache, you'll be removing all the cached results. **D** is incorrect because while you can execute the FLUSH procedure to free up space in the result cache, you don't have to do it.

12. ☑ **C** is correct because you can override the default behavior of the database when you set the `auto` option, which is to cache a query result based on its frequency of execution, by specifying the `no result cache` hint in a query.

☒ **A, B,** and **D** are incorrect. **A** is incorrect because the database doesn't make a determination as to which queries to cache. It simply caches all queries wherever it is possible to do so. **B** is incorrect because you don't have to set the `result cache` hint in the statements; the database determines which queries to cache. **D** is incorrect because you don't need to specify the `result_cache` hint when you set the `result_cache_mode` parameter to `force`. Under the `force` option, the database will cache all results wherever it's possible to do so.

Adaptive Cursor Sharing

13. ☑ **A** is correct. If, during its observation of the initial values of the bind variable, the database determines that the various values could potentially result in a different execution plan, it marks the cursor as bind sensitive, The IS_BIND_SENSITIVE column in the V$SQL view shows whether the optimizer will generate multiple execution plans based on the bind variable values. If the column shows Y as the value, it means that the database considers the cursor bind sensitive.

☒ **B** is incorrect because the database doesn't use the same execution plan for a bind-sensitive query. **C** is incorrect because a bind-sensitive query doesn't mean that its results depend on the bind variable values. Even a query that's not bind sensitive will depend on the bind variable values. **D** is incorrect because a bind-sensitive query will actually benefit from the use of different execution plans.

14. ☑ **D** is correct. If you're using SQL Plan Management, the database adds all new plans for a query to the plan history for that statement. The database will mark these new plans for verification and will mark them as accepted plans only after it successfully verifies that the new plans offer better performance than the plan or plans already in the plan baseline.

☒ **A** is incorrect because while the very first plan in the plan baseline is always marked as an accepted plan, it isn't the only plan that the database uses. The database may also use any new plans that it finds because it verifies that they offer superior performance. **B** is incorrect because when the database finds new plans, it doesn't automatically make them part of the SQL plan baseline for a statement. A plan becomes a part of the SQL plan baseline only after its verification by the database. **C** is incorrect because the database doesn't automatically use a new plan. It uses a new plan only after it verifies it first. The verification may lead to the acceptance of the new plan into the SQL plan baseline or its rejection, if the new plan doesn't offer the required improvement in performance.

15. ☑ **C** is correct. Under adaptive cursor sharing, if the new bind values fall in the selectivity cube, the database doesn't see any need to create a new execution plan. It reuses the same execution plan and performs a soft parse instead of a hard parse for the next execution of the cursor.

☒ **A** is incorrect because the database uses the same execution plan when the new set of bind values doesn't differ much from the original set of values. **B** is incorrect because the database performs a soft parse if the new bind values fall in the selectivity cube. **D** is incorrect because the database will always use an explain plan. The big question is whether it will use the same execution plan or a new plan. If the new sets of bind values aren't that much different from the old set of values, there isn't any need to change the execution plan.

LAB ANSWER

Follow these steps to use the deferred statistics publishing feature in Oracle Database 11g. I use the HR schema and the EMPLOYEES table to demonstrate the feature.

1. Execute the SET_TABLE_PREFS procedure to keep the optimizer from automatically publishing the statistics for the EMPLOYEES table as current statistics.

```
SQL> exec dbms_stats.set_table_prefs('hr','employees',
     'publish','false');
```

2. Collect the statistics for the EMPLOYEES table.

```
SQL> exec dbms_stats.gather_table_stats('hr','employees');
```

The statistics are stored in the pending area instead of the data dictionary.

3. In order to test the new pending statistics before making them public, you must execute the following statement:

```
SQL> alter session set optimizer_use_pending_statistics=true;
```

4. You can now issue various queries that refer to the HR.EMPLOYEES table to test performance.

5. If you're satisfied with the test results, you can make the pending statistics on the EMPLOYEES table public using the PUBLISH_PENDING_STATS procedure.

```
SQL> exec dbms_stats,publish_pending_stats('hr','employees');
```

The pending statistics on the EMPLOYEES table will be current (published) statistics now.

7

RMAN and Flashback Enhancements

CERTIFICATION OBJECTIVES

7.01	RMAN Enhancements	✓	Two-Minute Drill
7.02	Recovery Catalog Management	Q&A	Self Test
7.03	New Flashback-Related Features		

Thi chapter discusses the enhancements to Oracle's backup and recovery tool, the Recovery Manager (RMAN), and the additions to the flashback feature, which Oracle introduced in the Oracle9i release. There are two major enhancements to Oracle's flashback capability: the *flashback data archive* feature lets you archive all changes to a table and the *flashback transaction backout* feature enables you to back out a transaction with a single click.

CERTIFICATION OBJECTIVE 7.01

RMAN Enhancements

RMAN includes several interesting new features, including the following:

- Active (network-based) database duplication
- Parallel backup and restore of large files (multisection backups)
- Archival (long-term) backups
- Fast incremental backups
- Improved lock media recovery performance
- New persistent configuration parameters
- Backup failover to non-flash recovery areas

I start with a discussion of RMAN's exciting active database duplication feature.

Active (Network-Based) Database Duplication

Oracle Database 11g extends the well-known `duplicate database` command to let you duplicate a database over the network without any need for prior backups of the source database. This feature is called *active database duplication* or *network-aware database duplication*. Using the active duplication method, you can duplicate a live or active database, with a minimal network and CPU overhead. You can perform the duplication on the same or a different server in your network. You don't need to make any copies of the source database, which saves you time and storage space. You can use active database duplication techniques to clone a database or create a standby database. You can use either RMAN to perform the backup or use Database Control.

The source database can remain open to the users while you're performing the active database duplication. This means that you don't have to suffer any downtime to perform the database duplication. RMAN always performs an incomplete recovery when you use the active database duplication method because it doesn't copy the online redo log files to apply them to the duplicate database. RMAN can recover only up to the most recent archived redo log on the source database.

Requirements

You must satisfy the following requirements in order to perform active database duplication:

- You must make sure you can connect to both the target and the duplicate databases through Oracle Net.
- Both the target and the duplicate databases must use an identical operating system platform.
- You must use password files on both databases to register the SYSDBA password.
- You can run the source database in the mount or open state. If it is in the open state, it must be in the archivelog mode.
- You can make the database automatically copy the source database password file to the server hosting the duplicate database by specifying the `password file` clause in the `duplicate database` statement.

exam
Watch

You must understand all the important clauses you use in the `duplicate database` command when performing active database duplication.

What's the relationship between the `set` clause and the `db_file_name_convert` and the `log_file_name_convert` parameters?

In order to name the files of the duplicate database, you can use one or more file naming techniques. Oracle recommends that you specify the new clause `spfile` to name the duplicate database's datafiles. You can supplement this file-naming technique with one or more other file-naming techniques, such as specifying the `db_file_name_convert` parameter. The following are various options you can use to set filenames for the duplicate database:

- `spfile...parameter_value_convert 'string_pattern'`
  Specifies conversion strings for all initialization parameters specifying path

names, except the `db_file_name_convert` and `log_file_name_convert` parameters. You can also specify the `parameter_value_convert` clause to update string values.

- `spfile...set 'string_pattern'` Enables you to specify the `log_file_name_convert` parameter for the online redo log files. The `set` clause enables you to specify initialization parameters such as `sga_target`, for example. The `set` clause in effect stops the duplication process midway and alters the initialization parameter values in the restored parameter file by issuing multiple `alter system set` statements. Because the `set` clauses are processed after the `parameter_value_convert` clause, the value you set for a parameter using a `set` clause will override the values for the same parameters set through the `parameter_value_convert` clause.

- `db_file_name_convert 'string_pattern'` Enables you to specify file-naming rules for creating the duplicate database's datafiles and tempfiles.

Specifying the `spfile` clause is straightforward and simple. The following example demonstrates how to specify the `spfile` clause within the `duplicate database` command to name data files and log files for the new database you're creating from the source database.

```
RMAN> duplicate database to dupdb
   2> from active database
   3> db_file_name_convert '/u01/app/oracle','/u05/app/oracle'
   4> spfile
   5> parameter_value_convert '/u01/app/oracle','/u05/app/oracle'
   6> set log_file_name_convert '/u01/app/oracle',
      '/u05/app/oracle'
   7> set sga_max_size '3000m'
   8> set sga_target '2000m';
```

In the example,

- The `from active database` clause specifies that the files for the duplicate (or standby) database must be provided directly from the source database and not from the source database backups.

- The `db_file_name_convert` clause substitutes the string /u05/app/oracle in the names of the duplicate database's datafiles (and tempfiles).

- The `spfile` clause copies the server parameter file from the source database to an operating system–specific default location on the server hosting the duplicate database. This means that an SPFILE and not a text-based initialization parameter file must be in use by the source database instance. RMAN will use the SPFILE to start the auxiliary instance for creating the duplicate database. The database will process all remaining options in the `duplicate database` command after it starts the new duplicate database instance (auxiliary instance) with the source database's SPFILE.

■ The `parameter_value_convert` clause in the example specifies the string `/u05/app/oracle` to be used in all initialization parameters that specify filenames for the duplicate database, except the `db_file_name_ convert` and `log_file_name_convert` parameters.

■ The `set` clauses specify initialization parameters, including the `log_file_ name_convert` parameter, which specifies the substitution of `/u05/app/ oracle` in the filenames of the duplicate database's online redo log files.

Oracle has enhanced the well-known `duplicate database` command to enable you to perform active database duplication. To perform network-based duplication, add the new clause `from active database` to the `duplicate database` command. The following command creates a duplicate database on a different server using the same directory structure as the source database:

```
RMAN> connect target sys/oracle@prod1
RMAN> connect auxiliary sys/oracle@prod1
RMAN> duplicate target database to dupdb
  2> from active database
  3> spfile
  4> nofilenamecheck;
```

The `spfile` clause directs the database to copy the target database's spfile to the duplicate database. All the initialization parameters you specify for the source database in its spfile will also apply to the duplicate database. However, this is an exception because you usually want to alter some parameters, in which case you specify the `set` clause to specify the values of the parameters right in the `duplicate database` command. The following examples demonstrate how to use the `set` clause to specify parameter values:

■ `set db_file_name_convert '/disk1','/disk10'`
■ `set log_file_name_convert '/disk1','/disk10'`
■ `set sga_max_size '500m'`
■ `set sga_target '250m'`

If you specify the same parameter in both the SPFILE and the `set` clause, the values you specify in the `set` clause will override those in the SPFILE for that initialization parameter. You must use the `nofilenamecheck` clause because the two databases are on different hosts and you want the database to bypass the needless checks to ensure that the datafile and online redo log file names in the primary and the duplicate databases are different. You worry about filenames on the source and the target being identical only when you are duplicating a database to the same host. If the two databases are on separate hosts and you want the duplicate database filenames to be the same as the source database files, you must specify the `nofilenamecheck` clause.

An Active Database Duplication Example

Let's learn how to use the active database duplication technique by duplicating a database on the same server. This means, of course, that you must have different datafile names for the target and the duplicate database. Because you're using network-enabled duplication, you must first ensure that both databases are known to Oracle Net. Use the following steps to perform the network-enabled duplication of a database:

1. Add the name of the duplicate instance, which is test1 in this example, to the listener.ora file on the host of the source database.

```
SID_LIST_LISTENER =
(SID_DESC =
(GLOBAL_DBNAME = prod1)
(ORACLE_HOME = /u01/app/oracle/product/10.1g/)
(SID_NAME =prod1)
    )
(SID_DESC =
(GLOBAL_DBNAME = test1)
(ORACLE_HOME = /u01/app/oracle/product/11.1/)
(SID_NAME =test1)
   )
   )
```

2. Restart or reload the listener after making the changes shown here. Make sure you also update the tnsnames.ora file with the information about the duplicate database, test1.

```
test1 =
(DESCRIPTION =
(ADDRESS_LIST =
(ADDRESS = (PROTOCOL = TCP)(HOST = prod1)(PORT = 1521))
)
(CONNECT_DATA =
(SERVER = DEDICATED)
```

```
(SERVICE_NAME = test1)
  )
  )
```

3. When you execute the `duplicate database` command with the `spfile` clause, you must have already started the auxiliary instance with a text-based initialization parameter file. Create an initialization parameter file for the duplicate databases with just the db_name parameter in it. The new database will use the db_file_name_convert and the log_file_name_convert parameters in the `duplicate database` command to specify filenames. The text-based initialization parameter file for the duplicate database then will contain just one parameter:

   db_name=test1

   Since I specify the `spfile` clause in the `duplicate database` command, RMAN will copy the source database's SPFILE to the server hosting the auxiliary instance, make changes to the initialization parameters according to the parameter settings specified in the `spfile` clause, and then restart the auxiliary instance with the modified SPFILE.

4. Create a password file to connect to the auxiliary instance during the database duplication. The password you specify for SYSDBA in the password file must be the same as the password in the source database.

   ```
   $ orapwd file=orapwtest1 password=<sys_pwd>
     entries=20  ignorecase=n
   ```

   You can also specify the `password file` clause in the `duplicate database` statement to copy the source database's password file to the target database.

5. Start the auxiliary instance in the nomount mode, as shown here:

   ```
   $ sqlplus /nolog
   SQL> connect sys/sammyy1 as sysdba
   Connected to an idle instance
   SQL> startup nomount
   Oracle Instance started.
   Total System Global Area       113246208 bytes
   Fixed Size                       1218004 bytes
   Variable Size                   58722860 bytes
   Database Buffers                50331648 bytes
   Redo Buffers                     2973696 bytes
   SQL>
   ```

You don't yet have a control file for the auxiliary instance and therefore can't mount the new database. The `startup nomount` command uses the SPFILE to start the auxiliary instance in the `nomount` mode. The `spfile` clause specifies that RMAN copy the entire SPFILE belonging to the source database to the server hosting the auxiliary database.

6. Connect to the target database using the RMAN client. The source database must be running in the archivelog mode for you to duplicate it.

```
$rman target sys/sammyy1@eleven
connected to target database: ELEVEN (DBID=3481681133)
```

7. Once you connect to the target database, establish a connection to the auxiliary instance, as shown here:

```
RMAN> connect auxiliary sys/sammyy1@test1
connected to auxiliary database: TEST1 (not mounted)
RMAN>
```

8. Issue the `duplicate target database` command to create the duplicate database. The `from active database` clause tells RMAN to copy the source datafiles over the network to create the duplicate database.

```
RMAN> duplicate target database
     2> to test1
     3> from active database
     4> spfile
     5> parameter_value_convert
         '/u01/app/oracle/eleven','/u10/app/oracle/test1'
     6> set log_file_name_convert
         '/u05/app/oracle/eleven', '/u10/app/oracle/test1'
     7> db_file_name_convert '/u10/app/oracle/eleven',
         '/u10/app/oracle/test1';

Starting Duplicate Db at 28-DEC-07
using target database control file instead of recovery
 catalog
contents of Memory Script:
{
  sql "declare worked boolean;
   begin worked := dbms_backup_restore.networkFileTransfer(
   ''auxdb'', null, null,
...
executing Memory Script
...
Starting backup at 28-DEC-07
...
```

```
Finished backup at 28-DEC-07
...
contents of Memory Script:
{
   set until scn  901715;
   recover
   clone database
   delete archivelog
   ;
}
...
starting media recovery
...
media recovery complete, elapsed time: 00:00:01
Finished recover at 28-DEC-07
...
database opened
Finished Duplicate Db at 28-DEC-07
RMAN>
```

When you issue the `duplicate target database` command, RMAN updates the SPFILE of the duplicate database using the values you supply through the `parameter_name_convert` and the `set` clauses. RMAN then starts the auxiliary instance using this SPFILE and starts copying the source datafiles over the network. After it completes the copying of the datafiles, RMAN performs a recovery of the duplicate database and opens it.

During the database duplication, RMAN

- Copies the datafiles
- Doesn't copy the flash recovery area files
- Copies the archived redo logs if they are necessary for the duplication
- Copies the SPFILE to the server where you are creating the duplicate database, if you specify the `spfile` clause
- Copies the password file if you specify the `password file` clause
- Re-creates the control files
- Re-creates the tempfiles in the directory you specify with the `db_create_file_dest` parameter
- Re-creates the online redo logs

As you can see from our example, active database duplication offers an attractive alternative to the traditional backup-based RMAN database duplication technique; you don't have to use any backup files or incur any downtime for the duplication.

Parallel Backup and Restore of Large Files

Oracle Database 11g enables you to back up and restore large files in sections, with a section-level backup known as a multisection backup. A section is a contiguous set of blocks in a file. Each backup piece in a backup set will contain blocks from a file section. The multisection backup capability enables you to easily handle larger datafile size standards by breaking up a large file into sections and backing up or restoring each section separately. When faced with large file sizes such as 32 GB, multisection backups offer faster backups, because you can back up the different sections in parallel.

Since each RMAN channel backs up a different section of a datafile under multisection backups, you can get better performance when backing up large data files with multiple channels. If your backup of a large file fails midway, you can back up only the sections that weren't backed up, after resuming the backup. RMAN creates uniform-sized sections for all but the very last section, which may or may not be of the same size as the other sections. You can create as many as 256 sections per datafile. RMAN allows you to specify different section sizes for different datafiles in the same backup job.

e x a m

ⓦatch   *Demonstrate that you can make a multisection backup using the new section size attribute.*

Performing Multisection Backups

You must specify the backup command clause section size for RMAN to create a multisection backup. You must specify a value for the section size parameter. If you omit a value for the section size parameter, RMAN assigns a default value for section size. Each section corresponds to a backup piece in the backup set for a backup.

The following example shows how to specify the section size clause to perform a multisection backup.

1. Connect to the target database:

   ```
   $ rman target sys/<sys_password>@target_db
   ```

2. In order to take advantage of parallelism, configure multiple channels. In this example, I use a parallel setting of four and create four SBT channels.

   ```
   RMAN> run
   {{allocate channel c1 device type sbt
    parms 'env=(ob device 1=testtape1)';
   allocate channel c2 device type sbt
   ```

```
    parms 'env=(ob device 2=testtape2)';
allocate channel c3 device type sbt
parms 'env=(ob device 3=testtape3)';
 {allocate channel c4 device type sbt
 parms 'env=(ob device 4=testtape4)';
             }
```

3. Issue the `backup` command, specifying the `section size` parameter:

```
RMAN> backup
   2> section size 200m
   3> tablespace example;
```

If the tablespace EXAMPLE uses a single datafile that's 800m, RMAN backs it up into four sections, each 200m in size, with each section in a different backup piece.

on the job ***You can't specify the `section size` attribute along with the `maxpiecesize` attribute.***

In addition to the `backup` command, you can also specify the `section size` clause with the `validate datafile` command, as I show later in this chapter.

Managing Multisection Backups

You can query the V$BACKUP_DATAFILE and the RC_BACKUP_DATAFILE views to get information about multisection backups. The SECTION_SIZE column in both of these views reveals the size of each section in a multisection backup, in blocks. If this column shows a zero value, it means that it's a whole file backup and not a multisection backup. You can query the V$BACKUP_SET and the RC_BACKUP_SET views to see which backups are multisection backups, as shown by the following query on the V$BACKUP_DATAFILE view:

```
SQL> select piece, multi_section from v$backup_datafile;
PIECES              MUL
-------             ----
1                   NO
2                   YES
7                   YES
4                   NO
SQL>
```

The two backup pieces, 2 and 7, show a value of YES for the MULTI_SECTION column and are multisection backups.

Archival (Long-Term) Backups

Oracle Database 10g offered the backup . . . keep command to enable you to override the configured retention policies for a backup. In Oracle Database 11g, you can use the refined backup . . . keep command to create long-term backups called archival backups, which you can retain for years if you want. An archival backup contains all the files necessary to restore and recover a database. You can create an archival backup for testing purposes or to retain data for long periods to satisfy regulatory requirements.

In Oracle Database 10g, you can specify the keep and nokeep options to determine if a backup was exempt from RMAN's configured retention policies. The forever and until time clauses enable you to specify the length of time for which RMAN must exempt a backup from a retention policy. Thus, the keep . . . forever option within a backup command meant that RMAN kept a backup forever without removing it. You could specify the logs and nologs options to specify whether RMAN should keep or not keep the archived redo logs necessary to recover a database.

In Oracle Database 11g, you can't specify the logs or nologs options with the keep command. However, you now have a new option, restore point, which you can specify with the keep command. You can specify the restore point option to tell RMAN to create a restore point corresponding to the SCN up to which RMAN must recover the database in order to make the database consistent. Thus, the restore point determines the time point to which RMAN can restore an archival backup.

In Oracle Database 11g, the main reason for using the backup . . . keep command is to create a self-contained archival backup. This archival backup is all-inclusive, meaning it contains all the backups and the archived redo logs necessary to restore and recover the database. Of course, the archival backup is immune from any retention policies you may have configured, but that's not the main purpose behind using the backup . . . keep command—it's to create archival backups. It's important to understand that when you create an archival backup, your goal is to save the backup of the database along with a set of archived redo logs necessary to restore and recover the database. RMAN doesn't have to save all archived redo logs from the time you create the archival backup because the purpose behind making an archival backup isn't to perform a point-in-time recovery. Of course, this means that RMAN needs far less storage space to save the backup and the set of archived redo logs to recover a consistent database. You must store the archival backups in a non-flash recovery area because you may fill up the flash recovery area quickly if you store the archival backups in that location.

Creating an Archival Backup

You can issue the `backup ... keep` command to create a new archival backup from the database files. You can also change the status of an existing backup to that of an archival backup, by issuing the `change` command.

Specify the `keep until time` option to create an archival backup and store it for a specified period of time, as shown in the following example:

```
RMAN> backup database
   2> format 'c:\archives\db_%U.bkp'
   3> tag quarterly
   4> keep until time 'sysdate + 365'
   5> restore point firstquart07;
Starting backup at 29-DEC-07
using channel ORA_DISK_1
backup will be obsolete on date 29-DEC-08
archived logs required to recover from this backup will be backed up
channel ORA_DISK_1: starting full datafile backup set
channel ORA_DISK_1: specifying datafile(s) in backup set
input datafile file number=00001
...
channel ORA_DISK_1: backup set complete, elapsed time: 00:00:08
Finished backup at 29-DEC-07
RMAN>
```

The `keep until time` clause in the previous example dictates that RMAN keep the backup for a year (365 days). If you want to create an archival backup that RMAN stores forever, you use the `keep forever` clause, as shown in this example:

```
RMAN> backup database
   2> format 'c:\archives\db_%U.bkp'
   3> tag quarterly
   4> keep forever'
   5> restore point finyear2007;
RMAN>
```

The keep forever clause specifies that RMAN never treat the backup as obsolete. When you issue a backup ... keep command with either option (forever or until time), this is what happens:

- The database switches the redo logs so it can archive the current online redo log. RMAN needs the current redo information to make the database consistent upon a database restoration.
- RMAN backs up all the datafiles, archived redo logs, the control file, and the server parameter file.
- RMAN backs up only those archived redo logs necessary to recover the database to a consistent state.
- If you specify the optional restore point clause, the database will create a restore point that captures the SCN at the time the RMAN backup completes.
- The control file autobackup stores the restore point so RMAN can utilize it when you restore the control file.

on the **Job**

You can create archival backups only if you are using a recovery catalog.

Instead of creating a brand-new archival backup as shown in the previous example, you can simply alter the status of a normal RMAN backup to that of an archival backup by using the change command, as shown in this example:

```
RMAN> change backup
   2> tag 'weekly_bkp'
   3> keep forever;
```

The change command in this example alters the status of a normal weekly backup into an archival backup that RMAN will store forever (keep forever). The backup's status never becomes obsolete, thus making it immune to any configured RMAN backup retention policies.

You can change the status of an archival backup to a regular backup that's subject to the configured retention polices by using the change ... nokeep command, as shown here:

```
RMAN> change copy of database controlfile nokeep;
```

The previous change ... nokeep command will make the backup of the database and the control file eligible for the obsolete status again, and thus also make it eligible for eventual deletion. You can't issue the change ... keep command to alter the status of backups that RMAN has stored in the flash recovery area.

Restoring an Archival Backup

You can issue the `duplicate database` command to restore an archival backup. Here are the steps to restore and recover the database using an archival backup:

1. Create an auxiliary instance after creating the usual password file and the parameter files. Connect to the auxiliary instance and start it.

2. Connect to the recovery catalog, the target, and the auxiliary instances, as shown here:

```
RMAN> connect target sys/<sys_password>@prod1
RMAN> connect catalog rman/rman@catdb
RMAN> connect auxiliary /
```

3. Issue the `list restore point all` command to find out the name of the restore points that are available.

```
RMAN> list restore point all;

SCN        RSP Time    Type    Time         Name
-------    -------------  ----------   ------------
3074299                            30-DEC-07    FIRSTQUART07

RMAN>
```

4. Issue the `duplicate database` command, making sure you specify the correct restore point name to restore the database to the point in time the restore point stands for.

```
RMAN> duplicate database
  2> to newdb
  3> until restore point firstquart07
  4> db_file_name_convert='/u01/prod1/dbfiles/',
  5>'/u01/newdb/dbfiles'
  6> pfile = '/u01/newdb/admin/init.ora';
```

The restore point you specify in the `duplicate database` command and the SCN that corresponds to it are recorded in the target database control file as well as the recovery catalog, if you're using one. The `duplicate database` command doesn't restore the target database control file, but rather creates a new control file instead. You must therefore use the recovery catalog or the target database control file to get the SCN corresponding to the recovery point, until the point in time to which RMAN will recover the database.

Fast Incremental Backups

The block change tracking feature introduced by Oracle in the previous release helps back up a file faster because RMAN will back up the change data blocks during an incremental backup. By instituting block change tracking, you let RMAN avoid scanning the entire file looking for changed data. By tracking the changed blocks in a special file, RMAN can quickly find out which data blocks have been changed.

In Oracle Database 11g, you can enable block change tracking on a physical standby database. When you do this, RMAN will track the changed blocks during a standby managed recovery. The result is faster incremental backups of physical standby databases.

Improved Block Media Recovery Performance

Oracle's block media recovery feature helps you recover from data block corruption by restoring just the corrupted blocks in a datafile. Recovery is thus faster because you are recovering only the corrupt blocks and not the entire datafile. Database availability is enhanced by the block media recovery feature because you don't have to take affected datafiles offline. The block media recovery feature is an attractive alternative to the traditional restore and recovery of a datafile to fix a few corrupted data blocks. In a block media recovery, RMAN restores the good data blocks from the database backups to replace the corrupted data blocks. Once it restores the good data blocks, it performs a recovery using archived redo logs. Because you have to restore and recover only the few corrupted blocks, the entire restore and recovery process is much faster than a normal datafile restore and recovery operation.

In Oracle Database 10g, the `blockrecover` command helped you perform a block media recovery. In Oracle Database 11g, the new `recover...block` command replaces the `blockrecover` command, which is no longer available. The `recover...block` command is more efficient than its predecessor, the `blockrecover` command, because it searches the flashback logs before looking in the backup files. It's much faster to read the flashback logs than to read an archived database backup when the database is looking for a good copy of corrupted data block. This means that you must implement the Flashback Database feature, which enables the database to make use of the flashback logs to fix data block corruption quickly.

The database must be either open or in the mounted state for you to issue the `recover...block` command. Because RMAN makes use of archived redo logs to perform the block recovery, the database must be in the archivelog mode. You can use either full or level 0 backups, but not proxy copies when performing a block recovery with the `recover...block` command.

Identifying the Corrupt Blocks

Block media recovery helps you repair physical or media corruption, which occurs when a database fails to recognize the corrupted data blocks. You can use one of the following commands to discover block corruption:

- `analyze table and analyze index`
- `list failure`
- `validate`
- `backup...validate`
- `export to dev/null?`

Each time one of the preceding commands reveals a database corruption, the database logs the information in the V$DATABASE_BLOCK_CORRUPTION view. You can also use the *dbverify* utility to reveal block corruption. A message such as the following accompanies a typical block corruption in the database:

```
ORA-01578: ORACLE data block corrupted (file # 2, block # 4)
ORA-01110: data file 2: '/u01/app/oracle/prod1/data01.dbf'
ORA-01578: ORACLE data block corrupted (file # 3, block # 95)
ORA-01110: data file 3: '/u01/app/oracle/prod1/data01.dbf'
```

Use the new `recover...block` command to recover the corrupted data blocks, as I explain in the following section.

Using the Recover...Block Command

You can fix each corrupted block separately by issuing the `recover...block` command for a data block or set of data blocks, or fix all corrupted blocks with a single execution of the command. To recover a specific database block or a set of data blocks, specify the datafile number and the corrupted data blocks in the `recover...block` command:

```
RMAN> recover datafile 2 block 24
      datafile 4 block 10;
```

You can specify the exact backup from which you want RMAN to recover the corrupt data blocks by specifying the backup tag with the `recover...block` command, as shown here:

```
RMAN> recover datafile 2 block 24
      datafile 4 block 10
      from tag=sundaynight;
```

The from tag clause in the recover...block command specifies that RMAN should get copies of the corrupted blocks from backup with the tag sundaynight.

Instead of fixing each corrupted data block one data block at a time, you can choose to fix all corrupted data blocks in one step. To do this, first execute the validate database command so the database populates the V$DATABASE_BLOCK_CORRUPTION view with all corrupt data block information. Here's an example:

```
RMAN> validate database;
Starting validate at 30-DEC-2007
allocated channel: ORA_DISK_1
channel ORA_DISK_1: SID=174 device type=DISK
channel ORA_DISK_1: starting compressed full datafile backup set
channel ORA_DISK_1: specifying datafile(s) for validation
input datafile file number=00002 name=C:\ORCL11\APP\ORACLE\ORADATA\ORCL1101.DBF
input datafile file number=00001 name=C:\ORCL11\APP\ORACLE\ORADATA\ORCL1101.DBF
input datafile file number=00003 name=C:\ORCL11\APP\ORACLE\ORADATA\ORCL11S01.DBF
input datafile file number=00005 name=C:\ORCL11\APP\ORACLE\ORADATA\ORCL11E01.DBF
input datafile file number=00004 name=C:\ORCL11\APP\ORACLE\ORADATA\ORCL111.DBF
channel ORA_DISK_1: validation complete, elapsed time: 00:12:05
List of Datafiles
=================
File Status Marked Corrupt Empty Blocks Blocks Examined SCN
---- ------ -------------- ------------ --------------- --------
1    OK     0              12499        72960           12591563
   File Name: C:\ORCL11\APP\ORACLE\ORADATA\ORCL11\SYSTEM01.DBF
   Block Type Blocks Failing Blocks Processed
   ---------- -------------- ----------------
   Data       0              48999
   Index      0              9146
   Other      0              2316
File Status Marked Corrupt Empty Blocks Blocks Examined SCN
---- ------ -------------- ------------ --------------- --------
2    OK     37             20609        91976           12673599
   File Name: C:\ORCL11\APP\ORACLE\ORADATA\ORCL11\SYSAUX01.DBF
   Block Type Blocks Failing Blocks Processed
   ---------- -------------- ----------------
   Data       0              26850
   Index      0              22864
   Other      0              21653
channel ORA_DISK_1: specifying datafile(s) for validation
including current control file for validation
channel ORA_DISK_1: validation complete, elapsed time: 00:00:02
List of Control File and SPFILE
===============================
```

```
File Type    Status Blocks Failing Blocks Examined
------------ ------ -------------- ----------------
Control File OK     0              594
Finished validate at 30-DEC-07
RMAN>
```

The `validate database` command reveals that file 2 has some data blocks that are marked corrupt. Issue the `recover corruption list` command to recover all corrupted data blocks, as shown here:

```
RMAN> recover corruption list;
Starting recover at 31-DEC-07
using channel ORA_DISK_1
channel ORA_DISK_1: restoring block(s)
channel ORA_DISK_1: specifying block(s)
 to restore from backup set
restoring blocks of datafile 00002
channel ORA_DISK_1: reading from backup piece
 C:\ORCL11\APP\ORACLE\PRODUC0\DB_1\DATABASE\5SIFHTAF_1_1
...
channel ORA_DISK_1: restored block(s) from backup piece 1
channel ORA_DISK_1: block restore complete,elapsed time:00:00:12
channel ORA_DISK_1: restoring block(s)
channel ORA_DISK_1: specifying block(s) to restore from bkup set
restoring blocks of datafile 00002
channel ORA_DISK_1: reading from backup piece ...
starting media recovery
starting media recovery
media recovery complete, elapsed time: 00:00:01
Finished recover at 31-DEC-07
RMAN>
```

After the database recovers the corrupt blocks, it will delete the information about them from the V$DATABASE_BLOCK_CORRUPTION view.

New Persistent Configuration Parameters

There are a couple of new persistent configuration parameters in Oracle Database 11g for RMAN. The following output for the `show all` command shows the new configuration parameters.

```
RMAN> show all;
using target database control file instead of recovery catalog
RMAN configuration parameters are:
```

```
CONFIGURE RETENTION POLICY TO REDUNDANCY 1; # default
CONFIGURE BACKUP OPTIMIZATION OFF; # default
CONFIGURE DEFAULT DEVICE TYPE TO DISK;
CONFIGURE CONTROLFILE AUTOBACKUP OFF; # default
CONFIGURE CONTROLFILE AUTOBACKUP FORMAT FOR DEVICE TYPE DISK
TO '%F'; # default
CONFIGURE CONTROLFILE AUTOBACKUP FORMAT FOR DEVICE TYPE SBT_TAPE
TO '%F';default
CONFIGURE DEVICE TYPE DISK BACKUP TYPE TO COMPRESSED
 BACKUPSET PARALLELISM 1;
CONFIGURE DEVICE TYPE 'SBT_TAPE' BACKUP TYPE TO COMPRESSED
 BACKUPSET PARALLELISM 1;
CONFIGURE DATAFILE BACKUP COPIES FOR DEVICE TYPE DISK
 TO 1; # default
CONFIGURE DATAFILE BACKUP COPIES FOR DEVICE TYPE SBT_TAPE
 TO 1; # default
CONFIGURE ARCHIVELOG BACKUP COPIES FOR DEVICE TYPE DISK
 TO 1; # default
CONFIGURE ARCHIVELOG BACKUP COPIES FOR DEVICE TYPE SBT_TAPE
 TO 1; # default
CONFIGURE MAXSETSIZE TO UNLIMITED; # default
CONFIGURE ENCRYPTION FOR DATABASE ON;
CONFIGURE ENCRYPTION ALGORITHM 'AES128'; # default
CONFIGURE COMPRESSION ALGORITHM 'ZLIB'; # default
CONFIGURE ARCHIVELOG DELETION POLICY TO NONE; # default
CONFIGURE SNAPSHOT CONTROLFILE NAME TO 'C:\ORCL11\APP\ORACLE\
11.1.0\DB_1\DATABASE\SNCFORCL11.ORA'; # default
RMAN>
```

The two major changes pertaining to RMAN configuration are the new
archivelog deletion policy configuration and the enhanced compression algorithm
configuration. In the following sections, I discuss the two major new RMAN
configuration parameters.

New Compression Algorithm

You now have a choice between two compression algorithms. In the previous release
you could only use the default BZIP2 compression algorithm. In Oracle Database
11g, you can also choose the new ZLIB compression algorithm, which Oracle claims
can be 40 percent faster than the older BZIP2 algorithm. The following query
on the V$RMAN_COMPRESSION_ALGORITHM view shows the differences
between the two compression algorithms you can choose from:

```
SQL> select algorithm_name,algorithm_description, is_default
  2  from v$rman_compression_algorithm;
```

```
ALGORITHM   ALGORITHM DESCRIPTION                      IS_DEFAULT
---------   ---------------------------------------    ----------
ZLIB        fast but little worse compression ratio    YES
BZIP2       good compression ratio but little slower   NO
SQL>
```

The new compression algorithm, ZLIB, is the default algorithm in Oracle Database 11g. The ZLIB compression algorithm is 40 to 50 percent faster than the older BZIP2 compression algorithm, according to Oracle. However, the BZIP2 compression algorithm provides a better compression ratio. Oracle's real-world data warehousing database study showed that the BZIP2 algorithm had a compression ratio of 2.0:1, compared to a ratio of 1.68:1 with the ZLIB algorithm. You can choose the configuration algorithm you want to use by executing the configure command, as shown here:

```
RMAN> configure compression algorithm 'bzip2';
new RMAN configuration parameters:
CONFIGURE COMPRESSION ALGORITHM 'bzip2';
new RMAN configuration parameters are successfully stored
RMAN>
```

As mentioned earlier, ZLIB is the default compression algorithm.

Archived Redo Log Deletion Policy

In Oracle Database 11g, you can configure a persistent parameter to specify an archived redo log deletion policy. By default, the value of the configure archivelog deletion policy parameter is set to NONE, meaning there's no archived redo log deletion policy by default. Configuring an archived redo log policy allows you to specify when the archived redo logs become eligible for deletion. The configured deletion policy applies to all archived redo logs stored on disk, regardless of the destination, including the flash recovery area.

Criteria for Deleting Archived Redo Logs   RMAN uses criteria such as the number of backups it made of a certain archived redo log and whether it has successfully moved the archived redo logs to their destinations, to decide if the archived redo logs are eligible for deletion. If you don't configure an archived redo log deletion policy, Oracle will mark an archived redo log for deletion when the log satisfies the following conditions:

- If you specify the log_archive_dest_n initialization parameter, the database must first successfully transfer the archived redo log to all the specified remote destinations.

■ The archived redo log must be backed up at least once or it must be obsolete. The current backup retention policy in force determines whether the archived redo log is obsolete.

Note that regardless of RMAN's backup retention policy, RMAN won't mark a backup as obsolete under the following circumstances:

■ If an archived redo log is necessary to support a guaranteed restore point
■ If an archived redo log is needed to support the Flashback Database feature

Once you configure an archived redo log deletion policy, both the `backup...delete` and the `delete...archivelog` commands will take the policy into account. In addition, the flash recovery area will also comply with the archived redo log deletion policy that you configure.

Configuring an Archived Redo Log Deletion Policy   You configure an archivelog deletion policy by executing the following `configure` command.

```
RMAN> configure archivelog deletion policy
   2> to backed up 2 times to sbt;
new RMAN configuration parameters:
CONFIGURE ARCHIVELOG DELETION POLICY TO
 BACKED UP 2 TIMES TO 'SBT_TAPE';
new RMAN configuration parameters are successfully stored
RMAN>
```

The `configure` command shown here specifies that all archived redo logs are eligible for deletion after they are backed up at least twice to tape (sbt). Once you create an archived redo log policy as shown here, the policy comes into force immediately. To disable the policy, issue the following command:

```
RMAN> configure archivelog deletion policy to none;
```

The previous command will let RMAN revert to the default setting of no archived redo log policy.

You can also execute the `configure archive log deletion policy` command to specify an archived redo log deletion policy in a Data Guard setup. You can specify a deletion policy for any standby destination or only for mandatory standby destinations.

Backup Failover to Non-Flash Recovery Areas

RMAN backs up the redo logs from the flash recovery area for archiving. When RMAN discovers that an archived redo log file in the flash recovery is either corrupt or missing, it automatically uses an archived redo log from a non-flash recovery area location. This automatic failover to a non-flash recovery area destination is new in Oracle Database 11g. This feature guarantees that an RMAN backup of the flash recovery area won't fail even if a disk on which the flash recovery area resides is damaged.

CERTIFICATION OBJECTIVE 7.02

Recovery Catalog Management

There are two important innovations in the way you manage the recovery catalog in Oracle Database 11g. The first of these is the ability to merge catalogs with the new `import catalog` command. You can also use this command to move a recovery catalog to a different database. The second big innovation is the concept of a virtual private catalog, which lets you limit a user's access to only part of the recovery catalog instead of the entire catalog. Let's start with a discussion of the merging of recovery catalogs with the `import catalog` command.

Merging Recovery Catalogs

In prior releases, the only way to combine the contents of two or more recovery catalogs was to use the export and import utilities (or Data Pump) to migrate data between two recovery catalogs. Oracle Database 11g lets you combine multiple recovery catalogs into a single catalog schema for several databases through the new `import database` command. Using the `import catalog` command, you can completely merge two or more recovery catalogs or just the metadata for specific databases.

In the following example, the `list incarnation` command shows two databases as being registered in the recovery catalog stored in database rman11.

```
RMAN> list incarnation;
List of Database Incarnations
DB     Inc   DB Name  DB ID        STATUS    Reset SCN   ResetTime
---    ----  ------   ----------   --------  ----------  ---------
192    207   ELEVEN   3481526915   PARENT    1           22-NOV-06
192    193   ELEVEN   3481526915   CURRENT   909437      13-MAR-07
1      15    ORCL11   3863017760   PARENT    1           22-NOV-06
1      2     ORCL11   3863017760   CURRENT   909437      03-MAR-07
RMAN>
```

Let's say you have an Oracle Database 10.2 release recovery catalog schema with just a single database (named TENNER) registered in it, as shown here:

```
RMAN> list incarnation;
List of Database Incarnations
DB    Inc    DB Name   DB ID        STATUS   Reset SCN   ResetTime
------ --    ------    -----------  -------  ---------   -----------
1      8     TENNER    1166569509   PARENT   1           30-AUG-05
1      2     TENNER    1166569509   CURRENT 534907       13-MAR-07
RMAN>
```

Let's see how you can merge the two recovery catalogs—one from the 10.2 release and the other from the 11g release—into a single recovery catalog schema that will register all three databases. Here are the steps to perform the merge using the `import catalog` command.

1. Connect to the destination recovery catalog.

   ```
   $ rman
   RMAN> connect catalog rman/rman@rman11
   ```

2. Issue the `import catalog` command while connecting to the recovery catalog you want to import to the target you've connected to in Step 1.

   ```
   RMAN> import catalog rman1/rman1@rman10;
   Starting import catalog at 08-JAN-08
   connected to source recovery catalog database
   import validation complete
   database unregistered from the source recovery catalog
   Finished import catalog at 08-JAN-08
   RMAN>
   ```

3. Issue the `list incarnation` command to verify that the two recovery catalogs have been correctly merged.

   ```
   RMAN> list incarnation;
   RMAN> list incarnation;
   List of Database Incarnations
   DB Inc DB       Name     DB ID        STATUS   ResetSCN Reset Time
   ----- -----    -------  -----------   ------   -------- --------
   1411  1418     TENNER    66569509     PARENT   1        30-AUG-05
   1411  1412     TENNER   1166569509    CURRENT 534907    13-MAR-07
   192   207      ELEVEN   3481526915    PARENT   1        22-NOV-06
   192   193      ELEVEN   3481526915    CURRENT 909437    13-MAR-07
   1     15       ORCL11   3863017760    PARENT   1        22-NOV-06
   1     2        ORCL11   3863017760    CURRENT 909437    03-MAR-07
   RMAN>
   ```

The `import catalog` command imports the metadata for all databases that are registered in the source recovery catalog. You can limit the import to a specific database or databases by specifying the DBID or database name, as shown here:

```
RMAN> import catalog rman10/rman10@tenner
        dbid = 123456, 123457;
RMAN> import catalog rman10/rman10@tenner
        db_name = testdb, mydb;
```

After the `import catalog` command finishes executing, the source database from which you imported the TENNER database won't show any database registered in it, as the following list incarnation command reveals:

```
RMAN> list incarnation;
RMAN>
```

Importing all the databases from the source recovery catalog means that the source recovery catalog will now be empty.

By default, when you merge two recovery catalogs with the `import catalog` command, RMAN automatically deregisters all databases from the source recovery catalog after it imports those databases to the target catalog. You can, however, override this default behavior by specifying the `no unregister` clause when you issue the `import catalog` command, as shown here:

```
RMAN> import catalog rman1/rman1@rman10 no unregister;
```

exam

Watch

| Show how to import metadata from one recovery catalog schema into another recovery catalog. | What does the `no unregister` clause do in this connection? |

Using the `no unregister` clause tells RMAN not to remove the imported databases from the source recovery catalog after importing them to the target catalog.

on the Job

If the same databases are registered in more than one recovery catalog, you must remove it from one of the catalogs by unregistering it, before issuing the `import catalog` command.

In order to use the `import catalog` commands, the source database must be from the same version as the RMAN client. Otherwise, you must first upgrade the source recovery catalog schema. If a global stored script has the same name in different catalogs, RMAN renames the source catalog script using the format `copy of script_name`.

In addition to merging multiple recovery catalogs, you can also use the `import catalog` command to move the recovery catalog to a different database. To move a recovery catalog, you must first create an empty recovery catalog in the destination database. You must then connect to the destination recovery catalog and issue the `import catalog` command. The following example shows this:

```
$ rman
RMAN> connect catalog rman/rman@target_db
RMAN> import catalog rman10/rman10@source_db;
```

The `import catalog` command imports the source_db recovery catalog contents to a catalog in the target_db database.

Virtual Private Catalogs

In previous releases, if a user needed access to even a single database in the recovery catalog, you were forced to grant that user access to the entire recovery catalog. You can now restrict access to all databases in the recovery catalog by granting access to a subset of the recovery catalog, known as the `virtual private catalog` or `virtual catalog`. You can create a virtual catalog for one or more users. The central or source recovery catalog itself is now also referred to as the *base recovery catalog*. Oracle recommends that you merge all the recovery catalogs in your system into a central base recovery catalog. You can then create multiple virtual catalogs to grant access to one or more databases to a user or users.

The virtual private catalog doesn't exist as a separate entity, like the base recovery catalog. The virtual private catalog is merely a set of synonyms and views based on the central catalog. The main or base recovery catalog owner must grant the privilege to the virtual catalog owners to connect to one or more databases or even register the databases on their own. Once a virtual catalog owner logs into the virtual catalog, all recovery catalog functions remain the same as in the base recovery catalog. The virtual recovery catalog owner can, however, operate with only a limited set of databases compared to the base catalog owner, who has access to all the databases registered in the base catalog.

Creating a Virtual Private Catalog

In order to create a virtual private catalog, you must create a virtual private catalog user, who will own the virtual catalog. Follow these steps to create a virtual private catalog:

1. Create a new database user, who you will designate as the owner of the virtual private catalog.

```
SQL> connect sys/<sys_password> as sysdba
SQL> create user virtual1 identified by virtual1
     temporary tablespace temp
     default tablespace vp_users
     quota unlimited on vp_users;

User created.
SQL>
```

2. Grant the new user you created, VIRTUAL1, the privileges to work with a virtual recovery catalog in the next step. You first grant the `recovery_catalog_owner` role to the new user from the SQL*Plus interface, as shown here:

```
SQL> grant recovery_catalog_owner to virtual1;
Grant succeeded.
SQL>
```

The `recovery_catalog_owner` role grants the new user privileges to use the new private virtual catalog you're going to create.

3. Start the RMAN client and connect as the base recovery catalog owner. Grant the new user privileges to work with various databases. You do this with the `grant register database` and the `grant catalog` statements, as shown here:

```
$ rman
RMAN> connect catalog rman/rman@nick
connected to recovery catalog database
RMAN> grant register database to virutal1;
RMAN> grant catalog for database test1, test2 to virtual1;
Grant succeeded.
RMAN>
```

The first execution of the `grant` command (`grant register database`) grants user VIRTUAL1 the ability to register any database in the virtual private catalog. The `grant catalog for database` statement grants user VIRTUAL1 access to databases in the base recovery catalog, in this case providing access to a subset of two databases in the base catalog, TEST1 and TEST2. You may specify the DBID for a database instead of the database name when granting access to them with the `grant catalog for database` statement.

on the Job

As a virtual catalog owner, a user can create only local stored scripts and not global scripts. However, the virtual catalog owner has read-only rights to global stored scripts.

4. Log in as the virtual catalog owner to the base recovery catalog and create the virtual catalog, as shown here:

```
RMAN> connect catalog virtual1/virtual1@catdb
connected to recovery catalog database
RMAN> create virtual catalog;
found eligible base catalog owned by RMAN
created virtual catalog against base catalog owned by RMAN
RMAN>
```

User VIRTUAL1, who owns the new virtual catalog, can access two databases from the base recovery catalog—test1 and test2. Thus, these two databases are registered in the private recovery catalog as well, as you can see with the list incarnation command:

```
RMAN> list incarnation;
List of Database Incarnations
DB   Inc  DB Name  DB ID       STATUS    Reset SCN   Reset Time
----------  -------  ----------  --------  ----------  ---------
192  207  TEST1    3481526915  PARENT    1           22-NOV-06
192  193  TEST1    3481526915  CURRENT   909437       3-MAR-07
1    15   TEST2    3863017760  PARENT    1            2-NOV-06
1    2    TEST2    3863017760  CURRENT   909437      03-MAR-07
RMAN>
```

exam Watch

You must understand the correct sequence of steps you need to follow in order to create a virtual private catalog. Which commands are issued by the base catalog owner and which by the virtual private catalog owner?

In order to use the virtual private catalog, the virtual catalog owner must log in to the base recovery catalog (catdb) by specifying the VIRTUAL1 schema in the connect catalog command. The following example shows how the virtual catalog owner registers a new database in the catalog:

```
RMAN> connect target / catalog virtual1/virtual1@catdb;
RMAN> register database;
```

Once the virtual private catalog owner registers the database, she can use her virtual private catalog that's stored in the VIRUTAL1 schema in catdb (the base recovery catalog) to perform a backup of the database, as shown here:

```
RMAN> connect target /catalog virtual1/virtual1@catdb;
RMAN> backup database plus archivelog;
```

The backup metadata for the target database will be stored in the VIRTUAL1 schema in the base recovery catalog, catdb. The virtual private catalog owner will be able to perform all RMAN operations on those databases in the base recovery catalog that have been registered by the virtual private catalog owner.

Managing Virtual Private Catalogs

When you create a virtual private catalog owner, that owner has no access to the base recovery catalog. You use the `grant` command to grant privileges for a virtual recovery catalog schema to a user.

After you create the new Oracle database user that will own the virtual private catalog schema, first grant that user the `recovery_catalog_owner` role. Then, connect to the base recovery catalog as the base recovery catalog owner (RMAN) and use the `grant` command to assign privileges on the recovery catalog to the new virtual catalog owner. Once you grant the privileges, you create the virtual catalog schema for the new user.

You can issue the `grant` command with the clauses `catalog for database` or `register database`. The `grant catalog` (for database) command grants recovery catalog access for a specific database to a user. Here's an example:

```
RMAN> grant catalog for database test1 to virtual1;
```

You can grant access to any of the databases that are currently registered in the base recovery catalog with the `grant catalog` command. You may also grant access to databases that aren't currently registered in the base recovery catalog. This will enable the virtual private catalog owner to register those databases. Note that you must specify the DBID of the database instead of the database name when granting access to databases that aren't currently registered in the base recovery catalog.

You can also grant a user the ability to register and unregister target databases (that is, databases that aren't currently known to the base recovery catalog) by issuing the `grant register database` command, as shown here:

```
RMAN> grant register database to virtual1;
```

When you grant the `register database` privilege to a user, you implicitly grant the `catalog for database` privileges for any databases that the user registers in the recovery catalog. Any database that a virtual catalog owner registers in a virtual private catalog will automatically be a part of the base recovery catalog as well. The base recovery catalog owner can unregister any database registered by the virtual catalog owner.

You can issue the `revoke` command to revoke a virtual catalog owner's privileges. Issue the `revoke catalog for database` command to revoke a virtual catalog owner's access to a specific database. Here's an example:

```
RMAN> connect catalog rman/<password>@catdb;
RMAN> revoke catalog for database test1 from virtual1;
```

You may also use the `revoke register database` command to revoke the ability of the recovery catalog owner to register new databases, as shown here:

```
RMAN> connect catalog rman/<password>@catdb;
RMAN> revoke register database from virtual1;
```

The `revoke register database` command will keep a virtual catalog owner from registering new databases. However, if the user still has the `catalog for database` privilege, that user can still register and unregister the specific databases for which the `catalog for database` privilege was granted.

Finally, you can issue the `revoke all privileges from` command to revoke both the `catalog` and the `register` privileges in the same command, as shown here:

```
RMAN> revoke all privileges from virtual1;
```

As a result of revoking all privileges on the virtual catalog to the user virtual1, that user can no longer register a new database in the catalog or even log into a currently registered database.

Dropping a Virtual Private Catalog

A virtual private catalog owner can drop the catalog by issuing the `drop catalog` command, as shown here:

1. Log in as the virtual catalog owner to the base recovery catalog:

   ```
   RMAN> connect catalog virtual1/<password>@catadb;
   ```

2. Issue the `drop catalog` command:

   ```
   RMAN> drop catalog;
   ```

The issuing of the `drop catalog` command results in the removal of all metadata for the virtual catalog schema from the base recovery catalog.

The previous `drop catalog` command works only for an Oracle Database 11g or higher release. If you're using a pre–Oracle 11g release RMAN executable, you must issue the following command to work with a virtual private catalog:

```
SQL> exec
     base_catalog_owner.dbms_rcvcat.create_virtual_catalog;
```

The previous command doesn't actually create a virtual private catalog. You need to issue this command before working with any pre–Oracle 11.1 release databases.

And to drop a virtual catalog, you must issue the following command:

```
SQL> exec
     base_catalog_owner.dbms_rcvcat.drop_virtual_catalog;
```

Dropping the virtual catalog doesn't have any impact on the base recovery catalog. All databases that were part of the virtual catalog will remain in the base recovery catalog.

CERTIFICATION OBJECTIVE 7.03

New Flashback-Related Features

One of the best new features of the Oracle Database 9i and 10g releases was the set of flashback-related features, which let the DBA retrieve older data without having to perform a time-consuming traditional recovery operation. Oracle Database 11g offers significant enhancements in the flashback area by introducing two major flashback-related features—*flashback data archive* and the *flashback transaction backout* feature. A flashback data archive is a logical container for storing older versions of data over a long period of time. You can use the archive to retrieve an older version of a table or to perform queries involving data from the past. The flashback transaction feature provides the capability to easily back out a transaction, including its dependent transactions. Let's start with a review of the flashback data archive.

Flashback Data Archive

While you can rely on the undo data in the undo tablespace to query older versions of a row or even perform a logical recovery, there's a limit on how far back you can go. Because the main purpose of the undo data is to provide data consistency, you can't expect to find very old versions of a row in the undo segments. Undo tablespaces are usually sized by the DBA to provide read consistency for the longest transactions run in a database. The undo tablespace was never meant to be a historical repository of all the changes made to a row in a table.

In addition, the undo tablespace contains all the data changes made in the database, not just changes for a specific table. If you want to go back, say, two years in time to find out what values a certain table's row had then, the undo tablespace can't help you. Your only choice was to maintain the change records in separate tables and maintain them yourself. Oracle Database 11g's new *flashback data archive* feature enables you to automatically store changes made to a table's data over time. The flashback data archive lets you store data changes for any length of time you want. An undo tablespace can only help you if the SCN of the transaction you are interested in exists in one of the undo segments. A flashback data archive has nothing to do with the SCN of the transactions—it will simply store the data for the period of time you specify. Once the retention period is up, the archive will purge the older data automatically. Thus, the archive imposes hardly any administrative burden on you. You simply create the flashback data archive and walk away from it! You don't turn on the flashback data archive for the entire database, as you do with automatic undo management. You specify the table or tables for which you want the archive to track and store changes.

In order to satisfy regulatory requirements of legislative acts such as HIPAA and Sarbanes-Oxley, many organizations must maintain historical data. In addition, financial concerns all too often have a need to keep older data for a specific number of years. Using traditional solutions to implement a historical data management system is not only tedious, but it also doesn't provide any built-in safety features. The flashback data archive is easy to implement and has built-in safety features to protect the historical data. You can use the flashback data archive feature for change tracking, information lifecycle management (ILM), auditing and regulatory compliance, and for generating reports that use historical data.

One of the problems with querying data from a past period of time is that the data you're looking for may have been overwritten by the database, which results in the familiar "snapshot too old" error. With a flashback data archive you can confidently query data from the past, a period that could be as far back in the past as you want. The database automatically deletes data beyond the time period you specified, thus enforcing a built-in digital shredding. Aged data will simply disappear from the table, without any intervention from the DBA.

on the Job

You can't modify any data stored in a flashback data archive, but you are allowed to purge data from it.

Flashback Data Archive and Flashback Database

The flashback data archive is quite different from the Flashback Database feature, although both involve some kind of flashing back to a previous state of the database. However, the two features are quite distinct, as follows:

- The Flashback Database feature lets you take the database back in time. A flashback data archive doesn't change the current data. That is, the database remains in its current state—the flashback data archive simply lets you access the data from a previous point in time.
- You must enable table tracking for the flashback data archive to function, whereas you must configure the Flashback Database feature.
- The flashback data archive is an online feature, while the Flashback Database is an offline feature.
- You can use the Flashback Database only at the database level, whereas you can enable the flashback data archive at the table level.
- A Flashback Database operation enables you to take back the entire database to the same point in time in the past, whereas the flashback data archive feature enables you to go to different points in time for different tables.

How Flashback Data Archiving Works

The flashback data archive itself is a logical container for historical data for one or more tables in the database. The archive contains the data itself along with the retention and purging policies for the data. The flashback data archive stores its data in one or more tablespaces that you assign to the archive. In order for the database to archive a table's changes, you must first enable that table for the flashback archiving. Once you do this, the new Oracle background process *fbda* (Flashback Data Archiver) writes the changed data in the tables to the flashback data archive.

You should be aware of the following aspects of the flashback data archive feature:

- A flashback data archive can contain data from multiple tables.
- You can set different retention periods for different tables, by assigning them to different flashback data archives.
- You can create multiple flashback data archives. In fact, Oracle recommends that you do this so that you can dedicate one flashback area, say, for long-term storage, such as five years, and the other flashback data archive for a shorter period, such as a year or six months.
- You can assign one of the flashback data archives as the default flashback archive for the database. Any table for which you don't specify a flashback data archive will then use the default flashback archive for archival storage.
- The database automatically purges the flashback data archive by deleting the necessary data a day after the expiration of the retention period you set for that table.

■ Once you enable a table for flashback data archiving, the database creates an internal history table for that table to hold the historical data. In addition to the columns of the original table, the historical table will have a few additional columns showing the time stamp of the transactions in order to track transactions.

An insert operation won't cause the database to add any rows to the historical table because that row doesn't have a before change image. But when you update or delete a row in the original table, the fbda process marks the undo records corresponding to these operations for archival. The fbda records the pre-commit image of the row that was affected by the delete or update operation in the history table. The fbda process first tries to use the undo in the buffer cache. If the undo is gone from the buffer cache already, fbda will read the necessary values from the undo segments. At system-determined intervals (default is 5 minutes), the fbda process wakes up and copies the necessary undo data to the history table. To enable the functioning of the flashback data archiving process, the database ensures that any undo records that the fbda has marked for recording to the history table aren't recycled. The database automatically adjusts the sleep time of the fbda process by lowering it when the database is generating a large amount of undo data, thus enabling fbda to read frequently from the buffer cache. Because the fbda doesn't work continuously, there will be a lag between the time an update or delete operation commits and the time the changed data shows up in the history table.

Let's use some simple examples to demonstrate how the flashback data archive feature works. Let's first insert a new row into the DEPARTMENTS table owned by the user HR.

```
SQL> insert into hr.departments
     values (300,'New Department',200,1700);

1 row created.
SQL> commit;
Commit complete.
SQL>
```

Because it involves an insertion of a new row, the preceding transaction won't result in the addition of a history record to the history table. But let's say a user updates a row in the DEPARTMENTS table, as shown here:

```
SQL> update departments
     set department_name='Last Department'
     where department_id=300;

1 row updated.
SQL> commit;
```

The fbda background process will mark this transaction as a candidate for recording in the history table. As soon as it can, fbda will add a record to the history table showing the pre-change value of the DEPARTMENT_NAME column. Let's next delete the row that was just updated in the previous transaction:

```
SQL> delete from hr.departments where department_id=300;
1 row deleted.

SQL> commit;
Commit complete.
SQL>
```

If you query the history table, which is given a system-generated name, you'll see that the fbda process has successfully tracked and recorded all versions of the row with the DEPARTMENT_ID value of 300.

```
SQL> select department_id, department_name, manager_id,
       location_id from hr. SYS_FBA_HIST_70308;

DEPT_ID    DEPT_NAME          MANAGER_ID    LOCATION_ID
-------    ----------------   ----------    ------------
300        New Department     200           1700
300        Last Department    200           1700

SQL>
```

The historical table shows both the pre-delete and the pre-update values of the row with the DEPARTMENT_ID value of 300. You can use these values for a query or to fix the values in a row. I show you some scenarios of the usage of the flashback data archive later in this chapter, to illustrate how you can take advantage of this feature.

Benefits of Using a Flashback Data Archive

The flashback data archive feature provides the following important benefits:

- You can set a common retention policy for a related group of tables.
- The database automatically purges older data from the flashback archive.
- Instead of writing your own administrative interface, you can use a centralized management interface to manage the data archive.
- You can use the as of flashback query to retrieve historical data.
- The database makes the retrieval of historical data efficient by automatically partitioning the internal history tables using a range-partitioning scheme.
- You don't need to make any application changes to implement the feature.

■ There is a very small overhead for implementing data archiving because the fbda process archives the data so efficiently.

■ The database stores the archived data in a compressed format, saving storage space.

■ Archiving data is safe because no one, including the DBA, can directly update the historical data—they can only query it. Because you can't modify the archived data, the archive remains tamper proof, which is a big objective behind using the archive. In fact, the data in the archive is safer than the original data because the archived data is tamper-proof.

Creating a Flashback Data Archive

A user must either have the DBA role or have the `flashback archive administer` system privilege in order to create a flashback data archive. The `flashback archive administer` privilege allows a user to execute the following statements:

■ `create flashback archive`
■ `alter flashback archive`
■ `drop flashback archive`

You can query the DBA_SYS_PRIVS view, as shown here, to find out which users have the `flashback archive administer` privilege.

```
SQL> select * from dba_sys_privs where privilege like '%FLASH%';
GRANTEE               PRIVILEGE                        ADM
-----------           --------------------             ----
SYS                   FLASHBACK ANY TABLE              NO
DBA                   FLASHBACK ANY TABLE              YES
DBA                   FLASHBACK ARCHIVE ADMINISTER     YES
SQL>
```

You grant the `flashback archive administer` privilege to a user as follows:

```
SQL> grant flashback archive administer to hr;
Grant succeeded.
SQL>
```

It's probably a good idea to designate a DBA or some other user as your flashback data archive administrator and grant the `flashback data archive privilege` to that user alone in order to make the archive secure. The `flashback archive` `administer` system privilege allows a user to execute the following statements pertaining to the administration of the flashback data archives.

- `create flashback archive`
- `alter flashback archive`
- `drop flashback archive`

Later in this chapter, you'll see how to use the three statements listed here to create, alter, and drop a flashback archive.

You allow a user access to a specific flashback data archive by granting the `flashback archive` object privilege on that flashback data archive to the user, as shown here:

```
SQL> grant flashback archive on flash1 to oe;
```

The previous `grant flashback archive` statement confers the privilege to the user OE to use the flashback archive flash1. Once you grant the `flashback archive` object privilege to a user, that user can enable flashback archiving for a specific table in the flashback archive for which the user was granted the `flashback archive` privilege. You must also grant the users the `flashback` and `select` privileges on all the objects referenced in a query, so the users are allowed to access to those objects. You must also grant a user the `execute` privilege on the DBMS_FLASHBACK feature, so the user can use the DBMS_FLASHBACK.ENABLE and DBMS_FLASHBACK.DISABLE procedures to enable and disable the flashback data archive for which they've been granted the `flashback archive` object privilege.

Use the `create flashback` statement to create a flashback data archive. Remember that the flashback data archive, while it's a database object, is only a logical construct. The tablespace you assign to the archive stores the data. Thus, you first create a new tablespace to assign to the flashback data archive you're about to create. You may also use an already available tablespace for this purpose because the archive doesn't require a dedicated tablespace.

When creating a flashback data archive with the `create flashback` statement, you can specify the following:

- A flashback data archive name
- Whether the flashback data archive is the default archive for the database (you don't have to create a default archive)
- The name of the tablespace to which you want to assign the flashback data archive

You must first create the tablespace that will host the flashback data archive. You may specify the following things while creating a new flashback data archive:

- A *quota* for the flashback data archive in the tablespace you're assigning for the archive: If you don't assign a quota, the archive can take up all the space available in that tablespace.
- A *retention period* for the archive: This is a mandatory attribute, because it determines how long the database must retain the data in the archive before purging it.

The following example demonstrates how to create a flashback data archive in the FLASH_TBS1 tablespace:

```
SQL> create flashback data archive flash1
     tablespace flash_tbs1
     retention 4 year;
Flashback Data Archive created.
SQL>
```

The clause `retention 4 year` specifies that the database must retain the data in the new flashback data archive flash1 for four years before purging it. The absence of the `quota` clause means the flash1 archive can occupy the entire tablespace FLASH_TBS1. If you want to limit the archive to only a part of the tablespace, specify the `quota` clause, as shown here:

```
SQL> create flashback data archive flash2
     tablespace flash_tbs1
     quota 2000m
     retention 4 year;
Flashback Data Archive created.
SQL>
```

You size the flashback data archive based on the amount of transactions you anticipate the database will be archiving and the length of time for which you want the archive to retain the data. If the flashback data archive runs out of space, Oracle issues an out-of-space alert and marks it in the archive log for the database. You can then either purge older data to free up space in the archive or add space to the tablespace that you assigned for the flashback data archive.

Use the `drop flashback archive` statement to drop a flashback data archive, as shown here:

```
SQL> drop flashback archive flash1;
```

When you drop the flashback data archive, the data stored in that archive will be gone for good, but the tablespace remains.

Altering a Flashback Data Archive

You can alter flashback data archive attributes such as the length of the retention period, or you can add space to an archive by issuing an `alter flashback archive` statement. The following examples show you how to use the `alter flashback archive` statement to modify different attributes of a flashback data archive.

```
SQL> alter flashback archive flash1
     set default            # makes flash1 the default archive

SQL> alter flashback archive flash1
     add tablespace
     flash_tbs1    # adds space to the flashback archive

SQL> alter flashback archive flash1
     modify tablespace
     flash_tbs1 quota 10G;   # changes the quota for the archive

SQL> alter flashback archive flash1
     modify retention
     2 year;   # changes the archive retention time

SQL> alter flashback tablespace flash1
     add tablespace flash_tbs2; #adds a tablespace to an archive

SQL> alter flashback tablespace flash1
     remove tablespace
     flash_tbs2; #removes a tablespace from an archive

SQL> alter flashback archive flash1
     purge all;                    # purges all archived data

SQL> alter flashback archive flash1
     purge before
```

```
         timestamp (systimestamp - interval '2' day); # purges data
                                                    older than 2 days

SQL> alter flashback archive flash1
     purge before scn 123456;            # purges all data before
                                          the specified SCN
```

on the

!

j o b

All tables in a flashback data archive are subject to the same flashback
archive attributes, such as the length of the retention period for data.

Although you can purge data from the archive yourself using any of the `purge`
clauses shown in the last three examples here, the database will automatically purge
all data in the archive a day after the expiration of the retention period for the
archive.

Enabling and Disabling Flashback Data Archiving

Once you create a flashback data archive, the database is set up for archiving
changes to a specified table or tables. As mentioned earlier, unlike in the case of
undo data, the database doesn't automatically store changes database wide. It does so
only for a table or tables for which you enable flashback logging. You must be either
the DBA or have the `flashback data archive` system privilege and the
`create tablespace` system privileges to turn flashback logging on for a table.

You can enable flashback logging in the flashback data archive for a table either
when you create the table or even later. Of course, if you enable it after you create
the table, only those changes made after you enable the table for flashback logging
will be stored in the archive.

You enable a table for flashback logging by including the `flashback archive`
clause in the `create table` statement:

```
SQL> create table test1 (
  2   name varchar2(30),
  3   address varchar2(50))
  4*  flashback archive fla4;

Table created.
SQL>
```

In the previous example, I specified the flashback archive fla4 for archiving changes
in the table TEST1. Because you can have more than one flashback archive in a
database, you can specify the appropriate flashback archive based on an attribute
such as the retention period—for example, for a certain table. However, you don't
have to specify the name of the flashback archive. If you have created a default

flashback data archive and want to use this for archiving the data, you can leave out the name of the flashback archive in the `create table` statement shown here. If you don't include the flashback archive name, the database will use the default flashback archive when you issue a `create table` or an `alter table` statement that includes a `flashback archive` clause.

You can query the DBA_FLASHBACK_ARCHIVE_TABLES view to find out information about all tables that are enabled for flashback data archiving, as shown here:

```
SQL> select * from dba_flashback_archive_tables;
TABLE_NAME      OWNER     FLASHBACK_ARCH_NAME    ARCH_TABLE_NAM
-----------     ------    -------------------    ------------------
EMPLOYEES       HR        FLASH1                 SYS_FBA_HIST_70313
```

The query shows that the user HR owns the EMPLOYEES table, which is enabled for flashback data archiving. The flashback archive name is FLASH1 and the history table where the database stores the archived data is given the system-generated name SYS_FBA_HIST_70313.

Instead of specifying the `flashback archive` clause when creating a table, you can enable flashback archiving for a table by issuing the `alter table` statement, as shown here:

```
SQL> alter table employees
     flashback archive;
```

The absence of the flashback archive name in the `flashback archive` clause means that the database will use the default flashback data archive. You can specify a specific flashback archive by providing the flashback archive name, as follows:

```
SQL> alter table employees
     flashback archive flash2;
```

You can disable flashback archiving for a specific table by executing the `alter table` command, as follows:

```
SQL> alter table employees
     no flashback archive;
```

When you include the `no flashback archive` clause, the database will remove all the flashback data for that table from the flashback data archive. The previous statement would only affect flashback logging for the EMPLOYEES table. The flashback logging for the other tables would continue and the flashback archive itself remains in place. In order to remove the flashback archive itself, you must use the `drop flashback archive` statement.

Flashback Data Archive Limitations

Following are the limitations on using the flashback data archive feature:

- You can't execute the `drop column` command, although you can execute the `add column` command. If you want to drop a column in a table for which you enabled flashback data logging, you must first turn off flashback logging for that table with the `alter table...no flashback` statement. However, you'll lose all the archived data for the table.

- You also can't use the `alter table` statement to rename or modify a column on a table enabled for flashback data archive.

- You can't use the `alter table` statement to perform a partition or subpartition operation or convert a LONG column to a LOB column on a table enabled for flashback data archive.

- You can't use the `drop table` or the `truncate table` statement on a table enabled for flashback data archive.

Monitoring Flashback Data Archives

You can use several new views to manage a flashback data archive. The following list offers brief descriptions of the new views:

- The DBA_FLASHBACK_ARCHIVE_TABLES view shows details about the tables that are enabled for flashback data archiving.

- The DBA_FLASHBACK_ARCHIVE view shows all flashback data archives that you've created.

  ```
  SQL>  select flashback_archive_name,retention_in_days
          from dba_flashback_archive;
        FLASHBACK_ARCHIVE_NAME      RETENTION_IN_DAYS
        ----------------------      -----------------
        FLASH1                            365
  ```

- The DBA_FLASHBACK_ARCHIVE_TS view shows details about the tablespaces hosting the flashback data archives.

  ```
  SQL> select flashback_archive_name, tablespace_name, quota_in_mb
          from dba_flashback_archive_ts;
        FLASHBACK_ARCHIVE _NAME      TABLESPACE_NAME   QUOTA_IN_MB
        ----------------------      ---------------   -----------
        FLASH1                      FLASH1_TBS          100
  ```

Using Flashback Data Archives: Examples

As I mentioned earlier in this chapter, you can use the flashback data archive feature for several types of tasks, including the querying of historical data, auditing, and even to recover from logical errors. The following examples illustrate the versatility of the flashback data archive feature.

Accessing Older Data You can use an `as_of` clause in your `select` statement to query historical data, as shown by this query:

```
SQL> select transaction_number, doctor_name, count
     from patient_info as of
     timestamp to_timestamp ('2007-01-01 00:00:00',
     'YYYY-MM-DD HH23:MI:SS');
```

You can use the `as_of` clause to recover from logical errors, by retrieving older data, even when you don't know the exact time when the wrong data entry was made. The following example shows how to use the `as_of` clause to correct wrongly updated data in a table.

The following query shows the current salary data for the employee with the `last_name` Zlotkey in the EMPLOYEES table owned by the user HR.

```
SQL> select salary from hr.employees where
     last_name='Zlotkey';
     SALARY
------------
     10500
SQL>
```

A user raises Zlotkey's salary by a wrong amount, by updating the SALARY column by 50000 instead of 5000.

```
SQL> update hr.employees set salary=salary+50000
     where last_name='Zlotkey';
1 row updated.
SQL> commit;
Commit complete.
SQL>
```

You can correct the error if you know the correct salary of Zlotkey before the database committed the results of the `update` statement. You don't know the exact time the user issued the `update` statement, but it doesn't matter. If you can roughly estimate when the error was made, you can still retrieve the pre-change data. If you know that the erroneous update was made about two hours ago, you can set Zlotkey's salary to its value at that time by using the following `update` statement.

```
SQL> update hr.employees set salary =
    (select salary from hr.employees
    as of timestamp (systimestamp - interval '120' minute);
    where last_name='Zlotkey')
    where last_name='Zlotkey';
1 row updated.
SQL> commit;
Commit complete.
SQL>
```

The update shown here uses historical values made possible by the use of the flashback data archive but the use of the flashback data archive is transparent. That is, in order to correct the logical error by retrieving the historical value of the SALARY column, you don't have to query the history table directly. The database will use that information automatically because you specified the `as of` clause in your `update` statement. The `systimestamp - interval '120'` clause tells the database to retrieve the values that prevailed two hours before for the SALARY column for the user Zlotkey. If you want, you can specify seconds, days, and months as well in the `systimestamp` clause, as shown here:

```
systimestamp - interval '60' second
systimestamp - interval '7' day
systimestamp - interval '12' month
```

Generating Reports You can use the historical data stored in the flashback data archive to create reports that span a long period of time in the past. Use the `versions between timestamp` clause as shown here to get values for a table's columns that prevailed during a time interval that you specify.

```
SQL> select * from patient_info
    versions between timestamp
    to_timestamp('2008-01-01 00:00:00','YYYY-MM-DD HH23:MI:SS')
    and maxvalue
    where name ='ALAPATI';
```

The query uses the `versions between timestamp` clause to capture all versions of the data in the PATIENT_INFO table between January 1, 2008 and today for the patient named ALAPATI.

Information Lifecycle Management You can also use the `versions between` clause to retrieve multiple versions of a row to satisfy the requirement of information lifecycle management (ILM) applications. Instead of your having to collect and store the multiple versions over time, you can simply enable flashback data archiving for the tables that you need to track for an ILM application. Here's an example that shows how you can specify the `versions between` clause to retrieve all versions of a table's rows during a specific interval of time.

```
SQL> select * from patient_info
     versions between timestamp
     to_timestamp ('2008-01-01 00:00:00',
     'YYYY-MM-DD HH24:MI:SS')
     and
     to_timestamp ('2008-06-01 00:00:00',
     'YYYY-MM-DD HH24:MI:SS')
     where name='ALAPATI';
```

The `select` statement shown here utilizes the flashback data archive to retrieve all versions of the rows in the PATIENT_INFO table for the first six months of the year 2008.

Flashback Transaction Backout

The flashback version query and the flashback transaction query features introduced in Oracle Database 10g helped you to correct logical errors in a table by first querying the data from the past and then updating it, thus undoing wrong transactions. Oracle Database 11g introduces the *flashback transaction backout* feature, which lets you perform logical recovery by undoing changes made by a transaction as well as its dependent transactions. It is easy to maintain data consistency because you can back out transactions that include a sequence of `insert`, `update`, and `delete` statements with a single execution of the TRANSACTION_BACKOUT procedure belonging to the DBMS_FLASHBACK package. You can do the same thing through the Enterprise Manager, which uses the TRANSACTION_BACKOUT procedure as well, to back out the changes made by a transaction or set of transactions with just a single click on your part.

A dependent transaction can have either a *write-after-write* or a *primary key constraint* relationship with the parent transaction:

- In a *write-after-write* relationship, the dependent transaction modifies the data that was previously modified by the parent transaction.

- Under a *primary key constraint* relationship, the dependent transaction reinserts the primary key deleted by the parent transaction.

In order to undo the changes brought about by a transaction, the database executes appropriate *compensating transactions* to return the data to its original state. Because the flashback transaction backout feature needs both the undo as well as the redo data generated for the undo blocks to execute the compensating transactions, you'll need the necessary undo data and the archived redo logs to undo a transaction.

Prerequisites for Flashback Transaction Backout

You must enable *supplemental logging* in the database to enable the flashback transaction backout feature. So, first issue the following statements to turn supplemental logging on in the database:

```
SQL> alter database add supplemental log data;
SQL> alter database add supplemental log data
     (primary key) columns;
```

You must also grant the following privileges to any user that wants to use the flashback transaction backout feature. The following statements grant the necessary privileges to the user HR:

```
SQL> grant execute on dbms_flashback to hr;
SQL> grant select any transaction to hr;
```

The first privilege grants the user HR the `flashback` system privilege and the second, the `select any transaction` privilege. If a user wants to perform a transaction backout operation in another user's schema, the first user must also have the necessary DML privileges on the table or tables in the second user's schema.

Using the DBMS_FLASHBACK.TRANSACTION_BACKOUT Procedure

You can use the new DBMS_FLASHBACK.TRANSACTION_BACKOUT procedure to back out transactions. Here's the structure of the DBMS_FLASHBACK.TRANSACTION_BACKOUT procedure:

```
PROCEDURE TRANSACTION_BACKOUT
   Argument Name        Type            In/Out     Default?
   ---------------      --------------  ---------  ----------
   NUMBEROFXIDS         NUMBER          IN
   XIDS                 XID_ARRAY       IN
   OPTIONS              BINARY_INTEGER  IN          DEFAULT
   SCNHINT              TIMESTAMP       IN
```

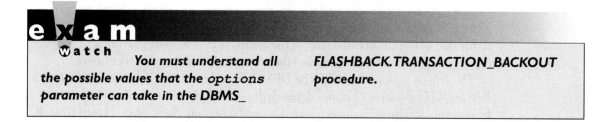

Here's a brief explanation of the four key parameters in the DBMS_
FLASHBACK.TRANSACTION_BACKOUT procedure:

- `numberofxids` is the number of transactions you want to back out in this operation.
- `xids`   A list of transaction identifiers that are passed as an array.
- `options`   Enables you to specify the order in which to back out the parent and the child transactions. You can use the following four values for the `options` parameter:

  - The `nocascade` value is the default and you use it when you don't expect a transaction to have any dependent transactions.

  - The `cascade` value backs out the dependent transactions before backing out the parent transaction.

  - The `nocascade_force` value backs out only the parent transactions. It ignores any dependent transactions.

  - The `noconflict_only` option backs out only those rows in the parent transaction that don't have any conflicts.

on the
ⓙob   *If you use the default value of `nocascade` for the `options` parameter,*
it means that you're expecting the parent transaction doesn't have any
dependent transactions.

- `scnhint`   You use the `scnhint` parameter to specify the SCN at the start of the transaction. The SCN must be before the start of the first transaction in the transaction set to be backed out.

Note that you can use several variations of the TRANSACTION_BACKOUT procedure. In our example here, I showed how you can use the `xids` parameter to specify an array of transaction identifiers to list the transactions. You can alternately use the parameter `txnames` to pass an array of transaction names. Similarly, you can replace the `scnhint` parameter with the `timehint` parameter, which enables you to provide a time hint on the start of the transaction. You must provide a `timehint` parameter if you're using transaction names instead of transaction identifiers.

The length of time for which the DBMS_FLASHBACK.TRANSACTION_ BACKOUT operation executes depends directly on the amount of redo generated by the transactions being backed out. Once you execute the DBMS_FLASHBACK. TRANSACTION_BACKOUT procedure, the transactions you name aren't automatically backed out by the database. The procedure checks the dependencies among transactions and performs the DML operations, but doesn't commit them. Instead, it provides you with a report of its work. In the meantime, it holds locks on the rows and the tables in order to keep new transactions from affecting the backout operation. In order for the transactions to be backed out for good, you must issue a `commit` statement.

EXERCISE 7-1

Using the TRANSACTION_BACKOUT Procedure

The following exercise shows you how to use the DBMS_FLASHBACK. TRANSACTION_BACKOUT procedure to back out a transaction along with its dependent transactions. Before you can execute the DBMS_FLASHBACK .TRANSACTION_BACKOUT procedure, you must first create a variable of an XID_ARRAY type. This array will hold a set of transaction identifiers as the starting point of the dependency search. Alternately, you can use a set of transaction names to identify the transactions.

```
declare
   trans_arr xid_array;
begin
   trans_arr := xid_array('030003000D02540','D10001000D02550');
   dbms_flashback.transaction_backout (
       numtxns          => 1,
       xids             => trans_arr,
       options          => dbms_flashback.nocascade
   );
end;
```

The column XIDS passes an array of transactions as input to the procedure. The default value for the options parameter is `cascade`, but I chose `nocascade` in this example. When you execute this procedure, the primary transaction and its dependent transaction are rolled back in one step.

Although the database names the backout operation, for auditing purposes, Oracle recommends that you name your backout operation. Successful execution of the TRANSACTION_BACKOUT procedure means that the database backed out a single parent transaction.

TRANSACTION_BACKOUT Reports

The TRANSACTION_BACKOUT procedure populates the views DBA_ FLASHBACK_TRANSACTION_STATE and DBA_FLASHBACK_ TRANSACTION_REPORT. Once the database successfully backs out a transaction, the database records the transaction in the DBA_FLASHBACK_TRANSACTION_ STATE view. You can query the DBA_FLASHBACK_TRANSACTION_REPORT view to get detailed reports about the transaction backout operations.

INSIDE THE EXAM

The exam will most certainly ask you at least one question about the new active duplication feature in RMAN. Be prepared to answer questions relating to the syntax of the active database duplication command, including the use of the set parameter. Is the use of the password file mandatory during active database duplication?

The new multisection backup feature is likely to appear in a question. Again, it's important to know the syntax of the command for creating a multisection RMAN backup. Other new RMAN features such as archival backups and the new archivelog deletion policy are likely to play a role in the test. How does the change . . . nokeep command affect the retention of a backup?

There are several key enhancements in recovery catalog management and you can expect to be tested on at least one of them. How do you import a catalog into another

catalog? What is the syntax for the import catalog command? You must know the precise sequence of steps to follow to create a virtual private catalog. Which commands can the virtual private catalog owner execute?

The two major flashback-related features—flashback data archive and transaction backout—are likely to appear on the exam. The exam is very likely to contain a question about creating a flashback archive. You must know the syntax of the create flashback archive command thoroughly. How do you set the retention period for a flashback archive? There probably will be a question on maintaining a flashback data archive, such as purging the archive. You are expected to understand how to enable and disable history tracking for a table. Do you have to specify the name of the flashback data archive when you enable history tracking for a table? In the flashback transaction feature, you must understand how to set the various options such as `nocascade`, `nonconflict_only`, and `cascade` when you execute the TRANSACTION_BACKOUT procedure. Which of these options must you specify, if you want to forcibly back out a set of transactions without paying attention to the dependent transactions?

CERTIFICATION SUMMARY

The first section of this chapter described the major RMAN enhancements. Active database duplication enables you to duplicate a database across the network without any prior backups for the source database. You can use the new `section size` clause to perform multisection backups and restores, which are much faster because you can parallelize the backup or restore. You can now use the `backup...keep` command to perform an archival backup, whose purpose is to enable you to restore a consistent version of the database. The `recover...block` command lets you recover corrupt data blocks faster because it searches in the flashback logs first before looking for the good blocks in the backup files.

You have a choice between two compression algorithms in Oracle Database 11g. The new compression algorithm ZLIB is much faster than the older BZIP2 algorithm. You can now configure an archived redo log policy, which controls the behavior of any commands that delete the archived redo logs. The new `import database` command in RMAN enables you to merge two recovery catalogs or import databases from one recovery catalog to another. The virtual private catalog feature enables you to control access to the base recovery catalog.

A flashback data archive stores the changes made to a table that you enabled for flashback archiving. You can use the historical data for auditing, querying older data, generating reports, and information lifecycle management. The flashback transaction backout feature enables you to easily back out a transaction along with all of its dependent transactions.

✓ # TWO-MINUTE DRILL

RMAN Enhancements

❑ Active database duplication doesn't use any backups for duplicating the database.

❑ You can perform active database duplication with the database open or in the mount state.

❑ When you perform active database duplication, you must use password files on both the source and the auxiliary databases so you can use the same SYSDBA password.

❑ Use the `spfile ... parameter_name_convert` clause to specify conversion strings for all initialization parameters except the `db_file_name_convert` and the `log_file_name_convert` parameters.

❑ The `set` clause in the `duplicate database` command enables you to specify initialization parameters for the new database.

❑ The `db_file_name_convert` parameter enables you to specify file-naming rules for creating datafiles and tempfiles.

❑ The `log_file_name_convert` parameter enables you to specify the file-naming rules for online redo log files.

❑ The `spfile` clause in the duplicate database statement specifies the copying of the source database's SPFILE to the duplicate database.

❑ Specify the `nofilenamecheck` clause in the `duplicate database` statement when duplicating a database to a different server.

❑ The `section size` backup command parameter enables RMAN to back up and restore a large datafile a section at a time.

❑ RMAN creates uniform-sized sections for all but the very last section size, which may or may not be the same size as the other sections.

❑ RMAN assigns a default value for section size, if you omit a value for the `section size` parameter.

❑ You can also specify the `section size` clause with the `validate datafile` command.

❑ You can use the revised `backup ... keep` command to create long-term archival backups.

❏ An archival backup contains all the backups and archived redo log files necessary to restore and recover a database.

❏ You can specify the `restore point` option with the `keep` command.

❏ The `restore point` clause determines the time until which RMAN can restore an archival backup.

❏ Specify the `keep ... until time` option to create an archival backup and store it for a specified period of time.

❏ Specify the `keep ... forever` clause to create an archival backup that RMAN stores forever.

❏ You can also alter the status of a normal backup to that of an archival backup by using the `change` (`change backup`) command.

❏ You can't use the `change ... keep` command to alter the status of backups stored in the flash recovery area.

❏ You can enable block change tracking on a physical standby database.

❏ The `recover ... block` command replaces the `blockrecover` command.

❏ The `recover ... block` command searches the flashback logs before the backup files, when it's looking for good copies of a corrupted data block.

❏ Each time a command such as `validate` or `backup ... validate` reveals a database corruption, the database logs that information in the V$DATABASE_BLOCK_CORRUPTION view.

❏ You can use the `recover ... block` command to recover a specific data block or all corrupt data blocks at once.

❏ Issue the recover `corruption list` command to recover all corrupt data blocks in the database.

❏ RMAN uses the new compression algorithm `ZLIB` as the default algorithm.

❏ The `ZIB` algorithm is faster than `BZIP2` but doesn't offer as good a compression ratio.

❏ An archived redo log deletion policy enables you to specify when an archived redo log becomes eligible for deletion.

❏ By default, no archived redo log deletion policy is set.

❏ The backup retention policy won't mark an archived redo log as obsolete if the log is necessary to support a guaranteed restore point or the Flashback Database feature.

❏ Both the `backup...delete` and the `delete...archivelog` commands will take an archived redo log deletion policy into account.

❏ RMAN automatically fails over to a non-flash recovery area when archiving a redo log, if an archived redo log file in the flash recovery area is missing or corrupt.

Recovery Catalog Management

❏ A virtual recovery catalog enables you to restrict a user to only a part of the base recovery catalog.

❏ The `import catalog` command enables you to merge recovery catalogs.

❏ By default, RMAN unregisters all databases from the source recovery catalog after it imports those databases to another recovery catalog.

❏ Use the `no unregister` clause if you want RMAN to retain the imported database in the source recovery catalog after importing them to another recovery catalog.

❏ If a global store script has identical names in different catalogs, RMAN will rename the source recovery catalog script.

❏ You can use the `import catalog` command to move a recovery catalog to a different database.

❏ A virtual private catalog is a set of synonyms and views based on the central base recovery catalog.

❏ The `catalog` privilege grants the user the ability to register and unregister a database from the recovery catalog.

❏ The `revoke catalog for database` command is used to revoke a virtual catalog owner's access to a database.

❏ You can use the `revoke register database` or the `revoke all privileges` command to revoke privileges from a virtual catalog owner.

New Flashback-Related Features

❏ A flashback data archive is a logical container for storing older versions of data over a long period of time.

❏ The flashback transaction feature lets you easily back out a transaction, along with its dependent transactions.

❑ The flashback data archive will automatically purge older data.

❑ The flashback data archive is an online feature.

❑ You must enable flashback data archiving at the table level.

❑ You can use different retention periods for different flashback data archives.

❑ You can create a default flashback data archive, but it isn't a requirement.

❑ You must first enable a table for flashback data archiving before the database can start archiving data for that table.

❑ The Oracle background process fbda writes the changed data to the flashback data archive.

❑ A flashback data archive can contain data from multiple tables.

❑ You can set different retention periods for different tables.

❑ If you don't specify a flashback data archive, a table will use the default flashback data archive.

❑ The database stores the history data in an internal history table it creates for each table it tracks.

❑ The database doesn't add any rows to the history table when you insert rows into the original table.

❑ The fbda background process marks the undo data for an `update` or `delete` command for archiving to the history table.

❑ The database automatically adjusts the sleep time of the fbda process.

❑ You can use the `as of` construct to retrieve flashback data.

❑ No one can update the history data. You can query the data but you can't modify it.

❑ You must grant the `flashback archive administer` system privilege for a user to be able to create a flashback data archive.

❑ You must always assign a retention period for a flashback data archive by specifying the `retention` clause in the `create flashback data archive` command.

❑ When you drop a flashback data archive, the archived data will be gone but the tablespace hosting the data archive remains intact.

❑ You must specify the `flashback archive` clause when you create a table in order to archive the changes to that table's data.

- ❏ You can also specify the `flashback archive` clause with an `alter table` statement in order to archive the changes made to a table.
- ❏ You can disable flashback archiving for a table by issuing the `alter table` statement with the `no flashback archive` clause.
- ❏ You can't issue an `alter table` statement to drop, rename, or modify a column on a table enabled for a flashback data archive.
- ❏ You can't execute the `drop table` or `truncate table` statement against a table enabled for a flashback data archive.
- ❏ You can back out transactions with the DBMS_FLASHBACK. TRANSACTION_BACKOUT procedure.
- ❏ In a write-after-write relationship, the dependent transaction modifies the data that was modified earlier by the parent transaction.
- ❏ In a primary key constraint relationship, the dependent transaction reinserts the primary key deleted by the parent transaction.
- ❏ In the flashback transaction backout feature, the database executes compensating transactions to return data to its original state.
- ❏ You must enable supplemental logging to enable the flashback transaction backout feature.
- ❏ In the TRANSACTION_BACKOUT procedure, the `nocascade` value for the `options` parameter is the default.
- ❏ The `nocascade` value for the `options` parameter is used when you don't expect any dependent transactions.
- ❏ The `cascade` value for the `options` parameter backs out the dependent transactions first.
- ❏ The `nocascade_force` value for the `options` parameter backs out only the parent transactions.
- ❏ The `noconflict_only` option for the `options` parameter backs out only those rows in the parent transaction that don't have any conflicts.

SELF TEST

RMAN Enhancements

1. The `set` clause in the `duplicate database` command lets you specify the
   A. Initialization parameters
   B. `log_file_name_convert` parameter
   C. `db_file_name_convert` parameter
   D. `parameter_value_convert` clause

2. The `password file` clause in the `duplicate database` command
   A. Copies the source database's password file to the target database
   B. Copies the target database's password file to the source database
   C. Isn't necessary if the SYSDBA password is the same in the source and the target databases
   D. Is mandatory when duplicating a database

3. When you perform a multisection backup,
   A. Each section corresponds to a backup piece in the backup set.
   B. Each section corresponds to a backup set in a backup.
   C. The very last section may or may not be the same size as the rest of the sections.
   D. You don't have to specify a value for the section size parameter.

4. An archival backup
   A. Includes all archived redo logs from the time the backup was taken
   B. Includes all archived redo logs necessary to make the backup consistent
   C. Is immune from any retention policies you may have configured
   D. Can include a `restore point` option

5. Which of the following statements is true?
   A. If an archived redo log is necessary to support a normal restore point, the backup retention policy won't make it obsolete.
   B. If an archived redo log is necessary to support a guaranteed restore point, the backup retention policy won't make it obsolete.
   C. The `delete...archivelog` command doesn't take a configured archived redo log deletion policy into account.
   D. An archived redo log deletion policy determines when RMAN can delete all archived redo log files.

6. What does the `parameter_value_convert` clause in the duplicate database command do?
   A. It specifies the string to be used in all initialization parameters that specify filenames, except the `db_file_name_convert` and the `log_file_name_convert` parameters.
   B. It specifies the substitution of the appropriate file path in the filenames of the duplicate database's online redo log files.
   C. It specifies all initialization parameters for the duplicate database.
   D. It substitutes the appropriate string in the names of the duplicate database's datafiles and tempfiles.

7. When you execute the `recover...block` command, the database
   A. Searches the archived redo logs first for the good data blocks
   B. Searches the online redo logs first for the good data blocks
   C. Searches the backed up data files for the good data blocks
   D. Searches the flashback logs for the good data blocks

Recovery Catalog Management

8. When merging two recovery catalogs with the `import catalog` command, the `no unregister` clause
   A. Instructs RMAN not to unregister the imported database in the destination recovery catalog
   B. Instructs RMAN not to register the imported database in the destination recovery catalog
   C. Instructs RMAN not to remove the imported databases from the source recovery catalog after their import to the target catalog
   D. Is always used by RMAN by default

9. A virtual catalog owner
   A. Can create only global stored scripts
   B. Can create only local stored scripts
   C. Can create both local and global stored scripts
   D. Has read-only rights to global stored scripts

10. The `grant catalog for database` command
    A. Grants recovery catalog access on a specific database to a user
    B. Grants recovery catalog access on all databases to a user
    C. Lets you grant access to only databases that are currently registered in the base recovery catalog.
    D. Lets you grant access to target databases that are not yet registered in the base recovery catalog.

11. The `grant register database to <username>` command
    A. Grants recovery catalog access to a specific database to a user
    B. Grants recovery catalog access to all databases to a user
    C. Grants the ability to a user to execute the `register database` command to register databases that are currently unknown to the database
    D. Grants the ability to execute the `register database` command to register a database currently known to the recovery catalog in that user's virtual private catalog

12. The DBMS_RCVCAT.CREATE_VIRTUAL_CATALOG procedure
    A. Creates a virtual private catalog when you're using a pre–Oracle 11g release RMAN executable
    B. Lets you work with a pre–Oracle 11.1 release database
    C. Must always be executed before you can start working with a virtual recovery catalog
    D. Is a procedure you must execute in order to create a virtual catalog

13. You must use the following set of commands in the correct sequence to create a recovery catalog and register a new database in that catalog, following the creation of the base catalog.
    1. grant recovery catalog owner to vpcowner;
    2. grant catalog for database test1 to vpcowner;
    3. register database;
    4. create virtual catalog;
    5. grant register database to vpcowner;
    Which of the following shows the correct sequence of steps?
    A. 5, 4, 3, 2, 1
    B. 1, 2, 3, 4, 5
    C. 1, 5, 2, 4, 3
    D. 1, 5, 4, 2, 3

14. When you execute the `import catalog` command to merge two recovery catalogs,
    A. You can only import metadata of a single database at a time.
    B. You can import the metadata of all registered databases in the source catalog.
    C. You can specify only the DBID of the databases you'd like to import.
    D. You can specify the database name or the DBID of the databases you'd like to import.

New Flashback-Related Features

15. A flashback data archive
   - **A.** Will store data up to the SCN you specify
   - **B.** Will automatically purge older data
   - **C.** Never purges data on its own
   - **D.** Can be activated for the entire database

16. How do you set different retention periods for tables when you use the flashback data archive?
   - **A.** By assigning the tables to different flashback data archives
   - **B.** By using the `alter table` statement to change the retention period for the tables
   - **C.** By purging the flashback data archive after the retention period for a table is over
   - **D.** By changing the retention period for the history table that the database maintains for each of the tables in the flashback data archive

17. Which of the following items must you specify when you create a flashback data archive?
   - **A.** Quota
   - **B.** Retention period
   - **C.** Flashback data archive name
   - **D.** Name of the tablespace

18. How can you free up space in the flashback data archive when it runs out of space?
   - **A.** Purge older data
   - **B.** Add space to the tablespace hosting the flashback data archive
   - **C.** Delete the history tables
   - **D.** Add space to the flashback data archive by executing the `alter flashback archive` statement

19. How do you enable flashback data archiving for a set of tables?
   - **A.** By creating a flashback data archive
   - **B.** By specifying the `flashback archive` clause when you create a table
   - **C.** By executing the `alter table ... flashback archive` statement
   - **D.** By using the initialization parameter `enable_flashback_archive` and setting it to `TRUE`

20. In the DBMS_FLASHBACK.TRANSACTION_BACKOUT procedure, the `nocascade` value for the `options` parameter
   - **A.** Is the default value for the `options` parameter
   - **B.** Backs out dependent transactions before backing out the parent transaction
   - **C.** Backs out only the parent transactions and ignores any dependent transactions
   - **D.** Backs out only those rows in the parent transaction that don't have any conflicts

21. In the DBMS_FLASHBACK.TRANSACTION_BACKOUT procedure, the `nocascade_` `force` value for the `options` parameter

    A. Is the default value for the `options` parameter

    B. Backs out dependent transactions before backing out the parent transaction

    C. Backs out only the parent transactions and ignores any dependent transactions

    D. Backs out only those rows in the parent transaction that don't have any conflicts

LAB QUESTION

Show how to create a virtual private catalog and enable a user to use that virtual catalog for a pre–Oracle Database 11g client.

SELF TEST ANSWERS

RMAN Enhancements

1. ☑ **A** and **B** are correct. **A** is correct because the `set` clause enables you to specify the initialization parameters directly in the `duplicate database` command, without specifying them in the SPFILE for the duplicate database. The values you set for any initialization parameters by specifying the `set` clause override the values for the same parameters in the SPFILE for the duplicate database. **B** is correct because the `set` clause enables you to specify the value for the `log_file_name_convert` parameter.
☒ **C** is incorrect because you must specify the `db_file_name_convert` parameter on its own, not by specifying the `set` command. **D** is incorrect because you specify the `parameter_value_convert` parameter separately, not as part of the `set` command.

2. ☑ **A** is correct because the `password file` clause enables you to copy the source database's password file to the duplicate database.
☒ **B**, **C**, and **D** are incorrect. **B** is incorrect because the `password file` clause copies the source database's password file over to the target database. **C** is incorrect because the need for the `password file` clause has nothing to do with the SYSDBA password being the same in the two databases. **D** is incorrect because the `password file` clause is optional, not mandatory.

3. ☑ **A** and **C** are correct. **A** is correct because each section in a multisection backup job corresponds to a backup piece in the resulting backup set. **C** is correct because all sections are of the same size, but the last section may or may not be.
☒ **B** is incorrect because each section in a multisection backup corresponds to a backup piece, not a backup set. **D** is incorrect because the `section size` parameter is mandatory—there's no default size for the section size parameter.

4. ☑ **B**, **C**, and **D** are correct. **B** is correct because an archival backup includes all the necessary archived redo logs that are necessary to make a backup consistent. The goal of an archival backup isn't to make a point-in-time recovery, but to create a consistent database from the backups. **C** is correct because an archival backup ignores any retention policies you might have configured for RMAN backups. **D** is correct because you can include an optional `restore point` option when creating an archival backup.
☒ **A** is incorrect because an archival backup doesn't include all archived redo logs from the time the backup was made. It simply includes the archived redo logs to make the recovery consistent, but not up-to-date.

5. ☑ **B** and **D** are correct. **B** is correct because when you configure an archived redo log deletion policy, RMAN won't mark a backup as obsolete if that archived redo log is necessary to support a *guaranteed* restore point. **D** is correct because when you configure an archived redo log policy, the policy determines when RMAN can delete all the archived redo log files.

   ☒ **A** and **C** are incorrect. **A** is incorrect because RMAN may mark as obsolete archived redo logs that are necessary to support a *normal* restore point. It will not, however, mark the archived redo logs necessary to support a *guaranteed* restore point as obsolete. **C** is incorrect because the `delete...archivelog` command takes the archived redo log policy that you configured into account when it deletes archived redo logs.

6. ☑ **A** is correct because the `parameter_value_convert` clause specifies the string names for all initialization parameters that specify filenames, with the exception of the `db_file_name_convert` and the `log_file_name_convert` parameters.

   ☒ **B, C,** and **D** are incorrect. **B** is incorrect because it's the `log_file_name_convert` parameter that specifies the string for the filenames of the duplicate database's online redo log files. **C** is incorrect because the `parameter_name_convert` parameter doesn't specify any initialization parameters or the duplicate database—it's the `set` clause in the duplicate database command that specifies the initialization parameters for the duplicate database. The `parameter_name_convert` clause merely specifies the string names for all initialization parameters that specify filenames, with the exception of the `log_file_name_convert` and the `db_file_name_convert` parameters. **D** is incorrect because it's the `db_file_name_convert` parameter that substitutes the string to be used in the names of the duplicate database's datafiles and tempfiles.

7. ☑ **D** is correct because when you issue the `block...recover` command, the database first searches the flashback logs for the good data blocks that it restores in place of the corrupted data blocks.

   ☒ **A, B,** and **C** are incorrect because the database first looks in the flashback logs for the good data blocks, which is why the `recover...block` command is more efficient than the old `blockrecover` command. The flashback logs are always online, and enable a quick restore of the corrupt data blocks.

Recovery Catalog Management

8. ☑ **C** is correct because the `no unregister` clause tells RMAN not to automatically unregister the database that it imported from the source recovery catalog database.

   ☒ **A, B,** and **D** are incorrect. **A** is incorrect because the `no unregister` clause deals with unregistering already registered databases from the source recovery catalog. **B** is incorrect because the `no unregister` clause deals with the unregistering of previously registered databases, not with the registering of new databases in either of the two recovery catalogs. **D** is incorrect because the `no unregister` clause is optional and RMAN doesn't use it by default.

9. ☑ **B** and **D** are correct. **B** is correct because a virtual catalog owner can create only local stored scripts. **D** is correct because even though the virtual catalog owner can't create any global stored scripts, the owner has read-only rights to global stored scripts.

☒ **A** and **C** are incorrect because the virtual catalog owner can't create any global scripts.

10. ☑ **A** and **D** are correct. **A** is correct because the `grant catalog for database...` command grants recovery catalog access on a specific database to a user. The command is used in the following way:

```
SQL> grant catalog for database test1 to vpcuser;
```

D is correct because you can grant access to databases that aren't yet registered in the base recovery catalog. You must grant access by using the DBID of the database in such cases.

☒ **B** and **C** are incorrect. **B** is incorrect because the `grant catalog for database` command doesn't grant access to all databases, but only to the databases that you explicitly specify. **C** is incorrect because the command lets you grant access to target databases that are not yet registered in the base recovery catalog.

11. ☑ **C** is correct because the `grant register for database...` command grants the ability to execute the `register database` command to register new databases in the virtual catalog, and therefore in the base recovery catalog as well.

☒ **A**, **B**, and **D** are incorrect. **A** is incorrect because the `register database` command doesn't automatically grant access to a database. **B** is incorrect because the `grant register database` command grants the privilege only on a specific database and not on all databases. **D** is incorrect because the `grant register for database` command grants the ability to register databases that are currently unknown to the database.

12. ☑ **B** is correct because you must execute the CREATE_VIRTUAL_CATALOG procedure from the DBMS_RCVCAT package before working with any pre–Oracle 11.1 release database.

☒ **A**, **C**, and **D** are incorrect. **A** is incorrect because the CREATE_VIRTUAL_CATALOG procedure doesn't actually create a virtual private catalog. **C** is incorrect because you have to execute this procedure only when you want to work with a pre–Oracle 11.1 release database. **D** is incorrect because you don't use this procedure to create a virtual catalog, but to work with one.

13. ☑ **C** is correct because it shows the correct sequence of steps.

☒ **A**, **B**, and **D** are incorrect because they all show an incorrect sequence of steps.

14. ☑ **B** and **D** are correct. **B** is correct because when you issue the `import catalog` command without either the database or the DBID clause, the command will import metadata for all databases from the source recovery catalog into the destination recovery catalog. **D** is correct because you can specify either the DBID or the database when naming the database or databases you want to import from the source database.

☒ **A** and **C** are incorrect. **A** is incorrect because you don't have to import one database at a time. When you issue the `import catalog` command without any database or DBID clauses, you import the metadata for all database registered in the source recovery catalog. **C** is incorrect because you can specify either the DBID or the database when naming the database or databases you want to import from the source database.

New Flashback-Related Features

15. ☑ **B** is correct because the flashback data archive will purge data automatically, based on the retention period that you specify for that archive.
    ☒ **A, C,** and **D** are incorrect. **A** is incorrect because the flashback data archive doesn't take into account any SCNs when storing historical data for a table. After you enable a table for the flashback data archive, the database simply records all changes made to that table until you disable archiving for the table. **C** is incorrect because the flashback data archive automatically manages the purging of its data, as explained earlier. **D** is incorrect because you can't activate flashback data archiving for the entire database. You can enable only specific tables for archiving, one table at a time. You can enable a table for archiving either when you create the table, or later on, with the `alter table` statement.

16. ☑ **A** is correct because you can assign tables to different flashback data archives, each of which is configured with a different retention period that's appropriate to a table.
    ☒ **B, C,** and **D** are incorrect. **B** is incorrect because you can't change the retention period with the `alter table` statement. You can change the retention period with the `alter flashback data archive` statement. **C** is incorrect because purging the flashback data archive removes all data for a table. **D** is incorrect because you can't change the retention period for the history table.

17. ☑ **B** and **D** are correct. **B** is correct because it's a mandatory attribute you must specify when creating a flashback data archive. **D** is correct because you must specify the name of the tablespace when creating a flashback data archive.
    ☒ **A** is incorrect because you don't have to specify the quota attribute. **C** is incorrect because the flashback data archive isn't mandatory—you can omit the attribute as long as you have already created a default flashback data archive for the database.

18. ☑ **A, B,** and **D** are correct because doing any one or all of these will create more free space in the flashback data archive for new history records for a table.
    ☒ **C** is incorrect because you can't delete the history table for a table that is enabled for flashback data archiving.

19. ☑ **B** and **C** are correct. **B** is correct because you can specify the `flashback archive` clause when you create a table with the `create table` statement. **C** is correct because you can also enable flashback data archiving for a table with the `alter table` statement.
    ☒ **A** is incorrect because you can't enable flashback data archiving by merely creating a flashback data archive. You must follow this by explicitly enabling a table for flashback data

archiving, either when you create the table or with the `alter table` statement later on. **D** is incorrect because there is no initialization parameter named `enable_flashback_archive`.

20. ☑ **A** is correct because `nocascade` is the default value for the `options` attribute. You use the `nocascade` value when you don't expect the transaction you're backing out to have any dependent transactions.
    ☒ **B, C, and D** are wrong. **B** is incorrect because it's the `cascade` value that backs out dependent transactions before backing out the parent transaction. **C** is incorrect because it is the `nocascade_force` value that backs out only the parent transaction while ignoring any dependent transactions. **D** is incorrect because it is the `noconflict_only` value for the `options` parameter that backs out only those rows in the parent transaction that don't have any conflicts.

21. ☑ **C** is correct because the `nocascade_force` value results in backing out only the parent transaction while ignoring any dependent transactions.
    ☒ **A, B, and D** are incorrect. **A** is incorrect because `nocascade` is the default value for the `options` attribute. **B** is incorrect because it is the `cascade` value that backs out dependent transactions before backing out the parent transaction. **D** is incorrect because it is the `noconflict_only` value for the `options` parameter that backs out only those rows in the parent transaction that don't have any conflicts.

LAB ANSWER

The process for creating a virtual catalog for a pre–Oracle Database 11g client is essentially the same as that for an Oracle Database 11g client, with one small difference. I show the sequence of steps here.

1. Create an RMAN base catalog and connect to it as shown here:

   ```
   RMAN> connect catalog rman/rman@catdb;
   ```

2. Grant the `recovery_catalog_owner` privilege to the new virtual catalog owner, virtual1:

   ```
   SQL> connect sys/sammyy1@catdb as sysdba
   SQL> grant recovery_catalog_owner to virtual1;
   ```

3. Grant one of the following privileges to the virtual catalog owner virtual1, after first connecting to the base recovery catalog as the recover catalog owner, rman.

   ```
   RMAN> grant register database to virtual1;
   RMAN> grant catalog for database testdb to virutal1
   ```

4. Create a virtual catalog for a pre–Oracle Database 11g client after first logging in as the virtual catalog owner, virtual1.

   ```
   SQL> connect virtual1/virtual1@catdb
   SQL> exec rman.dbms_rcvcat.create_virtual_catalog;
   ```

5. Register a new database in the catalog.

```
RMAN> connect target/catalog virtual1/virtual1@catdb
RMAN> register database;
```

6. Use the virtual catalog to create a backup of a database.

```
RMAN> connect target / catalog virtual1/virtual1@catdb;
RMAN> backup database;
```

8

Oracle SecureFiles and Miscellaneous New Features

CERTIFICATION OBJECTIVES

8.01   Oracle SecureFiles

8.02   Online Enhancements

8.03   Miscellaneous New Features

    Two-Minute Drill

Q&A   Self Test

T his final chapter of the book deals with Oracle SecureFiles, which is a newly re-engineered LOB data type for large objects. Oracle SecureFiles is a completely new storage infrastructure for data that's a drop-in replacement of Oracle's previous implementation of large object infrastructure. The Oracle SecureFiles architecture has been designed to offer improved performance and security while reducing disk usage with its advanced compression features. This chapter shows you how to create LOBs as Oracle SecureFiles and how to migrate from traditional LOBs to the new Oracle SecureFiles infrastructure.

The second part of this chapter is a quick round-up of miscellaneous new features in Oracle Database 11*g*. These features include several online enhancements such as locking enhancements and minimal invalidation of dependent objects during online redefinitions. The chapter shows how to replace your parameter file by using the parameter values currently in use by the instance. Online patching with the opatch utility offers several benefits, and you learn about this new feature as well. The new release also lets you create what are called *invisible indexes*, which the optimizer can't "see" until you explicitly make those indexes visible. You'll learn about the enhancements to temporary tablespace management. The chapter discusses the new method to easily enable you to set up native PL/SQL compilation in a database. You can now use table compression for OLTP databases and compress data during DML operations. The chapter concludes by introducing the Oracle Direct Network File System (NFS) implementation that offers you considerable benefits over using the kernel NFS layer.

Let's start by learning how to implement Oracle SecureFiles.

CERTIFICATION OBJECTIVE 8.01

Oracle SecureFiles

Contemporary organizations deal with data that includes traditional data stored in relational tables, semi-structured data such as XML and word processing documents, and unstructured data such as media and imaging data. Oracle has used LOBs since the Oracle 8*i* release to take care of semi-structured and unstructured data, but the implementation of LOBs suffered from several drawbacks, as follows:

- The LOBs were created for mostly "write once, read many times" operations and couldn't handle frequent updates.
- LOBs assumed low concurrent usage data.

- You had to control the amount of undo retained by setting the `retention` and `pctversion` parameters, which led to additional management burden.
- LOBs weren't expected to be very large in size.
- It was assumed that the LOB sizes were uniform. The chunk size could be only 32 KB at its maximum.
- LOBs were not planned with the concurrent usage requirements in Oracle RAC in mind.

The reality is that unstructured and semi-structured data today are very different from the way they were just a few years ago. Today's LOBs can be quite large, and they could come in all sizes. High concurrency in a LOB environment is quite common, and the LOBs in the previous release couldn't efficiently deal with highly concurrent RAC environments.

In Oracle Database 11g, Oracle offers a completely new way of handling unstructured data to address the concerns resulting from the way LOBs are currently implemented. The newly reengineered LOB data type is called Oracle SecureFiles. You can refer to the older LOB implementation as *BasicFiles*. Oracle SecureFiles offer intelligent compression and transparent encryption capabilities and improve performance while being easy to manage and implement.

Oracle SecureFiles use variable chunk sizes, which can be as large as 64 MB. By storing these chunks next to one another, Oracle also minimizes fragmentation. SecureFiles relieve the user from version control tasks by determining whether to generate full redo records or to generate them only for the changed data. Read and write performance is also higher with SecureFiles because they offer a new client/server network layer that allows fast data transfer. SecureFiles also maintain internal memory and space usage statistics that enable the database to maintain the SecureFiles with minimal specification of parameters by you.

Enabling SecureFiles

You can continue to create the older LOBs, which are now also referred to as BasicFiles. You must set the *compatible* initialization parameter to at least 11.0.0.0 in order to use SecureFiles. This means that when you set the compatible parameter to 11.0.0.0, you can create both BasicFiles and SecureFiles in the same database if you want. By default, the database allows the creation of SecureFiles. You can control the ability of the database to create SecureFiles by setting the `db_securefile` initialization parameter. The parameter can take the following values:

- `always` Creates all LOBs as SecureFile LOBs. However, if you use a tablespace that is not enabled for ASSM (automatic segment space management), the database can create only the traditional BasicFile LOBs.

- **force** Creates all LOBs as SecureFile LOBs, regardless of whether the tablespace in which the LOB is created is an ASSM-enabled tablespace or not.
- **permitted** This is the default value for the parameter, under which the database allows the creation of SecureFiles.
- **never** The database won't allow the creation of new SecureFile LOBs.
- **ignore** The database won't allow the creation of new SecureFile LOBs and also ignores errors caused by creating a BasicFile with SecureFile options.

on the **Job**

If you use any SecureFile options such as encryption, compression, and deduplication for a BasicFile, you'll get an error.

As you can see, only the `never` option will disallow the creation of SecureFile LOBs. If you don't specify a certain storage option when creating SecureFiles, the database applies the BasicFile defaults.

You can also use the Enterprise Manager to modify the SecureFile storage options. Simply access the Initialization Parameters link from the Server tab on the Database Control Home page to change the settings of the `db_securefile` initialization parameter. You can use the `alter system` and `alter session` statements to modify a SecureFile storage setting. The following example shows you how to issue an `alter system` statement to prevent the creation of SecureFile LOBs:

```
SQL> alter system set db_securefile = 'never' scope=spfile;
```

Once you execute the `alter system` statement shown here, the database will disallow any attempts to create SecureFiles.

Capabilities of SecureFiles

By implementing Oracle SecureFiles instead of the traditional BasicFiles, you can take advantage of three new advanced capabilities: compression, deduplication, and encryption. I explain each of these new capabilities here.

- **Compression** You can choose to compress SecureFiles. The database will uncompress only those blocks that are necessary for read and write operations.
- **Deduplication** This feature automatically detects duplicate data and saves only one copy of any duplicated data, thus saving disk storage space and lowering I/O. You can specify deduplication at the table or the partition level.

on the !job

You need to choose the Advanced Compression option if you want to use the deduplication feature. Similarly, you must use the Advanced Security Option if you want to employ encryption for SecureFiles.

■ **Encryption** SecureFiles offer transparent encryption, which the database can use for random reads and writes, thus enhancing database security. The database uses Transparent Data Encryption to encrypt the SecureFile LOBs on a per-column basis and uses an identical encryption algorithm for all partitions within a LOB column. You can specify the standard 3DES168, AES128, AES192, and the AES256 encryption algorithms for the encryption of SecureFiles. By default, the database uses the AES128 encryption algorithm.

You can set up the three advanced features—deduplication, encryption, and compression—either independently or together. If you adopt all three features, Oracle will first perform deduplication of the data and then compress it before encrypting the data.

exam ⚙atch *Show how you can specify the compression, deduplication, and encryption features when creating a table with a SecureFile LOB.*

Storage Options for SecureFiles

Specifying the old storage clauses `chunk`, `pctversion`, `freepools`, `freelists` and `freelistgroups` isn't necessary when you use SecureFiles. If you do specify any of these clauses, the database will parse but not interpret these clauses. Instead of these clauses, you now have the following new storage-related clauses.

■ `maxsize` Specifies the maximum LOB segment size.
■ `retention` Specifies the version control policy by telling the database which versions it must retain. Here are the options you can specify for the `retention` parameter:

  ■ `max` Specifies that the database start reclaiming the old version once a segment reaches its `maxsize` value.
  ■ `min` Specifies that the database retain old versions for at least the minimum time specified (in seconds).
  ■ `auto` Lets the database automatically determine the retention time. This is the default setting.
  ■ `none` Specifies that the database use old versions as much as possible.

You specify the storage attributes when you create a SecureFile object. However, you can issue the `alter table` statement to modify the storage settings, in which case the database will apply the new settings only to the space created after the database executes the `alter table` statement.

Creating SecureFiles

When you create a table with a LOB column or you add a LOB column to a table, you can specify whether the database must create the LOB as a traditional BasicFile or the new SecureFile. You can create a SecureFile by specifying the storage clause `store as securefile` in a `create table` statement to tell the database the storage type of the new LOB. You create a BasicFile (traditional LOB) by specifying the clause `store as lob`. If you don't specify any storage type clause, by default, the database will create a traditional LOB, now called a BasicFile.

The following example shows you how to create a SecureFile by specifying the `store as securefile` clause:

```
SQL> create table secure1    id number, doc clob)
     LOB(doc) store as securefile;
```

The database will store all documents in the SECURE1 table as SecureFiles. You can create SecureFiles with the deduplication option, as shown here, to specify that the database not store any duplicates for the LOBs.

```
SQL> create table secure2
     id number, doc clob)
     LOB(doc) store as securefile
     (deduplicate lob cache nologging);
```

The `deduplicate` clause, of course, specifies that the database not keep LOB duplicates. The `cache` clause specifies that the database cache the LOB upon reading it by placing the LOB pages in the buffer cache for speedier access. You can also specify the `nocache` option, the default for LOB caching, to specify that the database not store the LOB values in the buffer cache. The third caching option, `cache reads`, specifies that the database can store LOB values in the buffer cache only during read operations but not for write operations. The `nologging` clause specifies that the database not generate any redo during update operations.

In order to specify encryption of the LOBs, you can use either of the following two specifications, one specifying the encryption when declaring the CLOB and the other specifying encryption by using the `encrypt` storage clause.

```
SQL> create table secure2
     id number, doc clob)
     LOB(doc) store as securefile (ENCRYPT);

SQL> create table secure3
     id number, doc clob encrypt using 'AES256')
     LOB(doc) store as securefile;
```

The database encrypts the SECURE3 table with the encryption algorithm I specify, AES256. Because I didn't specify an encryption algorithm in the first case, the database uses the default AES128 encryption algorithm for the table SECURE2.

The following example shows you how to specify compression when creating a LOB as a SecureFile:

```
SQL> create table secure4
     id number, doc clob)
     LOB(doc) store as securefile
     (compress high keep duplicates);
```

The `compress high` clause specifies compression at the `high` level (you can also specify the `medium` level, which is the default option). In addition, the `keep duplicates` clause specifies that the database may store duplicates for the LOB column.

You can issue the `alter table` statement to alter Securefile storage options. The following examples show how to change various SecureFile storage options:

- Enable duplication by specifying the `keep duplicates` option:

  ```
  SQL> alter table test modify LOB(one)  ( keep duplicates);
  ```

- Disable duplication by specifying the `deduplicate lob` option:

  ```
  SQL> alter table test modify LOB(one)  ( deduplicate lob);
  ```

- Disable compression by specifying the `nocompress` option:

  ```
  SQL> alter table test modify LOB(one)  ( nocompress);
  ```

■ Enable a high level of compression by specifying the `compress high` clause:

```
SQL> alter table test modify LOB(one) ( compress high);
```

■ Specify encryption using the `3DES168` encryption algorithm:

```
SQL> alter table test modify
        (one clob encrypt using '3des168');
```

■ Specify encryption and build the encryption key using a password:

```
SQL> alter table test modify LOB
        (one clob encrypt identified by abcdef);
```

You can update the encryption algorithm or encryption key by using the `alter table rekey` syntax.

Managing and Monitoring SecureFiles

You can use the familiar DBA_SPACE and DBA_LOB packages to manage the new SecureFiles implementation of LOBs. You can use the LOB locator API to configure LOB column settings such as encryption and deduplication on a per-LOB level. However, you can't use the `LONG` API to configure the SecureFile LOB settings. Use the following new DBMS_LOB function and procedure to manage the setting of LOB functions:

■ The GETOPTIONS function gets you the LOB settings.

■ The SETOPTIONS procedure helps set the LOB features. You can use this procedure to override default LOB settings and set the attributes on a per-LOB basis.

You can use the SPACE_USAGE procedure of the DBMS_SPACE package to determine the amount of disk space used by all the LOBs in the LOB segment. You can use this procedure only for tablespaces with the ASSM (automated segment space management) feature.

The DBA_SEGMENTS, DBA_LOBS, DBA_LOB_PARTITIONS, and the DBA_PART_LOBS views have been enhanced to show information about SecureFiles usage. Here's a typical query using the DBA_SEGMENTS view.

```
SQL> select segment_name, segment_type, segment_subtype
     from dba_segments
     where tablespace_name = 'TEST_SECFILS'
     and segment_type = 'LOBSEGMENT';
```

```
SEGMENT_NAME                        SEGMENT_TYPE        SEGEMENT_SU
-------------------------           ----------------    ------------
SYS_LOB0000063424C00003$$           LOBSEGMENT          SECUREFILE
SQL>
```

The SEGMENT_SUBTYPE column shows if a LOB is implemented as a SecureFile.

Migrating to SecureFiles

You can use two basic methods to migrate to SecureFiles: *partition exchange* and *online redefinition*. Let's see how you migrate to SecureFiles using both of these approaches.

When you use partition exchange to migrate to SecureFiles, you have to make sure that a number of factors are taken care of such as ensuring you have enough space to accommodate the largest of the partitions of the table. The migration job takes a long time and therefore, you must have a long maintenance window to perform the migration. You must also maintain the indexes during the partition exchange. In addition, the table or partition must be offline in order for you to perform the partition exchange.

Oracle recommends that you use the online redefinition method to migrate to SecureFiles. Online redefinition means you don't take the table offline. You can perform the migration in parallel. You must rebuild global indexes and must have additional storage equal to the entire table. You can, however, cut back on the additional space requirements by performing the online redefinition on a partition basis.

Let me use a simple example to demonstrate how to perform online redefinition to migrate to SecureFiles from a traditional BasicFiles LOB implementation:

1. Create a table using BasicFiles:

   ```
   SQL> create table tab1 (id number not null, c clob)
        lob(c) store as lob);
   ```

   The `store as lob` clause creates a BasicFile LOB.

2. Insert some test data into the BasicFile-based table.

3. Create a new, interim table using SecureFiles, but with the same columns as the first table:

   ```
   SQL> create table tab2 (id number not null, c clob)
        lob(c) store as securefile);
   ```

   The `store as securefile` clause creates a SecureFile LOB.

4. Execute the DBMS_REDFINITION procedure to convert the BasicFile-based table into a SecureFile-based table:

```
begin
dbms_redefinition.start_redef_table
('scott','tab1','tab2','id id c c');
dbms_refinition.copy_table_dependents
('scott','tab1','tab2'
,1,true,true,true,true,false,error_count);
dbms_redefinition.finish_redef_table
('scott','tab1','tab2');
end;
```

You can perform the redefinition in parallel to make it faster.

CERTIFICATION OBJECTIVE 8.02

Online Enhancements

Oracle Database 11g provides several significant enhancements in the performing of online operations, which I summarize in the following sections.

Locking Enhancements

Oracle Database 11g provides more efficient capabilities relating to the implementation of object locking. These new capabilities include allowing a DDL lock to wait for a DML lock instead of failing if it can't get one right away. In addition, the database makes less use of exclusive locks.

Allowing DDL Locks to Wait for DML Locks

One of the problems with DDL statements is that if they can't immediately obtain a DML lock on the tables, they fail. In Oracle Database 11g, you can specify a time interval for which the DDL statement will wait for a DML lock, instead of the DDL failing automatically when it can't get an immediate DDL lock.

Use the new `ddl_lock_timeout` parameter to specify the length of time a DDL statement can wait for a DML statement. The default value of `zero` for this parameter produces the default Oracle behavior. Execute the `alter session` statement, shown here, to set the duration that the DDL statement can wait for a DML lock:

```
SQL> alter session set ddl_lock_timeout = 30;
Session altered.
SQL>
```

The `alter session` statement here will enable a DDL statement to wait for 30 seconds for a necessary DML lock, after which the DDL statement fails. You can set a value as high as 1,000,000 seconds (11.5 days) for the `ddl_lock_timeout` parameter.

Explicit Table Locking

In addition to the new feature that lets you control the time for which a DDL statement waits to obtain a DML lock, Oracle Database 11g also has enhanced the `lock table` statement so you can specify the time a statement will wait for a DML lock on that table. Any DDL statement you issue on a table, such as a statement that adds a column, needs to acquire an exclusive DML lock on the table. Currently, an attempt to add a column to a table will fail if the database can't immediately acquire an exclusive lock on the table.

If your users frequently update a table to which you are planning to add a column, the new `lock table` syntax provides a way to control the time for which your DDL statements will wait to acquire the necessary exclusive DML lock on the table. Here's the syntax of the enhanced `lock table` command:

```
lock table...in lockmode mode [nowait | wait  integer]
```

The `mode` parameter can take two values—`wait` and `nowait`. Here's how the two options affect the waiting behavior for a DML lock:

- The `nowait` option immediately returns control to you if the table is already locked by others.
- The `wait` option lets the statement wait for execution for the period you specify. You can set any value for the `nowait` parameter.
- If you omit the `mode` parameter altogether, the database locks the table once it becomes available and returns control to you. Thus, the default behavior now is for a DDL statement to wait until it gets an exclusive DML lock, however long the wait may be.

Reduced Need for Exclusive Locks

When you perform an operation such as online index creation or rebuild, there is a requirement for acquiring an exclusive DML lock. In a database that has heavy concurrent usage, this requirement of applying a DML exclusive lock to a table leads to a severe drop in performance, as user sessions are kept waiting for the online operation to complete. Oracle Database 11g removes the requirement for an exclusive lock on tables during the following operations:

- ■ `create index online`
- ■ `create materialized view log`
- ■ `alter table enable constraint novalidate`

Minimal Invalidation of Dependent Objects

In the previous release, Oracle automatically invalidated all dependent views and PL/SQL packages during an online redefinition, even if those objects weren't logically affected. For example, if you dropped a table column during redefinition, all procedures and views that referenced the table were automatically invalidated. Unlike in the previous releases, Oracle Database 11g invalidates only the logically affected objects such as views and synonyms during an online redefinition. It doesn't automatically invalidate all dependent views and PL/SQL packages as before. In the case of a dropped column, Oracle will invalidate a procedure or view only if the object used the dropped column. This new concept of minimal validation of dependent objects is called *fine-grained dependency management*, under which the database tracks object dependencies at the level of the element within a unit.

on the job

Triggers continue to be automatically invalidated as before during an online redefinition.

Objects such as views, synonyms, and other similar table-dependent objects aren't logically affected by a table redefinition and thus aren't invalidated. Thus, for example, if an object referenced during an online redefinition isn't modified during the redefinition, the object remains valid. All triggers that are defined on a redefined table will be invalidated, but the database automatically revalidates them when the next DML statement execution takes place.

The use of fine-grained dependencies leads to more precise dependency metadata. In Oracle Database 10g, the object dependency metadata was looked at from the object level. For example, let's say a view depends on a specific table. Even though the addition of a new column to the table has no bearing on the view, the database still invalidates the view because it treats the entire object as the unit of reference. In Oracle Database 11g, the fact that a new column has been added to a table doesn't invalidate a view that uses a table if the view doesn't use the newly added column.

Similar fine-grained dependency management applies to PL/SQL objects such as procedures and functions. If you add a new procedure or function to a package, that will invalidate other procedures and functions in that package only if those objects have a dependency on the altered or new procedure or function.

The fine-grained dependency management is easy to use, as it doesn't need any configuration on your part. Your application availability will be higher as a result, especially during an application upgrade.

Creating a Parameter File from Memory

You can now create a text initialization parameter file (PFILE) or a server parameter file (SPFILE) from the system-wide parameters currently in use by the instance. Here's how you generate the initialization parameter file from the settings in memory:

```
SQL> create pfile from memory;
File created.
SQL>
```

You can also create an SPFILE from the parameter settings in memory, as follows:

```
SQL> create spfile from memory;
File created.
SQL>
```

You can use this ability to create a text parameter file or an SPFILE from memory when you can't access your parameter file because it's corrupted or lost. The following example demonstrates this:

```
SQL> create pfile from spfile;
create pfile from spfile
*
ERROR at line 1:
ORA-01565: error in identifying file
'/u01/app/oracle/product/11.1/db_1/dbs/spfileauxdb.ora'
ORA-27037: unable to obtain file status
Linux Error: 2: No such file or directory
Additional information: 3
SQL>
```

The example shows that you can't create a new parameter file from the SPFILE because the database can't find the SPFILE. When you lose an SPFILE, it's easy to recover from it because of the new ability to re-create the SPFILE from memory. If the instance can't find the parameter file and you therefore can't create the new parameter file, you can execute the `create pfile from memory` statement instead to re-create an init.ora file from memory. The new file that you create from memory will have values for all the 150 or so initialization parameters, even though you haven't set the values for most of them in your parameter file when starting the database. Oracle uses the default value for all the parameters that you ignored.

Hot Patching

Traditional patching of database server code always involves downtime for the database. While the downtime doesn't pose any problems on a test database, it's not so easy when you are working with production databases. Hot patching (or online patching) enables you to apply bug fixes or diagnostic patches on a live database, without incurring any downtime. Live application of patches makes a lot of sense, especially when you are dealing with a small bug fix or a diagnostic patch. The *opatch* command-line utility lets you perform online patching. Using opatch, you can install, enable, and disable patches. You can continue to use the opatch utility as in the previous release to perform normal offline code patching. In Oracle Database 11g, you can use opatch to perform online patching as well.

Benefits of Hot Patching

Hot patching with the opatch utility offers the following benefits:

- No need to restart the database, thus preventing any downtime for patching.
- Quick installation and de-installation of patches. Unlike conventional patches, hot patches take seconds, not minutes to apply.
- Automatic listing in patch inventory.
- Ability to work in an Oracle RAC environment, which lets you perform a rolling patch application. You don't have to worry about whether the hot patch can be applied as a rolling upgrade or as an upgrade.
- Hot patches persist across instance shutdowns.

exam

ⓦatch   *Review the benefits and drawbacks of using hot patching. Do you need more or less memory for performing an online patch compared to an offline patch?*

Installing a Hot Patch

As mentioned earlier, you use the opatch utility to perform an online patching. Oracle automatically detects any conflicts between two hot patches. You can issue the following command to determine if a patch is a hot patch:

```
$ opatch query -is_online_patch <patch location>
```

You can also use this variant of the previous command for the same purpose:

```
$ opatch query -is_online_patch <patch location> -all
```

Once you confirm that a patch is indeed an online patch, you can use the opatch utility to perform the patching.

Considerations

Currently, hot patching is available only on some platforms such as Linux x86, Linux x86-64, and Solaris SPARC64. The opatch utility does consume extra memory depending on the size of the patch and the number of currently running concurrent Oracle processes. You'll need a minimum of one OS page of memory for each running Oracle process when you apply a patch. An OS page usually is 4 KB on a Linux x86 server and 8 KB on a Solaris SPARC64 system. If there are 500 Oracle concurrent processes running on a Solaris SPARC64 server, for example, you can expect to need only about 4 MB of memory for applying a small patch online.

CERTIFICATION OBJECTIVE 8.03

Miscellaneous New Features

In the last section, I summarize miscellaneous Oracle Database 11g new features, such as invisible indexes and PL/SQL native compilation.

Invisible Indexes

In Oracle Database 11g, you can create *invisible indexes*. An invisible index is similar to regular indexes in most respects. However, you can hide the index from the optimizer, thus making it invisible to the optimizer. You can also change the status of an index from visible to invisible any time you want, and you can set an initialization parameter at the database level to make all invisible indexes visible to the optimizer, thus treating the invisible indexes as any other regular indexes. You can use the invisible indexes feature to use a temporary index for specific operations without forcing all operations to use that index. You can also use invisible indexes to test the effects of removing an index before you get rid of an index for good.

You can create an invisible index by specifying the `invisible` clause, as shown here:

```
SQL> create index invib_idx1 on test_tab(name) invisible;
```

You can also modify a regular index into an invisible index by using the `alter index` statement, as shown here:

```
SQL> alter index indx1 invisible;
```

The database maintains an invisible index during DML statements.

The previous statement will make the index INDX1 invisible to the optimizer. Therefore, the optimizer disregards the index when creating an execution plan that involves the table column indexed by INDX1. Whether you create a new index as invisible or you modify a regular index to an invisible index with the `alter index` statement, you can make an index visible again by issuing the following statement:

```
SQL> alter index invisib_idx1 visible;
```

Once you issue the previous statement, the index becomes a regular index visible to the optimizer.

The new initialization parameter `optimizer_use_invisible_indexes` helps you enable or disable invisible indexes. You can make the cost optimizer take into account all invisible indexes in the database by setting the `optimizer_use_invisible_indexes` parameter to `true`. You can do this at the session or at the system level, as shown here:

```
SQL> alter system set optimizer_use_invisible_indexes = true
        scope=spfile;
```

When you set the `optimizer_use_invisible_indexes` parameter to `true`, the database treats all invisible indexes as visible (normal) indexes. The default value of the `optimizer_use_invisible_indexes` initialization parameter is `false`, which means that the optimizer doesn't consider any invisible indexes, although the database will maintain the invisible indexes through all DML operations, just as if they were normal indexes.

You can check whether an index is visible or not by issuing a query such as the one shown in this example:

```
SQL> select index_name, visibility from dba_indexes
        where index_name like '%NAME_IDX%';

INDEX_NAME          VISIBILITY
------------        -----------
NAME_IDX2           INVISIBLE
NAME_IDX1           INVISIBLE
SQL>
```

The VISIBILITY column in the DBA_INDEXES view shows whether an index is visible. In the preceding example, both indexes retrieved by the query are invisible to the optimizer.

Shrinking Temporary Tablespaces

When a large job that uses a temporary tablespace finishes executing, the database doesn't immediately release the space used by the job in the temporary tablespace, even after the job completes. You can get the free space back faster sometimes by dropping the temporary tablespace and creating a smaller one instead, but then it may not be easy to do this on a live database because users may require the temporary tablespace for various operations. Oracle Database 11g lets you shrink a temporary tablespace online, thus enabling you to control the space allocated to temporary operations in the database. You can shrink both temporary tablespaces and individual tempfiles.

Use the shrink space clause within an alter tablespace command to shrink a temporary tablespace, as shown here:

```
SQL> alter tablespace temp shrink space;
```

To shrink a tempfile, use the shrink tempfile clause, as shown here:

```
SQL> alter tablespace temp shrink
     tempfile '/u01/app/oracle/oradata/or11/temp01.dbf';
```

The shrink space command in the first example shrinks all tempfiles to a database-determined minimum size, 1 MB. The database takes into account the temporary tablespace storage requirements when determining the minimum size of the tempfiles. You can override this default behavior by specifying a minimum size for the temporary tablespace after a shrink operation, as shown here:

```
SQL> alter tablespace temp shrink space
     keep 100m;
```

The keep clause lets you specify the minimum value for the temporary tablespace named TEMP. The following examples illustrate how Oracle approaches a temporary tablespace shrinking operation. In this example, the temporary tablespace TEMP has two tempfiles, each sized at 1 GB, thus making the total size of the temporary tablespace 2 GB. You issue the following alter tablespace statement to shrink the temporary tablespace to 1 GB.

```
SQL> alter tablespace temp shrink space keep 1000m;
Tablespace altered.
SQL>
```

Because the combined size of the two tempfiles in the TEMP tablespace is 2 GB, you'd assume that Oracle would shrink both tempfiles to about 500 MB each, to get a total of 1 GB, when you issue the alter tablespace statement shown here. However, this isn't what happens, as you can see by issuing the following query:

```
SQL> select file#, name, bytes/1024/1024 MB from v$tempfile;

FILE#   NAME                                            MB
------  -------------------------------------------     --------
1       /u01/app/oracle/temp/temp01.dbf                 999.9375
2       /u01/app/oracle/temp/temp02.dbf
SQL>
```

Oracle does shrink the TEMP tablespace from 2 GB to 1 GB, but not by shrinking both tempfiles by an equal amount. It shrinks the file temp01.dbf by less than 1 MB and the file temp02.dbf by over 999 MB. You can specify a minimum space that the database must retain in a specific tempfile, by specifying the keep clause in the alter tablespace ... shrink statement, as follows:

```
SQL> alter tablespace temp shrink space
     tempfile '/u01/app/oracle/temp02.dbf'
     keep 500m;
Tablespace altered.
SQL>
```

This statement will shrink just the datafile temp02 and leave the other tempfiles in the tablespace alone.

You can query the new DBA_TEMP_FREE_SPACE view to get information about temporary tablespace usage, as shown in this example:

```
SQL> select * from dba_temp_free_space;

TABLESPACE_NAME   TABLESPACE_SIZE   ALLOCATED_SPACE   FREE_SPACE
---------------   ---------------   ---------------   ----------
TEMP              41943040          41943040          40894464
SQL>
```

The DBA_TEMP_FREE_SPACE view shows the total free space available, including the space currently allocated to a temporary tablespace and available for reuse as well as space that's currently unallocated.

Tablespace Option for Creating Temporary Tables

When you created a global temporary table in Oracle Database 10g, you didn't have to specify a tablespace. In Oracle Database 11g, you can specify a tablespace clause when creating a temporary table. If you omit the tablespace clause, the database creates the global temporary table in the default temporary tablespace for the database. The database also stores the indexes you create on the global temporary table in the same tablespace as the temporary table.

The ability to specify the tablespace when creating a global temporary table means that you can now assign a proper extent size for a temporary table to deal with its sort usage. Different tables might use the temporary space differently, and the capability to assign different extent sizes to them leads to better performance.

PL/SQL and Java Automatic Native Compilation

Up until the Oracle Database 11g release, the database always transformed PL/SQL code to C code first before executing it. This meant you needed a third-party C compiler to execute the C code. In Oracle Database 11g, the database skips the C compiler by directly translating PL/SQL source code to DLL for the server. The feature is called PL/SQL native compilation. Oracle also performs the linking and delinking itself and bypasses the file system directories for doing that. Oracle claims that its test show performance improvements as large as two-fold, with the native compilation of PL/SQL.

The really good news for DBAs is that it is extremely easy to take advantage of the native PL/SQL compilation capability. You simply set the appropriate value for the new initialization parameter `plsql_code_type` to turn automatic native PL/SQL compilation on, as the next section explains.

Using Real Native Compilation

Use the initialization parameter `plsql_code_type` to specify the compilation mode for PL/SQL library units. The parameter can take two values, `interpreted` and `compiled`. Setting the value of this parameter to `compiled` produces the default behavior where the database compiles PL/SQL code first to a PL/SQL bytecode format using the C compiler. The PL/SQL interpreter engine then executes the bytecode. By setting the parameter to the value `native`, you let the database compile the PL/SQL code to machine code and execute it natively without the need for an interpreter. The database stores the DLLs it generates from the PL/SQL source code in the database catalog, from where the Oracle executable loads the code directly without first using a file system to stage them.

By default, the `plsql_code_type` parameter is set to the value `interpreted`, and you can turn native PL/SQL compilation on in the database by setting the `plsql_code_type` parameter to `native`, as shown here:

```
plsql_code_type=native
```

You can check that the database is using the correct mode of PL/SQL compilation by issuing the following statement:

```
SQL> select name, value from v$parameter where
     name like '%plsql%;

NAME                         VALUE
--------------------         ------------
plsql_code_type              INTERPRETED
plsql_optimize_level         2
...
9 rows selected.
SQL>
```

You can also use the `alter system` or `alter session` statements to change the value for the `plsql_code_type` parameter dynamically, without restarting the database. Any PL/SQL units that are already compiled won't be affected by a change in the compilation mode. Also, even after you change the compilation mode, say from compiled to native, PL/SQL units that the database has already compiled will be recompiled in the original compilation mode.

EXERCISE 8-1

Setting Up a PL/SQL Program Unit for Native Compilation

In order to set up a single PL/SQL program unit for native compilation, you must change the value of the `plsql_code_type` parameter to `native` from its default value of `interpreted`, by making the change and restarting the database or by using the `alter system/session` statement to change the value of the parameter.

You can also issue the `alter <PLSQL unit type>` statement to enable native compilation for a single PL/SQL program unit. Let's use a simple example that illustrates how to do this:

1. First, create a simple procedure, called TEST_NATIVE.

```
SQL> create or replace procedure test_native as
  2    begin
  3    dbms_output.put_line('Test Procedure.');
  4*   end test_native;
SQL> /
Procedure created.
SQL>
```

2. Check the current PL/SQL compilation mode by issuing the following statement:

```
SQL> select plsql_code_type
  2  from all_plsql_object_settings
  3  where name='TEST_NATIVE';

PLSQL_CODE_TYPE
----------------
INTERPRETED
SQL>
```

The query shows that, currently, the procedure TEST_NATIVE is set for interpreted compiling and not native compilation.

3. Issue the following `alter procedure` statement to change the compilation mode to `native` for just the TEST_NATIVE procedure.

```
SQL> alter procedure test_native compile plsql_code_type=native;
Procedure altered.
SQL>
```

4. Confirm that the procedure TEST_NATIVE will now use native compilation, by issuing the following query on the DBA_PLSQL_OBJECT_SETTINGS view:

```
SQL> select plsql_code_type
  2  from all_plsql_object_settings
  3* where name='TEST_NATIVE';

PLSQL_CODE_TYPE
----------------
NATIVE
SQL>
```

The value of `native` for the PLSQL_CODE_TYPE column means that from here on, the database will use native compilation for the TEST_NATIVE procedure.

Recompiling a Database for PL/SQL Native Compilation

You can use the dbmsupgnv.sql script provided with Oracle Database 11g to recompile all the PL/SQL modules in the database to compile natively. Follow these steps to recompile all the PL/SQL modules:

1. Shut down the database using the `shutdown normal` or `shutdown immediate` commands.

   ```
   SQL> shutdown immediate;
   ```

   In the initialization parameter file, set the `plsql_code_type` parameter to `native` so it will allow native compilation.

   ```
   plsql_code_type=native
   ```

2. You must also check to ensure that the value of the `plsql_optimize_level` parameter is at least 2. The default value for this parameter is 2.

   ```
   plsql_optimize_level=3
   ```

   Because the value of the `plsql_optimize_level` parameter is more than 2, you don't have to change the setting of this parameter.

3. Start the database with the `startup upgrade` command, which you specify when upgrading to a new release of the Oracle database.

   ```
   SQL> connect sys/sammyy1 as sysdba
   Connected to an idle instance.
   SQL> startup upgrade
   ORACLE instance started.
   ...
   Database opened.
   ```

4. After the database is opened in the upgrade mode, execute the script dbmsupgnv.sql, located in the $ORACLE_HOME/rdbms/admin directory.

   ```
   SQL> @$ORACLE_HOME/rdbms/admin/dbsupgnv.sql
   OC>###########################################################
   DOC>###########################################################
   DOC>   dbmsupgnv.sql completed successfully.
   DOC> All PL/SQL procedures, functions, type bodies, triggers,
   DOC> and type bodies objects in the database have been
   DOC> invalidated and their settings set to native.
   DOC>
   DOC>   Shut down and restart the database in normal mode and
   DOC>   run utlrp.sql to recompile invalid objects.
   SQL>
   ```

When the dbmsupgnv.sql script completes executing, all PL/SQL procedures in the database are natively compiled.

5. Once the script finishes running, shut down the database and start it back up again. Run the utlrp.sql script located in the $ORACLE_HOME/rdbms/admin directory to recompile the invalidated PL/SQL program units.

```
SQL> shutdown immediate;
SQL> startup
ORACLE instance started.
...
Database opened.
SQL> @$ORACLE_HOME/rdbms/admin/utlrp.sql
...
SQL> Rem END utlrp.sql
SQL>
```

As a result of upgrading the database and compiling all PL/SQL units in the native mode, you don't need to individually enable PL/SQL procedures for native compilation. You can always change the compilation mode back to the default value of `interpreted` by reversing the recompilation process shown here. You follow a procedure similar to the one shown here to compile all PL/SQL program units in the interpreted mode by running the script dbmsupgin.sql, also located in the $ORACLE_HOME/rdbms/admin directory.

e x a m

Ⓦ a t c h *Be familiar with the sequence of steps to recompile an entire database for PL/SQL native compilation.*

Java Native Compilation

Oracle Database 11g uses the new initialization parameter `java_jit_enabled` to set the Java compilation mode. By default, the value of the `java_jit_enabled` initialization parameter is `true`, meaning Java native compilation is enabled in the database. As in the case of the PL/SQL native compilation, this feature allows the database to compile Java in the database natively without using a C compiler.

on the
Ⓙ o b *Oracle claims that native compilation offers a 100 percent faster performance for both pure PL/SQL and Java code.*

Oracle's Java native compilation is similar to that of the Java Development Kit and runs as an independent session in the server process that is transparent to the user. There's only one compiler session per Oracle instance and the database stores the Java code for future recompilations. Java native compilation offers you the high performance of pure Java execution and is very easy to implement because you can enable it for the entire database, not merely when you actually execute the Java code in the database. The absence of a C compiler means you save on licensing and other costs involved in maintaining the compiler.

OLTP Table Compression

In earlier releases, you could compress data only during bulk load operations such as during a direct load or a `create table as select` operation. You couldn't, however, compress data during a DML operation such as an insert operation. Oracle Database 11g extends its table compression capability to OLTP workloads, meaning you can now compress data during a data insertion job, for example. The compression technology Oracle uses works independent of the application, meaning you can use compression for packaged applications such as SAP and PeopleSoft.

OLTP compression saves you storage by reducing space consumption by 50 to 75 percent. A major concern when compressing data is the impact on performance, especially during read operations, when the database usually has to uncompress the data before reading it. Oracle's new OLTP compression technology doesn't degrade write performance, while improving the read performance. Write performance doesn't degrade because of Oracle's batched compression strategy. The read performance is better because Oracle reads compressed data directly without first uncompressing the data.

When new data comes in, the database inserts that data into a data block, but in an uncompressed format. Once the block reaches its PCTFREE level, Oracle compresses the data in the block. This compression strategy is efficient and also uses space efficiently by eliminating the holes made by the deleted data in the data blocks.

Setting Up Table Compression You can use either the traditional `compress` clause or the new `compress for direct_load operations` clause in a `create table` statement to let the database compress data during a direct load insert. The following examples show how to specify the `compress` and the `compress for direct_load operations` clauses in a `create table` statement:

```
SQL> create table sales_history ( ... )
     compress;
SQL> create table sales_history
     ( ... ) compress for direct_load operations;
```

The previous two `create table` statements show how to set up traditional compression for a data warehouse table. To enable the new compression for DML operations, you must specify the `compress for all operations` clause, as shown here:

```
SQL> create table sales_history ( ... )
     compress for all operations;
```

The `compress for all operations` clause compresses data during all DML operations.

Monitoring Table Compression   Use the columns COMPRESSION and COMPRESS_FOR in the DBA_TABLES view to find out information about whether compression is enabled for a table and, if so, the type of compression. Here's the query:

```
SQL> select table_name, compression, compress_for
     from dba_tables;

   TABLE_NAME      COMPRESS        COMPRESS_FOR
   -----------     --------        ------------------
   T1              DISABLED
   T2              ENABLED         DIRECT LOAD ONLY
   T3              ENABLED         FOR ALL OPERATIONS
```

The previous query shows that compression is enabled for tables T2 and T3. The COMPRESSED_FOR column shows that table T3 is enabled for compression for all operations including DML operations, whereas table T2 is enabled only for compression for direct load operations.

Direct NFS Client

NAS storage devices use the Network File System (NFS) to access data. In Oracle Database 10g, NAS devices were accessed using operating system–specific kernel NFS drivers. This required that you tune many parameters, and the configuration varied across the platforms. The NFS clients tended to be inconsistent across the different operating system platforms. Manageability wasn't easy because you had to contend with over 20 configuration parameters.

In Oracle Database 11g, the Oracle NFS implements the NFS Version 3 protocol in the Oracle RDBMS kernel. Implementing the Oracle Direct NFS offers the following benefits:

■ Avoids the bottlenecks and resource constraints by avoiding the kernel NFS layer.

- Provides a common NFS interface for Oracle for use on all operating system platforms and supported NFS servers.
- Provides load balancing across multiple connections to the NFS servers, thus improving performance.
- Performance is predictable because the Oracle NFS implementation enables you to completely control the input/output path to the Network File Servers.
- Easier management including simpler configuration and superior diagnosability.

Configuring Direct NFS

You don't have to configure much to implement Oracle Direct NFS Client. Specify the mount point you want Direct NFS to mount in the /etc/mtab file. Direct NFS will first attempt to mount the entries it finds in the /etc/mtab file, by default. You can also use the oranfstab file to specify any Oracle-specific options to Direct NFS such as additional paths to a mount point, but this is an optional step. You can use the oranfstab file to provide mount points for all Oracle databases, by placing the file in the /etc directory. In order to provide just the entries for a specific database, you must place the oranfstab file in the $ORACLE_HOME/dbs directory.

e x a m

ⓦ a t c h   *Review the correct lookup order for the oranfstab file.*

Direct NFS searches for the mount point entries in the following order:

- $ORCLE_HOME/dbs/oranfstab
- /etc/orafnstab
- /etc/mtab

The database uses the first match as the mount point. Oracle always requires that even when you use Direct NFS, the kernel NFS system must perform the mounting. For this reason, Oracle will always crosscheck the information about mount points in the oranfstab file with the operating system NFS mount points. If there's a mismatch, Direct NFS can't act as a client to the NFS server and stops serving the NFS server.

Enabling Direct NFS

You must follow these steps to enable Direct NFS:

1. You must mount all NFS mount points with your kernel NFS client. You must make sure you mount any file systems you plan on using through ODM NFS and make the file systems available to Oracle over regular NFS mounts.

2. If you want to specify Oracle-specific options to Direct NFS, you'll need an oranfstab file. This is an optional step. The oranfstab file must have the following attributes so the database can access all NFS servers through Direct NFS:

- `server` Provides the NFS server name.
- `mount` Provides the local mount point for the NFS server.
- `export` Provides the exported path from the NFS server.
- `path` Provides the network path to the NFS server. You can specify up to four network paths with an IP address or by name. Using multiple network paths enables the Direct NFS client to use an alternate path if the current path fails. Multiple paths also enable the client to perform load balancing.

A typical oranfstab file looks similar to the following:

- `server: TestServer1`
- `path: 130.33.34.11`
- `export: /vol/oradata1`
- `mount: /mnt/oradata1`

on the
Job

In order to remove an NFS path that the database is using currently, you must restart the database.

3. You must replace the standard ODM library, libnfsodm10.so, with the ODM NFS library, as shown here:

```
$ cd $ORACLE_HOME/lib
$ cp libodm11.so libodm11.so_stub
$ ln -s libnfsodm11.so libodm11.so
```

You can disable the Direct NFS client by using any of the following three methods.

- Delete the oranfstab file.
- Replace the ODM NFS library with the stub libodm11.so file.
- Modify the oranfstab file by deleting the specific NFS server or the network paths to the NFS server.

If the database can't open the NFS server using Direct NFS, it will use the operating system kernel client instead.

Monitoring Direct NFS

You can query the following views in order to manage Direct NFS:

- **V$DNFS_STATS** Shows performance statistics for Direct NFS.

- **V$DNFS_SERVERS**   Shows servers accessed by Direct NFS.
- **V$DNFS_FILES**   Shows files currently using Direct NFS.
- **V$DNFS_CHANNELS**   Shows the open network paths being used by Direct NFS.

Using LogMiner

The LogMiner tool helps you identify changes in the database and provides a way to roll back logical data corruptions and user errors. The LogMiner tool directly accesses the Oracle redo logs to enable you to use older data to correct logical errors.

In previous releases, you could manage LogMiner through SQL*Plus or through a special GUI interface, which required you to install a standalone Java console. In Oracle Database 11g, Enterprise Manager Database Control provides an interface to the LogMiner. Select Availability | Manage | View and Manage Transactions to access LogMiner. Figure 8-1 shows the LogMiner page in Database Control.

FIGURE 8-1   The LogMiner page

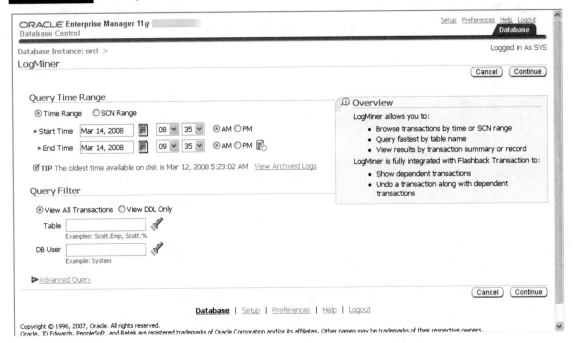

INSIDE THE EXAM

Oracle SecureFiles is a key new feature in the new release. You must understand how to set the `db_securefile` initialization parameter. You must understand what the setting of the values `ignore` or `permitted` for the `db_securefile` parameter implies regarding the ability to create LOBs as SecureFiles. You must also know how to take advantage of the important capabilities of SecureFiles such as deduplication. The exam might question you about the use of the various clauses such as `cache` and `duplicate` when creating SecureFile LOBs. There could be a question on the methods you use to migrate to SecureFiles. Which of the two methods, partition exchange or online redefinition, needs more space? You must know the steps involved in using the online redefinition method to migrate to SecureFiles.

In terms of online enhancements, the key topic is the new minimally dependent recompilation feature. What happens when an online redefinition operation drops a column that refers to only a few procedures and views? Review the new online enhancements that involve the use of the `ddl_lock_timeout` initialization parameter to control the time a DDL statement waits for a DML lock. You must also understand how to use the `lock table...in lockmode...` statement to control the wait time for a DML lock.

The exam will probably test you on how to create a text initialization parameter file or an SPFILE from the current values of the initialization parameters being used by an instance. Expect a question on performing online patching. Review how to use the opatch utility to perform an online code patch. You may also want to review the memory requirements for online patching.

You can probably expect the exam to ask you a question about the new invisible indexes feature. You must know how to set the initialization parameter that controls if an index is visible. In terms of native PL/SQL compilation, you must know how to set it up, including the initialization parameters you must set in order to enable native PL/SQL compilation in the database.

The exam will test your understanding of the new Direct NFS feature. Pay particular attention to the configuration of Direct NFS. You must understand the role of the oranfstab file in the configuration of Direct NFS and where the file is located. In which order does Direct NFS look for the mount points? The exam might test your understanding of the relationship between the kernel NFS system and the Direct NFS system. What happens if there's a mismatch between the kernel NFS mounts and the operating system NFS mount points? You are also expected to know the procedure to enable Direct NFS. For example, how do you replace the standard ODM library with the ODM NFS library?

CERTIFICATION SUMMARY

Oracle Database 11g offers SecureFiles to handle unstructured data. SecureFiles offer better performance than the traditional Oracle LOBs. In addition, SecureFiles offer compression, deduplication and encryption capabilities. SecureFiles are also easier to implement, needing only a minimal specification of parameters to maintain them.

You use the db_securefile initialization parameter to control the ability of the database to create SecureFiles. Old LOB storage clauses such as chunk, pctversion, and freepools are necessary when using SecureFiles. In order to create a table with a LOB as a SecureFile, you must add the clause store as securefile to the create table statement. You can modify the storage options by executing the alter table statement.

There are two basic methods to migrate to SecureFiles: partition exchange and online redefinition. Oracle recommends that you use the online redefinition method to migrate to SecureFiles.

The invisible indexes feature offers you a way to test the use of an index before making it available to the cost optimizer. You can make all invisible indexes visible to the optimizer by setting the initialization parameter optimizer_use_invisible_indexes to true. In Oracle Database 11g, you can shrink temporary tablespaces online. You can shrink both temporary tablespaces and tempfiles. You can also specify a tablespace clause when creating a temporary table, thus enabling you to assign the proper extent size for a temporary table to deal with its sort usage.

PL/SQL native compilation directly translates PL/SQL code to the DLL to the server. Native compilation provides considerable performance improvements over using a third-party C compiler. You set the initialization parameter plsql_code_type to the value native in order to turn on automatic native PL/SQL compilation. Use the dbmsupgrnv.sql script to recompile all the PL/SQL modules in the database for native compilation.

Oracle Database 11g allows DDL locks to wait for a DML lock. You can control the wait time by specifying the ddl_lock_timeout parameter. The new syntax for the lock table statement enables you to control the duration for which a DDL statement will wait for a DML lock. The database invalidates only the logically affected objects during an online redefinition in Oracle Database 11g, instead of automatically invalidating all dependent views and PL/SQL packages. This is called the fine-grained dependency management feature. Oracle Database 11g extends its table compression capability to OLTP jobs such as data insertion. Use the new compress for all operations clause when you create a table to set up compression for DML operations.

You can now create an initialization parameter file or an SPFILE from the system-wide parameters currently in use by the instance. This feature lets you easily recover from the loss of an SPFILE.

Implementing Oracle Direct NFS enables you to avoid the kernel NFS layer and provides load balancing and predictable performance while being easy to manage. You can configure Direct NFS by specifying the mount points in the /etc/mtab file and Oracle-specific options in the oranfstab file.

The hot patching feature enables you to apply bug fixes or diagnostic patches online. You can use the opatch utility to perform online patching.

In Oracle Database 11g, the Enterprise Manager provides an interface to the LogMiner tool.

✓ TWO-MINUTE DRILL

Oracle SecureFiles

- ❑ Oracle SecureFiles are a newly engineered LOB data type that is an alternative to the traditional LOB implementation.
- ❑ SecureFiles offer compression, encryption, and deduplication features.
- ❑ Oracle SecureFiles minimize fragmentation by using variable chunk sizes, with the chunks stored next to one another.
- ❑ SecureFiles provide better read and write performance than traditional LOBs.
- ❑ SecureFiles relieve the user from version control tasks.
- ❑ You enable the creation of SecureFiles by setting the `db_securefile` initialization parameter.
- ❑ The `db_securefile` parameter can take the values `always`, `force`, `permitted`, `never`, and `ignore`.
- ❑ Only the `never` option will disallow the creation of SecureFiles.
- ❑ The deduplication feature automatically detects duplicate data and saves only one copy of the duplicated data.
- ❑ You don't need to specify the old storage clauses such as `chunk`, `pctversion`, and `freelists` when using SecureFiles.
- ❑ You use the store clauses `maxsize`, `retention`, `max`, `min`, `auto`, and `none` when creating a SecureFile LOB.
- ❑ Use the `store as securefile` clause when creating a table with a LOB column as a SecureFile. Specify the `encrypt` clause to create a SecureFile with encryption.
- ❑ You can specify compression with the key word `compression`.
- ❑ You can specify compression at the high or the default medium level.
- ❑ The `keep duplicates` and `no keep duplicates` clauses specify whether the database can or can't store duplicates for the LOB column.
- ❑ You can use the partition exchange technique or the online redefinition method to migrate to SecureFiles.
- ❑ Oracle recommends that you use the online redefinition method to migrate to SecureFiles.

Online Enhancements

❑ You can use the new `ddl_lock_timeout` parameter to specify the time for which a DDL statement can wait for a DML statement.

❑ The `lock table...in lockmode...` statement lets you control the time for which a DDL statement will wait to acquire a necessary DML lock on a table.

❑ The `nowait` option for DML locks immediately returns control if the table is already locked by others.

❑ The `wait` option lets the statement wait for the period that you specify.

❑ There is no limit to the value you can set for the `nowait` parameter.

❑ The default behavior is for a DDL statement to wait indefinitely for an exclusive DML lock.

❑ There is no requirement for an exclusive lock on tables during the following operations: `create index online`, `create materialized view log`, and `alter table enable constraint novalidate`.

❑ Fine-grained dependency management invalidates only the logically affected objects during an online redefinition instead of invalidating all dependent views and PL/SQL packages as before.

❑ You can create a text initialization parameter file or an SPFILE from the initialization parameters in memory.

❑ Hot patching enables you to apply bug fixes and diagnostic patches online, without any downtime.

❑ You can use the opatch utility to perform an online patch.

Miscellaneous New Features

❑ An invisible index is like any normal Oracle index, but is hidden from the Oracle optimizer.

❑ You create an invisible index by specifying the clause `invisible` to the `create index` statement.

❑ You can change a normal index into an invisible index by issuing the `alter index` statement.

❑ By setting the initialization parameter `optimizer_use_invisible_indexes` to `true`, you can make all invisible indexes in a database visible to the optimizer.

❑ You can shrink a temporary tablespace and individual tempfiles in Oracle Database 11g.

❑ The keep clause enables you to specify a minimum value for the temporary tables.

❑ You can specify a tablespace clause when creating a temporary table.

❑ PL/SQL native compilation directly translates PL/SQL code into DLLs, thus eliminating the need to use a third-party C compiler for executing PL/SQL.

❑ Use the plsql_code_type parameter to set up native compilation.

❑ The default value of the pls_sql_code parameter is interpreted.

❑ You must set the plsql_code_type parameter to native to set up real native compilation.

❑ You can use the alter <PLSQL unit type>... statement to enable native compilation of a single PL/SQL program unit.

❑ You can recompile the entire database for native compilation by executing the dbmsupgnv.sql script.

❑ Use the java_jit_enabled parameter to set up Java native compilation in a database.

❑ You can compress data during an OLTP workload, such as an insert operation.

❑ You can enable compression for DML operations by specifying the compress for all operations clause in a create table statement.

❑ Oracle NFS implements the NFS Version 3 protocol in the Oracle RDBMS kernel.

❑ Oracle NFS provides load balancing and predictable performance, in addition to greater manageability.

❑ You can specify the mount points for the NFS mounts in the /etc/mtab file.

❑ Optionally, you can use the oranfstab file to specify Oracle-specific options to Direct NFS.

❑ Direct NFS searches for mount point entries in a specific order and uses the first match as the mount point.

❑ Even when you use Direct NFS, the kernel NFS system must perform the mounting.

❑ The oranfstab file has the following attributes that you can set: server, mount, export, and path.

❑ You can disable the direct NFS client by deleting the oranfstab file.

SELF TEST

Oracle SecureFiles

1. When you assign the value `force` for the `db_securefile` initialization parameter, the database
   A. Creates all LOBs as SecureFile LOBs, as long as you have an Automatic Segment Space Management tablespace enabled.
   B. Creates all LOBs as SecureFile LOBs.
   C. Allows the creation of SecureFiles.
   D. Will not allow the creation of new SecureFile LOBs; it also ignores errors that result from creating a BasicFile with SecureFile options.

2. When you assign the value `ignore` for the `db_securefile` initialization parameter, the database
   A. Creates all LOBs as SecureFile LOBs, as long as you use an ASSM-enabled tablespace.
   B. Creates all LOBs as SecureFile LOBs.
   C. Allows the creation of SecureFiles.
   D. Will not allow the creation of new SecureFile LOBs; it also ignores errors that result from creating a BasicFile with SecureFile options.

3. Which two of the following storage clauses are applicable to the new SecureFiles?
   A. `maxsize`
   B. `chunk`
   C. `retention`
   D. `pctversion`

4. Which of the following are valid SecureFiles caching options?
   A. `cache`
   B. `nocache`
   C. `cache writes`
   D. `cache reads`

5. How do you enable duplication in a SecureFile LOB?
   A. With the `duplicates` option
   B. With the `keep duplicates` option
   C. With the `deduplication` clause
   D. With the `no deduplication` clause

6. Which of the following are valid methods for migrating to Oracle SecureFiles?

A. Partition transfer

B. Partition exchange

C. Online redefinition

D. Online exchange

7. Which of the following methods does Oracle recommend for migrating to Oracle SecureFiles?

A. Partition transfer

B. Partition exchange

C. Online redefinition

D. Online exchange

Online Enhancements

8. Which of the following statement(s) is/are true with regards to allowing DDL locks to wait for a DML lock?

A. The default value is 0 for the `ddl_lock_timeout` parameter.

B. The default value is unlimited for the `ddl_lock_timeout` parameter.

C. By default, if a DDL statement can't get an immediate DML lock on the table, it will fail.

D. By default, a DDL statement will wait forever for a DML lock.

9. In the `lock table ... in lockmode mode ...` command, what happens if you leave out the mode parameter?

A. The attempt to lock the table will immediately fail.

B. The database locks the table once it becomes available and returns control to you.

C. It is the same as setting the `nowait` option for the `mode` parameter.

D. It is the same as setting the `wait` option for the `mode` parameter.

10. The opatch utility lets you

A. Enable patches

B. Disable patches

C. Install patches

D. Create patches

11. What does the `create pfile from memory` command do?

A. Creates the SPFILE from the current parameter values in use

B. Creates the text initialization parameter file from the current initialization parameter values in use

C. Creates the parameter file from the SPFILE in use

D. Creates a copy of the parameter file that is currently in use

12. Which of the following statements are correct, when a view (V) depends on a table (T)?

   A. If the addition of a new column to table T has no bearing on the view V, the database invalidates V.

   B. If the addition of a new column to table T has no bearing on the view V, the database doesn't invalidate V.

   C. The database invalidates V only if the view uses the new column.

   D. The database invalidates V only if the view doesn't use the new column.

13. When you create a new parameter file from memory,

   A. The file will have values for all the 150 or so initialization parameters, even if you haven't set values for all of them.

   B. The file will have values only for those parameters that you set.

   C. The file will use default values for all initialization parameters.

   D. The file will use default values for all parameters that you ignored.

14. When you hot patch with the opatch utility,

   A. You must always restart the database.

   B. It takes longer than conventional patches.

   C. You can't work in an Oracle RAC environment.

   D. The hot patches persist across instance shutdowns.

Miscellaneous New Features

15. Which of the following statements are true when dealing with invisible indexes?

   A. By default, all indexes are created as visible indexes.

   B. By default, all indexes are created as invisible indexes.

   C. You can make an index invisible only when you create an index.

   D. You can make an index invisible when you create the index or later on, with the help of the alter index statement.

16. When you create a global temporary table in Oracle Database 11g,

   A. You must specify a tablespace.

   B. You can specify a tablespace.

   C. The attempt to create the temporary table will fail if you omit the tablespace.

   D. If you omit the `tablespace` clause, the database creates the global temporary table in the default temporary tablespace for the database.

17. Which of the following clauses can you use with a `create table` statement to set up OLTP table compression?

    A. `compress for direct_load operations`

    B. `compress for OLTP operations`

    C. `compress`

    D. `compress for all operations`

18. Which of the following files does Direct NFS search for mount point entries first?

    A. $ORACLE_HOME/dbs/oranfstab

    B. /etc/oranfstab

    C. /etc/mtab

    D. $ORACLE_HOME/dbs/mtab

19. You can disable the Direct NFS client by

    A. Deleting the oranfstab file

    B. Replacing the stub libodm11.so file with the ODM NFS library

    C. Replacing the ODM NFS library with the stub libodm11.so file

    D. Deleting the specific NFS server by editing the oranfstab file

20. To set up native compilation for PL/SQL, you must

    A. Set the `plsql_code_type` parameter to `interpreted`

    B. Set the `plsql_code_type` parameter to `native`

    C. Set the `plsql_optimimize` level to at least 2

    D. Set the `plsql_native_compilation` parameter to `true`

21. Which of the following commands will shrink a temporary tablespace?

    A. `alter tablespace temp shrink space;`

    B. `alter tablespace temp shrink tempfile '/u01/app/oracle/tem01.dbf';`

    C. `alter tablespace temp shrink space keep 500m;`

    D. `alter tablespace keep 500m;`

Lab Question

Show how you would apply an online "hot" patch to a running database and roll the patch back without shutting down, using the opatch utility.

SELF TEST ANSWERS

Oracle SecureFiles

1. ☑ **B** is correct because the value `force` for the `db_securefile` initialization parameter forces the database to create all LOBs as Securefile LOBs, without any exceptions.
☒ **A, C,** and **D** are incorrect. **A** is incorrect because you must specify the value `always` create LOBs as SecureFiles, but only as long as they use an ASSM-enabled tablespace. **C** is incorrect because it is the value `permitted` (default value) that allows the creation of SecureFiles. **D** is incorrect because you must set the value to `ignore` for the database to disallow the creation of SecureFiles and the errors caused by creating BasicFiles with SecureFiles options.

2. ☑ **D** is correct because when you set the `db_securefile` parameter to `ignore`, the database won't allow the creation of new SecureFiles. It also ignores errors that result from the creation of BasicFiles with SecureFiles options.
☒ **A, B,** and **C** are incorrect. **A** is incorrect because you must specify that the value always creates LOBs as SecureFiles, but only as long as they use an ASSM-enabled tablespace. **B** is incorrect because it is the value `force` for the `db_securefile` initialization parameter that forces the database to create all LOBs was Securefile LOBs, without any exceptions. **C** is incorrect because it is the value `permitted` (default value) that allows the creation of SecureFiles.

3. ☑ **A** and **C** are correct. **A** is correct because you use the `maxsize` parameter to specify the maximum LOB segment size. **C** is correct because you use the `retention` clause to specify which versions the database must retain.
☒ **B** and **D** are incorrect because both of these parameters are old storage clauses that aren't necessary when you use SecureFiles.

4. ☑ **A, B,** and **D** are correct. All of these are valid caching options for SecureFiles.
☒ **C** is incorrect. It is not a valid caching attribute for SecureFiles.

5. ☑ **B** is correct. You enable duplication by specifying the `keep duplicates` option.
☒ **A, C,** and **D** are incorrect. **A** is incorrect because it is a nonexistent option. **C** is incorrect because the `deduplication` option specifies that the database not keep any LOB duplicates. **D** is incorrect because it refers to a nonexistent option.

6. ☑ **B** and **C** are correct because partition exchange and online redefinition are the methods you can use to migrate to Oracle SecureFiles.
☒ **A** and **D** are incorrect because both of these are nonexistent methods.

7. ☑ **C** is correct. Oracle recommends that you use online redefinition to migrate to SecureFiles.
   ☒ **A**, **B**, and **D** are incorrect. **A** and **D** are incorrect because they are nonexistent methods. **B** is incorrect because while partition exchange is a valid method to migrate to SecureFiles, it isn't the recommended method to do so.

Online Enhancements

8. ☑ **A** and **C** are correct. **A** is correct because the default value is 0 for the `ddl_lock_timeout` parameter. **C** is correct because, by default, a DDL statement will fail if it can't get an immediate lock on a table.
   ☒ **B** and **D** are incorrect. **B** is incorrect because the default value is 0, not `unlimited`. **D** is correct because, by default, a DDL statement doesn't wait, but fails immediately if it can't acquire a DML lock on a table.

9. ☑ **B** and **D** are correct. **B** is correct because the database locks the table once it becomes available and returns control to you. **D** is correct because omitting the `mode` parameter is the same as setting the `wait` option for the `mode` parameter because it's the default value for the `mode` parameter.
   ☒ **A** and **C** are incorrect. **A** is incorrect because the attempt to lock a table won't fail. The statement will wait indefinitely for execution. **C** is incorrect because leaving the `mode` parameter out is the same as setting the `wait` option, not the `nowait` option for the `mode` parameter.

10. ☑ **A**, **B**, and **C** are correct because the opatch utility lets you do all of these.
    ☒ **D** is incorrect because the opatch utility doesn't create patches, but helps you install them and enable or disable them.

11. ☑ **B** is correct because the `create pfile from memory` command creates a text initialization parameter file from the current parameter values being used by the instance.
    ☒ **A**, **C**, and **D** are incorrect. **A** is incorrect because the command creates a text initialization parameter file, not the SPFILE. **C** is incorrect because the database creates the parameter file from the parameter values in memory, not from the SPFILE. **D** is incorrect because the command doesn't make a copy of the current parameter file—it simply creates a new parameter file by using the parameter values in memory.

12. ☑ **B** and **C** are correct. **B** is correct because if the new column doesn't affect the view, the database won't invalidate the view. **C** is correct because the database will invalidate a view only if that view uses the new column.
    ☒ **A** and **D** are incorrect. **A** is incorrect because if the new column has no bearing on the view, the database doesn't invalidate the view. **D** is incorrect because if the view doesn't use the new column, the database doesn't invalidate the view.

13. ☑ **A** and **D** are correct. **A** is correct because the new parameter file that you create with the `create pfile from memory` command will contain values for all 150 or so initialization parameters, regardless of whether you've set values for all of those parameters. **D** is correct because the newly created file will use the default values for all the initialization parameters you didn't specify in the PFILE or the SPFILE.

    ☒ **B** and **C** are incorrect. **B** is incorrect because the file will have values for parameters, including those you haven't explicitly set. **C** is incorrect because the file will contain default values only for those parameters you haven't set.

14. ☑ **D** is correct because the hot patches that you apply will persist across instance shutdowns.

    ☒ **A, B,** and **C** are incorrect. **A** is incorrect because you don't have to restart the database after you apply a hot patch. **B** is incorrect because it actually is much faster to apply a patch online with the opatch utility than to apply a conventional patch. **C** is incorrect because you use the hot patching with the opatch utility in a RAC environment.

Miscellaneous New Features

15. ☑ **A** and **D** are correct. **A** is correct because, by default, all indexes are visible to the optimizer, as in the previous releases of the database. **D** is correct because you can make an index invisible either when you create it or later on, by issuing the `alter index` statement.

    ☒ **B** and **C** are incorrect. **B** is incorrect because, by default, all indexes are visible. **C** is incorrect because you can also make an index invisible after you create it, by issuing the `alter index` statement.

16. ☑ **B** and **D** are correct. **B** is correct because the specification of a tablespace is optional, not mandatory. **D** is correct because if you don't specify a tablespace when creating a global temporary table, the database creates the table in the database's default temporary tablespace.

    ☒ **A** and **C** are incorrect. **A** is incorrect because you don't have to specify the tablespace—it's optional. **C** is correct because you can create the global temporary table without specifying the tablespace.

17. ☑ **D** is correct because you must specify the `compress for all operations` clause to set up OLTP table compression.

    ☒ **A, B,** and **C** are incorrect. **A** is incorrect because you use this option for data warehouse compression only. **B** is incorrect because it is a nonexistent option. **C** is incorrect because the `compress option by default` command compresses only data warehouse workloads, not OLTP workloads.

18. ☑ **A** is correct because the Direct NFS first searches the $ORACLE_HOME/dbs/oranfstab directory for mount point entries.

    ☒ **B, C,** and **D** are incorrect because none of these is the first choice for a search by Direct NFS for mount point entries.

19. ☑ **A, B,** and **D** are correct because you can disable Direct NFS by doing any one of these.
☒ **C** is incorrect because you must actually do the opposite—replace the stub libodm11.so file with the ODM NFS library.

20. ☑ **B** and **C** are correct. **B** is correct because you must set the `plsql_code_type` parameter to `native` to set up PL/SQL native compilation. **C** is correct because you must ensure that the `plsql_optimize_level` parameter is set to at least 2 before the database can natively compile PL/SQL.
☒ **A** and **D** are incorrect. **B** is incorrect because you must set the `plsql_code_type` parameter to `native` to set up PL/SQL native compilation. **D** is incorrect. It isn't a valid option for the `plsql_code_type` parameter.

21. ☑ **A, B,** and **C** are correct because all of these commands will shrink a temporary tablespace.
☒ **D** is incorrect because you can't use this command to shrink a temporary tablespace. This is a command with an incorrect syntax that will fail.

LAB ANSWER

Let's assume you identified a code bug in your database. Let's also assume that the patch you must apply to fix the code bug is in the /u01/app/oracle/OP directory in the hotpatch.zip file. Here are the steps to apply the patch and, if necessary, to roll back the patch.

1. Unzip the hotpatch.zip file to retrieve the patch you must apply to fix the code bug.

   ```
   $ unzip hotpatch.zip
   ```

2. Check if the patch is indeed an online patch that you can apply while the database is running.

   ```
   $ $ORACLE_HOME/Opatch/opatch query -is_online_patch "pwd"
   ```

3. Once the `opatch query` command shows that the path is an online patch, proceed to the next step.

4. Apply the patch using the `opatch apply` command.

   ```
   $ $ORACLE_HOME/Opatch/opatch apply
   ```

5. Issue the `opatch lsinventory` command to ensure that the patch you just applied shows up in the patch inventory.

   ```
   $ $ORACLE_HOME/Opatch/opatch lsinventory
   ```

6. To roll back the patch, use the `opatch rollback` command, as shown here:

   ```
   $ $ORACLE_HOME/Opatch/opatch rollback -id1234567
   ```

Note that you must provide the patch ID as part of the `opatch rollback` command.

Appendix

About the CD-ROM

The CD-ROM included with this book comes complete with MasterExam and the electronic version of the book. The software is easy to install on any Windows 98/NT/2000/XP/Vista computer and must be installed to access the MasterExam feature. You may, however, browse the electronic book directly from the CD-ROM without installation. To register for a second, bonus MasterExam, simply click the Online Training link on the main page and follow the directions to the free online registration.

System Requirements

Software requires Windows 98 or higher and Internet Explorer 5.0 or above and 20 MB of hard disk space for full installation. The electronic book requires Adobe Acrobat Reader.

Installing and Running MasterExam

If your computer CD-ROM drive is configured to auto run, the CD-ROM will automatically start up upon inserting the disk. From the opening screen you can install MasterExam by pressing the MasterExam button. This will begin the installation process and create a program group named LearnKey. To run MasterExam, use Start | Programs | LearnKey. If the auto run feature did not launch your CD-ROM, browse to the CD-ROM and click the LaunchTraining.exe icon.

MasterExam

MasterExam provides you with a simulation of the actual exam. The number of questions, the type of questions, and the time allowed are intended to be an accurate representation of the exam environment. You have the option to take an open book exam, including hints, references, and answers; a closed book exam; or the timed MasterExam simulation.

When you launch MasterExam, a digital clock display will appear in the upper-left corner of your screen. The clock will continue to count down to zero unless you choose to end the exam before the time expires.

Electronic Book

The entire contents of this exam guide are provided in PDF format. Adobe's Acrobat Reader has been included on the CD-ROM.

Help

A help file is provided through the help button on the main page in the lower-left corner. An individual help feature is also available through MasterExam.

Removing Installation(s)

MasterExam is installed to your hard drive. For best results when removing programs, use the Start | Programs | LearnKey | Uninstall option to remove MasterExam.

Technical Support

For questions regarding the technical content of the electronic book or MasterExam, please visit www.osborne.com or e-mail customer.service@mcgraw-hill.com. For customers outside the 50 United States, e-mail international_cs@mcgraw-hill.com. If you would like clarifications regarding the questions or answers, you may reach the author directly at salapati@netbsa.org.

LearnKey Technical Support

For technical problems with the software (installation, operation, removing installations), please visit www.learnkey.com or e-mail techsupport@learnkey.com.

Glossary

Autotask Background Process (ABP)　A new Oracle background process that converts the automated scheduled tasks into Scheduler jobs.

ABP　*See* Autotask Background Process.

accepted plans　An accepted plan is a plan that is verified not to cause a performance regression. All accepted plans are integrated into the SQL plan baseline for a SQL statement.

access control list (ACL)　A group of directives that you define to grant appropriate levels of access to specific data for specific clients or groups of clients when they access the database through the network.

ACL　*See* access control list.

active database duplication　A database duplication process wherein you transfer files over the network instead of restoring backups of the target database.

adaptive cursor sharing　A new type of cursor sharing that allows for intelligent cursor sharing only for statements that use bind variables; offers a compromise between traditional cursor sharing and optimization.

adaptive metric thresholds   The adaptive metric thresholds feature enables the selection of better alert thresholds for database performance metrics and uses the AWR baselines as the source for metric statistics.

ADDM   *See* Automatic Database Diagnostic Monitor (ADDM).

ADR base   The ADR base is the ADR root directory. You set its location with the `diagnostic_dest` initialization parameter.

ADR Command Interpreter   The ADR Command Interpreter (ADRCI) is a command line–based tool that enables you to investigate database incidents and problems, view the database alert log and health check reports, and package and upload diagnostic data to Oracle Support.

ADR Home   An ADR home is the root directory for all diagnostic data for a particular instance of an Oracle product or component, such as a database, for example. With an ADR base, there can be multiple ADR homes.

ADR   *See* Automatic Diagnostic Repository.

ADRCI   *See* ADR Command Interpreter.

allocation unit   An allocation unit is the basic unit of allocation in an ASM disk group. An ASM file consists of one or more file extents with each extent consisting of one or more AUs.

AMBR   *See* ASM metadata backup and restore.

ASM metadata backup and restore   Consists of the `md_backup` command, which enables you to back up the metadata for ASM disk groups and the `md_restore` command, which helps you restore a disk group backup.

ASM disk group compatibility   ASM disk group compatibility, indicated by the value of the `compatible.asm` attribute, determines the minimum software version required to use the disk group for ASM.

ASM Fast Mirror Resync   This new ASM feature reduces the time to synchronize a failed disk by letting ASM quickly resynchronize the ASM disk extents.

ASM Preferred Mirrored Read   Under this feature, ASM reads from the closest extent (local copy), rather than always reading the primary copy. You can specify a list of failure group names by setting the `asm_preferred_read_ failure_groups` initialization parameter.

ASMCMD   An ASM command-line utility to view and manage files and directories within ASM disk groups.

AU   *See* allocation unit.

Automatic Database Diagnostic monitor (ADDM)   A tool to diagnose Oracle database performance; offers solutions to problems it identifies. It runs automatically after each AWR statistics capture.

automatic diagnostic repository (ADR)   A new repository for system-wide tracing and error logging. The repository is file-based and is used to store diagnostic information of all types, including alert log files.

automatic memory management   This is a new method of memory management that lets the database automatically manage and tune the memory allocated to the Oracle instance, including the SGA and the PGA components.

automatic plan capture   The setup where the database automatically creates and maintains the plan history for SQL statements.

automatic secure configuration   When creating a new database with the DBCA, the new automatic secure configuration feature lets you enable secure configuration settings by default. These settings include the password-specific settings in the default profile and auditing for specific database events such as connecting to the database.

Automatic SQL Tuning Advisor   This is an advisor that runs nightly during the default maintenance window, automatically invoking the SQL Tuning Advisor on selected high-load SQL statements captured by the AWR.

Automatic Storage Management (ASM)   Vertically integrates the file system and the volume manager, especially for Oracle database files; uses striping and mirroring capabilities to optimize performance.

AWR baselines   These are baselines that let you accurately compare database performance by letting you mark a representative time as the base against which you can compare performance during other periods in the future.

base recovery catalog   The base or central recovery catalog is the actual recovery catalog, based on which you can create a virtual recovery catalog.

basicfile   This refers to the original LOB implementation, which is supplemented by the SecureFiles implementation in Oracle Database 11g.

bind-aware   A cursor in the cursor cache that the database has marked to use bind-aware cursor sharing is called bind-aware.

bind peeking   The process where the query optimizer looks at the values of the user-defined bind variables when the database invokes a cursor for the first time.

bind-sensitive   A query for which a change in a bind variable value may lead to a different execution plan is called bind-sensitive.

capture files   Platform-independent transportable binary files in which the database tracks and stores all external client requests when using the Database Replay feature.

checker   *See* Health Monitor checks.

checks   *See* Health Monitor checks.

client_query result cache   The client query result cache (also called the OCI result cache) is separate from the server-side result cache and stores OCI application results that are shared across all sessions.

connect_time_scale   This parameter scales the elapsed time from the time the workload capture started to when the session connects with the specified value.

control_management_pack_access   This initialization parameter specifies which of the Server Manageability Packs should be active. There are two management packs: the diagnostic pack and the tuning pack.

custom packaging   A manual incident packaging method that involves more steps than the Quick Packaging method. Custom packaging offers more control over the packaging process, by enabling you to add or remove problems or incidents, trace files, and additional diagnostic data.

Data Recovery Advisor   A new automated data repair tool designed to reduce the mean time to recover from failures. It automatically diagnoses data failures, presents a report of the repair options, and, optionally, executes those repairs.

database ADDM   In this mode, ADDM analyzes all instances of the databases in a cluster.

Database Replay Is   A new change management tool that enables you to realistically test the effect of system changes on database workload. You capture the production workload and replay it on a test system, the simulation helping you assess the impact of the system change on performance.

db_securefile   This initialization parameter specifies whether the database will treat a LOB file as the new SecureFile or a traditional BasicFile LOB.

db_ultra_safe   This new initialization parameter sets the default values for the initialization parameters that control protection levels (db_block_checking, db_block_checksum, and db_lost_write_protect).

DBMS_SQLPA   This new Oracle-supplied PL/SQL package provides procedures and functions to use the SQL Performance Analyzer feature. The interface lets you compare and analyze the workload between two versions and isolate SQL statements whose performance is affected by making system changes.

ddl_lock_timeout   This initialization parameter specifies the time limit for which a DDL statement will wait to acquire a DML lock.

diagnostic_dest   This initialization parameter specifies the directory where the diagnostic information for an instance of an Oracle product is stored.

evolving SQL plan baselines   In this phase, the database evaluates the performance of new plans and adds plans with better performance into the SQL plan baseline for a SQL statement.

expression statistics   Statistics on an expression on a column, valuable to gather so the cost optimizer will have a better selectivity value.

extended statistics   Statistics on a group of columns (multicolumn statistics) or an expression on a column (expression statistics).

fixed SQL plan baselines   A SQL plan baseline that contains at least one enabled plan whose `fixed` attribute is set to Yes.

flashback data archive   A flashback data archive is a historical repository of the changes made to every row in a table for the duration of the row's lifetime.

flashback transaction backout   A feature that lets you selectively remove the effect of individual transactions.

forced dropping of diskgroups   You can drop disk groups that you are unable to mount by specifying the force option of the drop diskgroup command.

health check   *See* Health Monitor checks.

Health Monitor   A new framework for running diagnostic checks on the database.

Health Monitor checks   Health Monitor checks, also known as checkers or health checks, detect various types of database corruption and generate reports of findings as well as recommendations for resolving the problems causing the corruption. The database can run reactive checks automatically in response to a critical error or you can manually invoke a health check anytime.

I/O calibration   The I/O calibration feature in Oracle Database 11g enables you to assess the I/O performance of the storage subsystem and determine whether the problem lies in the storage subsystem or the database.

importing recovery catalogs   You can use the import catalog command to import one recovery catalog's metadata into a different recovery catalog schema, thus allowing you to maintain a single recovery catalog schema for all databases.

incident flood control   A strategy to avoid overloading the ADR with diagnostic data in the ADR for a single problem. After a problem is logged a certain predetermined number of times, the database applies a flood control mechanism. A flood controlled incident is an incident that is recorded in the alert logs, without generating new incident dumps in the ADR.

incident package   A collection of metadata pertaining to diagnostic data files both within and outside the ADR. After you create a package, you add one or more problems to it and the Support Workbench will automatically add the incident information and diagnostic data associated to the selected problems to the package. Only the first three and the last three incidents for each problem are added to a package.

Incident Packaging Service   A facility that automatically identifies all the required diagnostic files and adds them to an incident package. You can use the service to edit and modify the package and transmit the Zip file to Oracle Support.

incidents   An incident is a single occurrence of a database problem. The database creates an incident for each occurrence of a problem.

incremental statistics   A term used for a statistics collection strategy to save time when collecting statistics for large partitioned tables. If you set the incremental value for a partitioned table to TRUE and gather statistics for that table with the granularity set to auto, Oracle will gather statistics only on the new partition added since the last time statistics were collected for the table. Oracle updates the global table statistics with the statistics it collects for the new partition, thus saving time.

instance ADDM   In this mode, ADDM analyzes only a particular instance in a cluster.

interval partitioning   An extension of range partitioning, which tells the database to automatically create partitions of a specified interval when new data that is inserted into the table exceeds all the range partitions.

invisible index   An invisible index can't be used by the cost optimizer, although the database maintains it during all DML operations like a regular index.

IOPS   I/O per second.

IPS   *See* Incident Packaging Service.

large objects   Large objects (LOBs) are designed for storing data that is large in size and includes the following SQL data types: BLOB, CLOB, NCLOB, and BFILE.

latency   Describes the delay or the time it takes for a response.

ldap_directory_sysauth   Enables or disables directory-based authorization for the SYSDBA and SYOPER privileges.

lightweight job   An easy-to-create type of Scheduler job that is based on a job template that is the source of the privileges and the job metadata.

LOB   *See* large objects.

lsdsk   Command to list disks visible to ASM. Uses the V$ASM_DISK_STAT and the V$ASM_DISK views.

MBPS   Megabytes of I/O per second.

md_backup   Creates a backup file (named ambr_backup_intermediate_file) containing metadata for one or more ASM disk groups.

md_restore   Restores an ASM disk group backup.

memory_max_target   This initialization parameter provides the maximum value to which you can set the memory_target initialization parameter.

memory_target   This initialization parameter is used to specify the memory allocated to the Oracle instance when you use automatic memory management to automatically manage the SGA and the PGA components of memory.

merging recovery catalogs   You can use the import catalog command to merge one catalog schema into another. You can merge a complete recovery catalog schema or just the metadata for specified databases.

mixed workload resource plan   A predefined Oracle Scheduler resource plan that gives priority to interactive operations over batch operations.

moving window baselines   A moving window baseline corresponds to the entire set of AWR data covering the AWR retention period, which is eight days by default. A moving window baseline is particularly helpful when you're using adaptive thresholds. The database automatically maintains a system-defined moving window baseline with a default window size of eight days.

multicolumn statistics   Gathering statistics on a group of columns within a table to provide better selectivity value for the column group instead of generating selectivity values based on individual columns statistics.

multisection backups   An RMAN backup set in which each backup piece contains a section of the file that is being backed up. You create a multisection backup by specifying the section size parameter in the backup command.

Opatch   A platform-independent utility that helps you apply a patch, which is a small collection of files, the application of which results in an upgrade to the version of a product.

optimizer_capture_sql_plan_baselines   This initialization parameter enables and disables the generation of SQL plan baselines for repeatable SQL statements.

optimizer_use_invisible_indexes   This initialization parameter enables and disables the use of invisible indexes.

optimizer_use_sql_baselines   This initialization parameter enables or disables the use of the SQL plan baselines stored by the database in the SQL Management Base, when it compiles a SQL statement.

Oracle Direct NFS   You can use the Oracle internal Direct NFS client to take advantage of a network-attached storage (NAS) system.

Oracle wallet   A container that stores public key security credentials and can be read by the Oracle Database, Oracle Application Server 10g, and the Oracle Identity Management infrastructure.

OSASM   This is an optional operating system group, which you create if you want to grant the SYSASM system privilege.

partial ADDM   In this mode, ADDM analyzes a subset of the instances in a cluster.

partition exchange loading   A technique to improve performance when loading or purging data in a database.

pending statistics   Statistics that are not published for use by the optimizer. You can publish the statistics after a satisfactory test.

PL/SQL Function Result   This cache stores the results of PL/SQL functions in the SGA and makes them available to all sessions that use your application.

PL/SQL Native Compilation   Under PL/SQL native compilation, PL/SQL code units are compiled into native code and stored in the SYSTEM tablespace. The code runs faster than the traditional execution that consists of compiling into an intermediate machine readable code first and then interpreting it at runtime. You use the `plsql_code_type` initialization parameter to specify whether PL/SQL code is natively compiled or interpreted.

Problems   A problem is a critical error in the database such as an ORA-00600 or ORA-07445 error.

quick packaging   The simplest and fastest way to create an incident package; uses a minimum number of steps. You can't add, edit, or remove package files and other diagnostic data.

RDBMS compatibility   This is shown by the value of the disk group `compatible.rdbms` attribute; determines the minimum compatible database initialization parameter setting for a database instance that uses the disk group.

read-only table   You can use the `alter table` statement to make a table read-only even for the owner of the table.

Real Application Testing   This is a feature that helps you test the effect of system changes on applications before deploying the changes in production. Oracle Real Application Testing consists of the Database Replay and the SQL Performance Analyzer features.

reference partitioning A method of partitioning where the partitioning key is resolved through an existing parent-child relationship between two tables, with the relationship enforced by active primary key or foreign key constraints.

remap An ASM command that repairs a range of physical blocks on a disk that have read I/O errors.

remapping connections The process of using the connection strings used to connect to the production system to connect to the replay system during a database workload replay.

remote external jobs A remote external job that runs on a different server from the server on which the Oracle database that scheduled the job runs.

repeating baseline A baseline that repeats during a specific time interval over a specific period.

replay client The replay client, represented by the wrc executable, is a program used by Database Replay to submit a workload from a captured session.

restricted mount mode in ASM You can use the `startup restrict` command to restrict access to an ASM instance while you perform maintenance chores. Databases can't connect to the ASM instance because all ASM diskgroups are mounted in the restricted mode.

result cache The result cache is a part of the SGA memory that is used to cache the results of queries. The result cache consists of the SQL result cache and the PL/SQL function result cache.

result_cache hint This parameter determines if the SQL query results will be cached. If you set the value to `force`, the database will cache all results if possible. If you set it to `manual`, you must specify the `result_cache` hint in order for a particular result to use the result cache.

result_cache_max_result This initialization parameter specifies the percentage of the `result_cache_max_size` parameter that a single result can use.

result_cache_mode This initialization parameter specifies under what conditions the database splices the ResultCache operator into a query's execution plan.

ResultCache operator   The database inserts the ResultCache operator into the execution plan for a SQL statement when the statement contains the `result_cache` hint.

Scheduler agent   A Scheduler agent runs on a remote host and communicates with the Oracle database on a different host that originates a remote external job. The agent is responsible for starting the remote jobs and returning the execution results to the originating database.

sec_case_sensitive_logon   This initialization parameter lets you enable or disable password case sensitivity.

sec_max_failed_login_attempts   This initialization parameter specifies the maximum number of authentication attempts a client can make when connecting to a server before the connection is automatically dropped.

SecureFiles   A new paradigm for LOBs designed to supplement the original LOB implementation.

single baseline   A single baseline is captured at a single fixed-time interval.

SMB   *See* SQL Management Base.

snapshot standby database   A snapshot standby database is a fully updateable standby database. You can apply the redo data from the primary database to convert the snapshot standby database into a physical standby database, thus providing you with disaster recovery and data protection benefits just as a physical standby database does.

SQL Access Advisor   The SQL Access Advisor is a tool that helps you improve performance by recommending the creation of materialized views, table partitions, and indexes for a database workload.

SQL Management Base   Located in the SYSAUX tablespace, this is a repository for statement logs, SQL plan histories, SQL profiles, and SQL plan baselines. The database adds plans automatically to the SMB, which you can also do manually.

SQL Performance Analyzer   Helps you automate the testing of the effects of changes in the SQL workload on database performance. SQL Performance Analyzer's goal is to efficiently find out if SQL changes would lead to an improvement. SQL Performance Analyzer also provides tuning recommendations for SQL statements whose performance regresses following the changes.

SQL plan baseline   The set of all accepted plans in the plan history is the SQL plan baseline for a SQL statement.

SQL Plan Management   SQL Plan Management is a preventative mechanism designed to prevent performance regressions resulting from changes in the execution plans of SQL statements. It uses SQL baselines, composed of known efficient execution plans to preserve the performance of SQL statements in the face of system changes.

SQL profile   A SQL profile is additional information beyond the usual statistics that helps the query optimizer create an optimal execution plan for a SQL statement.

SQL Query Result Cache   A part of the result cache where the database caches the results of queries and query fragments.

SQL Repair Advisor   The SQL Repair Advisor analyzes a SQL statement that fails with a critical error and in many cases recommends a patch as a workaround for the failed statement. Applying the patch leads the optimizer to choose a different explain plan for future executions of the statement.

SQL Test Case Builder   The SQL Test Case Builder collects and packages all information necessary to reproduce a problem.

SQL Tuning Set   A SQL Tuning Set (STS) is a database object that includes one or more SQL statements along with their execution statistics and execution context.

STS   *See* SQL Tuning Set.

support workbench   The Support Workbench (formal name: Enterprise Manager Support Workbench) is a GUI tool that helps you investigate, report, and even repair some problems. You can save time in resolving problems by using the tool to gather diagnostic data and easily uploading diagnostic data to Oracle Support. You can view diagnostic information, run health checks, and package incident data with the help of the Support Workbench.

SYSASM   A new system privilege designed to separate the database administration tasks from ASM administration tasks.

system partitioning   Enables application-controlled data partitioning. The database merely provides the ability to break up the table into meaningless partitions, without using any partitioning key. The application controls all aspects of partitioning.

table compression   Table compression compresses data in a table by eliminating duplicate values in a database block. Oracle supports all DML operations such as insert, update, and delete on compressed tables in Oracle Database 11g, thus making compression viable for both OLTP and data warehousing applications.

tablespace encryption   Enables you to encrypt an entire tablespace to secure all the data stored in a tablespace.

think_time_auto_correct   This parameter corrects the think time between calls. The value is based on the value of the `think_time_scale` parameter.

think_time_scale   This parameter scales the elapsed time between two successive user calls from the same session.

throughput   A measure of the amount of data transferred in a specific amount of time, which is usually expressed as bits per second (bps).

transition point   In an interval partitioning, the range partitioning key value determines the high value of the range partitions and is called the transition point because the database creates interval partitioning beyond this point.

virtual column partitioning   A partitioning method that uses partitioning key columns defined on virtual columns of a table.

virtual private catalog   A virtual private catalog is a subset of the metadata in the base or central recovery catalog to which you grant access to a user, called the virtual catalog owner.

workload filters   You use these filters in Database Replay to specify that only a subset of the database workload should be captured or that certain session types should be ignored when capturing the workload.

wrc   *See* replay client.

INDEX

A

ABP (Autotask Background Process), 163, 493
accepted attribute, 236
accepted plans, 226, 232–234, 236, 493
accept_sql_profiles parameter, 219
access control lists. *See* ACLs
ACLs (access control lists)
    assigning to hosts, 192–193
    checking privileges/host assignments, 194
    creating, 191–194
    described, 191, 493
    host name evaluation, 193
    privileges and, 194
active database duplication, 384–391, 493
adaptive cursor sharing, 362–366, 493
adaptive metric thresholds, 494
add column command, 424
ADD_FILTER procedure, 36–37
ADDM (Automatic Database Diagnostic Monitor)
    advisor findings/directives, 325–327
    cluster-wide mode, 323
    database ADDM, 323–324, 497
    DBMS_ADDM package, 324–327
    described, 322, 495, 497
    enabling/disabling, 324
    instance ADDM, 323, 499
    managing, 324–327
    new views, 327
    partial ADDM, 323, 324, 502
    performance enhancements, 322–327
    Real Application Clusters, 322–324
    reports, 325
    tuning process and, 214, 216
ADD_STS_REF procedure, 241, 245
ADR (Automatic Diagnostic Repository), 80–88
    home subdirectories, 82
    homepath, 84, 85–86
    overview, 5, 78, 80–81, 495
    structure of, 81–83
    viewing incidents, 88
    viewing locations, 82–83
ADR base directory
    ADRCI and, 84
    described, 494
    location of, 5
    path for, 83
    setting, 11
    shared storage and, 82
    vs. ADR home, 81

ADR Command Interpreter. *See* ADRCI
ADR home directory
    ADRCI commands and, 84
    described, 80, 494
    location of, 5
    multiple, 84, 86
    path for, 83
    setting homepath for, 85–86
    single, 86
    vs. ADR base, 81
ADR homepath, 83, 84, 85–86
ADRCI (ADR Command Interpreter), 83–88
    batch mode for, 86–87
    IPS management via, 91
    overview, 79, 83–84, 494
    packaging incidents with, 92–95
    starting, 84–85
    viewing alert log contents, 87–88
    viewing heath check reports, 109–110
    viewing incidents, 88, 92
ADRCI commands
    help for, 84–85
    listing, 84–85
    script file for, 87
    types of, 86
ADRCI scripts, 87
advise failure command, 120–123, 124, 128, 129
AES128 encryption, 453
alert directory, 81, 82
alert logs. *See also* log files
    location of, 81, 82
    text-based, 5, 82, 104
    versions, 5
    viewing with ADRCI, 87–88
    viewing with Support Workbench, 104
    XML-formatted, 5, 81, 82, 83, 104
alert thresholds, 148, 152–155
alerts, 79, 96–98. *See also* errors
allocation units (AUs), 265, 272, 279, 494
alter diskgroup command, 267, 268, 277–278, 281–282
alter flashback archive statement, 421–422
alter profile statement, 18, 189
alter session statement, 340–341, 452, 458–459
alter system statement, 195, 348, 452
alter table statement, 294, 299, 300, 455, 489, 490
ALTER_SQL_PLAN_BASELINE procedure, 236–237
always value, 451

AMBR (ASM metadata backup and restore), 284, 286, 288–289, 494
ANALYZE_DB procedure, 324, 325
ANALYZE_INST procedure, 324, 325
ANALYZE_PARTIAL procedure, 324, 325
APEX (Application Express), 7
Application Express (APEX), 7
applications
    debugging, 34
    OLAP, 164
    OLTP, 164
    testing. See Real Application Testing
archival backups, 394–397
archived redo logs, 394, 403–405
archives. See flashback data archives
arrays. See job arrays
as of clause, 417, 425
ASM (Automatic Storage Management), 264–289
    architecture, 264–265
    compatibility issues, 275–278, 494
    described, 495
    disk failures, 265–266, 267, 270
    fast mirror resync feature, 265–269
    group attributes, 279–280
    manageability options, 280–289
    new features, 264–289
    performance, 272–274
    preferred mirror read feature, 269–272, 495
    restricted mount mode, 281–282, 503
    role/privilege changes, 7–8
    scalability, 272–274
    SYSASM privileges, 8, 9, 20, 274–275, 506
    using Enterprise Manager with, 269, 271–272
ASM disk groups
    backing up/restoring data, 286–289
    compatibility issues, 275–278, 494
    copying files between, 284
    described, 264
    dropping, 282–283, 498
    mount options, 281–283
ASM disks, 284–286
    adding, 267
    damaged, 266, 267, 282–283
    described, 264
    dropping, 266–267
    failures, 265–266, 267, 270
    mirrored, 265–272
    offline, 266
    repairing, 266–269, 279, 281, 283
ASM Fast Mirror Resync, 494

ASM files, 265, 272–273, 284
ASM metadata backup and restore (AMBR), 284, 286, 288–289, 494
ASMCMD utility, 283–288, 495
asm_diskgroups parameter, 281, 282
asm_preferred_read_failure_groups parameter, 270–272
ASSIGN_ACL procedure, 192–193
ATO (Automatic Tuning Optimizer), 214, 215, 216. See also Automatic SQL Tuning Advisor
attribute clause, 274, 279–280
attribute_name parameter, 230
attribute_value parameter, 230–231
audit-related security settings, 18
audit_trail parameter, 18
AUs (allocation units), 265, 272, 279, 494
au_size attribute, 274
automated maintenance tasks, 158–167
    clients, 160–161
    converting to Scheduler jobs, 163
    default, 163, 164
    details about, 160
    enabling/disabling, 160, 161–162
    implementing, 163
    I/O calibration, 164–167
    maintenance windows, 159
    managing, 159–162
    operations, 160–161
    overview, 158–159
    priority, 163, 164
    resource allocation for, 163–164
automatic balancing, 265
Automatic Database Diagnostic Monitor. See ADDM
Automatic Diagnostic Repository. See ADR
automatic memory management
    DBCA and, 333–334
    monitoring, 332–333
    overview, 13, 328–329, 495
    performance enhancements, 328–334
    setting up, 331
    using, 331–332
Automatic Memory Management option, 19
automatic plan capture, 495
automatic secure configuration, 13, 495
automatic session switching, 169–172
Automatic SQL Tuning Advisor, 214–224. See also Automatic Tuning Optimizer; SQL Tuning Advisor
    configuration, 219–220
    data dictionary views, 224
    limitations, 217

managing, 220–223
overview, 158, 214–215, 495
recommendations, 218
reports, 223–224
SQL profiles, 215, 216–224
tuning process, 217–223
automatic storage management. *See* ASM
automatic switching, 169–172
Automatic Tuning Optimizer (ATO), 214, 215, 216. *See also*
  Automatic SQL Tuning Advisor
Automatic Workload Repository. *See* AWR
auto-open wallets, 195
`auto_purge` attribute, 236
Autotask Background Process (ABP), 163, 493
auxiliary instance, 387, 389–391, 397
AWR (Automatic Workload Repository)
exports, 48
tuning process and, 215, 217–221, 229, 231
AWR baselines
creating, 149
described, 148, 496
details about, 157–158
dropping, 149
enabling, 149
expiration period for, 149
loading statements, 53
managing new features, 156–158
metric threshold settings, 152–155
modifying, 149
moving window, 148–149, 155–156, 501
naming, 149–152
new features, 148–158
static, 148
templates, 149–152, 156–157
types of, 148–149
working with, 149
AWR snapshots
described, 148
exporting, 48
loading statements with, 53
tuning process and, 220, 229
workload replay and, 48

B

`background_dump_dest` parameter, 11
`backup` command, 458, 459
backup failover, 404–405
`backup ... keep` command, 394–396
backups
archival, 394–397

ASM metadata backup and restore, 284, 286, 288–289, 494
disk group compatibility and, 277
fast, 398
incremental, 398
long-term, 394–397
`md_backup` command, 277, 286, 288–289, 500
multisection, 392–393, 501
obsolete, 404
redo log files, 404–405
RMAN, 392–398
base recovery catalog, 408–412, 496
baselines. *See also* snapshots
AWR. *See* AWR baselines
moving window, 148–149, 155–156, 501
repeating, 503
single, 504
SQL plan. *See* SQL plan baselines
BASELINE_TYPE column, 158
BasicFiles, 451–452, 454, 457, 496. *See also* SecureFiles
batch_group, 172–173
bdump directory. *See* ADR
`bdump` parameter, 80
bind peeking technique, 363, 496
bind sensitivity, 364, 496
bind-aware cursor, 364–366, 496
block change tracking feature, 398
block media recovery feature, 398–401
`blockrecover` command, 398
BSLN_MAINTAIN_STATS_SCHED schedule, 153
buffer cache, 416
bug fixes, 462–463
BYPASS procedure, 352–353
BZIP2 compression algorithm, 402–403

C

cache
buffer, 416
cursor. *See* cursor cache
parameters for, 11
result. *See* result cache
`cache` clause, 454
`cache reads` clause, 454–455
CALIBRATE_IO procedure, 166–167
calibration, I/O, 164–167
CANCEL_TASK procedure, 247
capture directory, 37
capture files, 35, 496
capturing client requests, 34–35
capturing/replaying workloads, 35–51

cascade value, 429, 430
catalog for database privileges, 411–412
catdwgrd.sql script, 30
catproc.sql script, 6
catupgrd.sql script, 21, 23, 27, 28, 32
catuppst.sql script, 22, 23, 28, 32
CCR (Customer Configuration Repository). See OCM
CD-ROM, included with book, 491–492
cdump directory, 80, 83. See also ADR
central recovery catalog. See base recovery catalog
change command, 395, 396
change failure command, 117, 120
change management, 2
change...nokeep command, 396
check command, 280–281
checker run reports, 82
checkers, 116. See also health checks
CHECK_PRIVILEGE function, 194
checksums, 132
client requests, 34–35
client_result_cache_lag parameter, 361
client_result_cache_size parameter, 361
CLIENT_RESULT_CACHE_STATS$ view, 362
clients
    automated maintenance tasks, 160–161
    replay, 40–44, 503
    result cache, 359–362, 496
client-side caching, 11
column groups, 342–345
commit parameter, 234
COMPARE_PERFORMANCE value, 57
compatibility issues, 21, 275–278, 502
compatible parameter, 26, 451
compatible.asm attribute, 275–278, 279
compatible.rdbms attribute, 275–278
compensating transactions, 428
compiled value, 467
composite partitioning, 307–309
compress clauses, 472–473
compress high clause, 455, 456
compression
    BZIP2, 402–403
    OLTP, 472–473
    SecureFiles, 11, 450–456, 504
    tables, 506
    ZLIB, 402–403
compression algorithms, 402–403
configuration
    new options for, 12–13
    persistent configuration parameters, 467–470
    Secure Configure option, 17

configure archive log deletion policy
    command, 404
configure archivelog deletion policy
    parameter, 403
configure command, 404
connect catalog command, 410–411
connect_time_scale parameter, 46, 496
control_management_pack_access parameter,
    12, 496
COPY_SQLWKLD_TO_STS procedure, 244
core_dump_dest parameter, 11
corrupted data blocks, 398–401
corruption, database, 131–133
corruption-checking parameters, 11
cp command, 284
CPU usage
    per session limits, 168–172
    resource groups based on, 169–172
    terminating sessions based on, 171–172
CPU_Pn parameters, 168
create database SQL statement, 10
create diskgroup command, 274, 277, 280
create flashback statement, 419–420
create pfile from memory command, 461
create profile statement, 18
create table as select (CTAS) operation,
    298, 472
create table statement, 291, 293, 300, 304, 472–473
CREATE_ACL procedure, 191–192
CREATE_BASELINE procedure, 149–150
CREATE_BASELINE_TEMPLATE procedure, 149, 150–152
CREATE_EXTENDED_STATS function, 341, 344, 346–347
CREATE_FILE procedure, 247
CREATE_JOB procedure, 175–177
CREATE_PLAN_DIRECTIVE procedure, 168, 170
CREATE_PRIVILEGE procedure, 192
CREATE_PROGRAM procedure, 174, 175
CREATE_RESOURCE_PLAN procedure, 169
CREATE_TASK procedure, 244
CREATION_TIME column, 158
credentials, 182, 186, 187
critical errors, 88, 89, 96–98
critical failures, 117, 119–120
CTAS (create table as select) operation, 298, 472
CTXXPATH index, 6
current statistics, 338
cursor cache
    loading SQL plans from, 230–231
    loading statements, 53
    SQL Access Advisor recommendations, 251–252
cursor sharing, 362–366, 493

`cursor_sharing` parameter, 362
Custom option, 334
custom packaging, 100–102, 497
Customer Configuration Repository (CCR). *See* OCM

D

daily maintenance windows, 159
data
    accessing older, 425–427
    archived, 394–397
    backing up. *See* backups
    flashback. *See* flashback data archives
    historical, 414, 415–417, 425
    moving with upgrades, 19
    replay, 44–45
    undo feature, 413–414
data blocks, 398–401
data dictionary views, 224
Data Guard, 184–185, 404
data integrity checks, 116. *See also* health checks
Data Mining option, 6
Data Mining Scoring Engine, 6
Data Pump, 405
Data Recovery Advisor (DRA), 115–133
    managing with Database Control, 130–131
    overview, 79, 115–117, 497
    repair options, 118–119
    restoring datafiles, 123–126
    RMAN and, 79, 117, 119–126, 134
    shared storage and, 82
Data Resource Manager, 169–172
data transfer rate, 164
database ADDM, 323–324, 497
Database Configuration Assistant. *See* DBCA
Database Control, 13, 130–131
database creation
    with DBCA, 13–19
    default security settings, 14, 17–19
    new features in, 10–19
    password-specific settings, 17–18
    Secure Configure option, 17
database failures. *See* failures
database health checks. *See* health checks
database identifier (DBID), 152, 407, 409, 411
Database Replay feature, 33–51
    client request capture, 34–35
    debugging applications with, 34
    managing, 50
    overview, 7, 33–35
    preprocessing workloads, 38–39

    RAC system and, 34–35
    testing system changes, 34–35, 39–48
    workload capture/replay, 35–51
    workload filters, 36–37
Database Resource Manager
    mixed workload resource plan, 172–173
    new resources, 167–173
    overview, 167–168
    session I/O limits, 168–172
Database Upgrade Assistant (DBUA), 21, 22, 31–32
`DATABASE_ROLE` attribute, 184
databases. *See also* Oracle Database
    compatibility issues, 21, 275–278, 502
    corruption, 131–133
    creating. *See* database creation
    downgrading, 30–31
    duplication of, 384–391
    exporting SQL patches to, 114–115
    initialization parameters, 10–12
    restarting, 35–36
    restricted mode, 36
    snapshot standby, 32–33, 36, 39, 504
    target, 387–392
datafiles. *See also* files
    corrupted blocks in, 398–401
    location of, 3, 4, 13
    missing, 123–126
    raw storage support for, 6
    restoring, 123–126
data-loss repair, 120
DBA_ADDM_FINDINGS view, 327
DBA_ADDM_INSTANCES view, 327
DBA_ADDM_TASKS view, 327
DBA_ADVISOR_EXECUTIONS view, 224
DBA_ADVISOR_FINDING_NAMES view, 325, 326–327
DBA_ADVISOR_FINDINGS view, 325, 327
DBA_ADVISOR_JOURNAL view, 246
DBA_ADVISOR_SQLPLANS view, 224
DBA_ADVISOR_SQLSTATS view, 224
DBA_AUTOTASK_CLIENT view, 160
DBA_AUTOTASK_OPERATION view, 160, 161
DBA_FLASHBACK_ARCHIVE view, 424
DBA_FLASHBACK_ARCHIVE_TABLES view, 423, 424
DBA_FLASHBACK_ARCHIVE_TS view, 424
DBA_FLASHBACK_TRANSACTION_REPORT view, 431
DBA_HIST_BASELINE view, 158
DBA_HIST_BASELINE_DETAILS view, 157–158
DBA_HIST_BASELINE_TEMPLATE view, 156–157
DBA_INDEXES view, 463–464
DBA_LOB package, 456

DBA_SCHEDULER_CREDENTIALS view, 183
DBA_SEGMENTS view, 456–457
DBA_SPACE package, 456
DBA_SQL_MANAGEMENT_CONFIG view, 238–239
DBA_SQL_PLAN_BASELINES view, 235
DBA_SQL_PROFILES view, 219
DBA_STAT_EXTENSIONS view, 342, 346–347
DBA_SYS_PRIVS view, 418
DBA_TAB_STATS_PREFS view, 337, 339, 340
DBA_TEMP_FREE_SPACE view, 466–467
DBA_USERS view, 29
db_block_checking command, 131, 132–133
db_block_checksum command, 131, 132
DBCA (Database Configuration Assistant)
    automatic memory management and, 333–334
    configuring database with, 14–19
    database creation, 13–19
    new features, 12–13
db_file_name_convert clause, 386
db_file_name_convert parameter, 385–386, 387, 389
DBID (database identifier), 152, 407, 409, 411
db_lost_write_protect command, 131, 132–133
DBMS_ADDM package, 324–327
DBMS_AUTO_TASK_ADMIN package, 160, 163, 220–222
DBMS_CRYPTO package, 194
DBMS_FLASHBACK feature, 419, 427
DBMS_FLASHBACK.TRANSACTION_BACKOUT
    procedure, 428–431
DBMS_HM package, 106
DBMS_NETWORK_ACL_ADMIN package, 191
DBMS_NETWORK_ACL_UTILITY package, 191
DBMS_REDEFINITION package, 242
DBMS_REDEFINITION procedure, 458
DBMS_RESULT_CACHE package, 350–353
DBMS_SCHEDULER package, 174, 175
DBMS_SPM package, 228–229
DBMS_SQLDIAG package, 111–115
DBMS_SQLPA package, 33, 52, 56–59, 497
DBMS_SQLTUNE package, 52, 219, 241
DBMS_STATS package, 336
dbmsupgnv.sql script, 470–471
DBMS_WORKLOAD_CAPTURE package, 33, 35, 36–37
DBMS_WORKLOAD_REPLAY package, 33, 39, 44–48
DBMS_XPLAN package, 237
DBMS_XPLAN.DISPLAY procedure, 232, 349
db_securefile parameter, 11, 451–452, 497
DBUA (Database Upgrade Assistant), 21, 22, 31–32
db_ultra_safe command, 131–133
db_ultra_safe parameter, 11, 497
dbverify utility, 399
dd command, 266, 283

DDL locks, 11, 458–459
DDL statements, 11, 57, 458–460
ddl_lock_timeout parameter, 458–459, 497
ddl_time_lockout parameter, 11
debugging applications, 34
deduplicate clause, 454, 455
deduplication feature, 452–453
default trace file, 83
deferred statistics publishing, 338–341
def_partition_tablespace attribute, 246
DELETE function, 324, 327
delete operation, 416
DELETE_FILTER procedure, 37
DELETE_FINDING_DIRECTIVE procedure, 327
DELETE_PENDING_STATS procedure, 341
DELETE_STS_REF procedure, 241–242
dependency metadata, 460
dependent objects, 460–461
dependent transactions, 427
deterministic keywords, 356
Diag Alert location, 83
Diag Cdump directory, 83
Diag incident location, 83
Diag Trace file, 83
diagnostic data
    collecting with Support Workbench, 98–99
    packaging/uploading, 100–102
diagnostic directories. See ADR
diagnostic pack, 12
diagnostic patches, 462–463
diagnostic_dest parameter, 5, 11, 13, 80, 81, 133, 497
Direct NFS, 473–476, 501
directories. See also ADR base directory; ADR home
  directory
    capture, 37
    cdump, 80, 83
    hm directory, 82
    incident directory, 82
    Oracle base, 3–4, 13
    Oracle home, 4
    rdbms, 5
    trace, 81, 82
disk groups. See ASM disk groups
disk_repair_time attribute, 266–269, 279, 283
DISPLAY_SQL_PLAN_BASELINE function, 237–238
DML locks, 458–460
DML statements, 57, 464
domain names, 193
DRA. See Data Recovery Advisor
drop after clause, 268
drop catalog command, 412–413

`drop column` command, 424
`drop diskgroup` option, 282–283, 498
`drop flashback archive` statement, 421, 423
`drop table` statement, 424
`DROP_BASELINE_TEMPLATE` procedure, 149, 152
`DROP_EXTENDED_STATS` procedure, 341, 345
dropping items
    disk groups, 282–283, 498
    disks, 266–267
    flashback data archives, 421, 423
    virtual private catalogs, 412–413
dump files, 89
`*_dump_dest` initialization parameters. *See* ADR
`duplicate database` command, 384, 385–391, 397
`duplicate target database` command, 390–391
DVDs, installing from, 8
dynamic performance views, 353–354
dynamic sampling, 342

E

electronic book, 492
`enabled` attribute, 236
`encrypt` clause, 455
encryption. *See also* security
    AES128, 453
    SecureFiles, 11, 450–458, 504
    tablespaces, 194, 196–198, 506
    Transparent Data Encryption, 194, 453
encryption keys, 456
encryption wallets, 195
Enterprise Manager
    accessing SQL Tuning Advisor, 220–223
    I/O calibration via, 165–167
    managing SPM with, 240
    modifying SecureFile options, 452
    using with ASM, 269, 271–272
    using with SQL Access Advisor, 249–251
    viewing incidents, 88
Enterprise Manager Java Console, 6
Enterprise Manager Support Workbench. *See* Support
  Workbench
environment variables, 26
ERROR_COUNT column, 158
errors. *See also* alerts; failures; problems
    critical, 88, 89
    diagnostic session workflow, 79
    SQL statements, 110–115
`estimate_percent` option, 338
EVOLVE_SQL_PLAN_BASELINE function, 233–235
evolving SQL plan baselines, 232–235, 497

exam simulation, 492
exclusive locks, 459–460
`exec` parameter, 86
EXECUTE_ANALYSIS_TASK procedure, 57–59, 61, 62
EXECUTE_TUNING_TASK procedure, 220
execution plans, 214, 216, 224–228, 232, 238
`execution_days_to_expire` parameter, 219
`execution_type` command, 57
EXPIRATION column, 157, 158
`EXPLAIN PLAN` value, 57
EXPORT_PENDING_STATS procedure, 341
expression statistics, 341, 345–347, 498
extended statistics, 341–347, 498

F

failure groups, 265
failures. *See also* errors; problems
    characteristics, 117–118
    closed, 117, 119, 120
    critical, 117, 119–120
    grouping, 118
    open, 117
    overview, 115–118
    priority, 117
    repair options, 118–119
    severity levels, 80
    status, 117
    sub-failures, 117, 119, 124
fast mirror resync feature, 265–269
fault diagnosability infrastructure, 78–81
fault management, 88
fbda (Flashback Data Archiver) process, 415,
  416–418
files. *See also* datafiles
    ASM, 265, 272–273, 284
    BasicFiles, 451–452, 454, 457, 496
    capture, 35, 496
    copying between disk groups, 284
    dump, 89
    LOB, 11
    log. *See* log files
    OMF, 15
    parameter, 461
    password, 26, 188–189, 385, 389, 391
    redo. *See* redo log files
    script, 87
    SecureFiles, 11, 450–458, 504
    tempfiles, 465–466
    trace, 83
filters, workload, 36–37, 506

finding directives, 325–327
fine-grained dependency management, 460–461
`fixed` attribute, 236
`fixed` parameter, 230
fixed SQL plan baselines, 235, 236, 498
flash recovery area, 3, 4, 404–405
`flashback archive` clause, 422, 423
Flashback Data Archiver process (fbda) process, 415,
   416–418
flashback data archives, 413–427
      advantages, 417–418
      altering, 414, 421–422
      creating, 418–421
      dropping, 421, 423
      enabling/disabling, 422–423
      examples, 425–427
      limitations, 424
      monitoring, 424
      names, 423
      new features, 413–427
      overview, 413–417, 498
      privileges, 418–419, 422, 428
      quotas, 420
      reports, 426
      retention period, 420
      size, 420–421
      vs. Flashback Database feature, 414–415
Flashback Database feature, 404, 414–415
flashback logging, 422
flashback transaction backout, 427–431, 498
flood control, 91
flood-controlled incident reporting, 88, 89
FLUSH procedure, 352–353
`force` option, 282–283, 498
`force` value, 452
`forever` option, 394
`from active database` clause, 386, 387, 390
`from tag` clause, 400

GATHER_TABLE_STATS procedure, 337, 345, 346
`generated always` clause, 299
GETOPTIONS function, 456
GET_PREFS function, 339
GET_RUN_REPORT function, 108–109
GET_TASK_REPORT function, 246–247
global statistics, 337, 339
global temporary table, 467
glossary, 493–506

`grant catalog` command, 409, 411
`grant` command, 409, 411
Grid Control, 13

H

health checks. *See also* Health Monitor
      described, 78, 116, 498
      manual, 105
      proactive checks, 126–130
      reactive, 105
      running, 106–110
      types of, 105–106
Health Monitor, 105–110. *See also* health checks
      checker run reports, 82
      overview, 78, 105–106
      reports, 108–110
`help` command, 85
help file, 492
historical data, 414, 415–417, 425
history table, 416–417
hm directory, 82
host assignments, 194
host names, 193
hot patching, 462–463
HTML DB. *See* Oracle Application Express

I

`ignore` value, 452
ILM (information lifecycle management), 426–427
`import catalog` command, 85, 405, 406–408, 500
`import database` command, 405
incident directory, 82
incident files and dumps retention policy, 89
incident flood control, 91, 499
incident metadata retention policy, 89
incident packages, 89, 90–95, 499
incident packaging service. *See* IPS
incident reports, 82
incidents, 88–95. *See also* problems
      automatic creation of, 89
      described, 88, 499
      packaging with ADRCI, 92–95
      status, 89–90
      viewing, 88, 92
incremental backups, 398
`incremental` option, 336
incremental statistics, 336, 337, 499
indexes, invisible, 450, 463–465, 499
information lifecycle management (ILM), 426–427

initialization parameters, 10–12, 190
`insert` operation, 416
`insert` statement, 296
INSERT_FINDING_DIRECTIVE procedure, 326–327
INSERT_PARAMETER_DIRECTIVE procedure, 327
INSERT_SEGMENT_DIRECTIVE procedure, 327
INSERT_SQL_DIRECTIVE procedure, 327
installing Oracle Database 11*g*, 3–10
instance ADDM, 323, 499
interactive_group, 172–173
`interpreted` value, 467, 468, 471
INTERRUPT_TASK procedure, 247
`interval` clause, 291, 297
interval partitioning, 290–295, 303, 499
interval-range partitioned tables, 307–308
invalid objects, 29, 460–461
INVALID status, 28
`invisible` clause, 463
invisible indexes, 450, 463–465, 499
I/O calibration, 164–167, 498
I/O latency, 265
I/O limits, 168–172
I/O per second (IOPS), 164, 500
IOPS (I/O per second), 164, 500
IOPS rate, 164
IP addresses, 193
IPS (incident packaging service), 79, 90–95, 499
`ips add incident` command, 95
`ips create package` command, 93, 95
IPS rules, 91
`ips set configuration` command, 91
IS_BIND_AWARE column, 365–366
IS_BIND_SENSITIVE column, 365–366
iSQL*Plus, 6

Java Development Kit (JDK) 1.4, 6
Java native compilation, 467, 471–472
`java_jit_enabled` parameter, 471
JDK (Java Development Kit) 1.4, 6
job arrays, 176–178
jobs, Scheduler. *See* Oracle Scheduler

K

`keep` clause, 466
`keep` command, 394
`keep duplicates` clause, 455
`keep forever` clause, 395–396
`keep` option, 394

`keep until time` clause, 395
keys
    encryption, 456
    partitioning, 290, 295–297, 301
    subpartitioning, 308, 350
keywords, deterministic, 356

L

large objects. *See* LOBs
LAST_COMPUTED column, 158
latency, 165, 500
ldap_directory_sysauth, 500
`ldap_directory_sysauth` parameter, 190
LearnKey group, 491
learnkey.com website, 492
lightweight jobs, 173–178, 500
`list failure` command, 117–120, 124, 127, 133
`list incarnation` command, 405–407, 410
`list restore point all` clause, 397
LOAD_PLANS_FROM_CURSOR_CACHE function, 230–231
LOAD_PLANS_FROM_SQLSET function, 228–229
LOAD_SQLSET procedure, 229, 244–245
LOB data types, 450, 451
LOB files, 11
LOBs (large objects), 450–457, 500
local external jobs, 178, 179
`lock table` statement, 459
locking enhancements, 458–460
locking tables, 458–459
locks
    DDL, 458–459
    DML, 458–460
log files, 385, 386, 387, 390. *See also* alert logs; redo log files
`log_archive_dest_n` parameter, 403
`log_file_name_convert` parameter, 385, 386, 387, 390
logical incident packages, 92–93
logical recovery, 427
LogMiner tool, 476
`logs` option, 394
lost writes, 132
`lsdsk` command, 284–285, 500

M

maintenance tasks. *See* automated maintenance tasks
maintenance windows, 159
manual checklist, 121, 123
MasterExam, 491, 492
`max_auto_sql_profiles` parameter, 219
`max_number_partitions` attribute, 246

max_sql_profiles_per_exec parameter, 219
MBPS (megabytes of I/O per second), 164, 500
MBPS rate, 164
md_backup command, 277, 286, 288–289, 500
md_restore command, 287–289, 500
megabytes of I/O per second (MBPS), 164, 500
memory
    automatic. *See* automatic memory management
    creating parameter files from, 461
    Custom option, 19
    manual, 19
    shared, 19
    Typical option, 19
memory monitor (MMON) process, 88, 89, 163
memory pool, 347
memory_max_target parameter, 11, 328–331, 500
MEMORY_REPORT function, 351
memory_target parameter, 11, 13, 328–331, 500
merge partitions clause, 294
merge statement, 293–294, 297
merging partitions, 293–294, 297
merging recovery catalogs, 405–408, 500
metadata, 460
MetaLink, 96, 99–100
metric value statistics, 152–155
MGMT_Pn parameters, 168
mirrored disks, 265–272
mixed workload resource plan, 172–173, 501
mkstore command, 195
MMON (memory monitor) process, 88, 89, 163
mode parameter, 459
MODIFY_BASELINE_WINDOW_SIZE procedure,
   149, 156
MODIFY_SNAPSHOT_SETTINGS procedure, 156
moving window baselines, 148–149, 155–156, 501
MOVING_WINDOW_SIZE column, 158
multicolumn statistics, 341, 342–345, 501
multisection backups, 392–393, 501

N

native compilation, 467–472, 502
native value, 467, 468, 469
net stop command, 26
Network File System. *See* NFS
network services, 190–194
network-aware database duplication, 384–391
never value, 452
NFS (Network File System), 473–476, 501
NFS client, 473–476
NFS server, 474–475

no flashback archive clause, 423
no unregister clause, 407
nocascade value, 429, 430
nocascade_force value, 429
nocompress clause, 455
noconflict_only option, 429
nofilenamecheck clause, 388
nokeep option, 394
nologging clause, 455
nologs option, 394
nomount mode, 389–390
non-flash recovery area, 404–405
no_result_cache hint, 350, 355, 360, 362
nowait option, 459
numberofxids parameter, 429

O

objects
    dependent, 460–461
    invalid, 29, 460–461
OCI (Oracle Call Interface), 359–360
oci_result_cache_max_rset_rows parameter, 361
oci_result_cache_max_rset_size parameter, 361
oci_result_cache_max_size parameter, 361
OCM (Oracle Configuration Manager), 6, 7, 96
ODM library, 475
ODM NFS library, 475
OFA (Optimal Flexible Architecture), 3–4
OLAP applications, 164
OLTP applications, 164
OLTP table compression, 472–473
OMF (Oracle-Managed Files), 15
online operations, 458–463
online patching, 462–463
online redefinition method, 457, 460
opatch utility, 462–463, 501
Optimal Flexible Architecture (OFA), 3–4
optimization. *See* performance
optimizer statistics collection, 334–347
optimizer_capture_sql_plan_baselines
   parameter, 12, 227, 231, 365, 501
optimizer_features_enable command, 57, 58,
   227–228
optimizer_use_invisible_indexes parameter, 12,
   464, 501
optimizer_use_pending_statistics parameter, 340
optimizer_use_private_statistics parameter, 12
optimizer_use_sql_baselines parameter, 12, 231,
   232, 501
options parameter, 429

Oracle Application Express (APEX), 7
Oracle base directory
    configuration of, 13
    diagnostic destination, 13
    location of, 3–4
Oracle Call Interface (OCI), 359–360
Oracle Clusterware home, 3
Oracle Configuration Manager. *See* OCM
Oracle Data Guard, 184–185
Oracle Data Mining option, 6
Oracle Data Mining Scoring Engine, 6
Oracle Database 10*g* Release, compatibility issues, 275–276
Oracle Database 11*g* Release. *See also* databases
    change management and, 2
    compatibility issues, 21, 275–278, 502
    configuration options, 12–13
    deprecated features, 6
    downgrading, 30–31
    installing, 3–10
    new features/components, 7, 10–19
    role/privilege changes, 7–8
    testing changes to. *See* Real Application Testing
    upgrading to, 19–32
Oracle Database Vault, 6, 7, 18
Oracle Direct NFS, 473–476, 501
Oracle Enterprise Manager Java Console, 6
Oracle home directory, 4
Oracle HTML DB. *See* Oracle Application Express
Oracle Real Application Testing, 2, 7
Oracle Scheduler, 173–185
    Data Guard, 184–185
    job arrays, 176–178
    job templates, 174–175
    lightweight jobs, 173–178, 500
    local external jobs, 178, 179
    monitoring jobs, 178
    new features, 173–185
    regular jobs, 173, 174, 176
    remote external jobs, 178–184, 503
Oracle SecureFiles, 11, 450–458, 504
Oracle SQL Developer, 7
Oracle Ultra Search, 6
Oracle Universal Installer, 4, 8–10
Oracle Wallet, 195–196
Oracle Wallet Manager (OWM), 195–196
Oracle Warehouse Builder, 7
Oracle Workflow, 6
Oracle XML DB option, 6, 179
ORACLE_BASE variable, 3, 4, 5, 81
Oracle-Managed Files (OMF), 15
oranfstab file, 475

orapwd command, 189
ORIGIN attribute, 236
OSASM group, 8, 9, 20, 502
osborne.com website, 492
OWM (Oracle Wallet Manager), 195–196

P

parameter file (PFILE), 461
parameter_name_convert clause, 391
parameter_value_convert clause, 385–386, 387
partial ADDM, 323, 324, 502
partition by reference clause, 304
partition by system clause, 296
partition clause, 291, 297
partition exchange, 457, 502
partition option, 246
partition pruning, 290
partitioned tables, 336–337
partitioning, 289–309
    composite, 307–309
    enhancements, 289–309
    incremental statistics, 337, 499
    interval, 290–295, 303, 499
    merging partitions, 293–294, 297
    partitioning keys, 290, 295–297, 301
    range, 290–295, 307–309
    reference, 301–307
    SQL Access Advisor, 242–243
    subpartitioning keys, 308, 350
    system, 295–298, 506
    transition point, 291, 293–295, 506
    virtual column, 298–301, 506
partitioning keys, 290, 295–297, 301
password file clause, 385, 389, 391
password files, 26, 188–189, 385, 389, 391
passwords
    case sensitivity, 12, 29, 186–189
    checking status of, 29
    default, 30
    encryption keys, 456
    expiration of, 17
    managing, 189–190
    new features, 186–190
    reusing, 17–18
    Scheduler agent, 180
    settings for, 17–18
    SYSDBA, 385, 389
    versions, 29
patches
    database server code, 462–463

patches (*continued*)
    diagnostic, 462–463
    SQL, 110–115
PCT_TOTAL_TIME column, 158
pctversion parameter, 451, 453
pending statistics, 335, 338, 502
Perform Recovery page, 130–131
performance, 321–366
    adaptive cursor sharing, 362–366, 493
    ADDM enhancements, 322–327
    alert thresholds, 152–155
    ASM, 272–274
    automatic memory enhancements, 328–334
    AWR baselines and, 148
    DML locks and, 459–460
    query result cache, 353–354, 505
    result cache, 347–362
Performance Analyzer, 2, 7
performance metrics, 152–155
performance regressions, 226–227, 228
permitted value, 452
persistent configuration parameters, 467–470
pga_aggregate_target parameter, 13, 328–331
physical incident packages, 94–95
plan history, 226
plan_hash_value parameter, 230
plan_list parameter, 234
plan_name parameter, 234
PL/SQL
    compilation, 11, 467–471
    function result, 502
    I/O calibration via, 166–167
    native compilation, 467–471, 502
    network access and, 190–191
    result cache, 350–353, 357–358, 503
    using with SQL Access Advisor, 243–249
PL/SQL code block, 175
PL/SQL objects, 460
plsql_code_type parameter, 11, 467–470
Post-Upgrade Status Tool, 21, 27–28
preferred mirror read feature, 269–272, 495
preprocessing captured workloads, 38
Pre-Upgrade Information Tool, 22–23
primary key constraint relationship, 427
Privileged Operating System Groups page, 9
privileges
    ACLs and, 194
    changes to, 7–8
    flashback data archives, 418–419, 422, 428
    recovery catalog, 411–412

storage management, 20
SYSASM, 8, 9, 20, 274–275, 506
SYSDBA, 8, 20, 274
SYSOPER, 20
virtual catalogs, 411–412
proactive checks, 126–130
problems, 88–95. *See also* errors; failures; incidents;
    troubleshooting
    described, 88, 502
    system-generated, 103–104
    user-reported, 103–104
    viewing details about, 98
production workload, capturing, 37–38
publish option, 335, 339
publish points, 243
publishing statistics, 335, 338–341
PUBLISH_PENDING_STATS procedure, 341
PURGE_SQL_PLAN_BASELINE procedure, 239

Q

query result cache, 353–357, 505. *See also* result cache
Quick Packaging method, 100, 502
quotas, 420

R

RAC environment, 34–35, 82, 352
RAC installations, 32
RACs (Real Application Clusters), 322–324, 502
range partitioning, 290–295, 307–309
range-range partitioned tables, 308–309
raw storage support, 6
RDBMS compatibility, 21, 275–278, 502
rdbms directory, 5
read-only tablespaces, 502
Real Application Clusters. *See* RACs
Real Application Testing, 32–61
    Database Replay. *See* Database Replay feature
    overview, 7, 32–33
    snapshot standby databases, 32–33, 36, 39, 504
    SQL Performance Analyzer, 51–61
real native compilation, 467–468
recover corruption list command, 401
recover...block command, 398–401, 465–467
recovery. *See also* Data Recovery Advisor; RMAN
    base recovery catalog, 408–412, 496
    block media recovery feature, 398–401
    catalogs. *See* recovery catalogs
    logical, 427
    Perform Recovery page, 130–131

recovery catalogs, 405–413
    importing, 498
    merging, 408–408, 500
    privileges, 411–412
    virtual private catalogs, 405, 408–413, 506
recovery_catalog_owner role, 409, 411
redo log files
    accessing via LogMiner, 476
    archived, 403–404
    backups, 404–405
    deletion policy, 403–404
    obsolete, 404
    standby database and, 33
reference partitioning, 301–307, 503
register database privilege, 411
regression, performance, 226–227, 228
remap command, 286, 503
REMAP_CONNECTION procedure, 45
remapping connections, 503
remote external jobs, 178–184, 503
RENAME_BASELINE procedure, 149, 152
repair failure command, 122, 126
repair failure preview command, 122, 125
repair script, 118, 121, 125–126
repairs
    automatic, 118, 121, 122, 124–125
    manual, 118, 121, 122, 123
repeating baseline, 503
REPEAT_INTERVAL column, 157
replace_user_sql_profiles parameter, 219
replay clients, 40–44, 503
replay driver, 40
replaying captured workloads, 39–48
REPORT_AUTO_TUNING_TASK function, 223–224
reports
    ADDM, 325
    Automatic SQL Tuning, 223–224
    checker run, 82
    flashback data archive, 426
    Health Monitor, 82, 108–110
    incident, 82
    SQL Performance Analyzer, 59–61
    TRANSACTION_BACKOUT, 431
    workload capture/replay, 48–51
REPORT_TUNING_TASK procedure, 220
resource allocation, 163–164
Resource Consumer Group, 167
resource limits, 169–172
Resource Manager. *See* Database Resource Manager
resource plan directives, 168
resource plans, 168, 172–173, 501

restarting database, 35–36
restore point clause, 394, 396
restore points, 394–397, 404
restoring
    archival backups, 397
    ASM metadata backup and restore, 284, 286,
        288–289, 494
    corrupted data blocks, 398–401
    Data Recovery Advisor, 123–126
    Recovery Manager, 124–126
restricted mount mode, 281–282, 503
result cache, 347–362
    caching SQL results, 348–350
    client, 359–362, 496
    DBMS_RESULT_CACHE package, 350–353
    described, 347, 503
    dynamic performance views, 353–354
    managing, 348
    memory pool, 347
    Oracle Call Interface, 359–360
    performance, 347–362
    PL/SQL, 350–353, 357–358, 503
    removing contents of, 352
    SQL, 353–357, 503, 505
result_cache hint, 349, 352, 355, 356, 503
ResultCache operator, 348–350, 354–355, 356, 504
result_cache_max_result parameter, 348,
    351, 503
result_cache_max_size parameter, 348, 351, 503
result_cache_mode parameter, 11, 348–350, 354–355,
    360, 503
result_cache_remote_expiration parameter, 348
RESUME_GATHER_STATS procedure, 339
retention 4 year clause, 420
retention parameter, 451, 453
retention period, 420
retention policy, 89
return parameter, 234
revoke all privileges from command, 412
revoke catalog for database command, 412
revoke command, 412
RMAN (Recovery Manager), 384–405
    active database duplication, 384–391
    archives, 394–397
    backups, 392–398
    block media recovery, 398–401
    DRA and, 79, 117, 119–126, 134
    enhancements, 384–405
    persistent configuration parameters, 467–470
    restoring datafiles, 124–126
    restoring files, 392–397

roles, changes to, 7–8
RUN_CHECK procedure, 106, 108
runInstaller script, 8

S

sampling techniques, 338
schagent executable, 181–182
Scheduler. *See* Oracle Scheduler
Scheduler agent, 179–183, 504
Scheduler jobs, 163
SCN (System Change Number), 394, 396–397, 414, 430
scnhint parameter, 429, 430
script files, 87
script parameter, 86, 87
scripts
    generating SQL scripts, 247–249
    repair, 118, 121, 125–126
    upgrade, 22–32
sec_case_sensitive_logon parameter, 12, 186, 190, 504
sec_max_failed_login_attempts parameter, 12, 190, 504
sec_protocol_error_further_action parameter, 190
sec_protocol_error_trace_action parameter, 190
section size parameter, 392–393
sections, 392
SecureFiles, 11, 450–458, 504
security
    default settings, 14, 17–19
    encryption. *See* encryption
    initialization parameters, 190
    new features, 185–198
    Oracle SecureFiles, 11, 450–458, 504
    Oracle Wallet, 195–196
    passwords. *See* passwords
    settings, 14
select any transaction privilege, 428
SELECT_BASELINE_METRICS function, 149, 152–153
Server Manageability Pack, 12
server parameter file (SPFILE), 385–391, 461
server-side caching, 11
service requests
    creating, 99–100
    tracking with Support Workbench, 102–103
session limits, 168–172
session switching, 169–172
set clause, 386, 387–388, 391
set homepath command, 85
SET_ATTRIBUTE procedure, 183, 184

SETOPTIONS procedure, 456
SET_PREFS procedure, 336
SET_SCHEMA_PREFS procedure, 339
SET_TABLE_PREFS procedure, 339
SET_TASK_PARAMETER procedure, 245–246
SET_TUNING_TASK_PARAMETERS procedure, 219–222
sga_target parameter, 13, 329–331, 347
shared cursors, 362–366, 493
shared memory, 19
show alert command, 87
show alert -tail command, 87, 88
show all command, 401–402
show hm_run command, 109–110
show homes command, 86
show incident command, 90
SHOW_EXTENDED_STATS_NAME function, 341, 344–345
shrink space clause, 465–466
shrink tempfile clause, 465
SHUTDOWN column, 157
shutdown immediate command, 26
single baseline, 504
SMB. *See* SQL Management Base
snapshot standby database, 32–33, 36, 39, 504
snapshots, 48, 148. *See also* baselines
source recovery catalog. *See* base recovery catalog
space_budget_percent parameter, 238, 239
SPACE_USAGE procedure, 456
SPFILE (server parameter file), 385–391, 461
spfile clause, 385–389, 391
SPM. *See* SQL Plan Management
SQL Access Advisor, 240–252
    creating SQL Tuning Sets, 244
    creating tasks, 244
    described, 240, 504
    enhancements, 240–252
    executing tasks, 246
    generating SQL scripts, 247–249
    linking tasks/workloads, 245
    new procedures, 240–242
    partitioning recommendations, 242–243
    publish points, 243
    SQL Workload and, 241
    task parameters, 245–246
    using cursor cache with, 251–252
    using Enterprise Manager with, 249–251
    using PL/SQL with, 243–249
    using SQL Tuning Advisor with, 240–241
    viewing recommendations, 246–247
SQL Developer, 7
SQL Management Base (SMB)
    configuring, 238–239

described, 238, 504
purging policies, 239–240
SQL patches, 110–115
SQL Performance Analyzer, 51–61
analyzing post-change SQL workload,
58–59
analyzing pre-change SQL workload, 57–58
capturing SQL workload, 54–61
comparing SQL performance, 58–59
creating tasks, 56
overview, 7, 51–53, 504–505
reports, 59–61
SQL Tuning Set, 52–61
testing performance changes, 51–52
workflow, 53–54
SQL plan baselines, 226–238
accepted plans, 226, 232–234, 236, 493
attributes, 235–237
capturing, 227–235
disabling, 236–237
enabled, 231, 233, 235–238
evolving, 232–235, 497
execution plans, 214, 216, 224–228, 232, 238
fixed, 235–236, 498
managing, 237–238
non-accepted, 232–235
overview, 226–227, 505
plan history, 226
plan loading, 228–231
selecting, 231–232
verified plans, 226, 236
viewing SQL plans in, 237–238
SQL Plan Management (SPM), 225–240
baselines. *See* SQL plan baselines
described, 214, 505
managing with Enterprise Manager, 240
SQL plans, 226–235, 239–240
SQL profiles, 215, 216–224, 505
SQL query result cache, 353–357, 505
SQL Repair Advisor, 110–115
DBMS_SQLDIAG package, 111–115
overview, 79, 110–111, 505
SQL patches, 110–115
using Support Workbench with, 111
SQL result cache, 503
SQL scripts, 247–249
SQL statements
loading STS with, 244–245
repairing statement failures, 110–115
tuning. *See* Automatic SQL Tuning Advisor; SQL
Tuning Advisor

SQL Test Case Builder
accessing from Support Workbench, 115
overview, 79, 505
SQL Tuning Advisor. *See also* Automatic SQL Tuning
Advisor
creating, 244
described, 214–215
evolving SQL plans with, 235
loading, 244–245
SQL Access Advisor and, 240–241
using, 54, 60–61
SQL tuning reports, 223–224
SQL Tuning Set (STS), 52–61, 228–231, 505
SQL workload, 51–61, 241
SQL_HANDLE attribute, 236
sql_handle parameter, 230, 234
sql_id parameter, 230
SQL_PLAN_NAME attribute, 236
SQL*Plus, 409
SQL_TEXT attribute, 236
sql_text parameter, 230
staging table, 114
stale_percent option, 335–336
standby databases, 32–33, 36, 39
startup nomount command, 390
startup restrict command, 36, 282, 503
startup upgrade command, 29
static baselines, 148
statistics
current, 338
deferred statistics publishing, 338–341
deleting, 341
exporting, 341
expression, 341, 345–347, 498
extended, 341–347, 498
global, 337, 339
incremental, 336
multicolumn, 341, 342–345, 501
optimizer statistics collection, 334–347
pending, 335, 338, 502
preferences, 334–337
private, 338
public, 335, 338, 340–341
publishing, 335, 338–341
stale, 335–336
status, 339–340
statistics_level parameter, 149, 219, 220
storage management privileges, 20
store as securefile clause, 454, 455, 457
store in clause, 291
striping, 265

STS. *See* SQL Tuning Set
subpartitioning keys, 308, 350
supplemental logging, 428
support, technical, 492
Support Workbench, 96–104
    closing incidents, 103
    diagnostic data, 98–102
    IPS management via, 91
    overview, 79, 96, 505
    packaging diagnostic data, 100–102
    problem details, 98
    repairs, 103
    service request creation, 99–100
    tracking service requests, 102–103
    user-reported problems, 103–104
    using SQL Repair Advisor with, 111
    viewing alert logs, 104
    viewing critical error alerts, 96–98
`switch_call` parameter, 168
`switch_estimate` parameter, 170
`switch_for_call` parameter, 170
`switch_group` parameter, 169
`switch_io_megabytes` parameter, 170
`switch_io_reqs` parameter, 170
`switch_time` parameter, 169
`switch_time_in_call` parameter, 168
`synchronization` parameter, 45–46
synchronized replay, 45–46
SYSASM privileges, 8, 9, 20, 274–275, 506
SYS_AUTO_SQL_TUNING_TASK procedure, 220
SYSAUX tablespace, 23, 163, 238, 239
SYSDBA password, 385, 389
SYSDBA privileges, 8, 20, 274
sys_group, 172
SYSOPER privilege, 20
System Change Number (SCN), 394, 396–397, 414, 430
system partitioning, 295–298, 506
system requirements, CD-ROM, 491
system-generated problems, 103–104
`systimestamp - interval '120'` clause, 426

table compression, 506
tables
    compressing, 472–473
    history, 416–417
    locking, 458–459
    OLTP, 472–473

    partitioned. *See* partitioning
    temporary, 467
tablespace clause, 467
tablespaces
    encrypting, 194, 196–198, 506
    flashback data archives, 419
    free space in, 466–467
    shrinking, 465–467
    temporary, 465–467
    undo tablespace, 413–414
target databases, 387–392
TCP ports, 193
TDE (Transparent Data Encryption), 194, 453
technical support, 492
tempfiles, 465–466
TEMPLATE_NAME column, 158
templates
    baseline, 149–152, 156–157
    redundancy, 279
    Scheduler job, 174–175
    striping attribute, 279
`template.tname.redundancy` attribute, 279
`template.tname.striping` attribute, 279
TEMPLATE_TYPE column, 157
terminology, 493–506
TEST_EXECUTE value, 57
testing. *See also* Real Application Testing
    SQL performance. *See* SQL Performance Analyzer
    system changes with Database Replay, 34–35, 39–48
text initialization parameter file (PFILE), 461
text-based alert logs, 82, 104
`think_time_auto_correct` parameter, 46, 506
`think_time_scale` parameter, 46, 506
throughput, 165, 506
`timehint` parameter, 430
`time_limit` parameter, 57–58
Total Replay feature, 51
trace directory, 81, 82
trace files, 83
TRANSACTION_BACKOUT procedure, 427
transactions
    backing out, 427–431, 498
    compensating, 428
    dependent, 427
transition point, 291, 293–295, 506
Transparent Data Encryption (TDE), 194, 453
troubleshooting, 77–146. *See also* errors
    Automatic Diagnostic Repository, 80–88
    Data Recovery Advisor, 115–133

Health Monitor, 105–110
incidents, 88–95
overview, 78–80
problems, 88–95
SQL Repair Advisor, 110–115
Support Workbench, 96–104
truncate table statement, 424
tuning. *See* Automatic SQL Tuning Advisor; SQL Tuning
  Advisor
tuning pack, 12
txnames parameter, 430
Typical option, 333

Ultra Search, 6
undo data feature, 413–414
undo tablespace, 413–414
update operation, 416
Upgrade Status Utility script, 23
upgrades, 19–32
  changes in process, 20–21
  compatibility issues, 21
  Database Upgrade Assistant, 21, 22, 31–32
  manual method, 22–31
  moving data during, 19
  new privileges, 20
  Post-Upgrade Status Tool, 21, 27–28
  Pre-Upgrade Information Tool, 22–23
  procedure for, 20–32
  scripts for, 22–32
  status of, 23
user_dump_dest parameter, 11
user-reported problems, 103–104
UTL_RECOMP package, 28–29
utlrp.sql script, 23, 28–29, 31, 32
utlu111i.sql script, 22–25, 31
utlu111s.sql script, 23, 27–28, 32

V

validate backupset command, 127
validate database command, 127, 400–401
V$ASM_DISKGROUP view, 274, 278
V$DATABASE_BLOCK_CORRUPTION view, 399,
  400–401
V$DIAG_INFO view, 82–83
V$DNFS_CHANNELS view, 476
V$DNFS_FILES view, 476
V$DNFS_SERVERS view, 476

verified plans, 226, 236
verify parameter, 234
verify_function command, 189–190
versions between timestamp clause, 426–427
V$HM_CHECK view, 105–106
V$IR_FAILURE view, 119, 123
V$IR_FAILURE_SET view, 123
V$IR_MANUAL_CHECKLIST view, 119, 123
V$IR_REPAIR view, 122–123
virtual column partitioning, 298–301, 506
virtual private catalogs, 405, 408–413, 506
V$MEMORY_CURRENT_RESIZE_OPS view, 332
V$MEMORY_DYNAMIC_COMPONENTS view, 332
V$MEMORY_RESIZE_OPS view, 332
V$RESULT_CACHE_DEPENDENCY view, 353
V$RESULT_CACHE_MEMORY view, 353
V$RESULT_CACHE_OBJECTS view, 353, 354
V$RESULT_CACHE_STATISTICS view, 353
V$RMAN_COMPRESSION_ALGORITH view, 402–403
V$SQL view, 365, 366
V$SQL_CS_HISTOGRAM view, 366
V$SQL_CS_SELECTIVITY view, 366
V$SQL_CS_STATISTICS view, 366

wait option, 459
Warehouse Builder, 7
workload capture/replay, 35–51, 241
workload filters, 36–37, 506
workload, SQL, 51–61
wrc. *See* replay clients
wrc executable, 41–43
write-after-write relationship, 427

X

xids parameter, 429, 430
XML DB option, 6, 179
XML-formatted alert logs, 81, 82, 83, 104
XMLIndex, 6

Z

ZLIB compression algorithm, 402–403

GET YOUR FREE SUBSCRIPTION
TO ORACLE MAGAZINE

Oracle Magazine is essential gear for today's information technology professionals. Stay informed and increase your productivity with every issue of *Oracle Magazine*. Inside each free bimonthly issue you'll get:

IF THERE ARE OTHER ORACLE USERS AT YOUR LOCATION WHO WOULD LIKE TO RECEIVE THEIR OWN SUBSCRIPTION TO ORACLE MAGAZINE, PLEASE PHOTOCOPY THIS FORM AND PASS IT ALONG.

- Up-to-date information on Oracle Database, Oracle Application Server, Web development, enterprise grid computing, database technology, and business trends
- Third-party vendor news and announcements
- Technical articles on Oracle and partner products, technologies, and operating environments
- Development and administration tips
- Real-world customer stories

Three easy ways to subscribe:

① Web
Visit our Web site at otn.oracle.com/oraclemagazine. You'll find a subscription form there, plus much more!

② Fax
Complete the questionnaire on the back of this card and fax the questionnaire side only to +1.847.763.9638.

③ Mail
Complete the questionnaire on the back of this card and mail it to P.O. Box 1263, Skokie, IL 60076-8263

ORACLE®

FREE SUBSCRIPTION

○ **Yes, please send me a FREE subscription to *Oracle Magazine*.**   ○ NO
To receive a free subscription to *Oracle Magazine*, you must fill out the entire card, sign it, and date it
(incomplete cards cannot be processed or acknowledged). You can also fax your application to +1.847.763.9638.
Or subscribe at our Web site at otn.oracle.com/oraclemagazine

○ From time to time, Oracle Publishing allows
our partners exclusive access to our e-mail
addresses for special promotions and
announcements. To be included in this program, please check this circle.

signature (required)   date

X

○ Oracle Publishing allows sharing of our
mailing list with selected third parties. If you
prefer your mailing address not to be
included in this program, please check here.
If at any time you would like to be removed
from this mailing list, please contact
Customer Service at +1.847.647.9630 or send
an e-mail to oracle@halldata.com.

name   title

company   e-mail address

street/p.o. box

city/state/zip or postal code   telephone

country   fax

YOU MUST ANSWER ALL TEN QUESTIONS BELOW.

① WHAT IS THE PRIMARY BUSINESS ACTIVITY OF YOUR FIRM AT THIS LOCATION? (check one only)
- □ 01 Aerospace and Defense Manufacturing
- □ 02 Application Service Provider
- □ 03 Automotive Manufacturing
- □ 04 Chemicals, Oil and Gas
- □ 05 Communications and Media
- □ 06 Construction/Engineering
- □ 07 Consumer Sector/Consumer Packaged Goods
- □ 08 Education
- □ 09 Financial Services/Insurance
- □ 10 Government (civil)
- □ 11 Government (military)
- □ 12 Healthcare
- □ 13 High Technology Manufacturing, OEM
- □ 14 Integrated Software Vendor
- □ 15 Life Sciences (Biotech, Pharmaceuticals)
- □ 16 Mining
- □ 17 Retail/Wholesale/Distribution
- □ 18 Systems Integrator, VAR/VAD
- □ 19 Telecommunications
- □ 20 Travel and Transportation
- □ 21 Utilities (electric, gas, sanitation, water)
- □ 98 Other Business and Services

② WHICH OF THE FOLLOWING BEST DESCRIBES YOUR PRIMARY JOB FUNCTION? (check one only)
Corporate Management/Staff
- □ 01 Executive Management (President, Chair, CEO, CFO, Owner, Partner, Principal)
- □ 02 Finance/Administrative Management (VP/Director/ Manager/Controller, Purchasing, Administration)
- □ 03 Sales/Marketing Management (VP/Director/Manager)
- □ 04 Computer Systems/Operations Management (CIO/VP/Director/ Manager MIS, Operations)
IS/IT Staff
- □ 05 Systems Development/ Programming Management
- □ 06 Systems Development/ Programming Staff
- □ 07 Consulting
- □ 08 DBA/Systems Administrator
- □ 09 Education/Training
- □ 10 Technical Support Director/Manager
- □ 11 Other Technical Management/Staff
- □ 98 Other

③ WHAT IS YOUR CURRENT PRIMARY OPERATING PLATFORM? (select all that apply)
- □ 01 Digital Equipment UNIX
- □ 02 Digital Equipment VAX VMS
- □ 03 HP UNIX
- □ 04 IBM AIX
- □ 05 IBM UNIX
- □ 06 Java
- □ 07 Linux
- □ 08 Macintosh
- □ 09 MS-DOS
- □ 10 MVS
- □ 11 NetWare
- □ 12 Network Computing
- □ 13 OpenVMS
- □ 14 SCO UNIX
- □ 15 Sequent DYNIX/ptx
- □ 16 Sun Solaris/SunOS
- □ 17 SVR4
- □ 18 UnixWare
- □ 19 Windows
- □ 20 Windows NT
- □ 21 Other UNIX
- □ 98 Other
- 99 □ None of the above

④ DO YOU EVALUATE, SPECIFY, RECOMMEND, OR AUTHORIZE THE PURCHASE OF ANY OF THE FOLLOWING? (check all that apply)
- □ 01 Hardware
- □ 02 Software
- □ 03 Application Development Tools
- □ 04 Database Products
- □ 05 Internet or Intranet Products
- 99 □ None of the above

⑤ IN YOUR JOB, DO YOU USE OR PLAN TO PURCHASE ANY OF THE FOLLOWING PRODUCTS? (check all that apply)
Software
- □ 01 Business Graphics
- □ 02 CAD/CAE/CAM
- □ 03 CASE
- □ 04 Communications
- □ 05 Database Management
- □ 06 File Management
- □ 07 Finance
- □ 08 Java
- □ 09 Materials Resource Planning
- □ 10 Multimedia Authoring
- □ 11 Networking
- □ 12 Office Automation
- □ 13 Order Entry/Inventory Control
- □ 14 Programming
- □ 15 Project Management
- □ 16 Scientific and Engineering
- □ 17 Spreadsheets
- □ 18 Systems Management
- □ 19 Workflow

Hardware
- □ 20 Macintosh
- □ 21 Mainframe
- □ 22 Massively Parallel Processing
- □ 23 Minicomputer
- □ 24 PC
- □ 25 Network Computer
- □ 26 Symmetric Multiprocessing
- □ 27 Workstation
Peripherals
- □ 28 Bridges/Routers/Hubs/Gateways
- □ 29 CD-ROM Drives
- □ 30 Disk Drives/Subsystems
- □ 31 Modems
- □ 32 Tape Drives/Subsystems
- □ 33 Video Boards/Multimedia
Services
- □ 34 Application Service Provider
- □ 35 Consulting
- □ 36 Education/Training
- □ 37 Maintenance
- □ 38 Online Database Services
- □ 39 Support
- □ 40 Technology-Based Training
- □ 98 Other
- 99 □ None of the above

⑥ WHAT ORACLE PRODUCTS ARE IN USE AT YOUR SITE? (check all that apply)
Oracle E-Business Suite
- □ 01 Oracle Marketing
- □ 02 Oracle Sales
- □ 03 Oracle Order Fulfillment
- □ 04 Oracle Supply Chain Management
- □ 05 Oracle Procurement
- □ 06 Oracle Manufacturing
- □ 07 Oracle Maintenance Management
- □ 08 Oracle Service
- □ 09 Oracle Contracts
- □ 10 Oracle Projects
- □ 11 Oracle Financials
- □ 12 Oracle Human Resources
- □ 13 Oracle Interaction Center
- □ 14 Oracle Communications/Utilities (modules)
- □ 15 Oracle Public Sector/University (modules)
- □ 16 Oracle Financial Services (modules)
Server/Software
- □ 17 Oracle9i
- □ 18 Oracle9i Lite
- □ 19 Oracle8i
- □ 20 Other Oracle database
- □ 21 Oracle9i Application Server
- □ 22 Oracle9i Application Server Wireless
- □ 23 Oracle Small Business Suite

Tools
- □ 24 Oracle Developer Suite
- □ 25 Oracle Discoverer
- □ 26 Oracle JDeveloper
- □ 27 Oracle Migration Workbench
- □ 28 Oracle9i/AS Portal
- □ 29 Oracle Warehouse Builder
Oracle Services
- □ 30 Oracle Outsourcing
- □ 31 Oracle Consulting
- □ 32 Oracle Education
- □ 33 Oracle Support
- □ 98 Other
- 99 □ None of the above

⑦ WHAT OTHER DATABASE PRODUCTS ARE IN USE AT YOUR SITE? (check all that apply)
- □ 01 Access
- □ 02 Baan
- □ 03 dbase
- □ 04 Gupta
- □ 05 IBM DB2
- □ 06 Informix
- □ 07 Ingres
- □ 08 Microsoft Access
- □ 09 Microsoft SQL Server
- □ 10 PeopleSoft
- □ 11 Progress
- □ 12 SAP
- □ 13 Sybase
- □ 14 VSAM
- □ 98 Other
- 99 □ None of the above

⑧ WHAT OTHER APPLICATION SERVER PRODUCTS ARE IN USE AT YOUR SITE? (check all that apply)
- □ 01 BEA
- □ 02 IBM
- □ 03 Sybase
- □ 04 Sun
- □ 05 Other

⑨ DURING THE NEXT 12 MONTHS, HOW MUCH DO YOU ANTICIPATE YOUR ORGANIZATION WILL SPEND ON COMPUTER HARDWARE, SOFTWARE, PERIPHERALS, AND SERVICES FOR YOUR LOCATION? (check only one)
- □ 01 Less than $10,000
- □ 02 $10,000 to $49,999
- □ 03 $50,000 to $99,999
- □ 04 $100,000 to $499,999
- □ 05 $500,000 to $999,999
- □ 06 $1,000,000 and over

⑩ WHAT IS YOUR COMPANY'S YEARLY SALES REVENUE? (please choose one)
- □ 01 $500, 000, 000 and above
- □ 02 $100, 000, 000 to $500, 000, 000
- □ 03 $50, 000, 000 to $100, 000, 000
- □ 04 $5, 000, 000 to $50, 000, 000
- □ 05 $1, 000, 000 to $5, 000, 000

100103